A HISTORY OF THE SOUTH

VOLUMES IN THE SERIES

Volume VII

THE CONFEDERATE STATES
OF AMERICA
1861–1865

A HISTORY

OF

THE SOUTH

Volume VII

EDITORS

WENDELL HOLMES STEPHENSON

PROFESSOR OF SOUTHERN HISTORY
AT TULANE UNIVERSITY

E. MERTON COULTER

PROFESSOR OF HISTORY AT THE
UNIVERSITY OF GEORGIA

The
Confederate States
of America
1861-1865

BY E. MERTON COULTER

Baton Rouge

LOUISIANA STATE UNIVERSITY PRESS

THE LITTLEFIELD FUND FOR SOUTHERN
HISTORY OF THE UNIVERSITY OF TEXAS

1950

PUBLISHERS' PREFACE

A HISTORY OF THE SOUTH is sponsored by Louisiana State University and the Trustees of the Littlefield Fund for Southern History at The University of Texas. More remotely, it is the outgrowth of the vision of Major George W. Littlefield, C.S.A., who established a fund at The University of Texas in 1914 for the collection of materials on Southern history and the publication of a "full and impartial study of the South and its part in American history." Trustees of the Littlefield Fund began preparations in 1937 for the writing of the history that Major Littlefield contemplated. Meanwhile, a plan had been conceived at Louisiana State University for a history of the South as a part of that institution's comprehensive program to promote interest, research, and writing in the field of Southern history.

As the two undertakings harmonized in essentials, the planning groups united to become joint sponsors of *A History of the South*. Wendell Holmes Stephenson, then professor of American history at Louisiana State University, and the late Charles W. Ramsdell, professor of American history at The University of Texas, were chosen to edit the series. They had been primarily interested in initiating the plans, and it was appropriate that they should be selected to edit the work. Upon the death of Professor Ramsdell in 1943, E. Merton Coulter, professor of history at the University of Georgia, was named his successor.

Volumes of the series are being published as the manuscripts are received. This is the fourth published volume; it follows Volume I. When completed, the ten-volume set will represent about twelve years of historical planning and research.

vii

AUTHOR'S PREFACE

THE war years in the South were a time of heroism, self-sacrifice, despondency, and destruction. Now the fight of Southerners to maintain a civilization against change appeared to them to be as fundamental as was the contest of a later generation of Americans to protect Western culture against Asiatic tyrannical regimentation. Defeat brought an end to an era and lent special meaning to the term ante-bellum or "before the war." Thereafter that war needed no name (despite some Southerners' insistence on "War Between the States"), for the sound in their ears of the word "war" could mean only one war.

These four years were of almost equal importance to all Americans, for what took place in the South reacted on the whole country with greater effect than that of any other four years in American history. It was only natural, then, that both Northerners and Southerners should set out to record the happenings of these eventful years. As it was human nature that they should write about what was most exciting and interesting, the logical result was a vast number of military and naval accounts. This, of course, made a full history of the war against the South and by the South, but took little note of the South itself. Only in recent times have historians begun to write of some of the many other aspects of the years 1861 to 1865.

This volume could not, of course, do otherwise than concern itself with the whole picture of the South, thereby relegating the war itself to its proper relative position. It is hoped that in these pages the war has not been made to recede too far from its high estate. Here was the opportunity as well as the necessity of writing a history of the South and not of the war principally. But, indeed, there was little, as will be seen, which was not related in some way to the war; and so in these pages, where the war is not, its shadow falls. With the space thus saved, it has been possible to light up some of the dark corners of the South during the war years.

The writer must here lament the loss suffered by the South as well as by the nation, in the death of Charles W. Ramsdell (1877–1942), who had been originally assigned this volume and who in this period was learned beyond all others. Were it the policy to dedicate volumes in the present series, this one would be inscribed to him.

E. M. C.

CONTENTS

CONTENTS

ILLUSTRATIONS

ILLUSTRATIONS

A Bummer of General Sherman's Army

Treasure Seekers

The Burning of Columbia, South Carolina, February 17, 1865

A Female Rebel in Baltimore—An Everyday Scene

Federal Steamer, Under a Flag of Truce, Unloading Refugees from New Orleans Within Confederate Lines on Lake Pontchartrain

Fraternizing of Confederate and Federal Pickets in the Rappahannock

Bar of the Spotswood House, Richmond, Virginia

Exterior View of the Libby Prison, Richmond, Virginia

Encampment of Union Prisoners at Belle Isle, Richmond, Virginia

Title Page of Confederate Sheet Music, "Riding a Raid"

Mr. Jefferson Davis Signing Acts of Government by the Roadside

Mr. Jefferson Davis Bidding Farewell to his Escort Two Days before his Capture

CHAPTER I

THE LOWER SOUTH SECEDES

AFTER forty years of mounting bitterness and misunderstanding between the Northern and Southern sections of the United States, in 1860–1861 a large segment of Southerners broke away from the Union and set up a government of their own. The South, which had long felt itself to be much apart from the rest of the nation, intended now to make itself so in fact.

It was not surprising that South Carolina should be the first state to act. Had she not sat at the feet of John C. Calhoun for many years, absorbed his doctrine of state rights, and nullified the tariff of 1832? It was Abraham Lincoln's election to the presidency in 1860 which precipitated the secession movement. Leaders in many portions of the South had openly threatened to leave the Union if this calamity should happen. So, the legislature of South Carolina, which alone of all such bodies in the American states continued to choose Presidential electors, immediately called for the election of a sovereign convention when it learned of Lincoln's victory. This convention met in Columbia on December 17, adjourned to Charleston, and unanimously adopted an ordinance of secession on the twentieth.

This quick action led some Southerners to charge South Carolina with showing little respect for the other slaveholding states. A newspaper editor in Arkansas chided her for having "whirled herself" out of the Union "without even passing the compliments of the season with her sister slaveholding States," an act which reminded him of the Irish wit's remark that "she has passed us by without even saying 'good morning, d——m your sowl.' " [1] Benjamin H. Hill of Georgia felt that South Carolina had acted hastily both in respect to her sister states and to the importance of the issue.

[1] Des Arc (Ark.) *Constitutional Union,* January 4, 1861.

"Rather," he queried, "has she not acted with abrupt discourtesy to the claims, wishes, and movements" of the other Southern states? [2]

Such charges were unfair, for secession had been talked all over the South with increasing persistency during the preceding ten years, and every one of the original seven Confederate States had authorized a sovereign convention before South Carolina seceded. Alabama had done so more than eight months before South Carolina acted, but she had been slow in ordering its election. In December, 1859, shortly after John Brown's Raid, South Carolina had tried unsuccessfully to secure a meeting of all the slaveholding states "to concert measures of united action," and Governor William H. Gist had more than a month before Lincoln's election written a confidential letter to various Southern governors informing them that his state would call a convention in the event the South should lose the election.[3] Sundry Southern leaders had urged South Carolina to proceed; and when her convention met, commissioners from Alabama and Mississippi urged her to secede. Furthermore, five days before the convention assembled, a large group of Southern Congressmen in Washington signed a manifesto declaring that the argument was exhausted "and that the sole and primary aim of each slaveholding State ought to be its speedy and absolute separation from an unnatural and hostile Union." [4]

These charges of precipitancy fell flat, and the secession movement, which was already spreading fast before South Carolina acted, increased its speed thereafter. On January 9, 1861, it leaped across intervening states to Mississippi, and on the tenth and eleventh, respectively, Florida and Alabama left the Union. Now only Georgia prevented a solid stretch of seceded territory from the southern border of North Carolina to the Mississippi River. Eight days later this so-called Empire State of the South seceded. Though time was passing fast and the inauguration of Lincoln was rapidly approaching, the movement had not yet spent itself. On January 26 Louisiana withdrew. Except for the half-settled state of Texas, the lower or

[2] Benjamin H. Hill, Jr., *Senator Benjamin H. Hill of Georgia. His Life, Speeches and Writings* (Atlanta, 1893), 39.

[3] James G. Randall, *The Civil War and Reconstruction* (Boston, 1937), 184 n. This work gives an excellent interpretation of the war period.

[4] Edward McPherson, *The Political History of the United States of America, during the Great Rebellion* . . . (2d ed., Washington, 1865), 37.

cotton South had now been accounted for. On February 1 Texas completed the sweep of secession to the Rio Grande. At this time the movement came to a definite halt, with seven states out of the Union.

Secession leaders confidently expected that all fifteen slaveholding states would secede.[5] In fact, the four states of South Carolina, Georgia, Alabama, and Mississippi sent commissioners to the other slaveholding states to urge them to act in this great emergency. And there had been much excitement in these nonseceding states. During January the legislatures of five of them (Tennessee, Virginia, Arkansas, Missouri, and North Carolina, in the order of their acting) provided for conventions, which were either voted down by the people or were hamstrung into inactivity by Unionist members. The legislatures in the three remaining states of Delaware, Maryland, and Kentucky could never bring themselves to the point of calling conventions.

The first wave of secession had spent itself on the Lower South where rampant democracy was much more deeply entrenched than in the Upper South. Here, too, the state-sovereignty teachings of Calhoun had sunk deepest. Reaching political maturity earlier, the Upper South had adopted a more conservative attitude on national as well as sectional issues, a position promoted by exposure to Northern influences, both cultural and economic. Here agricultural economy was becoming more like that of the North, and many small trading connections were having their effect.

There was strong opposition to secession, not only in the Upper South, but also in some parts of the Lower South, the very heart land of the future Confederacy. In every convention except South Carolina's there were votes against secession, and in Alabama and Georgia the opposition was considerable. Even in South Carolina there were Union leaders of long standing. Christopher G. Memminger, destined for important work in the Confederacy, opposed secession until Lincoln's election; James L. Orr, Benjamin F. Perry, and James H. Hammond had Union inclinations; and there was unyielding and unterrified James L. Petigru, who on South Carolina's seceding, sorrowfully remarked, "I have seen the last happy day of

[5] So confident was South Carolina that all fifteen slave states would secede and form another government that she adopted a flag with fifteen stars in it.

my life." [6] In Georgia, Alexander H. Stephens, Herschel V. Johnson, and Benjamin H. Hill gave up their fight for the Union only after their state had seceded and threatened to leave them behind. Texas had its Sam Houston, now governor of the state but ever mindful of the time when he had been the president of the Republic, tenaciously holding that his dignity and that of his state forbade him to follow the headstrong secessionists into withdrawing from the Union and erecting a bogus central government. His stern refusal to call a special session of the legislature led to an unofficial call for a convention, which took Texas out of the Union and deposed Houston.[7]

In their campaign to save the nation, the Unionists resorted both to argument and to delaying tactics. They played on national sentiments; the Revolution and its heroes; the flag; the phenomenal growth of the nation; the Constitution, which largely Southerners had made and which was sufficient for all needs if properly interpreted and enforced. Lincoln had been constitutionally elected, and his entrance into the presidency was no cause for seceding. He was only the executive, and could therefore pass no laws; neither would Congress enact hurtful legislation, at least not during the next two years, for the Republicans lacked thirty of having a majority in the House, and four in the Senate. Nor could Lincoln make executive appointments inimical to the South, for the Senate majority would not confirm them. Up to this time the South had generally dominated the government, either through Southern-born presidents or "dough-faces"—the cutting description of John Randolph of Roanoke for Northern men with Southern principles. Most of the justices of the Supreme Court had been Southerners, and the court at this time was dominated by the South. A majority of other high governmental officials from the days of George Washington had

[6] Lillian A. Kibler, "Unionist Sentiment in South Carolina in 1860," in *Journal of Southern History* (Baton Rouge), IV (1938), 365.

[7] Amelia W. Williams and Eugene C. Barker (eds.), *The Writings of Sam Houston, 1813–1863* (Austin, 1938–1943), VIII, 226, 230, 273; Charles W. Ramsdell, *Reconstruction in Texas* (New York, 1910), 11–20. The standard work on the secession of the Lower South is that of Dwight L. Dumond, *The Secession Movement, 1860–1861* (New York, 1931), who also edited *Southern Editorials on Secession* (New York, 1931). Special studies on states of the Lower South are Clarence P. Denman, *The Secession Movement in Alabama* (Montgomery, 1933); and Percy L. Rainwater, *Mississippi, Storm Center of Secession, 1856–1861* (Baton Rouge, 1938).

been Southerners. Turn about might be fair play. Wait until Lincoln's government had committed some overt act—then the South could move without the onus of precipitating conflict.

It should be remembered that there was a great body of Northern conservatives who were almost as much interested in the welfare of the South as were the Southerners—Northerners had been no less zealous in voting against Lincoln, and the numbers of such were a quarter of a million more than the Southerners. The tenuous hold Lincoln had on the country was well attested by the fact that his popular vote was almost a million short of a majority. The next election might well dethrone him. If the South should set up a new government, the cost of maintaining it would be much greater than continuing under the old.[8]

In fact, the whole idea of secession was illogical and wrong, it was argued. The process should be reversed. The North should do the seceding, for the South represented more truly the nation which the forefathers had set up in 1789. Therefore, the South should not allow itself to be driven out of its own home. Henry A. Wise of Virginia was especially vigorous in arguing this point of view. "Logically the Union belongs to those who have kept, not those who have broken, its covenants," he declared. If he ever had to fight he hoped it would be against a seceding North, "with the star-spangled banner still in one hand and my musket in the other." He would never "take any Southern cross or any palmetto" for his flag.[9]

Furthermore, secession could not be carried out peaceably, for the North would not permit it. Why not bear the ills of the times than fly to others unfathomable? "War I look for as almost certain," said Stephens in February, 1861.[10] It would come, not because some evil genius beyond the control of man had willed it, but "because there are not virtue, patriotism, and sense enough left in the country

[8] Alexander H. Stephens included many of these arguments in his speech before the Georgia legislature, November 14, 1860. See Henry Cleveland, *Alexander H. Stephens in Public and Private. With Letters and Speeches, before, during, and since the War* (Philadelphia, 1866), 694–713. Benjamin H. Hill, the next day at the same place, made additional Union arguments. See Hill, *Benjamin H. Hill*, 237 ff.

[9] Barton H. Wise, *The Life of Henry A. Wise of Virginia, 1806–1876* (New York, 1899), 267, 273.

[10] Richard M. Johnston and William H. Browne, *Life of Alexander H. Stephens* (Philadelphia, 1878), 387.

to avoid it." After the firing on Fort Sumter he said, "we shall be in one of the bloodiest civil wars that history has recorded." [11] Stephens, so unstable in his emotions, having predicted before Georgia seceded that she would do so, was already a defeatist. He moaned, "We are on the high road to ruin I verily believe." [12]

In addition to these arguments the Unionists resorted also to various obstructions. In some of the conventions, they tried to pass resolutions making secession inoperative until certain other states had seceded and also to submit secession ordinances to a vote of the people. Nowhere did the former plan prevail, and in only Texas, Tennessee, and Virginia did the latter. As a delaying tactic, Benjamin H. Hill argued that the North should be confronted with a flat demand for the enforcement of such laws as the fugitive-slave act; if then nothing came of it, the South would be unified by this refusal, and meanwhile the people would have time to make preparations for the new government that would then be necessary.

The best way to carry out such a program would be through the co-operation of all the slave states, and this could be best attained by a convention of these states. In this co-operative movement rested the South's greatest hopes of avoiding secession. First, the voice of fifteen states back of demands on the North would have a tremendously sobering effect on public opinion, far beyond the weak voice of each state as it seceded separately. It would also give time for the disintegrating forces in the Republican party to break up that unnatural conglomeration of factions, held together by nothing but their dislike of slavery. If the South had left the Union by the co-operation plan instead of by individual state action, the new government might have avoided the withering effects of the dissensions that came from the state-rights dogma, which were so powerful in destroying the Confederacy. This plan was brought up in the conventions in various states, but it was never successful.

It was not a far step from the co-operative movement to the idea of holding a national convention in which both the Northern and Southern states should come together to settle their difficulties and save the Union. While wrestling with the problem of secession, the

---

[11] *Autobiography of Col. Richard Malcolm Johnston* (2d ed., Washington, 1901), 152.

[12] Johnston and Browne, *Alexander H. Stephens,* 377.

Virginia legislature called such a conference to meet in Washington on February 4, 1861. Twenty-one states sent delegates at the appointed time, with the seven seceded Southern states, Arkansas, Michigan, Wisconsin, Minnesota, California, and Oregon, unrepresented. After weeks of fruitless discussion it adjourned on the twenty-seventh with seven propositions which it recommended to Congress as amendments to the Constitution, which the Senate promptly rejected.

These propositions presented practically the same plan which the Senate Committee of Thirteen had seen fall by the wayside. Appointed before South Carolina seceded, this Committee sought to compromise the sectional differences. One of its members, John J. Crittenden of Kentucky, presented to the Senate on December 18 his famous compromise measures and a few days later they were referred to his Committee. They consisted of six proposed amendments to the Constitution, the sixth making the preceding five and certain other parts of the Constitution unamendable. All of them dealt with slavery. The old Missouri Compromise line of 36° 30' would be restored, and all states whether north or south of this line would be admitted either slave or free as each pleased. Three proposals would restrict legislative authority: Congress should have no power to free slaves in regions controlled by the Federal government within slave states; it could not free slaves in the District of Columbia without the consent of Virginia and Maryland; and it should have no power to interfere with the interstate slave trade. The United States should pay for all fugitive slaves not returned because of interference by the people of the free states. In addition, four resolutions recommending the enforcement of the fugitive-slave act were included in the Crittenden plan. On Lincoln's advice, the Republicans refused to accept it. Various other compromise propositions were then presented to the Committee but it finally reported that it was unable "to agree upon any general plan of adjustment."

At the same time that the Senate appointed the Committee of Thirteen, the House set up a Committee of Thirty-three, which recommended to that body the so-called Corwin Amendment, named for its author Thomas Corwin of Ohio, forbidding any future amendment giving Congress the right to interfere with slavery

7

in a state. This resolution was passed by both House and Senate and was submitted to the states. If this thirteenth amendment had been ratified, it would, as far as its wording was concerned, have forever riveted slavery on the states except as they themselves should have dealt with the subject; the Thirteenth Amendment which was adopted after the war forever abolished slavery. Many other plans of compromise were suggested during 1861 by individuals, groups, and formal conventions; but all of them failed, for there were enough leaders North and South, either through desire or a lack of statesmanship, to prevent their acceptance. A disconsolate Virginian remarked in April, 1861, that it seemed to him *"honest* reflecting men could settle our difficulties without any dishonor to either section." [13] This was probably the feeling of a great majority of all people in both sections. Crittenden sought unsuccessully to have a national plebiscite on his compromise propositions.

But neither arguments on the part of Southern Unionists, nor their delaying tactics, nor the combined wisdom of both North and South exercising itself through compromise seemed able to save the nation from self-destruction. What mighty force lay back of this Southern movement, which by the beginning of February, 1861, had swept seven states out of the Union? An explanation early accepted and long held by the North made it simply the South's desire to protect slavery. Forty years of wrangling over this subject, fortified by many statements Southerners had made about it, gave ample proof that slavery had had much to do with getting the country into its predicament. The diverging attitudes of the two wings of the Democratic party on this issue in the national convention in 1860 had certainly been responsible for breaking up the party. And in most compromise plans, such as those of the committees of Congress and of the Washington Peace Conference, had not every item related to slavery? South Carolina in her secession declaration had made the North's interference with slavery her greatest grievance, and the subject had appeared equally large in other seceding states. Benjamin M. Palmer, the great Presbyterian theologian and pulpit orator, departed from a religious discourse to a political address in his famous Thanksgiving sermon in New Orleans on November 29,

[13] M. H. Effinger, Harrisonburg, Va., to William Massie, April 30, 1861, in William Massie Papers (University of Texas Library, Austin).

1860, and said that it was the duty of the South "to conserve and to perpetuate the institution of domestic slavery as now existing." [14] The North particularly liked this slavery explanation, for before Lincoln made emancipation a war aim, strategists felt that charging the South with fighting for slavery would secure friends in Europe.

Yet simple answers are never very satisfying, and in this case it was too simple to say that Southerners seceded and fought a four-year war for the surface reason of merely protecting their property in slaves. Had not the South spurned the Corwin Amendment, which guaranteed slavery in the states against all future interference by Congress? And what happened to the subject of slavery in the territories, which had loomed so big in the 1850's? Now it was forgotten by both the North and the South. It had served its purpose. Benjamin H. Hill charged in 1860 that slavery had become a whipping boy for designing politicians in both sections—it had long been "the hobby of the political demagogue." [15] It was something which made it easy to arouse emotions and secure attention. If slavery was the simple fundamental cause, the question immediately arises, why were two thirds of the Southerners, who owned no slaves, as interested in seceding and fighting the war as were the slaveholders? A Richmond editor seemed to be under no delusions when he said, "If there were not a slave from the Aroostock to the Sabine, the North and the South could never permanently agree." [16]

Slavery was undoubtedly a potent cause; but more powerful than slavery was the Negro himself. It was the fear of what would ultimately happen to the South if the Negro should be freed by the North, as the abolitionists seemed so intent on doing—and Southerners considered Republicans and abolitionists the same. This fear had worried Calhoun when he wrote in 1849 "The Address of Southern Delegates in Congress to their Constituents." It was not the loss of property in slaves that the South feared so much as the danger of the South becoming another San Domingo, should a Republican regime free the slaves. And it is no argument to say that Lincoln would never have tried to do this. The South believed that

---

[14] This sermon was printed in pamphlet form and widely circulated. It was also published in *De Bow's Review* (New Orleans, etc.), XXX (1861), 223–36.

[15] Hill, *Benjamin H. Hill*, 38–39.

[16] Richmond *Daily Whig*, April 23, 1862.

his party would force him to it if he did not do so of his own volition. If he were not himself an abolitionist, he had got his position by abolition votes. What Southerners believed to be the fact impelled them to action—not what the fact might have been.[17] A friend of Salmon P. Chase, Secretary of the Treasury, told him that the South's knowledge of what happened in San Domingo and "Self preservation had compelled secession."[18]

Southern leaders were careful not to let the nonslaveholders forget what would happen to them if the slaves were freed. Free Negroes would then overrun the land, claiming social and economic equality with the whites, going to their schools and churches, and taking white men's jobs. The richer whites could flee the country, but the poorer people must remain and endure their degradation. Furthermore, when the government should pay the former slave-owner for his slaves, the money would inevitably come from the taxes collected from the old nonslaveholding class. If the freed Negroes should be removed, then the mass of whites must do the work of the former slaves and would sink to the level of European peasants. Slavery gave to the nonslaveholders their position and standing. They were reminded by a Georgia editor that it was slavery that made "the poor man respectable." It gave the poor "an elevated position in society that they would not otherwise have."[19] That the nonslaveholders were sufficiently convinced of the dangers of Negro equality was eloquently attested by this expression of a North Carolina mountaineer: "To prevent this we are willing to spare the last man, down to the point where women and children begin to suffer for food and clothing; when these begin to suffer and die, rather than see them equalized with an inferior race we will die with them."[20] Joseph E. Brown of Georgia and Albert Gallatin Brown

[17] For the two points of view on this question, see Arthur C. Cole, "Lincoln's Election an Immediate Menace to Slavery in the States?" in *American Historical Review* (New York), XXXVI (1930–1931), 740–67; and J. G. de Roulhac Hamilton, "Lincoln's Election an Immediate Menace to Slavery in the States?" *ibid.*, XXXVII (1931–1932), 700–11.

[18] Richard Ela, Washington, D.C., to Salmon P. Chase, April 12, 1861, in Albert B. Hart (ed.), "Letters to Secretary Chase from the South," in *American Historical Review*, IV (1898–1899), 335.

[19] Atlanta *Southern Confederacy*, October 25, 1862.

[20] D. W. Siler, Franklin, N.C., to Zebulon B. Vance, November 3, 1862, in *War of the Rebellion: A Compilation of the Official Records of the Union and Confederate*

of Mississippi, two outstanding Southern leaders who had risen from the lower middle classes, were eloquent in these warnings.[21] The point that Stephens emphasized in his celebrated "Corner Stone Speech" in Savannah in March, 1861, was not that the mere ownership of slaves should be the cornerstone of the new structure, but that slavery solved the race issue and kept the Negro in the inferior position for which nature had designed him.

Palmer in his Thanksgiving address amplified slavery's role in the Southern structure. Southern civilization in its broadest aspects was economically and otherwise the balance wheel of the nation. Thus the issue went far beneath mere slavery. If the South did not protect itself against the North its whole way of life would be destroyed. It was what lay back of the institution of slavery and was made possible by it which mattered most to Southerners—not simply the money value of slaves.

The more Southerners viewed their own civilization the more they feared the dangers of its disintegration by the infiltration of Northern radicalism and its actual overthrow by continued Northern agitation and outright attack. They shuddered at the thought that they should ever be forced to embrace Northern ways. The deluge of European immigrants with their strange and dangerous ideas had made of Northerners another race. Even basically, it was held, Northerners and Southerners were of different origins. It was the openhearted Cavalier of the South against the tight-fisted Puritan of the North—"the advocate of rational liberty and the support of authority, as against the licentiousness and morbid impulse of unregulated passion and unenlightened sentiment." [22] As William H. Russell put it, Southerners believed that the "New Englander must have something to persecute, and as he has hunted down all his Indians, burnt all his witches, and persecuted all his opponents to the death, he invented abolitionism as the sole resource left to him for the gratification of his favorite passion." [23] In the North

---

Armies (Washington, 1880–1901), Ser. I, Vol. XVIII, 772. Cited hereafter as *Official Records*.

[21] James B. Ranck, *Albert Gallatin Brown; Radical Southern Nationalist* (New York, 1937), 208; Handbill of Joseph E. Brown's Letter of December 5, 1860. See also, *De Bow's Review*, XXX (1861), 67–77; Fayetteville *Arkansian*, March 8, 1861.

[22] *De Bow's Review*, XXXII (1862), 8.

[23] William H. Russell, *The Civil War in America* (Boston, 1861), 45.

there was corruption in state and municipal government; the rulers were King Numbers, agrarian mobs, lawless democracies, black and red Republicans. There were overgrown grimy cities filled with crime and poverty. Beggars were everywhere—not like the South where an Englishman had spent six months and could say, "I never saw a beggar." [24] There were free-soilism, abolitionism, freeloveism, Fourierism, Mormonism, a fanatical press "without honor or modesty," free thought and infidelity, "intemperance and violence and indecorum" of the clergy (where a preacher could be forgiving enough to hope that he might meet the Reverend Benjamin Palmer in heaven, but only after he had been hanged on earth). Northerners were a people "whose wisdom is paltry cunning, whose valor and manhood have been swallowed up in corruption, howling demagoguery, and in the marts of dishonest commerce." [25] Capital and labor were in perpetual conflict; there was neither the orderly relation which existed between master and slave nor the social security which the slave possessed. There was likely to be a violent social upheaval, not unlike the French Revolution, and the South did not care to be a part of the country undergoing it.

A Yankee was a man who would "ask you twenty questions in half an hour" and would "walk five miles to make a cent." [26] According to a Southern rhymster,

> Yankee Doodle is a knave,
>   And everybody knows it,
> And swindling is his natural trade,
>   For by his tricks he shows it.
> He'll go to church and sing and pray,
>   Be full of grace on Sunday,
> With wooden hams and paper shoes,
>   He'll cheat you on a Monday.[27]

[24] Rev. William W. Malet, *An Errand to the South in the Summer of 1862* (London, 1863), 212.

[25] Russell, *Civil War in America*, 44. See also, *Southern Literary Messenger* (Richmond), XXXII (1861), 334; XXXIII (1861), 241–48; *Southern Illustrated News* (Richmond), I (October 25, 1862), 2; Edward Mayes, *Lucius Q. C. Lamar; His Life, Times and Speeches, 1825–1893* (Nashville, 1896), 637.

[26] *The Burckmyer Letters, March, 1863–June, 1865* (Columbia, 1926), 31.

[27] Augusta *Weekly Chronicle & Sentinel*, April 7, 1863.

If the Southerners believed this picture of their Northern brethren, there should be little wonder that they wanted to get away as far as possible from them and fight not only for independence but for "all that is valuable in morals and legislation and religion." As a Southern clergyman said, "We have been selected to be a bulwark against the worst developments of human nature, fanaticism, democracy, license, atheism." [28] The Southerner wanted his own country, one that he could love and take pride in. In fact, the Southern movement was a revolt of conservatism against the modernism of the North. It was the normal reaction of an isolated landed civilization against the world currents of trade and industry.

So when Lincoln was elected and it seemed that he and his party would attempt to remake Southerners in the image of the North, it needed little further argument to induce them to leave the Union. It was not simply the fact of Lincoln's election that induced the South to secede and it was not solely the fact that he had been elected by the people of one section of the country; it was the fact that a sectional party with a sectional program dangerous to the other section had come into power. That had never happened before. A new nation would give the South a chance to profit from its own wealth and prevent the North from siphoning away an estimated $100,000,000 annually. It would also relieve the South from helping to pay for the special privileges which the North alone enjoyed, such as bounties on fisheries and such aids to commerce as harbor works and lighthouses. The South would save enough on cotton to pay the cost of a new government. According to the Declaration of the South Carolina convention, the South stood "exactly in the same position toward the Northern States that our ancestors in the Colonies did toward Great Britain." Southerners had a high sense of honor; they could not bear to be deprived of their equal position in the Union which the North would do by excluding slavery from the territories. Southerners would really take few slaves into the remaining territories, but they deeply resented a principle which said they could not. In early December, 1860, Howell Cobb

[28] *Gideon's Water-Lappers. A Sermon Preached in Christ Church, Savannah, on Friday, the 8th Day of April, 1864, the Day set apart by the Congress of the Confederate States, as a Day of Humiliation. Fasting and Prayer* (Macon, 1864), 20–21.

of Georgia said, "Equality and safety in the Union are at an end.
. . . This issue must now be met, or forever abandoned," [29] and the
South Carolina secession convention declared in its Address that the
Constitution of the United States had been "absorbed by its pre-
amble" and that the tyranny of the majority prevailed—"The very
object of all constitutions in free popular government, is to restrain
the majority." After a few states had seceded the Unionists' argument that Lincoln's party did not have a majority in the House and
Senate disappeared, for the withdrawal of Southern Congressmen
soon gave the Republicans that fatal majority. To wait for an overt
act by Lincoln was to wait until he had riveted chains of bondage
on the Southerners, making it impossible for them to act thereafter.
They should strike while the iron was hot. Even Stephens said that
if secession must come it ought to come quickly.

This same argument answered the co-operation movement. It was
purely a scheme to delay action and confuse the Southerners. And
there was this additional reason against that method: The Constitution forbade states to contract alliances among themselves or to
make treaties. Southerners' inborn respect for legalism made them
resort to secession rather than to radical revolution. Secession, they
argued, was constitutional, for it had not been forbidden by the
Constitution; and as Jefferson Davis later ingeniously argued, the
present Union had grown up through secession from the old Confederation.[30] Memminger said in May, 1861: "The South has always exhibited the example of communities in which law prevails;
and the secession of the Southern States gives to history a splendid
illustration of peaceful Revolution." [31]

The secessionists were at great pains to impress the fact that secession and war were not the same, and that secession would never
lead to war. Robert Barnwell Rhett is said to have remarked in a
Charleston theater that he would eat the bodies of all people slain

[29] Ulrich B. Phillips (ed.), *The Correspondence of Robert Toombs, Alexander H. Stephens, and Howell Cobb,* in American Historical Association, *Annual Report,* 1911, II (Washington, 1913), 515; *De Bow's Review,* XXX (1861), 356.

[30] Message to Congress, January 12, 1863, in James D. Richardson (comp.), *A Compilation of the Messages and Papers of the Confederacy, Including the Diplomatic Correspondence, 1861–1865* (Nashville, 1906), I, 278.

[31] Christopher G. Memminger to John Boston, Collector of Customs at Savannah, May 1, 1861, in "I CSA Treasury 1861" (Division of Manuscripts, Library of Congress).

in a war following secession, and James Chesnut, Jr., was likewise reported to have said that he would drink all the blood shed.[32] A common saying during these days was: "A lady's thimble will hold all the blood that will be shed." A month after Fort Sumter, Cobb was still hopeful. "If we can go forty days without a conflict," he said, "there will be no war—I stand to that opinion still & find others begin to concur." [33] In a spirit of banter, some Southerners said a Yankee could never be made into a soldier, for before pulling the trigger of his gun he would shut his eyes and turn his head away. What one should do if he met a Northern soldier provided a joke that early went the rounds: "If I should see a yankee with his gun levelled and looking right at me, I will draw out my pocket book and ask him what he will take for his gun, and right there the fight would end." [34]

Secession came and the people celebrated—as if a great burden had suddenly rolled off their shoulders. In one small town there was a salute of a hundred guns, a balloon was sent up, and the houses were illuminated. Similar celebrations took place throughout the South, including street parades with blaring bands, torchlight processions, and fireworks. Variegated cockades (called "badges of treason" by the Unionists) were worn from Maryland to the Gulf of Mexico. People should not celebrate and fiddle while Rome was burning, warned Benjamin H. Hill. "But is it not strange," he exclaimed, "that we should fire cannons, illumine cities, raise bonfires, and make noisy the still hours of night with shouts over the destruction of a government infinitely greater than Rome ever was!" [35] The inevitable poet added his mite, as an untamed literary genius from Texas demonstrated in this stanza:

> *Assassins and demons, a joyful good-bye;*
> *Ye ghouls and hyenas, howl on till ye die;*
> *Disgraced and degraded, polluted with crime,*
> *Be the scoff and the scorn of the world*
> *throughout time!* [36]

[32] Charleston *Daily Courier,* October 27, 1863.
[33] Howell Cobb, Montgomery, to his wife, May 11, 1861, in **Howell Cobb Papers** (in private possession).
[34] Macon *Daily Telegraph,* April 23, 1861.
[35] Hill, *Benjamin H. Hill,* 39–40.   [36] Richmond *Daily Whig,* August 12, 1862.

Was the charge true, so often made and so long believed in the North, that secession was the work of a dozen or two conspirators? [37] Outside of a few very wealthy and a few extremely poor, the contagion of secession swept the Lower South in the spring of 1861. And many of the very lowly were filled with unspeakable zeal. An illiterate Alabama father wrote his son in Mississippi who had turned secessionist, "It was disgusting to me to think that I had Raised a child that would Cecede from under the government that he was born and raised under." Had he forgotten his Revolutionary ancestors? "Tha have got you puft up with Cecessionism as tight as a tode   I dont See what you nede to Care for   you hant got no Slaves." The son, equally illiterate, scrawled across this letter: "Henry Bell Is my Name and fite I will before I will submit to black republican princibles lose my life I will first." [38] Another Alabama father wrote his son, "Alas to my sorrow you have proved to be a cesessionist." [39] Secession was more likely to sweep the young off their feet, but leave the old people doubting or disconsolate. A venerable old South Carolinian exclaimed, "I have lived too long. I should have died ere these evil days arrived." [40]

Secession was certainly regarded as a people's movement by the Southerners of 1861. Mrs. James Chesnut, Jr., keen observer of conditions in the South, said that the people everywhere had "been complaining bitterly of slow and lukewarm public leaders." [41] To the governor of Mississippi came the opinion of a fellow citizen,

[37] The irrepressible William G. Brownlow, Unionist from East Tennessee, extended the number of conspirators to make it include abolitionists as well. In a speech in Cincinnati, in April, 1862, he said, "If I had been authorized, some two or three years ago, to select about two or three hundred of your most abominable anti-Slavery agitators in the North, and an equal number of our God-forsaken and most hell-deserving Disunionists at the South, and had marched them to the District of Columbia, hanged them on a common gallows, dug for them a common grave, and embalmed their bodies with *jimson-weed* and *dog-fennel,* there would have been none of this trouble, nor should I have been here tonight!" Cincinnati *Daily Commercial,* April 7, 1862.

[38] J. B. Bell to son Henry, April 21, 1861 (Alabama State Archives, Montgomery).
[39] Unsigned letter from Tensaw P.O., April 21, 1861, *ibid.*
[40] William H. Russell, *My Diary North and South* (Boston, 1863), 117.
[41] Isabella D. Martin and Myrta Lockett Avary (eds.), *A Diary from Dixie, as Written by Mary Boykin Chesnut, Wife of James Chesnut, Jr., United States Senator from South Carolina, 1859–1861, and Afterward an Aide to Jefferson Davis and a Brigadier-General in the Confederate Army* (New York, 1905), 2.

"Sure as you live the people are a long way in advance of those they have honored with the posts of Leadership." [42] A Georgia editor declared that the politicians had not made secession in his state: "The act of seceding from the United States was done by the people, and by them alone." [43] Any persons of prominence, especially those found on passing trains, were besieged by the people with demands for speeches. An acquaintance of Salmon P. Chase, in Augusta, Georgia, reported to him in March, 1861, that there were not "in the Confederate States, one thousand men, who" would not "sacrifice all"; and another in New Orleans the following May reported to Chase that the South was a unit for independence. [44] An Englishman, traveling through the Confederacy a year later, declared he found the people equally determined to be free. [45]

Most Southerners who had been Unionists before secession gave up this position after the act. Especially old Whigs, like Stephens, were in this class. Legalistic Southerners had a strong feeling of allegiance to their state. They believed that their national citizenship (not yet clearly defined in American jurisprudence) came through their state citizenship. When their state seceded they lost their national citizenship, and not to go along with their state made them traitors or men without a country.

In the early days of the movement there was much talk and some fear that the people did not consider secession permanent. It was merely taking a position of vantage, from which a trade or compromise could be made to bring them back into the Union. Thus, in the very beginning, did the word *reconstruction* gain currency. In fact, one of the luring arguments of the secessionists had been, "We can make better terms out of the Union than in it." Stephens believed that Thomas R. R. Cobb, an emotional Georgia secessionist and brother of Howell Cobb, had used this argument with telling force. There was in reality slight vitality in the sentiment of returning to the Union—though Stephens never gave up the secret hope that the Union would be "reconstructed." The South had too long

[42] Charles D. Fontaine to Gov. J. J. Pettus, November 12, 1860 (Mississippi State Archives, Jackson).

[43] Sandersville *Central Georgian*, March 6, 1861.

[44] J. McCormick, Augusta, Ga., to Chase, March 6, 1861, in Hart (ed.), "Letters to Secretary Chase from the South," *loc. cit.*, 332.

[45] Malet, *Errand to the South*, 36–37.

dreamed of the day when it would have its own government. Even without the slavery issue there was enough feeling of separateness to set many of the people to longing for independence from the North. William Porcher Miles, South Carolinian, said never again would he live within the old Union; Rhett admitted that he had hoped for Southern independence for thirty years; Lawrence M. Keitt, another South Carolinian, said, "I have been engaged in this movement ever since I entered political life"; [46] and it had long been a passion with William L. Yancey, born in South Carolina but now living in Alabama. To smother any movement for compromise that might crop up, South Carolinians formed The 1860 Association, an organization which issued propaganda pamphlets until they were no longer needed.

Secession had in fact merely recognized a division of the country that was already almost complete except for the bonds of government. The churches of the masses, the Methodists and Baptists, had broken away from the North fifteen years previously; the Democratic party crumbled in 1860; the Republicans had never had any support in the South; John Brown's Raid made many reluctant Southerners admit what they had previously refused to see—that there was no longer a union of hearts and souls between North and South. Verily, as Howell Cobb had said, "Black Republicanism" had "buried brotherhood in the same grave with the Constitution." [47]

The North had, in the eyes of the Southerners, assumed a nagging and holier-than-thou attitude. Nothing Southern seemed to please some Northerners. Being proud of their personal integrity and of the worth of their own civilization, Southerners set a limit to the insults and vilification they would endure. It was never in their minds that they could be goaded into fighting their traducers, except on a personal basis, which they always stood ready to do as only gentlemen could do, in the duel. They would as a people withdraw their presence from that part of the country that delighted in insulting them. They would secede—not engage in an unseemly brawl.

[46] *American Annual Cyclopaedia and Register of Important Events of the Year 1861* (New York, 1866), 122.

[47] Phillips (ed.), *Correspondence of Toombs, Stephens, and Cobb,* 516.

CHAPTER II

THE CONFEDERATE STATES
OF AMERICA

B Y THE beginning of February, seven states—the heart land of the South—had left the Union. These states now claimed to be independent nations, and some of their citizens, reveling in their newly got importance, used in their correspondence "Republic of Mississippi," "Republic of Georgia," and so on. More seriously, their governments began to act in their sovereign capacities by seizing Federal forts and other property, sending agents to Europe, organizing armies, setting up customs barriers, and as did Mississippi, providing for a postmaster general. Thus was Calhoun's state rights, which they had been brought up on, running riot.

There was little likelihood, however, that these states would not cluster themselves into some sort of a central government, for the Southern movement had long had this as its logical conclusion. When South Carolina seceded, she urged that departing states band themselves together as soon as possible into a new union to secure protection and added strength. And she suggested Montgomery, Alabama, as the meeting place. It was the special desire of Robert Barnwell Rhett that Montgomery be selected, for there he would have the strong support of Alabama's William L. Yancey in erecting a permanent government that would never turn back. Practically all the secession conventions, the commissioners from one state to another, and the twelve Southern Senators in their conference in Washington on January 5, fell in line with the idea. The Senators had urged that the states meet not later than the fifteenth of February.[1]

[1] *Official Records*, Ser. I, Vol. I, 443–44. For garbled accounts, see Edward A. Pollard, *Life of Jefferson Davis, with a Secret History of the Southern Confederacy, Gathered*

19

There was great need to hurry, for Abraham Lincoln would become President on March 4, and thereafter the Southerners might have harder days ahead than they had been enjoying under President James Buchanan, who had said that states had no right to secede but he had no constitutional power to force them back. Alabama's secession convention called the meeting for February 4 in Montgomery—giving this new South one month to organize a government and take on strength before a Republican should seek to direct its destiny. Despite the need for speed there was a scattered feeling that the seceded states were moving too fast, for some of the states of the Upper South had not yet called sovereign conventions and to them it might well appear that the Lower South was attempting to control the destiny of the whole section by setting up a government and putting its own leaders into the offices. The old love for the Union was not yet dead in the hearts of many who were active in the secession movement. To them, setting up a new government would make reconciliation thereafter the harder. In December, 1860, Lucius Q. C. Lamar, who was later to father the secession ordinance in Mississippi, devised an ingenious plan whereby the South could secede and still keep the old Union. Having seceded it would meet in convention and adopt the Constitution of the United States and all its treaties and laws, even taking the name of United States of America and calling the rest of the country the United States of North America. As soon as this had been done the governors of the states would provide for the election of a congress and a new president to take the place of Lincoln.[2] As foolish as this might sound, it tended to satisfy a deep longing in the hearts of many Southerners, high and low, and was somewhat an equivalent of Wise's idea that the North should secede—not the South. There was long the fear on the part of some Southerners that Lamar's plan might be extended into an all-devouring movement which would be made to bring into the maw of the Southern government most of the states of the North—all except New England, which would be sternly rejected. And thus the South would restore the Union by this method of accretion.

"Behind the Scenes in Richmond" (Philadelphia, 1869), 61–66; *American Annual Cyclopaedia . . . 1861*, pp. 125–26.

2 Mayes, *Lucius Q. C. Lamar*, 88, 637, 638.

Kentucky-born George N. Sanders, promoter, revolutionist, adventurer, and subsequent Confederate agent, appeared at the Montgomery Convention, supposedly an agent now of Stephen A. Douglas, to see that the free states were not excluded from joining this new government-in-the-making. That devoutly passionate Southerner Thomas R. R. Cobb declared, "The game, now, is to reconstruct *under our* Constitution."[3] The equally irreconcilable Rhett stood out against the new government admitting free states, voicing this same fear. The South wanted to be let alone, to be itself without any dilutions from the North.

In regard to providing for the Montgomery Convention and in supporting it, the feeling was almost universal at this time that the least possible break with the past should be made. There must be nothing done which would suggest that a violent revolution was in progress, for fear not only that enthusiasm for the new day might die down in the seceded South but that it would be prevented from ever growing up in the Upper South and the Border states. Thus it was that from every quarter came the cry that the old Federal Constitution should be adopted with only the most necessary changes. Southerners had never had a quarrel with this document, interpreted as they saw it. Stephens had refused to become a delegate to the Montgomery meeting until the Georgia Convention recommended the old Federal Constitution. Also the flag and the laws should be kept, as far as possible. In these early days there was a slight trace of opinion to the effect that the meeting in Montgomery should be only advisory and should do very little toward erecting a government. In this opinion even the old Confederation had had too stringent a government. There was already too much government; why make more? The states could get along as semi-independent entities.[4] If the general government were kept weak and poor, the inevitable consequence would be that "the prime talent of the Confederation" would be "engaged by the States, and not by the General Congress."[5] The ghost of Calhoun was walking again.

[3] Thomas R. R. Cobb, Montgomery, to his wife, March 6, 1861, in Thomas R. R. Cobb Letters (typescripts in University of Georgia Library).

[4] Augusta *Chronicle & Sentinel,* which claimed to be one of the most widely circulated journals in the Confederacy, thought so. See also, Athens *Southern Watchman,* February 7, 1861. [5] Atlanta *Gate City Guardian,* February 14, 1861.

Strangely enough there was some feeling now, and later to grow much stronger, that there should be little framework of government, but for the opposite reason: To make possible a strong dictator, even a Cromwell or a Napoleon to forge the South into a mighty thunderbolt in the approaching war that many foresaw. As Yancey looked back, he believed this would have been the better policy. How could a government, born fighting for its life, be expected to give heed to every little punctilio observed in peacetime? The weakness of this argument is evident when it is noted that the people at this stage would never have followed such a government, and the Upper South and Border states would have remained aloof.

The Montgomery Convention met according to call, on February 4, composed of delegates selected by the secession conventions, varying in number from three representing Florida to ten from Georgia. The tendency was to keep the number about the same as the state's representation had been in Congress, though Texas, with four Congressmen, sent seven delegates. The number was not of great importance, as each state, being a sovereign, had only one vote. Some of the delegates had been recent members of Congress who had made their farewell addresses and returned home; the total number in Montgomery at any one time varied from forty-one to fifty. They constituted the best the South had to offer. Few who were well known nationally were not there; and these were soon to be levied upon for high office, either in the civil service or the military. Surprisingly, Yancey was not a member, but he was an onlooker. One observer remarked that they were "plain farmer looking, serious men, invested with a sort of unaffected revolutionary simplicity." [6] As another saw them, they were "grave and reverend looking." There was Stephens, "a little sallow, dried-up looking fellow"; the awful fire-eater Rhett, yet mild-looking with his gold-rimmed spectacles; Benjamin H. Hill of Georgia, with his great physique and fine open countenance; Howell Cobb, "fat, pussy, round-faced, jolly looking fellow"; his brother Thomas, of "youthful look, with a clear face and long hair"; and the others, each mostly as nature made him.[7]

[6] Richmond *Daily Examiner*, July 22, 1861.
[7] Huntsville *Southern Advocate*, February 20, 1861.

They immediately set to work, for time was of the very essence of their existence. Howell Cobb was made president by acclamation, and the next day a committee was appointed to draw up a constitution. It was reported two days later, February 7, and, after a day's debate with some minor amendments, was adopted unanimously. The constitution was to be provisional only and should not continue more than a year. The immediate need was to provide offices to be filled so that the government might begin to function at once. Being largely an adaptation of the Federal Constitution, it had been made in record time.

Everything had run so smoothly up to this time, in these honeymoon days of the Confederacy, that the leaders were doubly determined that nothing should mar the equally important task of filling the two high offices of the presidency and vice-presidency. Only one name for each office should be voted for. No one should be formally nominated, but the states would vote instinctively for one name. In this excessive zeal for unanimity and harmony seems to lie the explanation of why Jefferson Davis instead of Robert Toombs was elected President. Various leaders were in a receptive mood for this position, but there was no semblance of a campaign for it. Rhett felt that his long service in the forefront of the Southern movement fitted him for the office, and though there were other fire-eaters in the Convention they were never able to direct the proceedings—Rhett got nowhere. The other great fire-eater, Yancey, had long stood out in the popular imagination as the logical president of a Southern nation. It was claimed by some who thought they knew, that Yancey was eliminated with his own consent, when it appeared that Virginia would find it very difficult to secede and join a government presided over by so dangerous a person as Yancey—a man who would be certain to stir up a war with the North. So to save Virginia, Yancey stepped aside.[8] Was this why Yancey never fulfilled his earlier promise of leadership, was shunted off to England, and died at the height of the Confederate struggle?

[8] John W. Du Bose, *The Life and Times of William Lowndes Yancey. A History of Political Parties in the United States, from 1834 to 1864; Especially as to the Origin of the Confederate States* (Birmingham, 1892), 588; A Memoir by F. M. Gilmer, one of Alabama's commissioners to Virginia, in the secession movement, written about May, 1880, in "Collection. Autograph Letters, Documents, Manuscripts, etc., Relating to the Confederacy, 1861–1865," Case IV (University of Texas Library).

Howell Cobb had a large following, but he was still tainted by his Unionism of the early 1850's, which eliminated him; and besides he was already president of the Convention. He told his wife, at least, that he did not want to be President of the Confederacy.[9] Stephens confided to some of his friends that he wanted no position in the new government, but so uncertain were his emotions that he was never known to have refused an office. The presidency was not offered him. Robert Toombs, able and ambitious, ponderous of body and keen of mind, had a burning desire for the position. In passing him by, the Confederacy lost the great talents of this man, destined to disintegrate more and more as a feeling of frustration gripped him when he saw his suggestions ignored. After the war his friend Stephens said, "But of all the men in the Confederate States, I thought Mr. Toombs was by far the best fitted for that position, looking to all the qualifications necessary to meet its full requirements." [10]

Then, there was Jefferson Davis of Mississippi but more strictly of nowhere in particular, so much had he moved around, who had been somewhat of an extremist in the early fifties but who had become much more conservative of late. He had been early, frequently, and widely mentioned for the presidency. Virginians liked him; his farewell address on leaving the Senate in January, 1861, had greatly pleased them. They much preferred him to Yancey. But Davis had also been mentioned as a possible commander in chief of the Confederate armies; and this pleased him, for he still remembered his services in the Mexican War and his term as Secretary of War under President Pierce. A fellow Mississippian on asking him whether he would take the presidency if it were offered to him received the reply that he would rather be commander in chief of the armies, but that he would serve wherever directed.[11]

9 Cobb, Montgomery, to his wife, February 6, 1861, in Phillips (ed.), *Correspondence of Toombs, Stephens, and Cobb*, 537.

10 Alexander H. Stephens, *A Constitutional View of the Late War Between the States; its Causes, Character, Conduct and Results. Presented in a Series of Colloquies at Liberty Hall* (Philadelphia, 1868–1870), II, 332–33.

11 *Ibid.*, 329 ff.; Johnston and Browne, *Alexander H. Stephens*, 389; Alexander H. Stephens, *The Reviewers Reviewed; A Supplement to the "War Between the States,"* etc., *with an Appendix in Review of "Reconstruction," So Called* (New York, 1872),

So, as there must be no contest on the floor of the Convention, it was necessary for the various state delegations to agree on a name beforehand. The word was soon abroad that Georgia would have a candidate to present; and some of the delegations, assuming that Howell Cobb would be the person, let it be known that they would oppose Georgia. Before the confusion could be cleared up, that Toombs and not Cobb was the Georgia candidate, Davis had been endorsed by the various delegations, meeting in different places the night before the election. The next day Davis was unanimously elected. Georgia, in withdrawing her candidate Toombs, submitted Stephens for the vice-presidency, and he also was elected unanimously. The elections took place on February 9.

These men were highly in keeping with this revolution that was not a revolution but more a counterrevolution—both were conservatives and Stephens was always a Unionist at heart. Enthusiasm was now running high in Montgomery and throughout this new nation. "Three cheers and a tiger for the new Government!" exclaimed one editor;[12] another reminiscently observed that it was the "posthumous child" of John A. Quitman, that Mississippi firebrand of the fifties.[13] Both President and Vice-President were accepted openly almost unanimously as the best possible choices; but privately there were some sour feelings about Stephens. The sensitive, hypercritical Thomas R. R. Cobb wrote his wife that his fellow Georgian was "a bitter pill to some of us but we have swallowed it with as good grace as we could."[14] Wryly he wrote that

---

147. Another explanation, of little or no validity, was that Toombs attended a dinner party given by some of the members of the convention and took too much wine. The spectacle he made led people to believe he would not make a dependable President. Johnston, *Autobiography*, 124–25. William H. Trescot observed that the possibility of Stephens' becoming President was an unpleasant thought. "I think there can be no doubt," he wrote, "that the popular expectation is that Cobb will be President and Davis Lieut. General." William H. Trescot, Charleston, to William Porcher Miles, Montgomery, February 6, 1861, in William Porcher Miles Papers (University of North Carolina Library, Chapel Hill). These and other manuscripts at this depository are in the Southern Historical Collection.

12 Grove Hill (Ala.) *Clarke County Democrat*, February 14, 1861.

13 Natchez *Mississippi Free Trader*, February 18, 1861.

14 Cobb, Montgomery, to his wife, February 9, 1861, in Thomas R. R. Cobb Letters. P. G. T. Beauregard, in New Orleans, writing to Jefferson Davis, at Montgomery, February 10, 1861, in Pierre Gustave Toutant Beauregard Papers (Manuscript Division, Duke University Library, Durham), wished "to express to you the universal

the man who had fought against the South's rights and liberties was selected "to wear the laurels of our victory." That night Stephens with most of the celebrities in Montgomery was serenaded, but his health, which he long used as one of his most clever strategies, forbade his making a long speech. On February 11 he was inaugurated in a simple, unheralded ceremony; and as became the occasion he made only a few remarks, none relating to policies.

Eager to set the new government going, the Convention inaugurated Stephens before Davis could arrive. In the rose garden on his plantation below Vicksburg, Davis had been notified of his election. With mixed emotions he immediately set out for Montgomery, but the absence of a railway from Meridian on to Montgomery led him to make a roundabout trip from Vicksburg to Jackson, north to the Memphis and Charleston Railroad in Tennessee, eastward to Chattanooga, south to Atlanta, and west to Montgomery. This long trip gave him an opportunity to show himself to the multitudes who came out in masses at every station shouting their greetings, firing off guns by day and setting off bonfires by night. He made at least twenty-five short speeches. On arriving in Montgomery he was taken in hand by Yancey, who ended his speech of welcome at the Exchange Hotel with these famous words, "The man and the hour have met. We may now hope that prosperity, honor and victory await his administration." [15]

The people were hungry for a display, and they now got it in Davis' inauguration on the eighteenth. With Stephens and Howell Cobb he entered an elegant carriage drawn by six iron-gray horses "driven by that veteran 'whip' Prof. Snow," and to the tune of "Dixie," now first set to a band performance, proceeded up the commanding hill to the capitol, amidst thousands of cheering Confederates.[16] The day was propitious, balmy and flooded with sunshine. Nearly six feet tall, slight of frame and frail, but straight as an Indian chief, with thin lips and sharply defined features, with agreeable, unassuming, easy manners, an "indescribable charm in his voice," though shrill in oratory, an air of easy command—in

---

sentiment of approval that this choice has been greeted with here & elsewhere— everyone feeling convinced that the honor & prosperity of the country shall be safe in your Jacksonian hands."

[15] Montgomery *Weekly Mail*, February 22, 1861.   [16] *Ibid.*

fine an unaffected gentleman—Davis was now about to assume command. No President of the United States ever had a more difficult task. Washington had inaugurated a new government, but in peacetime; Lincoln had a government of long standing and strength; Wilson was to have a bigger theater in which to operate, but he had the richest government on earth and the resources of nearly all the world back of him. From the portico of the Alabama capitol, Davis delivered his inaugural address. This was no revolution; it was merely a transfer of rulership. He hoped for peace, but he was resolved on independence for the South, and if war must come, the South would accept it. The London *Times* declared, "The inaugural ceremonies today were the grandest pageant ever witnessed in the South," and, to show how important it regarded the occasion, published the text of his address.[17]

All of what had taken place up to this point was provisional; President Davis and Vice-President Stephens were merely provisional officers, elected only for a year at most. The constitution under which they assumed office was provisional, only a stopgap until a permanent constitution could be written. Of course, most of its provisions were to be taken over into the new constitution and amplified, but some of its features were unique. Under it, the congress consisted of one house, that congress being the Convention itself. The president and vice-president were to be elected by the states, each casting one vote; the supreme court should be made up of the judges of the district courts; the capital would be Montgomery until the congress should change it; and this constitution could be amended by a two-thirds vote of the congress. The next day after the adoption of this constitution, a committee had been appointed to report the text of a permanent document, and for the next month it gave much attention to this task. On February 28, Congress took up the discussion of the text which had been presented by the committee, and each day, resolving itself into a constitutional convention, discussed and amended this document until finally on March 11 the Convention adopted it by a unanimous vote.[18]

[17] London *Times*, March 7, 1861. The most accessible source of this address is Richardson (comp.), *Messages and Papers of the Confederacy*, I, 32–36.

[18] The proceedings of the convention may be found in *Journal of the Congress of*

The Permanent Constitution of the Confederate States of America has remained one of the most interesting documents of fundamental law in America, not for its underlying principles, for they as well as most of the language coincided with the Federal Constitution, but for its clarifications and additions. All of the twelve amendments of the old document were worked into the text of this one and "Almighty God" was included in the pre-amble.[19] The President and Vice-President should serve for terms of six years and the President should be ineligible for re-election; [20] the President should have the right to veto separate items in an appropriation bill; and he must report his reasons to the Senate for the removal of any officers except cabinet members and diplomatic officials. With the consent of Congress, cabinet members might have seats upon the floor of either house to discuss measures relating to their respective departments.[21] Congress could not grant bounties, foster any branch of industry by a protective tariff, levy an export tax except by a two-thirds majority, provide money for internal improvements, nor make any appropriations without a two-thirds majority unless asked for in the Presidential budget, excepting its own expenses and the just claims against the Confederate government. No law should relate to more than one subject, which must be clearly expressed in the title. The general-welfare clause, the source of so much elasticity in the Federal

the Confederate States of America, 1861–1865 (Washington, 1904–1905), I, 851–96. The original vellum manuscript Permanent Constitution with the signatures of all the signers is in the University of Georgia Library; the original Provisional Constitution is in the Confederate Museum in Richmond.

19 It was an ardent desire of Thomas R. R. Cobb to include in the Constitution a reference to the Deity. He also wanted a provision against Sunday mails, but he failed in this endeavor. Many of the clergy and other deeply religious Americans had long bemoaned the absence of a reference to God in the Federal Constitution.

20 A presidential succession bill passed by the Confederate Congress became law on April 19, 1862. It provided for the succession, after the Vice-President, through the president *pro tempore* of the Senate and the speaker of the House. James M. Matthews (ed.), *Public Laws of the Confederate States of America, Passed at the First Session of the First Congress, 1862* (Richmond, 1862), 46–47.

21 This seems to have been the idea of Stephens and Toombs, who were admirers of the British parliamentary system. Burton J. Hendrick, *Statesmen of the Lost Cause; Jefferson Davis and his Cabinet* (Boston, 1939), 102. The *Illustrated London News* (London), XXXVIII (March 30, 1861), 284, in referring to this parliamentary innovation queried, "Is this a step towards the adoption of some of the so-called aristocratic customs of the old country?"

Constitution, was left out. The Post Office Department must after its first two years be self-sufficient. Unlike that of the Federal Constitution, the prohibition against foreign slave trade was strengthened and made mandatory,[22] and the bald words "slave" and "slavery" were used instead of the circumlocutionary expression "those bound to Service for a Term of Years." The right to slavery was guaranteed in the territories. To prevent unnaturalized foreigners from voting as they did in the old government, the Constitution withheld suffrage from all who were not citizens. As a special recognition to the rights of the states, Confederate officials whose duties lay wholly within one state were subject to impeachment by the state legislature; also, where a river flowed between or crossed two or more states, they might enter into an agreement to improve its navigation. Furthermore, in the preamble a salute to state sovereignty was made in these words, "each State acting in its sovereign and independent character." New states might be admitted by a vote of two thirds of all the Representatives and Senators, the Senate voting by states.[23]

All power of amending this Constitution was taken out of the hands of Congress. Any three states agreeing on amendments made it mandatory on Congress to call a convention of all the states, and should this convention agree on these amendments, voting by states, it must submit them to the states, and if two thirds of them through their legislatures or conventions agreed, then the amendments should become part of the Constitution.

Though the right of a state to secede was being bitterly disputed by the Federal government at this time and though there was discussion of this point in the Confederate Convention, the Constitution was left silent on this point. President Davis declared that this Constitution "admits of no coerced association" and that this rule of voluntary union had great merit by making the central government doubly regardful of the rights of the states. This

[22] The states and territories of the United States were excepted from this provision, as a gesture of friendship for the slave states which had not yet seceded; but Congress was given the right to apply the exclusion principle. This power could be used to induce the slave states to secede and join the Confederacy.

[23] There was great opposition in South Carolina to this principle, as it permitted the admission of free states. There were even threats that South Carolina might secede from the Confederacy. Athens *Southern Watchman*, April 3, 1861.

was an admission that a state had the right to secede. Yet as time went on and tempers wore thin, there were frequent demands that the right to secede be put into the Constitution.[24] In 1863 Herschel V. Johnson, Senator from Georgia, developed an ingenious scheme of definitely allowing secession as a method of strengthening the Confederacy. Forgetting how to amend the Confederate document, but remembering the old Federal method, he introduced resolutions in Congress, somewhat reminiscent of Calhoun's nullification doctrines, providing that when a state declared a Confederate law unconstitutional, a national convention should be called to discuss the issue. Whether it declared the law constitutional or not, a dissatisfied state might secede. This was a slowing-down process that might save the state for the union. When it was pointed out that this was not the way to amend the Constitution, Johnson withdrew his resolutions.[25] Very soon people with grudges against some Confederate official were suggesting various other amendments. The editor of the Richmond *Whig* was a chronic amender, and letter writers in his paper echoed his sentiments. He thought the old Articles of Confederation would have been ideal. He would have the President elected by the state legislatures; to get rid of disliked cabinet members he would give Congress the right to force their resignation by a two-thirds vote. No official should receive more than $1,000 a year, and the President and Congressmen should serve without pay—the honor should be enough for any patriot. The President should appoint only cabinet members, foreign ministers, and members of the Confederate Supreme Court; the Supreme Court should appoint district judges, who should appoint officers of the courts, and district attorneys should appoint customs officials and postmasters—this was to clip the power of President Davis. The House should have five hundred members to represent fully all the interests of the Confederacy, and

[24] There was long an erroneous opinion widely held in the Confederacy that Virginia, in ratifying the constitution, had reserved the right to secede. It grew out of the fact that a clause in the Virginia ratifying ordinance stated that this ratification should be void if the popular vote on secession should be unfavorable. Atlanta *Southern Confederacy*, July 2, 1861; Athens *Southern Watchman*, July 20, 1864.

[25] *Southern Historical Society Papers* (Richmond), XLVIII (1941), 59–60; Athens *Southern Watchman*, March 4, 1863; Percy S. Flippin, *Herschel V. Johnson of Georgia, State Rights Unionist* (Richmond, 1931), 243–44.

the Confederacy should have neither army nor navy—the states should have these. The Richmond *Examiner* thought it had been a terrible mistake to adopt a Chinese copy of the Federal Constitution—a "servile plagiary." [26]

Nevertheless, at the time the Confederate Constitution was made, it was generally received with acclaim. President Davis proudly noted how nearly like the old Federal Constitution it was: "The Constitution framed by our Fathers is that of these Confederate States"; [27] Benjamin H. Hill declared that "we hugged that Constitution to our bosom and carried it with us"; [28] and Howell Cobb proudly observed that this new document was the "ablest instrument ever prepared for the government of a free people." [29] Having adopted it, the Convention submitted it to the states, and each adopted it either by its secession convention, if still sitting, or by its legislature. Some took it unanimously as did Georgia, and some with considerable opposition as did South Carolina. Nowhere was it submitted to a vote of the people, for the mania for unanimity was still uppermost; for to have submitted it to a referendum would have brought on a commotion and fatal delay. It was so much like the constitution under which they had been living, why should it be readopted?

Yet there was objection to this procedure and in general to the way in which the people had been left out of the movement. Objectors felt that the people would have adopted it overwhelmingly and would thus have silenced Northerners who were claiming that this was not a popular revolution. The leaders undoubtedly had no fear of the people; they were now fighting against time and the day Lincoln would be inaugurated. At this early day there were Jeremiahs, voicing their lamentations for the most part privately; later they would shout from the housetops so all might hear. Rhett went back home disgruntled; Toombs was halfway sulking; Yancey assuredly must have felt hurt at being left out; and privately Thomas R. R. Cobb was bitter. What right, after all, did the

[26] Richmond *Daily Whig*, November 13, 18, 1861; January 12, 1863; Charleston *Daily Mercury*, April 11, 1862; *Southern Literary Messenger*, XXXIV, (1862), 68; XXXVII (1863), 61–62.

[27] Richardson (comp.), *Messages and Papers of the Confederacy*, I, 36, 184.

[28] Hill, *Benjamin H. Hill*, 42.

[29] *Journal of the Congress of the Confederate States*, I, 153.

Montgomery Convention have to select a President and Vice-President? asked Rhett. As a sop to state-rightsism and a left-handed compliment to Davis, he was referred to as the "President of the Six Nations" before Texas had joined the Confederacy to make the seventh. Thomas R. R. Cobb was "sick at heart with the daily manifestations of selfishness, intrigue, low cunning and meanness among those who at this critical moment should have an eye single to the protection of their people." [30] Yea, flecks of storm clouds menacing the future of the Confederacy were flying at its birth.

[30] *Southern Historical Society Papers,* XXVIII (1900), 282, 285.

CHAPTER III

SECESSION RUNS ITS COURSE

BEING "President of the Six Nations" or even of the seven, with the admission of Texas into the Confederacy, did not fulfill the expectations of Jefferson Davis and the Confederate people. The less impulsive Upper South had coolly calculated that the election of Lincoln was not a sufficient reason for leaving the Union.[1] But there were many problems yet to be settled, and when Lincoln should take his seat he might well precipitate new disturbances—the revolution evidently had not yet run its course.

In preparing for these eventualities, Davis had filled out his administration immediately after his inauguration by appointing a cabinet and taking charge of the defense of the Confederacy. His most important problem was to come to terms with his northern neighbor, the United States of America. So, in pursuance of Congressional resolutions, he appointed on February 25 André B. Roman of Louisiana, Martin J. Crawford of Georgia, and John Forsyth of Alabama, to represent the Confederacy in Washington and specifically to obtain the recognition of the Confederacy, secure the possession of all Federal forts, arsenals, and other public property in the Confederacy, and to negotiate in the most friendly manner a settlement of all matters of indebtedness and other points that might arise.

---

[1] There had been some resentment in the Upper South against the precipitancy with which the Cotton States had run away with the secession movement, organizing a Confederate government and compromising the position of other Southerners. C. C. Jones of Lenoir, N.C., February 4, 1861, wrote Zebulon B. Vance that it was "deeply humiliating (or ought to be) to any citizen of a Border state if they will allow these august Cotton olygarchys [sic] south of them to dragoon them into their service." Zebulon B. Vance Papers (North Carolina State Archives, Raleigh), I.

It was evident that the most immediate danger of trouble lay in inducing the United States to abandon the few forts it still held in the Confederacy, for it was intolerable that a foreign power should be permitted to violate Confederate sovereignty in such a fashion. The various states immediately on their secession had pounced upon Federal forts and arsenals, and some had not even waited to secede before doing so. Governor Joseph E. Brown of Georgia, on January 3, 1861, more than two weeks before the state seceded, seized Fort Pulaski at the mouth of the Savannah River; Florida occupied Fort Marion at St. Augustine, Fort Clinch at Fernandina, and the Chattahoochee Arsenal, and in conjunction with Alabama troops took Fort Barrancas which guarded Pensacola, causing the Federal troops to move to Fort Pickens on Santa Rosa Island; Alabama took possession of Fort Morgan on the edge of Mobile Harbor, and Mount Vernon Arsenal forty-five miles north of Mobile; Mississippi seized Fort Hill which guarded Vicksburg on the north; and Louisiana occupied Fort Jackson and Fort St. Philip on the Mississippi River below New Orleans, and the Baton Rouge Arsenal.[2] None of these places had been fully garrisoned and most of them had only caretakers; happily there was no bloodshed. As a result of these actions there remained only a few forts in Federal possession, any one of which might be, however, the powder keg blowing up into a war. Fort Taylor at Key West, so far away, never led to trouble, and it remained in Federal possession throughout the war. The points of danger were Fort Pickens near Pensacola, and Fort Sumter at the entrance to Charleston Harbor. Circumstances were so directed as to leave the former to the side, to remain, like Fort Taylor, in continuous Federal possession; and so it came about that Fort Sumter was catapulted into fame.

When South Carolina seceded she sent her commissioners to President Buchanan to secure the forts within her borders and got the promise that nothing would be done to change the situation; yet on the day after Christmas (1860) Major Robert Anderson, in charge of Fort Moultrie, moved his forces to Fort Sumter, which was easier to defend. On Buchanan's refusal to order Major Anderson back, South Carolina charged bad faith and became much

[2] For many documents regarding the seizing of forts and arsenals, see *Official Records,* Ser. I, Vol. I, 318–691.

excited. She immediately took menacing possession of Fort Moultrie and also fortified the islands on the southern side of Fort Sumter. Troops were moved into the Charleston area, and demands were made for the evacuation of Sumter. Buchanan, who had been vacillating as he tried to steer a course to avoid war in his attempt to please both North and South and who was characterized by a Georgian as being "incapable of *purpose* as a child," [3] had by January fallen more into the hands of his Northern advisers. The Southern members got out of his cabinet, and on January 5 he sent a merchantman, the *Star of the West,* with supplies (and troops hidden under the hold) to relieve the fort. South Carolina fired upon the vessel and forced it to return. When the Confederacy took charge of national defenses, it inherited this ugly situation, made worse by South Carolina's insistence that Sumter must be evacuated, and by all means before Lincoln's inauguration. The Confederacy placed General Pierre G. T. Beauregard, Louisiana Creole, in charge of the troops there.

The scene now shifted to Washington, where opportunism, indecision, chicanery, confusion, and Machiavellian deception of the worst sort were inextricably combined—never, it seems, to be certainly unraveled. The age of Lincoln settled down upon the country with his inauguration on March 4—in fact, his shadow had fallen heavily over the land and upon Buchanan since the election in the preceding November. During these four months and until the firing on Fort Sumter, Lincoln showed less understanding of conditions in the South and gave less evidence of broad statesmanship than was ever again to characterize him. When he might have made some clear unequivocal statement following his election which could have reassured the South of his real intentions toward that region—a statement that was frequently called for and many hungered for—he dismissed the subject by advising inquirers to read what he had already said. Having said nothing to head off secession, when it came he failed to realize its strength and widespread support. To him and other Republican leaders, it was a movement of a few disgruntled and disappointed conspira-

[3] Martin J. Crawford, Washington, D.C., to Robert Toombs, March 3, 1861, in Robert Toombs Letterbook (South Caroliniana Collection, University of South Carolina Library, Columbia).

tors, and it need not be taken seriously. The Southern people would snuff out secession as soon as an election afforded opportunity to register their position. Thus was the true Southern position misunderstood.

The feeling that possessed many Republicans up to the time of actual secession, that the South was bluffing, and afterwards that secession would soon fall of its own weight, played an important part in the North's refusal to entertain any thoughts of compromise. A modern authority on the secession movement has declared, "Had the Republicans, therefore, deliberately sought the most efficient method of furthering the secession movement they could have found none better than their refusal to listen to methods of conciliation." [4] The conglomerate composition of the Republican party was also another important element in forming the attitude Lincoln held toward the secession movement. As various groups of Republicans stood for various things, Lincoln must be careful to weld his party into a permanent unity—it was not as bald a decision in Lincoln's mind as to say that he was willing to see his country disintegrate, but never his party. He did not believe that signs of his country's disintegration were serious; he would hold his party together as well as his country. As opposition to the extension of slavery seemed to be the basic factor in the rise of the Republicans, Lincoln was determined not to budge an inch in weakening it. He could write his old-time fellow Whig, Alexander H. Stephens, that he was not moving against slavery in the states but that he and his party thought slavery *"wrong and ought to be restricted,"* while Stephens thought it *"right and ought to be extended."* But Stephens replied that the Republicans had made slavery their touchstone, and though he did not believe the Republicans would "attempt to interfere *directly* and *immediately* with slavery in the States," yet the long-time threat of strangulation was there.[5] Southerners who thought they knew Lincoln believed that his party was bigger than he was and that what the Republican party had announced as its principles was more important than what Lincoln might say. Whether his contemporaries believed it or not, later generations were to find out that Lincoln

[4] Dumond, *Secession Movement,* 168.
[5] Cleveland, *Alexander H. Stephens,* 151–54.

36

was bigger than his party, when the days of indecision before Sumter were past.

The actors in the tragedy leading up to the firing on Fort Sumter were heterogeneous. There were Lincoln himself; his Secretary of State, William H. Seward; the Confederate commissioners; Supreme Court Justices John A. Campbell of Alabama and Samuel Nelson of New York, self-appointed intermediaries between Seward and the Confederate commissioners, since Seward would not personally see them; Major Anderson at Fort Sumter; various runners, messengers, and advisers of Lincoln's who were to keep him informed on Sumter; Francis W. Pickens, governor of South Carolina; the crouching lion Pierre G. T. Beauregard, eyeing the fort; and Davis and his cabinet in Montgomery. The question which has troubled subsequent generations is whether Lincoln was the marplot and bungler or the cunning villain and provocateur; whether he stumbled into war at Sumter or whether he planned it.

Having refused to recognize secession and the Confederacy as facts, Lincoln refused to receive the Confederate commissioners; but Seward, believing at this time that he more than Lincoln was President, negotiated with the commissioners through Campbell and Nelson and led the Confederates to believe that Sumter would be evacuated. Through a tortuous course of developments, it turned out later that Sumter would not be evacuated but instead would be relieved with food and soldiers, and Lincoln sent his messenger to tell Governor Pickens so. If Lincoln had wanted successfully to relieve the fort, why did he tell the Confederates of the expedition which had set out? Because previously he had promised to do so? Was this promise more important than successfully relieving the fort? Had not Seward broken his promise, or Lincoln broken it for him, that the fort would be evacuated? Some would answer by saying that Lincoln thus deliberately provoked the Confederates to fire on Sumter. Others say that Lincoln had got caught in his own web of confusion and blundered into a war that he by no means planned or wanted. It is safe to say that in such a complicated affair, lasting over a month and more, a simple answer will not suffice. Undoubtedly Lincoln wanted no war, but with equal zeal he wanted to save the Union, and if war were the last resort he would use it. And if war must come, how much more valuable it would be to have the enemy strike the first blow! It would unite all diverging factions. Lincoln saw this after the blow had been struck, and well must he have sensed it before. Campbell believed the "equivocating conduct of the [Lincoln] Administration" was "the proximate cause of the great calamity," [6] and Davis bitterly commented: "The crooked paths of diplomacy can scarcely furnish an example so wanting in courtesy, in candor, and directness as was the course of the United States Government toward our commissioners in Washington"; and in the light of the fact that a Federal fleet was off the bar, it was an "unfounded pretense that the Confederate States . . . [were] the assailants." [7]

In the emotional situation which had developed, Fort Sumter had become the symbol of Federal authority and dignity for all the country to behold—to lower the flag there was to recognize the Confederacy; it had also become a like symbol for the integrity, existence, and independence of the Confederacy—the flag must come down. In Montgomery, Davis and his cabinet, who wanted no war, awaiting every delaying action which might lead to evacuation, reluctantly ordered the reduction of the fort rather than see it reinforced. The hotheads were glad. Gray-haired old Edmund Ruffin, disgusted with the supineness of his native Virginia, had come to South Carolina, land of action, and tradition early in the making awarded him the honor of firing the first gun; and Roger A. Pryor, fellow Virginian equally disappointed in his native state, declared that if the South struck the blow it would awaken the people and that it would put Virginia "in the Southern Confederacy in less than a hour by Shrewsbury clock." [8]

Dramatically the process of bringing down the United States flag on Sumter began at 4:30 o'clock in the morning of April 12,

[6] Richardson (comp.), *Messages and Papers of the Confederacy*, I, 96.

[7] *Ibid.*, 71, 118–19. For various documents and accounts of the Fort Sumter negotiations, see *ibid.*, 84–98; *Southern Historical Society Papers*, XLII (1917), 30–38; Henry G. Connor, *John Archibald Campbell, Associate Justice of the United States Supreme Court, 1853–1861* (Boston, 1920), 109–48. For the point of view that Abraham Lincoln lured the South into firing on Fort Sumter, see Charles W. Ramsdell, "Lincoln and Fort Sumter," in *Journal of Southern History*, III (1937), 259–88; John S. Tilley, *Lincoln Takes Command* (Chapel Hill, 1941). For the point of view that Lincoln blundered, see David M. Potter, Jr., *Lincoln and his Party in the Secession Crisis* (New Haven, 1942), 1–19, 142 ff.

[8] *American Annual Cyclopaedia . . . 1861*, p. 137.

1861, when batteries on Morris Island opened with shells sweeping across the sky and bursting on the fort. The next day at 7 P.M. the flag was lowered, after the irrepressible South Carolina-born Texan, Louis T. Wigfall, with a few Negro oarsmen had set out in a small boat for the fort, and with a handkerchief on a saber as a flag of truce, made his way through a breach in the walls and induced Major Anderson to surrender.[9] In this long bombardment providentially no one on either side was killed; but when Major Anderson ordered a salute to the flag as it came down, an ammunition dump exploded and killed two men.

The firing on Sumter clarified the atmosphere everywhere, relieving the tension that had gripped Northerners and Southerners alike. Most hesitating people now saw where their loyalties lay, whether they showed it by wildly celebrating the end of uncertainties or by solemnly beholding the inevitable end of an era, however much they might regret its passing. But a second bombshell, which struck with especial force that part of the South which had not yet seceded, was Lincoln's call for 75,000 militia to be provided by the states on a quota basis. Though Lincoln did not imply in his proclamation a full declaration of war, for the probable service of these troops would likely lie in repossessing "the forts, places, and property" which had been seized by the Confederates, yet to all Southerners it meant coercion against those who had seceded and a forced participation in a cruel and unnatural war against their brethren for those Southerners who had not seceded. An unhappy choice was now forced upon the Upper South, which had cried out equally against coercion and secession.

For most Southerners the choice had now been made easier, even for the mass of Unionists of the Upper South. If the firing on Fort Sumter had not electrified the Upper South into seceding, Lincoln's call for troops could not possibly have missed doing so. It seemed unbelievable that Lincoln would call on Virginians, Tennesseans, and North Carolinians to fight against their own

9 Mrs. Louise (Wigfall) Wright, *A Southern Girl in '61. The War-Time Memories of a Confederate Senator's Daughter* (New York, 1905), 45–46. For many documents relating to activities around Fort Sumter and Charleston Harbor, see *Official Records*, Ser. I, Vol. I, 1–317; Samuel W. Crawford, *The Genesis of the Civil War. The Story of Sumter, 1860–1861* (New York, 1887).

kith and kin—had some strange obsession seized him? A North Carolina Unionist who had believed that Lincoln's inaugural address breathed "peace to any candid mind," now could see nothing but base ingratitude or worse in thus crushing the Unionists in the South: "He did more than all the secessionists to break up the Union, but whether he did this, not being statesman enough to comprehend the effect of his measures; or whether his purpose was to drive all the slave States into rebellion, thinking he could bring against us men enough, with the aid of a servile insurrection, to overthrow us and abolish Slavery, we are in doubt." [10] Had Lincoln misjudged the South again? Just because only seven states had seceded, had he been lulled into the belief that the others could not be jolted out by any measures? Possibly. Lincoln had seen Virginia call a convention in January, to be elected and to meet the next month, which had dillydallied and done nothing; he had seen North Carolina in January set an election for the next month in which the people were to choose the delegates to a convention and at the same time decide whether the convention should meet, and had seen the people vote it down and hold no convention; and he had seen Tennessee act on a like time schedule and had noted that the Tennesseans had rejected the convention. In January Arkansas had asked her people to vote for a convention in February, and Lincoln had seen that convention meet the day he was inaugurated President; it had voted against secession and hesitatingly had submitted the question to the people in the following August. To some minds these developments might mean that the Upper South would not secede under any circumstances.

But to Virginians it did not mean anything of the sort. Back in the latter part of March, Southern sentiment had overcome a great concourse of people in Richmond, who had shown it by erecting a Confederate flag at the head of Mechanicsville Turnpike and had saluted it by speechmaking and musketry.[11] The news of Fort Sumter had caused pandemonium to break loose. Three thousand Virginians, quickly forming, marched to the Tredegar Iron Works in Richmond to see a Confederate flag run up and to hear

[10] J. G. de Roulhac Hamilton (ed.), *The Correspondence of Jonathan Worth* (Raleigh, 1909), I, 150. See also *ibid.*, 134, 143.

[11] Richmond *Semi-Weekly Enquirer*, March 26, 1861.

speeches informing the Tredegar workers that it was cannon which they had made that had breached the walls of Sumter. Seizing artillery pieces in the state arsenal, they dragged them to Capitol Square and fired a salute of one hundred guns. Facing around to Union-loving Governor John Letcher's mansion, they heard a dampering speech, not sufficient to prevent them from hoisting a Confederate flag atop the capitol—to be secretly taken down during the night. The air became resonant with the inspiring music of "Dixie." That night torchlight processions threaded the streets of Richmond amidst a hundred burning tar barrels, whirling rockets, and buildings illuminated from garret to cellar. Thus would the doddering convention be brought back to life.[12]

Governor Letcher answered the call for troops with the statement that since Lincoln had "chosen to inaugurate civil war," he could have no troops from Virginia. The next day (April 17) the convention passed a secession ordinance, and in the words of one of the historians of the Confederate war, Edward A. Pollard, "She turned around, and walked out of the Union, with the step of an old Queen." [13] Secession called for more celebrations, and in answer the principal street in Richmond was illuminated for more than a mile.

The contest for Virginia was now over; the Confederacy had won. Some of Lincoln's Fort Sumter diplomacy seems to have been affected by his desire to keep Virginia in the Union. There yet remained the popular vote on secession, May 23, which the convention had ordered. Not until then would Virginia legally be out of the Union; but for all practical purposes she was already out, and contingent on the vote in May she ratified the Confederate Constitution on April 25, and was admitted into the Confederacy on May 8. Of such transcendent importance to the Confederacy was Virginia's adherence to it that Vice-President Stephens was dispatched to Richmond immediately, after the state had seceded, to

[12] *Ibid.*, April 16, 1861; William S. White, "A Diary of the War, or What I Saw of it," in *Contributions to a History of the Richmond Howitzer Battalion* (Richmond, 1883), No. 2, pp. 90–91; Bela Estván, *War Pictures from the South* (New York, 1863), 34–35.

[13] Pollard, *Jefferson Davis*, 119. For a special study on the secession of Virginia, see Henry T. Shanks, *The Secession Movement in Virginia, 1847–1861* (Richmond, 1934).

bring about union.[14] There was really no danger that Virginia would remain independent, though there were some who argued for it.

The long-standing sectionalism between the eastern and western parts of Virginia came to a head in the secession movement. The western counties voted against secession both in the convention and in the popular election in May and began a new-state movement which finally resulted in the division of the Old Dominion and the admission of West Virginia into the Union of the United States in 1863.

The guns of Sumter were heard in Arkansas, but even louder came Lincoln's call for troops. Governor Henry M. Rector indignantly replied: "The people of this Commonwealth are freemen, not slaves, and will defend to the last extremity, their honor, lives, and property, against Northern mendacity and usurpation." [15] The convention, which had refused to secede, now came back to life and on May 6 passed an ordinance of secession with only one dissenting vote.

Governor John W. Ellis of North Carolina answered Lincoln with the statement that his state would send no troops and would "be no party to this wicked violation of the laws of the country, and to this war upon the liberties of a free people." He immediately seized the three Federal forts in the state and the Fayetteville Arsenal, called for thirty thousand volunteers, and promised the Confederacy a regiment. On May 1 the legislature called a convention, which was elected on the thirteenth. On the twentieth it met and passed unanimously a secession ordinance.[16]

Governor Isham G. Harris informed Lincoln that Tennessee would "not furnish a man for purposes of coercion, but 50,000, if necessary, for the defense of our rights, and those of our Southern brothers." The legislature on May 1 authorized the Governor to appoint commissioners to treat with the Confederacy. On the sixth, exercising the right of revolution, it declared Tennessee inde-

[14] Richardson (comp.), *Messages and Papers of the Confederacy*, I, 62; Cleveland, *Alexander H. Stephens*, 729–46.

[15] *American Annual Cyclopaedia . . . 1861*, p. 23.

[16] J. G. de Roulhac Hamilton, *Reconstruction in North Carolina* (New York, 1914), 20 ff.; J. Carlyle Sitterson, *The Secession Movement in North Carolina* (Chapel Hill, 1939).

pendent, and the following day ratified a league agreement with the Confederacy and the Confederate Constitution and provided that the people should vote on these matters June 8 following. The people accepted by a large majority.

These four new Confederate states added to the original seven made eleven stars for the Confederate flag. Would there be others? How far north would the Confederacy spread?

It was easy enough for a person in the Lower South far from the influences and arguments of Northerners to convince himself of the righteousness of the South and of the secession movement, and there it was safe to act on such convictions or whims. The farther northward a person lived, the more likely it was that he would be played upon by influences and arguments less evident to the Lower Southerners; economic forces and social considerations made it more gainful and politic for him to weigh the seriousness of secession, both from the standpoint of making a living and even of continuing to live at all. For he was now more in the orbit of the North, and if secession should lead to war, he would be on the fields where the first clashes of arms would take place.

Even so, he was Southern in those deep emotions born of long-standing family ties and associations. He could not help being profoundly disturbed by any movement which interfered either with his going his way as a Southerner or his continuing to enjoy the advantages of living in the American Union. He wanted both and did not see why he should not be allowed to retain them. Hence it was that all of the states of the Upper South had developed persistent movements for compromise and for delaying the evil day in every other way possible. But the cruel choice which Lincoln forced upon these states by his call for troops led four of them to take secession as the lesser of the evils.

In the Border slave states, a fringe running from Delaware westward through Maryland, Kentucky, and Missouri, the choice was harder to make.[17] Either through the development of circumstances which they could not control, through attempts to remain apart from the quarrel between South and North, or through long-

[17] Virginia, in one sense, was a Border state; but the counties west of the mountains had long considered themselves a distant region, and when the Old Dominion seceded, they broke away to form another state.

43

standing feelings of national patriotism, all of them finally remained in the Union.

Delaware had few of the characteristics of the South except her tenacious clinging to the institution of slavery. Not being strategically situated, and weak besides, she was not much belabored by either side. Some of the Southern states sent commissioners, who were received but not heeded. Lincoln's call for militia did not much disturb the state, for as Governor William Burton replied, Delaware had no militia, and, therefore, could not comply.[18] He recommended that militia be organized, and added that if any of them wanted to offer their services to the United States, they might do so. The legislature never entertained the idea of seceding. A flourish of Confederate emotionalism punctured this matter-of-fact atmosphere when one of the state's cadets at West Point resigned, joined the Confederate army, and soon fell in battle.

Maryland, to the westward, was in quite a different position. Here there was genuine Southernism, not only on the Eastern Shore but all around Chesapeake Bay through Baltimore and to the south, and what was more important to Lincoln, Maryland was of extreme strategic importance. If Maryland should secede, the capital of the United States would be in the Confederacy. Governor Thomas H. Hicks, believing neither in secession nor in coercion, played with the idea of state neutrality. The Southern element called for a convention, but in vain. The Governor responded to Lincoln's call for troops by refusing to send any except to defend Washington. On April 19 the so-called Baltimore Massacre took place as Massachusetts troops attempted to pass through that city to Washington, and other expressions of sympathy for the South manifested themselves. As soon as possible Lincoln occupied key points with Federal troops; he suspended the writ of habeas corpus and ordered the arrest of prominent Southern sympathizers, including various members of the legislature.[19] The hard realities of military occupation were now upon the state, and thus Maryland was saved for the Union.

[18] Frank Moore (ed.), *The Rebellion Record: A Diary of American Events, with Documents, Narratives, Illustrative Incidents, Poetry, etc.* (New York, 1861–1868), I, 155 (documents).

[19] For various arrests in Maryland, see *Official Records*, Ser. I, Vol. V, 193–97.

About this time James Ryder Randall, far from his native state, wrote "My Maryland" with its ringing first line, "The despot's heel is on thy shore, Maryland!" First sung by Jennie Cary, a belle of Baltimore, it became a rallying cry of the Confederacy and emotionalized the sad plight of that state. Jennie Cary and her sister and many other Confederate sympathizers were soon fleeing Maryland for Virginia. Marylanders became the heroes and heroines of everyone in Richmond. The Confederate Congress resolved that no peace would ever be concluded with the United States which did not give Maryland the right to choose the Confederacy if she wanted it.[20] A regiment of Marylanders soon arose in Virginia, and before the war ended an estimated twenty thousand Marylanders fought for the South.

But Marylanders outlasted their popularity with many Virginians. Too many made Richmond their footstool, to enter business instead of the army, and some so-called "plug-uglies" from Baltimore made their more worthy fellows suspect. A Confederate Congressman declared they were "always ready to break out into the strains of 'Maryland, My Maryland,' but unwilling to strike a blow for the Confederacy";[21] and another Congressman said they should be compelled "to fight as well as to sing hymns for Maryland."[22] As these Marylanders were not citizens of the Confederacy, but merely resident refugees, they claimed exemption under the Confederate conscription laws, and many who were forced into the army got release through the Confederate District Court in Richmond.

Kentucky with her tradition of Henry Clay and compromise found it exceedingly difficult to make up her mind. Here especially the forces of North and South worked with great effect. But Governor Beriah Magoffin was a thoroughgoing secessionist and made every effort to take his state out of the Union. In answer to Lincoln's call for troops, he tartly replied, "I say, emphatically, Kentucky will furnish no troops for the wicked purpose of subduing

[20] James M. Matthews (ed.), *The Statutes at Large of the Provisional Government of the Confederate States of America, from . . . February 8, 1861, to . . . February 18, 1862 . . . and the Treaties Concluded by the Confederate States with the Indians* (Richmond, 1864), 281; *Journal of the Congress of the Confederate States,* I, 589.

[21] *Southern Historical Society Papers,* XLVII (1930), 120.

[22] Richmond *Daily Examiner,* January 6, 1864.

her sister Southern States." [23] The contending forces finally agreed on a policy of neutrality, and on May 20 Magoffin issued a proclamation warning both Confederate and Federal troops not to enter the state. Though neutrality was as unconstitutional as secession could have been, yet Lincoln, knowing his native state, respected this policy and bided his time; for so strategic was Kentucky's position on the Middle Western frontier that Lincoln was said to have remarked, he hoped to have God on his side, but he must have Kentucky.

Davis equally felt the necessity of having Kentucky. Respecting her neutrality, he accepted all troops leaving Kentucky for the Confederacy and set up recruiting camps on the southern border. In late August, 1861, the Confederate Congress appropriated $1,000,000 to be used in aiding Kentucky and securing her for the Confederacy. [24]

As was well known by both Lincoln and Davis, Kentucky's neutrality could not last long. By early September each had violated it sufficiently to lead the other to poise for seizing the prize. The Confederates marched in first, giving the Unionist element an excuse for abandoning neutrality and calling on the Federals to help drive the Confederates out. Federal troops swarmed across the Ohio River and soon seized half the state. On November 18 two hundred delegates from sixty-five counties met at Russellville, and, exercising the "natural right resting upon the law of God," declared the state independent. Doubly sealing its act, the convention, exercising the "civil right founded upon the Constitution," passed an ordinance of secession. The assembly organized a provisional government consisting of a governor and a council of ten, awaiting the time when the Federals could be driven out of the state and a fully-organized government instituted. On December 10, 1861, the Confederate Congress admitted Kentucky into the Confederacy. Thereafter throughout the war a steadily increasing number

[23] *American Annual Cyclopaedia . . . 1861*, p. 396.
[24] Charles W. Ramsdell (ed.), *Laws and Joint Resolutions of the Last Session of the Confederate Congress (November 7, 1864–March 18, 1865) Together with the Secret Acts of Previous Congresses* (Durham, 1941), 159–60. As all of this money had not been expended before Kentucky joined the Confederacy, the governor later tried to collect the remainder of it. Dunbar Rowland (ed.), *Jefferson Davis, Constitutionalist, His Letters, Papers and Speeches* (Jackson, Miss., 1923), VI, 157.

of Kentuckians were to rue the day they had taken into their bosom this nest of "Federal vipers." [25]

Beyond Kentucky lay Missouri, much a product of the Bluegrass State and equally as strategic in the contest between North and South. Claiborne F. Jackson was the governor. He advocated secession, and he had no good reason to doubt its success; for in the election of 1860 Lincoln had polled slightly more than 17,000 votes while his opponents got more than 148,000. There was great Southern strength in Missouri, but St. Louis with its large Unionist German population was not to be ignored. With Jackson's support the legislature on January 15, 1861, called a sovereign convention which met on February 28 in Jefferson City, but soon thereafter it moved to St. Louis where a Union atmosphere prevailed. It refused to pass a secession ordinance and on March 22 adjourned. Despite this refusal to take Missouri out of the Union, Governor Jackson answered Lincoln's call for troops in a most decisive manner, using a flood of invective adjectives suggestive of his just having laid down Peter Mark Roget's *Thesaurus:* "Your requisition is illegal, unconstitutional, revolutionary, inhuman, diabolical, and cannot be complied with." [26]

The Union cause in Missouri was in the hands of Francis P. Blair, Jr., a member of the powerful Blair clan of Maryland, who had Lincoln's ear. He was determined that the secessionists should not get control of the Federal arsenal in St. Louis. Before Lincoln's inauguration he had Nathaniel Lyon detailed as commander of the arsenal, and thereupon Lyon moved much of the valuable war material over into Illinois. In early May, Governor Jackson assembled an encampment of part of the state militia at Camp Jackson, on the outskirts of St. Louis, for their annual training. Ludicrously dressed in the clothing of Blair's blind mother-in-law and riding in her carriage, Lyon spied out the situation, and on

[25] Matthews (ed.), *Statutes at Large of the Provisional Government of the Confederate States, 1861–1862,* p. 222; *Journal of the Congress of the Confederate States,* I, 537–43. For an extended account of Kentucky during the secession movement and the war, see E. Merton Coulter, *The Civil War and Readjustment in Kentucky* (Chapel Hill, 1926).

[26] McPherson, *History of the . . . Rebellion,* 115; Benson J. Lossing, *Pictorial History of the Civil War in the United States of America* (Philadelphia, 1866–1868), I, 338.

47

May 10, at the head of seven thousand Federal troops, many of them the recently enlisted Wide-Awake Germans, seized outrageously the seven hundred militia. On the way back a riot was precipitated, in which Lyon's troops shot and killed fifteen citizens.

This precipitated civil war in Missouri. Sterling Price, who up to this time had been a Union supporter, took charge of the pro-Southern state troops, making a peace agreement with General William S. Harney, commander of Federal troops in the Department of Missouri. Blair had Harney removed and the implacable and passionate Lyon put in charge. Calling for fifty thousand volunteers, Governor Jackson and Price retreated up the Missouri River and were defeated at Boonville in June. Continuing into southwest Missouri, Price defeated Lyon on August 10 at Wilson's Creek, an engagement in which Lyon was killed. Price now surged back into northern Missouri, won the battle of Lexington in September, but by superior numbers was forced to retreat back into southwest Missouri. Meanwhile, the old convention assembled again, outlawed the Jackson government, and set up a provisional government. On October 21 a remnant of the Jackson legislature met at Neosho and declared Missouri out of the Union, and on November 28 the Confederate Congress admitted Missouri as a state in the Confederacy. Up to this time the Confederacy had been co-operating with the Southern movement in Missouri and aiding it through an appropriation of $1,000,000 made by the Confederate Congress in August. "Old Pap" Price had not found Missourians as ready to join his forces as he had thought when he issued his flaming proclamations calling for fifty thousand troops, in which he had tried to stampede them into joining with such grandiloquent words as these: "Do I hear your shouts? Is that your war-cry which echoes through the land? Are you coming? Fifty-thousand men! Missouri shall move to victory with the tread of a giant. Come on, my brave boys, 50,000 heroic, gallant, unconquerable Southern men! We await your coming." He continued to wait, and got fewer than five thousand.[27]

---

[27] *Official Records*, Ser. I, Vol. VIII, 695–97. Handy accounts of what was happening in Missouri may be found in *American Annual Cyclopaedia . . . 1861*, pp. 477–97; Basil W. Duke, *Reminiscences of General Basil W. Duke, C.S.A.* (Garden City, 1911), 32–45 ff.; Eugene M. Violette, *A History of Missouri* (Boston, 1918), 322 ff.

Determined to drive the Confederates completely out of the state, the Federals gathered together an army, which pushed Price across into Arkansas and defeated him in the battle of Pea Ridge, or Elkhorn Tavern, March 6–8, 1862. In this battle Ben McCulloch, the Texas Ranger and hero, was killed. Price and his army were soon thereafter transferred east of the Mississippi, and Missouri was left to her fate—not to be seriously molested again until 1864. The high Confederate authorities had not realized the importance of Missouri in the full picture of Confederate military strategy. By giving up this dangerous threat to the Federal flank in Kentucky, they made possible the Federal thrust down through Kentucky and Tennessee in the spring of 1862, which did not stop until it had pierced the heart of the Confederacy in northern Mississippi.

The South, having lost the fight in Kansas in the 1850's, made no effort to try battle there now that it had become a state in January, 1861, but to the south was a prize well worth fighting for. In a region called the Indian Territory, later to become the state of Oklahoma, lived the five civilized Indian nations, the Cherokees, Creeks, Choctaws, Chickasaws, and Seminoles, and various other tribes of wild Plains Indians, such as the Comanches, Osages, Senecas, Shawnees, and Quapaws. As early as January, 1861, a Georgian had thought of them as "an important element of strength in the western wilds . . . who might be converted into an invaluable arm of defense—into cossacks of the Don & Volga—that would entirely stop the S. W-n progress of the cowardly abolition hordes." [28] Moreover, in this region north of the Red River was great natural wealth, timber, minerals, and rich agricultural lands, for the Confederacy later to exploit—oil had not yet been suspected.

Setting out early to win over the Indians, President Davis appointed Albert Pike, Maine-born Arkansan, later to be more famous as poet and Mason than Indian commissioner and warrior, to make treaties of alliance. These negotiations were facilitated by the fact that many of the Indians of the civilized nations were slaveholders, and also because the superintendent, with his headquarters at Fort Smith, Arkansas, was a Southerner, as were his agents dispersed among the various tribes. Even so, before Pike arrived

[28] James M. Green to John B. Lamar, January 21, 1861, in Howell Cobb Papers.

49

the Chickasaw Nation had issued a declaration of independence and had sought to have other nations adhere, and the Cherokees, under their testy and tricky old chief John Ross, had declared their neutrality. Passing the Cherokees by, Pike went on to the other civilized nations. He made his first treaty with the Creeks on July 10, and two days later he made a treaty with the Choctaws and Chickasaws. In August he negotiated a treaty with the Seminoles. Before returning to the Cherokee Nation, he went on to the Plains Indians and during August and October made treaties with all of them. The Cherokees, rather than be left out, agreed to a treaty on October 7.

The treaties with the five civilized tribes were much the same. The Confederacy formed alliances offensive and defensive with these Indians and assumed all the annuities and other obligations which the United States had owed them. The Choctaws and Chickasaws together might send a delegate to the Confederate Congress, the Creeks and Seminoles might do likewise, and the Cherokees might send one. What was much more remarkable, the Choctaws and Chickasaws might form a state and apply for admission into the Confederacy, and any one or all of the other three civilized nations might become a part of this state. The nations promised to provide varying numbers of troops for the Confederate armies. The treaties with the Plains Indians were much more elementary. They took these Indians under the protection of the Confederacy, assumed the former obligations of the United States, gained a pledge from the Indians to forsake their wild life on the plains and settle down; in return the Confederacy promised them various materials and services, such as furnishing them with houses and wells. These Indians were not called upon to provide troops (the Confederacy could not imperil its standing by employing wild troops which might engage in barbarous warfare), nor were they given the right to send delegates to the Confederate Congress or become a state in the Confederacy.[29]

President Davis objected to the clauses providing for delegates and statehood as not coming within the purview of treaty making and hence unconstitutional, but the treaties were ratified as they

[29] For the texts of these treaties, see Matthews (ed.), *Statutes at Large of the Provisional Congress of the Confederate States, 1861–1862*, pp. 289–411.

stood. All sent delegates, who were seated; but no move was ever made toward statehood. The most prominent of these delegates was Elias Cornelius Boudinot, representing the Cherokees. A Bureau of Indian Affairs, set up in the War Department, administered the treaty obligations, providing money, services, and protection; and toward the end of the war, when Confederate currency became almost worthless, the Indians were paid in cotton delivered at a Gulf port. Two district courts were set up for them.[30]

On their part the Indians provided the Confederacy with troops whose chief activities were confined to the Indian Territory, where they engaged in war against pro-Union Indians and Kansas raiders. In this internecine conflict, the half-breeds were largely pro-Confederate while the purebloods stood with the Union. The Cherokee Nation divided, with Chief Ross going over to the Union and Stand Watie setting up a rival Confederate regime with himself as chief. Stand Watie remained to the end a loyal Confederate. He was finally made a brigadier general and did not formally surrender until a month after the war ended.[31] The only other

[30] For various statutes relative to the Confederacy's dealings with the Indians, see *ibid.*, 32, 68, 232–37, 239–40, 271–75; James M. Matthews (ed.), *Public Laws of the Confederate States of America . . . Fourth Session of the First Congress; 1863–4* (Richmond, 1864), 175; Ramsdell (ed.), *Laws and Joint Resolutions,* 25, 75, 94–95, 158–59. For a report on the Commissioner of Indian Affairs, see *Official Records,* Ser. IV, Vol. II, 352 ff.

[31] Matthews (ed.), *Statutes at Large of the Provisional Congress of the Confederate States,* 1861–1862, p. 284; Richardson (comp.), *Messages and Papers of the Confederacy,* I, 149–51, 295, 477–79; William M. Robinson, Jr., *Justice in Grey; A History of the Judicial System of the Confederate States of America* (Cambridge, Mass., 1941), 331 ff.; Annie H. Abel, "The Indians in the Civil War," in *American Historical Review,* XV (1909–1910), 281–96. For an interesting account of the part played by the Cherokees, see Edward E. Dale and Gaston Litton, *Cherokee Cavaliers; Forty Years of Cherokee History as Told in the Correspondence of the Ridge-Watie-Boudinot Family* (Norman, Okla., 1939). The Cherokee National Council, after the battle of Pea Ridge, earnestly recommended to its troops that they "avoid any acts toward captured or fallen foes that would be incompatible with . . . the usages of war among civilized nations." *Official Records,* Ser. I, Vol. XIII, 826. Elias C. Boudinot, the Cherokee delegate to the Confederate Congress, claimed that the Cherokees sent a greater proportion of their population to the army than did any Confederate state. Richmond *Daily Enquirer,* December 19, 1863. But the Choctaws seem to have been the most loyal to the Confederacy and to their treaty obligations. In the summer of 1861, 200 Choctaw warriors were encamped near Fort Smith, Arkansas, and 1,800 more were expected soon. This led the editor of the Fort Smith *Daily Times and Herald,* July 8, 1861, to observe: "These noble sons of the west, armed with their long rifles, Tomma-hawks

Indian who received outstanding military honors from the Confederacy was John Jumper, principal chief of the Seminoles, who was made an honorary lieutenant colonel in the Confederate army and presented with a uniform, saber, rifle, and a liberal amount of ammunition. The chief military activity in which the Indians participated outside their territory was the battle of Pea Ridge, where they were charged by the Federals with having engaged in some scalping.

There were two remnants of Indian tribes which had never migrated to the West. They were the Seminoles in the Florida Everglades and the Cherokees in the Great Smoky Mountains of western North Carolina. These Seminoles played no part in the war, but the Cherokees, who were much more numerous, enlisted to the number of a few hundred and engaged in scouting, especially in East Tennessee. As loyal Confederates, when they heard of the victory at Corinth they gave a war whoop which reverberated through their mountain home. In 1864 a delegation headed by Chief George Bushyhead made a visit to Richmond, where it was lionized by high Confederate officials.

West of Texas was the Territory of New Mexico, extending to California. Here was a prize which if secured would place the Confederacy almost on the Pacific. President Davis as Secretary of War in President Pierce's cabinet had come to understand the importance of the West. With the possibilities of securing California, or at least the southern part of it, and of annexing some of the states of northern Mexico, it was of outstanding importance for the Confederacy to secure New Mexico. There had long been a movement to divide this region by an east-west line and erect the southern part into a territory to be called Arizona. With the coming of the secession movement, the inhabitants of the southern part seized the opportunity to declare their independence of the United States and their adherence to the Confederacy, making the thirty-fourth parallel their northern boundary. To support this movement, Lieutenant Colonel John R. Baylor marched out of

---

and scalping knives, swear that nothing but the scalp of the Yankee will satisfy their vengeance, for intruding on their southern brothers." Only about half of the Creeks, Seminoles, and Cherokees remained loyal to the Confederacy. Richmond *Daily Whig,* February 24, 1863.

Fort Bliss at Franklin (El Paso) a few months later, organized the territory, declared himself governor, and sent Granville H. Oury as a delegate to the Confederate Congress. The Congress created the territory on January 24, 1862, and a few days later seated Oury. After the inauguration of the permanent government of the Confederacy on February 22, a new delegate was sent to Richmond and was seated on March 11. This bold move aroused the Federal authorities to the danger of this Confederate thrust into the Southwest. Forces from Colorado and California converged on this Arizona movement, which had successfully surged northward to embrace Albuquerque and Santa Fe. Federal soldiers under Major John M. Chivington on March 28, 1862, defeated the Confederates led by Brigadier General Henry H. Sibley at Glorieta Pass, twenty-three miles east of Santa Fe, and snuffed out the Territory of Arizona.

The Arizona movement represented the most serious Confederate penetration into the West and Southwest. For a time there was fear that a Confederate movement in southern California, aided by the activities of pro-Southern Senator William M. Gwin, might lead to a Confederate state on the Pacific, but this hope was soon ended by Federal troops. In the Territory of Nevada, Confederate sympathizers seized Virginia City and raised the Confederate flag, but they were soon driven out. Loud-shouting Southern miners scared the Federal authorities for a time in the Territory of Colorado and the Montana part of the Territory of Idaho, but they soon subsided. Clever and designing Brigham Young, head of the Mormon Church in Utah, gave the Confederate movement no chance in his dominions.

During the first year following the secession of South Carolina, there were widespread hopes that the Union might disintegrate far beyond the slave South, that a Pacific Republic might form, that the Northwestern states might organize a republic, even that New York City, which had long been disgruntled over the treatment it received from the state, might secede and set itself up as a free city. In fact, Fernando Wood, mayor of the city, suggested such a move in January, 1861. In those troubled and uncertain waters the Confederacy was willing to fish. To woo the Border slave states and even the states northward, the Confederate Congress

early declared the Mississippi River free and open to the navigation of all states touching it or its tributaries; President Davis in his
proclamation of May 6, 1861, recognizing hostilities with the
United States, exempted all the Border slave states, the Indian
Territory, and the Territory of Arizona; and the constitution
makers refused to restrict the admission of new states to those which
possessed slaves.

But the Confederacy had reached the height of its territorial
expansion in 1861; thereafter it suffered contraction through military occupation by the enemy. Counting the Border slave states
and the many inhabitants of the lower parts of Ohio, Indiana, and
Illinois, who had Southern background and proclivities, the Confederacy was never able to embrace within its territory half of the
Southern Americans. The recession of the Confederacy was not
only to play havoc with its attempt to include such doubtful states
as Kentucky and Missouri, but with the passing of time it was
even to hamper the Confederacy's efforts to control its own heart
land as it came to be occupied by Federal troops. The Confederate
Congress, by 1863, was passing laws to make it possible for these
invaded states to maintain their representation in Richmond. In
Louisiana representatives in Congressional districts occupied by the
enemy might be elected by qualified voters living in other parts of
the state. Arkansas was allowed to provide a general ticket without
reference to Congressional districts. In Tennessee the election
should likewise be by general ticket, and qualified Tennesseans
anywhere in the Confederacy might vote. A similar arrangement
was allowed for Kentucky and Missouri. It turned out that these
makeshift elections could be decided by the qualified voters who
might be stationed at Macon, Georgia, at Camp Lee, Virginia, or
anywhere else in the Confederacy.

Since these elections were decided by soldiers, the Congressmen
so elected were almost uniformly supporters of the Davis administration and its unpopular measures such as conscription, impressments, and the suspension of the writ of habeas corpus. Critics of
the Davis administration became bitter against these fugitive Congressmen, and sought to have invaded states excluded from representation in the Confederate government.

The question logically arises: Were there eleven or thirteen

Confederate States? The number thirteen had a charm about it in American history, and though the superstitious might consider it unlucky, the Confederate government on occasion clung to the claim of thirteen. There were thirteen stars in the Confederate flag; there were seats for thirteen states in the Confederate Congress. Yet on other occasions the Confederacy did not act as if it recognized the flimsy claims of the make-believe states of Kentucky and Missouri. As neither one of these states had been admitted when the election for the permanent government of the Confederacy took place in November, 1861, of course no votes were to be counted from those states. Thus only eleven states voted for Jefferson Davis and Alexander H. Stephens. In a message to Congress in 1863 President Davis either unwittingly or by design referred to the eleven states as forming the Confederate Union. And when the war was over and the seceded states were to be treated to a reconstruction, the United States ignored Kentucky and Missouri.

Secession had been a popular movement; cruelly so, for it had trodden down many who were hesitant and had stampeded others who were easily influenced. Secession was action, promising brilliant new experiences, the romance of a new country, a future with wide horizons; Unionism could offer little more than a continuation of the evil days which had beset the South for a generation. Southerners who opposed secession were run over roughshod, and even though there can be no doubt that in the states which seceded the movement was supported by the majority, yet this virile, militant majority had already used clinching tactics where the question was submitted to a popular vote, not so much for fear of the results as to save precious time, which was fast running out. In the three states of Texas, Virginia, and Tennessee, where the people were allowed to vote on secession, in every case the state had, previous to the vote, committed itself to the Confederacy either by a military alliance, sending delegates to the Confederate Congress, or by admission into the Confederacy. The futility of voting against secession under these circumstances was evident, and in every case it carried by large majorities.[32]

[32] In two of the states, Tennessee and Missouri, the legislatures (a remnant in the latter state) passed secession ordinances. In the other states sovereign conventions acted, and in some of these states, notably North Carolina, South Carolina, and

Georgia, these conventions continued to sit long after there seemed any need for them, tending to usurp the powers of government belonging to the legislatures. In South Carolina the convention continued for two years amidst many complaints of the people. See Charleston *Daily Mercury*, February 11, 1862; Atlanta *Southern Confederacy*, September 5, 1861; September 23, 1862.

CHAPTER IV

A NEW DAY DAWNS

FOR almost half a century Southerners had let their imaginations play upon the establishment of a Southern Confederacy,[1] but not until the 1850's did fancy turn into burning desire. By this time the South had come to look upon the North as little less than a millstone around its neck, making further progress all but impossible. So, with the coming of the Confederate States of America, a wave of optimism seized the people, making them look forward to their destiny with the enthusiasm of a child about to come into a heritage left as a gift by Santa Claus. "We are in the dawn of an Era of prosperity and happiness unprecedented in the annals of Nations," exclaimed a Georgian;[2] "We cannot hope to make this a real land of Beula; but near approaches are not denied to us," wrote another Southerner to Secretary of the Treasury Salmon P. Chase.[3] Lucius Q. C. Lamar, speaking in June, 1861, from the balcony of the Spotswood Hotel in Richmond, told the assembled multitude that they now had a beloved country—"for, thank God! we have a country at last . . . to live for, to pray for, to fight for, and if necessary, to die for." A voice from the crowd answered back, "Yes, I am willing to die for it a hundred times over."[4]

It was a country not only to love, but one in which to grow rich and powerful. An Alabamian saw the South "destined to become the proudest and most powerful country that ever flourished in the

[1] For example, Darien (Ga.) *Gazette,* April 22, June 22, 1824.
[2] J. C. Edwards, Macon, Ga., to Cobb, February 6, 1861, in Howell Cobb Papers.
[3] McCormick, Augusta, Ga., to Chase, March 6, 1861, in Hart (ed.), "Letters to Secretary Chase from the South," *loc. cit.,* 333.
[4] Mayes, *Lucius Q. C. Lamar,* 96.

tide of time"; [5] and a Louisianian echoed that there was "no country upon the face of the globe" that combined "all the elements of greatness, power and wealth so beautifully" as were "embraced within the limits of the slave States." [6] After three years of war Robert M. T. Hunter of Virginia still saw "peace, liberty, independence, unrivalled opportunities for moral, material, and social development, and a renown which the proudest nations of the earth might admire and envy." [7] The South was now to enter a richer material life in which commerce and manufactories, as well as agriculture, would play their part. And why not? It was as large as any European nation, excluding Russia and Turkey; it had five times the population that had won independence from Great Britain; it had provided four fifths of the exports of the former United States; and it had a homogeneous white population uncontaminated by foreigners. Unlike the French Revolutionists, it would not remake the calendar; it would not declare 1861 the Year One; yet a movement, persistent but unsuccessful, broke out to abolish the Yankee system of weights and measures, inherited from the English, and to establish the more exact and sensible metric system. Had not Thomas Jefferson gone part of the way when he set up the decimal system for American money?

Here was an all-embracing enthusiasm which might easily weld together a Southern nationality. What should this new nation be called? Since there were questions of more importance to be settled in Montgomery, in a matter-of-fact way the constitution makers called it the Confederate States of America. Yet there were suggestions that it be called the Republic of the Southern United States of America, and Thomas R. R. Cobb wanted to call it the Republic of Washington. As time went on sundry other names were suggested, such as Appalachia, Alleghania, Chicora, Panola, or even just Southland. The Federals liked to call it Secessia, which did not displease the Richmond *Whig* editor too much, for he felt that the United States might well be renamed Servia, as it was a land of serfs made so by Lincoln's tyrannies. But this editor and

5 Montgomery *Weekly Mail*, January 11, 1861.

6 E. Delony, in *De Bow's Review*, XXXI (1861), 522.

7 *Journal of the Congress of the Confederate States*, III, 795.

other strongly state-rights Southerners wanted none of these names—not even Confederate States of America, for that indicated a nationality. They hated the word *national* when applied to the South; there was no Southern nation, they argued. There were eleven nations in the South; they hated the word *state,* as it was a Yankee term. They would compromise on *commonwealth;* but the term "League of Nations" should be applied to the whole, or "The Allied Nations" or the "Allied Republics." Imperialistic South-erners felt that the name Confederate States of America was well chosen, for, "huge in its dimensions, wealthy, powerful, and mighty in its influence," it might include in time to come states in Central and South America.[8]

As for the people, historically they came to be called Confederates and most of them and their descendants considered this their proper appellation; and though their enemies delighted in calling them "rebels," [9] the Southerners took up this term very early and gloried in it. They liked to recall that George Washington was the first great American rebel and that Martin Luther was another great rebel. They argued that the greatest world progress had been brought about by rebels and remembered the old proverb, "Re-bellion, if successful, is sacred; if not, is treason." As the states were seceding, some newspapers kept the tally under the title, "Roll of the Rebel States," and used the term otherwise instead of "South-ern" or "Confederate." In fact, *Southern* was especially disliked by some, as it indicated merely the southern part of the old Union. Units of the Confederate army used the term in their names, as Albany Rebels, Irish Rebels. A South Carolina Irishman said he preferred the name "rebel" because his ancestors had "been so called for more than six hundred years." [10] Of course, the poets had to hallow the name in their rhymes: So, sang one,

> *Then call us rebels, if you will—*
> *We glory in the name;*
> *For bending under unjust laws,*

[8] Natchez *Daily Free Trader,* February 16, 1861.

[9] General Ulysses S. Grant often referred to them as Confederates; but implacable Edwin M. Stanton used the word "rebels."

[10] Charleston *Daily Mercury,* January 8, 1862.

And swearing faith to an unjust cause,
We count a greater shame.[11]

And another penned this as one of his stanzas in a poem of five:

Yes, call them rebels! 'tis the name
Their patriot fathers bore,
And by such deeds they'll hallow it,
As they have done before.[12]

When war came, a name had to be found for it, too. Just as Thomas R. R. Cobb had wanted to call the new nation Washington, most Southerners liked to refer to the war as the "Revolution." But in doing so they were at great pains to impress on the world that their movement was not revolutionary in the sense of being radical, anarchical, agrarian, or touched with the "powder-cask abstractions" which accompanied some revolutions. Stephens emphasized to the Virginians, when he went to Richmond in early 1861 to induce them to join the Confederacy, that the new government was no "wild scheme of revolution." This Confederate Revolution was much like the American Revolution; each sought release from tyranny. According to George Fitzhugh, the Southern sociologist and philosopher, it was "the grandest, most momentous event since the days of Luther and of Calvin." [13] It was a profound conservative movement; it was, in fact, a counterrevolution against the excesses of Northern demagoguery, mob rule, and dangerous fanaticisms imported from Europe. Moreover, when dark days of defeats came, it was of psychological value to keep Southerners remembering the Confederate Revolution in relation to the American Revolution, for the Americans sank to lower depths of despair and defeat than ever the Confederates were to acknowledge for themselves. The Confederates were never to admit until after the war that they had had a Valley Forge.

Southerners used also other names for this conflict. One of the first was "War of Independence." Another, strangely enough in

[11] Frank Moore (ed.), *Songs and Ballads of the Southern People, 1861–1865* (New York, 1886), 62.

[12] New Orleans *Daily Picayune*, May 26, 1861.

[13] George Fitzhugh, "The Revolutions of 1776 and 1861 Contrasted," in *Southern Literary Messenger*, XXXVII (1863), 723.

the light of later history, was "Civil War." One Confederate wrote a book entitled *War for Separation*. The North, of course, soon denominated it the "Rebellion" or "War of the Rebellion," terms which nearly became permanent, until finally for subsequent generations "Civil War" became most common, except among some Southerners, who preferred the cumbersome title "War Between the States." The last term, not used until the conflict was over, was popularized by Stephens, who employed it as part of the title of his book, *A Constitutional View of the Late War Between the States,* the first volume of which was published in 1868. Many Southerners took up this term as relieving them from the apparent admission that the Confederacy had not been an independent nation, implied in the term "Civil War." [14] A more descriptive term later used infrequently was "The War of the Sections."

Another postwar name based on a sentimental truth but never popularized was "The Brothers' War." Here was suggested the conflict of brother against brother, father against son, kith against kin of every degree, former friend against former friend. There was scarcely an end that could be made to the accumulation of examples of this pathetic fact. Throughout the Upper South and especially in the Border slave states, the division of families was commonplace. At Hilton Head on the coast of South Carolina, Percival Drayton, commander of a Federal gunboat, fought against his brother, Brigadier General Thomas F. Drayton, who led the Confederate forces there. Likewise, Franklin Buchanan, who commanded the *Virginia* (*Merrimac*), fought against his brother McKean, who was on the *Congress,* which was destroyed in the engagement at Hampton Roads. James Ewell Brown (Jeb) Stuart, in his famous ride around General George B. McClellan's army, was pursued by his Federal father-in-law, Philip St. George Cooke, but not captured. In another conflict a Confederate soldier actually captured his own father. Attorney General Edward Bates of Lincoln's cabinet had a son in the Confederate army. John J. Crittenden of Kentucky had sons fighting in both the Confederate and Union armies, and the Breck-

[14] In reality, this term has the same implication as "Civil War," for "War Between the States" suggests a conflict between the Northern and Southern states of the Union. And Stephens' record before and during the war affords no argument that, except for a brief period, he really wanted the South to become a permanent independent nation.

inridges, from the same state, were badly divided. Robert E. Lee's cousin, Samuel P. Lee, was in charge of a Federal fleet of gunboats blockading the James River; General George G. Meade's wife was a sister of former Governor Henry A. Wise of Virginia; Lincoln's wife as a young girl had been a playmate of John C. Breckinridge in Lexington, Kentucky, and her brother, three half-brothers, and three brothers-in-law fought in the Confederate armies. In fine, Mrs. Lincoln was Southern, of the bluest Bluegrass aristocracy, and Abraham Lincoln was born a Kentuckian; while Mrs. Jefferson Davis was of Northern antecedents, her grandfather having been governor of New Jersey. So must it be when a people who were one were divided by war.

Indeed, so little was the Confederacy a revolutionary movement in the generally accepted sense that rumors were early started to the effect that the South would ultimately set up a monarchy. William H. Russell, the British diarist and newspaper correspondent of the London *Times,* claimed to have heard Southerners on various occasions, on his trip through the Confederacy in 1861, make the remark that they would like to have a British prince as their ruler. Other rumors had it that they would take a member of the Bonaparte House. These charges were so persistently leveled against the South as to force note to be taken of them and denials and explanations made. Senator Alfred Iverson of Georgia replied that "there is not one man in a million, as far as I know and believe, in the State of Georgia, or elsewhere in the South, who would be in favor of any such principle." [15] A South Carolinian said that he had heard of but two people who said such foolish things, and both were extremely eccentric, with minds that zigzagged and ran upstream. The keen-minded Mrs. Chesnut believed the rumor arose out of the fact that "Every man wants to be at the head of affairs himself. If he can not be king himself, then a republic, of course." [16] A fellow countryman of Russell's believed that he had misunderstood what he heard—Southerners really meant that they would take a British prince or live under British rule again in preference to being conquered.[17] Yet a British subject, long domiciled in Georgia, declared:

[15] Rowland (ed.), *Jefferson Davis, Constitutionalist,* V, 27.

[16] Martin and Avary (eds.), *Mrs. Chesnut's Diary from Dixie,* 66.

[17] Malet, *Errand to the South,* 172. George A. Lawrence, a British subject who spent some time in Maryland in 1863, said he had frequently heard people say that as a

"I was astonished by Russell's So[uth] Ca[rolina] letter—but believe myself that a Constitutional monarchy is better than a Repu[blican] Govt—although costs more—in half a century or less there will be none of the latter in No America." [18] Also, as late as 1864 a Federal prisoner in conversation with his Confederate captor "first heard, what I afterwards found to be quite a popular opinion in the South, that a republican form of government is a failure, and cannot endure; and if they succeed in the war, which they surely would, they would not continue six months a republic, but would make Lee dictator, until they could select a royal family by ballot. As preposterous as this thing seemed to a Northerner, this man, who evidently did some thinking of his own, spoke of it with great earnestness and faith." [19] Lamar told an Atlanta audience in 1864 that he had often been asked (since his return from Europe) whether his observations of monarchies had not impaired his faith in republics and he had replied that a monarchy could not be transferred to this country.[20]

There was, in fact, a strong and persistent segment of Southern opinion that a Caesar or a Napoleon would be a godsend to the war-ridden Confederacy. As the Richmond *Examiner* said, "No power in Executive hands can be too great, no discretion too absolute, at such moments as these. We need a Dictator." [21] George Fitzhugh believed that ordinary liberties should be suspended until the end of the war, and others felt that it had been a mistake to make a constitution.

---

choice between being conquered by the North or reverting to British rule, they "would infinitely prefer becoming again a colonial subject of England to remaining a member of the Federal Union." [George A. Lawrence], *Border and Bastile* (New York, 1863), 257–58. As victory seemed farther away with Confederate defeats, at least one Virginia lady felt that the American Revolution might have been a mistake and that Washington's glories were in vain. "Had he been gifted with prophetic vision, in addition to his great powers, we would still remain a British colony," she said. [Judith Brockenbrough McGuire], *Diary of a Southern Refugee during the War. By a Lady of Virginia* (New York, 1867), 194. She made this statement on February 22, 1863.

[18] Godfrey Barnsley, Woodlands, Ga., to William Duncan, June 25, 1861, in Godfrey Barnsley Papers (University of Georgia Library, Athens).

[19] John Vestal Hadley, *Seven Months a Prisoner* (New York, 1898), 47.

[20] Mayes, *Lucius Q. C. Lamar*, 645.

[21] Frederick S. Daniel, *The Richmond Examiner during the War; or, The Writings of John M. Daniel. With a Memoir of his Life* (New York, 1868), 14–15.

But such ideas almost prostrated dogmatic Alexander H. Stephens—"That would never do . . . —not even for a day." And Stephens represented by far the wider point of view. It was the concentration of authority in the central government that was objected to, rather than its concentration in the states. State rights was the shibboleth in the South, argued by Jefferson and hallowed by the memory of Calhoun, the doctrine on which the South had grown away from the North, the panacea for every Southern ill. As an expression it would elicit a thousand thrilling emotions to one that the word "Confederate" would produce—it was only after the war that "Confederate" became a word to conjure with. A strong central government was as dangerous as the old Union had been: "Shall we wade through fire and blood only to substitute King Stork for King Log? Again, I ask, what are we fighting for?" queried a correspondent in the Richmond *Whig*.[22] The central government ought to be so conducted that "its citizens, so far as their personal interests would be thereby effected, would not even be aware that we had any Government." [23] The President should be incidental or accidental and should secure his position through the casting of lots. There ought not to be a capital district as provided for in the Confederate Constitution. There ought not to be a permanent capital—the Confederate government ought to migrate from state capital to state capital.

Then there was a growing opinion among Southerners that a proper concept of eternal law was the bulwark of all liberty. Universal suffrage would never be able to discover and conserve this law. Universal suffrage in the North was "organized confiscation, legalized violence and corruption . . . a moral disease of the body politic." It was mob government, radical democracy, "the willing instrument of consolidation in the hands of an abolition oligarchy," which had perverted the old Union. It was this the South was fighting against. The individual must be buried in the institution. The mob did not know what it was voting for, except to obtain money for doing it or to get a drink of whisky. Calhoun had recognized the tyranny of majorities and had sought remedies

22 Richmond *Daily Whig*, September 20, 1861.
23 Correspondent in Atlanta *Southern Confederacy*, May 9, 1861.

against them. The South had never believed in democracy; it had worked with the Democrats in the North only to secure a place of power in the government. Most positions should be appointive and not remunerative. Officers would serve without pay, if they were patriots. Now every petty sheriff, whisky-drinking constable, and justice of the peace must be elected and get a fee. All of this was Yankeeism, which the South should cast out—all this "universal suffrage—elective Judges—biennial Legislatures—and many other features of policy—all tending to degrade government and corrupt the people." [24]

Many Southern leaders had long since discarded Jefferson, excepting his state-rights arguments. Without so stating it, they had embraced Alexander Hamilton and John Adams. They believed in an aristocracy. Only an aristocracy could safeguard the liberties of all. An aristocracy afforded an "adequate embodiment of that regulated liberty beyond the control of ignorant and fanatical mobs; of that perfect order which reposes in security in that virtue, intelligence, and interested attachment, which the experience of all nations tell [sic] us are the only reliable safe-guards of liberty." [25] An observant Federal prisoner sensed Southern sentiment thus: "They will tell you that what we want is an aristocracy. That's what we are fighting for. That's what our training and mode of life demands. That's what we will have, and nothing short of that will satisfy the ambition of Southern chivalry." [26]

This aristocracy must be bred up to arms and empire, for after the Confederate victory at First Manassas the feeling grew that the Yankees were humbugs, "that the *white people* of the slaveholding States are the true masters—the real rulers of this continent." In fact, the Yankees were "little better than Chinese. They lay the same stress on the jingle of their dollars, that the Celestials do on the noise of their gongs." The editor of the Richmond *Whig* continued, "The art military should constitute a leading part of every white man's education. The right of voting should be a high priv-

[24] This point of view was widely expressed by Southern leaders, journalistic, governmental, and religious. For quotation, see Richmond *Daily Whig*, July 6, 1861.

[25] Frank H. Alfriend, "A Southern Republic and a Northern Democracy," in *Southern Literary Messenger*, XXXVII (1863), 285.

[26] Solon Hyde, *A Captive of War* (New York, 1900), 45.

ilege to be enjoyed by those only who are worthy to exercise it. In a word, the whole white population of the South should be wrought into a high-toned aristocracy." [27]

As here suggested, the Southern aristocracy was not to be restricted by any system of caste—the ideal was for all white Southerners ultimately to become aristocrats. It was exactly this which Stephens had in mind in his much-quoted "Corner Stone Speech," in which he said that the new government's cornerstone rested "upon the great truth, that the negro is not equal to the white man," that slavery for the black man made true freedom for the white man possible, and, by implication, that here lay the road to that universal aristocracy of the white man. A Richmond editor stated the same idea in these words: "We believe that it is not impossible, and that it is desirable, that our Confederacy should consist exclusively of gentlemen and negroes. By a wise system of government, encouraging the virtues which make the gentleman, and discouraging the vices which constitute the blackguard, the result is feasible. The object is worthy of the best efforts of our statesmen; for one pure, high-toned Southern gentleman, weighed in any scales, human or divine, is worth more than the entire twenty millions of Yankees." [28]

These adornments of state rights were argued only by the more philosophically-minded Southerners; it was not to be expected that Congressmen and other office seekers would be so bold as to come out openly for these aristocratic arguments. Yet they now and then appeared in the debates in Richmond. State-rights dogmas flourished openly like the proverbial green bay tree.

The democratic point of view must have been widely held by the mass of Southerners who thought of such subjects at all, but seldom did it find expression. Against the movement to restrict the suffrage, a voice was raised in Georgia, where it was argued that even the preachers were giving it support. Nine tenths of the soldiers were fighting for their political rights, so an Athens editor argued; but he admitted that there were dangers in going to either extreme: "On the one side we shall be threatened with an aristocratic form of government, tending toward monarchy; on the

[27] Richmond *Daily Whig*, July 23, 1861.
[28] *Ibid.*, December 19, 1861.

other extreme, with red republicanism, tending to anarchy." [29]

Had the South won its independence, it would undoubtedly have developed more toward a conservative aristocracy. Being denied peace in which to work, it developed a government of increasing centralization, much the same as Lincoln gave the North.

In line with its conservatism, the Confederacy debated much the abolition of the naturalization laws which it had inherited from the old Union and which had made possible the infiltration of masses of foreigners with their "dangerous European radical ideas." The repeal of the naturalization laws would bring about the "cessation of this poisonous infusion of bad races, worse habits, and fatal principles, which had so long weakened, and which would have soon destroyed, all the original characteristics of the republic." [30] Especially would they exclude Yankees. Representative John B. Clark of Missouri declared that he would "as soon admit to citizenship a devil from hell." He advocated a law banishing any Southerner who should marry a Yankee.[31] The South should grow its own citizens. In August, 1861, Congress passed a law giving the full protection of citizenship to any foreigners in the service of the Confederacy; but the next year it repealed the naturalization laws in a bill which President Davis vetoed on the ground that it denied citizenship to the many foreigners in the Confederate armies and, besides, was out of accord "with the civilization of the age." But as there were many aliens in the Confederacy who did not join the armies, there were widespread grumblings that they might become citizens of a country they would not defend.[32]

Also, there was the same question as in the old Union, whether there could be a national citizenship apart from state citizenship. Southerners generally had held that national citizenship could not exist apart from states—hence their quandary on what happened to

---

[29] Athens *Southern Watchman,* October 28, 1863. See also, *ibid.,* June 3.

[30] Richmond *Daily Examiner,* April 29, 1863.

[31] *Ibid.,* April 26, 1863.

[32] Governor Joseph E. Brown of Georgia issued a proclamation in 1864 banishing all aliens of military age who would not enlist. Augusta *Daily Constitutionalist,* July 30, 1864. The Mississippi legislature in 1863 passed a law banishing all aliens between eighteen and forty-five years of age who refused to enlist. James W. Garner, *Reconstruction in Mississippi* (New York, 1901), 27.

a person who refused to go along with his state when it seceded. Would he not be a man without a country? This feeling helped to induce many legalistically-minded Southerners to follow their states. A few of the Confederate states passed citizenship laws. In 1861 Georgia decreed that all resident aliens were citizens unless they made a positive declaration to the contrary within three months, and the next year Florida declared that no citizen of the United States might ever become a citizen of that state.

But it was with a light heart that most Southerners entered into the secession movement, for they felt that there would be no war; when the war came, they entered it lightheartedly, for they felt that they would surely win. The fact that the remaining area of the United States was about three times as large as the Confederacy, and its population almost four times as large as the number of white Southerners, did not in the beginning discourage them. Northerners would be poor soldiers compared with Southerners; and the more than 700,000 square miles of the Confederacy would be space enough in which to draw out Federal forces to their ultimate defeat, as surely as the immensity of Russian territory, as much as the Cossacks, had defeated Napoleon.[33] And though Southern manufactories were almost nonexistent as compared with Northern industry, Southerners ignored this woeful insufficiency as they pointed to their vastly strong agricultural establishment, whose cotton alone, in the opinion of Benjamin H. Hill, would pay for a successful war, if it took a hundred years to fight it. Many Southerners considered agriculture an element of strength and stability rather than a weakness, for thereby there was no concentration to be easily attacked and destroyed by the enemy as would be the case if the Confederacy's strength lay in its cities. "It is not

[33] The total white population in the eleven Confederate states in 1860 was about 5,400,000, and for the rest of the United States, about 21,200,000. There were about 3,500,000 slaves in the Confederacy and about 130,000 free Negroes. The Confederacy had about $6,740,000,000 of real and personal wealth, while the rest of the country had about $12,230,000,000. The Confederacy raised about half as much corn as the rest of the country, about a fourth as much wheat, about an eighteenth as much hay, and had about a tenth as much invested in manufactories. There were about 9,800 miles of railroads in the Confederacy to 19,000 beyond its limits. The Confederacy's 221 banks had about a fourth as much banking capital as the 1,421 elsewhere. Ernest A. Smith, *The History of the Confederate Treasury* (Harrisburg, Pa., 1901), 114-15.

the cities which raise cotton," said a Richmond editor, "they are small affairs at the best, and made up in great part of Yankees." [34] Even if the Confederacy should be overrun, thought another, it would take 500,000 troops to police it and cost $500,000,000 a year.

The Confederacy took on an attitude of good cheer, from President Davis on down to the most lowly citizen. Time and again from the beginning to the final collapse there were voluble leaders who insisted that the Confederacy had sufficient resources to win the war. James D. B. De Bow, in his well-known *Review*, promised that the South would be "more than a match, when fighting upon her own soil and in sight of her own homes, for any twenty million that could be organized against" it.[35] Davis' early messages to Congress radiated confidence; a former Unionist of North Carolina declared that the "cartridge box is preferred to the ballot box," and that the "very women and children are for war." [36] The masses everywhere became war-minded, and some even said war was a great institution, bringing out the best in the people. War-minded Southerners thought they heard the guns of battle as far as 150 miles away; a Huntsville, Alabama, girl came into possession of some hairs from the tail of Beauregard's horse and to some of her special friends she sent a few; war-consciousness ruled people's minds. A Georgian said, "the climate will fight for us in summer and we will *try* in winter." [37]

To serious-minded Southerners, in their calmer moments, it was evident from the beginning that if the victory depended entirely on material resources, the South must inevitably lose; but, rightly, they held that other, intangible, factors were involved. They remembered from Biblical lore that the race was not always to the swift nor the battle to the strong. They also knew that it was the actual use made of resources and not merely their possession that counted. In fine, it was not only skill in handling resources, but morale—the will to win. If the South possessed enough of this, it could not lose. Davis said, "Liberty is always won where there

---

[34] Richmond *Daily Dispatch*, March 13, 1862.

[35] *De Bow's Review*, XXX (1861), 681–82.

[36] Jonathan Worth to Gaius Winningham, May 20, 1861, in Hamilton (ed.), *Correspondence of Jonathan Worth*, I, 149.

[37] Barnsley, New Orleans, to John R. Gardner, May 4, 1861, in Barnsley Papers (University of Georgia Library).

exists the unconquerable will to be free, and we have reason to know the strength that is given by a conscious sense not only of the magnitude but of the righteousness of our cause"; [38] Stephens knew that no Northern army could ever defeat a people "determined never to submit"; and the Richmond *Whig* declared that a "virtuous and gallant people in a good cause never have failed." [39]

Having less of every other war resource, the South must excel in one thing especially—morale. If it should ever have less of this the war would be lost. Without the will to win, George Fitzhugh said, all the money in the world would be of no avail; and the Richmond *Examiner,* somewhat discouraged by 1864, said, "The country will never be unable, if willing, to supply the wants of its Government, but it may easily become unwilling; and then no pressure of legislation will be of any value." [40] As the war wore on, people in their private correspondence began to give way to such expressions as these: "The discouraging spirit of despondency, is to be dreaded more than the power of the enemy"; and "Our great danger and only one, is that the spirit of the people may give way." [41] And herein, actually, lay the fundamental cause for the collapse of the Confederacy.

Propaganda techniques, as they were later to be developed, were never used by either the South or the North in this war. Yet without any central organization or direction, sundry devices grew up to hold and increase enthusiasm and to steel the hearts of the people. Songs were written and sung, and patriotic stationery, whereon Confederate flags, symbols of liberty, and fervent poetry carried their messages, was widely used. On one envelope was this: A man sitting on a bale of cotton, with these words, "Our Throne. Cotton defeated Packenham, and cotton will defeat 'Ape Lincoln.' " On another was this stanza:

> *Stand firmly by your cannon,*
> *Let ball and grape-shot fly,*

[38] Richardson (comp.), *Messages and Papers of the Confederacy,* I, 144.

[39] Athens *Southern Watchman,* February 3, 1864.

[40] Richmond *Daily Examiner,* December 29, 1864.

[41] John A. Gilmer to Vance, February 14, 1865, in Vance Papers (North Carolina State Archives, Raleigh), VI; Vance to John H. Houghton, August 17, 1863, *ibid.,* III.

And trust in God and Davis.
But keep your powder dry.

To popularize Davis and the principal military leaders, their pictures were offered for sale; and the only instance in American history where a picture of a living person has appeared on a postage stamp was Jefferson Davis on Confederate stamps. Many Confederates who had never seen Davis before the war and were never to see him during the conflict saw a poor likeness of him on these stamps.

For a time it was somewhat of an enigma as to what should be done about those two patriotic days of old, the Fourth of July and Washington's Birthday; but it did not take long for most Confederates to appropriate them and turn their celebration into good propaganda. "The Confederate States of 1861 are acting over again the history of the American Revolution of 1776," said the New Orleans *Picayune*. "To them, therefore, belongs the most sacred right of property in the memories of Independence Day, as the loyal inheritors of its principles and its glories." [42] A Mississippian said the Yankees need not think that they could cheat the Confederacy out of this possession: "We trust the day may never come when the people of the Confederate States will cease to celebrate with becoming marks of respect and reverence this great and glorious Anniversary." [43] It was celebrated every year throughout the war with guns booming, Confederate flags raised high, fireworks by night, military organizations parading, bands playing, speechmaking, and with newspapers suspending their issue for that day, having in the previous number published the Declaration of Independence. Only in 1864 Richmond, the beleaguered city of the Confederacy, was less enthusiastic, and the *Examiner* reported: "No windy orator beat his bosom and sawed the air in the Capitol Square, and gauged his patriotism by the amount of gin in his glass. No bunting flapped in your face; no American eagle screamed; nobody got drunk because it was the fourth day of July. We are glad to record the fact, and to know that all such exhibitions

---

[42] Moore (ed.), *Rebellion Record*, II, 252 (documents).
[43] Paulding (Miss.) *Eastern Clarion*, July 12, 1861.

of rank liberty run to seed is [sic] now of purely Yankee cultivation." [44]

As for Washington's Birthday, it now had a double significance, for it was on this day that the permanent Confederate Government was inaugurated and so it now became the natal day of the Confederacy. Moreover, Washington had been a rebel, and would have been a Confederate, it was held, had he lived in 1861. This day was observed as a holiday in the Confederate capital.

Confederate heroes, living and dead, greatly aroused enthusiasm for the cause and determination to win final victory. "Shouts of victory and wails for the dead were strangely blended," thought a Virginia refugee. The first hero was a live one, General Beauregard, who had reduced Fort Sumter; but very soon, vying with him for first honors was a Shanghai rooster, which the Confederates in a bantering spirit erected high and which some suggested should be made the emblem of the Confederacy. The rooster came to fame in this fashion: In an insignificant bombardment of Aquia, in northern Virginia, early in the war, the report was spread that warships expended $6,000 worth of ammunition and succeeded in killing only one setting hen. Whereupon a rooster mounted a dung heap and crowed defiance as each shot was fired. Its owner was soon offered $50 for it but replied that he would not sell it for its weight in gold. There soon followed two dead heroes: James W. Jackson, who slew Elmer Ellsworth as he attempted to remove a Confederate flag from the Marshall House in Alexandria, Virginia, and who himself was killed by the invading Federal troops, was long remembered; pamphlets were written about him, and collections were taken up for his widow and children. Under somewhat similar circumstances William B. Mumford was hanged in New Orleans when on the fall of that city in 1862, he removed a United States flag, which had been prematurely run up on the Mint Building. Benjamin F. Butler was given credit for this atrocity, and hatred of Butler for this and other reasons was as powerful in arousing the Confederacy as memory of the martyr. Governor Thomas O. Moore in an address "To the People of Louisiana" told how Mumford had been shown the gallows and offered his liberty if he would swear allegiance to the United States.

[44] Richmond *Daily Examiner*, July 5, 1864.

"Scorning to stain his soul with such foul dishonor," continued the Governor, "he met his fate courageously and transmitted to his countrymen a fresh example of what we will do and dare when under the inspiration of fervid patriotism." [45]

Every Confederate officer of any prominence became somebody's hero, but like Jackson and Mumford, his fame spread if he were killed. "Old Pap" Price of Missouri early became a hero far beyond the borders of his own state, and though rumor killed him as many times as a cat has lives, to increase his fame he lived through the war. A hero whose renown early became so great that his death in 1864 could not increase it was John H. Morgan, the intrepid Kentucky cavalry leader. His playground was Tennessee and Kentucky, but he extended his activities in a raid across the Ohio River into Indiana and Ohio, where in 1863 he was captured and imprisoned in the penitentiary like a common felon. Making his escape, he returned to the Confederacy and made a grand entry into Richmond, where he was given a reception which was attended by high Confederate generals and at which flowed, in bumpers of health-drinking, ten gallons of apple brandy. There followed a dance at the Ballard House, an entertainment at the Presidential Mansion, honors by the Virginia legislature, and a gift of a "massive and elegant pair of solid silver spurs." Books were written about his exploits, which would "go far to make up the romance of this war," songs were composed, such as "John Morgan's Raid," and Paul Hamilton Hayne wrote a poem about him. Soldiers deserted the armies in Virginia to join Morgan. In September, 1864, killed by treachery in East Tennessee, he was returned to Richmond to be given a state funeral and interment in Hollywood Cemetery.

One of the earliest and most pathetic state funerals was that of O. Jennings Wise, son of former Governor Henry A. Wise, killed

---

[45] Sources of the two quotations, respectively, [McGuire], *Diary of a Southern Refugee,* 179 (January, 1863); *Official Records,* Ser. I, Vol. XV, 509. One of the most heroic figures of the war, whose pathetic execution, little heralded during the war, proved strongly appealing to later generations, was the twenty-one-year-old Sam Davis. A private in the First Tennessee Infantry, he was captured back of the Federal lines with information of enemy strength. Rather than divulge the name of the Federal officer who had given him that information, he went to his execution by hanging. A statue of him was erected on the capitol grounds at Nashville.

on Roanoke Island early in 1862. The next year the greatest of the Confederate dead lay in state in Richmond. Stonewall Jackson, remindful of "Cromwell or some old Covenanter," had antedated Lee as a living hero. Now that he was dead of wounds at Chancellorsville, his death was announced with "feelings of sorrow inexpressible." "From the Rio Grande to the Potomac will go up one wild wail of lamentation over the great departed. All Israel will mourn, for truly a great and good man has fallen." [46] The Confederacy was frequently treated to these great emotional outpourings. In early 1862 Ben McCulloch, the six-foot, athletic former Texas Ranger, looking much like Garibaldi, the cynosure of all eyes, was killed. Soon there followed blond John Pelham of Stuart's cavalry, the idol of many a Confederate girl, then Turner Ashby of Jackson's army, and in 1864 the great Jeb Stuart himself. Meantime, Thomas R. R. Cobb and Maxcy Gregg had been killed at Fredericksburg in December, 1862. Concerning the death of these two the editor of the *Southern Literary Messenger* said, "The annihilation of the entire Yankee nation . . . would hardly compensate for the death of the meanest Southern private, much less such heroic spirits as Gregg and Cobb." [47] Francis S. Bartow and Bernard E. Bee had fallen at the very beginning, at First Manassas, and the Confederacy was made to mourn dead generals and other high officers to the end, even Ambrose Powell Hill, just before Appomattox. In all, the Confederacy lost seventy-eight generals, killed in the war.

All these deaths meant sorrow in the hearts of the people, but not despair. Their mournings were sublimated into a determination to fight on with renewed vigor. The leader that was to typify the embattled Confederacy, sacrosanct from the time he took command in Virginia in 1862 throughout the rest of the war and ever thereafter, was Robert E. Lee. By the middle of 1862 an editor could say that his "reputation now overshadows all others. His fame has been nobly won." [48] At the same time another could say,

---

[46] Sandersville *Central Georgian*, May 13, 1863. The editor of the Richmond *Daily Enquirer*, May 11, 1863, said, "The hero of the war, the great genius, that noble patriot, the support and hope of this country, is no more."

[47] *Southern Literary Messenger*, XXXVII (1863), 56.

[48] *Ibid.*, XXXIV (1862), 504.

"The rise which this officer has suddenly taken in the public confidence is without a precedent." [49] He was presented with a house in Richmond, which he refused, golden spurs, hats, and other articles expressive of esteem. His name alone kept his armies together for the last six months of the war.

Morale was, of course, highest at the beginning of the war. Then and for some time following, this enthusiasm for the war expressed itself in impressive and unusual ways. Now, more than ever after, the Confederacy appeared as one great family; people felt obligated to each other and to their government like loyal members of that family. To the governments, state and Confederate, the people, high and low, poured out their contributions. Large planters offered the free services of their slaves; an Arkansas widow gave the Confederate government 400 bales of cotton; a Charleston lady gave her silverware; and a Charleston gentleman donated $10,000 in gold. A lady schoolteacher gave her full salary, and the students of Lucy Cobb Institute in Athens, Georgia, sought to save the Confederacy from bankruptcy by a donation of $120. At the suggestion of a Georgia clergyman, on a Fast Day in the summer of 1861 the churches took up a collection for the Confederacy, amounting to $5,278.88, which the Congress appropriated for sick and wounded soldiers. A private killed in action willed his estate to the Confederate government, and a Georgian offered to be one of 100,000 people to give $1,000 apiece for building a Confederate navy. A New Orleans merchant gave a Mississippi county a battery of six cannon, worth $40,000, to stimulate recruiting; a Georgia lumber mill offered to saw free 20,000 feet of lumber for pike handles; and the railroads gave reduced rates on all Confederate business. So the story went, of strong citizens lifting up weak governments.

Attracting even greater concern were the soldiers. No one could be so mean as not to do something for a soldier—every civilian ought to adopt one. Many wealthy men equipped whole companies, whether their own or units which they had adopted. A Georgian not only equipped a company, but subscribed his whole cotton crop for Confederate bonds and promised a $50,000 prize for the victory which won Southern independence. A patriotic blacksmith

[49] Richmond *Daily Dispatch*, July 9, 1862.

equipped a company with bowie knives which he had made; twenty-nine girls in Wesleyan Female College at Macon, Georgia, donated to the soldiers blankets from their own beds; and Joseph Henry Lumpkin, Chief Justice of the Georgia Supreme Court, gave $1,000 a year out of his salary for the transportation of indigent soldiers on their way home. Hotels gave free meals and beds to traveling soldiers; a Richmond hotel turned itself into a hospital; and the proprietor of the famous Spotswood House in Richmond, a foreigner too old for the army, offered his full time to be used in any way possible.

The scarcity of metals for casting cannon suggested to General Beauregard that a supply might be had from the bells of churches, plantations, and courthouses. Immediately churches throughout the Confederacy began to donate their bells. In some towns a strange silence pervaded the Lord's Day—all of the bells had gone to war. "Let these bells in future be rung with powder and balls, and toll the death-knell of every Yankee who comes within their range," said a patriot; [50] and another observed, "No bell in our Confederacy has ever chimed more sweetly or more acceptably to Heaven, than when cast into cannon." [51] Some of the churches insisted that the batteries made of their bells be given the name of the church, as the Second Baptist Church Battery. Thus rang the bells in rhyme:

> Melt the bells, melt the bells,
> That for years have called to prayer,
> And, instead, the cannon's roar
> Shall resound the valleys o'er,
> That the foe may catch despair
> From the bells.[52]

Old brass kettles, andirons, and other household equipment, worn-out printing presses, and the odds and ends of old machinery helped to make up the scrap heap. On the fall of New Orleans a sad note was added to some of the Confederate bells, for 418 of them collected there fell into the hands of the Federal forces, who sent

---

[50] Atlanta *Southern Confederacy*, March 29, 1862.
[51] Richmond *Semi-Weekly Enquirer*, April 1, 1862.
[52] Moore (ed.), *Songs and Ballads of the Southern People*, 47.

them to Boston where they were sold for $30,000, either to be melted down or to ring forth mockery at the rebels.[53]

Benjamin H. Hill declared in 1861 that every man, woman, and child had become an assistant quartermaster or assistant commissary, and Robert M. T. Hunter as late as 1864 could ask the rhetorical question: "When has the world beheld a nobler spectacle than that of a whole people springing to arms in defense of their liberties, and maintaining the war for three long years by levies en masse—the living pressing forward with unflinching will and unfaltering devotion to take the places of the dead who fell where they held the front ranks of battle?" [54] And De Bow declared that this was nothing more than should be expected: "The country is entitled to the services of every man, woman, and child within its limits; and upon no other theory of duty can any be exempted in a period like this of terrible trials and necessities." [55] The Virginia legislature resolved that a Book of Honor should be kept in which to record the especially meritorious services of Virginia citizens and corporations. A modern historian of the Confederacy said that evidences of kindly generosity "run like threads of gold through the woven tapestry of any adequate account of the history of the people of the Southern Confederacy." [56]

Naturally it helped morale to be told that the war would be short. "How long will the war last" was constantly on the minds of the people. A few weeks after Fort Sumter, Howell Cobb wrote his wife, "Toombs agrees with me that we will come to a settlement without much if any fighting—others think differently." [57] But Lee about this time wrote his wife that the war might last for ten years; some thought this revolution, like the old Revolution, might take seven years; and another thought that it was going to be "a *big war,* & we have but one course left us, & that is to whip

---

[53] Columbus (Ga.) *Weekly Enquirer,* August 19, 1862. General Benjamin F. Butler's forces seized some of these bells from the churches.

[54] *Journal of the Congress of the Confederate States,* III, 795.

[55] *De Bow's Review,* XXXIV (1864), 48.

[56] Charles W. Ramsdell, *Behind the Lines in the Southern Confederacy* (Baton Rouge, 1944), 121.

[57] Cobb, Montgomery, to his wife, April 29, 1861, in Howell Cobb Papers. Cobb, in Montgomery, May 11, 1861, wrote Williams Rutherford, *ibid.,* "I indulge the hope & conviction that the struggle will be a short one."

it or die in the attempt." [58] After First Manassas, in July, 1861, Cobb, the perennial optimist, thought it could not last much longer, but many others were not carried away by this widespread feeling. By 1862 Stephens, tired of hearing the question, answered, "I believe it will last until it is ended." [59] Others, more explicit, took comfort in the fact that modern methods of fighting now made hundred-year wars impossible. After three years of war, the question became more insistent. An impatient editor said that fifty times a day had he been asked for the answer. In reply he would say that it reminded him of the man who dreamed that he had slept fifty years and that when he awoke he saw seventeen men on the south bank of the Rapidan River and was told that they were Lee's Army of Northern Virginia, and that the Federal army of twenty-one men was on the other bank, but he was assured that the Confederates expected to get the advantage of position, whip the Yankees, and end the war immediately. [60] Another editor offered this wholesome advice, "If we organize for a war which may be prosecuted until the year 1900 we may hope, with God's favor, to see the end of it in the present year." [61] The American Revolution was a great comfort for the Confederates to point to; newspapers published histories of the Revolution to refresh the memories of the people on how long it had lasted and on what reverses had been endured—much worse than the Confederates had ever suffered. Even on April 15, 1865, six days after Appomattox, a South Carolinian, not having heard of the end, remarked that conditions had been much worse in the Revolution.

The most exhilarating tonic and the most cruel poison were combined in the simple word *rumor*. Rumors arose because of poor news service and the Confederate policy of giving out little information, through the efforts of well-meaning patriots to put the best interpretation on events, and by the sly work of spies and traitors. The people were lifted to the skies by the exhilaration of good news and dropped into the depths of despondency by the real

[58] Crawford, Columbus, Ga., to Cobb, July 15, 1861, *ibid.*
[59] Charleston *Daily Courier,* February 12, 1862.
[60] Richmond *Daily Enquirer,* August 10, 1864.
[61] Augusta *Weekly Chronicle & Sentinel,* January 20, 1864.

facts of defeat later learned. Frequently the people were led to believe that England and France had recognized the independence of the Confederacy, that Cincinnati, St. Louis, Baltimore, and other Federal cities had been captured, that Lincoln and Grant were dead. At Fort Donelson the Confederates had won a great victory, proved by the newspaper headlines, "Clouds Lifting," "A Complete Victory. 1,000 Hessians Taken Prisoners." A little later the newspapers had recaptured New Orleans; but the grandest victory was at Gettysburg. General Meade was killed: "Complete Route [sic] of the Yankees at Gettysburg! Forty Thousand Prisoners Taken!!!" Lee would soon take Philadelphia, and Washington was on the verge of falling. All was untrue, and one observer remarked, "it is astonishing what people can bring themselves to believe if they try." [62]

On the other hand, rumors of bad news, untrue, spread. Davis was dead—had committed suicide—had died a natural death. Rumor felled Vicksburg almost every day during May and June, preceding its actual fall in July, 1863. General John B. Hood had been killed at Chickamauga, and newspapers published laudatory biographies of him, only to retract the next day when it was learned that he had merely been wounded. The charge, perennial in every war, passed the rounds of how the socks knit by the fingers of devoted wives, sisters, mothers, and sweethearts for their brave soldiers were actually being sold by the Quartermaster Department. As early as 1861 a Georgian concluded that there were "so many false statements published it is difficult to get at the truth and the lies printed in our papers are scarcely exceeded by those which appear in the U.S." [63] A Texan declared that he had "become sick of rumors, reports, extras, and newspapers, all lies, lies from beginning to end." Even the newspapers admitted their shortcomings; one entitled a column "News and Rumors." Another confessed that people were "too busy now contriving how they shall live and keep warm next winter to take the time to fabricate sensation stories."

[62] Fitzgerald Ross, *A Visit to the Cities and Camps of the Confederate States* (Edinburgh, 1865), 94.

[63] Barnsley, Woodlands, Ga., to Lucien Barnsley, July 22, 1861, in Barnsley Papers (University of Georgia Library).

Flour at $75 a barrel and beef at $1.75 a pound were "sensations sufficient for the public without taxing their imagination for others." [64]

But there was true news of many victories which had its lasting effect on the people's morale. The tally the newspapers kept for propaganda showed that by the end of the year 1861 the Confederates had won 53 victories to 8 by the Federals and that the Confederates had lost 6,000 men while the Federals' losses were 21,000. In the light of this, no wonder the Charleston *Courier* could say on January 1, 1862, "The face of this day that ushers in another year is bright and clear."

Confederate morale took its first sharp dip in the spring of 1862. On February 8 Roanoke Island fell; on the sixteenth there was disaster at Fort Donelson, followed by the fall of Nashville a week later. In early May, New Orleans fell, while McClellan's armies were beseiging Richmond. By summer the Federal flag was flying in every Confederate state. There was much brave talk but also deep despondency and fear of the approaching end. But the Confederacy rebounded as McClellan was driven back and as victories followed at Second Manassas and at Fredericksburg near the end of the year.

Confederates everywhere looked upon 1863 as the year of fate; in January Davis declared, "we have every reason to expect that this will be the closing year of the war." [65] Chancellorsville, in early May, gave them confidence that the year was theirs, but in early July came simultaneously the double thud of defeat at Gettysburg and Vicksburg. A few days after these battles, John Beauchamp Jones, sedulously keeping his *Rebel War Clerk's Diary* with an eye to its future publication, wrote, "This is the day of fate— and, without a cloud in the sky, the red sun, dimly seen through the mist (at noonday), casts a baleful light on the earth. It has been so for several days." [66] Now, for the first time, doubts of ultimate victory took deep root. There was "gloom of almost despondency,"

[64] Richmond *Daily Examiner*, October 29, 1863.

[65] Richardson (comp.), *Messages and Papers of the Confederacy*, I, 277.

[66] John B. Jones, *A Rebel War Clerk's Diary at the Confederate States Capital* (Philadelphia, 1866), I, 375.

thought a Richmond editor. "Many faint-hearted regard all as lost." [67] From Alabama came the sad conclusion, "We are without doubt gone up; no help can be had"; [68] and even President Davis could say, "We are now in the darkest hour of our political existence." [69] This dreadful year came to an end on this note: "to-day closes the gloomiest year of our struggle." [70] Yet in 1864 people were to take heart again.

All along, looking away from their own troubles, Southerners took comfort in Northern weaknesses and magnified them. Without the balance wheel of the South, democratic mobs would soon pervert and destroy the old United States; the lack of cotton would bring on it economic and financial collapse; grass had by the summer of 1861 begun growing in the streets of Northern cities, and, to prove it, weeds plucked in the streets of New York were put on display in Selma, Alabama. The North was spending three times as much on the war as was the Confederacy; it was soon costing the Yankees $2,000,000 a day; such a debt must surely crush the government without the Confederate armies having to give the final blow.

Also, hatred of the Yankees would add strength to the Confederacy. The atrocities committed by their invading armies were played high. "Yankee" became "henceforth and forever an *odious* name," and "damyankee," so celebrated in later generations, originated as early as 1861 when a Negro slave forcibly taken away from his master called his abductors "de d'yam Yankees." [71] According to a religious paper, vandalism had been supplanted by a new term: "This war will give to the pages of history another word,

[67] Richmond *Semi-Weekly Examiner*, August 13, 1863.

[68] E. S. Dargin, Mobile, Ala., to James A. Seddon, July 24, 1863, in *Official Records*, Ser. IV, Vol. II, 664.

[69] Davis to General E. Kirby Smith, July 14, 1863, in Rowland (ed.), *Jefferson Davis, Constitutionalist*, V, 554.

[70] Richmond *Daily Examiner*, December 31, 1863.

[71] Atlanta *Southern Confederacy*, July 24, 1862; Richmond *Daily Whig*, November 30, 1861. Hatred of the Yankees will be further discussed in connection with atrocities. The *Illustrated London News*, XLIII (August 22, 1863), 181, said, "The South, with no advantage except that of 'immortal hate'—which is a better provocative of valour than all the wealth and bounty-money in the world—has maintained the contest with a heroism that has carried men's hearts captive with admiration."

expressive of a still deeper dye of depravity than Europe ever dreamed of. It is Yankeeism." [72] And the Texas legislature resolved that, "Army, Government, and people, have united to make the name of *Yankee,* suggestive as it was before, of fraud, now the synonym of *barbarism* and *baseness.*" [73] Remembering again the American Revolution, Southerners liked to call the Federal soldiers Hessians.

Closely akin emotionally to hatred is terror. The South would use this weapon, too, to build up morale. Representative Pryor of Virginia told the Confederate Congress that this war was no pastime, no tournament, "no holiday rehearsal of war"; it was a "red, wrathful and consuming war" in which the issue had to be victory or death. By the North's two Confiscation Acts, the Federals were laying plans not only to dispossess Southerners of their lands and other wealth, but to Africanize the South by setting their slaves over them. The Confederate Congress resolved that Southerners would "never, on any terms, politically affiliate with a people who are guilty of an invasion of their soil and the butchery of their citizens"; [74] and a Richmond editor pictured the people turned out of their property "while Doodle is to cock his legs over our fire places, snort hallelujahs in our churches, and abolish slavery by whipping the negroes to death, if they do not kill themselves by hard work in six months after they have fallen into his hands." [75] The people were implored to remember the fate of Ireland and Poland. The embittered Texas legislature in 1864 charged that the Northerners were "lying to themselves, and pretending to the rest of the world that" they were "fighting the battle of freedom for four millions of happy and contented negroes," but they were in fact "attempting the enslavement of eight millions of freemen." [76] Before the war was six months old the editor of the Richmond *Whig* pictured the terrors of invasion and conquest by the Northerners: "They have sworn that our roofs shall be given to the

[72] Tuskegee (Ala.) *South Western Baptist,* October 13, 1864.

[73] Broadside of Texas Resolution of November 12, 1864 (Texas State Library, Austin).

[74] Matthews (ed.), *Public Laws of the Confederate States,* 1 Cong., 1 Sess., 1862, p. 53.

[75] Richmond *Daily Dispatch,* May 6, 1862.

[76] Broadside of Texas Resolution of November 12, 1864.

flames and our bodies to the eagles, and they have made good the oath wherever they have had the power. They refuse to treat us as belligerents, but hold us as rebels and traitors, for whom the gibbet waits. They war upon women and children, forbid medicine to the sick, seek to incite slaves to insurrection, carry handcuffs and halters for their masters, and show us by all they do that our only safety is in victory. We cannot afford to be defeated by such an enemy. The war that they are waging strikes at everything dear to us— our institutions, our civilization, our society, our existence. Nothing so helpless as to awaken their mercy—nothing so venerable as to command their respect." [77]

Morale was the most potent weapon the South had; and with all of the Confederates' unco-ordinated efforts at building it up and maintaining it, they lost this weapon, and, therefore, the war.

[77] Richmond *Daily Whig,* October 28, 1861.

CHAPTER V

ENEMIES, SPIES, AND TRAITORS
—AND RECONSTRUCTION

DESPITE the apparent unanimity of feeling that in the beginning prevailed over large sections of the South, there was, of course, no universal support of secession and of the young Confederate government in any part of the South, and in considerable areas there was never majority support. The great thrust of the Appalachian Highlands, extending as far south as northern Georgia and Alabama, and including the western parts of Virginia and North Carolina and the eastern sections of Kentucky and Tennessee, was primarily Union in sentiment. There had been an unsympathetic feeling within the South between these mountainous regions and the plantation country, especially of the Lower South, based on a feeling of isolation on the part of the former growing out of lack of transportation connections, a lack of influence in the state governments, and on the presence of only a small slave population—all of which gave rise to a lack of identity of general interests. There were also other parts of the South, not mountainous but of the thinner soils, which maintained strong Union sentiment. The greatest common denominator was the fear of what might happen to all if the slaves, in the course of time, were ever made free.

The most spectacular Union movement within the South was the breakaway of the western part of Virginia in 1861, its organization into another state, and its ultimate admission into the Union in 1863 as West Virginia. This rape of Virginia's western counties remained in the minds of Virginians and of the Confederate Congress a wrong to be righted before peace should ever be agreed to. Rather than see this disruption become permanent, Congress would uphold

Virginia's authority "to the uttermost limits of her ancient boundaries, at any and every cost." [1]

At the same time that West Virginia was a-borning, mountainous East Tennessee sought to make itself a state; but it found much more difficulty, for there was no easy road for Federal troops to go to its aid, as they had done for West Virginia. Abraham Lincoln, longing to free the East Tennesseans from Confederate control, attempted to send troops through both Virginia and Kentucky, but not until 1863 did aid arrive. By this time the course of events made it inexpedient for East Tennessee to attempt statehood. Also there was talk in northern Alabama of erecting that region into the State of Nickajack, but the movement never attained strength.

Assisted by Confederate deserters and urged on by growing war-weariness, certain other regions became disaffected. It did not take much to wean away Tishomingo County in northern Mississippi, though Jones County in the southeastern part of the state became more famous, as it took on the popular name, Republic of Jones. The erroneous tradition arose that it had seceded from Mississippi; but after the war so ashamed were the people of its record that the legislature changed the name of the county to Davis and the county seat to Leesburg, though the original names were later restored.[2] In Texas the Germans, who had settled there in the 1840's, formed nests of Unionism which gave the Confederate authorities much trouble. In eastern North Carolina there was a considerable sprinkling of Unionists, sometimes called Buffaloes, who joined the Federal armies when they marched into the state in 1861–1862.

But apart from group or regional reactions there were individual Southerners who went against the current, wherever they might be. Of course, the major sentiment in the Upper South had been Unionist until Lincoln's call for troops, when the great majority, like Zebulon B. Vance of North Carolina, deserted their Unionism.

[1] *Journal of the Congress of the Confederate States*, I, 689–90; James M. Matthews (ed.), *Public Laws of the Confederate States of America. . . . First Session of the Second Congress; 1864* (Richmond, 1864), 285; Matthews (ed.), *Public Laws of the Confederate States*, 1 Cong., 1 Sess., 1862, p. 53.

[2] Natchez *Weekly Courier*, July 12, 1864; John K. Bettersworth, *Confederate Mississippi, The People and Policies of a Cotton State in Wartime* (Baton Rouge, 1943), 216 ff.; Georgia Lee Tatum, *Disloyalty in the Confederacy* (Chapel Hill, 1934), 98.

Unionists in the Lower South, like Stephens, went with their states when secession came; but the unique case of a Unionist who did not change when his state seceded and yet maintained the respect and love of his fellow man to the end was James L. Pettigru of South Carolina. When he died in 1863, he was memorialized not only in South Carolina but also in the North.[3]

Andrew Johnson of East Tennessee was the only member of Congress from a seceding state who refused to resign and return home. However, the most notorious uncompromising Unionist in the Confederacy was William G. Brownlow, popularly called "Parson Brownlow," from the same part of Tennessee. The sharp, cutting, grotesque language of vituperation against Confederates, which he used in his Knoxville *Whig*, finally got him into trouble. Fleeing into the Great Smoky Mountains for refuge, he was induced to return to Knoxville, and rather than make a martyr of him, which he craved, the Confederate authorities pushed him through the Federal lines. The speech which he had memorized to be delivered from his gallows thus came to be so many wasted words.[4]

The martyr role had an appeal for Southern Unionists. In Mississippi, John H. Aughey, a New York-born Presbyterian preacher who refused to support the Confederacy, was driven from the state; but appearing to fear that he might not be able to escape and might be hanged, he wrote a lugubrious farewell letter to his wife, his obituary, a curious address to his own soul, and, obligingly, his soul's answer.[5]

A people can believe so thoroughly in law and order that they violate their fundamental convictions in attempting to maintain them. As long as times were normal, the South believed its own order was fixed and permanent; but with the abnormalities of

[3] Charleston *Daily Courier*, May 12, 1863.

[4] E. Merton Coulter, *William G. Brownlow, Fighting Parson of the Southern Highlands* (Chapel Hill, 1937), 134–207. It was charged at this time in the South that Andrew Johnson's grandfather had been hanged as a Tory spy and marauder during the American Revolution; that a cousin had been hanged as a horse thief; and that Andrew himself had hurried away from his North Carolina home to Tennessee to escape a like fate for some similar crime. Sandersville *Central Georgian*, July 2, 1862.

[5] See John H. Aughey, *The Iron Furnace; or, Slavery and Secession* (Philadelphia, 1863).

secession there grew up widespread fear that spies and traitors might upset this order—that the South was sitting on the proverbial powder keg. Of course, their great terror was the possibility of a servile insurrection. There was the patrol system, designed to control the slaves, but it had fallen into disuse except in times of excitement. As the revivifying of the patrols was not now considered sufficient, a more closely knit and quicker-acting organization sprang into existence throughout the South. Unlike the patrol system it was extralegal, though legal in the sense that it represented the deepest convictions of a substantial element of the people; yet it was dangerous, as it tended to undermine all government.

In early January, 1861, people in Columbia County, Georgia, formed what they called Fredonia Guards, pledged to defend one another, their families, their homes and property. However, the more typical organization represented a smaller area and a smaller personnel and was called a Vigilance Committee. In Montgomery, Alabama, the committee consisted of twenty-four citizens; in Greene County, Georgia, it was made up of ten men; whereas in Washington County, Georgia, there was a central committee composed of one representative from each militia district, who could call to his aid as many men as needed for any emergency. In these committees there was represented a sort of revolutionary local government, not invisible but representing the will of an inflamed and half-terrorized people. "Every town and neighborhood," said a Georgia editor, "should organize a vigilance committee of its most discreet men, and a patrol of its most active men." [6] There was no

6 Macon *Daily Telegraph*, April 23, 1861. Dr. Hiram F. Nichols was driven from Atlanta for being a "Black Republican" and abolitionist. Atlanta *Southern Confederacy*, June 2, 1861. Notice of a reward of $250 was carried in this same paper, May 28, 1861, for George Martin, "dead or alive, charged with uttering treasonable sentiments against the Southern Confederacy, and admitted by him—and for an attempt to take the life of Lieut. Carruthers, when under arrest." The Sandersville *Central Georgian*, May 22, 1861, advised that suspicious strangers should be closely watched, and "Should they be caught aiding our enemies, or tampering with our institutions, let their doom be sealed upon the nearest tree." The following sentiment, expressed in a letter from a Georgian to Alexander H. Stephens, had it been known to the local vigilance committee, would undoubtedly have produced quick action against the author: "This war of destruction *must* be stopped. Reconstruction is better than fire and sword. . . . My God what has the nation come to?" D. F. Brandons (?), Thomasville, Ga., to Stephens, July 11, 1861, in Alexander H. Stephens Papers (microfilm in the University of Texas Library, from original in Division of Manuscripts, Library of

appeal from its decision. Suspecting a John Brown in every stranger they saw, these committees watched railway stations as well as the country villages and districts and arrested suspicious strangers or local citizens considered traitors to the Confederate cause. They arrested people, tried them, and punished them by whipping, banishing, or hanging. When they began to let their activities touch business affairs and trivialities, as was always the danger in such extralegal government, they lost their popular support and gradually disappeared as the war wore on. A Georgia editor declared the vigilance committee was "an illegal, irresponsible organization, usurping all the power it pretends to exercise"; [7] and an outraged Virginian exclaimed: "A Vigilent Committy! Great God! and has it come to this that the friend[s] of the union are to be harrassed by a Vigilent Commity? then let us have a Robespier to fill up our cup of iniquities that the vengeance of heaven may fall upon us at once; and give us a Merciful Bonaparte." [8]

The underlying feeling which seemed to pervade Southerners that their constituted government could not act heroically had a further expression in their habit of appointing a Committee of Safety to take charge on the approaching fall of a city. When New Orleans was in danger a Committee of Safety was appointed, which raised $1,250,000 for the defense of the city. Like committees were appointed for Mobile and other Southern cities.

With the disappearance of the vigilance committees, the regularly constituted authorities, civil and military, took over the work of dealing with dangerous Unionists, spies, and traitors. It was difficult to draw a distinction among these classes of people, for any one was potentially one or both of the others. Men and women suspected of Northern proclivities or birth were arrested, and anyone admitting that he was a Republican would likely be taken up, for Republicans were considered as being more of a conspiracy against the South than a political party. On arresting a Republican near Lynchburg and sending him on to Richmond, an officer ex-

---

Congress). In Camden, Arkansas, the vigilance committee seized goods worth about $8,000 belonging to a suspicious "Dutch Jew." Kie Oldham Papers (Arkansas State Archives, Little Rock), May 18, 1861.

[7] Atlanta *Southern Confederacy*, October 20, 1861.

[8] William Fitzgerald to Massie, May 1, 1861, in Massie Papers.

plained to Governor John Letcher that the person "may intend no harm but I dont think any man professing to belong to the party to which he claims to belong ought to be permitted to travel through the country." [9]

Political prisoners were sent to various prisons, either improvised warehouses or established jails. Most of the Unionists arrested in East Tennessee were taken to Tuscaloosa, Alabama. Other well-known prisons were in Raleigh and Salisbury, North Carolina. The best-known place for the detention of political prisoners was the so-called "Castle Thunder," in Richmond. Also another in Richmond, soon merged with Castle Thunder, was Castle Lightning. Castle Thunder soon became a bedlam, filled as it was with "the murderer, the robber, the deserter, the substitute deserter, the pickpocket, and worst of all the skulker—the man who by his skulking endangers his comrades, therefore worse than the murderer—the spy, the reconstructionist, the disloyal." The death of an inmate created scarcely a flurry among the rest of the prisoners. A newspaper correspondent, in recording the fact that a prisoner had dropped dead, remarked that it led to no more excitement "than if it had never occurred! One simply stretched out his limbs with an 'I'll be d——d if he aint dead!' While another placed a billet of wood under his head, and notified the guard with the jocose remark—'There's a fellow here got his discharge, and wants to get out.' " [10] So persistent were reports of the fearful conditions prevailing that the Confederate House of Representatives ordered an investigation of the commandant, G. W. Alexander, resulting in a majority report clearing him of any cruelty.[11]

Richmond, being the capital of the Confederacy, was naturally the center of spy rings, and here and in the vicinity a great many arrests were made. The provost marshal and virtual military commander of Richmond was General John H. Winder, a former major in the United States army and a Marylander, who collected a force of detectives and police, charged with being and long to

9 W. D. Branch, Lynchburg, Va., to Gov. John Letcher, June 14, 1861, in Virginia Executive Papers (Virginia State Archives, Richmond). For various arrests, see *Official Records*, Ser. II, Vol. II, 1361–1557.

10 Quotations respectively: *Official Records*, Ser. II, Vol. V, 917; Richmond *Daily Examiner*, March 23, 1863.

11 *Official Records*, Ser. II, Vol. V, 871–924.

be remembered as plug-uglies from Baltimore. His men arrested many petty suspects and lawbreakers, but failed to bring in the most dangerous spies. Such news items as this frequently appeared in the Richmond newspapers: "H. P. Derby, Thomas A. Case, and Joseph Dawson, were arrested yesterday for using treasonable language. William Devine, of Fluvanna, was also arrested on the charge of disloyalty." [12] Now and then such expressions as "The Scorpion of Secession—it has stung itself" and "Nationals, arise and gird on your strength!" were written on buildings, and Winder's men made more arrests. Among those arrested was Dr. George Rogers Clark Todd, the brother of Mrs. Abraham Lincoln, who, on not receiving promptly a promised appointment as surgeon in the Confederate army, remarked in a saloon while under the influence of a drink that President Davis had treated him "damned rascally." With proper explanations the next morning, he was released. He got his appointment and served the Confederacy loyally.

One of the most celebrated examples of the arrest of a Virginia Unionist was that of John Minor Botts. Charged with treasonable intercourse with the enemy, he was lodged in the Negro jail, where he remained for a few weeks until a court of inquiry disposed of his case by allowing him to reside in Lynchburg, Danville, Raleigh, or any other agreed-upon place in the interior. He should not depart more than five miles from the place and must promise to express no opinion or do no act which would injure the Confederacy. Botts bought an estate in Culpeper County and settled down there for the war, to suffer visitations from both Confederate and Federal forces who seized his livestock, burned his fences, and pastured his fields.[13]

The arrest of William Henry Hurlburt attracted much attention throughout the Confederacy. Born in Charleston, he remained there until he was four years old, grew up in the North, and became a person of some note as a journalist. Resigning his position

---

[12] Richmond *Daily Whig*, March 6, 1862.

[13] *General Orders from Adjutant and Inspector-General's Office, Confederate States Army, from January, 1862, to December, 1863 (Both Inclusive)* (Columbia, S.C., 1864), Ser. 1862, pp. 32–33; *Official Records*, Ser. II, Vol. II, 1545–47; John Minor Botts, *The Great Rebellion: Its Secret History, Rise, Progress, and Disastrous Failure. The Political Life of the Author Vindicated* (New York, 1866), xiii, 279 ff.; Richmond *Daily Examiner*, March 3, April 29, 1862.

on the New York *Times* in the summer of 1861, he made his way
to Richmond, and after a conference with high Confederate officials, he offered his services to the South. He soon turned up in
Charleston, and on being threatened by the local vigilance committee left the city. He was arrested in Atlanta as a spy and sent to
Richmond, to reside for a time in one of General Winder's jails.
Finally released, he slipped out of the Confederacy on a forged
passport. His original intentions were doubtless friendly, but exaggerated zeal in spy-catching turned him against the Confederate
cause.[14]

The Reverend Alden Bosserman, a Universalist preacher in
Richmond and a native of Maine, seems to have had no intention
of acting as a Federal spy, but he was unwise enough to show his
extreme Unionism by refusing to observe in his church thanksgiving for the victory at First Manassas and by expressing his contempt
for the Confederacy in foolishly praying that "this unholy rebellion should be crushed out." He was arrested and jailed.

Women in all wars have engaged in effective spy service. A female spy, whose case long remained before the courts in Richmond,
was Mrs. Patterson Allan, a Cincinnati-born lady who had married
a son of Edgar Allan Poe's benefactor. When not residing on her
husband's plantation in near-by Goochland County, she often
visited in the home of the Reverend Moses D. Hoge of Richmond.
The interception of some letters she had written to friends in the
North, in which she ungratefully asked the arrest of her host on
his return from a trip he was then making to Europe in quest of
Bibles for the Confederacy, and the burning of Secretary of War
James A. Seddon's plantation the next time Federal raiders appeared in the vicinity clearly marked her as a spy. Winder's men
arrested her, but instead of subjecting her to the indignities of
imprisonment in Castle Thunder, they placed her under duress
in the St. Francis de Sales Hospital. When her case came before
the Confederate District Court she was admitted to bail in the
extent of $100,000. Time and again her trial was set and equally

14 *Official Records,* Ser. II, Vol. II, 1490–1500; Richmond *Daily Examiner,* July 6,
1861; Richmond *Daily Dispatch,* November 7, 1862; Richmond *Semi-Weekly Enquirer,* January 10, 1862: Richmond *Daily Whig,* July 3, 1861; January 9, November
6, 1862.

often postponed, and so skillful was her lawyer, George W. Randolph, former Confederate Secretary of War, that the war ended without a decision being reached.[15]

Another Richmond lady, Elizabeth Van Lew, was in fact a spy but successfully covered up the fact and escaped arrest by posing as merely a friend of the Federal prisoners in Libby Prison. Though born in Richmond, she was the daughter of Northern parents. Her father had become a Richmond merchant and at his death had left his widow, Mrs. John Van Lew, and their daughter a small fortune and a stately home. She communicated information to the Federal forces besieging Richmond, which led to Benjamin F. Butler's abortive efforts to take the city in 1864 and to the raid against the Confederate capital resulting in the death of the Federal officer Ulric Dahlgren.[16]

But not all of General Winder's work was in vain. There were bona fide spies caught, tried, and hanged. Timothy Webster appeared in Richmond as a noble and true defender of the Confederacy. He was in fact one of the most trusted agents of Allan Pinkerton, head of General McClellan's secret service. Ultimately a situation developed which exposed his work; he was arrested and hanged at Camp Lee on the outskirts of Richmond.[17] Not so unfortunate was Lafayette C. Baker, who was later to become the chief secret service agent of Lincoln's War Department. After the First Battle of Manassas he appeared in Richmond but was soon arrested and imprisoned. According to his story, he argued himself out of prison, got into Davis' presence a number of times, and, loaded with military information, made his way back to the North. The Confederacy, and especially Richmond, unknowingly harbored many Northern spies. After the war S. Emma E. Edmonds claimed to have entered frequently the Confederate lines, variously

[15] Richmond *Daily Examiner*, February 22, September 13, October 28, December 19, 1864; Richmond *Daily Whig*, July 20, 1863; February 22, 1864; Augusta *Daily Chronicle & Sentinel*, July 24, 1863; Clifford Dowdey, *Experiment in Rebellion* (Garden City, 1946), 302–303, 336.

[16] Mrs. John Van Lew was also an important figure in the picture. Charles Lanman (ed.), *Journal of Alfred Ely, a Prisoner of War in Richmond* (New York, 1862), 158–88.

[17] Richmond *Daily Examiner*, April 30, 1862; Mrs. Sallie A. (Brock) Putnam, *Richmond during the War; Four Years of Personal Observation* (New York, 1867), 211.

disguised—once as a Negro boy, having blacked herself and donned a kinky wig, and another time as an Irishwoman selling cakes and pies.[18] In carrying out a law of Congress, Davis on August 8, 1861, issued a proclamation requiring all males over fourteen years of age who did not offer allegiance to the Confederacy to depart within forty days or be treated as enemy aliens. An exodus began which extended far beyond the forty days, as passports were easy to get— so easy that spies secured them repeatedly. Either dressed to look the part or actually so or merely targets of patriotic Confederate anger, these people were described by one observer as "the scurviest looking wretches the earth ever produced," one of whom was "enough to infect a whole neighborhood with hog cholera." [19]

Southern credulity and ordinary friendliness toward newcomers who appeared worthy made it easy for spies to operate with much success. They came into Richmond and other Southern towns, set up businesses, and while profiting in various speculations as well as in honest practices, acted as spies. In the spring of 1861, while the Confederacy was being organized, correspondents of such hated Northern newspapers as the New York *Tribune* (so detested in Georgia that a grand jury recommended a law fining and imprisoning anyone who subscribed for it) and the New York *Times* secretly covered on the spot the important events that were happening. As more and more evidence of spy activities came to light, Southerners began to look beneath the surface of the bespoken friendship for the Confederacy; they were awakening to the fact that the Cape Cod Yankees "were running rings around them." But as late as 1864, one Richmond editor seemed doubtful that the South would ever fully realize the spy danger: "We are doomed to be fooled out of existence, and there is no help for it, for we are incurably honest and unsuspecting." [20]

In contradistinction to the vengeance of vigilance committees and in addition to Southern credulity was the exaggerated zeal of certain Confederate District Court judges in giving those charged

[18] Lafayette C. Baker, *History of the United States Secret Service* (Philadelphia, 1867), 56–70; S. Emma E. Edmonds, *Nurse and Spy in the Union Army* . . . (Hartford, 1865), *passim.*

[19] Richmond correspondent of the Charleston *Mercury,* quoted in Natchez *Weekly Courier,* October 30, 1861.

[20] Richmond *Daily Whig,* April 22, 1864.

with crime a fair trial. Judge James D. Halyburton, of the court sitting in Richmond, became the most famous of this class. As an example of his activities, in 1863 he released on a writ of habeas corpus a group of prisoners who were held by the military authorities on the charge of discouraging enlistments. The Confederate Commissioner, believing that the evidence of their guilt was conclusive, immediately rearrested them and prepared to send them into the jurisdiction of another Confederate District Court for trial. Meanwhile, they had been lodged in Castle Thunder, much to the chagrin of Judge Halyburton, who ordered Commandant Alexander to release them. On Alexander's refusal, the judge cited him for contempt of court and secured the prisoners' release. Judge Halyburton had a long record of obstructing Confederate authority by using the writ of habeas corpus to free prisoners charged with treason and desertion from the Confederate armies.

After a few years of war, disaffection and war-weariness spread widely over the Confederacy, and as Federal armies marched farther they brought great areas under Federal control. What should be the attitude of the people in these conquered regions toward the United States? Simple expediency and general economic advantage exerted a powerful pull on people so situated. In 1862 United States Quartermaster General Montgomery C. Meigs ordered the armies to pay immediately for property taken in invaded regions from inhabitants of known loyalty and to give certificates to be paid after the war to persons who took the oath and remained loyal thereafter.[21] True enough, this practice was not to be honored in the long run, but it must have had a powerful immediate effect. It offered a strong incentive to inhabitants of the Confederacy to take the oath of allegiance to the United States, and it carried out Lincoln's desire to ameliorate the harsh terms of the two Confiscation Acts of 1861 and 1862, promoted by a growing radicalism in the American Congress with which Lincoln disagreed. The first act provided for the confiscation of any property used for insurrectionary purposes and the forfeiture of any claims to slaves owned by persons aiding the Confederacy but did not state that the slaves were thereby freed. The second punished by death, heavy fine, or imprisonment anyone guilty of treason or aiding the rebellion,

21 *Official Records,* Ser. III, Vol. II, 806.

provided for the immediate confiscation of property owned by military officers or civil leaders and the property of all others aiding the insurrection after at least two months, and announced the freedom of all slaves of such persons. As both laws applied only to the future, they were designed to lead to an immediate collapse of the Confederacy through the people's prompt cessation of opposition in order to retain their property. Then, on December 8, 1863, as part of a Reconstruction program Lincoln issued his Amnesty Proclamation, in which he definitely promised to restore citizenship and property except in slaves to all who took the oath of allegiance. These were powerful weapons in building up treason against the Confederacy, and many Confederates in conquered regions succumbed to them. Within less than six months after the fall of Nashville, in February, 1862, seven hundred people there had taken the oath, and in the conquered city of New Orleans, within an equal length of time, the rigors of Benjamin F. Butler had induced sixty thousand people to take the oath. Confederates did not judge all of them too severely, for there was a feeling that an expedient act did not change their fundamental attitude.

Yet it was only natural that many people in the path of invading armies should forget their heroics and cringe in fear, hoping to avert the worst. They waved from their homes white flags and banners with the word Union written on them. Thomas R. R. Cobb noted in September, 1861, that the York Peninsula below Richmond was "filled with *white flags* flying over houses where the inhabitants profess to be neutral." "My Heavens! For a Government to admit of such neutrality," he exclaimed. "God helping me, I will tear them down wherever I meet them and arrest the Traitors." [22] Later, with the coming of war-weariness and defeatism, the spirit of submission became more marked. When Sherman took Atlanta in 1864 many of the municipal officials and the principal businessmen took the oath and embraced the enemy, and later in the year Savannah, with more reason, when Sherman appeared received him in a co-operative spirit. One who was not under the yoke of occupation vented his anger in this scathing denunciation of the Savannah people: "If there is one sink lower than any other in the abyss of degradation the people of Savannah have reached

[22] Cobb to his wife, September 28, 1861, in Thomas R. R. Cobb Letters.

95

it. . . . The brave and generous everywhere deplore such a decay of lofty sentiment and patriotic emotion as are presented by these miserable Sycophants." [23] The Wilmington people capitulated in March, 1865, apparently satisfied with their conquerors.

To combat this threat to the integrity of the Confederacy, a widespread clamor was raised against this growing practice. No true Southerner could thus desert his government. "Choose the dungeon and scaffold a thousand times," advised the Presbyterian preacher-statesman Benjamin M. Palmer, "rather than transmit the taint of this leprosy to your offspring." [24] The Georgia legislature passed a law making it valid grounds for divorce for any woman if her husband entered the service of the United States or offered it aid and comfort.

Many Southerners in the occupied territory held out to the bitter end. William H. Seward was asked, after visiting the Winchester region of northern Virginia, what he thought of Union sentiment there. "Well," he replied, "all the men were gone to war, and all the women were she-devils." [25] The stolid Anglo-Saxon could erect himself as a Rock of Gibraltar against the enemy; not so the Latin Louisianians: "those vain, passionate, impatient little Creoles were forever committing suicide," declared the diarist Mrs. Chesnut.[26]

Governing occupied territories presented an immediate problem for the Federal authorities. According to Lincoln's theory the states were not out of the Union, and, hence, it was only a matter of setting up loyal regimes to supplant the rebel governments. But the occupying armies were in immediate control, and they acted on the assumption that martial law should normally prevail—an assumption which found expression in General Orders No. 100, "Instructions for the Government of Armies of the United States in the Field," promulgated in April, 1863. Yet it would relieve the armies of many troubles if civil government could be re-established as soon as possible. For the most part local govern-

[23] Editorial in Augusta *Weekly Constitutionalist*, March 1, 1865. See also, Richard H. Shryock (ed.), *Letters of Richard D. Arnold, M.D., 1808–1876, Mayor of Savannah, Georgia, First Secretary of the American Medical Association* (Durham, 1929), 112–20.

[24] Little Rock *Arkansas Patriot*, May 9, 1863.

[25] Edward [James Stephen] Dicey, *Six Months in the Federal States* (London, 1863), II, 78.

[26] Martin and Avary (eds.), *Diary from Dixie*, 346.

ments were not supplanted where the officials agreed to co-operate; it was the state governments, always fleeing on the approach of the enemy, which must be reconstituted. Before the end of the war, in four states, Virginia, Tennessee, Louisiana, and Arkansas, fictitious governments were set up which Lincoln recognized but which the Radicals in Congress refused to countenance, with the exceptions of those in Virginia and in Louisiana for a short time.

The Virginia recognized by the United States was a sort of by-product of the establishment of West Virginia. Union Virginia, claiming a continuous descent from the secession of that state when the Union leaders of the western counties enthroned themselves as Virginia and moved the capital to Wheeling, migrated to Alexandria when West Virginia was admitted in 1863. Here Francis H. Pierpont eked out an inglorious existence as the governor of a state, little of which he was ever able to control.

The other three states traveled a different road to their uncertain statehood, a road which led first through the appointment of a military governor whose duty it was to organize a civil government. Lincoln began this process by appointing Andrew Johnson military governor of Tennessee on March 3, 1862, immediately after the fall of Nashville; [27] followed in June, on the capture of New Orleans, by the appointment of George F. Shepley for Louisiana; and in July, after the fall of Helena, by John S. Phelps for Arkansas. Not until near the end of the war was Johnson able to install a civil governor for Tennessee, the amazing Parson William G. Brownlow; Louisiana organized herself for civil government and elected Michael Hahn governor in early 1864; about the same time, Arkansas set up a civil government with Isaac Murphy as governor. None of these governments pleased the Radicals in Congress, who a little later passed the Wade-Davis Bill, making the process of re-entering the Union more difficult than did Lincoln's plan, which had been set forth in his Amnesty Proclamation of December 8, 1863. They further showed their displeasure by refusing to

[27] In the following July, Johnson wrote in a letter to Secretary of War Stanton those words which were destined to be frequently repeated: "The rebels must be made to feel the weight and ravages of the war they have brought upon the country. Treason must be made odious and traitors impoverished." *Official Records*, Ser. I, Vol. XVI, Pt. II, 216.

97

count the electoral votes of these reconstructed states in the Presidential election of 1864.

In North Carolina, in the fall of 1861, an incipient and fruitless effort was made to set up a loyal state government by citizens in a few of the eastern counties after the landing of Federal troops at Fort Hatteras. Marble Nash Taylor, a Methodist minister from the panhandle of Virginia, was elected provisional governor, and Charles H. Foster, formerly of Maine, was elected to Congress. Foster was refused his seat, and the movement soon collapsed for want of support anywhere. The next year a new movement broke out, this time engineered by Lincoln, when on May 19 he appointed Edward Stanly, a former North Carolina Congressman, military governor. Stanly tried to set up a conservative government, but, receiving little support in his conservatism from either Lincoln or Congress, he resigned in March, 1863. Thereafter, no further effort was made to establish a loyal government in North Carolina until after the war. To organize in Florida a loyal government in time for it to participate in the Presidential election of 1864, Lincoln directed an expedition to invade that state early in the year. General Quincy A. Gillmore landed at Jacksonville and marched westward into the interior, where he suffered a crushing defeat at Olustee or Ocean Pond on February 20. This marked the end of wartime efforts to put Florida back into the Union.

Naturally the Confederacy looked with great hostility on these efforts to make traitors of its citizens and to disrupt its government. About the time Johnson was appointed military governor of Tennessee, reports were circulated in the South that the United States Congress was planning to legislate the Confederate states into Federal territories and direct the appointment of its chief politicians as governors—Charles Sumner for South Carolina, Benjamin Wade for Tennessee, John Sherman for Georgia, and so on. Southerners declared that Lincoln's 10 per cent plan, set forth in his Amnesty Proclamation, was a most amazing absurdity but well in keeping with the kind of democracy the North supported—they would have one tenth of the people domineer over the other nine tenths. All good Confederates agreed with Governor Henry W. Allen of Louisiana when he offered this counsel to his fellow citizens on the proposition of entering into the loyal Louisiana government movement: "Spurn all propositions for compromise of any kind; spit upon the insulting proposal for a bastard State Government." [28]

A nation born in war with no time to consolidate a national sentiment, the Confederacy might well have considered itself fortunate in maintaining the loyalty of its citizens as long as it did.

[28] Richmond *Daily Examiner,* March 18, 1864.

CHAPTER VI

CONSOLIDATING THE GOVERNMENT

THE Southern leaders had selected Montgomery as a centrally located place in the Lower South where they might meet to organize their new government, but they had no intention thereby of designating it the permanent capital of the Confederacy. The constitution makers, contemplating an arrangement like that of the old government, gave Congress exclusive rule over a district of not more than ten miles square which one or more states might cede. Later, when the Upper South joined the Confederacy, it was the general expectation that the capital would be moved farther northward; yet some cities and states of the Lower South did not lose hope that the seat of government would remain somewhere within the original seven states.

Georgia quickly offered a district for the capital, and Atlanta, mindful that she was not the capital of the state, made a bid for the bigger prize. This city had good railroad connections, was free from yellow fever, could supply the most wholesome foods, "and as for 'goobers,' an indispensable article for a Southern Legislator, we have them *all* the time," the *Gate City Guardian* explained.[1] Opelika, Alabama, put in a claim, calling attention to its central location, railroad connections, healthfulness, and near-by supply of coal and iron for manufactories and of building materials of wood and stone necessary for governmental structures.[2] James H. Smith, who owned a large tract of land north of Montgomery around Shelby Springs, offered the Confederacy five hundred acres as a gift and lots for any members of Congress who wanted to build

[1] Atlanta *Gate City Guardian*, February 16, 1861.
[2] Leaflet, "Opelika Ala. In Nomination for the Capitol" (in possession of the writer).

there. The town that would grow up he would call Calhoun. He was especially anxious that the Upper South not get the capital.[3] Other places, so small as never to have been heard of outside of their localities, put in claims. With a broader vision, one Southerner early suggested that Washington, D.C., must become the capital, as Virginia and Maryland would soon secede.

Montgomery was not averse to remaining the capital, and after Tennessee joined the Confederacy, Memphis invited the Congress to hold its sessions there; but it was almost inevitable after Virginia seceded that Richmond would be chosen. In fact, Stephens had practically promised Virginia that the capital would be moved there when she joined the Confederacy. In May Congress decided to remove the government to Richmond, and on the twenty-first it adjourned to meet in the Virginia capital two months later. This move was dictated both by political expedience and by military strategy. It was in recognition of the Upper South, for the Confederacy up to this time had largely been the work of the Lower South, which was to continue to be looked upon somewhat as dominating the government. Strategically, removal of the capital to Richmond would show defiance and strength. It was early felt that the war must be fought in Virginia, and the government should be close to the field of operations; besides, Virginia was a great storehouse of grain, other foods and feed, and the raw materials for war supplies. It must be held at all hazards.

Yet there were military strategists who argued that it was a mistake to put the capital so close to the frontier. It made the enemy's lines of communication short and easy to defend, and it made the capital from the beginning a beleaguered city. There would be less chance for large-scale war movements if Richmond must be held, more as a symbol of the Confederacy than of any transcending military value. If Chattanooga, even Nashville, or some other centrally located city had been chosen, Federal forces would have been coaxed away from easy water lines of communication, which they could always more easily defend, and forced to deploy their forces over long and tortuous roads which could be easily attacked and harassed. It would have required many more troops for the North to have carried on such warfare. Moreover, the Confederacy

[3] Leaflet, without title (in possession of the writer).

might thereby have been led to attach greater importance to the defense of the West. But others answered that thus opening up the South would have led to the early destruction of vital Confederate resources, including the loss of such munitions works as the Tredegar factories in Richmond, and brought about an early defeat.

Richmond, however, was never made the permanent seat of government. Virginia gave over the use of the state capitol to the Confederate Congress, and the city provided various buildings and warehouses in the vicinity for housing the rest of the government; but the Confederacy never acquired permanent property there, though Congress considered for a time the purchase of the Exchange Hotel for its meeting place. As the war wore on and Richmond became crowded and prices began soaring, a definite dislike for Richmond developed, leading such Congressmen as Henry S. Foote, the irascible representative from Tennessee, to argue that the capital should be moved to some other city. In fact, more than once it looked like the Federal armies would force the removal. The governmental archives were made ready for transportation southward in the early summer of 1862; in 1864 Congress gave the President the right to remove the executive department and call Congress to meet elsewhere; and in 1865 this permission was renewed.[4]

On July 20, 1861, Congress, welcomed by the ringing of church bells, settled down in the old Virginia capitol, designed by Thomas Jefferson, opening its session with prayer and great solemnity. Later the halls were to be refurnished and more room provided when on the inauguration of the Permanent Government the Congress would become a two-chambered body; but the Congressmen would be forced to forgo walking on fine Brussels carpet, for one thousand yards ordered from Europe for the capitol was destined to be captured as Confederate blockade-runners sought to bring it into Wilmington.[5] Outside the halls, in the rotunda, "negresses, some of them as hideous as death at the gates of hell," held sway as they dispensed their cakes and ale, peanuts and cooked mutton—until later they were to be driven away from this time-honored business of serving the legislators.

4 Ramsdell (ed.), *Laws and Joint Resolutions*, 139, 172.
5 Richmond *Daily Examiner*, November 25, 1863.

In late May, President Davis made his entry into Richmond amidst great rejoicing. Accompanied by Louis T. Wigfall and Toombs, he had come by train from Montgomery, through Atlanta, Augusta, Wilmington, and Goldsboro, welcomed at every stop and called on for speeches. At Goldsboro, as he dined at the hotel, he was surrounded by a group of ladies who fanned him and attended to his smallest want. In Richmond he was given a gigantic reception at the New Fair Grounds, where, already sick and exhausted, he went through a siege of handshaking. For the next few days his time was taken up with reviewing troops, making speeches, and receiving visitors at the Spotswood Hotel, where he was first to reside.[6]

As the Provisional Government should function for one year or less, Congress provided that elections should be held on the first Wednesday in November, 1861, for President, Vice-President, and Congressmen. Now for the first time the people would have the right to choose their officials. Would they ratify the choice of Congressmen whom the state conventions had sent to Montgomery and of the President and Vice-President whom the Congress had selected? Was Thomas R. R. Cobb right when only a few days after Davis' original selection he said, "Many are regretting already his election"?[7] There was hardly a thought otherwise than that Davis should be continued, though a few professed to believe that General Beauregard might be a better choice and there was some feeling that Robert M. T. Hunter of Virginia might have ambitions for the position. Others argued that the electoral college should exercise its right and elect whom it pleased. But, as for Vice-President Stephens, there were some strong misgivings. He had never favored secession and he was still a reconstructionist at heart; if Davis should die, what would happen to this Southern Revolution with Stephens at the head? It would be a "public calamity," declared a Richmond editor. Then, too, the Upper South, which had entered the Confederacy late, deserved more recognition. Stephens should give way. James M. Mason or John B. Floyd of Virginia, John Bell of Tennessee, or Claiborne Jackson of Missouri—any one of these would be a good choice, it was

6 Richmond *Semi-Weekly Enquirer*, May 31, June 4, 1861.
7 *Southern Historical Society Papers*, XXVIII (1900), 282.

argued. The Richmond *Examiner* carried on a persistent campaign against Stephens.

Obsessed with the feeling that there should be harmony, the Confederacy provided only one ticket, and, of course, Davis and Stephens were re-elected. Still eschewing all ideas of political parties, nevertheless the people in many of the Congressional districts had a choice between two candidates. For instance, there were contests in six out of the seven districts in Mississippi. But everywhere the leaders begged the people to go to the polls and vote, even if there were only one candidate; for only in this way could the Confederacy show the world that it rested on a popular foundation. Some of the states passed laws providing for their soldiers to vote. Yet this election attracted no great popular attention.

On February 22, 1862, Jefferson Davis was again inaugurated President of the Confederacy—this time for six years. But Richmond was not Montgomery; there was no balmy weather to presage a glorious future. Instead there was a cold, dreary winter day, with "a mean hateful rain," which came down in torrents on a mass of people in Capitol Square, trying to protect themselves under a sea of somber black umbrellas while President Davis under an improvised shelter at the base of the Washington equestrian statue recited his inaugural, heard by only a few. He referred to Washington and the American Revolution; the Confederacy wanted peace, but it must choose to defend itself against unholy attack; Confederate armies had suffered defeats on the battlefields, but victory would surely come; and the South would secure its liberties, though bought at a dear price. James D. Halyburton, Confederate District Judge, who was to give the Confederacy much trouble in using his court to liberate its soldiers, administered the oath to the President, and Robert M. T. Hunter, president pro tempore of the Senate, swore in Vice-President Stephens. A Bible printed in the Confederacy was used in the ceremonies. After the inaugural the President and Mrs. Davis held a levee attended by many people, though the rain continued "to trickle, pour, and drip." [8]

8 For Davis' Inaugural Address, see Richardson (comp.), *Messages and Papers of the Confederacy*, I, 183–88. See also, Richmond *Daily Whig*, February 24, 1862; Rev. J. William Jones, *Christ in the Camp; or, Religion in Lee's Army. Supplemented by a Sketch of the Work in the Other Confederate Armies* (Richmond, 1888), 148; Jones,

The American Revolution had its Washington; the Southern Revolution had its Davis. Therein lay in part the historic fact that the one succeeded and the other failed; but not to the extent that Davis' enemies charged—that the Confederacy "Died of Davis." Davis was as heroic as Washington and his will was as indomitable, but except in the honeymoon era of the Confederacy he was never a popular figure. Had he been, he might have built up a powerful national *esprit de corps,* not only among the masses but among the major and lesser leaders. He might have made the word "Confederate" a powerful shibboleth to arouse the people to that atmosphere of heroism in which Davis himself lived; he might have made it as moving during the struggle as it was to be thereafter, for the Confederacy never became an emotional reality to the people until Reconstruction made it so after the war had been lost. The petty leaders of the states siphoned off the enthusiasm that should have been labeled Confederate, caused the people to revel the more in the name Georgian or Carolinian or Alabamian, and made the word Confederate a label for a tyranny bent upon the destruction of the people's liberties. Wigfall, later guilty of the same criticism he was making, said in 1863, "It seems to me that the people do not properly realize the fact that their interests are identical with those of their government," [9] and the next year, Congress, equally guilty, resolved against internal feuds and factious tempers and called for "harmonious and unselfish and patriotic co-operation." [10]

President Davis himself was unwittingly the cause of much of the internal dissensions which early beset the Confederacy. The effect of health on history was well illustrated in Davis, and those who first selected him should have realized its importance, for they knew he was not a well man. His health had not been robust for years, and a facial paralysis had caused him to lose the sight of one eye. In the words of his wife, he was "a nervous dyspeptic by habit," and if he ate anything while excited he might be ill for days. His

---

Rebel War Clerk's Diary, I, 111; Pollard, *Jefferson Davis,* 197; Edwin A. Alderman and Armistead C. Gordon, *J. L. M. Curry. A Biography* (New York, 1911), 162.

[9] *Record of News, History and Literature* (Richmond), I (October 15, 1863), 165.
[10] Matthews (ed.), *Public Laws of the Confederate States,* 1 Cong., 4 Sess., 1864, p. 238.

trip north to Richmond had exhausted him, frequently he was unable to appear at the executive offices, and once his ill-health kept him away for a month. Now and then rumors that he was dead upset the people and lent hope to the North.[11] "Mr. Davis himself is troubled with blindness," said an Alabama newspaper in 1863, "is very dispeptic and splenitic, and as prejudiced and stubborn as a man can well be, and not be well." [12] Such a person could never become a popular hero, however much the people might respect him. Had he had the bodily vigor of a Toombs he might have captured the imagination of his people; the Confederacy badly needed such a leader. His ill-health made him extremely sensitive to disapprobation and led to an uneven temper. Even the disapproval of a child could upset him. And yet with such a temperament, he had the opposite qualities of tenacity, determination, and will power which stirred up lasting opposition. He made little effort to court popularity. Almost like an Adams, he spurned it as showing a departure from high principles. He had a spiritual rigidity which involved him in quarrels and in an unbending attitude toward people. People must agree with him if they would get along with him. He loved his friends and stood by them unendingly, just as he found it hard to shake off an enemy. He was as "unforgiving as a Spaniard to those whom he fancies his foes," remarked a contemporary.[13] His archenemy Edward A. Pollard of the Richmond *Examiner* declared that he was "careless of public opinion at home," but courted it abroad.[14] In addition to his set temperament in that direction, there was the fact that the Confederate Constitution gave the President only one term of six years, making it unnecessary for him to court popular favor for further service. Davis believed

[11] Mrs. Jefferson Davis, *Jefferson Davis, Ex-President of the Confederate States of America. A Memoir by his Wife* (New York, 1890), II, 161; Jones, *Rebel War Clerk's Diary*, I, 312; Rowland (ed.), *Jefferson Davis, Constitutionalist*, V, 102; Richmond *Daily Examiner*, September 10, 30, 1861; Charleston *Daily Courier*, December 24, 1864.

[12] Mobile *Tribune*, quoted in Richmond *Daily Examiner*, June 9, 1863.

[13] *Southern Literary Messenger*, XXXIV (1862), 583. Josiah Gorgas wrote of Davis, August 10, 1863: "The President seems determined to respect the opinions of no one; and has, I fear, little appreciation of service rendered, unless the party enjoys his good opinion. He seems to be an indifferent judge of men, and is guided more by prejudice than by sound, discriminating judgment." Frank E. Vandiver (ed.), *The Civil War Diary of General Josiah Gorgas* (University, Ala., 1947), 58.

[14] Edward A. Pollard, *The Second Year of the War* (New York, 1863), 286.

that this was a wise provision and that it had been adopted "for the express purpose of imparting stability to Government and of withdrawing all motive for courting popular favor at the expense of duty." [15] Yet now and then the warmth of a popular reception led Davis to say that he regretted that the cares of office were so great that he did not have more time to enjoy social intercourse with the people and that he hoped when peace came he might see them more.

Knowing these characteristics of Davis, some like Judah P. Benjamin, the ingratiating, smiling Louisianian, capitalized heavily on them. To others, friends of his without their working at it, Davis clung, braving the most stinging and widespread criticism. In addition to Benjamin, he liked Theophilus H. Holmes, whom he placed in command of forces west of the Mississippi River, and Thomas C. Hindman, a "Davis pet" in the same region. He also esteemed Lucius B. Northrop, whom he kept at the head of the Commissary Department almost to the end, throughout a storm of criticism, and Braxton Bragg, who rose the higher in Davis' estimation and appointments the more he was detested by the rest of the army. On the other hand, Davis held to Albert Sidney Johnston until his death at Shiloh, when the President's most bitter critics came to agree with him, and he showed superb good sense and good judgment of men by selecting Robert E. Lee for high position when others thought it a mistake. He never had any warm feeling for Joseph E. Johnston or Pierre G. T. Beauregard for reasons that may not have been to his discredit—these two generals made themselves difficult by their exaggerated opinions of themselves. Disliking certain uncalled-for parts of the latter's report on First Manassas, he wrote Beauregard that it was "an attempt to exalt yourself at my expense." [16]

"I wish I could learn just to let people alone who snap at me; in forbearance and charity to turn away as well from the cats as the snakes," Davis wrote his wife in 1862.[17] It was not conceit, as Pollard asserted, that "seemed to swallow up every other idea in his mind," but a high unbending sense of public duty that occasionally made Davis so brusque. In refusing a commission to an ac-

---

[15] Rowland (ed.), *Jefferson Davis, Constitutionalist*, VI, 460.
[16] *Ibid.*, V, 157.   [17] *Ibid.*, 246.

quaintance, Davis objected "to your recital of services rendered to me . . . because personal obligations do not form my standard in the appointment of officers." The appointing power was "a public trust to be exercised for the public welfare, and not a private fund with which to discharge personal obligations." [18] He could be brutally curt and frank in dealing with people of all ranks. He rightly accused Albert Pike of "an impropriety" in addressing the President through a printed circular. Under army rules it was "a grave military offense," and if the purpose was to abate an evil "the mode taken was one of the slowest and worst that could have been adopted." [19] To the letter of resignation of Secretary of War George W. Randolph, a grandson of Thomas Jefferson, who was stung by a remark of the President, Davis replied, "As you have thus without notice and in terms excluding inquiry" resigned, "nothing remains but to give you this formal notice of the acceptance of your resignation." [20] To Wade Keyes, later to be a member of the cabinet, Davis wrote in 1862, "I do not admit the propriety on the part of a subordinate officer of the government to interpose his criticism on the intercourse between the President and members of the cabinet." [21] Theodore O'Hara, made famous by his poem, "The Bivouac of the Dead," on not getting a desired brigadier-generalship declared that quite a few held the opinion "that our President will rather persist in an act of injustice, however plainly demonstrated, than practically acknowledge by repairing it that he has done a wrong act; and that you cannot do more to embitter & *set him* against you than by showing him wherein he has wronged you." [22]

President Davis lessened his efficiency as an executive by trying to attend to too many details. Stephens thought that Toombs could do in twenty minutes what it would take the President an hour to handle. Frequently behind with his duties, Davis would apologize for his delay; in one instance he explained to Governor Joseph E. Brown of Georgia that it was "through no want of respect, personal or official, but from the pressure of events which have prevented an earlier response." [23] Had Davis attended more to his civil

[18] *Ibid.*, 144.   [19] *Ibid.*, 315.   [20] *Ibid.*, 374.   [21] *Ibid.*, 383.
[22] Theodore O'Hara, Columbus, Ga., to Judah P. Benjamin, January 30, 1864, in John T. Pickett Papers (Division of Manuscripts, Library of Congress), Box 92.
[23] Rowland (ed.), *Jefferson Davis, Constitutionalist*, VI, 260.

duties and less to his constitutional prerogatives as commander in chief of the Confederate armies, he would have had more time and have saved himself from many criticisms. But he was military-minded, and he had never wanted to be President anyway. This attitude was heightened by frequent calls from the West for him to assume active command; after the fall of Fort Donelson and of Nashville even General Albert Sidney Johnston begged him to take charge: "Were you to assume command, it would afford me the most unfeigned pleasure to help you to victory and the country to independence." [24]

Davis' firm determination was one of his most positive characteristics, and in this respect he did the Confederacy an outstanding service—even so recognized by the enemy. His "energy, sagacity, and indomitable will," declared a Northerner in 1864, was all that kept the Confederacy going. "Without him the Rebellion would crumble to pieces in a day." [25] There was nothing of the barbarian in Davis, even under the strongest provocation. Though he threatened retaliation on various occasions, he never carried out his threat, and Postmaster General John H. Reagan declared that Davis never approved a death sentence for desertion or any other military offense. Reagan reported the President as saying that "the poorest use that could be made of a soldier was to shoot him." [26] Davis was often condemned for being too lenient.

Through his rigidity there frequently beamed the kindest and most considerate informality. On his way to the hotel from the train that brought the Davises to Richmond, a little girl threw a

[24] *Official Records,* Ser. I, Vol. VII, 260. See A. B. Bacon, Algiers, La., to Davis, February 25, 1862, in Jefferson Davis Papers (microfilms in the University of Texas Library, originals in Duke University Library). Gorgas wrote of Davis, January 15, 1865: "I have cherished and long ago expressed my conviction that the President is not endowed with military genius, but who would have done better? It is impossible to get anyone to say who." Vandiver (ed.), *Civil War Diary of General Josiah Gorgas,* 165.

[25] Edmund Kirke [James Roberts Gilmore], *Down in Tennessee, and Back by Way of Richmond* (New York, 1864), 269 ff. "Cold, reserved, imperious, he could be the tool of no man." "Ever audacious, yet never rash, inflexible in his purpose, yet versatile in the use of his means . . . of a temper and soul incapable alike of undue elation or despondency, of tireless industry, and of first rate executive ability." Quoted from New York *Times,* in Athens *Southern Watchman,* September 9, 1863.

[26] John H. Reagan, *Memoirs, with Special Reference to Secession and the Civil War,* ed. by Walter F. McCaleb (New York, 1906), 164.

bouquet to Mrs. Davis, which missed the carriage and fell to the ground. The President stopped the vehicle, alighted, and recovered it. Spurning the trappings of bodyguards, Davis walked through Richmond's streets unaccompanied or often rode on horseback to inspect near-by camps. One day a North Carolina soldier, somewhat drunk, stopped him on the Capitol Square and asked, "Sir, mister, be'ent you Jefferson Davis?" "Sir," replied the President, "that is my name." And, repeating the stock joke, the Tarheel warrior is said to have remarked, "I thought so, you look so much like a Confederate postage stamp." Commenting on these informalities, Jones, the "Rebel War Clerk," wrote in his diary that Davis evinced "little prudence, for it is incredible that he should be ignorant of the fact that he has some few deadly enemies in the city." [27] As an example of his simplicity of manner, he greeted with a handshake forty Negro workmen employed in a pistol shop in Griswoldville, Georgia.

Davis was showered with gifts, by all classes of people. Former governor Henry A. Wise of Virginia gave him two fine horses, a soldier presented him with a set of chessmen carved by himself, others gave him bridle bits and spurs, and an old lady in Mississippi knit him a pair of warm socks for a Christmas present.

To defend the President's policies and to popularize him, some of his chief supporters like Benjamin H. Hill and Lucius Q. C. Lamar made speaking trips, and Davis himself made three extensive trips. He entered upon these journeys primarily to carry out military inspections, but he did not neglect to show himself to the people and make frequent speeches. In December, 1862, he went to Chattanooga and on into Middle Tennessee, and, accompanied by General Joseph E. Johnston, he continued to Jackson, Mississippi, where he made a speech an hour and a half long before a vast throng filling up and extending far beyond the Hall of the House of Representatives. He defended his administration against his critics and called for the people's confidence. In Mobile he reviewed troops by moonlight, and at the Battle House received the greetings of serenaders. On his return to Richmond in early January he was welcomed by a large concourse and given a serenade. During October and November of 1863 Davis made another trip,

27 Jones, *Rebel War Clerk's Diary,* II, 16.

primarily to straighten out the military tangle which followed Bragg's defeats around Chattanooga. He was accompanied northward from Atlanta by Governor Brown and by Generals Howell Cobb, James Longstreet, John C. Breckinridge, and John C. Pemberton. He went as far west as Meridian, Mississippi, and returned by way of Atlanta, Macon, Savannah, Charleston, and Wilmington, making many speeches on the way. At Macon he spoke from the balcony of the Lanier House; at Savannah he was received with a torchlight procession and an enthusiasm declared to have been unequaled by anyone ever to have visited the city; and at Charleston he rode in a carriage, along streets lined with cheering people, to the City Hall, where he spoke. From Wilmington northward to Richmond he shared his train with a fine Arabian steed, recently presented to him by admirers abroad.

His final extensive trip before his flight after the fall of Richmond was made in September and October of 1864. His chief purpose now seems to have been to counterbalance the defeatism of Brown, Stephens, and Toombs by building up the morale of the sinking Georgians. After a conference with General John B. Hood at his headquarters at Palmetto, west of Atlanta, he went on to Montgomery, where he addressed the Alabama legislature. Returning by way of Macon, he here made the most famous of his speeches on this trip. He lashed out at his critics who were charging him with abandoning Georgia, denying it in the most pointed language: "Miserable man. The man who uttered this was a scoundrel. He was not a man to save our country." [28] And everybody knew this was a reference to Governor Brown. The termagant Foote called this speech "a harangue, the most disgusting specimen of fustian and billingsgate oratory that has ever been uttered outside of an insane asylum." [29] At Augusta, accompanied by Generals Beauregard, Cobb, and William J. Hardee, he was received with the most unfeigned enthusiasm, with the ladies pressing forward to kiss his hand. Again he defended the Confederate administration and predicted victory. He returned to Richmond by way of Columbia. Had President Davis taken time to show himself more frequently to the people he might have increased his popularity and strengthened the determination of the people to hold out.

[28] Athens *Southern Watchman*, October 5, 1864.   [29] *Ibid.*, November 30, 1864.

In his wife President Davis found consolation and strength, and in his children he found relaxation. "My ease, my health, my property, my life I can give to the Cause of my country," he wrote Mrs. Davis after he had sent her and the children away from Richmond when its fall seemed imminent in May, 1862, but he added, "The heroism which could lay my wife and children on any sacrificial altar is not mine." [30] Born in Natchez, Mrs. Davis was seventeen years younger than her husband and was his second wife. She was not "a coarse Western woman," as Mrs. Wigfall described her, nor was the President "notoriously governed" by her, as Pollard charged. A brunette, she had a full round face, and was inclined to be heavy. She had a warm heart and a sensitive nature; she was witty, clever, and tactful; she could successfully spar with Benjamin; and she could be blunt and caustic at times. She conducted her social obligations with grace and ease. Her life revolved around her husband and her children. She bore a daughter during the life of the Confederacy and she underwent the sorrows of the loss of a young son. Former Governor Robert F. W. Allston of South Carolina reported to his wife in the summer of 1861 that he had paid his respects to the Davises and found the President looking "very feeble," but "Mrs. Davis has not lost any flesh since you saw her and is as animated as ever. She moves about, receives and talks, as in a triumph, and is strong in having her country women about her as a sort of court." [31] Some of the Richmond ladies may have been a little puzzled over how to take Mrs. Davis, but the cabinet wives with a few exceptions got along well with her. Wives reflected toward Mrs. Davis their husbands' attitudes toward the President. Hence, Mrs. Toombs regarded her with a jealous fury, and Mrs. Joseph E. Johnston, who at first was intimate enough to go for a drive with her which ended in a carriage accident, later became lukewarm. Gossips claimed that Quartermaster General Abraham C. Myers was superseded because his wife quarreled with Mrs. Davis.[32] Mrs. Mary Boykin Chesnut, of diary fame, remained her lifelong friend.

[30] Rowland (ed.), *Jefferson Davis, Constitutionalist*, V, 277.

[31] J. Harold Easterby (ed.), *The South Carolina Rice Plantation As Revealed in the Papers of Robert F. W. Allston* (Chicago, 1945), 178.

[32] James L. Orr, Richmond, Va., to James H. Hammond, January 3, 1864, in James H. Hammond Papers (Division of Manuscripts, Library of Congress).

The White House of the Confederacy, infrequently called the Grey House to keep from aping the Yankees but popularly called by Richmonders during wartime the Presidential Mansion, was a commodious home not far from Capitol Square, which the city bought and presented to the Confederacy. The government, not wanting to impose this burden on Richmond, did not accept it, but instead used it and paid a rental. Here the social life of governmental circles centered, with frequent receptions thrown open to all who cared to come. New Year's receptions especially were looked forward to and were well attended. It was from the high porch of this home that Davis' young son Joseph fell and was killed. Hollywood Cemetery presented a lot in which he was buried, amidst widespread sympathy for the Davis family.

Davis was not the ideal leader for the Southern Revolution, but in the light of the characters of the other outstanding men as they developed during the struggle, he showed fewer weaknesses than any other. How others might have developed had they been at the head might alter judgments; but it is hard to see how Toombs could have developed the necessary stability; or Cobb, the qualities of leadership; or Lee, the will to accept; or such early secessionists as Yancey and Rhett, the constructive ability. However admirable Stephens might have been in other periods of his life, he showed no qualities necessary for leading a revolution. A judicious selecting of characteristics from all the Southern leaders and endowing one man with them would have produced the perfect composite leader —but it was not within the realm of man to do this.

It became a widespread obsession in the early days of the Confederacy that there should be neither partyism nor sectionalism in this new nation. There must be no Upper South and Lower South, and the old party distinctions of Democrat and Whig, somewhat forgotten in the movement leading up to secession, must remain forgotten—at least until the war had been won. Even old personal animosities, like those between Benjamin H. Hill and Alexander H. Stephens, must be remembered no more—and in this case the people were shown that they ceased to exist. The first public utterance Davis made on his arrival in Montgomery to assume the presidency was: "For now we *are* brethren not in name merely, but in fact— men of one flesh, of one bone, of one interest, of one purpose, and of identity in domestic institutions"; [33] and later as President he called for "harmony, energy, and unity of the States." [34] After two and a half years of war he could say, though not with entire truth, "We have been united as a people never were united under like circumstances before." [35] On Davis' second election, in November, 1861, Governor Brown declared he would "be the last man in Georgia to attempt to create any division" by opposing the President,[36] and a little earlier Vice-President Stephens, not being able to foretell that he would be a chief offender, issued this warning: "If unwise counsels prevail—if we become divided—if schisms arise—if dissensions spring up—if factions are engendered—if party spirit, nourished by unholy personal ambition shall rear its hydra head, I have no good to prophesy for you." [37]

So fearful of party division were the leaders that some suggested dispensing with popular elections, and others advocated that multiple candidates for an office be "called up in a row and interrogated" that they might "recite the same political chatechism [sic] with the uniformity of a Sunday school." [38] Or, "Give us an old-fashioned, honest scrub race" where every man would "run who feels inclined, and let every man vote for whoever he feels inclined, whether he be a candidate or not." [39] Partyism would bring on a situation reminiscent of the old government: "God forbid, that Richmond, or the Capital of our Confederate Government, should become the den of beasts, the nest of obscene birds—the buzzard's roost—that Washington was in the last corrupt, dying days of the old United States." [40] The old issues which separated the people into parties were now dead; but when independence should come, "We may safely form political parties and revel in our former joys of canvassing, candidacy, elections and stump-speaking—when we may luxuriate again in self-laudation and in villifying our opponents." [41]

[33] Montgomery *Weekly Mail*, February 22, 1861.
[34] Richardson (comp.), *Messages and Papers of the Confederacy*, I, 296.
[35] *Ibid.*, 382.
[36] Phillips (ed.), *Correspondence of Toombs, Stephens, and Cobb*, 577.
[37] Cleveland, *Alexander H. Stephens*, 725.
[38] Richmond *Daily Examiner*, May 28, 1863.
[39] Atlanta *Southern Confederacy*, August 13, 1861.
[40] Richmond *Daily Whig*, July 6, 1861.
[41] Augusta *Weekly Chronicle & Sentinel*, January 6, 1863.

But, alas! it did not take long for these Confederates to find out that human nature never changes much. Soon charges were raised against President Davis that he appointed no one to office who had been an old Whig, and that the Democrats were in complete control of the government; then arose the cry for parties. By 1864 the Richmond *Whig* was agreeing that parties were "necessary to good government" and that to erase all party lines was "to create a one-man power." By then a reaction had taken place in North Carolina, which had at that time in Congress a delegation entirely made up, with one exception, of old Whigs. In fact, there had never died out the division between those who wanted a strong central government and those who insisted on the states having most of the power —and it was along these lines that two strong and bitter factions grew up in the Confederacy.

Complaints were soon arising that civil service was on no higher plane than it had been under the old government, though at first it seems that there was much informality in the governmental offices and that pure democracy reigned. Within a year the critical Charleston *Mercury*, edited by sour Robert Barnwell Rhett, was saying that incompetency weighed "heavily on the efficiency of the public service, while nepotism and partisanship" reigned triumphant.[42] A Texan thought "nimble-jointed carpet cavaliers" danced "around the Government sanctuaries" [43] and red tape ran rampant. The Richmond *Examiner* declared that it took eight or ten days of traveling around through a dozen offices, dealing with impolite clerks, to get an account of a few hundred dollars settled. Throughout an existence of two thousand years, the Roman Empire had not accumulated "as many records as our young Confederacy has done in twelve months." [44] "An automaton musket holder" ornamented "the entrance of every Government Department," and

[42] Charleston *Daily Mercury*, January 25, 1862.

[43] Richmond *Daily Whig*, September 30, 1861.

[44] Richmond *Daily Examiner*, March 24, 1862. A Congressman, in describing how Benjamin H. Hill had tried to get a furlough for a sick soldier, said, "Having walked himself down, going from one office to another, he had been obliged to hire a hack to continue the rounds." But the day ended while his efforts were still uncompleted. The next morning when he resumed his task and finally reached the proper hospital, he was informed "it was too early in the day to attend to such business." *Southern Historical Society Papers*, XLVI (1928), 223–24.

after putting the would-be entrant through a catechism, lowered his musket like a fence rail, if he were acceptable.[45] Thomas J. Foster, an irate Representative from Alabama, introduced a mock resolution asking for the "court etiquette for the use of members in their intercourse" with the governmental offices; he had often been forced to stand with hat under arm, "dancing attendance upon, and being treated cavalierly by the governmental officials." [46] Representative Foote, who reveled in captious condemnation of the Davis administration, announced himself as the champion of the people against the corruptions of the government.

Apart from certain treasury clerks who stole about $1,000,000, there was little dishonesty among Confederate civil officials; though carping critics never ceased to make shining targets of them, and, thereby, tended to cause people in general to lose faith in the integrity of their public servants. Though a great many women worked in the government service, especially in the Treasury Department, most clerks were men, and a considerable number of them were within the military age. In this respect they came in for much condemnation for not abandoning their "bomb-proof" jobs and joining the army. Albert Gallatin Brown, Senator from Mississippi, became bitter on this subject: "While the young men of the country were day after day enduring uncomplainingly the hardships of the camp, parching under the noonday sun or wet with the dews of night, eating the commonest of food, wearing the coarsest apparel, aye, traveling barefoot over the flinty hills in pursuit of the enemy, and content with eleven dollars a month, these clerks were quartered in snug apartments and employing their time in drawing up petitions for an increase of pay, and a consequent increase of comforts and luxuries." They sat behind mahogany desks, complacently reading "of the dangers by flood and field" which they "had so successfully shunned." [47]

And it was particularly unworthy of them to be asking for an increase in salary. Rather, Senator Williamson S. Oldham of Texas declared, "Our immediate business should be to stop the further depreciation of the currency and not the raising of salaries.

[45] Richmond *Daily Examiner*, June 18, 1863.
[46] *Southern Historical Society Papers*, XLV (1927), 76–77.
[47] *Ibid.*, XLVII (1930), 101.

Unless we accomplish the former work we might go on increasing wages every month, day and hour, until a wagon load of treasury notes would not buy a pair of shoe strings, to say nothing of shoes." [48] But there was genuine need for increasing the salaries of clerks, if the depreciation of the currency could not be stopped, for many public servants were not receiving enough to pay their house rent. "Rebel War Clerk" Jones complained almost every day in his diary of how he was unable to pay his expenses because of high prices.

The President received $25,000 annually and house rent; the Vice-President and cabinet members, $6,000; members of Congress, at first $8.00 a day while in session, and later when the Senate was added under the Permanent Government, $2,760 annually; while most clerks received from $1,200 to $2,000. Inflation soon made these salaries ridiculous, but not until 1864 were there such increases as one third for clerks, 100 per cent for Congressmen, and to $9,000 for heads of departments and the Vice-President. In 1865 there were increases of 100 per cent for almost all governmental officials and workers.

As no government can be considered fully organized without a flag, the Montgomery Congress, a week after it convened, appointed a committee on flag, seal, coat of arms, and motto. Immediately men, women, and children began sending in a flood of designs and suggestions for the flag. The hold the old flag had on Southerners was tremendous—to one it was as "the dead body of a friend." Design after design was an adaptation of the Stars and Stripes. A Mississippi delegate introduced a resolution to make the flag "as similar as possible to the flag of the United States"; but William Porcher Miles, chairman of the committee, declared he had detested the old flag from his boyhood as representing a hostile government. As the flags of Liberia and the Sandwich Islands were similar to the Stars and Stripes, naturally the committee did not want to borrow "what had been pilfered and appropriated by a free negro community and a race of savages." [49]

On March 4, the day Lincoln was inaugurated President of the United States, the Confederacy adopted its first flag, hoping to

[48] *Ibid.*, 102.
[49] *Journal of the Congress of the Confederate States*, I, 102.

raise it on the capitol dome in Montgomery as Lincoln delivered his address in Washington. The exercises did not take place, however, until four in the afternoon, when a granddaughter of John Tyler, the only living former President in the Confederacy, hoisted the flag, amidst the playing of bands and the firing of a seven-gun salute. The design consisted of three bars, red, white, and red, with a blue union containing a circle of seven white stars, to be increased as new states should be admitted. This came to be called the Stars and Bars. It was soon waving from flagstaffs all over the Confederacy.

Though the committee did not think it looked much like the Stars and Stripes, yet it had the same colors as the old flag, and at a distance there was difficulty in determining which flag it was. At the First Battle of Manassas this was true, and almost tragically so. Immediately afterwards, Beauregard and other Confederate generals in the fight determined that there should be a new flag to be carried in battles. A new design was worked out and recommended to Congress, but failing of action there, the military authorities submitted it to the War Department, which gave its approval on October 1, 1861. This flag was a perfect square, divided symmetrically by a St. Andrew's cross, which enclosed the stars, one for each state. The colors were still red, white, and blue. This was the so-called "Battle Flag," sometimes called the "Southern Cross," supplanting the Stars and Bars only on the battlefield.

Though no longer to be confused in military operations, the Stars and Bars still was not liked. Some said it looked too much like the United States flag—"and that is enough to make it utterly detestable"; others thought it looked like a pair of suspenders. Mounting dislike of it led to another flood of designs and suggestions embracing such insignia as snakes, beehives, temples of liberty, and the constellation of the Southern Cross (though it could not be seen in the skies over any part of the Confederacy). There were also various designs of the sun with radiating rays, each representing a state. It was suggested that a white field crossed diagonally by a wide black bar would get away from every vestige of resemblance to the United States flag—the white representing the ruling race and the black, the eternal principle of slavery. Or a white field with a black horse on it would do—a fitting representation of the equestrian South. Finally, on May 1, 1863, Congress adopted a new flag—a white field, with the Battle Flag superimposed in the upper left corner.

But this second official flag did not prove to be entirely satisfactory, for having so much white, it looked like a flag of truce, when draped or drooped, or a mere tablecloth, and, besides, it was easily soiled. Congress now set to discussing another flag, and not until March 8, 1865, when the Confederacy was within a month of collapse, did the lawmakers succeed in agreeing on a third one. This flag was merely the old one changed by the addition of a red bar extending down the outer width of the field. But from First Manassas to Appomattox, the flag used in military operations was the Battle Flag or Southern Cross.[50]

Throughout the life of the Confederacy there were various state and regimental flags used on occasion, flags with red stars, blue stars, stripes, cotton bolls, cotton stalks, shamrocks, palmettoes, magnolias, with various mottoes, and there was the famous Bonnie Blue Flag with the white star. In the early days of the war scarcely a regiment or company departed for the battlefields without flag presentation exercises, in which a young lady presented the flag, usually made by the ladies of the community, and a representative of the soldiers replied in his politest oratory.

This new nation must also have a great seal, which would include the national symbol and motto. The Provisional Government adopted a seal which was a simple device representing a scroll with the word "Constitution" written above it and "Liberty" beneath, but a more elaborate work of art must be made to signify the Permanent Government. Lawmakers and other citizens set their imagination and ingenuity to work and presented almost as many suggestions as were made for the flag. One selected a single star as the symbol, saying that it represented the nature of the Confederacy, which reflected light or power from the states, like a star receiving the same from the sun. Another insisted on the live oak, representing sturdiness and perennial youth. No one seemed to want the eagle, liberty cap, lion, or other symbols already in use by other nations. Finally, on April 30, 1863, Congress agreed on a

---

[50] For a history of the Confederate flags, see Mrs. Lucile L. Dufner, "The Flags of the Confederate States of America" (M.A. thesis, University of Texas, 1944).

great seal, which represented the equestrian statue of Washington (to be seen just outside the legislative halls), flanked by a wreath of the chief agricultural products of the Confederacy, cotton, tobacco, cane, corn, wheat, and rice. Around the outer edge were the words, "The Confederate States of America. 22 February 1862" and the motto "Deo Vindice." This seal, engraved in England and run through the blockade in the fall of 1864, was never used, as part of the equipment necessary for operating it was captured at sea. The Confederacy continued to use the old Provisional Government seal, and when at the end Benjamin was fleeing the country, he dropped it in the Savannah River to prevent its capture.[51]

Although a cabinet was provided only by implication in the Confederate Constitution as in the Federal document, the Provisional Congress early established executive departments and President Davis instituted a cabinet of the heads of these departments. Disregarding entirely personal friendship or even acquaintanceship, Davis appointed the original members of his cabinet on the basis of political and geographical considerations. He chose Robert Toombs of Georgia (which was already represented by Vice-President Stephens), Secretary of State; Christopher G. Memminger of South Carolina, born in Germany, Secretary of the Treasury; Leroy P. Walker of Alabama, Secretary of War; Stephen R. Mallory of Florida, born in Trinidad, Secretary of the Navy; Judah P. Benjamin of Louisiana, born in St. Croix in the Danish West Indies, Attorney General; and John H. Reagan of Texas, Postmaster General. Thus, every one of the seven states provided a cabinet member, except Mississippi, which had been honored with the Presidency. Strangely enough this cabinet, with three foreign-born members, little represented the old native planter aristocracy. Only two members, Mallory and Reagan, continued in their original positions throughout the war. Benjamin remained in the cabinet to the end, but he held successively three different posts. There were four secretaries of state, five attorneys general,

[51] James M. Matthews (ed.), *Public Laws of the Confederate States of America . . . Third Session of the First Congress; 1863* (Richmond, 1863), 167; *Southern Historical Society Papers,* XLI (1916), 20–33. This seal is now in the Confederate Museum in Richmond.

two secretaries of the treasury, and six secretaries of war. These frequent changes made for instability in a continuing policy except as the President directed it, but, harassed as he was by carping Congressmen and petulant newspaper editors, Davis kept throughout a cabinet of respectable standing and efficiency.[52]

The Confederacy was to have the distinction of being first to set up a Department of Justice, presided over by an attorney general, with cabinet rank. It was given some of the duties of the old Federal Department of the Interior, which the Confederacy abandoned because it savored too much of centralization. In view of the fact that Southerners had long considered their chief interests to be agricultural, it is noteworthy that they did not establish a Department of Agriculture, though such a department was early advocated by agricultural journals and planters' conventions.

Placed in the Department of Justice were the Bureau of Printing, the Patent Office, and territorial affairs. Also, the attorney general should prosecute all suits before the Supreme Court and execute the Sequestration Act. Benjamin continued as attorney general only until November, 1861, when he was succeeded by Thomas Bragg of North Carolina, a representative of the Upper South and a former Union man. In March of the following year he gave way to Thomas H. Watts of Alabama, an old Whig and Unionist, who remained until October, 1863, when he became governor of Alabama. Wade Keyes, another Alabamian, succeeded under an ad interim appointment until January, 1864, when George Davis of North Carolina became the final attorney general.

The only active Confederate courts were the district courts. Many writs of habeas corpus, relating especially to soldiers seeking to avoid military service, were handled in these courts. The Confederacy provided for no cumbersome circuit courts. It did set up a court of admiralty to sit in Key West, but as the Confederacy never secured possession of this city, the court was not organized. Congress was never able to agree on setting up a supreme court, though the Permanent Constitution required it to perform this duty. The Provisional Constitution provided that all of the district judges should constitute the personnel of the supreme court; but

[52] Rembert W. Patrick, *Jefferson Davis and his Cabinet* (Baton Rouge, 1944), is a scholarly treatment of Davis' cabinet.

the court was never organized under this document, and when the Permanent Constitution copied the language of the Federal document, Congress wrangled throughout the life of the Confederacy on how to carry it out and finally dissolved without having acted.[53]

The principal point of dispute was the clause in the Judiciary Act of March 16, 1861, granting the contemplated supreme court appellate jurisdiction in cases arising in state courts. The fear of centralization as well as a long-standing dislike of the United States Supreme Court led Southerners to steer clear of the pitfalls which they considered had had a large part in bringing about the necessity of secession. To allow appellate jurisdiction was to degrade the state courts and strike a dangerous blow at state rights. It was courting the creation of another John Marshall, who would subvert the Confederate Constitution, as the old John Marshall had done for the Federal document. A Confederate Senator declared that if John Marshall had been a weakling instead of having the "unimpeachable character" and "great intellect" which characterized him, the old Supreme Court would never have developed the power it did, and the old Union would now be in existence.[54]

The fear of the court's personnel was thus closely mixed in with the dislike of the appellate jurisdiction clauses. Those who were hostile to Davis visualized a court filled with his puppets, bent on assisting him in establishing a tyranny over the states. Davis' bitter enemy, Foote, declared that he would "never consent to the establishment of a supreme court of the Confederate States so long as Judah P. Benjamin shall continue to pollute the ears of majesty Davis with his insidious counsels." [55] Some opposed the establishment of the court because they believed Davis would appoint as chief justice John A. Campbell, formerly on the United States Supreme Court, and that he would become the John Marshall of the Confederacy. Those who fought hardest against setting up the court were Yancey, Wigfall, Foote, Robert W. Barnwell of South Carolina, Henry C. Burnett of Kentucky, and Herschel V. Johnson of Georgia. The most active supporters were Benjamin H. Hill,

[53] For a definitive study of the Confederate judiciary, see Robinson, *Justice in Grey.* See also, J. G. de Roulhac Hamilton, "The North Carolina Courts and the Confederacy," in *North Carolina Historical Review* (Raleigh), IV (1927), 366–403.

[54] *Southern Historical Society Papers*, XLVII (1930), 206–211.

[55] Richmond *Daily Examiner,* December 17, 1863.

Augustus H. Garland of Arkansas, and James Phelan of Mississippi.

It was unfortunate for the Confederacy that it never possessed a supreme court. There was much work for such a court, such as settling questions relating to taxation and the conscription and impressment laws, and generally asserting the supremacy of the Confederacy over the individual states in national affairs. There continued much confusion as to the meaning of Confederate legislation, with the result that interpretations varied with the states, though few state supreme courts ever declared a Confederate law void. Individual judges, however, like Richmond M. Pearson, chief justice of the North Carolina Supreme Court, gave no end of trouble. The Confederacy was fortunate in not having its military supremacy upset in any state by the decisions of the highest state court.

Another constitutional tribunal which the Confederacy never set up was the court of claims; but the work which this court would have handled was done by the various executive departments over which cabinet members presided, by the Board of Sequestration Commissioners, and by the district courts. One of the first acts of belligerent nations is to sequester or confiscate enemy property and debts. In May, 1861, the Confederate Congress passed a law sequestering all debts owed to individuals and corporations in the United States; and on August 30 as an act of retaliation against the First Confiscation Act, passed by the United States, the Congress enacted another sequestration law for seizing the property of alien enemies and for indemnification of Confederate citizens suffering under this Federal law. To execute these laws, agents were appointed to ferret out the property of aliens and advertise it for sale. There was nothing too small or too large to be seized and sold. Ships, slaves, houses, pianos, warehouses, city lots, plantations, stocks of banks, of railroads, and of other corporations, horses, buggies—whatever could be uncovered was seized. Two millions of dollars' worth of tobacco impounded in Richmond warehouses, claimed by French citizens but suspected of belonging to New York brokers, was finally released by the Confederate District Court. Three hundred thousand acres of land in Florida were seized and offered for sale, and it was asserted that during the latter part of 1861 an average of $500,000 in alien property in Richmond was being sequestered daily. One of the most interesting cases related to Monticello and its 360 acres of land, formerly the property of Thomas Jefferson but now owned by Uriah P. Levy of New York, who was in the United States navy. The Confederacy seized it in 1861, but sequestration proceedings were not completed until September, 1864, when Judge Halyburton of the Confederate District Court ordered its sale, despite the attempt of Levy to save it by willing it to the United States to be used as a school.[56]

Some guessed that there was enemy alien property worth $300,-000,000 in the Confederacy, in addition to the debts of Southerners owed to the North, which were estimated from $40,000,000 to $400,000,000. Undoubtedly these guesses were greatly exaggerated; probably the Southern debts lacked much of being $40,000,000.[57] The amount realized by the Confederacy was about $6,000,000 in depreciated Confederate currency, and the amount obtained by the states, for there were also state sequestration laws, was of no consequence. From January to October, 1863, the amount received by the Confederate Treasury was $1,862,550.

One reason why the program did not materialize more fully was the lack of entire agreement among important Southerners. John A. Campbell opposed it, and many other people allowed themselves to be made the means of saving enemy alien property by claiming its ownership. Practically no one who owed Northern debts went to the trouble to pay them either to the Confederacy or to the states, but when the war was over Southerners settled their accounts with their Northern creditors.

The Post Office Department was the last Federal agency to be taken over by the Confederacy. Not until June 1, 1861, more than a month and a half after Fort Sumter, did the United States cease to carry the mails in the South and the Confederacy take control.

So large a business undertaking was the carrying of mails that

[56] Richmond *Daily Dispatch*, September 2, 1862; Richmond *Semi-Weekly Enquirer*, October 11, 1861; Richmond *Daily Enquirer*, September 28, 1864; Richmond *Daily Examiner*, September 28, 1864; Richmond *Daily Whig*, November 20, 1862, May 13, 1864; Jackson *Weekly Mississippian*, October 30, 1861.

[57] Richmond *Daily Examiner*, September 2, 1861; John C. Schwab, *The Confederate States of America, 1861-1865. A Financial and Industrial History of the South during the Civil War* (New Haven, 1913), 110 ff.; *American Annual Cyclopaedia . . . 1861*, p. 147.

President Davis found great difficulty in securing a Postmaster General. Two of his fellow Mississippians refused the post, and twice did John H. Reagan of Texas reject the offer before he was finally prevailed upon to accept it. But once he entered upon the work, he remained to the end, being, in fact, the last member of the cabinet to leave Davis on his flight after the fall of the Confederacy. In his preparations to assume control, Reagan worked a sort of *coup d'état* by sending secretly to Washington an agent who succeeded in enticing many of the high postal officials to join the Confederacy, bringing with them their forms, postal maps, contracts, books of instructions, and other needed postal information.[58]

On May 31, 1861, the postmasters, postal clerks, carriers, and other postal officials in the eleven Confederate States worked their last day for the United States government. The next day they became the Confederate postal establishment; yet they were the same people with the same contracts. The principal difference now was that, having been recommissioned, they should receive their salaries from the Confederate government—in the case of the postmasters it was from 10 to 50 per cent of their postal receipts—and they should no longer accept letters bearing United States stamps. All unused stamps and stamped envelopes were sent to Washington, but the money on hand was kept to meet the last expenses not paid by the Federal government.[59]

Under the old government, the post office had not been self-sustaining; in 1860 it had had a deficit of almost $2,000,000 in the eleven states which were to make up the Confederacy. Southerners had believed that carrying the mail for less than it cost was in effect a subsidy to the business interests of the North, who made the most use of the mails. So, the Montgomery Convention inserted in the Confederate Constitution the clause that required the Confederate

[58] Reagan, *Memoirs*, 124–25, 129; Francis B. C. Bradlee, *Blockade Running during the Civil War and the Effect of Land and Water Transportation on the Confederacy* (Salem, Mass., 1925), 278; Post Office Department Circular Letter, No. 1. Confederate Post Office Department, May 13, 1861 (no date or place of publication given).

[59] Matthews (ed.), *Statutes at Large of the Provisional Government of the Confederate States*, 1861–1862, pp. 199–200; Walter F. McCaleb, "The Organization of the Post-Office Department of the Confederacy," in *American Historical Review*, XII (1906–1907), 66–74.

Post Office Department to be self-sufficing after March 1, 1863. This provided a troublesome problem for Reagan, who tried to meet it in various ways. First, he reduced the number of post offices, discontinuing the smallest ones and those most isolated. He decreased the number of mails received by some of the post offices and induced the railroads to make new contracts lowering their compensation for carrying the mails. He reduced the franking privilege to the point where letters were carried free only for the Post Office Department itself. And what was a more serious matter for the mass of people, postal rates were increased. Instead of the old three-cent rate, letters of one-half ounce weight now must pay five cents for the first five hundred miles and five cents more for any additional distance. In 1862 these rates were doubled and made to apply without regard to distance. Congressmen and soldiers were allowed to post letters without paying postage, but recipients must pay the proper amount before the letters would be delivered. Soldiers must write on the envelope their names, companies, and regiments.

It was comparatively easy for Reagan to transform the Federal postal establishment in the South into a Confederate system, but the simple little matter of providing new stamps he found much more difficult. As there were no engravers in the Confederacy who could provide plates for printing stamps, he was forced to look abroad for help. In the meantime, until stamps could be provided, letters might be mailed without stamps, upon the sender's paying the proper amount when he mailed them. Some postmasters devised crude stamps or impressions of their own, known as "local stamps," and affixed them. Reagan first sought contracts for stamps and plates in the North, but before these could be completed hostilities intervened. Luckily he found a firm in Richmond, Hoyer & Ludwig, who could make crude stamps by the lithographing process. He made a contract with them, and it was this firm which printed the first Confederate stamp. This was a five-cent denomination, done in green, and bearing the picture of Davis as a propaganda measure to popularize the Confederate President. The stamp was first used on October 16, 1861.

To provide a more artistic stamp, in the fall of 1861 Reagan sent to England an agent who made a contract with the well-known engravers, De La Rue & Company of London, to execute plates and print a few million stamps. The first shipment, including plates, was captured in the attempt to run the blockade; but new plates were made and successfully brought in. Thereafter the Confederacy was able to supply itself with a sufficiency of stamps. In 1862 the stamp bureau was transferred to Columbia, South Carolina, where the Confederate stamps were printed until February, 1865, when Sherman's army destroyed the city together with the supply of stamps on hand and the plates. This brought an end to printing Confederate stamps, a few months before the Confederacy itself ended.

Besides the five-cent Davis stamp, there were various other denominations designed and printed. There was a one-cent stamp, with the likeness of Calhoun; but as no use was ever found for the stamp, it was never issued. The first ten-cent stamp appeared in November, 1861, a crude design of Thomas Jefferson lithographed by Hoyer & Ludwig. The next year a two-cent stamp bearing the likeness of Andrew Jackson was issued, to be used for letters called for where mailed. A new ten-cent Davis stamp was issued, which was generally used throughout the Confederacy. Finally there appeared in 1863 a twenty-cent stamp bearing the likeness of Washington. This design had originally been intended for the first stamp, but the fact that the United States was using Washington on its stamps made the Confederacy defer for a time. The Washington stamps were frequently cut in half and used as ten-cent stamps on letters. They were also much used for small change, taking the place of five-cent stamps which had heretofore been so used and had become "a greater nuisance every day." [60]

People had some difficulty in sending their mail beyond the limits of the Confederacy, as the United States Post Office refused to handle Confederate mail and Federal commanders attempted to stop all communication across the lines from the South. In the early days before the Federal invasion of Kentucky and Tennessee, the

[60] *Report of the Postmaster General . . . November 27, 1861* (Richmond, 1861), 21–25; Richmond *Semi-Weekly Enquirer*, October 17, 1861; Richmond *Daily Examiner*, April 21, June 4, 1863; Robert S. Henry, *The Story of the Confederacy* (Indianapolis, 1931), 92, 93. The definitive work on the postage stamps of the Confederacy is August Dietz, *The Postal Service of the Confederate States of America* (Richmond, 1929).

Southern Express Company agreed to take letters to Louisville where they would be mailed or turned over to the Adams Express Company, which would see that they reached their destination. The cost was twenty-five cents. The American Letter Express Company, with offices in Nashville and Louisville, was organized especially for carrying mail across the border both ways. To send a letter out of the Confederacy, a person should enclose it and money sufficient to buy another envelope with United States postage, in an envelope bearing the required Confederate postage. It would be opened in Louisville and forwarded to its destination by United States mail. The charge for this service was ten cents, which should also be enclosed in the envelope and might be in the form of United States postage stamps.[61]

As these openly announced methods of communicating with the North did not last long, clandestine ways came to be employed. Adventurers could always be found who would carry letters across the border for prices ranging from one to three dollars.[62] An enterprising private mail carrier used a kite, when wind and other conditions were favorable, to convey his letters across the lower Potomac into Maryland. After large stretches of the Mississippi Valley had been overrun by Federal invasion, Absalom Grimes, a Kentucky-born Missourian, acted as a semiofficial mail carrier for this region, making it possible for soldiers and their families to communicate with one another.[63] The transmission of inoffensive mail, whose authors were willing to have it submitted to the censors, was provided by agreement between the Confederate and Federal authorities. This was the well-known flag-of-truce mail, which was regularly carried by boat on the James, between Richmond and Fortress Monroe. Such letters must not be over a page in length and must be placed in unsealed envelopes which should bear both the required Confederate and United States stamps. Each authority canceled its own stamps. The need for United States stamps for this flag-of-truce mail, especially in writing to Confederate prisoners of war in the North, led Congress to pass a law authorizing the

[61] New Orleans *Daily Picayune,* June 19, 1861 (afternoon edition).

[62] On one occasion a thousand contraband letters were captured and brought back to Richmond. Richmond *Daily Enquirer,* May 4, 1863.

[63] Milo M. Quaife (ed.), *Absalom Grimes, Confederate Mail Runner* (New Haven, 1926).

Post Office Department to secure United States stamps and make them available at the principal post offices. Mail destined for Europe could either take its chances in running the blockade or be dispatched to Mexico, where it would find unobstructed passage to its destination. During the first year of the war a resourceful promoter named Antonio Costa, with the approval of the post-master at New Orleans, arranged for a mail twice a month from that city to Tampico, Mexico, whence the British Mail Steamers carried it to the West Indies and European ports. The charge was one dollar a letter to be paid in Confederate postage.[64]

A clever way for Southerners and Northerners to communicate with one another, short of writing letters, was through the use of "personal" advertisements in the newspapers. This was effective as there was a constant exchange of Northern and Southern papers. The two which became the principals in carrying out this method were the Richmond *Enquirer* and the New York *News*. Each copied the other's "personals" by request made in the advertisement, though occasionally additional papers were called upon to copy. These messages were generally of the agonizing type, in which some father was searching for a lost soldier son; but many, such as this one in the New York *News*, were cryptic enough to lead the Federal authorities to stop such advertisements: "Mr. C. M. Kulp and George Blessing, Richmond, Va.—My poor Pet died January 1, 1864. She received all the attention possible. I am almost crazed. Break it softly to her mother. Answer through Richmond 'Enquirer,' for Personal of New York 'News,' and I will send all the particulars. J. K." The *Enquirer* charged $2 for eight lines or less for each appearance. It denied heatedly that these were spy messages, explaining that a better method of passing spy ciphers would be through the "Help Wanted" columns and openly admitting that this latter method had been used by Confederate agents in their attempts to rescue Confederate prisoners of war.[65]

The kind of service afforded by the Post Office Department would of necessity have a profound effect on the morale of the people, for no Confederate activity, outside of raising armies, touched the

[64] Charleston *Daily Mercury*, January 8, 1862.
[65] For examples, see Richmond *Semi-Weekly Enquirer*, January 22, 1864; Richmond *Daily Enquirer*, August 13, 31, 1864; February 8, 1865.

ordinary citizen so closely. Reagan no doubt realized this fact when twice he refused the postmaster-generalship, and he was made to feel it more keenly throughout the existence of the Confederacy. A psychological blunder was made in the beginning when the postal rates were made first almost twice what the people were accustomed to, and a little later more than three times as much. Further criticism arose when the service was curtailed and many post offices were discontinued; but the endless, long-drawn-out complaints were due to the uncertainty and slowness of the mails. Within less than two months after the Confederacy took over the mails, complaints were arising over bad service, and the newspapers, especially, cited example after example of the inefficiency of the Post Office Department. A correspondent of a Columbus, Georgia, newspaper mailed a dispatch to his paper. He left for that city two days later and arrived a day before his dispatch. In 1862 a Mobile editor complained that no mail from Virginia had arrived at that city for the past several days; and in 1863 a Richmond editor noted the receipt of a Lynchburg paper, mailed ten days earlier, which led him to comment sarcastically, "Is this the best the Post Office Department can do—ten *days* from Lynchburg, when the travel is made in some seven or eight hours. An ox cart could do better." [66] The next year a Georgia editor complained that in "point of facility and dispatch" the postal service had "retrograded at least two centuries since the war began," [67] and a Congressman in Richmond declared that Congress had been in session about a month and yet no letters had arrived from home.

In desperation many people stamped their letters and sent them through the Southern Express Company, but a postal regulation soon forbade the express companies to carry mail. Postal regulations even forbade the sale of newspapers on trains unless postage had been paid on them. The postal laws were "an outrage on a free people," complained a Georgia editor.[68] Soldiers' mail was long a source of contention. Each regiment had a mail carrier, who collected the mail and took it to the nearest post office and brought back the mail for the regiment; but when armies were moving it

[66] Richmond *Daily Examiner*, March 14, 1863.
[67] Augusta *Daily Chronicle & Sentinel*, December 4, 1864.
[68] Atlanta *Southern Confederacy*, July 30, 1862.

was difficult to keep correspondents informed on mailing addresses, and frequently mail was addressed to soldiers with no indication of the regiment. As a result great stacks of soldier mail collected in Richmond and in other centers. Reagan, once importuned by a lowly soldier for aid in searching for his mail, accompanied him to the Richmond post office and succeeded in recovering a half-dozen letters. There was nothing that soldiers longed for more than letters from home. Constantly were they disappointed, and their morale dipped with each disappointment. But there was little that Reagan could do to better the situation; the weaknesses were inherent.

There had long been a sentiment, expressed by certain people of strong religious convictions, against carrying the mails on Sunday. As this movement had never been able to turn the United States from the practice, the Southern element sought to have the Confederacy adopt the prohibition. Thomas R. R. Cobb tried unsuccessfully to have such a provision inserted in the Confederate Constitution, and some members of Congress later carried the fight to the floors of that body. At least one of Reagan's postmasters threatened to resign if the mails were continued on Sunday.[69] As Reagan's service was already too slow, he never gave any comfort to those who would delay it still further. Congress took note of the slowness of the mails, and in a law of May 1, 1863, provided for a fast service to apply only to letters and government dispatches that bore the increased rate of $1.00 for a half ounce.

But for ordinary mails the service became increasingly worse. A fundamental cause of the poor service was the policy which provided that the Post Office Department must be self-supporting. It was impossible for Reagan to provide service as complete, fast, and efficient as the United States had done, without losing money; but he was to blame in adopting a policy of exceeding constitutional requirements by trying to make a surplus. Late in 1863 he had a surplus of $675,000, in which he took pride. This amount had been built up not only by discontinuing post offices and services, but also by zealously forcing down the amount the railroads should receive in their contracts for carrying mail. Six months after he had taken control, he had succeeded in making new contracts with

69 "C.S.A., P.O. Route Va.," I (Division of Manuscripts, Library of Congress).

only fifteen of the ninety-one railroad lines and branches. Though the railroads were continuing to carry the mails under their old contracts, it was with much turmoil, confusion, and inefficiency. He had a dispute with the Virginia Central Railroad, lasting more than a year, over deductions he was making from what the road claimed it should receive.[70]

But most of the delay incident to carrying the mail was beyond Reagan's control. The outer fringes of the Confederacy were invaded immediately on the outbreak of war, and as the Federal armies marched farther they upset the whole system of mail routes. Where large areas were permanently conquered, Reagan, of course, stood to save money, since mail services there were entirely discontinued; but too frequently raiding parties passed through regions, burning bridges and upsetting transportation routes which must be restored again. Federal soldiers took special delight in demolishing post offices and carrying off equipment. Then, too, a new nation in the pangs of birth amidst war and invasion should not be compared in its postal services, as well as in other performances for that matter, with a nation at peace. Trains were run primarily to haul military supplies and transport soldiers, and their schedules were largely at the mercy of military commanders. Such trains could not be delayed to make connections with incoming mails. These factors weighed heavily in slowing down the Confederate mail service. In 1862 Adjutant General Samuel Cooper aided Reagan slightly by issuing an order requiring troop trains to carry mail cars, but not to wait for connections.[71] When in 1863 the Trans-Mississippi part of the Confederacy was severed by the fall of Vicksburg and Port Hudson, regular mail connections with this region were discontinued; but Reagan soon instituted a special service whereby letters would be carried back and forth for forty cents a half ounce. Private individuals who had set up a service in which they charged $3.00 a letter were warned that such activities were in violation of the law.

[70] *Correspondence between the President of the Virginia Central Rail Road Company and the Postmaster General, in Relation to Postal Service* (Richmond, 1864); Augusta *Weekly Chronicle & Sentinel*, August 31, 1864; Richmond *Daily Dispatch*, January 15, 1862; Richmond *Daily Enquirer*, August 22, 1864.

[71] *General Orders from Adjutant and Inspector-General's Office, Confederate States Army, 1862–1863*, Ser. 1862, p. 27.

Most of the mail routes of the Confederacy were not on railways, but over rough country roads, by horse and buggy or horseback. As man power became upset with the conscription of soldiers, Reagan was forced to hire as mail carriers such persons as he could find. In explaining the failure of the mails on one Virginia route, a postmaster stated that the carrier was "a trifling Boy and should be dismissed from the service." Other causes of poor service were "careless contractors, careless riders, and poor horses." [72] Later laws liberalized exemptions of postal workers from conscription as soldiers, but this action helped the service little and actually led to the evil of draft dodgers finding safety in Reagan's department.

Reagan began on June 1, 1861, with 8,411 post offices; within six months he had discontinued 111. The recession continued steadily as the territory of the Confederacy crumbled away, and by the time of Lee's surrender at Appomattox the number had almost vanished.

[72] "C.S.A., P.O. Route, Va.," I.

CHAPTER VII

THE CONFEDERATE CONGRESS

THERE were three Congresses during the life of the Confederacy. The original Convention in Montgomery, which wrote the two Confederate Constitutions and organized the government, was called the Provisional Congress. With members appointed by the state secession conventions, it met on February 4, 1861, and ended its existence on February 17, 1862, having held five sessions in all. The first body elected by the people, and called the First Congress, met the next day and adjourned sine die exactly two years after the end of the Provisional Congress. It held four sessions. The so-called Second Congress, actually the third and last to meet, held two sessions before the approaching collapse of the Confederacy brought its final adjournment on March 18, 1865. The Provisional Congress had only one house; the Congress of the Permanent Government, like its Federal prototype, was composed of a House and a Senate.

There were in all 267 men who served in the Confederate Congress, of whom slightly less than a third had at one time or another been members of the United States Congress. Also some had gained experience in state legislatures. During the four years of the Confederacy there was a rapid turnover in membership, only a few more than a tenth (twenty-seven, to be exact) serving continuously. But of those members of continuous service there were such outstanding leaders, either for good or evil, as Thomas S. Bocock and Robert M. T. Hunter of Virginia, William W. Boyce and William Porcher Miles of South Carolina, Benjamin H. Hill of Georgia, and Louis T. Wigfall of Texas. Other famous characters such as the "silver-tongued" Yancey of Alabama and Henry S. Foote of Tennessee, with his "colicky delivery," served only for a part of the life of the Confederacy. Until his death in January, 1862, a former President of the United States, John Tyler, was a member of the Provisional Congress.

Some of the most able members served only a short time, either because, overcome by their military ardor, they secured commissions and entered the army or because, failing to satisfy their constituency, they were defeated for re-election. Howell Cobb and Robert Toombs succumbed to military glory, and Jabez L. M. Curry of Alabama fell before the rising peace sentiment in his state. There were two who actually turned traitor to their government. Williamson R. W. Cobb of Alabama, elected by the disaffected citizens in the northern part of the state, never appeared to take his seat, and his name was dropped from the rolls of the House.[1] The other was the incorrigible, eccentric, irascible, voluble, and restless Foote. Consumed by hatred of Davis, longstanding from the time when the two opposed each other in Mississippi, Foote had hied himself away to California, later to return to Tennessee and get himself elected to the Confederate Congress. Opposing almost every Confederate policy, he was charged as early as the spring of 1864 with plans to "go over to the Yankees." Veering from an early position of utter desolation for the Yankee homeland to a seeker for peace at any price, he mysteriously left the halls of Congress in December, 1864, and early in the following January he was arrested by the Confederate military authorities as he tried to make his way across the Potomac. He was on his way to Washington to make peace and save the people of the Confederacy from Davis' despotism, so he maintained. Brought on a writ of habeas corpus into Judge Halyburton's Confederate District Court, where he acted as his own lawyer, he was released by the War Department from its custody, thereby leaving nothing for the court to do. He made his way to the House of Representatives, where he was given permission to explain his actions. After a long harangue he was cut short by the Speaker and made to take his seat. A motion to expel him was lost for want of the required two-thirds majority, but his arrest was pronounced proper by a

---

[1] Richmond *Daily Examiner*, May 4, 1864; Bessie Martin, *Desertion of Alabama Troops from the Confederate Army; A Study in Sectionalism* (New York, 1932), 110 ff.; Tatum, *Disloyalty in the Confederacy*, 6..

unanimous vote. Leaving Richmond again he successfully made his escape to the North, but, learning that the Federal authorities did not receive his peace proposals with favor, he took boat for Europe. In London he issued a manifesto to his Tennessee constituency, asking them to secede from the Confederacy and re-enter the Union. After his final escape the House expelled him unanimously.[2]

Howell Cobb was the President of the Provisional Congress and Thomas S. Bocock was Speaker of the House of Representatives of the Permanent Government throughout its existence. Speaker Bocock was a statesman of ability and integrity, whose past services in the United States Congress fitted him well for his post. His valedictory at the end of his first term, a ringing address calling on his countrymen to gird themselves for the final victory, marked him as a forceful speaker and clear thinker.

Stephens was the President of the Senate by virtue of his position as Vice-President. Forever sick and ailing in both mind and body, with an almost humped back, chest bowed inward, sallow pinched features, wrinkles radiating in every direction, harsh gray hair, ashen lips, eyes that sparkled and fascinated and restlessly blazed with excitement, and an effeminate, boyish, yet melodious and well-modulated voice, he looked like the handiwork of the Florida agues, fevers, and mosquitoes. War-clerk Jones thought one might suppose him "to be afflicted with all manner of diseases, and doomed to speedy dissolution," but, he added, "he has worn this appearance during the last twenty years." [3] His appearance and the state of his health served him well in playing on the sentiments of the people.[4] Torn asunder by psychological storms, he found his greatest love and consolation in his dog Rio and his half brother Linton, both of whom remained in Georgia except for Linton's short mili-

---

[2] *Journal of the Congress of the Confederate States,* VII, 454, 465–67, 659; *Official Records,* Ser. I, Vol. XLVI, Pt. II, 124, 126, 505, 561; Richmond *Daily Whig,* April 16, 1864; Richmond *Daily Examiner,* December 19, 21, 1864; January 17, March 22, 1865; Athens *Southern Watchman,* February 15, 1865; Henry S. Foote, *War of the Rebellion; or, Scylla and Charybdis. Consisting of Observations upon the Causes, Course and Consequences of the Late Civil War in the United States* (New York, 1866), 376–433; Jones, *Rebel War Clerk's Diary,* II, 359.

[3] Jones, *Rebel War Clerk's Diary,* I, 306.

[4] Cleveland, *Alexander H. Stephens,* 785.

tary service. Looking into his own soul he declared, "I have in my life been one of the most miserable beings, it seems to me, that walked the earth—subject to occasional fits of depression that seemed well-nigh bordering on despair. Without enjoyment, without pleasure, without hope, and without sympathy with the world." [5]

Thomas R. R. Cobb thought that Stephens had "the ear of Davis" in the early days of the Confederacy, and Cobb was probably right; but after this short honeymoon Stephens considered himself and his advice neglected by the President. He soon withdrew into a sullen isolation, deserted his post of duty in Richmond for his Georgia home, and became the most outstanding obstructionist in the Confederacy. He showed less practical statesmanship at this time than in any other period of his life. During 1863 and 1864 he was away from his duties as President of the Senate for a year and a half. When Stephens was sojourning in Georgia, Robert M. T. Hunter presided over the Senate and became in effect the Vice-President of the Confederacy. Stephens was often begged by his wiser friends, but without avail, to go to Richmond and perform his duties.

The Vice-President took an extreme dislike for Davis. He explained that it was not an aversion to him personally but a disagreement with his policies, which he held were driving the Confederacy into a dictatorship destructive of all the liberties the people were fighting for. "My hostility and wrath (and I have enough of it to burst ten thousand bottles) is not against him, or any man or men," he protested, "but against the thing—the measures and the policy which I see is leading us to despotism." He had "no more feeling of resentment" toward Davis than he had "toward the defects and infirmities of my poor old blind and deaf dog." [6] Such was the high plane which he reasoned himself into thinking he had attained. Stephens was inordinately ambitious for high position and adulation, without always seeming to realize that it was this ambition which made him act as he did. He toyed with the idea now and then of his becoming President, either through the death or removal of Davis. At one time he even thought out his

[5] Johnston and Browne, *Alexander H. Stephens*, 451.
[6] *Official Records*, Ser. IV, Vol. III, 280.

line of procedure if he should become President, and sensing the impossibility of carrying it out, shrank away in cowering fear—"I wish never to advert to this subject again." [7] Even once, going to the other extreme, he had a strong inclination to resign the vice-presidency, but he still clung to it like a child to a Christmas toy.

Stephens was, in fact, a fast prisoner of his own dogmas. He could never forgo for a moment any accustomed peacetime liberty or right in order to assure first the winning of independence and the restoration of every right the people wanted. Principles were fixed and never changed. He adopted as his motto: "Times change and we often change with them, but principles never." Stephens evidently regarded himself as more of an abstract principle than a man. Also deep down in Stephens was the feeling that the Confederacy was a mistake. He never really gave up the idea of the old Union. He was always a reconstructionist, and Mrs. Chesnut charged him to his face with being halfhearted and continually looking back.[8]

It is remarkable that Stephens remained throughout the period of the Confederacy almost sacrosanct to most of the people, though not to all. He had a few bold open critics. The all-seeing Thomas R. R. Cobb soon decided that Stephens did not have Davis' ear, and by January of 1862 was charging Stephens with "openly opposing the administration and trying to build up an opposition party" [9]—the very thing he had early cried out against so loudly. He was now "a poor selfish demagogue." A Virginian observed in 1864: "The truth is, the people of the Confederacy have been fooled in Mr. Stephens, and he owes it to himself, as an honorable man, and to them, to resign and give us an opportunity to elect one in whom we can place confidence." [10] And the sharp-tongued Pollard declared that Stephens "had blown hot and cold in the war" and that the "reputation of this man is a striking example of how difficult it is in all parts of America for the people to distinguish between a real statesman and an elaborate demagogue." [11]

7 Johnston and Browne, *Alexander H. Stephens*, 449.

8 Martin and Avary (eds.), *Diary from Dixie*, 49.

9 *Southern Historical Society Papers*, XXVIII (1900), 289, 290.

10 Richmond *Semi-Weekly Enquirer*, April 29, 1864.

11 Edward A. Pollard, *The Lost Cause; A New Southern History of the War of the Confederates. Comprising a Full and Authentic Account of the Rise and Progress of the Late Southern Confederacy* . . . (New York, 1866), 682.

The Confederate Congress, like all deliberative bodies, felt that its debates and proceedings were important and should be properly preserved and published. Although its laws, save those passed during its last session, were officially issued, none of its debates and proceedings were thus honored.[12] The amending and repealing of laws soon made it difficult for anyone to determine what the law was at any given time. And to add to this difficulty, no one could be sure which of the body of United States laws taken over by the Confederacy in the beginning had been superseded. Not sure whether the famous Force Bill passed in 1833 to coerce South Carolina in the Nullification movement had been inherited by the Confederacy, Senator Herschel V. Johnson of Georgia moved in 1863 to repeal it. A committee was appointed to codify the laws of the Confederacy, but it was soon discharged and its work came to nothing.[13] Now and then the Senate dallied with the idea of having all its proceedings taken down verbatim by a stenographer, but it was never able to find one. There were plans for issuing a Congressional record much like the old United States Congressional *Globe,* but this project also was abandoned.[14] Apart from its session statutes, the only records of the proceedings of Congress published contemporaneously were the accounts taken down by the newspaper correspondents.[15]

In the beginning the salary of Congressmen was $8.00 a day and ten cents a mile for the distance traveled in going to the place of meeting and returning home. In 1862 salaries were increased to $2,760 a year and the mileage rate to twenty cents. This slight increase brought on a storm of opposition. One editor bitterly

[12] The laws and resolutions of the last session of the Confederate Congress together with certain secret acts of previous congresses were edited by Charles W. Ramsdell and published in 1941 as *Laws and Joint Resolutions of the Last Session of the Confederate Congress (November 7, 1864–March 18, 1865) Together with the Secret Acts of Previous Congresses.* The official journals of the House and Senate were published by the United States government, in seven volumes, as *Journal of the Congress of the Confederate States of America, 1861–1865.*

[13] Richmond *Daily Enquirer,* February 19, 1863.

[14] Richmond *Daily Examiner,* November 7, 1864; Augusta *Daily Constitutionalist,* August 5, 1864; Macon *Daily Confederate,* July 24, 1864; *Official Records,* Ser. IV, Vol. III, 1015–18.

[15] The *Southern Historical Society Papers* is in the process of publishing in its occasional volumes the proceedings of the Confederate Congress as they were written by newspaper reporters of the Richmond press.

complained that a Congressman would get "more pay in one day than the poor soldier on the tented field receives in two months!" [16] and another recalled that the great Washington had served his country for seven years without pay. Why could not Congressmen be as patriotic? [17] Yet as prices went up and money thereby became correspondingly more worthless, Congress braved all opposition and raised its pay again, doubling it in 1864, and near the end it made further increases.

Frequently throughout the war, sessions of Congress were held in secrecy. The secret session, in fact, had been a time-honored practice in American history. The old Continental and Confederation Congresses had been held in secrecy and the United States Senate had not opened its doors until 1800. "The discussions of the Confederate Congress must be secret," declared the Richmond *Examiner.* "Its halls must not become the theatre of polemic oratory nor the banquet of popular curiosity." [18] Secrecy would keep down buncombe and demagoguery, so often indulged in in the old United States Congresses to please the gaping galleries, and it would prevent the enemy from obtaining desired information.

Within a year, when critics of all things Confederate began raising their voices, it was only natural that they should find a shining object to attack in the custom of holding secret sessions. The same Richmond *Examiner* which had recently been praising this practice could now say, "The members of the old Provisional Congress locked themselves from the newspapers that they might drink whiskey and give their votes, excluded from the observations of the world." [19] The people wanted to know what was going on in their legislative body; they feared that Congressmen were plotting against their liberties, that they were hiding their incompetency behind closed doors, that they distrusted the ability of the people to maintain their stamina in the face of disasters aired in Congress. "Nothing but motions to adjourn, tinker the currency, or appoint days of fasting and prayer, is done in open sessions," declared a Georgia editor.[20] Yancey in the Senate and Foote in the House

---

16 Sandersville *Central Georgian,* March 19, 1862.
17 Tuskegee *South Western Baptist,* April 10, 1862.
18 Richmond *Daily Examiner,* July 20, 1861.   19 *Ibid.,* July 7, 1862.
20 Augusta *Weekly Chronicle & Sentinel,* February 8, 1865.

were strong opponents of secrecy and made frequent and futile efforts to have it abolished. A sarcastic editor reported the perfection of a new invention which would automatically declare Congress in secret session without the formality or delay of motions and votes. Speaking of the First Congress, Stephens said it was "a weak and contemptible body." "They sat with closed doors," he said. "It was well they did, and so kept from the public some of the most disgraceful scenes ever enacted by a legislative body." [21]

Though Stephens' charges were not only somewhat true of this Congress but also of the next, he could ill afford to complain, for he was seldom present to offer a restraining hand. Revolutionary bodies had never been sedate assemblages, and even the ante-bellum United States Congress had presented some stormy scenes. The Confederate Congresses were no exception. Personal encounters took place not only among members of Congress but also among officials of that body. In April, 1863, Robert E. Ford of Elizabethtown, Kentucky, the journal clerk of the House, murdered Robert S. Dixon of Columbus, Georgia, the chief clerk. The encounter took place on Capitol Square, just outside the Congressional halls, where the two men met and shot it out. The trouble arose when Dixon dismissed Ford for negligence in preparing the journal for the next day's session. Ford was tried for murder, convicted, and sentenced to eighteen years in the penitentiary. He appealed his case and was given a new trial, which was postponed time and again until it was lost in the collapse of the Confederacy. [22]

In a wordy debate in the Senate, Hill threw an inkstand at Yancey, who had made some charges against him, hitting the Alabamian on the cheekbone and bringing forth blood splattered with ink. Sometime thereafter Yancey died, and Hill's enemies charged him with having indirectly killed Yancey, though in fact his death was due entirely to other causes. [23] Yancey also had a

---

[21] Johnston, *Autobiography*, 161. This is part of a rabid editorial which appeared in the Athens *Southern Watchman*, December 14, 1864: "If these enemies of Liberty and Republican Government refuse to do so [resign], there is still a remedy—a desperate one we admit—but dangerous cases require desperate remedies. *Let the enemies of public liberty be hung like egg-sucking dogs!*"

[22] Richmond *Daily Examiner*, April 25, 1863; February 2, 24, April 27, October 6, 20, December 7, 1864; January 20, March 29, 1865.

[23] Hill, *Benjamin H. Hill*, 43–44.

bitter word encounter with James Phelan of Mississippi, which lasted for two hours and involved such explosive matter that newspaper correspondents refused to report it for fear of their own personal safety.[24] Though Pollard was never a member of Congress, his vitriolic pen led him close to a duel with Daniel C. De Jarnette, a Virginia Congressman, when he described the latter as having a "reputation for snorting and coliky eloquence in the House, and his invocation to 'My Maryland' was, probably, intended only to relieve his own bowels of some windy rhetoric." To avert a duel, both were brought before the Mayor's Court and placed under a peace bond.[25] Another outsider, a woman, actually used force and violence to intrude herself on the House as it was assembling and proceeded to cowhide George G. Vest of Missouri. Her grievance was that Congress was about to force all government clerks to divulge their ages, incident to enforcing the Conscription Act. The woman was demented, and the House voted its confidence in Vest.[26]

The prince of Congressional villains of disorder was Foote. According to Pollard, he had "the most indecent itch for notoriety," [27] and as his harangues and antics made good news, the newspapers gave him much space. Also his venom against the President pleased the anti-Davis editors. A Richmond correspondent of an Alabama paper reported in January, 1864, that Congress had been in session for nine days and had "done nothing thus far but listen to Mr. Foote," who was a "universal talker . . . talks about every thing; and to little purpose upon any [thing] . . . —a verbose talker, a loose and inaccurate thinker." [28] Foote not only hated Davis, but he hated Davis' cabinet—Benjamin, Mallory, Memminger, and Seddon being his especial aversions. He claimed credit for having forced the resignations of Memminger and Seddon. In the beginning he would rake the North with fire and sword and win the war if it cost 1,000,000 men and $2,000,000,000, securing "indem-

24 Southern Historical Society Papers, XLVII (1930), 34.

25 Richmond Daily Examiner, January 21, 28, 1864.

26 Jones, Rebel War Clerk's Diary, II, 347–48; Journal of the Congress of the Confederate States, VII, 332. For the rule on divulging ages, see Memphis Daily Appeal, December 28, 1864.

27 Pollard, Jefferson Davis, 204–208.

28 Tuskegee South Western Baptist, January 14, 1864.

nity for the past and security for the future," and yet, as has appeared, he later advocated peace at any price and deserted the Confederacy before the end.

He fought with his fists as well as with words and threatened with dueling pistols. In the course of a speech by Congressman E. S. Dargan of Alabama, Foote interrupted to call him a "damned rascal," whereupon Dargan lunged at him with a bowie knife and was prevented by other members from assassinating Foote. In a committee hearing on the Commissary and Quartermaster Departments Foote ridiculed with laughter the testimony of Thomas B. Hanly of Arkansas. They immediately came to blows, which resulted in Foote tearing off Hanly's shirt bosom and knocking Commissary General Lucius B. Northrop into a corner. Another disgraceful affair was participated in by three actors. John Mitchel, a famous Irish patriot and exile on the staff of the Richmond *Examiner,* called on the House to expel Foote. Mitchel's challenge to a duel was carried to Foote by Congressman William G. Swan, a Tennessee colleague but bitter enemy. On entering Foote's rooms at the Ballard House, Swan was insulted by Foote with the remark that he was no gentleman, whereupon Swan hit him over the head with an umbrella. Foote then sought unsuccessfully to shoot Swan. All three were brought into the Mayor's Court and placed under bond to keep the peace.[29]

As has already been noted, Foote brought his role as Confederate Congressman to an inglorious end by deserting to the North. In the last days when tempers no less than patriotism had worn thin, a few Foote imitators, in their heroics, put on their hats and got as far as the door; but at least one, Congressman William R. Smith of Alabama, took permanent leave—not to try to make peace with the North, but to return home.

As a body the Confederate Congress was a disappointment; it did not maintain the standards of statesmanship which the people had expected. These civil leaders never received the acclaim which came to military officers, but it was much in the nature of things that this should be so. Military glory drew to the battlefield much talent that would have found an outlet in civil administration had

<hr>

[29] Richmond *Daily Examiner,* November 24, 1864; New York *World,* November 28, 1864; Jones, *Rebel War Clerk's Diary,* II, 337.

the Confederacy been allowed to establish itself in peace. And it was an old custom to give the soldier more praise than the civilian. It soon became the fashion to hold Congress and Congressmen in contempt, and Congressmen added to the turmoil by berating one another—as much so as abusing the Yankees, observed Mrs. Chesnut. Pollard declared that the Provisional Congress was "ignorant and unsavory" and that the succeeding one was "a weak, sycophantic, and trifling body," [30] and War-clerk Jones said there were "not a dozen [Congressmen] with any pretensions of statesmanship." This First Congress had just got well started in its work when General McClellan's march up the Peninsula made Richmond seem unsafe. Congress decided to adjourn and thereby brought down upon itself much condemnation and ridicule. Though the lawmakers claimed they had finished their work, their critics charged them with cowardice in running from the enemy. The Richmond *Whig* derisively described them as fleeing by canal boat, drawn by sweet-tempered mules, with a regiment of ladies armed with popguns of the longest range to protect them from snakes and bullfrogs. Their protectors were to escort them "to a secluded cave in the mountains of Hepsidam and leave them there in charge of the children of the vicinage." [31]

As sessions came and went, Congressmen were almost continuously charged with doing nothing but wasting their time on trivialities. They spent long hours debating on a time to adjourn, which on one occasion led a member to remark: "If the House would adjourn and not meet any more, it would benefit the country." [32] A Georgia editor said, "We daily publish their proceedings, but we daily question ourselves if they are worth the trouble." Congress had spent a year debating on a device for a seal. This editor suggested "A terrapin *passant*, 'Never in haste.' " [33] When Richmond was endangered by a cavalry raid in the spring of 1863, a company of Congressmen volunteered for local defense. A correspondent of the Richmond *Examiner* gave the news thus: "If a goose served for a sentinel when Rome was to be defended, why should not a Con-

[30] Edward A. Pollard, *The First Year of the War* (New York, 1863), 351.

[31] Grove Hill (Ala.) *Clarke County Democrat*, May 8, 1862, quoting Richmond *Daily Whig*.

[32] *Southern Historical Society Papers*, XLVIII (1941), 120.

[33] Augusta *Weekly Chronicle & Sentinel*, March 3, 1863.

gressman be fitted for the same duty when the Capital of the Confederacy is beleaguered?" [34] As the First Congress came to a close, a critic gave this estimate of it: "Never has any representative body of men met with more general censure from the great body of their constituency." [35]

Yet Congress was better than its critics made it. It showed a boldness of imagination as it faced unprecedented problems. It passed a system of conscription with exemptions for industrial reasons, a much more logical and just system than was later established by the United States; it set up a tax in kind, unheard of in American law; it provided for impressment of farm products for the army at fixed prices; it passed other outstanding laws and wrestled with gigantic problems. True enough, it was bitterly criticized for these very acts; and it is true that some of these acts were not properly executed, but that was not the fault of Congress. War was upon the land, and directly or indirectly almost all acts of Congress were predicated on that fact.

It was natural that Congress should want all the information it could get relating to military operations and that it should even attempt some direction of military affairs; but it never harassed the Executive and army commanders as much as the United States Congress did through its Committee on the Conduct of the War. An incipient effort to form such a committee to consist of one member from each state was defeated. Congress frequently asked Davis for military reports, some of which either were secret or had not yet been compiled, and when the President did not comply there were critics to condemn him. Congressmen were much upset by General Albert Sidney Johnston's retreat in the West in 1861–1862, and on the fall of Fort Donelson and Nashville many demanded his recall. When, about the same time, Roanoke Island on the coast of North Carolina was lost, the House appointed a committee of investigation, which later found "that the whole

[34] Richmond *Daily Examiner*, May 6, 1863. The editor of the Athens *Southern Watchman*, January 27, 1864, declared that Congress "contains material which but for the very small number of men of sense in it, would precipitate the country into untold evils. Indeed, we are afraid they will do so, any way. . . . What good can be expected from such a body? What hope can the People entertain from the legislation of *servants* who have impudently assumed to be their MASTERS?"

[35] Augusta *Weekly Constitutionalist*, February 24, 1864.

command did their duty." [36] But many still felt that General Benjamin Huger was largely responsible for the disaster, and later, when he seemed to show little resourcefulness in opposing McClellan's march up the Peninsula, the ever ready critic Foote said there was enough evidence against Huger "to convict a thousand criminals," that Rome had its Cataline, the Revolution, its Benedict Arnold, "and we have our Huger." [37]

Congressmen long sought to rid the army of General Braxton Bragg. On his retreat from Corinth, Mississippi, in 1862, he was charged with the execution of a soldier who had, against orders, made a noise by firing his gun at a chicken; then Bragg had had three soldiers executed without trial. But opposition mounted when he had failed in his Kentucky campaign in the early fall of 1862, and especially when the next year he lost the battles of Lookout Mountain and Missionary Ridge. So great was the outcry against him both in Congress and in the army, that Davis removed him, after the disaster in East Tennessee, but brought him to Richmond as his military adviser, to the greater embitterment of those who disliked the General. On the other hand, many Congressmen took the part of General Joseph E. Johnston in his alleged mistreatment by the President.

During January and February of 1864 Congress showed its appreciation of the services of various army units and commanders by passing resolutions of thanks. Being, of course, as desirous of winning the war as any other branch of the government, Congress issued joint addresses and manifestoes and its presiding officers made ringing speeches on certain occasions. Notable were the joint address issued at the end of the First Congress and Robert M. T. Hunter's speech delivered at the same time.

Relations between President Davis and Congress varied with the stresses of the times. Despite his bitter Congressional critics, Davis dominated Congress throughout most of the war, though near the end he almost completely lost control. He did not, however, wield more power than "George III ever aspired to [in his] palmiest days," as one critic charged,[38] for he was no perpetual censor over

[36] *Journal of the Congress of the Confederate States*, V, 241.

[37] *Southern Historical Society Papers*, XLV (1925), 197.

[38] *Southern Literary Messenger*, XXXIV (1862), 698, quoting P. W. Alexander in the Savannah *Republican*.

Congressional conscience and action. Only when Congress passed bills which were unconstitutional or manifestly unwise did Davis resort to the veto, but even so he exercised it thirty-nine times, and in many of these instances he showed intelligence superior to the mass mind of Congress. It was to the credit of Congress that it upheld Davis' veto with only one exception, although frequently either the House or the Senate overrode a veto. The exception was the bill which allowed newspapers addressed to soldiers to go free of postage. In his veto messages Davis mercilessly showed the careless haste and muddled thinking of Congress. On almost elementary matters Congress passed bills which were clearly unconstitutional, sometimes bills relating to officers who did not exist or amending laws that had never been passed. It is interesting to note, but to be expected, that the one-chambered Provisional Congress passed more unconstitutional or careless and unwise bills than in an equal length of time were passed by the two-chambered Congresses, where such bills got a double screening.

There were frequent outbursts in Congress against Davis, and there was always a well-knit minority which seized every advantage to attack the President. Thomas R. R. Cobb, pessimistically and mistakenly, charged near the end of the Provisional Congress that Davis had lost his power over Congress—that he was "as obstinate as a mule." A little later Cobb observed that the new Congress was in a furor and was "debating secretly the propriety of deposing him," adding, *"He would be deposed* if the Congress had any more confidence in Stephens than in him." [39] Near the end of 1863 his brother Howell wrote his wife: "The state of feeling between the President & Congress is bad—could not be worse. To one less hopeful and sanguine than myself it would cause desperation." [40] Vice-President Stephens, for reasons of his own, had no respect for the Congress sitting in the spring of 1864. He declared that he would stake his head on a bet that this Congress could not carry ten districts throughout the South.[41] The First Congress, which adjourned sine die February 17, 1864, took a slap at Davis for the unprecedented step of assuming power to call the new Congress

[39] Thomas R. R. Cobb to his wife, March 16, 1862, in Thomas R. R. Cobb Letters.
[40] Howell Cobb to his wife, December 17, 1863, in Howell Cobb Papers.
[41] Stephens to Herschel V. Johnson, April 8, 1864, in *Official Records,* Ser. IV, Vol. III, 280–81.

into special session the following May instead of awaiting its normal meeting time in December. Some considered this a usurpation and unconstitutional. When the special session met, Davis sent only a short message, cleverly answering the old Congress by saying that so short a time had elapsed since the First Congress had adjourned that there was little to be done.

Davis had certain stanch supporters in Congress who never deserted him; there were others who supported him loyally on certain outstanding policies. Senator Hill of Georgia never wavered; the less able Senator Phelan of Mississippi and Ethelbert Barksdale of the same state could generally be counted upon to support Davis, and even the twin fire-eaters Wigfall and Yancey came to Davis' rescue occasionally.

CHAPTER VIII

MONEY, BONDS, AND TAXES

MONEY, bonds, and taxes are inextricably interrelated in the financing of a government and the proper balancing of one against another is the test of success. Here the Confederacy was to enter a morass, and through the lack of proper wisdom and guidance, to flounder on deeper into the mire until it was finally engulfed in confusion and disaster. One of the most fundamental causes of the ultimate failure of the Confederacy lay in its unwise financial policies. Likewise, the assumption that the Confederacy was a firmly established government instead of merely one in the making was nowhere more fatal than in the field of finance. It was a country blockaded and cut off from the rest of the world, making foreign trade and financing almost impossible, and its own territory was soon deeply invaded and so disorganized that taxes could not be collected and bonds marketed.

The man selected by President Davis to carry out the impossible task of successfully directing the finances of the Confederacy was Christopher G. Memminger, born in Germany but nurtured in South Carolina, a man of sound instincts but weak will power, though antagonistic enough to make his dealings with others difficult and largely futile. He had received some training in finance in his political career in South Carolina, but his appointment was not for this reason so much as for giving his state a position in the cabinet. Some consideration had been given to Toombs, and it has been thought by a few that the Georgian would have used his admitted financial talents to good advantage as Secretary of the Treasury; but Toombs's valid criticisms of Confederate finances came after fatal mistakes had been made and their effects evident to all.

The period of Memminger's tranquil official life was short; his attempts to meet the financial problems of an infant nation at war soon made him an easy target for faultfinders. They blamed Memminger for what Congress did rather than for what he recommended that Congress should do. Foote with all his venom was soon upon him; Wigfall was saying that Memminger seemed to think he could finance the Confederacy by passing around the hat; and the hostile editor of the Richmond *Whig* could say by 1863: "A second rate lawyer in Charleston, famous for the energy and persistence with which he collected small bills and dunned petty debtors, his elevation to the head of the Treasury was a stroke of fortune which must have astonished the good man very much. He has done his best, but he has been overtaken—that is all." [1]

When Memminger first announced his program, no one could know that a devastating four-year war lay ahead. Consequently he made no plans for raising a large revenue—what he suggested might have done well enough for the first year of a young nation at peace. He called for a few minor taxes, a small bond issue, and the establishment of a uniform paper currency. He began operations in an unswept room in Montgomery, without desk, chair, or a sheet of paper, and with no funds. His own private bank account was drawn upon by his chief clerk Henry D. Capers in assembling furnishings for his headquarters.[2] Like Reagan and his postal clerks, Memminger was fortunate in enticing away from Washington important Treasury officials, who brought with them instruction books and printed forms.[3] In May, 1861, he accompanied the rest of the government to Richmond and occupied the first floor of the old United States customhouse, with President Davis and the Department of State on the second. Lady clerks, the largest part of the force working in his department, were kept busy signing, clipping, and numbering the treasury notes, for the Confederate Treasury soon came to be the greatest money factory in the world. Contrary to general belief, it was felt that each lady's signing her own name would make the notes harder to counterfeit. Memminger, who saw no protection in this device, wanted the names

[1] Richmond *Daily Whig*, September 25, 1863.

[2] Henry D. Capers, *The Life and Times of C. G. Memminger* (Richmond, 1893), 310.

[3] Smith, *History of the Confederate Treasury*, 3-4.

printed on the notes but he was never able to induce Congress to agree. The ladies, many of them society belles working for $500 a year, found release for their pent-up patriotism in this activity. As the cost of living increased and Richmond became more crowded, the Treasury Note Bureau was moved to Columbia, South Carolina, in 1864. Most of the ladies then resigned, but about a hundred with cooked rations for three weeks set out by rail for their new abode. In February, 1865, when the Federals burned Columbia, some of the equipment was saved and moved to Richmond and a part to Anderson, South Carolina; but by this time Confederate money was not worth the cost of printing and signing.[4]

The first credit the Confederacy received was the loan by Alabama, of $500,000, accepted by the Montgomery Convention four days after it had met; but the first actual cash to jingle in Memminger's coffers was $389,267, made up of the United States bullion fund in the New Orleans Mint, and of $174,519 in the New Orleans customhouse—all seized by Louisiana and turned over to the Confederacy. A small amount of bullion and customs funds were later secured in the assay office in Charlotte, North Carolina, and in the mint at Dahlonega, Georgia. The amount of specie of all nationalities in the banks of the Confederacy in 1861 was about $26,000,000, with about half of it in the banks of New Orleans, which had been the greatest financial center in the Southern states. Naturally this money was not confiscated by the Confederacy, though in other ways it was to secure most of it.[5] When New Orleans fell in 1862, the Confederacy seized about $2,500,000 in the banks there and paid for it in Confederate notes. The specie the Confederacy was able to secure throughout its existence amounted to about $27,000,000.[6] It consisted of almost every kind of coin imaginable. In a small Treasury shipment in 1862 there were the following coins: 28 Spanish dollars, 24 Spanish quarter dollars, 8 Spanish half dollars, 8 English sovereigns, 3 Napoleons, 385 United States half

---

[4] Richmond *Daily Whig*, November 7, 1862; April 19, May 5, 1864; Richmond *Daily Examiner*, April 19, 1864; Martin and Avary (eds.), *Diary from Dixie*, 162; Capers, *Life and Times of C. G. Memminger*, 337; Dallas D. Irvine, "The Fate of Confederate Archives," in *American Historical Review*, XLIV (1938–1939), 834–35.

[5] Schwab, *Confederate States of America*, 145.

[6] *Ibid.*, 43.

dollars, and 988 United States quarter dollars.[7] The Treasury Department needed specie not only to pay interest on certain of its bonds, but also to pay for foreign purchases. Less than a month before the downfall of the government, Congress, seeming to think that there was a plenitude of specie in the Confederacy, in banks and in private possession, passed a law trying to raise $30,000,000 in this form of currency to be used in increasing the value of the paper notes by buying them up on the market. A few days later, in desperation, it called on the people for $3,000,000 in specie with which to buy supplies for the army, and if they did not respond to the amount of a fourth of what was in their possession, then that amount should be confiscated by a 25 per cent tax on it.

With a considerable amount of bullion on hand and with what it hoped would be mined in Georgia and North Carolina, the Confederacy planned to coin money in the New Orleans and Dahlonega mints; but because of the scarcity of engravers and other skilled workers it soon reduced these mints to assay offices, and with the exception of four half dollars struck in New Orleans it gave up its plans for coining money. Nevertheless, the movement to mint Confederate coins was slow in dying; in 1862 the Senate passed a bill to coin $5,000,000 in copper currency of five-, ten-, and twenty-five-cent pieces, and a patriotic Alabama lady offered President Davis her silverware to be coined.

Although there were to be no Confederate coins, there was naturally an indeterminate but considerable amount of United States coins—estimated at $20,000,000—remaining in the pockets of the people. These coins, however, were immediately hoarded and did not come out except in rare instances. Some specie reached the Confederacy in the purchase of bonds but more escaped to make purchases in foreign markets In 1863 a patriotic South Carolinian gave the Charleston Arsenal 520 copper coins, weighing 12 pounds, and a Richmond editor in 1864, when $1.00 in gold was worth $20.00 in Confederate notes, wondered why more copper and nickel coins did not make their appearance. "There must be any quantity of them stored away," he observed.[8] To increase its circulating medium, before it loosed the flood of paper money on the country,

[7] "II CSA Treasury 1862 Jan–June" (Division of Manuscripts, Library of Congress).   [8] Richmond *Daily Whig*, April 27, 1864.

Congress made United States silver coins legal tender up to $10, and gave full monetary standing with fixed values stipulated to English sovereigns, French Napoleons, and Spanish and Mexican doubloons.

Although Memminger's financial plans included bonds, a paper currency, and taxes, Congress soon embarked on the easy road of paying its debts in unsecured paper and bonds. But the first problem was to secure a sufficient amount of circulating medium—the very opposite of what was later to plague the Confederacy to its death. Before it could get its own money printed, the Confederacy borrowed state bank notes for its current needs; but later, to give uniformity to Confederate notes which the state bank notes did not possess, the latter were relegated into the background as far as possible, especially by the device of inducing the issuing banks to suspend specie payment on them. The first Confederate notes provided for, in March, 1861, bore interest and were modest in amount—only $1,000,000 and in denominations of not less than $50—later to be increased and to bear a higher rate of interest. These notes were, in fact, more like bonds, as they must be endorsed each time they were passed. They would circulate little, as people would hold them for their interest. But after the First Battle of Manassas, in July, 1861, when the war began to take on serious proportions, the Confederacy embarked full blast on its downward road to ruin through an inflated currency. The following August it issued $100,000,000 in notes, in denominations of $5.00 and above, and at the same time provided for $100,000,000 in 8 per cent bonds. It was felt that the bonds would act as a brake on a redundant currency, since people would convert this money, if it became too cheap, into bonds and receive the high rate of interest. The following year millions of notes under $5.00 were issued. Like the drunkard who could not stay away from his drink, the Confederacy in 1863 passed a law allowing the Treasury to issue $50,000,000 monthly, still futilely hoping that the amount outstanding could be controlled by the people's converting the notes into bonds. Memminger thought in 1862 that the amount of money needed for all commercial transactions was $200,000,000; but the next year it was decided that $175,000,000 would be enough, and a law attempted to fix it at that amount.

With the disappearance of small coins it became an exceedingly troublesome problem to make change for amounts less than $1.00. Banks advised their depositors to make their checks in multiples of $5.00, and some newspaper editors returned subscriptions rather than make change where small amounts were involved. Many people resorted to the unsatisfactory sticky postage stamps, making use especially of those of twenty-cent denomination, which they often cut in two; but the greatest vogue was the so-called shinplaster. These were small paper notes, generally in denominations from five cents to fifty cents, though one person claimed to have seen a two-cent note redeemable in persimmons. They were issued illegally by merchants, railroads, taverns, saloons, butchers, bakers, almost every other kind of business, and even by individuals. To provide small notes which might be accepted with confidence, states issued them and gave cities as well as specified railroads and other private businesses authority to do so. Richmond had by 1863 issued them to the amount of $500,000. The Confederacy issued fractional currency in the denomination of fifty cents.

Shinplasters issued by unauthorized individuals and firms became an outstanding evil, for many of them were fraudulent in that the firm issuing them could never be located. "Great God what a people—" exclaimed a Mississippi editor, "two hundred and fifty different sorts of shinplasters, and not one dime in silver to be seen!" [9] A Georgia editor averred that shinplasters "hop out upon us as thick as the frogs and lice of Egypt, and are almost as great a nuisance," and a Virginian declared, "We are cursed with the most infernal currency in the world. The State is literally overrun with trash, that may be wholly worthless, certainly it is emitted without any authority of law." [10] Soon shinplasters were not worth the effort to counterfeit, and by the middle of 1863 beggars were spurning fifty-cent shinplasters, one in Richmond remarking that she already had plenty of "that truck" and that she would be satisfied with nothing less than a $5 bill.

Another kind of money which began to make its way into the Confederacy in 1863, brought in by invading Federals and prisoners

[9] Raymond (Miss.) *Hinds County Gazette,* February 5, 1862.
[10] Atlanta *Southern Confederacy,* August 27, 1862; Richmond *Daily Whig,* September 17, 1861.

of war, was the United States greenbacks, which began to compete with Confederate notes. Although both were fiat money, the greenbacks early circulated at a premium of two for one, and after the Battle of Gettysburg it took four Confederate dollars to buy one greenback dollar. This situation was so humiliating and invidious that Congress passed a law in 1864 forbidding anyone to buy, sell, or accept greenbacks in any transaction; but as there was genuine need for this currency on the military frontiers, the Confederate government itself gradually collected a supply.

From the beginning, efforts were made to popularize Confederate notes and induce people to accept them over bank notes and state notes, which were being issued in great amounts. A bank convention in Richmond, in July, 1861, recommended that Confederate notes be received by all banks, railways, merchants, and all other businesses and individuals. Other bank conventions were held, making similar recommendations and asking in addition state, county, and city treasurers to receive them. People were reminded that Confederate money was as safe as any other kind of property, land, buildings, or what not; for if the Confederacy failed, the people stood to lose all their possessions through confiscation. Anyone who refused to accept Confederate money was looked upon as a traitor. Some states by law made Confederate notes legal tender, and all through practice made them so. Patriotic Southerners in advertising property for sale specified that Confederate money would be accepted. Within four months of the fall of the Confederacy a Georgian offered to accept Confederate money for 1,500 acres of land which he offered for sale. It was a tribute to Confederate patriotism that this money was accepted generally until almost the end, though naturally there were some traders and speculators who refused it amidst the scorn of their community. "The currency of the Confederacy is its life blood," a Richmond editor declared, "and the man or corporation who would discredit or injure it reduces his patriotism to a question of dollars and cents, and ends with poisoning the public confidence in the success of our armies and the integrity of our cause." [11]

11 Richmond *Daily Examiner*, May 18, 1863. While John A. Campbell was still a private citizen, after his resignation from the United States Supreme Court and before he became Assistant Secretary of War, he advised his wife to spend her Con-

It should be noted that, unlike the United States with its greenbacks, the Confederacy never made its notes legal tender, though there was a widespread outcry for doing so. Much discussion in favor of it ensued in Congress, where on one occasion the excitable Foote declared that anyone refusing to accept Confederate notes was "deserving of the Penitentiary"; but both Davis and Memminger held that such a law would be unconstitutional and also unnecessary, for the people's patriotism was leading them to accept this money. General Beauregard threatened military arrest of anyone in the Memphis area who should refuse to accept Confederate money, and Secretary of War George W. Randolph suggested to commanders that they arrest anyone, "as hostile to the Confederacy," who refused to take it in any regions of military operations.[12]

Secretary Memminger in the beginning had difficulties in getting his paper money printed, on account of the scarcity of engravers as well as of suitable paper. He first let a contract to the American Bank Note Company, in the North, but most of the notes printed by it were seized on their way into the Confederacy. A printer in New Orleans made such a crude product that he was soon abandoned, and Memminger now found in Richmond the lithographers Hoyer & Ludwig, who were printing postage stamps for Reagan. All these lithographed notes were crudely done, and not until engravers were later found did Confederate money become attractive in appearance.[13]

There was one supposed advantage found in these crudely lithographed notes: The counterfeiters improved on the originals,

federate money first, as it "may be worthless" if the war should be lost. She should next spend her Georgia and Virginia bank notes, and should hold her coins until all other kinds of money could not be spent. Campbell, New Orleans, to his wife, April 23, 1862, in Clement Claiborne Clay Papers (Manuscript Division, Duke University Library).

[12] *Official Records*, Ser. IV, Vol. II, 116. A. M. Buchanan, New Orleans, writing to Senator Thomas J. Semmes, March 20, 1862, in Thomas Jenkins Semmes Papers (Manuscript Division, Duke University Library), claimed that many people refused to accept Confederate money and that this fact caused the money to depreciate and prices to go up. He wanted Congress to pass a law making Confederate money legal tender.

[13] Richmond *Semi-Weekly Enquirer*, May 27, 1862; Smith, *History of the Confederate Treasury*, 10–22; Capers, *Life and Times of C. G. Memminger*, 336–37; William W. Bradbeer, *Confederate and Southern State Currency* (Mount Vernon, N.Y., 1915), 16.

thereby making a product easy to detect. So extensively were these lithographed notes counterfeited that all of them were called in and canceled, and so bold were the counterfeiters that an agency for the Confederate government, Payne & Company, used over $100,000 in counterfeit in payment for cattle purchased in Texas. Jewish peddlers were often accused of spreading this money over the country. One counterfeiter, John Richardson, alias Louis Napoleon, was hanged; many others were arrested. By Confederate law, though counterfeiters of notes were subject to execution, those who counterfeited bonds were punishable by not more than ten years in prison and a fine of not more than $5,000. In the North clever Yankees began counterfeiting Confederate notes and selling them at a small price to Federal soldiers. These counterfeits were boldly advertised for sale in the Northern press, and so widely were they scattered that many dead Federal soldiers were found with a supply in their pockets. The danger of thus destroying the Confederate currency by this flood of Northern counterfeits led one Congressman to remark that the Yankees were to be feared more for their "frauds than their forces." In 1862 Congress passed a law imposing death by hanging, on anyone caught having these counterfeits with intent to pass them.[14]

The slow paralysis of inflation crept deeper into the vitals of the Confederacy and began to alarm not only Davis and Memminger but also the mass of newspaper editors, bankers, and people in general who thought about public questions. As the Confederacy

---

[14] Ramsdell (ed.), *Laws and Joint Resolutions,* 97-99; Atlanta *Southern Confederacy,* October 7, 1862; "Confederate States Treasury Department. Letters Received Jan. 3, 1862–March 6, 1863" (Division of Manuscripts, Library of Congress). In *Harper's Weekly* (New York), VII (1863), 80, appeared these two advertisements of Confederate counterfeit money ("fac-similies") money for sale:

"CONFEDERATE MONEY.

$20,000!—TWENTY THOUSAND DOLLARS in *fac-simile* REBEL NOTES of different denominations sent, post-paid, to any address, on receipt of $5, by S. C. UPHAM, 403 Chestnut Street, Philadelphia."

and

"CONFEDERATE [REBEL] MONEY.
Fac-simile Confederate Treasury Notes.

So exactly like the genuine that where one will pass current the other will go equally well. $500 in Confederate Notes of all denominations, sent free by mail on receipt of $5, by W. E. HILTON, 11 Spruce Street, New York."

shrank and needed less money, the amount increased. By the first of 1863 Memminger was saying that the Confederacy's needs could be satisfied with $150,000,000, yet the amount outstanding at that time was $410,000,000. At the end of the year he reported that the currency was five times too much; in fact, in the summer of 1862 he had warned that issuing notes was "the most dangerous of all the methods of raising money." [15] Now, by the end of 1863, Davis had become alarmed. The cheapening currency had led to high prices, speculation, and the moral degradation of the people.

The public had early sensed that there was too much money being issued and that it was becoming progressively more worthless. It was referred to as "rags" and "fodder" and likened to the French assignats and the old Revolutionary Continental currency. If something were not done soon, its value would sink so low "that at last no butcher's boy" would accept it "for an ounce of cat meat." [16] "An oak leaf will be worth just as much as the promise of the Confederate treasury to pay one dollar," declared a Georgian in 1863,[17] and a wise Texan concluded that "to the depreciation of our currency may be traced nearly every serious trouble our Confederacy has had to complain of." [18] A facetious Virginian declared that the most prolific plant in the South was the *"Symplethonia Memingeri Gigantea"* or in more common language "Memminger's Mammoth Skunk Cabbage." [19] Paraphrasing a stanza of Thomas Campbell's "Hohenlinden," a versifier wrote:

> *In Richmond when the cash was low,*
> *And "promises" were all the go,*
> *Then rapid, constant, was the flow*
> *Of the paper currency.*[20]

The Confederacy had never planned to finance the war by issuing paper money; it had started out on a peacetime program of finances, and when war came with its tremendous costs the government issued more paper money to pay its debts while it was de-

---

15 Capers, *Life and Times of C. G. Memminger*, 341.
16 Macon *Daily Telegraph*, February 18, 1864.
17 *Ibid.*, October 12, 1863.
18 Galveston *Tri-Weekly News*, January 6, 1864.
19 Richmond *Daily Examiner*, November 12, 1863.
20 *Ibid.*, March 9, 1864.

vising revenue measures. Since the people could make more profits by keeping their money free to use in speculation by converting it into land or commodities than they could by converting it into bonds bearing 8 per cent interest, the bonds went begging, and the amount of the currency steadily increased.

A method frequently advocated to control the amount of the currency was to base it on cotton and tobacco, for these commodities represented actual values, and as their amount must stay within definite limits the Confederate currency could thereby have been limited and faith maintained in it. This was not a bizarre idea, for the Confederate government used cotton to lend value and strength to certain of its bond issues, which it marketed in European countries on the strength thus attained; and, also, some of the states based their currency issues on cotton. As a matter of fact, the Confederacy adopted no standard of value, but the people, themselves, instinctively measured Confederate currency in gold; and thus gold for all practical purposes became that standard. The people clamored for gold as the safest commodity to hoard away; they used their currency in buying it and thus steadily ran the price of currency down. Many people cried out against this trading in gold and called on Congress to outlaw it. But the Confederate government itself needed gold or its equivalent, sterling exchange, to be used in making foreign purchases, and it accumulated both as far as it could. In September, 1861, Secretary Memminger was able to purchase £20,000 sterling for $100,000 in Confederate currency and almost a year later he secured £12,999 for $115,551. Of course, it was not the amount of Confederate money that was solely responsible for its fall in value, but rather the lack of faith and confidence in the government's ability to win its independence; for even if Confederate money had been based on gold or cotton, it would have become worthless with Confederate defeat, which everyone believed would be followed by confiscation. And, of course, the supply of commodities affected prices and, hence, the value of money. Some people became so heroic and correct in their thinking that they advocated a government levy on the resources of the country for whatever was necessary to fight the war—not only for men, which was done, but also for resources.

Apart from the rising fear that Confederate currency might become worthless because of final defeat, growing suspicion arose, evident by 1863, that the Confederacy might deliberately repudiate all of its debts and start anew in its financing. Some people were actually advocating this policy. Color was lent to these suspicions by laws singling out certain note issues which must be funded into lower interest-bearing bonds after a fixed date and which at a subsequent date could not be used at all in buying bonds. Though people were using little money to buy bonds, they feared the limiting of their opportunity to do so. Further proof that repudiation might be contemplated was seen in the tardiness of the Treasury in paying interest on its bonds. "It is just as easy for a Government to be honest as it is for a man," declared a Georgian, "and it is a heap more important." [21]

On February 17, 1864, a highly complicated law provided a last desperate measure to reduce the currency and increase its value. Various issues and denominations of notes were given different positions and rights in the refunding and exchange plan. All non-interest-bearing notes larger than $5.00 must be exchanged for 4 per cent bonds before the following April 1 (July 1 west of the Mississippi), and if this were not done those of $100.00 denomination should immediately be reduced one third in value and thereafter reduced one tenth monthly until they were valueless. All other non-interest-bearing notes should likewise be exchangeable for 4 per cent bonds up to April 1, and thereafter they could be exchanged for new money at the rate of three old dollars for two new dollars or at two-thirds their face value for bonds, except that after January 1, 1865, if this exchange had not been made they became worthless. To prevent the currency from being contracted too fast, all old $5.00 notes were to continue to circulate at full value until July 1 (October 1 west of the Mississippi), when they should be reduced one third in value. This act took away the right of the Secretary of the Treasury to issue additional money, except in exchange for old money at the two-thirds rate. It was expected that this act would reduce the currency to much less than two thirds of the old amount; for all of the non-interest-bearing $100 bills must be exchanged for bonds or become worthless, and much of the old

[21] [Charles H. Smith], *Bill Arp, So Called. A Side Show of the Southern Side of the War* (New York, 1866), 122.

smaller currency would be exchanged for bonds rather than suffer a one-third loss by waiting to be converted into new currency. The $100 interest-bearing notes were by this act deprived of the privilege of circulating as money.[22]

The amount of currency outstanding before the reduction operations began was $973,000,000. When April 1 arrived the first part of the reduction operations (exchanging money at face value for 4 per cent bonds) was ended. All old money still in existence was now worth a third less, and, excepting the non-interest-bearing $100 notes, which became worthless, could be exchanged at the reduced rate for new money or 4 per cent bonds. As this operation progressed, the amount of currency would be automatically reduced one third when exchanged for new money or 100 per cent when exchanged for bonds. The financial experts calculated that up to April 1 the currency had been reduced by from $177,000,000 to $300,000,000; but, since a great part of the old currency had been lost or destroyed during the previous years, the actual amount circulating was estimated at less than $300,000,000. But the records were so incomplete and confused, and were to become more so as time went on, that there was little certain knowledge to be had. "Bill Arp" (Charles H. Smith), a humorist of the times, reporting on the situation, said Secretary Memminger "war axed to say bout how much he thought war in sirkulation; and he said he hadnt charged his memory partikler, but akkordin to the best of his rekelekshun, thar war six hundred miliyuns or six thousand miliyuns— he warent sure which." [23]

President Davis predicted that the amount of old currency exchanged for new would be about $300,000,000, but he greatly feared that this would still leave too much money afloat. In November, 1864, he thought methods should be devised to reduce the amount outstanding to $150,000,000; and in the following March, when Congress, sentimentalizing over the tardy pay of the soldiers and sailors, abandoned this money policy by passing a bill to issue $80,000,000 more notes, Davis vetoed it. Vice-President Stephens

[22] By a law passed June 14, 1864, the $5.00 notes were declared worthless after January 1, 1865; but by a law passed December 29, 1864, Congress declared that all notes which would become worthless after January 1, 1865, should have the time limit extended to July 1, 1865.

[23] Richmond *Daily Whig*, May 5, 1864.

had long before given up hope; in April, 1864, he had privately declared to Secretary of War Seddon, "Our finances are now a wreck. Past all hope, in my judgment." [24] And about the same time Congressman William W. Boyce of South Carolina affirmed that the credit of the Confederacy was irretrievably gone.

All old money received by the Treasury was mutilated by a machine which bit out a semicircular hole and was then consigned to the furnace; but even so, now and then, a bill was secretly extracted on its road to destruction, patched up, and passed. The new money was much like the old, but the critical editor of the Richmond *Examiner* could not forgo lampooning it. To see the faces on the notes "with that unchanging expression of ineffable melancholy which the engraver has given to all of them, (for on the best specimens of the Confederate currency Davis is doleful, and Stephens saturnine, Hunter is heavy, and Clay clouded with care, Memminger is mournful, and even Benjamin the buoyant is *bien triste*), and to have constantly in sight the evidence of the country's trav[a]il and impecuniosity, were enough to drive even a well-regulated mind to lunacy." [25] Chivalry forbade him from remarking on the contracted features of Mrs. Francis W. Pickens of South Carolina, who adorned the $100 notes.

So confusing and complicated were the terms of the law that the people could not be blamed for first being thrown into a panic and then receding into a position of indifference as to whether it was old or new money which they possessed. In fact, the old money continued to circulate to the bitter end and frequently commanded as much value as the new; and there is reason to believe that the government actually paid out again some of the old money which had been received in exchange for the new.[26] But while the Con-

---

[24] Cleveland, *Alexander H. Stephens*, 788.

[25] Richmond *Daily Examiner*, February 16, 1864.

[26] It has been estimated that the amount of Confederate currency printed was about $1,550,000,000, but so imperfect were the records during the last year of the Confederacy and so little were the financial laws regarded, that probably $2,000,000,000 was actually printed. Including all the currency issued by the Confederacy, the states and local governmental divisions, railroads, banks, insurance companies, and other organizations, the amount was about $2,250,000,000. Smith, *History of the Confederate Treasury*, 100; Bradbeer, *Confederate and Southern State Currency*, 27–28.

federacy was in the midst of beginning the change from one money to the other, there was great confusion as to prices and the wisdom of offering commodities for sale. James H. Hammond, the South Carolina statesman, went to Augusta to make some purchases, but found it impossible to transact business, as no prices for anything had been established. The first effect was not uniform over the country; but in most places there was a sharp recession of prices. People generally had assumed that prices, in the "grand tumble," would fall uniformly one third; in a few places they did not change at all, but more widely they receded from 10 to 50 per cent. Hats in Richmond were off 10 per cent, while theater tickets dropped from $5.00 to $2.00, and tobacco fell from $3.00 to $1.65 a pound. Flour declined $50.00 a sack in Macon, to a $75.00 low. Butter dropped in Mobile from $10.00 to $5.00 a pound. Within a short time, however, prices were rising again until finally Confederate money would buy nothing after Appomattox. In January, 1865, a silver dollar was auctioned for $64.00.

To add to the financial confusion of the Confederate government, the different states issued great amounts of currency and followed the unsound practices of the Confederacy in their attempts to maintain it, although in the end it became as worthless as Confederate money.

Although Memminger was not wholly to blame for the collapse of the Confederate currency, public clamor forced him to resign in the summer of 1864, to be succeeded by George A. Trenholm, a well-known South Carolina banker and businessman.[27] Memminger defended himself by saying that he had been forced "to administer plans which I neither originated nor approve. You know how anxiously I endeavored to provide means to prevent a Redundant Currency. I have always disliked the supporting of the Government by Treasury Notes. But Congress would give nothing

[27] George A. Trenholm had early entered the trading house of John Fraser and Company and later became head of it. He developed a European branch in Liverpool under the name of Fraser, Trenholm and Company, which acted as the financial agent of the Confederacy in its purchases in the European markets. During the war he controlled as many as fifty blockade-runners, which carried out much cotton. He was most likely the richest man in the Confederacy. His appointment was received with enthusiasm.

but Notes & Bonds—and when we failed to pay specie for Interest the Bonds lost their availableness." [28]

Bonds played as inglorious a part as paper currency in the financial history of the Confederacy. With the passing of time the Treasury issued them in such large amounts that the people, losing faith in the ability of the government to redeem its bonds, ceased to buy them.

On February 28, 1861, Congress made a conservative start by allowing the President to borrow not over $15,000,000 through an issue of 8 per cent bonds, with both interest and principal guaranteed by an export tax of one eighth of a cent a pound on cotton. The Treasury first offered only $5,000,000, which was oversubscribed $3,000,000 by the banks during the first two days. When war seemed evident after the firing on Fort Sumter, the remaining $10,000,000 was offered; but the response was not as quick as was expected, for the banks had paid much of their specie for the original loan, and the people were reluctant to use theirs. The Upper South now joined the Confederacy and helped to absorb the rest. The city government of Richmond subscribed $50,000 and individuals all over the Confederacy came to the rescue. By the late fall the full amount had been taken. For a time the Treasury paid the interest on these bonds in specie, and they long continued to command a higher market price than any other Confederate bonds. It should be remembered that Confederate notes had not yet been issued.

To provide a loan which the people could buy with something else than money, which the Confederacy had not yet been able to supply, Congress passed the so-called Produce Loan act of May 16, 1861. In pursuance of this law the Treasury was permitted to issue $50,000,000 in 8 per cent bonds, increased to $100,000,000 by an act of the following August 19, which should be paid for in specie, military supplies, or in the proceeds from the sale of agricultural products or of manufactured articles. Benjamin H. Hill of Georgia claimed credit for having thought out this ingenious scheme of short-circuiting the use of money in the purchase of

28 Memminger to J. P. Boyce, March 31. 1864, in Christopher Gustavus Memminger Papers, 1860–1865 (microfilms in the University of Texas Library, originals in the University of North Carolina Library).

bonds and in the acquisition by the government of the sinews of war. He declared that it was unique in the history of the world, and that if the people sustained the plan, they could forget about any further taxes.[29]

The nearest approach to a bond drive ever inaugurated in the Confederacy began in May after the adjournment of Congress, when each Congressman became an agent to popularize this loan in his state. In addition, official agents were appointed with James D. B. De Bow, the well-known economist and editor, at their head. Congressmen made speeches to great throngs, explaining the law, and inducing planters to pledge the proceeds from the sale of farm products, generally cotton. Vice-President Stephens, now buoyant and in a fighting mood, secured the pledge of 2,000 bales after his speech at Washington, Georgia, the home of Robert Toombs. At that meeting Toombs, himself, subscribed 100 bales.[30] At Columbus, Georgia, the people subscribed 1,510 bales of cotton, 3,000 bushels of corn, and $3,050 in specie, and a farmer near Atlanta subscribed 200 bushels of corn and 125 bushels of wheat. On July 20 President Davis asserted that the people had already pledged $50,000,000 in cotton alone. By the end of the year 400,000 bales of cotton had been offered, 1,000 hogsheads of tobacco, 5,000 bushels of wheat, 270,000 bushels of rice, 1,000 hogsheads of sugar and molasses, $1,000,000 in produce of other kinds, and $1,000,000 in Confederate currency and state bank notes.[31] The Cotton Planters' Convention, meeting in Macon, July 4 and 5, and attended by such leaders as Duff Green and Charles S. Morehead, former governor of Kentucky, resolved that the planters should subscribe a half of their cotton crop for this loan and added this further recommendation, which was to be long agitated, that the government buy outright the whole cotton crop and pay for it in these bonds or in currency.

The attempt to collect these pledges dragged along until 1864, when the Treasury's final report showed that the people had subscribed in proceeds of farm products $34,476,000 out of a total

[29] Atlanta *Southern Confederacy*, June 25, 1861; Athens *Southern Watchman*, July 3, 1861.

[30] Atlanta *Southern Confederacy*, June 12, 1861.

[31] Schwab, *Confederate States of America*, 13; Smith, *History of the Confederate Treasury*, 18–19.

of $100,000,000 authorized in 1861; but more than $11,000,000 of the amount pledged could not be collected as the products had been destroyed through the exigencies of war or because of the outright refusal of people to redeem their pledges. This loan could, therefore, be considered a definite failure; and Hill's great discovery could be written off as a liability to his fame.

Cotton planters made strenuous efforts from the very beginning to have the government buy outright the whole cotton crop, and either hold it in the country as a basis of value for bonds and currency, or send it abroad to establish foreign credits before the blockade closed around the ports too tightly to be run. This was argued not only as good national policy but also as an absolute necessity in establishing a market for the planters, who otherwise would find themselves without money with which to pay their taxes or their ordinary debts. Buying up the cotton crop and sending it abroad was strongly recommended by Stephens, Benjamin, Joseph E. Johnston, and other leaders, civil and military. Since the South had a monopoly in cotton, some leaders felt that the steadily increasing price would yield a profit to the Confederate government sufficient to finance the war and absorb any other national debt that might accumulate.

This policy did not seem as simple to Secretary Memminger as to its proponents. In the first place, the government should not prefer the cotton planters over other producers of wealth, whether agricultural or industrial; and, furthermore, where could he find the money for such a great outlay, he queried. It would be state socialism and, besides, it was unconstitutional. In answer to those who insisted that the cotton should be bought and exported immediately, Memminger reminded them that the large amounts which they suggested, 4,000,000 or 5,000,000 bales, did not exist at that time, as the crop of 1860–1861 had been largely exported before the Confederacy had been set up, and that, even had it existed, where could the ships have been found to transport it? [32]

If instead of neglecting to get control of at least a part of the cotton during the first year of the war and of discouraging the exportation of it while the blockade was easy to run, the Con-

[32] Capers, *Life and Times of C. G. Memminger*, 352; Reagan, *Memoirs*, 113; Samuel B. Thompson, *Confederate Purchasing Operations Abroad* (Chapel Hill, 1935), 48–49.

federacy had taken an opposite course, it might well have made King Cotton an early source of credit at home as well as abroad and have strengthened the value of Confederate currency. "The greatest mistake that has been made in our policy," declared a Texas editor in 1864, "was the failure of the government from the beginning to acquire the control of the entire cotton crop in the Southern States." [33] Some of the states, notably Texas, Mississippi, and North Carolina, early toyed with the idea of basing their credit on cotton, and later when the Confederacy changed its policy, it became a rival of those states which had entered this field, and even developed a mild conflict with them.

There was validity in the cotton planters' complaints that they could not meet their obligations to buy bonds under the Produce Loan if they could not sell their cotton; for by this law the Confederate government accepted for bonds the proceeds of the sale of farm products, not the farm products themselves. To meet these objections and to gain actual possession of large amounts of cotton, tobacco, and other farm products, which would be consumed by the military forces as well as sent abroad to secure credits, Congress on April 21, 1862, passed a law allowing the people to exchange for bonds any articles which the government might need, and, what was more, those who had promised the proceeds of their cotton and other farm products under the Produce Loan law, might now give the government the produce itself at prices agreed upon with the purchasing agents.

Under this law and others subsequently passed, the Confederate government came into possession of large amounts of cotton, which

[33] Galveston *Tri-Weekly News*, February 3, 1861. John Fraser and Company, Charleston merchants, were strongly opposed to withholding cotton from exportation. They wrote Secretary of War Benjamin, September 30, 1861, expressing the opinion that withholding cotton would result "in a rapid and extravagant advance in the price of foreign exchange or, what is the same, a rapid depreciation of the currency of the country." *Official Records*, Ser. IV, Vol. I, 633. Secretary of the Treasury Memminger's position must not be misunderstood. Although he believed that the whole cotton crop of 1861 could not be suddenly exported, yet he had a strong feeling that as much as possible should be sent out, for he agreed with John Fraser and Company that foreign exchange was of first importance to the Confederacy and he knew that the chief source of it was in the exportation of cotton. See Memminger to Governor Francis W. Pickens, April 15, 1862, in Memminger Papers (University of North Carolina Library).

it pledged as payment for bonds. Imperfect records show that throughout the war the government bought at least 474,471 bales; but there was considerably more than this, as sales to the Confederacy made in the states of North Carolina, Tennessee, and Virginia are not included in these figures.[34] Most of this cotton was stored on the plantations where it was raised, though some of it was brought to warehouses in towns. Some was run through the blockade to Europe; some was permitted under special arrangements to go through the military lines into the United States to be exchanged for badly needed supplies; a great deal was destroyed incidentally in military activities and purposely to prevent it from falling into the hands of the Federal troops; little of it remained to be confiscated after Appomattox, for practically no cotton was bought by the Confederacy in 1864 or 1865. This was so because little was now being raised, and by this time the dispirited people had no desire to sell what little they had to a crumbling government when they could speculate with it to much greater advantage.

Cotton provided a basis on which bonds might be issued not only at home but also abroad. Erlanger and Company, financiers of great influence in France, suggested to John Slidell, the Confederate commissioner, a foreign loan which would be offered to the bond-buying public in the various countries of Europe. Congress agreed to this on January 29, 1863, to the extent of borrowing 75,000,000 francs through issuing 7 per cent bonds secured by cotton and payable after twenty years. These bonds were made attractive to the Erlangers, who were allowed to buy them at a discount of 23 per cent and to receive various commissions, and the public became interested by the fact that the bonds were secured by cotton at the very low price of sixpence a pound when the market price was more than four times that amount. But there was one disadvantage: The cotton was in the Confederacy, and if this new nation failed to establish its independence the bonds would become worthless. At first there was great enthusiasm, but soon military defeats and the manipulations of United States agents brought on a price decline. To boost the price and thereby keep the loan in popular

---

[34] *Cotton Sold to the Confederate States*, Senate Documents, 62 Cong., 3 Sess., No. 987, Serial No. 6348 (Washington, 1913), 314 pp. The total is the result of the writer's calculation.

favor, the Confederacy bought back over half of the issue, and actually made them more valuable on the European markets than United States bonds. It also underwent further outlays by redeeming according to agreement a fortieth of the loan twice a year and paying interest on all outstanding bonds, its last interest payment being made March 1, 1865. With all these deductions the Confederate government actually got about $2,599,000 out of bonds backed by $45,000,000 worth of cotton; but even so it was the winner over those who held the bonds, for, with the Confederacy crashing, none of the holders of the Erlanger bonds received any cotton or any other value for them.

As investment bankers, however, the Erlangers did not lose in this financing. In fact, they made an additional contract for financing a loan of 125,000,000 francs, which Congress agreed to on February 17, 1864; but the Confederacy in January, 1865, canceled this agreement and at the same time authorized raising a £15,000,000 loan. The plan contemplated the setting up by certain interested European financiers of a bank, to be known as the Franco-Confederate Bank, in Europe, with a branch in the Confederacy. Its solvency was to rest in the last analysis on cotton to be transported to Europe and sold there at fifty cents a pound, instead of being stored in the Confederacy according to the Erlanger plan, and one of its principal purposes was to reduce the Confederate currency to the actual amount needed. Part of the Duncan F. Kenner mission to Europe in 1865 was to assist in setting up this bank, but the Confederacy crashed before anything practical resulted.[35]

The attempt the Confederate government made on February 17, 1864, to extricate itself from the mire of too much currency, whereby new currency was to be issued for old, contemplated financing the government by bonds rather than by paper money. The Treasury was given permission to issue $500,000,000 in 6 per cent bonds. These were to be in addition to the 4 per cent bonds into which it was hoped the people would convert most of their old

35 Ramsdell (ed.), Laws and Joint Resolutions, 164–65; Frank L. Owsley, King Cotton Diplomacy; Foreign Relations of the Confederate States of America (Chicago, 1931), 396–404; Schwab, Confederate States of America, 29; Smith, History of the Confederate Treasury, 43–46; Thompson, Confederate Purchasing Operations Abroad, 56 ff.; Louise B. Hill, State Socialism in the Confederate States of America (Charlottesville, 1936), 25–28.

money. Much like these 6 per cent bonds were certificates of indebtedness, provided by this same law, which also bore 6 per cent interest and could be used in the payment of debts where the creditor would accept them. General Lee was anxious to have them to meet the debt requirements of his army.[36]

Bonds had never been a popular investment in the Confederacy and these 6 per cent securities were no different, though they were made nontaxable both in principal and interest, and the interest was to be guaranteed by export and import duties—and hereafter import duties must be paid in specie, sterling exchange, or in the coupons of these bonds. With no demand for these securities on the exchange market, the Treasury offered $5,000,000 in bonds at auction in Richmond in an attempt to set a market price. By February 1, 1865, only $44,500,000 had been sold. So uncertain were values in the last year of the Confederacy that people would not tie up their credits in rigid bonds; they must have their resources in the fluidity of currency or else in gold or personal property and real estate. Bonds were unpopular also because people were never sure if or when the government would pay the interest on them, to say nothing of their doubts that the principal would ever be paid.

Bonds and credit of the states were always higher than of the Confederacy. In March of 1863 bonds of the various states were selling from 130 to 150, whereas Confederate securities were ranging from 100 to 112. In January, 1864, state securities were selling from 200 to 620; Confederate bonds, from 98 to 185. This higher financial position of the states early led Virginia, in May, 1862, to suggest that the states should guarantee the Confederate bonds, thereby increasing their value and ensuring a wider market for them both in this country and abroad. South Carolina and Alabama were enthusiastic, the former passing an act to guarantee her proportional quota. All the other states with the exception of Georgia and North Carolina were agreeable to the idea; so determined was Governor Brown never to be guilty of enhancing the standing of the Confederacy at the possible expense of his state that he resolutely refused to have Georgia take part in the scheme. Vice-

[36] Charleston *Daily Courier*, October 8, 1864; *Official Records*, Ser. IV, Vol. III, 253, 255.

President Stephens was equally opposed. As unanimity was necessary, the plan was abandoned.[37]

If there was a financial wizard in the Confederacy, it was Trenholm. When he took charge of the Treasury in the summer of 1864 there were hopes that he would build up the Confederacy's credit. Resolutely setting himself against issuing more currency, he tried to induce the people to buy bonds and Congress to provide additional taxes. He hastened the exportation of cotton to secure foreign credit, which he would sell to people in the Confederacy for paper currency to be used in paying soldiers their monthly pittance, now so far behind, and to meet the many other debts, equally far behind. The little matter of paying the rental on the buildings of South Carolina College, which had been leased for a hospital, had not been attended to since the day they were first occupied in 1864. And now it was the middle of April, 1865, and the rent amounted to $80,000.[38] Trenholm wondered throughout the period of his secretaryship why the people could never see and think of the Confederacy as part of themselves—not something far away—and why they as one great family did not come to the rescue.

A month before the end he began to see some answer to his wonderment and the fruition of his hopes. His pleadings with the people to think of the Confederacy as they would of their own parents led Congress to pass a law permitting the Treasury to be financed in as strange and desperate a way as was ever thought out by man for any government—by patriotic citizens' "donations of money, jewels, gold and silver plate, and public securities." He himself set the pace by donating $200,000 in currency and securities. To contradict the general gloom and defeatism that had irrevocably and inexorably settled down upon the Confederacy, people came forward in many shining examples of a last heroic

---

37 *Message of his Excellency, Joseph E. Brown, to the General Assembly, Convened in the Capitol by his Proclamation, March 25th, 1863* (Milledgeville, Ga., 1863), 11; Richmond *Daily Examiner,* January 10, December 5, 1863; *Southern Historical Society Papers,* XLVII (1930), 135; XLVIII (1941), 265; Johnston and Browne, *Alexander H. Stephens,* 430, 441; Schwab, *Confederate States of America,* 50; Smith, *History of the Confederate Treasury,* 46–47.

38 W. F. De Saussure to Governor Andrew G. Magrath, April 15, 1865, in "South Carolina Correspondence, 1860–1865" (South Carolina State Archives, Columbia).

display of patriotism to present their contributions. In Staunton, Virginia, the people subscribed 130 barrels of flour, 7,100 pounds of bacon, and $150,000 in bonds; and so it went in other parts of the Confederacy where the people donated their gold, silver, jewelry, heirlooms, and food.[39] But all of this was a mere trickle of what would have been necessary to save the Confederacy; for when it succumbed it was owing current floating debts estimated between $400,000,000 and $600,000,000—owing soldiers their pay for many months and obligated to almost everybody for materials, rentals, or services, and for interest on the public debt.

It was much easier to finance the Confederacy by printing money and bonds than to devise tax measures and collect a real revenue. In the beginning there was the expectation that there would be no war or only a short one, and as taxes do not produce a quick return, a resort should be made to paper currency and bonds. Then, too, there was the feeling that a wartime tax system would need to be overhauled with peace, and it would therefore be better to await a later day to raise a large fund, if needed, by that method. There was also the genuine fear that the people, who had never paid a large tax under the old government, might react unfavorably to a new government which started out with a heavy tax program involving tax gatherers in addition to those of the states. In fact, both Stephens and Hill tried to popularize the Produce Loan by promising the people that if it were a success they would be relieved for a long time from taxation, which returned neither interest nor principal. Many believed that whatever taxes there were should be the hidden, indirect kind; for people would rather "give ten dollars which they have never seen than one they have had in their pockets," according to Lawrence M. Keitt of South Carolina.[40] And, of course, during the first few months of the Confederacy, there was little money in existence which could have been used to pay taxes.

Yet there was a bolder point of view which held that the government should immediately provide for taxes—all kinds, but particularly direct, for the people knew that what was worth having was worth paying for, and a direct tax would be effective in making

[39] Richmond *Daily Examiner*, March 30, 1865.
[40] Lawrence M. Keitt to Hammond, February 13, 1861, in Hammond Papers.

the government frugal. Gazaway B. Lamar, a Georgia banker with New York City connections, said at the very beginning that the Confederacy should tax property, polls, and income; [41] and before the end of the summer of 1861 voices were raised in favor of the levying of substantial taxes by Congress. The editor of the Richmond *Enquirer* declared that he would not disparage the people "by supposing that there would be even a reluctant payer of taxes south of the Potomac for the defense of our country, while men north of the Potomac are paying direct taxes to raise means for our invasion." [42] Memminger's instincts were correct though he was timid and halting in the matter of taxation; yet he was bold to say in May, 1861, that a certain fixed revenue was necessary and that this could be maintained only by a direct tax.[43]

Actually the first Confederate tax was the American tariff, inherited by virtue of the first law that Congress passed, which continued in force all laws of the United States not inconsistent with the Confederate Constitution; but as the Confederacy soon made the tariff more a matter of commercial and industrial policy than a revenue producer, it is not here treated primarily as a tax. Although in the beginning many believed that a tariff, which the Constitution forbade as protection, might be devised to bring in a large revenue, the blockade of Confederate ports, announced April 19, 1861, dried up these hopes. At first (February 18) the old American law was amended to allow free trade in foods and war materials, but not in other manufactured articles. Then on March 15 a duty of 15 per cent was established on various manufactures of iron and wood, foolishly including railroad materials and coal. Finally on May 21 a general and comprehensive tariff law, becoming effective the last day of August, was passed, setting up five schedules bearing ad valorem rates from 5 to 20 per cent. Another schedule bore specific duties such as $1.50 a ton on ice and two cents a bushel on salt. There was an extensive free list which included educational and artistic objects, gold and silver bullion, implements and munitions of war, and most household necessities and foods. The tariff throughout the history of the Confederacy

[41] Phillips (ed.), *Correspondence of Toombs, Stephens, and Cobb,* 557.
[42] Richmond *Semi-Weekly Enquirer,* August 16, 1861.
[43] Capers, *Life and Times of C. G. Memminger,* 419.

probably produced little more than $1,000,000 measured in specie.

Even before the blockade dried up the business of the Confederate customhouses, the Secretary of the Treasury determined to make the service as frugal as possible—at most not more than half the expense under the United States. In May, 1861, at New Orleans, the greatest customs port in the Confederacy, five clerks were doing the work formerly done by fifty. They worked ten hours a day instead of the customary six, and they were not to enjoy ice water nor keep a carriage and horses for transferring specie and for other uses—"The luxury or amusement of this species of pleasure riding can not be allowed at the public expense." [44]

Apart from customs the only taxes to be raised during the first two years of the Confederacy were mere nibbles at the main problem and represented nothing more than an attempt to raise money to bolster up bonds by allocating this revenue to the payment of the interest and principal on these securities. The first touch of this taxation appeared in the $15,000,000 bond act of February 28, 1861, and marked a unique experiment in American history. It was a tax of an eighth of a cent a pound on all cotton exported, the proceeds to be applied to these bonds. Cotton planters became somewhat embittered by thus being singled out from all producers of wealth to bear this burden.

The first large bond issue—$100,000,000 on August 19 carried another kind of bolstering tax, the so-called War Tax of one half of one per cent on the taxable wealth of the Confederacy, such as real estate, slaves, merchandise, livestock, such personal possessions as gold watches, gold and silver plate, pianos, pleasure carriages, and all sorts of securities, excepting Confederate bonds. This tax, partly direct, was permissible under the Provisional Constitution, still in effect, which did not include the provision in the United States Constitution (but incorporated in the Permanent Constitution) against levying a direct tax except according to population. Memminger estimated the gross value of property in the Confederacy to be $5,202,000,000. If the rate set up could be collected on

[44] *Official Records,* Ser. IV, Vol. II, 310; Richmond *Daily Examiner,* December 12, 1863; Richmond *Daily Whig,* January 28, 1864; Schwab, *Confederate States of America,* 240. For quotation, see Lewis Cruger to F. H. Hatch, May 1, 1861, in "Confederate States Treasury Department Letters Received Mar. 23, 1861–April 3, 1862" (Division of Manuscripts, Library of Congress).

this amount, it would bring in more than $26,000,000. As an inducement to the states to collect this tax and thereby relieve the Confederacy from appointing tax gatherers, the law permitted a 10 per cent reduction on the amount if the state assumed the tax. All of the states did this except Mississippi and Texas; but instead of adding this one half of one per cent to their own tax rate and collecting it for the Confederacy, they issued bonds or their own notes and relieved their people from paying the tax. Their excuse for issuing bonds was that there was not yet enough money in circulation, a charge that many planters were eloquently seconding.

This was the first Confederate tax to be felt by the people and they reacted variously. One planter, complaining that he had plenty of cotton but no money, was outspoken in his condemnation of Congress for passing the law: "This Government belongs to the people, and not to a little self-assuming Congress, who had no more right to levy such a tax than you and I have." [45] But a more patriotic citizen declared, "It may be burdensome to our people to pay it, but it will be paid most cheerfully." [46] This tax was to be levied only once and should be paid by May 1, 1862, but as certain states had been invaded and upset by this time, provision was made to excuse them in part or altogether. Missouri and Kentucky were exempted entirely. Other states, as South Carolina, sought partial exemption; the canny Brown, governor of Georgia, sought unsuccessfully to pay his state's amount before it was due, and collect 7 per cent interest. Final attempts to collect the tax were not given up until 1863, when the amount secured was about $18,000,000.[47] The tax was hardly a success and certainly did not fulfill the hopes expressed in the law that it would not only take care of the bonds but help support the government otherwise.

As the government continued its effort to support itself by printing more money and bonds, taxes receded to where they did not meet the interest on the public debt. As more money meant cheaper money and, therefore, an increase in prices, a widespread outcry

---

[45] Athens *Southern Watchman*, October 16, 1861.

[46] Atlanta *Southern Confederacy*, August 21, 1861.

[47] L. C. Elmore, Richmond, to Boston, Savannah, February 22, 1862, in "II CSA Treasury 1862" (Division of Manuscripts, Library of Congress); *Official Records*, Ser. IV, Vol. II, 324–34; Schwab, *Confederate States of America*, 285 ff.; Smith, *History of the Confederate Treasury*, 24.

went up for tax legislation. There now developed the unusual spectacle of a people begging to be taxed—reversing the old principle to representation without taxation. "If something be not done," said a Richmond observer in 1863, "we shall soon have to pay $27,000 for a barrel of flour. It is now $30 and beef 85 cts a pound." [48] Said a Georgia editor, "The error in the beginning was in not taxing heavily and severely enough to have kept prices down to a specie standard." [49] A Virginia editor believed the people were willing to support the war by taxes alone; Senator Herschel V. Johnson of Georgia warned that unless taxes were resorted to, "universal ruin would be the consequence"; Toombs declared that the government must cease issuing money; and disgruntled Stephens thought that $120,000,000 could be raised in taxes annually. President Davis called on Congress for taxes, and Memminger declared that the people were "fully prepared for the payment of a high tax" and that he favored a tax on general property and incomes—not one on occupations and other activities involving stamps, excises, and licenses which would be complicated and hard to collect. [50]

A veritable onset was made against Congress for its criminal timidity. "They are afraid to pass a good tax bill & nothing else can save us from ruin," said William M. Browne, a former Acting Secretary of State; they were "men of small calibre and most of them *politicians*—not statesmen," declared another; "the Congressman who is afraid of taxing the people, is, and ought to be regarded as a public enemy," wrote a Georgia editor. "Did ever nation before crave and pray to be heavily and immediately taxed as this people is craving now?" queried the editor of the Richmond *Enquirer*, who had long been waging a campaign for taxes. "For God's sake tax us." Governor Brown of Georgia asked his legislature to pass a resolution praying Congress to pass a tax act. Congress was brow-

[48] William M. Browne, Richmond, to Cobb, February 12, 1863, in Howell Cobb Papers.

[49] Augusta *Daily Chronicle & Sentinel*, April 3, 1863.

[50] Richmond *Daily Examiner*, March 26, 1863; Richmond *Daily Enquirer*, March 3, 1863; Richardson (comp.), *Messages and Papers of the Confederacy*, I, 259, 293; Phillips (ed.), *Correspondence of Toombs, Stephens, and Cobb*, 619; *Southern Historical Society Papers*, XLVIII (1941), 118; Capers, *Life and Times of C. G. Memminger*, 445, 447; Johnston and Browne, *Alexander H. Stephens*, 432.

beaten into at least discussing an act in the fall of 1862.[51] Still hesitating, the House in January, 1863, entertained for a time a resolution to levy on the states for $112,000,000, apportioning it on the basis of $1,000,000 for each Congressman.

To devise tax legislation was not as simple as many people imagined, for the Confederacy by slavishly following the United States Constitution had made it impossible to levy a direct tax without apportioning it according to population. The War Tax, which was a direct tax, was constitutional, since it was passed under the Provisional Constitution, which had no limitation on levying a direct tax. The Permanent Constitution required a census to be taken within three years after that document became effective, but war precluded a census. Hence a direct-tax law could not be constitutionally passed until the number of people in the Confederacy should be known and used as the basis. In order to raise much money, a direct tax would be necessary, for two thirds of the wealth of the Confederacy was in land and slaves; and it had long been the interpretation of a direct tax that it was one levied on land and polls only. But according to Memminger's reasoning, even if the census had been taken it would be unwise to apportion a direct tax according to population, as large areas of some of the states were now in the hands of the enemy, and it would be manifestly unjust to force the people not in the invaded region to pay on the basis of all their population and property.

As a result of the popular clamor and the limitations set by the Constitution, Congress, on April 24, 1863, passed an ingenious comprehensive tax act—the first one in the history of the Confederacy. Side-stepping a direct tax on land and slaves, it sought out every other source of revenue it could imagine. There was an ad valorem tax of 8 per cent on all farm and forest products and a tax of one per cent on all money held on the first day of July following. This tax would not be levied thereafter. Next, there was an exhaustive series of occupational and license taxes ranging from $500 for bankers to $40 for bowling alleys, and where sales

[51] *Message of his Excellency, Joseph E. Brown, to the General Assembly . . . March 25th, 1863*, p. 17; Barnsley to Alfred A. Marsh, March 7, 1863, in Barnsley Papers (University of Georgia Library); Browne, Richmond, to Cobb, March 4, 1863, in Howell Cobb Papers; Athens *Southern Watchman*, March 25, 1863; Richmond *Semi-Weekly Enquirer*, March 17, 1863.

of materials were involved an additional tax varying from 10 per cent of gross sales in the case of retail liquor dealers to one per cent for butchers. Hotels were thrown into five classes, based on the value of the structure, paying from $500 to $30. Also, an income tax was set up with the rates varying according to the source of the income and the amount. Salaries, excepting those derived from military and naval services, should bear a rate of one per cent on all over $1,000 up to $1,500 and 2 per cent on all over $1,500. On other kinds of income there should be no tax up to $500, but on all over that amount there should be a tax varying from 5 per cent up to 15 per cent, the highest bracket beginning on all income over $10,000. To strike the speculators, a flat 10 per cent tax was levied on all profits, except in a regular retail business, gained in the sale of farm products, clothing, and other objects commonly dealt in by speculators. The last tax was to apply to the year 1862 only, and would, therefore, not be included in the income tax for 1863.

In this general scheme for income taxes, the earnings and profits from land were exempted. This was so because Congress devised another kind of tax which touched the agriculturalists only; it was the unique tax of one tenth of farm produce, to be collected in the product itself—the tax in kind. Those articles which must be shared with the government to the extent of one tenth were carefully enumerated: wheat, corn, oats, rye, "buckwheat or rice," sweet and Irish potatoes, hay and fodder, sugar, molasses, cotton, wool, tobacco, peas, beans, and ground peas. In order not to take necessary foods from the farmers, each might reserve 50 bushels each of sweet potatoes, Irish potatoes, and wheat, 100 bushels of corn, and 20 bushels of either peas or beans. Also, each farmer must give $3/50$ of all pork, in the form of cured bacon. On all cattle, horses, and mules not used in cultivation and on all asses, he must pay a tax of one per cent. Assessors would estimate the amount of farm products in bins and containers and the ungathered amounts in the field, and if there was disagreement then the assessor and the taxpayer would each select a disinterested citizen of the vicinity, and if they could not agree, then these two would select a third. The farmer must deliver all products, in sacks and other containers furnished by the government, to depots if not more than eight miles away.

The administration of the tax in kind was given over to the Secretary of War and the Secretary of the Treasury. The former should divide his quartermaster service into two groups, the post quartermasters who should see to the gathering together of the material at certain depots, and the distributing quartermasters who should see that these products were conveyed to army supply points. All cotton, wool, and tobacco should be sent to the Secretary of the Treasury, who would hold it for sale or export or to guarantee Confederate bonds. Should some of these farm products be deposited where they could not be used or might spoil, the quartermaster must sell them and deposit the proceeds with the Treasury; and if there were certain districts where for any reason it was impractical to make collections, the quartermaster should notify the Treasury, which should then send agents there to collect the money value of those articles.

This tax-in-kind act was variously amended later to allow a person to pay a money tax instead of giving a part of his sweet potatoes raised in the year 1863; to keep all corn under 200 bushels; to substitute salt pork for cured bacon and to require no tax where less than 250 pounds of pork was slaughtered; to give full credit for all products accidentally destroyed by fire or by enemy action; and to exempt all products of incapacitated soldiers or of farmers who had no slaves. By a general revision of the tax act on February 17, 1864, no one paid a tax who was not worth over $500 with credit of $100 allowed for each minor child and $500 for each minor son who had entered the war service, and no soldier or sailor worth less than $1,000 or widow of such person was taxable.

The tax-in-kind idea had long been advocated as the best method of provisioning the army without printing money for the purpose, and had it been adopted earlier it might have largely averted the redundancy of the Confederacy currency. But it was difficult to administer and left much bitterness among many small farmers who had never before paid a tax of any kind. It was not uniformly collected, as isolated districts went free of it while easily accessible regions made most of the contributions. Much material rotted at the depots or was stolen, and the whole system opened up wide possibilities for dishonesties by the quartermaster agents as well as by impostors. The government found great difficulty in supplying sacks for grain, and it was almost impossible to gather hay on the small farms where there were no methods of baling it. It set up a small army of agents who were generally looked upon as slackers and tormenters. With Virginia, North Carolina, South Carolina, and Georgia paying most of the tax in kind, it yielded about $145,000,000, not more than $40,000,000 of which reached its proper destination, Stephens asserted. Yet, with all its faults, Hill declared that this method of securing provisions had kept the Confederate armies from starvation.

The tax act of April 24, 1863, was confusing in its terms and so complicated as to methods of assessment, with three different times from which various taxes should be reckoned and at which they should be paid, that people could not be blamed for becoming disgusted. Toombs declared that it was "partial, unequal, and complex; fosters vulgar prejudices, and will gather an abundant harvest of frauds and perjuries." [52] Farmers asserted that they were hardest hit, and people in the Upper South charged that the law favored the interests of the Cotton South. The law was undoubtedly widely evaded. Richmond merchants selling millions of dollars worth of goods reported returns of from $30,000 to $60,000. A Richmond trader listed his income at $3,000 when it was $25,000.[53] Yet, naturally, there were those who defended the law as being better than none; the editor of the Richmond *Examiner* declared that "no one who has two grains of common sense, can fail to see that the only chance of the Confederacy currency rests on these taxes." [54]

This tax act was practically a failure, bringing in during the first year about $82,000,000. Debts were mounting higher and the whole financial structure was becoming more unsteady. Evidently there was more work for Congress to do, but did it have wisdom and determination to do it? "The truth is," observed an Alabama editor, "we need more courage in Congress now, than we do in the field." [55] Now boldly forgetting constitutional limitations on a direct tax, and with the advice and approval of President Davis, who was willing to forsake the Constitution in this instance, Congress in an

52 Phillips (ed.), *Correspondence of Toombs, Stephens, and Cobb*, 626.
53 Richmond *Daily Examiner*, January 8, April 2, 1864.
54 *Ibid.*, August 17, 1863.
55 Tuskegee *South Western Baptist*, December 3, 1863.

act of February 17, 1864, placed a 5 per cent tax on "Property, real, personal, and mixed, of every kind and description" with the following exceptions: the tax in kind could be deducted from the tax on property employed in agriculture, and a rate of 10 per cent should be levied on jewelry, gold and silver plate, watches, and similar items. The same rate (later 40 per cent) was laid on all profits made in trading in farm and manufactured products, in an attempt to catch the speculators. Also a fourth was exacted of all profits in excess of 25 per cent made by banks, insurance companies, express companies, railroads, telegraph companies, and all joint-stock companies. All taxes in this law were in addition to the taxes in the old law of April 24, 1863, which was repeated almost without change in another tax act passed on this same day, February 17, 1864. The tax on land and slaves was based on their valuation in 1860, which would mean a low rate in real value, for this assessment would be in old Federal money, and the tax would now be paid in depreciated Confederate currency. But, again, to catch the speculators, it was provided that land, slaves, cotton, and tobacco bought since January 1, 1862, should be assessed at the price actually paid by the owner. Another new departure was the taxation of Confederate bonds. This led to charges of breach of contract and dishonesty, as in many cases the government had not paid interest on these bonds and yet was taxing the owners of them. And as all bonds were taxed on their face value rather than their market value, a holder of a $100 Confederate bond worth 100 on the market paid as much tax as the holder of a $100 railroad bond worth 500 on the market. In the following June, Congress ordered an increase of a fifth on the present tax levy to be used in paying a slight increase ordered in soldiers' pay.

These acts displeased many people as much as the old tax act. Stephens declared that they were "neither proper, wise or just," and Memminger made the understatement that their "flagrant injustice would provoke severe criticism, if we were in quiet times." [56] It was left for a Georgian to say the worst: "Thousands will be utterly ruined by this taxation. . . . Thousands will be reduced to beggary and starvation. . . . But I will not comment farther

[56] Memminger to Boyce, March 31, 1864, in Memminger Papers (Division of Manuscripts, Library of Congress); Cleveland, *Alexander H. Stephens*, 765.

upon the spawn of Congress whose members generally have merited the curses and contempt of every one." [57]

And still taxes did not come in. In January, 1865, Secretary Trenholm in desperation begged Congress to devise some tax means to raise the stupendous sum of $750,000,000; and the next month President Davis in an urgent and imploring message to Congress urged it to pass some kind of tax law, even an ill-advised one rather than none, to raise money necessary to keep together the army, now about to embark on the spring campaign. On March 11, less than a month before the end, Congress, being unable to think of anything new to tax, raised the rates in the old law. But the Confederacy was now sinking fast, financially, militarily, and spiritually. Taxes certainly, even if it had had them, could not now save it. The Confederacy raised throughout its existence about one per cent of its income in taxes! "Too late" could be written in more than one instance in Confederate policy, but in none more appropriately than in taxation.[58]

[57] Athens *Southern Watchman*, June 8, 1864.

[58] The states paralleled the Confederacy rather closely in their tax policies and thereby aggravated the general situation. See "Letter Books, Governors, April 22, 1861–1865 May 9 Joseph E. Brown" (Georgia State Archives, Atlanta); Garner, *Reconstruction in Mississippi*, 44; Bettersworth, *Confederate Mississippi*, 115; Hamilton, *Reconstruction in North Carolina*, 74; Ramsdell, *Behind the Lines in the Southern Confederacy*, 74 ff.; Schwab, *Confederate States of America*, 303 ff.; Milledgeville *Southern Recorder*, March 15, 1864.

CHAPTER IX

DIPLOMACY

THE Confederacy was organized in a time of peace and its leaders hoped and expected that their new government would be received into the family of nations, unaccompanied by the alarms of war. Their attempt to establish friendly relationships with the United States failed and greatly complicated their efforts to obtain recognition from the rest of the world. Had peace prevailed, the Confederacy would easily have secured its place among the nations of the earth, for it had all the requirements—an organized government, a homogeneous people, and a large and definite territory. Instead, it was forced to prove to foreign nations its ability to win and maintain its independence; and one of its greatest handicaps was the blockade which President Lincoln announced on April 19, 1861. And so, in addition to its efforts to win recognition, it must be equally concerned with having the blockade removed both by inducing foreign nations not to accept it and by having them provide the ships and sinews of war necessary for the Confederacy to break it.

To establish its peaceful intentions, Howell Cobb, the president of the Montgomery Convention, announced on the first day of the new government's existence that it wanted "the most peaceful and friendly relations" with the world, and President Davis later declared: "We feel that our cause is just and holy; we protest solemnly in the face of mankind that we desire peace at any sacrifice save that of honor and independence; we seek no conquest, no aggrandizement, no concession of any kind from the States with which we were lately confederated; all we ask is to be let alone; that those who never held power over us shall not now attempt our subjugation by arms." [1] To prove its responsibility as a new power and its acceptance of international law, Congress adopted the position which the United States had assumed relative to the Declaration of Paris: that neutral countries might carry enemy commerce except contraband, that neutral countries might ship on enemy vessels all commerce except contraband, that a blockade to be binding must be effective, but, like the United States, it refused to give up the right of privateering.

Failing to obtain recognition from the United States, the Confederacy got, instead, a war; but there were other countries which might be more amenable to Confederate reasoning. The principal nations of the Old World whose recognition was worth while were England, France, Spain, and Russia; and such minor countries as Belgium, Holland, the Scandinavian powers, the German states, and the Papacy. In the New World, Mexico and the English possession of Canada were of immediate importance; and Brazil, being a slave country, was worth wooing. But all the other countries of the earth might be ignored, if the Confederacy could secure recognition from England and France.

Long before the Confederacy had been organized, Southerners had come to believe that their greatest diplomatic weapon would be cotton rather than men. The world must have cotton and they held a monopoly in it: the United States must have it both to spin and to send abroad to maintain its credit, for more than half of the value of American exports was in cotton; and the cotton mills of England and France must lie idle unless they could get Southern cotton. It would "bring more wooing princes to the feet of the Confederate States than Penelope had"; or as Benjamin H. Hill said in describing Southern power, "we point to that little attenuated cotton thread, which a child can break, but which, nevertheless *can hang*

1 Davis' Message to Congress, April 29, 1861, in Richardson (comp.), *Messages and Papers of the Confederacy*, I, 82. The principal printed sources of the diplomatic documents of the Confederacy are *ibid.*, II; and *Official Records of the Union and Confederate Navies in the War of the Rebellion* (Washington, 1894–1922), Ser. II, Vol. III. The standard secondary work on Confederate diplomacy is Owsley, *King Cotton Diplomacy*. An earlier and less complete work is James M. Callahan, *Diplomatic History of the Southern Confederacy* (Baltimore, 1901). There is much unpublished diplomatic material in the James M. Mason Papers and in the Pickett Papers (both in Division of Manuscripts, Library of Congress).

the world." [2] It was a miracle weapon; "Cotton can be made to sustain our Government," said an Alabama editor, "support our army, supply our people, and secure our independence." [3] Even an Englishman admitted that cotton could do anything "from the establishment of an empire to the securing of a shirt button. It is at once king and subject, master and servant, captain and soldier, artilleryman and gun." [4] So much was it on the minds of everyone that a Mobile minister in reading his text, confusing "Cotton" for "God," read "Cotton is King."

Though cotton was deified as king, it could not act without the manipulations of a department of state and the efforts of foreign representatives. Toombs, as the first Secretary of State, mapped out the Confederate argument to be used by the first envoys bound for Europe; but his impetuosity soon got the better of him in a situation so mild as merely writing letters, and he resigned in July, 1861, for an army career. He was succeeded by Robert M. T. Hunter of Virginia, who remained only until he could get elected to the Senate, with the hopes of succeeding Davis in the presidency if the Confederacy should last so long. When the permanent government was inaugurated in February, 1862, Judah P. Benjamin, the Hebrew wizard from Louisiana, became Secretary of State and remained in that position to the end, enjoying the special favor of President Davis and the biting hostility of many of the other high governmental officials. His work was vigorous but futile, for it was soon apparent that if the independence of the Confederacy was to be established it must be done on the battlefield with its own arms. "It is a pity," said the editor of the Richmond *Examiner,* "that an entire Department of a great Government should have no occupation whatever but to draw pay." [5]

Less than a month after the organization of the Confederacy, three commissioners to the principal European countries were appointed and were soon on their way, arriving in April. They were William L. Yancey of Alabama, Pierre A. Rost of Louisiana, and

2 Atlanta *Southern Confederacy,* July 18, 1861.

3 Montgomery *Daily Post,* August 14, 1861.

4 Russell, *Civil War in America,* 64.

5 Richmond *Daily Examiner,* June 13, 1863. The best biography of Benjamin is Robert D. Meade, *Judah P. Benjamin, Confederate Statesman* (New York, 1943).

A. Dudley Mann of Georgia. None of these was well fitted for the post. Yancey was a great and convincing orator but not a diplomat in any sense; Rost, a French-born friend of Benjamin's, had been a judge in Louisiana; and Mann had had some minor diplomatic experience in Europe and was socially charming but egotistical and naïve. They were charged with presenting to Europe the might and power of the Confederacy, gaining recognition, getting the blockade declared illegal, and negotiating treaties of commerce and friendship. They went first to England, where they found the government cold and calculating, and then to France to receive the good wishes of Napoleon III and the promise to recognize the Confederacy if England could be induced to lead the way. Soon sensing the futility of expecting favors in Europe, Yancey resigned in the early fall and after a short time returned to the Confederacy. On his return he made a speech in New Orleans in which he warned that Europe had no sympathy or appreciation for the Confederacy, and would never do a favorable turn until the South won its independence on the battlefield. Subsequently he became a Senator from Alabama and died in 1863.

To supplement the work of these commissioners and to attach envoys to definite countries, Davis accredited James M. Mason to England and John Slidell to France in August, 1861. Mann was sent to Belgium and Rost to Spain. Mason was a Virginia aristocrat, a grandson of George Mason of Revolutionary fame, and, although he may have chewed tobacco as was charged, a man of culture and charm; however, he possessed little diplomatic skill. Slidell, a New Yorker who had gone to live in Louisiana, was more subtle, pugnacious, daring, and aggressive, and withal possessed of a dignity and suavity that made for success as a diplomat. As England was the key to Confederate diplomacy, Slidell should have been sent to that country.

But before these envoys reached Europe, unwittingly they came near achieving a much greater success than they were ever to attain after they arrived. Sailing out of Cuba on an English merchantman, the *Trent*, they were taken from this vessel by an American warship, the *San Jacinto*, and lodged in Fort Warren prison in Boston Harbor. This indignity was too much for Queen Victoria's government to bear. The British made immediate preparations for war and sent an ultimatum demanding the release of the Confederate envoys. The United States complied and thereby averted a possible conflict with the British. Mason often regretted that he and Slidell had been released, for he felt that this victory made the British more arrogant and harder to deal with, and he might well have added that under the circumstances he and Slidell were much more effective agents in prison than out. Yet this diplomatic defeat for the United States afforded the Confederates much satisfaction, as was so rudely yet eloquently expressed by the editor of the *Southern Literary Messenger:* "The Yankees have licked the spittle that fell from the British lion's mouth as he uttered his first wrathful growl, and now they squirm and writhe in the dust of a national humiliation unexampled in history—despised of mankind, the loathed and ridiculous vermin of civilization." [6]

The most determined thrust in Confederate diplomacy came with the arrival of Mason and Slidell, though considerable groundwork had been laid beforehand and important developments had taken place. On May 14, 1861, England and France, working in harmony at the moment, recognized the belligerency of the Confederacy, which was nothing more than a recognition that a war rather than a street fight was in progress and that the rules of war were now in effect. These were as important for neutrals as for belligerents, for nations not fighting in a war had rights and duties no less than those fighting. Nations must now recognize the Confederate flag on the high seas and must not consider Confederate seamen as pirates, but it also followed that the United States won the right to institute a blockade, which she could not logically set up if this commotion was not a war. In fact, this move favored the United States more than the Confederacy; yet the former always considered it a gross insult and an unneutral act.

King Cotton was to do its work through the creation of a cotton famine in England and France which would force those countries to break the blockade in order to secure the staple. As a means to this end, the Confederacy promoted the policy that the blockade, not yet effective, should be reinforced by withholding cotton from all the Southern ports. And as an additional phase of its cotton policy, the Confederacy encouraged neutrals to accumulate large

[6] *Southern Literary Messenger,* XXXIV (1862), 65.

supplies in the Confederacy, which, of course, could be got out only by breaking the blockade. It was believed that England would be forced to act to prevent a cotton famine, which would be followed by civil unrest. These well-laid plans failed because England had a large surplus of raw cotton on hand, sufficient to last her almost through 1862, as well as a large supply of finished cloth which she could market at an immense profit on a rising market. The embargo also led the British to try to fulfill fond hopes, long entertained, of breaking the Southern cotton monopoly by encouraging its growth in India and Egypt. Before the end of the war, they had succeeded in securing large supplies from these regions. This attempt to destroy the Southern monopoly helps to explain England's hostility to slavery, as she felt that the South could not raise cotton without slave labor.

But the Confederacy had another string to its bow against the blockade. It would resort to accepted international law by demanding that England and France declare the blockade illegal because it was not effective. In proof of the ineffectiveness of the blockade, the Confederate envoys, both the first commissioners as well as Mason and Slidell, assembled an array of statistics to show how many ships had run the blockade. They declared that four hundred vessels had passed through during the first four months of its existence. The British were not impressed because they had long cherished a paper blockade, and the United States was now defending a principle which had helped to drive it into the second war with Great Britain. The British had another reason: Secretary of State Seward had through grave threats and blandishments made the British afraid that the United States would declare war on them if they interfered. On the other hand, Davis publicly threw out the hint to England that if the blockade forced the Confederacy into giving up much of its cotton raising to enter manufacturing, by which at least four men in the industrial nations of Europe would be thrown out of employment to one in the Confederacy, then those nations would have themselves to thank.

At the same time that the Confederacy was attempting to make Europe break the blockade, it was also using every effort to obtain recognition of its independence. Even if recognition did not stir up war between European nations and the United States, to the great advantage of the Confederacy, it would give the Confederacy a standing, financial and otherwise, which would be of inestimable value. At times England seriously considered recognition, and in the fall of 1862 there was an excellent chance that the cabinet might so order. General George B. McClellan was driven back from Richmond in the summer, and soon thereafter the Federals were severely defeated in the Second Battle of Manassas and General Benjamin F. Butler's "Woman Order" in New Orleans aroused bitter resentment.[7] Convinced that the Confederacy was about to win the war, Lord Palmerston, the prime minister, and Lord John Russell, the foreign minister, agreed that a cabinet meeting should be called in October at which mediation and subsequent recognition of the Confederacy might be adopted. But before the time for that meeting arrived a number of disturbing events took place: William E. Gladstone, a member of the cabinet, made a premature speech at Newcastle virtually foreshadowing recognition; Lee's invasion of Maryland was stopped at the Battle of Antietam; and on the heels of strategic defeat for the Confederacy Lincoln issued his preliminary Emancipation Proclamation. The meeting was postponed, and this golden opportunity for recognition of the Confederacy was forever lost—largely as a result of Antietam.

Diplomacy, ever devious, was more so in Europe at this time; yet there was a widespread sympathy in England for the Confederacy. Southerners were fighting for their just right to independence, if they wanted it; the movement was distinctly a conservative one and appealed especially to the upper classes and to the government; Southerners with their plantation aristocracy had ever attracted Englishmen more than the restless Northerners had; the success of the Confederates would end the domination of the New World by the United States and with it the Monroe Doctrine; the Confederacy, believing in a low tariff, would provide a market for British manufactures and a source of raw products. In much of this, indeed, there was more of self-interest than regard for the Confederates, and the British were ever careful that the former should outweigh the latter. In Parliament there was an impressive

---

[7] Regarding Butler's order Lord Palmerston said, "Any Englishman must blush to think that such an act has been committed by one belonging to the Anglo-Saxon race." Quoted in Owsley, *King Cotton Diplomacy,* 323-24.

array of friends of the South, Lords and Commoners, who frequently debated recognition and blockade breaking, among them W. H. Gregory, John A. Roebuck, William S. Lindsay, Sir James Ferguson, the Marquess of Lothian, and others. Outside of Parliament were James Spence, author of the pro-Confederate *American Union* and fiscal agent of the Confederacy, Thomas C. Grattan, publicist, lecturer, and editor of the London *Times,* and many other newspapermen. The Confederacy, representing definitely a conservative movement, disliked by the Red Republicans of France, England, and the German States and the Black Republicans of the United States, greatly appealed to Tories everywhere, the Church of England, the government, the aristocracy, and slightly to the conservative Thomas Carlisle, who could express his impatience with people who were "cutting each other's throats, because one half of them prefer hiring their servants for life, and the other by the hour." [8] Irrespective of sentiment, the government, always haunted by the fear of war with the United States, was careful never to give the offense which might have precipitated it.

At the same time that Mason was promoting recognition in England, Slidell was attempting to effect the same end in France. Napoleon knew he could not embark on a policy which would bring him into collision with the United States unless he had British backing, even though he was at this time playing for high stakes in his Mexican venture. Hence he refused to move unless England led the way. Pinning more hopes on France than seemed warranted, Benjamin in April, 1862, instructed Slidell to offer admittance of French goods into the Confederacy free of duty "for a certain definite period," [9] and to present Napoleon 100,000 bales of cotton or as much as was necessary to lead him to break the blockade by coming for it. Napoleon dared not make such a move without Britain joining in, something she refused to do. Hoping to enlist other support than England's in moves to break the blockade, demand an armistice, or grant recognition, France approached Russia, Belgium, and Spain. Russia would like to see the war stopped, but she refused to join in any of these moves; Belgium

8 Quoted in Donaldson Jordan and Edwin J. Pratt, *Europe and the American Civil War* (Boston, 1931), 73.

9 *Official Records of the Union and Confederate Navies,* Ser. II, Vol. III, 386–90.

and Spain were willing to follow France in these particulars; but France would not act without England.

In the fall of 1862 France attempted to have England join her in proposing to the Confederacy and the United States a six-month armistice with the Southern ports opened, during which time efforts at mediation would be made. Napoleon had assured himself of the strength of the Confederacy and its determination to fight on to independence, through a visit of Count Henri Mercier, the French minister in Washington, to Richmond the previous April. England refused Napoleon's proposition, but the Confederate victory in the Battle of Fredericksburg in December, 1862, so impressed the French Emperor that the next month he ordered Mercier to offer mediation in the name of France alone. Secretary Seward rejected it.

From the beginning there were a few Confederates who believed that no help could be got from Europe—not even a respect for the Confederacy's lawful rights—and by the middle of 1863 the opinion had become general that this was so. Thomas R. R. Cobb hated England for her cold superciliousness, and he could not make up his mind which was meaner, Old England or New England. Governor Pickens of South Carolina believed that England and France hoped that both the Northerners and the Southerners would fight themselves into exhaustion, so that those two nations might pounce upon what was left and restore it to its former colonial status.[10] The Confederacy felt that it had reason to expect sympathy and honorable treatment from Europe. Had not European nations poured out their sympathy and aid for such struggling peoples as the Irish, the Belgians, the Greeks, the Hungarians, and even at the moment the Poles? But, as an Englishman replied, "it may be that the charity of the European Powers is exhausted in Poland, and that neither pity nor shame will induce them to break a thankless neutrality, here."[11]

It was now time for the South to realize that its only salvation lay within its own self. Too long had it failed to put forth its full strength, awaiting the recognition and help of England and, like a

[10] Pickens to Memminger, September 27, 1861, in "Correspondence, 1860–1865," (South Carolina State Archives).

[11] [Lawrence], *Border and Bastile*, 291.

silly child, looking across the big water, expecting the British lion with one bound to leap the Atlantic and with a mighty thrust of its paw crush the blockade.[12] Hunter pointed out that "when we have achieved the victory and won our independence, it will be a proud thing to know that we shall owe them only to God and ourselves, and that we are under no obligation to any other nation for alliance and assistance." [13] A wit suggested as a design for the Confederate seal, a man paddling his own canoe with the motto: "D——n England and France." The Confederacy would owe Europe nothing, but Europe would find herself paying the Confederate debt, for when the war was over Congress ought to place an export tax on cotton, rice, tobacco, and naval stores—articles which those nations must have.

President Davis had by 1863 become sternly critical of Europe's treatment of his country. Both England and France had "assumed a character positively unfriendly." They had recognized a blockade which was illegal by the recognized principles of international law; they had, in fact, been unneutral. Congress was also losing its patience; Foote, in the House, introduced a resolution advising Davis to recall the envoys from every country which had not recognized the Confederacy by May 1. In March, Davis nominated as commissioner to Russia Lucius Q. C. Lamar, who immediately set out on his assignment. He spent some time in England and France, but never proceeded to St. Petersburg, for Congress had by this time come to the conclusion that the Confederacy should wash its hands of Europe. The Senate refused to confirm his appointment and he returned.[14]

Another element in the mounting impatience which the Confederacy was developing toward Europe related to the foreign

[12] Selma *Daily Reporter*, March 13, 1862. J. C. Hunt, Richmond, Va., May 21, 1861, to Massie, in Massie Papers, said, "England & France we learn are sending fleets to the southern waters to protect their commerce & this we think is taking the starch out of the Yankees."

[13] *Journal of the Congress of the Confederate States*, III, 795. In the same tone, the editor of the Richmond *Daily Examiner*, April 2, 1863, wrote, "They have been forced to the stern Conclusion, that their country is alone on the earth; that they have no friend but God, who is afar off, and no hope but in their own swords."

[14] Richardson (comp.), *Messages and Papers of the Confederacy*, I, 311–12; Wirt A. Cate, *Lucius Q. C. Lamar, Secession and Reunion* (Chapel Hill, 1935), 91 ff.; Mayes, *Lucius Q. C. Lamar*, 109.

consuls residing in the South. When the Confederacy was established the principal European nations had a total of about twenty-five consuls within its borders. There was much criticism against their continuing to communicate with their respective ministers in Washington and their failure to secure new credentials from the Confederacy, but in one instance the Confederate government was recognized, when the Duke of Saxe-Coburg and Gotha applied for an exequatur for a consul he was sending to Texas.[15] These consuls, especially the British, who were the most important, tended to take on more diplomatic than commercial duties, since the blockade made the latter of little importance. Governor Brown of Georgia had a quarrel with Allen Fullarton, the British vice-consul at Savannah, over the enlistment of British subjects, and Governor Milledge L. Bonham of South Carolina had a like contest with the British vice-consul at Charleston; but the trouble that brought the issue to a head was the case of George Moore, the British consul at Richmond. Moore protested against enrolling in the Confederate army some Irishmen in Virginia, a subject within his province, but when he became embroiled with the State Department over the exercise of such authority in Alabama, as if he were a minister to the Confederacy, Secretary Benjamin in late 1863 called a meeting of the cabinet in the absence of President Davis, who was visiting the army in the West, and expelled all the British consuls. The others were not interfered with except that earlier, June 10, 1863, Benjamin had forbidden them to continue to communicate with the ministers of their countries in Washington.

England had become the country against whom there was the greatest enmity, for it was evident that in whatever direction Europe might go, the British lion would lead the way. Despairing of the devious and wily diplomacy of Palmerston and Russell, Mason left England for France in the early fall of 1863.

About the same time, A. Dudley Mann, who had been residing at Brussels, was sent on a special mission to the Vatican to thank the Pope for having written letters to the archbishops at New Orleans and New York urging them to work for peace. Mann had a few pleasant conferences with the Pope and came away bearing a letter from His Holiness to President Davis with the salutation, "Presi-

15 *Journal of the Congress of the Confederate States*, V, 422.

dent of the Confederate States of America." Mann jubilantly took this to be a recognition of the independence of the Confederacy but Benjamin saw no significance in the expression, though Lamar held that the Pope had "pronounced us right, and recognized the title which we have assumed among the nations." [16] In the spring of 1864 the Confederacy sent Bishop Patrick N. Lynch as a special commissioner to the Vatican to conclude a treaty on all matters of common interest. He was received in several audiences by the Pope, but nothing resulted beyond the transaction of routine ecclesiastical matters.

For those who could get little consolation out of the kind of recognition the Pope had given the Confederacy, there was another example which Poland had provided. In August, 1861, a delegation of three Poles arrived in Richmond on a mission looking toward Polish recognition of the Confederacy; but as Poland herself was unrecognized, there was even less consolation in this than in what the Pope had done.[17]

As the war took a more furious turn in the summer of 1864 with Grant's campaign against Richmond, Congress formulated a manifesto to the world in which it still seemed to prize the good opinion of Europe and to desire that European nations understand how determined the Confederates were to win their independence, and how they would rather die free than live as conquered slaves. A little later Davis, without begging again for recognition, warned Europe that their failure to recognize the Confederacy was only prolonging the war, which the Confederates would ultimately win. The editor of the Richmond *Whig* declared that "the question of recognition has long since passed the bounds of argument and reason, as it has, happily for ourselves, passed also beyond the lines of anxiety or expectation." [18] By 1865 the fear of subjugation seized many people and made some suggest the bizarre course of "repealing" the Declaration of Independence, which they held would automatically place the Confederacy back under England, and this would lead to war with the United States when England attempted to act on it. As a final dying diplomatic gasp, the Confederacy in

[16] Mayes, *Lucius Q. C. Lamar*, 645.
[17] Richmond *Daily Examiner*, August 31, 1864.
[18] Richmond *Daily Whig*, February 22, 1864.

the spring of 1865 sent Duncan F. Kenner, a Louisiana Congressman, on a hurried mission to England to offer as a last bid for recognition the freeing of the slaves. Mason now returned to London and saw Lord Palmerston and later Lord Donoughmore to whom he made the definite proposition of freeing the slaves. He was informed that it was then too late.

Out of a sort of nostalgic sentimentalism reminiscent of the American Revolution, many Southerners seemed to cling tenaciously to the feeling that just as France had saved America then, she might save the Confederacy now. Though the mass of French people supported the North, the government favored the Confederacy and it was the government and not the people that ruled. If France would not make an alliance with the whole Confederacy, then, some argued, let her resume control of that part of the Confederacy which had been in the Louisiana Purchase (all west of the Mississippi including Texas), for it was held that the United States had violated the treaty of cession of 1803.[19]

In addition to the diplomatic representatives, the Confederacy sent abroad a variety of financial, purchasing, and propaganda agents and some of the states added to the list; in fact, so many of one kind or another went to Europe that Lamar thought many of them ought to be back "at home fighting." The first ones to go were Caleb Huse, a Massachusetts-born West Pointer who was on the faculty of the University of Alabama, sent by the Ordnance Bureau, and James D. Bulloch, a Georgian, sent by the Navy Department. Huse was especially successful in buying small arms, heavy artillery, and ammunition. In addition to many purchases in England, he secured 100,000 rifles and 60 cannons from Austria.[20] Bulloch confined his chief interest to the building of fast cruisers such as the *Alabama* and *Florida*. His attempt to secure ironclads and especially the Laird ironclad rams failed because of threats of war the United States made against England if these vessels were allowed to sail. James Spence, an Englishman, acted as a financial agent until he overshot the mark by opposing

19 Major John Tyler to the Governor of Texas, October 27, 1863, and various other letters in "Governors Letters Jan–Dec 1863" (Texas State Archives, Austin).

20 Caleb Huse, *The Supplies of the Confederate Army, How they were Obtained in Europe and how Paid for. Personal Reminiscences and Unpublished History* (Boston, 1904), 36 pp.

slavery. With so many rival Confederate agents working at cross-purposes, the Confederacy, to bring order out of chaos, sent over in 1864 as sole financial agent Colin J. McRae, who for the remainder of the war made a remarkably successful record.

The two outstanding propaganda agents of the Confederacy were Henry Hotze, of Swiss birth, who had had some diplomatic experience and who had worked on a newspaper in Mobile, and Edwin de Leon, who had been American consul general to Egypt and also had had newspaper experience. By far the more successful was Hotze, who, arriving in England in January, 1862, immediately gained the confidence of the principal editors and publicists by his deft propaganda touches. Soon he was setting forth in the London *Times* and other journals the power and glory of the Confederacy, and on May 1, 1862, he began the publication of a dignified weekly journal called the *Index*, which ran for the remainder of the war and presented the Confederacy to good advantage. He extended his activities to Ireland, which was pouring out many of its citizens to the United States, ultimately to find themselves in the Federal armies. To Dublin he sent Father John Bannon to set the Irish aright on the indignities the United States was accustomed to show the Roman Catholic religion. De Leon was sent to France, but he was so unsuccessful in his propaganda efforts, in which he made an enemy of Slidell, that Hotze himself took over the work there.

The chief diplomatic activities of the Confederacy in the New World centered in Canada and Mexico. Ventures in the latter country were tied up with the activities of Napoleon, who was now setting up a puppet empire under Maximilian, and were much more successful commercially than diplomatically. As a special agent to checkmate the activities of Thomas Corwin, the United States minister, and to gain the good will of Mexico, whose long Rio Grande border was of outstanding commercial importance, Davis sent John T. Pickett. Though widely experienced in filibustering and other adventures and as consul at Vera Cruz, he was the worst possible choice for this mission, as he was undiplomatic in his acts and so volatile and flighty by nature that he ended up in a Mexican jail before he had been in the country very long. Instead of attempting further diplomatic efforts in Mexico City, the Confederacy early centered its attention on the Texas border, where

Santiago Vidaurri as governor of Neuvo León and Coahuila held power until 1864 and paid no attention to Benito Juarez, president of that part of Mexico opposing Maximilian and his Empire, or to Maximilian himself. As its agent to Vidaurri, the Confederacy sent Juan A. Quintero, a Cuban-born long-time resident of Mexico, who in some fashion had become a citizen of Texas. His dealings were equally successful whether with Vidaurri, Juarez, or Maximilian; for before the end, each of these authorities was to control for varying times the lower Rio Grande valley with the port of Matamoros.

There were also considerable bandit activities interspersed among these regimes, for the trade crossing the Rio Grande was of immense value—bandits such as Antonio Carvajal, Juan N. Cortina, and Octaviano Zapata. The Confederacy was able to do business with all of them, but not with the United States army, which held Brownsville from November, 1863, to July, 1864, leaving a small garrison thereafter at Brazos Santiago, some miles to the northward. To stop the European trade in and out of Matamoros through the application of the continuous voyage principle, the Federal navy seized the *Peterhoff,* an English vessel bound for that port; but Matamoros was left open in anticipation of the Supreme Court decision, which did not come until after the war, that the blockade did not extend to the Rio Grande inland frontier. Large amounts of cotton were sent out of Texas across the Rio Grande and thence to Europe through Matamoros, to pay for large amounts of powder, sulphur, mercury, lead, cloth, and for many other importations from Europe, which brought in import duties of more than $100,-000 a month to the Mexican authority controlling the border. This traffic supplied the armies of the Trans-Mississippi Department, but, as there were no railroads reaching from Texas to the rest of the Confederacy, the armies east of the Mississippi River profited little from this source.

Canada, though a possession of Great Britain, was largely free from the major implications of British policy toward the Confederacy, because the problem here was largely one of a land frontier rather than the application of rules relating to blockades and other maritime law. C. C. Clay, Jr., and Jacob Thompson were the principal Confederate agents operating in Canada, and their main purpose was to develop trouble in the rear of Federal armies. A specimen of these activities appeared in a conspiracy developed with Clement L. Vallandigham, an Ohio Copperhead, and his Order of American Knights or Sons of Liberty, wherein they were to aid in liberating the Confederate prisoners at Camp Douglas, outside Chicago, Johnson's Island, in Lake Erie, and at other camps. To accomplish the release of the Johnson's Island prisoners, John Y. Beall headed an attempt to seize the Federal vessels on Lake Erie. After some initial success he failed, and was captured, tried, and hanged. This being the year of the Presidential election of 1864, the Confederate agents in Canada hoped by the free but secret use of a large sum of money to bring about the defeat of Lincoln through encouraging the peace movement that had of its own accord attained considerable strength. Again there was failure. Another plan to disrupt conditions in the United States was to send secret agents to fire some of the large border cities such as Detroit and Buffalo. Fires were actually started simultaneously in eight hotels in New York City, but no great damage resulted.[21] The most successful attempt from Canada against the United States was the raid of Bennett H. Young with about thirty followers against St. Albans, Vermont, in October, 1864. They shot up the town in wild West fashion, robbed three banks of more than $200,000, escaped to Canada, and evaded conviction in a Canadian court on a technicality, as well as through the fact that the vast majority of Canadians sympathized with the Confederacy. The furor, panic, and indignation aroused in the United States over these incidents led to a sharp letter of rebuke from Lord Russell to the Confederate commissioners in Europe, Mason, Slidell, and Mann; but before more serious developments could arise out of the Canadian troubles, the war had ended and the Confederacy no longer existed to be either kicked or caressed.

[21] New York *World*, November 26, 28, 29, 1864; Athens *Southern Watchman*, December 21, 1864; Memphis *Daily Appeal*, December 27, 1864.

CHAPTER X

WAR SUPPLIES AND MANUFACTORIES

THAT the South had neither the desire nor the expectation of needing to fight a war for its independence is eloquently attested by the lack of preparations for such an eventuality. True enough, it had a martial spirit of long standing, which had made Southerners regard highly an army career and which had led to the founding of various military schools, but this feeling existed apart from any thought of armed conflict with the North. There was not a shipyard or ship owned by any Southern state nor were there in the South any munitions works or manufactories easily transformed into them, apart from the Tredegar Iron Works in Richmond and a few smaller establishments, which were serving the purposes of peace. The charges long held against John Floyd, Secretary of War under Buchanan, that he had stocked the United States arsenals in the South with an oversupply of small arms, on investigation proved to be unfounded. The arms he had sent to the Southern arsenals were muskets which had been shipped North for alterations and were now being returned.

But when secession actually began, it was the part of wisdom for the seceding states to provide themselves with the means of defending themselves. In line with this policy, they sent their purchasing agents to the North and to Europe, and each state on seceding seized the war supplies in the Federal arsenals, barracks, and forts within its borders. Louisiana obtained more than 47,000 small arms at the Baton Rouge Arsenal; North Carolina, 37,000 at Fayetteville; Georgia, nearly 23,000 at Augusta; and South Carolina, Alabama, and Arkansas seized smaller amounts at Charleston, Mount Vernon, and Little Rock, respectively.[1] On Virginia's seced-

[1] Claud E. Fuller and Richard D. Steuart, *Firearms of the Confederacy; The Shoulder Arms, Pistols and Revolvers of the Confederate Soldiers, including the Regular United*

ing, the Federal authorities burned both the armory at Harpers Ferry and the Gosport Navy Yard at Norfolk, but the machinery in the former and the many heavy guns at the latter remained undamaged. The machinery soon found its way to Richmond and Fayetteville arsenals and the Gosport guns were used on Confederate ships and elsewhere. Including arms early taken from Federal troops in Texas, the total haul of arms of United States ownership amounted to about 190,000. As soon as the Confederacy was formed, in theory it succeeded to all this war material; and although the states in joining the Confederacy agreed to turn it over, some of the governors never did so completely.

In addition to arms seized from the Federal government, there were in the Confederacy probably more than 300,000 arms, of varying degrees of antiquity and disrepair, which the states owned, and an undeterminable number of old muskets and shotguns which belonged to private individuals. Some of the latter were carried into the Confederate service, but few of the state arms found their way there, for many of them were unserviceable, and, too, governors like Joseph E. Brown of Georgia sternly forbade anyone to take these arms out of the state. As an example of the outpouring of private weapons, a person brought to Richmond an old duck gun about eight feet long, "for which a tea-cup full of buck shot would be a small load." [2] Some people believed that shotguns were especially desirable, because they spread the shot and did not waste as much lead as rifles and muskets.

Confronted from the beginning by the threat of war, the Confederacy sought every possible source of war materials. Seizing Federal arms inspired confidence but gave no hope of a sufficiency if war should come. President Davis in February, 1861, sent Raphael Semmes, later to become famous as commander of the *Alabama*, to the North to make purchases. [3] Other agents soon followed, and before hostilities actually broke out, war munitions were trickling into the Confederacy from that region, as Northern munitions

States Models, the Imported Arms and those Manufactured within the Confederacy (Huntington, W. Va., 1944), 19.

[2] Richmond *Daily Examiner*, March 8, 1862; Atlanta *Southern Confederacy*, July 30, 1861.

[3] Rowland (ed.), *Jefferson Davis, Constitutionalist*, V, 54–56.

makers had no scruples against selling to all buyers. On March 4, the day on which Lincoln was inaugurated President, there arrived in Macon, Georgia, for Howell Cobb, head of the Confederate Congress, an express package from Colonel Samuel Colt, then head of a well-known arms-manufacturing company, containing two pistols, one, a horse pistol for Cobb, and the other, an ivory-handled revolver for Mrs. Cobb. The implications of these gifts were plain enough. Even after Fort Sumter and First Manassas, large amounts of war material crossed the border into the South, much of it coming through Kentucky, whose neutrality, continuing until September, 1861, afforded an open road to the Confederacy. The blockade cut off a freely flowing supply of war materials from Europe, but the amount received from this source as well as the trade that went on between the lines and across the Northern border did much to tide the Confederacy through its four years of warfare.

Captures made on the battlefields were another source of supply. According to a rhymer,

> Want a weapon? Why capture one!
> Every Doodle has got a gun,
> Belt and bayonet, bright and new;
> Kill a Doodle, and capture two! [4]

A Confederate officer remarked, "In every battle we fight we must capture as much ammunition as we use." [5] In the Seven Days' Battles the Confederates captured about 35,000 small arms and at Second Manassas about 20,000. It was estimated that they captured during 1862 about 100,000 stands of arms. Much captured material could not be used, whether small arms or ammunition, because bullets did not always fit arms; but many of these captured rifles were sent to Confederate arsenals to be altered, and others were stacked up to rust away. One of the most serviceable Federal weapons, the Spencer rifle, a breach-loading repeater using a copper cartridge, was of little use to the Confederates, for although they captured many of them they were never able to produce the necessary cartridges. [6]

[4] This is one of eight stanzas, in Macon *Daily Telegraph*, April 5, 1862.

[5] Lieutenant Colonel [Arthur James Lyon] Fremantle, *Three Months in the Southern States: April–June, 1863* (New York, 1864), 241–42.

[6] *Ibid.*, 221; Memphis *Daily Appeal*, December 29, 1864.

The most dependable source of the Confederacy's war materials was her own manufactories. Starting out with no munitions works, she had a gigantic task in setting them up. The government itself not only went into the manufacture of war supplies, but through contracts with private firms it whipped into life businesses already in existence and led many others to spring up. To provide the armies with war material was the duty of the Ordnance Bureau of the War Department, whose head was Josiah Gorgas, the most successful and able organizer in the Confederacy. Gorgas was a Pennsylvanian and a West Pointer, but long residence in the South and his marriage to a daughter of John Gayle, an early governor of Alabama, led him to cast his lot with the Confederacy. Of his success in providing the Confederacy with munitions it could be said that "the supply never failed to be equal to the actual emergency, and no disaster was ever to be attributed to its scantiness." [7]

The South had the potentialities of practically all materials necessary for waging war. It had supplies of coal and iron in Virginia, North Carolina, Georgia, and Alabama; it had lead mines in Virginia, East Tennessee, Arkansas, and southwestern Missouri; it had scattered deposits of all other ingredients of munitions except mercury. It was only necessary to bring these deposits into production, by speeding up the blast furnaces and rolling mills already in existence, waking to life dormant ones, and beginning new establishments.

To aid businesses with which contracts had been made for war materials, Congress allowed the government to lend one half of the expenses of setting them up, and in order to build up large supplies of iron and coal it might advance a third of the value of the contemplated output. To hold prices within reasonable bounds, no business was allowed more than 75 per cent profit, later to be reduced to 33⅓ per cent; and to guarantee that the government receive an ample part of the output of materials other than ordnance supplies, where there would be a civilian demand, such as quartermaster supplies of cloth and wagons, these factories were required to sell to the government two thirds of their production. The gov-

---

[7] *Southern Historical Society Papers,* XI (1883), 113. See also, J. W. Mallet, "Work of the Ordnance Bureau of the War Department of the Confederate States, 1861–5," *ibid.,* XXXVII (1909), 1–20.

ernment enforced these regulations by refusing to detail workmen and allow transportation facilities to those who would not conform. It was able to exercise this control through the conscription acts and laws giving it authority over the railroads. As the government tended to establish a monopoly in cotton through purchases, it had the additional club over textile mills of withholding this raw supply.[8]

These arrangements did not always work smoothly, for by allowing a profit based on cost of production, the government unwittingly held out an invitation to mills to make their expenses as high as possible, since the profits would be correspondingly greater. By deliberately doubling the costs on a given output, a manufacturer thereby doubled his profits. To check this practice, contracts were later made for products at a fixed price—as iron at $180 a ton; but constantly rising prices made this plan unsatisfactory and led to an arrangement whereby arbitrators might periodically set new prices.[9] Government contracts, by forcing factories to give up most of their production, left little for the mass of civilians. There was such a dearth of iron for home use that finally the government allowed iron producers to sell half their output to private industry. Another difficulty the government encountered was competition with the states. Ever too watchful of their own interests apart from the general good, states sought to duplicate the efforts of the Confederacy in providing supplies for their own soldiers, especially clothing. As a result they contracted for so much of the output within their own boundaries as to leave little for the Confederacy, which must supply soldiers whether they came from states which had factories or not. By the end of 1864, out of the eighty textile factories still left in the Confederacy, half were in North Carolina, whose governor was pre-empting every yard of cloth made there, with the result that, according to Quartermaster General Alexander R. Lawton, "while all the other States of the Confederacy were contributing generously to the common cause, North Carolina alone

[8] Charles W. Ramsdell, "The Control of Manufacturing by the Confederate Government," in *Mississippi Valley Historical Review* (Cedar Rapids), VIII (1921–1922), 231–49.

[9] An original contract form is preserved in "Collection. Autograph Letters, Documents, Manuscript, etc. Relating to the Confederacy 1861–1865," Case III, Folder 3 (University of Texas Library).

husbanded her resources for North Carolina troops." [10] But only a few months earlier Lawton was complaining that Florida controlled the output of the only factory in that state, Georgia controlled part of hers, and that other states were trying to do likewise. [11]

Under governmental stimulation as well as patriotic impulse, a widespread industry in war materials sprang up. In one announcement in early 1862, Gorgas invited bids on 300,000 tons of iron and 1,000 pieces of artillery from 9-pounder field guns to 10-inch columbiads and 18-inch coast mortars. [12] Unlike the situation in the North, there seem to have been few dishonesties practiced or fortunes made by government contractors, though choleric Foote, in Congress, was sure that Hexall, Crenshaw & Company, who ran flour mills in Richmond, would make a $1,000,000 profit out of a government contract they held. On the other hand, Nelson and Amos Tift, Connecticut Yankee brothers who had early migrated to the South, held large government contracts with only modest compensation for making flour, hardtack, and barrels in their establishments in Albany, Georgia. In fact, government contracts in time came to be avoided rather than sought by many businesses, because of the tardiness of the government in making payments.

By the end of 1864 Alabama was producing four times as much raw iron as any other state, but on account of poor railway facilities the Tredegar works were unable to obtain it for manufacture into cannon and other war materials. The chief coal mines of the Confederacy lay in Virginia, west of Richmond, in the Deep River region of central North Carolina, in Tennessee around Chattanooga, and in central Alabama, north of Montgomery.

Lead had been mined around Wytheville, Virginia, since the Revolution, and this source should be added to the 2,000,000 pounds imported. It was these mines that afforded the Confederacy most of the domestic production. The output at times was from 100,000 to 150,000 pounds monthly. The mines near Neosho, in southwestern Missouri, early in the war had been lost through Federal occupation. John LeConte, one of the few scientific Southerners, directed mining operations around Spartanburg, South Carolina, but without much success. The Confederacy always felt that it was

---

[10] *Official Records*, Ser. IV, Vol. III, 691.
[11] *Ibid.*, 557.   [12] Charleston *Mercury*, March 12, 1862.

on the verge of a lead shortage, which it attempted to make up by appealing now and then to the people to strip their houses and premises of all articles made of lead, such as pipes, window weights, roofs, cistern linings, and various common utensils.[13] Most of the copper which did not reach the Confederacy through the blockade came from Polk County, in southeastern Tennessee, until 1864 when that region was occupied by Federal troops. After this calamity the Confederacy denied itself many of the former uses of copper, such as an alloy in cannon metal, and confined its use to percussion caps. During the last year of the war, copper from stills, mostly in North Carolina, was exclusively used for this purpose. Mexico provided most of the mercury, until the fall of Vicksburg cut the Confederacy in two and made communications with Texas difficult. Grindstones, so necessary for sharpening tools, especially in arsenals and armories, were found in the Deep River region of North Carolina and around Talladega, Alabama.

In the beginning the Confederacy was seized more severely by the nightmare of a shortage of powder than of any other military necessity. Powder was made of niter or saltpeter, charcoal, and sulphur, in the proportions by weight of 15, 3, and 2 respectively. The best charcoal was made from willow wood, which was easily available. Before the war sulphur had generally been imported from Italy, and its chief use in the South was in the sugar-making industry. A large amount on hand in Louisiana when the war broke out supplied the first needs of the powder mills, and thereafter, apart from some imports, the source of sulphur was iron pyrites. So successful were the small factories which roasted sulphur from pyrites, under government contract, that George W. Rains, who had been appointed by Gorgas to take charge of powder production, declared by the end of 1861 that he feared no sulphur shortage.

The greatest problem in powder making was the obtaining of niter. Though the Confederacy imported 2,700,000 pounds, it set feverishly to work to create a supply at home, and before the end it had produced about 3,000,000 pounds and had potentialities for

[13] Macon *Daily Telegraph,* April 3, 1862. As an indication of the large amounts of lead imported through the blockade, see the cargo manifests listed in Frank E. Vandiver (ed.), *Confederate Blockade Running through Bermuda, 1861–1865; Letters and Cargo Manifests* (Austin, 1947), 109–48.

an almost unlimited supply. Niter was present in the soil in cellars and under houses and especially in caves. An immediate survey of mountain caves was made by both governmental agents and private persons, and the caves in East Tennessee and northern Alabama were soon in production.[14] In 1862, after the loss of many of these caves through Federal occupation, the Niter and Mining Bureau was set up to intensify the production of niter as well as coal, copper, lead, iron, and other minerals. The Bureau now resorted to a method of production, familiar to Europeans, which involved the development of niter beds, or "nitriaries" as they came to be called. Pits two feet deep were dug and filled with carcasses, stable manure, and decaying vegetable matter, and as decomposition progressed, putrid water and organic liquids collected from the towns and neighborhood were sprinkled over the beds. Eighteen months later, after occasional mixing operations, this soil was put in hoppers and water drained through it. The niter was recovered from this drainage. Stray dogs afforded many of the carcasses used, which led a wit to remark, "Soldiers using this powder are said to make a peculiar *dogged* resistance." [15] Every community in the Confederacy was urged to develop niter beds. Jonathan Haralson, superintendent of the Selma, Alabama, region, was so efficient and persistent in his duties that a bit of contemporary doggerel addressed to him made him famous among the soldiers of the Confederacy.[16] By the end of 1864 there were almost a million cubic feet of niter beds, with the Richmond region standing first, claiming 256,000 cubic feet. The "nitriaries" had great potentialities, but the Confederacy fell before scarcely any niter could be obtained from this source.

No powder was made in the South when the Confederacy was set up, and only two inactive powder mills were within its limits, one at Nashville and the other at Walhalla, South Carolina. Rains, on

[14] Executive Papers, 1861 (Virginia State Library); George W. Rains, *History of the Confederate Powder Works* (Newburg, N.Y., 1882), 6; Richmond *Semi-Weekly Enquirer*, April 3, 1863; Richmond *Daily Whig*, April 2, 1863.

[15] Montgomery *Weekly Mail*, August 22, 1862. See also, "Public Improvements" (South Carolina State Archives); Columbus *Weekly Enquirer*, August 12, 1862; Richmond *Daily Enquirer*, May 4, 1863; Richmond *Semi-Weekly Enquirer*, January 1, 1864; Montgomery *Weekly Mail*, November 15, 1862.

[16] Selma *Daily Reporter*, June 5, July 1, 21, August 14, 1862.

his appointment as head of powder production, began a development at Augusta, which resulted in the largest powder manufactory in the Confederacy if not on the continent and which manufactured throughout the war 2,750,000 pounds.[17] Other powder mills were set up, notably at San Antonio and Petersburg. A substitute for powder, frequently talked about but never manufactured in the South, was guncotton, which had a much greater explosive power but which cost four or five times as much to produce. As it was made by soaking cotton in "monohydrate of azotic acid," its production would help to alleviate the demands for sulphur and niter. Disadvantages in addition to the cost were the danger that it might blow up the guns in which it was being used and that it left a troublesome amount of water after its explosion.

The war industries which grew up in the Confederacy were remarkable for a region which had long frowned on manufactories. They were a tribute to Gorgas and his organization of the Ordnance Bureau. These war industries were both privately and governmentally owned. Gorgas scattered over the Confederacy armories and arsenals (terms which were used interchangeably), where weapons of war were altered, repaired, manufactured, and stored. There were arsenals at Richmond, Fayetteville, Charleston, Macon, Augusta, Atlanta, Columbus, Montgomery, Selma, Jackson in Mississippi, Little Rock, San Antonio, and at other places.[18] Richmond was the greatest center of war manufactories in the Confederacy. Here the Tredegar Iron Works, a sort of scientific headquarters for the Confederacy, made torpedoes, submarines, plates for ironclad ships, propeller shafts, cannon, the great Brooke rifled naval guns, machinery for war production, and many other things both great and small.[19] Here also were the Richmond Armory with a capacity

[17] Rains, *Confederate Powder Works*, 24.

[18] Fuller and Steuart, *Firearms of the Confederacy*, 142, 150; Bettersworth, *Confederate Mississippi*, 143; Richmond *Daily Enquirer*, November 24, 1864; *General Orders from Adjutant and Inspector-General's Office, Confederate States Army*, 1862–1863, Ser. 1863, pp. 9–10; *General Orders from the Adjutant and Inspector-General's Office, Confederate States Army, From January 1, 1864, to July 1, 1864, Inclusive* (Columbia, 1864), 82.

[19] Kathleen Bruce, *Virginia Iron Manufacture in the Slave Era* (New York, 1931), 331, 347, 348. General Lee in September, 1863, suggested to President Davis that munition works and arsenals be scattered over the Confederacy as much as possible "so that if Richmond should fall we would not be destitute." *Official Records*, Ser. I,

for making five thousand small arms a month, the largest in the Confederacy,[20] and the Confederate States Laboratory which made percussion caps and cartridges, fixed ammunition, signal rockets, grenades, a million percussion caps, gun carriages, 12-pounder Napoleons, small arms, and canteens. Atlanta and Selma were other outstanding centers.

Small arms—the smoothbore muskets at first but later rifles—were made in many places in the Confederacy. They were all, however, muzzle-loading. The Minié balls and powder were wrapped in a paper cartridge, which the soldier tore open, often with his teeth, to discharge the contents down the barrel. Machine guns were still in the future, but someone in Macon claimed to have invented a gun which would shoot fifty times by merely pulling a lever. Another Confederate tried to interest Davis in a "seven shooting gun."

Pistols and revolvers, which every raw volunteer thought he must possess to be fully armed, were for sale before the war in all the principal towns of the South; but these arms were of Northern make, and the supply soon dried up. Many were then imported from Europe, and factories for making them were set up in the Confederacy. The well-known LaMat revolver, though patented by a Southerner, Dr. J. A. F. LaMat of New Orleans, was manufactured abroad and imported; but by November of 1863 factories in the Confederacy were turning out five hundred revolvers a month, and according to a prediction made by Gorgas at that time the number would be doubled within three or four months.[21] A North Carolinian invented a double-cylinder revolver which would shoot twenty-four times without reloading, but this weapon was more of a freak than a utility. Swords were hammered out in blacksmith-shops, where a half dozen a week was generally the capacity; more graceful ones were made in factories. A factory in Columbus turned out one hundred a week. Any blacksmith-shop could make bayonets, but soldiers disliked these weapons as they interfered with the use of the muzzle-loading rifles to which they were attached.

Vol. XXIX, Pt. II, 711. On March 1, 1865, Congress passed an act to set up a national foundry and arsenal in the Deep River region of North Carolina. Ramsdell (ed.), *Laws and Joint Resolutions*, 73.

20 Fuller and Steuart, *Firearms of the Confederacy*, 131.

21 *Official Records*, Ser. IV, Vol. II, 957.

A weapon suggestive of the bayonet was the pike, which had a brief and inglorious vogue. The shortage of rifles and muskets during the first year of the war led to the advocacy of this weapon, which was nothing more than a spear on the end of a pole six or seven feet long. Governor Brown put great faith in the pike. Declaring that the Federals could have been defeated at Fort Donelson if this weapon had been used against them, he called on mechanics throughout Georgia to begin their manufacture. Many were made in Macon, where one shop advertised for twenty thousand feet of ash lumber to be used in turning out the poles or staffs. Troops paraded, armed with pikes, and Congress authorized the raising of companies, battalions, and regiments to be armed with this weapon. A special kind of pike had a hooked knife attached which could be used to pull the enemy from his horse; it could also be removed and used as a bowie knife. A Baptist preacher from Tennessee devised a pike ten feet long, to be attached to the rifle, but to be folded up when not in use.

Among the early recruits bowie knives were even more desirable than revolvers or pistols, but when serious war began they disappeared. They were made in large numbers in blacksmith-shops and small factories. Their lease on life was lengthened a little by rumors that a Louisiana battalion at First Manassas had thrown away their rifles and with flourishing bowie knives had put the Yankees to flight. The inventive genius of someone devised what was called a "lasso-knife," which consisted of a bowie knife attached to the end of a rope to be thrown at the enemy.

In war plants there was always the danger of explosions and fires. A large part of the Tredegar Iron Works burned in 1863, but it was soon rebuilt; a unit of the powder works at Augusta blew up with 18,000 pounds of powder, killing nine men; the magazine in Jackson, Mississippi, exploded and killed about thirty-five men, women, and children; but the greatest disaster of this kind was the explosion which destroyed the Confederate Laboratory in Richmond, with from forty to fifty women reported killed.

Soldiers must not only be equipped with guns and ammunition; they must also be clothed and shod. For the first year the soldiers themselves provided their clothing; thereafter the government attempted to supply them through the Quartermaster Department.

Preparations were made in the summer of 1861, when the Clothing Bureau set up a large factory in Richmond, where the cloth was cut and farmed out to women who sewed together the uniforms in their homes. By the end of 1862 two thousand women were engaged in this work in Richmond, and many more were so employed in branch factories from Virginia to Mississippi. The chief quartermaster supply depot in the Lower South was Atlanta,[22] where by April, 1863, three thousand women were engaged in sewing soldiers' uniforms. Atlanta was also the seat of the main button manufactory of the Confederacy. Brass was rolled into sheets and then divided into strips from which buttons were cut by a die with the proper design.

The problem of providing shoes for soldiers, as well as for civilians, was never completely solved. Leather was always scarce, largely because of the carelessness of people in not saving the hides of slaughtered animals; but of the amount produced, the government requisitioned two thirds. Much of the leather came from Tennessee as long as the Confederates controlled that region. Contracts for shoes were made with private factories, which were aided by government exemption of cobblers from military service. The Quartermaster Department ran a shoe factory in Richmond which was producing 800 pairs a day in June, 1864; but the largest establishment of this kind in the Confederacy was in Columbus, Georgia, where 5,000 pairs a week were being made in November, 1863. A shoe factory was set up in Atlanta the same year, which accumulated enough leather from Middle Tennessee to produce 40,000 pairs during the first month of its existence.[23]

The war made Southerners as ingenious as Yankees. With ordinary leather scarce, they turned to squirrel skins for ladies' shoes and declared that such shoes were better than those made from calfskin. In Louisiana shoes and boots were made of alligator leather, and in many places the faithful dog was levied upon for its hide. A cobbler in Georgia offered a dollar apiece for dogskins. As early as 1861 canvas tops were used for shoes, and the next year a resourceful North Carolinian began the manufacture of wooden shoes.

22 *Ibid.*, Ser. I, Vol. XXIII, Pt. II, 772–73.
23 *Ibid.*, 767; Richmond *Daily Whig*, October 28, November 9, 1863; Richmond *Daily Examiner*, June 3, 1864; *Southern Cultivator* (Augusta, Athens, Atlanta), XXII (1864), 69; Ramsdell, "Control of Manufacturing by the Confederate Government," *loc. cit.*, 245.

He made them out of gum and poplar wood and insisted that they would last "until the next war." He turned out a hundred pairs a day and was still unable to supply the demand. It was reported that a Texan invented a wooden shoe with a hinge in the sole, for easy walking.

The impetus and enthusiasm for manufacturing war materials might easily carry over into the realm of manufactories in general as a policy to be adopted by the Confederacy not only in war but to be continued when peace should come. In fact, the rise of industrial enthusiasm went on contemporaneously with the rise of war industries. The South had long been aware of its industrial weakness, and some men, like William Gregg, the South Carolina factory master, were bold enough to cry out for remedies. Many rued the day they had refused to heed him, for now the people scurried around to find those manufactories which they had refused to provide for themselves, content to pay tribute to the North in these matters. "We were so poor, and so helpless," said a Mississippi editor, "the Yankees had to take care of us like so many children, or so many dependents. . . . Let us resolve never more to be dependent on that people who are murdering us, and stealing our substance, and burning our homes." [24] The hum of machinery, the white sails of the merchant ship, and the smoke of the steam frigate should be as pleasant as the whistle of the plowboy. The day when agriculture monopolized the South's interest would soon be over, and the rise of manufactures and a mechanical class would teach the Southerner to rise above the position "to which elegant indolence and aristocratic conceit had assigned him." [25] Just because the North had made industrialism its god, the South should not be blinded to its advantages. The Confederacy would now begin to make the many articles "heretofore imported from the North"—all except wooden nutmegs and cucumber seeds of which the Yankees were welcome to continue a monopoly. Congressman John Perkins, Jr., of Louisiana declared, "Political independence, without commercial independence, will be an abstraction"; [26] and Alfred O. P. Nicholson, Tennessee statesman, editor, and judge, made this prophecy in

24 Jackson *Daily Mississippian,* April 14, 1863.
25 Charleston *Daily Courier,* February 19, 1864.
26 Charleston *Mercury,* January 14, 1862.

1861: "We shall have our own navy, our own commercial marine, our own seamen, our own factories, our own manufactures, our own bankers, and reap from our own products those immense profits which the North has so long enjoyed. . . . No people ever had such brilliant prospects after victory.—Along with our political, commercial and financial independence, we will have all that can make a nation great, powerful and happy." [27]

In the fall of 1861 the *Merchants and Manufacturers Journal* sprang up in New Orleans to promote this new industrialism. In February of the preceding year the Direct Trade and Cotton Spinners' Convention of Georgia had met in Atlanta to promote trade with Europe. The following April it reconvened and after electing the industrialists William Gregg president and Daniel Pratt vice-president, and changing its name to the Manufacturing and Direct Trade Association of the Confederate States, determined to send a cargo of goods to Europe. It appointed a committee to urge Congress to allow the importation of cotton machinery duty-free for two years. A commercial convention, made up of four hundred delegates from nine states, met in Macon in October, 1861, to promote trade and manufactures. Even the old agriculturalists were capitulating; the officers of the Planters' Convention of the South, which had convened previously in Nashville and in Holly Springs, in planning a meeting in Memphis for early 1862 proposed the encouragement of commerce and manufactures equally with agriculture. Congress finally passed an act in 1863 allowing the importation of all machinery for cotton and wool manufactures duty-free for the duration of the war.

Southerners everywhere habitually boasted of every new manufactory they heard of, magnified its importance, and invariably announced that the product was superior to its Yankee prototype by far. In November, 1861, Secretary Memminger sent out a circular to towns and cities asking for information on all new manufactories started since the war and on all old ones that had been enlarged. Newspapers frequently carried stories and statistics of the various articles being manufactured and where; but out of all of this information noised around, the actual product that might have been of most value to the Confederacy, had it been able to

[27] Richmond *Daily Whig*, October 28, 1861.

establish its independence, was not the rudimentary manufactories that were getting started but rather the changed attitude of the people toward manufactories—an enthusiasm that might well have made the South a region of balanced economy in peacetime. As the war wore on and unstable prices made speculation thrive, people with money did not invest it in factories to make new things but rather in trading in what already existed. In 1864 Gregg declared that not one new cotton mill had been established during the war.[28]

The most substantial new manufactories were those that produced for war needs; yet factories whose output satisfied both military and civilian requirements, such as textile mills, did greatly increase their production. Gregg's mills in South Carolina and the Eagle Manufacturing Company in Columbus were outstanding examples of such establishments. Cotton was, of course, plentiful; the chief concern of the textile mills was the wool supply. Before the fall of Vicksburg and the severance of the Confederacy, wool from Texas came in abundance to the mills of Virginia and the Carolinas, but thereafter the small flocks of sheep east of the Mississippi must fulfill the needs. Farmers were begged not to kill their sheep for mutton, but to save them for their wool.

There was a standing scarcity of paper, which grew more severe with the passing of time. People and the government resorted to every conceivable device to satisfy this need. For writing and print paper they used crude brown paper, wrapping paper, leaves out of old ledger books, wallpaper, and backs of old letters. They turned old envelopes inside out to serve again; after filling all available space they often turned the sheet around and wrote crosswise; and some wrote in a small, almost undecipherable script. They wrote on paper captured from the enemy, and sometimes knowingly or not they used letter paper blaring forth in its watermarks such patriotic symbols as the United States shield or the screaming American eagle. One editor wrote his editorials on an old slate he had used as a schoolboy. Most newspapers by 1862 had resorted to the half sheet. Various paper mills were set up and paper was imported, but the need was never satisfied. In 1863 there were twenty paper mills in the Confederacy, calling for rags which they never received

---

[28] Augusta *Weekly Constitutionalist*, April 2, 1862; Augusta *Daily Chronicle & Sentinel*, May 26, 1864.

in sufficient quantities. A Georgia editor suspected that paper could be made from wood pulp, but no one acted at this time on the suggestion; an Alabamian tried to promote the manufacture of paper from cotton stalks.

The lack of a sufficient supply of good paper did not prevent Blanton Duncan from setting up a large establishment in Columbia to engage in lithographing and fine printing. He secured in Europe skilled engravers and workmen, but his services were largely monopolized by the Confederate government in printing its currency. A few of his lithographic caricatures of Yankees were exhibited in the show windows of stores in Richmond.

An industry which had long thrived and was to continue to do so through the war was the manufacture of chewing and smoking tobacco. It was confined almost entirely to Virginia, with Richmond and Lynchburg as the chief centers. As marching armies interfered with the raw supply, some of the manufacturers undoubtedly stretched out their product through adulterations, which led a South Carolina editor to call for a chemist to analyze the product and let him know what he was smoking. He believed it was a combination of sumac, Jimson weeds, moss, and fodder, with a slight sprinkling of tobacco. To aggravate the shortage in Manchester, across the river from Richmond, a fire in 1864 consumed a large tobacco factory, its warehouses filled with Confederate-owned tobacco, entailing a loss of about $4,000,000. Some of the well-known brands of smoking and chewing tobacco of the time were Killickinick, Sally Ward, Dixie, Rose Bud, Parlor Luxury, Okefenokee, Southern Star, Mattaponi, Wedding Cake, Dominion, Diadem of Old Virginia, Nelly Gray, Honey-dew, Christian's Comfort, Heart's Delight, Cousin Sally, and Perfect Love. Cigarettes made their appearance about the end of the war, an importation from Europe, but those who had grown up on the pipe and the plug got little satisfaction from this new way of using tobacco.[29]

To meet the needs for oil both for lubrication and illumination, Southerners resorted to many makeshifts and "remarkable discoveries of products better than what the Yankees formerly sold." Railways, factories, and newspaper plants were soon in dire need of

[29] Charleston *Daily Courier*, February 25, 1862; March 24, 1864; Richmond *Daily Examiner*, September 12, 1864; Richmond *Daily Whig*, April 13, 1864.

lubricating oil, as the petroleum products and sperm oil of the North were cut off. There were known petroleum deposits on the Little Kanawha in Virginia, but during the war there was neither time nor ability to develop them. For lubricants, apart from any that might run the blockade, the Confederates used oils made from castor beans, peanuts, cottonseed, and fish. As for illumination, many people did as they had always done; they went to bed soon after darkness; but for those who were accustomed to lighting their homes with coal-oil (kerosene) lamps, there were many hardships in store. Some, like the residents of Chapel Hill, North Carolina, never solved the riddle, as a resident of that village recorded the fact that she could walk the whole length of the town at night and not see lights in a half-dozen houses.[30] Unaffected were those who used candles made of beeswax or from the myrtlewax, bayberry, or candleberry shrub; but for those who enjoyed lamps cottonseed oil and palmetto oil were developed. A lamp was constructed which, it was asserted, would successfully burn lard. In 1862 the newspapers began to carry this advertisement: "Eureka! Eureka! A Substitute for Coal Oil!" It was distilled from pitch and could be burned in an ordinary lamp.[31] But the most persistently popularized oil was something called "terebene," distilled from rosin but containing some turpentine (which could be used alone, though it left an unpleasant odor). It was claimed that terebene might be burned in kerosene lamps and that it left no smell. Most Southern cities continued to be lighted with gas, now made from pine knots instead of coal as formerly.

Before the war no friction (lucifer) matches had been made in the South. Now with the Northern supply cut off, enterprising Southerners from Richmond to Galveston undertook their manufacture. A merchant in Jackson, Mississippi, frankly told his customers that not one in five would strike, though these so-called "Rebel Matches" were advertised as better than the Yankee product.

The many articles which Southerners had formerly bought from

[30] Cornelia P. Spencer, *The Last Ninety Days of the War in North Carolina* (New York, 1866), 244.

[31] Macon *Daily Telegraph*, April 10, 1862; Kate Cumming, *A Journal of Hospital Life in the Confederate Army of Tennessee, from the Battle of Shiloh to the End of the War . . .* (Louisville, 1866), 122.

the North must now be made in the South, and few there were which were not advertised as manufactured there. Cards for preparing cotton to be spun into thread were in great demand and were widely manufactured, as were spinning wheels which completed the process. Sacks, much in demand for grain, were made in Columbus; towels, in Troup County, Georgia; blankets, in Montgomery; socks for soldiers, in Columbus and Columbia; wooden buttons, in Columbus; and bonnet frames, in Newberry, South Carolina. A shoe-peg factory in Staunton could convert a maple tree into pegs before a stammering man could say "Jack Robinson," reported a Richmond paper in 1863; and in Columbus a machine was making knitting needles "almost as fast as a man can pick them up," having already, in 1864, made sixty thousand sets. In Montgomery a factory was turning out a thousand hats a week for the government, which was also taking all the hats made by a factory in Scottsville, Virginia; two hat factories in Richmond were making better hats than those "rushed into the market by Jew blockade-runners"; in many homes ladies' hats were being made of pine needles, palmetto leaves, straw, and corn shucks; and Joseph A. Turner, a planter and editor of Putnam County, Georgia, was making hats from the fur of rabbit, coon, fox, otter, mink, beaver skins, "and all other skins that have fur upon them." [32]

Though soap was widely made in the household, a shortage was soon felt, and to satisfy this need soap factories sprang up in Dalton, Augusta, and Little Rock. Though they made a "superior article," they never made enough, and in January, 1865, General Lee was complaining of the great suffering of his army for soap: "The neglect of personal cleanliness has occasioned cutaneous diseases to a great extent in many commands." [33] Large kaolin deposits in Augusta County, Virginia, led to the organization of a company which promised soon to be making plates, pitchers, cups, saucers, and other chinaware. A factory in Sandersville, Georgia, was manufacturing two hundred cyprus buckets a day by 1862—all for the government. A need for glassware was keenly felt but difficult to

[32] Columbus *Times*, December 28, 1864; Putnam County (Ga.) *Countryman*, October 27, 1862. Hats were also made in Statesville, North Carolina, and in Jackson, Mississippi.

[33] *Official Records*, Ser. I, Vol. XLVI, Pt. II, 1099.

satisfy. Hospitals and medical purveyors were almost frantic in their appeals for bottles, vials, and other articles made of glass. By 1862 Columbus, so prolific as a manufacturing center, had set up a glass factory soon to be followed by one in Savannah. Before the end of 1863 a glass factory, which produced bottles, windowpanes, lamp chimneys, and other glassware, had begun operations in Richmond. The steeple of the old Presbyterian Church in Petersburg was converted into a shot tower from which two thousand to four thousand pounds of lead were dropped a week.

Nature favored Northerners in only one respect, the Southerner thought; it gave them a monopoly of ice. But not quite so, for Virginia and even regions farther south had winters cold enough to make possible the harvesting of this article. The great fear that the hospitals would be left without ice led to a campaign in Virginia to induce people to save as much of it as possible. By-passing the climate, ice machines developed about this time by Captain Camille Girardey began making ice in Augusta—a ton a day in 1864. It sold for $5.00 a pound.

In New Orleans a factory began building streetcars in 1861; the little village of Lynchburg, South Carolina, made from fifty to seventy-five wagons a year; Enterprise and Canton, towns in Mississippi, made wagons and ambulances—about sixty a week; and Spartanburg made pleasure carriages.

Lead pencils, "as good as Faber's," were made in Greensboro, Alabama; knives and forks, in Macon and Raleigh; brooms, in the village of Davidson College, North Carolina; blacksmith bellows and all sorts of household furniture, in Macon; lampblack, umbrellas, and looking glasses, in Charleston. Baby carriages, each one "worth two of the yankee concerns heretofore purchased," were manufactured in Sandersville, Georgia.[34]

This enthusiasm for manufacturing everything made in the North or devising a substitute for it found additional expression in the large number of applications for patents. The Confederacy set up the Patent Office in the Department of Justice, and soon applications for patents numbered about seventy a month. In all, the num-

[34] Newspapers were sprinkled with items on manufactories. Another kind of enterprise which rapidly expanded was life insurance, nineteen companies being incorporated in Georgia alone.

ber granted was about 266, though the number of applications was more; many people had bizarre ideas which were worthless. "There are at least forty inventions, each of them infallible, for totally demolishing the Yankee fleet and army," declared the Richmond *Enquirer*.[35] In fact, a large number of the applications for patents had to do with weapons of war—thirteen small-arms patents were taken out. A machine was invented which would turn out 120 Minié balls a minute by the simple operation of a boy turning a crank; another machine was designed, to be operated by three men, which would make 42,500 percussion caps an hour.

Indeed, the South had become Yankeeized, at least in its own mind. In trying to beat the Yankees on the battlefield, it would also beat them at home. It could make anything produced in the North —the one hundred and one articles, and if necessary, one hundred and two. As impressive as the list of articles made in the Confederacy seemed, some of them were more talked about than real; for when the war was over there were no great factories, either for war or peace, that could be pointed to as the solid basis on which a New South would rest. They had never existed.

[35] Richmond *Semi-Weekly Enquirer*, March 13, 1863.

CHAPTER XI

PRICES, PROFITS, AND LABOR

THE steady rise in the price of everything for sale came to be the root of almost all evil in the Confederacy. Although the oversupply of money was the chief cause of high prices, there were other factors; for even before paper money came to flood the markets, prices began to advance. Because the supply of commodities, as well as the supply of money, affects prices, the announcement of the blockade threw people into a panic. They feared all imported articles might now become scarce. Those who would raise prices could now easily make the blockade the scapegoat. This excuse spread so widely that it became a joke. A Negro fiddler in defending his advance from $1.00 to $1.50 explained that since the blockade "de price ob rosum had riz"; and the mountaineer who brought his chestnuts down to Atlanta in the fall of 1861 and charged twenty-five cents a peck instead of the customary fifty cents a bushel answered the question of why he had increased the price with "yes, but dad fetch it, there wan't that infernal block-*cade* on 'em then." [1]

By the autumn of 1861 prices were becoming disturbed in a few commodities, and thereafter more articles were drawn into the whirlwind until by the middle of 1862 almost everything had been caught up. Prices skyrocketed still further as fear of defeat led to a lack of faith in Confederate money, thus adding another factor to its oversupply and the scarcity of commodities. Near the end, prices became fantastic and meant nothing. Not only were prices high but, on account of transportation difficulties, they were not uniform. This situation led to more discontent. Thus, in 1864 prices in Columbia were about a fifth of what they were in Richmond, where

[1] Atlanta *Southern Confederacy*, November 3, 1861.

219

they were always the highest in the Confederacy. The disparity between country districts and cities was even greater. In 1864 corn in some of the rural communities of South Carolina was selling for $2.00 a bushel while in Charleston it was bringing $20.00. Syrup could be had in the cane region of Georgia for $1.00 a gallon; the same amount in Richmond would cost $50.00. So uncertain were prices even within a given region, that a person in a Georgia town discovered that one cobbler would make him a pair of shoes for $5.00, whereas another wanted $15.00 for a like pair.

As has been noted, prices did not rise uniformly over the Confederacy, nor did the prices of all articles begin rising at the same time. The first to respond to the unsettled times, and most violently, was salt, so necessary to human welfare and now cut off by the blockade. In Athens, Georgia, it was selling in January, 1861, for eighty cents a bushel. The following August it rose to $1.25, and by the end of the year it was $3.75. The next month it doubled, and by the following May (1862) it was selling for $25.00 a bushel; at the end of 1862 it brought $30.00. On the other hand, cotton was one of the last articles to respond. On this same market it consistently remained from seven to ten cents a pound until December, 1862, when it jumped to seventeen cents. It continued to rise until by the middle of 1863 it was about forty cents. Thereafter regular quotations on everything were given up everywhere, as market conditions were too uncertain to make any quotation reliable.

Eventually it became a matter of news, chagrin, or gossip as to what any particular article might be selling for. In 1863 oranges were selling for $2.00 apiece in Richmond, chestnuts at fifty cents a dozen in Lynchburg, and peanuts at one cent apiece in Georgia. The next year coconuts cost $10.00 apiece in Mobile. "I saw a *ham* sell today for $350" in Richmond, War-clerk Jones wrote in his diary, February 20, 1864. In fact, the price of meat began to rise in the fall of 1861, when bacon, which customarily sold for twelve cents a pound, rose to thirty cents. By the fall of 1862 a Tennessean, having decided that meat was too high to buy, advertised in a newspaper for a dog "to hunt our meat with," and the editor observed, "A dog that will hunt coons, possums, kill a sheep occasionally will command a good price." [2] In the summer of 1862, bakers in Rich-

[2] Putnam County (Ga.) *Countryman,* November 17, 1862.

mond were charging $1.25 apiece for their loaves, and as the Confederacy neared its end in March, 1865, with flour at $1,200.00 a barrel, they made three sizes to sell at $1.00, $2.00, and $3.00 apiece—"The first is only visible by microscopick aid; the second can be discerned with the naked eye, and the third can be seen with outline and shape distinct." [3]

The prices which were momentarily prevailing in Richmond on December 21, 1863, were: apples, $65.00 to $75.00 a barrel; onions, $30.00 a bushel; Irish potatoes, $6.00 to $9.00 a bushel; corn, $11.00 a bushel (a soldier's pay for one month); wheat, $20.00 a bushel; sugar, $3.50 a pound; bacon, $3.00 a pound; butter, $4.00 a pound; beef, $1.50 a pound; and eggs, $3.00 a dozen.[4] Six months later these prices had doubled or more; and a felt hat would now cost $125, a gentleman's suit of clothes, $1,500; a lady's bonnet, $250; and a gallon of whisky, $100. But to buy the last article by the drink at a saloon would be much more expensive; a soldier wrote home in 1863, "It would cost about fifty Dollars to get tight here." A party of nine dined sumptuously at a Richmond restaurant in the fall of 1863, for they had various kinds of soups, fish, oysters, vegetables, meats, and such fowls as partridges, robins, plovers, and woodcocks, and also wines, liquors, and cigars. The cost of the evening's repast was $631.50.[5] The salary of a Confederate private had he begun his services before Fort Sumter in 1861 and continued to Appomattox in 1865 would not have paid for this dinner. In 1864 a cup of coffee at some of the restaurants in Richmond sold for $5.00. This price seemed exorbitant to a news reporter, who calculated the profit on a pound of coffee, which cost at this time $10, to be $240. "This literal reduction of facts to figures," he wrote, "we put upon record as part of the history of the times, and for the astonishment of generations yet to come. The *acme* of extortion is reached in this if it never was before. And yet the extortioners can look you in the face without blushing." [6]

Prices of slaves were most confusing, for two conflicting forces clashed. The more likely the Confederacy was to lose the war, the

---

[3] Richmond *Daily Examiner*, March 29, 1865.
[4] *Ibid.*, December 21, 1863.
[5] Ross, *Visit to the Cities and Camps of the Confederate States*, 194–95.
[6] Richmond *Daily Examiner*, March 18, 1864.

more worthless its money became; but at the same time the value of a slave should tend to vanish, for if the North won he became free. Yet in the summer of 1864 an eight-year-old girl sold in Augusta for $2,650, and one eighteen years old brought $4,250. A Negro man sold for $3,980. Slave prices might be considered a barometer of faith in ultimate victory and conversely an indicator of the worthlessness of Confederate money.

The constantly rising prices led hotels to resort to the "European plan," as they were unwilling to risk setting a table for patrons who would pay a fixed rate by the week or month. It was a joke of the times that a certain hotelkeeper had not allowed Robert Toombs to pay for his night's lodging before retiring, on the grounds that prices might rise during the night. As prices of commodities rose, naturally the prices of services likewise advanced. Rents became excessively high. Physicians doubled their fees by 1864; in the summer of that year some Virginia doctors raised their rates for a visit from $6.00 to $45.00 "to keep up with the price of wheat and corn." At this time Richmond barbers, mostly mulattoes, charged their customers $1.00 for a shave, $2.00 for a haircut, and $4.00 for a beard trim and haircut. Even beggars went up on their demands. In earlier times it was "Mister, give me a penny"; in 1865 it was "Mister, give me a dollar." Express charges became extremely high, especially on valuables. A citizen on calculating the cost of expressing $15,000 in bonds from Kingston, Georgia, to Montgomery, discovered that it would be more than the expenses of a person taking them there by train. Near the end of the war a person paid $2,500 for the hire of two scrubby mules and a ramshackle wagon to take him a distance of twenty-five miles—this was at the rate of $100 a mile!

Most people could not display as much lighthearted good nature on the rise of prices as the versemaker who wrote in 1862:

> *O! goodness me, what times these is—*
> *They cut us deep with want's dull scissor;*
> *All sorts of things to live on's riz,*
> *And clothes and shoes and hats is riz-er:*
> *So they is.*[7]

[7] Columbus *Weekly Enquirer*, September 9, 1862.

People saw the value of their money vanishing in high prices. Why must there be high prices, especially on commodities produced within the Confederacy? Who had hatched this conspiracy against the welfare of the Confederate people? These questions were asked as early as the fall of 1861 and various answers were given. Some said that agents of the army's Commissary Bureau, people who had no more business sense than the "Comanchee Indians knew of mathematics," had gone through the country buying up anything at any price, and had thus started the rise in prices. Others said that the merchants had first increased their prices, but the merchants denied that they had done so until the farmers had begun to charge more for country produce. The farmers pointed the finger of accusation at the merchants, the manufacturers, and the traders, and charged them with having begun this vicious circle. Pollard, the Virginia critic of all that made up the contemporary scene, declared that the initiative was taken "by Jews and foreign adventurers who everywhere infested the Confederacy." [8]

In fact, anyone who bought and sold commodities was in the movement which made high prices, for basically money was becoming cheaper and cheaper as the amount of it increased and as faith in it was lost with the approach of defeat. There was the further fact that supplies of many articles were growing smaller, either because they were cut off by the blockade or because upset conditions at home prevented their production. With prices mounting, anyone who bought an article and held it for a short time could sell it for much more than he had paid for it. What many critics did not see was the fact that though the trader may have sold it for much more than it cost, he got the higher price in cheaper money, and that in reality he may have received less purchasing power than he had originally paid. Everyone who engaged in business was in a sense a speculator, for as a Richmond factor wrote his principal in December, 1862, "no one can tell what will be the price of any article even the next day." [9]

Such a situation was an open invitation to speculators, who would not simply accept the opportunities for quick gains that naturally came, but who would make opportunities. It held out a terrible

[8] Pollard, *Second Year of the War*, 237.
[9] Hunt & James, Richmond, to Mrs. Massie, December 10, 1862, in Massie Papers.

temptation leading to a widespread corruption of public morality and to the disruption of the general welfare. John Milton, governor of Florida, wrote Secretary of War Seddon in January, 1864, of the decadence of public and private virtue. "The corruptions of office, manifested by suddenly acquired wealth," he declared, "have generated a wide spread desire for speculation and wealth, which have overcome the obligations of patriotism and endangered the very existence of the Confederate States. Notwithstanding the alleged depreciation of the currency, people of all ages and conditions seem wild in its accumulation, regardless of consequences and careless as to the result, though it lead to the destruction of their liberties." [10] A soldier wrote a friend in early 1862 that he expected "to speculate a little in a safe way," and a South Carolinian informed his wife that he had been speculating in stocks and bonds and only in that way had he made money. Most emphatically he had not been speculating in food and articles of clothing: "I should despise myself if in this time of our country's need I should do anything to put up the price of a single article of necessity. I leave that to the Jews and extortioners of whom there are unfortunately too many among us." Yet he knew a group of speculators who had made about $300,000 in dealing in food and clothing, and there was "a good deal of hard feeling and hard talk about them." [11]

The way of the speculator was to get control of as much of a commodity as possible in a city or given community, drive the people into a panic by the cry of shortages, and then raise his prices to any extent he pleased. Outcries were shouted against engrossers of commodities as early as the fall of 1861. Speculators began on salt, and by the end of 1862 they were busily getting control of all the cotton possible, expecting that the blockade would be broken or that the Confederacy would win its independence soon. Claiming to be agents of the Confederate government, they went through the country districts buying up cotton and other commodities. Such warnings as this were soon spread against them: "If you do not know them to be 'O.K.,' better not trust them." [12] Cotton was con-

---

[10] John Milton to James A. Seddon, January 11, 1864, in "Commissary Activities and War Correspondence, 1863–1865" (Florida State Archives, Tallahassee).

[11] *Burckmyer Letters, March, 1863–June, 1865*, pp. 236, 238.

[12] Sandersville *Central Georgian*, May 13, 1863.

sidered a safer investment than Confederate bonds by the speculator as well as by the careful investor. "It is a favorite article with Jews," said an Englishman living in Georgia, "and the country swarms with them—and other speculators." [13] The governor of Louisiana seized coffee and pork, which speculators had bought up in New Orleans, and Governor Brown of Georgia seized a large amount of salt. Six months after war started, speculators in Richmond bought up the nail supply and increased the price from $4 a keg to $10. Richmond speculators also tried to get control of the wheat crop in that vicinity in 1863, which led to this blast from the editor of the Richmond *Examiner:* "Had these contemptible wretches the power, they would bottle the universal air and sell it at so much a bottle." [14] The fishmongers of Richmond combined, set the price of their product, and sent "plug-uglies" to beat any dealers who dared to undersell. As soon as the news of the fall of Vicksburg reached Richmond, "the speculators broke to the streets, like vultures after carrion, ransacking and buying up every barrel of sugar that could be found." [15] Gambling on the probability of a great battle in the spring of 1862, speculators bought all the mourning goods in New Orleans, it was charged.[16] There was nothing too small or too large to escape them, and every community seemed to have had a few. A Richmond editor declared that "every man in the community is swindling everybody else, and everybody else swindling him." [17] Frequent and widespread accusations against railroads charged that they were catering to these speculators by making available to them most freight space not taken up by the government and that sometimes they managed to deny the government shipping space in order to sell it to the speculators at a higher price.

Farmers early came in for sharp criticism. They were charged with holding back their crops from the markets to create a shortage and secure higher prices. Senator Wigfall of Texas accused them of being the worst extortioners of all. He admitted, though, that cheap

[13] Barnsley to John R. Reid, March 26, 1863, in Barnsley Papers (University of Georgia Library).

[14] Richmond *Daily Examiner,* August 27, 1863.

[15] *Ibid.,* July 16, 1863.

[16] Charleston *Daily Mercury,* March 22, 1862.

[17] Richmond *Daily Examiner,* March 31, 1863.

money had made them speculators. "Make money cheap and you make men cheap," he exclaimed.[18] The hostility of city people toward the rural areas became widespread and marked. Country people resented the charges of extortion and defended their prices by citing the high cost of all articles bought in the towns and cities. A Richmond factor for a Virginia planter wrote in 1863, "Every thing is selling so high now that you can have any quantity of money if you will send down apples, Flour, Bacon, Potatoes, Peas, Cabbage or indeed anything to eat, of which I suppose you have plenty." [19] Another reason why farmers were loath to bring their products to market was the fear that this material would be seized by government agents who had the right to impress farm products for about half the market price.[20] Undoubtedly some farmers became sullen and refused to raise more than enough for their own needs; yet generally they were co-operative, and some, like the farmers of Washington County, Georgia, condemned high farm prices and called for conventions of farmers to set uniform prices for the state.

Although there was no general prejudice against the Jews in the Confederacy, there were a few sources of a bitter hostility to them, based largely on the charges that they were merciless speculators, army slackers, and blockade-runners across the land frontiers to the North. Outstanding opponents of the Jews were the Richmond *Examiner* and a sprinkling of other newspapers; John B. Jones, the war clerk who kept a diary; and Congressman Foote. The *Examiner* declared that the Confederacy was overrun by them and that they were buying up everything that was worth speculating on. In 1863 it charged that they had bought up two thirds of the cotton in Alabama, that they had seized practically all the mercantile business in Richmond, as, indeed, in many other towns, and that they "have

---

[18] *Ibid.*, December 31, 1863.

[19] Hunt, Richmond, Va., to Mrs. Massie, February 10, 1863, in Massie Papers.

[20] The Athens *Southern Watchman*, March 1, 1865, quoted the following prices paid on the market at Athens, Georgia, and the prices the government paid through impressment:

Flour, barrel	$200.00—$65.00		Wheat, bushel	$30.00—$12.50	
Bacon, pound	5.00—	2.25	Lard, pound	6.00—	2.25
Beef, pound	2.00—	.70	Sweet potatoes, bushel	15.00—	2.75
Corn, bushel	25.00—	3.50	Irish potatoes, bushel	25.00—	7.00
Meal, bushel	25.00—	3.50			

the chief seats in every Main street and Broad street throughout the land." [21] The *Examiner* knew a Jew who in 1861 had started a business in Richmond "with a stock in trade consisting of a few plugs of 'pig-tail' and a jug of whiskey." He had sold out for $300,000 recently and gone back North. Of Richmond business during the war another observer remarked: "Israel and David, and Moses and Jacob, and Hyman and Levy, and Guggenheimer and Rosenheimer, and other names innumerable of the Ancient People, were prominent, instead of the old Anglo-Saxon which had designated the most important business firms of Richmond." [22] It was a common saying that one would "meet more Jews in Charleston than . . . in Jerusalem," gathered there to buy goods that had run the blockade.[23] Foote declared that nine tenths of all traders in the towns of the Confederacy were Jews and that, if nothing were done about it, "the end of the war would probably find nearly all the property of the Confederacy in the hands of Jewish Shylocks." Robert B. Hilton, Congressman from Florida, charged that Jews "had swarmed here as the locusts of Egypt. They ate up the substance of the country, they exhausted its supplies, they monopolized its trade. They should be dragged into military service." [24] Jones said that since Jews had no nationality, all wars were harvests for them, and he charged that they had injured the Confederate "cause more than the armies of Lincoln." [25]

They were especially charged with evading military service, and when Richmond now and then seemed near capture and all men were being pressed into local defense units, Jewish traders made desperate efforts to secure passports for the North from Judah P. Benjamin, the Jewish Secretary of State, or from John A. Campbell in the War Department. Many of them succeeded and some failed, but in either case at considerable expense to themselves. It was not unusual for them to pay as high as $10,000 for conveyances and bribery of frontier guards to get across the Potomac. In 1863, $3,000 was paid "by a couple of fleeing Israelites, whose principal baggage

21 Richmond *Daily Examiner,* December 5, 1863.
22 Putnam, *Richmond During the War,* 105.
23 *Two Months in the Confederate States, Including a Visit to New Orleans under the Domination of General Butler. By an English Merchant* (London, 1863), 126.
24 *Southern Historical Society Papers,* XLVII (1930), 122, 123.
25 Jones, *Rebel War Clerk's Diary,* I, 221.

was gold and 'greenbacks.' " [26] The next year Lewis Hyman, a Richmond Jew who had sold out his business, was seized by pickets as he attempted to make his way North and was relieved of $20,000 in gold. These Jewish traders were even more detested by the Northern armies of invasion, for in their trading activities they often supplied the South with much-needed commodities.[27] In the Virginia region Jewish traders, with passes given by the Confederate authorities, carried on a traffic which War-clerk Jones estimated at $50,000 a day.[28]

The great influx of Jewish traders of German and Polish origins during the secession and early war days gave all Jews an evil reputation. Yet both Jew and Gentile came to the defense of the old Jewish population of culture and standing, many of whom were descendants of colonial ancestors. "Do you now know," inquired a Jew, "that there are in all the large cities, both North and South, Jews of the highest character, natives of the soil, who would scorn a mean action as much as any Christian in the land?" [29] A Charleston editor reminded his readers that there were extortioners and speculators other than Jews, and an Augusta editor declared that nobody could "impugn their patriotism in this war." Henry Hirsch, a Jewish merchant of Marietta, Georgia, refused to sell his salt to Atlanta speculators at $65 a sack but let the people in his own community have it at $50; a Jewish congregation in Richmond gave $1,230 for the support of soldiers' families; and a group of Jewish

26 Richmond *Daily Examiner*, December 31, 1863.

27 General Grant forbade trains to carry Jewish traders south. He declared they were "such an intolerable nuisance that the department must be purged of them." *Official Records*, Ser. I, Vol. XVII, Pt. II, 337. Voicing this prejudice, the Memphis correspondent of the Chicago *Times*, quoted in the Augusta *Daily Chronicle & Sentinel*, July 17, 1862, said: "The Israelites have come down upon the city [Memphis] like locusts. Every boat brings a load of the hooked-nosed fraternity, with mysterious boxes under their arms, and honied words on their tongues. Anything in the line of trade, up to a box of cigars, or a dozen papers of needles, may be obtained of these eager gentlemen at ruinous prices, for the purchaser."

28 Jones, *Rebel War Clerk's Diary*, I, 283. An Englishman observed that if the Jews "did not decamp from the Confederacy altogether, they found a thousand and one excuses for not bearing arms for the country that had enriched them, and in which perchance they had been born." "An English Combatant," *Battle-Fields of the South, from Bull Run to Fredericksburg; with Sketches of Confederate Commanders, and Gossip of the Camps* (London, 1863), 22.

29 Richmond *Daily Examiner*, January 5, 1863.

children in the same city decided that all the money they had been saving for a picnic should be used to aid wounded soldiers. Jews in Montgomery gave at the outbreak of the war $700 for the aid of soldiers' families, and so the story went.

The estimate that the Jews supplied ten thousand soldiers to the Confederate armies [30] was no doubt an exaggeration, but it could not be gainsaid that many Jews became Confederate soldiers and gave up their lives fighting for Confederate independence. In 1861 it was reported by newspaper correspondents that most regiments in the Virginia military area contained from twenty to fifty Jews; and the Jews in Columbus, Georgia, defended their patriotism by declaring that of the sixty-eight members of their faith of military age there, forty had volunteered.[31] Proof that the mass of Southerners had not hated the Jews as a race was evidenced in the strong hold that they acquired and maintained after the war in almost every small town of the South.

The manufacturers were no less caught up in this web of speculation than the farmers, the merchants, and the Jewish traders. On account of the rising cost of everything the manufacturer used, he was forced to raise the prices of what he produced and sold. The Manufacturers and Direct Trade Association of the Confederate States, with William Gregg as president and Enoch Steadman as secretary, declared in a session in Augusta, in November, 1862, that manufacturers could no longer sell to the Confederate government at prices fixed for a greater period than one month. As they generally sold to the government at a loss, they found it necessary to make up this deficit by charging a much higher price to civilians. But a Richmond editor pointed to the shameful fact that a bale of cotton which cost $40 sold for $210 when manufactured into cloth. Dr. John Bachman, a prominent Lutheran minister of South Carolina, became a greater crusader against the extortionate manufacturers than against the wicked devil himself.[32] Voices in many

---

[30] Augusta *Daily Constitutionalist*, August 4, 1864; Richmond *Daily Whig*, October 16, 1862; Meade, *Judah P. Benjamin*, 285.

[31] Columbus *Weekly Enquirer*, October 7, 1862.

[32] Charleston *Daily Courier*, May 16, October 22, November 24, 1862; Richmond *Semi-Weekly Enquirer*, June 14, 1864. The Manufacturers and Direct Trade Association of the Confederate States changed its name in 1864 to Manufacturers' Association of the Confederate States.

parts of the Confederacy warned grasping manufacturers that they were losing the good will which had earlier developed in the South for manufacturers and that their exorbitant prices would be remembered when peace came, for then foreign goods would be bought.

The manufacturers defended themselves by declaring that their real profits were very small and at times nonexistent. Their machinery was wearing out and it could not be replaced in wartime, and money which might be reserved for that purpose was currently expended as profits. They asserted that by the end of the war most mills would be worn out, with bankruptcy staring the owners in the face. Proof that manufacturing was not a lucrative business was seen in the fact that little capital was being invested in it. Joseph A. Turner, who manufactured hats in addition to running a newspaper on his plantation in Putnam County, Georgia, declared that everybody labeled as traitor and terrible extortioner anyone who made a living wage out of his business. "Our capitalists don't embark in manufactures," he explained, "because they do not believe either their reputations or their capital will be safe in such enterprise." [33] And Gregg, recalling with wounded feelings, that he had spent his life administering to the industrial welfare of the South and had trained two of his sons in the textile business and had planned to prepare a third, announced that he now advised all of them to go into some other occupation where they would not be called "rogues, thieves, and extortioners." [34] Some merchants, righteously indignant, announced that they were going out of business.

But, in fact, many manufacturers were making large profits, and one of the main reasons why more factories were not set up was the impossibility of getting machinery and skilled workmen for them. A stockholder in one of Gregg's factories reported in 1863 that it had "been making an immense amount of money during the war . . . and paid very large dividends in cash." He recently had sold stock of the par value of $500 for $4,750.[35] Mills in Petersburg, Virginia, were declaring from 50 per cent to 100 per cent dividends early in 1864, and the Manchester Cotton and Woolen Company,

[33] Putnam County (Ga.) *Countryman*, December 1, 1862.
[34] Charleston *Daily Courier*, December 12, 1862.
[35] *Burckmyer Letters, March, 1863–June, 1865*, p. 234.

near Richmond, declared a dividend of 25 per cent during the first quarter of 1862.[36] In 1863 the Virginia legislature investigated the profits of some large businesses in that state. It found that the Crenshaw Woolen Factory had declared during the previous year dividends of $530,000 on a capital of $200,000, holding undivided $100,000, and that the Belvidere Manufacturing Company, which made paper, had declared dividends of $175,000 in 1862 on a capital of $41,000. Since the war began a stockholder had received dividends amounting to $6,450 on a stock of $1,000.[37] These profits appear larger than they really were, as money was constantly depreciating.

A Georgia editor, who was barely able to meet the expenses of publishing his paper, believed that any business that could keep going in wartime was doing well enough. "No man should hope or ask to do more," he said, "when so many of his fellow-citizens are carrying the musket for eleven dollars a month." And then he uttered a wise saying, which nations seem never willing to accept as long as time and wars shall last: "It is doubtful if any man in these times, can pursue a speculative or money-making business, consistently with his duty to his country." [38]

The more discerning people drew a logical distinction between the manufacturer and the established merchant or trader on the one hand and the simon-pure speculator on the other. It was against this last person, who produced nothing and had no standing in any community as a businessman, that the choicest invectives were leveled. As early as October, 1861, a Georgian issued this blast against speculators: "If h—ll has any hotter place than another, or any particular corner especially heated, my prayer to God is, that every man (or pretended man) shall be consigned to that department, who speculates in food or clothing, and the necessaries of life, in these troublous times." [39] War-clerk Jones believed their avarice and cupidity "could only be excelled by ravenous wolves"; another critic used the epithet, "little whipper-snapper blear-eyed speculators"; President Davis declared "the attempt of groveling

[36] Richmond *Daily Whig*, April 10, 1862; January 22, 1864.
[37] Richmond *Daily Enquirer*, March 3, 1863.
[38] Macon *Daily Telegraph*, April 10, 1862.
[39] Athens *Southern Watchman*, October 23, 1861.

speculators to forestall the market and make money out of the life-blood of our defenders" had been responsible for high prices and shortages; and the inevitable versemaker had his say:

> *No beast, of which we ever read,*
> *Would prey upon his like;*
> *Whose craven heart, to feeling dead,*
> *Would 'gainst his species strike;*
> *'Tis left to man, man's high estate,*
> *To do the deed he'd execrate.*[40]

Some people advised the vigilance committees to proceed against the speculators, who, it was suggested, should forever be held as people apart. All money-makers should be grouped as speculators, and the future badge of distinction should be service to country, not to self; "property will be a despised thing, fortunate if it is not taken as a mark of the extortioner, and the reward of infamy." [41] That no one might forget, another suggested, "It would not be a bad idea to get up a Black Book, which should contain the names, in full, of all the great extortioners and Government swindlers, so that the mark of Cain might rest upon them and their descendants forever." [42]

High prices and speculation so upset the markets that many of the old, established mercantile businesses went out of existence. As stocks disappeared and could not be replenished business after business shrank in size or closed out. Before the end of 1862 only one of the three druggists of Warrenton, Virginia, was still in business; a bookstore in Augusta was said to have kept its last book and refused to sell it, though still remaining open. Business advertisements, which had customarily taken up a large space in the newspapers, first announced that all sales were for cash, and then soon disappeared altogether. A Georgia editor vividly described business conditions in his small town as they had developed by the beginning of 1864: "Nothing disturbs the 'solemn stillness' except now and then a rickety ox-cart whose unlubricated axles made melancholy music! Our great thoroughfare which once was crowded with country wagons laden with the rich products of a generous soil, is

[40] One of five stanzas, signed "Quixotte," *ibid.*, January 1, 1862.
[41] Richmond *Daily Examiner*, September 16, 1863.
[42] *Southern Literary Messenger*, XXXVII (1863), 182.

now bare and desolate—its stores closed—the noise of trade hushed —nothing to break the stillness, save now and then the voice of some descendant of Abraham 'jewing' a countrywoman, whose butter and eggs he considered too high at $3 per pound and $1.35 per dozen!" [43]

Instead of the customary methods of trade, cash and credit, primitive systems began to creep back out of the past. Now that money began to mean very little if anything definite, barter took its place. Manufacturing establishments partly paid their employees in food and raiment for which they had bartered some of their own output, whatever it might be. The Tredegar Iron Works swapped ironware to planters for food products, and a factory in Macon offered to exchange cotton yarn for six thousand pounds of bacon. Now and then a business that had something not of its own manufacture which could easily be swapped for something else did so: the armory at Selma announced that it would give one pound of sugar for two pounds of bacon; a dealer offered to swap salt for pork; and another offered to exchange three pounds of ice for one pound of butter. Even the Confederate government resorted to barter; in the latter part of 1864 it offered three hundred sheep for bacon at the ratio of one sheep for twenty pounds of bacon. Physicians, editors, and other professional men accepted their pay in country produce, and canal and railroad companies took such articles in payment for tickets.

Even more destructive of ordinary business methods was the auction, twin demon of speculation, defended by some as the only method of fixing a price for any article. The auction, in fact, scared people either into paying a third to a half more than a thing should have sold for or into not buying it at all. The old-line merchant now gave way to the auctioneer with his red flag. Anything that could be sold went under his hammer—farms, plantations, merchandise, and blockade goods of all kinds, cloth, needles, pins, tobacco. Manufacturers found it necessary to sell their output by auction; the wine

[43] Athens *Southern Watchman*, January 27, 1864. See also, Catherine C. Hopley [Sarah E. Jones, pseud.], *Life in the South; from the Commencement of the War. By a Blockaded British Subject. Being a Social History of those who Took Part in the Battles, from a Personal Acquaintance with them in their Homes. From the Spring of 1860 to August 1862* (London, 1863), II, 185; Ross, *Visit to the Cities and Camps of the Confederate States*, 173.

cellar of the late former President Tyler was sold at auction and brought $6,000; even the prices of stocks and bonds were established through auction sales.

Was there not some way to control prices? Many people anxiously asked this question. They might refuse to buy, as some suggested, and almost starve and wear rags; or they might lose their tempers and threaten violence to those asking exorbitant prices, as a mob did to a Baptist preacher in Richmond who attempted in 1864 to sell a barrel of flour for $500 and three bushels of meal for $100 a bushel. Various methods of regulation were seriously tried. Before the end of 1861 loud demands were made on Confederate, state, and municipal governments to fix prices. New Orleans did regulate the price of bread and the military authorities in Richmond regulated the price of many articles. In 1862 South Carolina attempted unsuccessfully to interest North Carolina and Georgia in establishing maximum prices for the necessities of life, but the next year the South Carolina legislature rejected the proposition as unworkable and unwise, as it defied the natural laws of trade—supply and demand. In Virginia there was great unrest over high prices, and War-clerk Jones warned that the "flames of insurrection may at any moment wrap this slumbering government in its destructive folds." None of the states attempted to regulate prices except as a part of the movement to suppress speculators and extortioners. They attempted to do this by forbidding the monopolizing of any of the necessities of life, or, in the words of the Georgia act, "receive exorbitant, unjust, or unreasonable prices" for such articles. All of these laws were unenforcible. In a few instances city ordinances against extortion resulted in punishment, as in Mobile where in 1864 a trader was convicted, fined $500, and sentenced to jail for three months. A determined effort was made in Congress in 1864 to regulate prices by extending to all purchasers the provisions of the act which fixed prices for articles purchased or impressed by the Confederate government. It was opposed on the ground that Congress had no constitutional right to pass such a law and in addition it would cause the mass of people throughout the Confederacy to cease producing more than their own needs.

Largely denied governmental protection against high prices, the people attempted to devise means of their own. Associations which would buy for their members without profit were formed. One of the best known of these efforts was the so-called "Danville Plan," whereby members bought shares in the association at $50 apiece, each share giving a right to buy a fixed amount. As a patriotic flourish with an anticipated practical turn, citizens of Enterprise, Mississippi, formed an organization in 1863 called the Confederate Society, and sought to popularize it throughout the Confederacy through the organization of chapters. Its members promised to buy and sell at low prices and to accept Confederate currency. This movement received the special blessings of President Davis. A few chapters were organized elsewhere but it secured no practical results.[44] In Virginia a movement grew up in 1863 to popularize what came to be called the Albemarle Platform, and it spread as far as Georgia before it also was engulfed by the swift current of events leading to financial, economic, and military collapse. According to this plan, adherents agreed to sell all surplus products at government prices and to report anyone refusing to do so, whereupon his surplus would be impressed by government agents; to sell nothing to speculators or distillers; to invest all surplus money in Confederate bonds; and to discourage desertion and help to restore deserters to the service. Some individual manufactories made efforts to hold down prices. In 1862 the Macon Manufacturing Company refused to sell its cloth to any merchant unless he promised not to dispose of it for more than twenty cents a yard.

Other elements in the population vitally concerned with economic conditions were wage earners and salaried workers. The latter suffered greater hardships than the former, for many of them worked for the Confederate government, which was very slow to adjust salaries to rising prices; and those who worked for state governments were no better placed. Jonathan Worth, treasurer of North Carolina, did not receive as salary a sixth of his living expenses by the end of 1864. Many of the skilled laborers in factories and ironworks, on railroads and in the telegraphic service, were natives of the North, and many returned home soon after the Confederacy was set up. Even had they remained, there still would have been a shortage of skilled workers in the Confederacy. Gregg

[44] Rowland (ed.), *Jefferson Davis, Constitutionalist*, VI, 40; Charleston *Daily Courier*, October 6, 16, November 8, 1863.

had a twelve-hour day in his factories and he offered workmen double wages for two more hours. A few laborers were secured from Europe, but some of them, and others, were later driven out by threats of the conscription laws. Wages varied according to skill and location, but a dollar a day was a common wage for many workers. For almost a year it still remained at that level, though the cost of manufactured products advanced in some cases as much as 1,000 per cent. In some factories wages increased a third or more during the first year. By 1862 wages in the larger towns and in all skilled work were from $10 to $15 a day.

Labor organizations and strikes were "Yankee innovations" and "abominations" and were practically unknown to the South until high prices during the Confederacy turned the laborer's mind in that direction, and before the war was over a keen labor consciousness had developed in some of the trades. Some Irish workmen in the Tredegar Iron Works struck for higher wages in the fall of 1861, setting off a series of strikes in the Confederacy which led to considerable agitation in various states to outlaw this method of intimidating employers. After the first year of the war, the Confederate government had a handy weapon which it did not refrain from using against strikers—the conscription act. In 1862 thirty workmen in a government harness factory struck because wages were not paid to them while they were being transferred to a new location. The same year, machinists in the Virginia and Tennessee Railroad shops in Lynchburg struck for $15 a day, which was refused them. They were enrolled in the army, but arrangements were later made for them to return to their work. In 1863 cobblers, who had been exempted from military service and were getting $16 a pair for making shoes, struck for $18. The editor of the Richmond *Examiner* advocated conscription if they were "not content with reasonable profit on their labour." [45]

Women were as vigorous as the men in fomenting strikes. In

[45] Richmond *Daily Examiner*, December 10, 1863. A shoemaker exempted from military duty was required to sign a form stating that "the product of my labor while exempt from military service shall not be sold, exchanged or bartered for a price exceeding the cost of production and seventy-five per cent. profit thereon." One of these forms may be found in "Civil War Period—Letters and Folders" (University of Texas Library), No. 6.

December, 1863, the women workers at the Confederate States Laboratory, who were getting only $2.40 a day, struck for $3.00. Their wages were raised so that by October, 1864, unmarried women were receiving $5.00 a day and married women $7.00. The former now demanded the same wages as the latter and struck to enforce their demands. The married women supported the strike, all were dismissed, and three hundred new workers were sought.[46] This was a strike against the government, but it was not quite as serious as the case of the Richmond postal clerks—civil servants of the government—who were admittedly not making a living wage and struck for higher pay. The editor of the Richmond *Examiner* declared that Postmaster General Reagan was "both a fool and a coward" if he yielded. The trouble was adjusted, and the clerks continued their services. In 1863 a number of workmen detailed from military service to work in the Richmond armory at $3.00 a day went on strike. They were promptly sent back to the army at $11.00 a month with the likelihood of getting killed in battle or dying of disease. In 1862 some lithographers who had been exempted from military service struck and for their pains got themselves arrested and locked up in a military prison. The same year the Virginia authorities used a different method in breaking a strike of Irish gravediggers in Richmond. Negroes were sent to take their places. The Irish returned, beat the Negroes' heads, and drove them away. But the Irish lost the strike when a crew from the penitentiary was set to work digging graves.

All of these strikes were the result of spontaneous agreement rather than the planning of labor organizations, but in the printing business and in the telegraph service there were attempts to develop such organizations. In 1862 the newspaper typesetters, who were organized in the Richmond Typographical Society, struck for higher wages and a recognition of the principles set up in the society's constitution. These principles required all typesetters in Richmond to join the society and forbade members to work in any establishment where there were nonmember typesetters. These closed-shop principles were considered by the Richmond authorities to be a conspiracy and therefore punishable by the laws

[46] Richmond *Daily Examiner,* December 7, 1863; October 13, 1864.

237

of Virginia. A grand jury brought an indictment against the society for unlawful and pernicious combination and conspiracy, but it was thrown out of court on account of certain technicalities.

In October, 1863, the telegraph operators formed in Augusta the Southern Telegraphic Association, which, as far as the public knew, was designed to raise their standing in the estimation of the public. They considered themselves a little more than common workmen, since they knew all the secret private and official dispatches which went over their lines. Not until the latter part of January, 1864, did the public really learn the main purpose of this organization when the newspapers exposed it as "a secret league." At this time they struck for higher wages, shorter hours, and a closed shop. The telegraph companies dismissed from the service all who had joined this union, and the military authorities immediately drafted them into the Confederate armies. These actions effectively broke up the union. Before the end of the war, however, the telegraphers developed two organizations, which were not labor unions at all, but purely social and benevolent clubs, the South-Western Telegraphic Association, founded at Meridian, Mississippi, in May, 1864, and the Confederate States Telegraphic Club, at Charleston in January, 1865.[47]

Cheap money had led to high prices, which had set in motion speculation and extortion and a widespread decay of the ancient virtues. People became embittered, one group against another, the country against the city, the rich against the poor; and they began to wonder whether the Confederacy, which had brought all these woes upon the country, was worth its continuing cost. Defeatism set in and the morale of the people crumbled. Innumerable little pieces of paper bearing the words, "The Confederate States of America will pay to the bearer on demand," had had much to do with the downfall.

[47] Charleston *Daily Courier*, January 5, February 18, 1864; Richmond *Daily Whig*, February 23, 1864; Richmond *Daily Examiner*, January 30, 1864; William R. Plum, *The Military Telegraph during the Civil War in the United States, with an Exposition of Ancient and Modern Means of Communication, and of the Federal and Confederate Cypher Systems; also a Running Account of the War between the States* (Chicago, 1882), 116–20.

CHAPTER XII

AGRICULTURE, SUBSISTENCE, AND NEGROES

IN PROMOTING manufactories the South did not intend to desert agriculture, its first love and most substantial interest. Providing food was both good military strategy and common sense, for the people must be fed, in the army as well as at home. In the beginning they had no fear that they would be unable to defeat all armies that might march against them; it was the specter of hunger and starvation that was their greatest enemy. Therefore, they must speed up their food crops, reorganize their agriculture and put it on a war footing, and forever end all dependence upon the North—stop "importing Hay from Maine, Irish Potatoes from Nova Scotia, Apples from Massachusetts, Butter and Cheese from New York; Flour and Pork from Ohio, or Beef from Illinois." [1] The battle cry went up:

> Yankee Doodle, now, good-bye!
> We spurn a thing so rotten;
> Proud independence is the cry
> Of Sugar, Rice and Cotton. [2]

So exuberant were some Southerners in their prospective agricultural independence that they could hardly tolerate the industrialization of the South during the war. When peace should come they would not be "shop-keepers, common-carriers and cobblers for mankind," for agriculture was their favorite and natural pursuit.

Emphasis must now be put on food crops and especially on corn. King Cotton must be dethroned, and King Corn and his satellites

[1] See E. Merton Coulter, "The Movement for Agricultural Reorganization in the Cotton South during the Civil War," in *Agricultural History*, I (1927), 3–17. Quotation from *Southern Cultivator*, XIX (1861), 15.

[2] Paulding (Miss.) *Eastern Clarion*, October 18, 1861.

enthroned. As the crops for 1861 were already in the ground before the dangers of war were apparent, the movement to limit or prohibit outright the planting of cotton, as well as tobacco, did not get started until planting time in 1862. Naturally opposed to legal restraints of individual rights, Southerners first sought to effect agricultural reorganization by building up public sentiment for it through voluntary acquiescence. Planters held meetings in which they resolved to limit the cotton acreage, and in some places they appointed committees of safety to enforce their decisions on recalcitrant citizens. Some advocated planting only a fourth as much as previously; others suggested four acres or less per hand. Governor Brown opposed planting a single acre more than was necessary to clothe the people, and the comptroller general of Georgia required all tax collectors to list the amount of land planted in cotton. The newspapers took up the cry against cotton. "O, that *every* planter could *realize* the immeasurable amount of mischief which the devil can sow in 'only *four* acres of cotton,' " one exclaimed and added, "If even 'four acres of cotton to the hand' is planted, the devil will do the picking." [3] Said another, who felt the limitation movement was not spreading fast enough, "Go on and raise your cotton, and the abolitionists will come and take it at their own price, which is nothing, and then take you and your plantation besides. O that planters would wake up to this subject." [4]

From the very beginning in some of the states the movement was not left in the hands of planters and committees of safety. Arkansas in March, 1862, passed a law limiting cotton to two bales per hand; other states did not pass laws against cotton until too late to affect the 1862 crop; and two states, Louisiana and Texas, did not act at all. The Confederate Congress took up the subject and debated it extensively, but arrived at the conclusion that it could not constitutionally infringe on state rights by passing limitation legislation, though it did recommend in a resolution that the people should plant food crops instead of cotton and tobacco. The state limitations ran from three acres per hand in Georgia to one in South Carolina. Alabama imposed a tax of ten cents a pound on all cotton beyond 2,500 pounds per hand. In some states where

[3] "Putnam," in Macon *Daily Telegraph,* March 27, 1862.
[4] *Ibid.,* February 19, 1862.

laws had not yet been passed, planters who ignored public sentiment found themselves the objects of bitter hostility. Forty women
were reported to have banded together in Calhoun County, Alabama, bent on chopping to pieces all cotton they could find, and a
committee of safety condemned Toombs for planting 560 acres of
cotton on his plantation in southwestern Georgia. Resenting this
interference in his private affairs, he replied, "You may rob me in
my absence, but you cannot intimidate me." [5] Other unco-operative
planters raised food crops on their lands near highways but planted
their cotton in out-of-the-way places. Alexander H. Stephens, who
conformed to public sentiment and to the law, nevertheless thought
more cotton ought to be raised.

President Davis issued a proclamation at planting time in 1863
calling on the people to discount a certain buoyancy in the air,
caused by rumors that peace was near, and to continue to forgo
the raising of cotton and tobacco. The Richmond *Examiner* declared about this time: "If all citizens were intelligent and patriotic,
not another leaf of tobacco or pod of cotton would be seen in the
fields of the South until peace is declared, and a harvest of those
necessaries on which our existence as a nation depends, would be
ripened by the next summer's sun, such as was never before seen
in the land." [6] Virginia, the chief tobacco-raising region of the Confederacy, set a maximum of 2,500 plants to each hand, but the law
seems to have been widely evaded, for a patriotic Virginian recommended that transgressors should have half their crop taken by the
government, their names entered on a Roll of Dishonor, and themselves drafted into the army and made to fight separately from
respectable soldiers.[7]

The movement to limit cotton production was highly successful,
though this success must not be attributed wholly to Confederate
patriotism, for invading armies and other war confusions upset
agriculture generally. The crop harvested in the fall of 1861, before the limitation movement got started, amounted to about
4,500,000 bales; the next year it dropped to about 1,500,000; in

[5] Atlanta *Southern Confederacy,* June 17, 1862; Milledgeville *Southern Recorder,*
September 30, 1862.

[6] Richmond *Daily Examiner,* March 10, 1863.

[7] Richmond *Daily Whig,* May 24, 1864.

1863 it was somewhat less than 500,000; and the next year it was about 300,000. By the planting season of 1865, the Confederacy was tottering and no one thought of limitation; the harvest in the fall of 1865, after the war had ended, amounted to over 1,500,000. A tribute to Confederate self-denial is seen in the fact that the New York prices of cotton steadily increased, running from thirteen cents in 1861 through thirty-one cents in 1862, sixty-seven cents in 1863, and $1.01 in 1864 to a peak of $1.90 in 1865.[8]

In the light of this keen demand for cotton, it required an excessive strain on patriotism for planters to obey the law of Congress requiring owners to destroy all cotton, tobacco, naval stores, and other property helpful to the enemy if it was in danger of falling into their hands. There was much complaining and some evasion of the law; yet it has been estimated that 2,500,000 cotton bales were destroyed either by the owners or by Confederate armies, for the military authorities as well as the owners were required to burn it.

It became the custom for travelers to remark on the absence of cotton fields and on the profusion of corn. A woman traveling in 1862 from Corinth, Mississippi, to Mobile, a distance of 250 miles, declared that she saw corn everywhere, scarcely an acre of cotton; a newspaper editor the next year on a trip from Atlanta to Augusta affirmed that he had not seen a stalk of cotton; and another observer saw what appeared to be almost a solid cornfield reaching from Demopolis, Alabama, to Selma.[9] A Federal soldier who had been besieging Vicksburg was so struck by the size of Mississippi cornfields that he reported them in square miles, not acres. With some exaggeration he affirmed that many of them contained "from ten to twelve square miles"; in fact, it was "impossible to find the limits of the cornfields, for almost every square foot of arable land . . . [was] in with corn." [10] President Davis in his annual message

[8] Ramsdell, *Behind the Lines in the Southern Confederacy*, 76; Douglas S. Freeman (ed.), *Lee's Dispatches; Unpublished Letters of General Robert E. Lee, C.S.A., to Jefferson Davis and the War Department of the Confederate States of America, 1862–1865* (New York, 1915), 323.

[9] *Southern Cultivator*, XXII (1864), 127; Atlanta *Southern Confederacy*, April 7, 1863; Cumming, *Journal of Hospital Life*, 36.

[10] Thomas H. Parker, *History of the 51st Regiment of P.V. and V.V., from . . . 1861, to . . . 1865* (Philadelphia, 1869), 376. One of the officers with Sherman on his march through Georgia noted the thousands of acres of corn and remarked that it was "surprising to see how the planters have carried out the wishes or orders of the Rebel

to Congress in January, 1863, proudly noted that Southern "fields, no longer whitened by cotton that . . . [could not] be exported, . . . [were] devoted to the production of cereals and the growth of stock formerly purchased with the proceeds of cotton." [11] General William T. Sherman the next year, on his invasion of Georgia, banteringly wrote: "Convey to Jeff. Davis my personal and official thanks for abolishing cotton and substituting corn and sweet potatoes in the South." He added, "These facilitate our military plans much, for food and forage are abundant." [12] So corn-conscious were the people that a trickster sought to humbug them into buying a miraculous Egyptian corn, which grew in the form of a tree, bore as many as twenty-two ears on a stalk, and yielded flour equal in color and fineness to that of wheat.[13]

But agricultural enthusiasm did not extend to corn alone. The raising of all sorts of food crops was promoted, and a great many articles which could be produced on the farms and plantations were offered as substitutes for those formerly imported. This campaign was, in fact, only an intensification of a movement for diversification which had long been going on, and which had developed such planters as William Mercer of Adams County, Mississippi, who in 1860 produced in addition to his 1,500 bales of cotton, 28,000 bushels of corn, 300 bushels of oats, 100 pounds of wool, 1,300 bushels of peas and beans, 4,000 bushels of Irish potatoes, 10,000 bushels of sweet potatoes, $500 worth of orchard fruits, 20 tons of hay, and $900 worth of meats.[14] The cultivation of sugar and rice should be extended into regions which had not heretofore been given over to these products, an expansion especially important after the coastal rice flats and Louisiana cane fields had been lost to the enemy. The sorghum, often referred to as the Chinese sugar cane, was now becoming popular as a substitute for sugar cane, as it could be grown much more widely. Not only could sugar and syrup be made from its juice, but its seed could be ground into a yellowish flour which was said to be better than buckwheat

Government." George W. Nichols, *The Story of the Great March* . . . (26th ed., New York, 1866), 81.

[11] Richardson (comp.), *Messages and Papers of the Confederacy*, I, 297.

[12] *Official Records*, Ser. I, Vol. XXXIX, Pt. III, 369.

[13] *Southern Cultivator*, XXII (1864), 87, 112.

[14] See Herbert Weaver, *Mississippi Farmers, 1850–1860* (Nashville, 1945). 90.

for hot cakes and the seed could be parched and used as a substitute for coffee.

In the country agricultural leaders advocated more extensive kitchen gardens, and in the cities newspaper editors called for war gardens on any "unoccupied piece of ground, large enough to spread a blanket upon." The problem of securing garden seeds was serious from the beginning, but it was partly solved by sending agents to Europe to secure a supply, and by the unexpected interest which the Ordnance Bureau showed in importing from Bermuda a large amount best suited for the climate of the Confederacy.[15] Onions, "this vegetable *aromatique*," was especially liked by the soldiers, and should, therefore, be produced in great quantities. "We say, therefore, plant Onions," exclaimed a patriot, "the soldiers say plant Onions; the generals join in the request, and let therefore go forth in trumpet tones throughout the length and breadth of the land, *plant Onions*." [16] Farmers should raise more peanuts, for they were excellent food and their oil was more valuable than sperm. People were cautioned against forgetting to plant sweet potatoes and begged to remember that Francis Marion and his men largely subsisted on them in the Revolution. Southerners were advised to raise broomcorn and to produce mustard needed for medicinal purposes. The newspapers started a movement to induce the ladies to plant poppies, so much needed in producing opium for the hospitals.

The land was a veritable seedbed for substitutes for articles now cut off by the blockade. They became so numerous that the word *Confederate* applied to any replacement and generally with the implication that it was better than that originally imported from the North. There were "Confederate needles" from the hawthorn bushes; "Confederate cork" from cypress knees or black-gum roots; "Confederate leather" from cotton cloth for bridle reins and shoe tops; shoe blacking from the boiled juice of chinaberries mixed with soot from lampblack or pine wood; soda from the ashes of burnt corncobs; rope from Spanish moss, okra stalks, or cotton

[15] Thomas Carter to Stephens, July 12, 1861, in Stephens Papers (microfilms in University of Texas Library, originals in Division of Manuscripts, Library of Congress); *Southern Cultivator*, XXII (1864), 32.

[16] *Southern Cultivator*, XXII (1864), 127.

saturated in tar. As a substitute for hops in yeast for bread, peach leaves were recommended; and as for tea, the leaves of blackberries, huckleberries, roses, or holly would taste as well. A Virginia lady baked mince pies from a concoction made by mixing "some of every thing sweet she had," but it did not have "a single ingredient of regular mince meat."

The perfect substitute for coffee was sought longest and most assiduously. A famous "Confederate coffee" was made in Richmond of parched peas and corn ground together. Other substitutes eloquently recommended were toasted rye and wheat, chicory, parched garden beets, okra seeds, yams, pumpkin seeds, and acorns. So absurd were some of the substitutes that now and then a disgusted coffee drinker would remark, "Anything will do, if you don't want coffee." "In fact, all that is wanted is something to color the water," remarked a Georgia editor, "and you can fancy and call the concoction what you please. It is coffee or it is dirty water just as you please to imagine." [17] As a substitute to end all coffee substitutes, a wit devised this mixture: "Take tan bark, three parts, three old cigar stumps and a quantity of water, mix well, and boil fifteen minutes in a dirty coffee pot, and the best judges cannot tell it from the best Mocha." [18]

As for colors, red could be got from figs, black from pomegranate, blue from wild indigo, and purple from red sumac. The most fruitful source of coloring matter was copperas got from soaking old iron in a cask of water impregnated with salt and vinegar. Many Confederate soldiers in the early days wore "copperas breeches," so called because they were colored from this dye.

The grain-growing region of the Confederacy was the Upper South, much of which early fell under Federal control or was fought over by the armies and thereby was lost as far as its products were concerned. The consequent scarcity of wheat forced the people at home to be content with corn bread, while the flour was sent to the armies in the form of hardtack or otherwise. An experimenter with foods in Charleston developed a soup cake or bouillon which he claimed made excellent soup when placed in boiling water, but it never reached practical production.

17 Macon *Daily Telegraph,* April 7, 1862.
18 Macon *Southern Confederacy,* December 31, 1864.

The Upper South was also the chief source of the meat supply of the Confederacy. Residents of the Shenandoah Valley of Virginia informed President Davis in 1861 that there was "perhaps no valley in America of the same extent that produces more fat cattle and hogs than the valley of the South Branch." [19] Though the planters throughout the Confederacy kept some hogs, in many parts of the Lower South many people had a prejudice against raising swine, probably because they thought it was not dignified. "It is one of the enigmas of the planting race that it hates to raise hogs, which are the first article of prime necessity," declared a Georgia editor. "Planters had rather raise a pound of cotton at three cents than a pound of bacon at a dollar." [20] The greatest source of beef was Texas, which, however, had the disadvantage of being far away from the main markets. In the early part of the war herds of Texas cattle were driven across Louisiana, Mississippi, and farther eastward. A Richmond editor reported in the autumn of 1862 that 20,000 Texas cattle had crossed the Mississippi for delivery to the army and more were on the way. A newspaper correspondent noted about this time that a herd of 600 Texas cattle had passed through the little Mississippi town of Raymond, and that "Texas Beeves in great numbers continue to pass through this place" in herds of from 400 to 600. [21] John A. Wilcox, a Texas Congressman, declared that his state could "furnish the whole army with beef during the war, and charge nothing for it," if the Confederacy would pay the expenses of driving the cattle. [22] Not all Texas cattle walked to market. A slaughterhouse in Alexandria, Louisiana, packed large quantities of salt beef, and contracted to furnish 100,000 barrels of it to the Confederate armies. [23] After the Mississippi River fell under the control of the Federals in the summer of 1863, Texas supplies were largely cut off from Confederate armies to the eastward.

With the greatest meat-producing parts of the Confederacy either

[19] *Official Records*, Ser. I, Vol. V, 845–46.
[20] Macon *Daily Telegraph*, March 5, 1862.
[21] Raymond *Hinds County Gazette*, September 17, 1862.
[22] *Southern Historical Society Papers*, XLV (1925), 138.
[23] Richmond *Whig and Public Advertiser*, November 8, 1861; Jefferson D. Bragg, *Louisiana in the Confederacy* (Baton Rouge, 1941), 83.

occupied by the enemy or cut off by them, the armies turned to Florida as the best source still remaining. Though this state was not as far away from the center of activities as was Texas, still it was like Texas in that it had no railway connections with the remainder of the Confederacy. A patriotic citizen suggested that the Confederate armies turn to the teeming fish of the seas and rivers for a substitute for beef, remembering the Biblical command, "Let the waters bring forth abundantly." He suggested that ten thousand men beyond military age and wounded soldiers turn fishermen. By using "traps, seines, floats and hooks, trot-lines, nets, spears, gigs, hooks, &c." they could set up fisheries along the rivers and coast which would supply the Confederate armies with salted sea food.[24] Before the end of the war many fisheries were established along the coasts, but there was always the hazard of destruction by raiding parties from Federal gunboats.

Basic in the food problems of the Confederacy was salt, so matter-of-fact and insignificant until it was once missed. Before the blockade most of it had been imported from Europe and the West Indies, with a fourth of all importations coming in at New Orleans; but when it was cut off and became scarce, a veritable panic seized the people. The price skyrocketed, and to bring it within reach methods were devised both to produce it inside the Confederacy and to regulate its price. Salt water along the fringe of seacoast could be evaporated; and in the course of time important works were set up there, but they were frequently raided and destroyed by crews from Federal gunboats. To escape this menace, all known inland salt springs were rapidly developed and rewards offered for the discovery of new ones. The most valuable salt wells were at Saltville, in southwestern Virginia, and states of the eastern part of the Confederacy made contracts to boil salt there. There were various salt springs in Alabama, and in 1862 a wild rumor spread that rock-salt mines had been discovered near Opelika. It turned out that some pieces of rock salt, which had fallen from a car, had been found in a railway cut near this place. The Confederacy was salt-mine conscious at this time, because there had been recently opened up vastly rich salt mines on Avery Island in southern

24 *Official Records,* Ser. IV, Vol. II, 916.

Louisiana. For the year preceding their capture by Federal troops in 1863, these mines produced 22,000,000 pounds of rock salt. The Confederacy was able to supply its salt needs, though not evenly and completely. Now and then meat spoiled, hides rotted, and herds of cattle died for want of salt.[25]

In the minds of many people whisky was almost as necessary as salt, if not for satisfying a thirst, then for medicinal uses in hospitals. But there was a gauntlet of temperance sentiment which this article had long been forced to run, and in addition there was the fact that now when the supply from the Upper South had been cut off, there arose opposition to using the grain in the rest of the Confederacy for the many small distilleries which sprang up. With whisky thus bearing the stigma of a moral evil as well as an instrument that promoted starvation, various states began to prohibit its distillation from grain and later from potatoes, molasses, and other farm products. South Carolina imposed a fine of $10,000 and a year's imprisonment for those distilling whisky from grain except under contract with the Confederate government for hospital use. In March, 1862, Governor Brown issued a proclamation, later enacted into law, forbidding the use of corn in making whisky, that "burning liquid stream of death, which is spreading desolation and ruin throughout the whole length and breadth of the land." To help enforce prohibition laws, which were constantly violated, railroads were induced to refuse to accept whisky as freight and in some places, as in Statesville, North Carolina, indignant women took it upon themselves to break open barrels of whisky and spill it.

The Confederate government needed whisky as an ingredient in medicines and for other hospital uses—and even for rationing to the soldiers and sailors on occasion. To provide a supply, it made contracts with distilleries throughout the Confederacy, but so strong was the sentiment against distilling grain that in some states, notably Georgia and Virginia, the governors sought to prevent the

25 Charleston *Daily Courier,* June 30, 1862; Jackson *Daily Mississippian,* April 23, 1863; Macon *Daily Telegraph,* March 6, April 10, 1862; Richmond *Daily Examiner,* March 23, 1863; Richmond *Daily Whig,* December 1, 1862; Jones, *Rebel War Clerk's Diary,* I, 183; *American Annual Cyclopaedia . . . 1864,* p. 10; Ramsdell, *Behind the Lines in the Southern Confederacy,* 69 ff. The standard work on salt in the Confederacy is Ella Lonn, *Salt as a Factor in the Confederacy* (New York, 1933).

contracts from being carried out. In 1864 the Confederate government set up its own distilleries.[26]

"Our battle against want and starvation is greater than against our enemies," declared a subsistence officer in 1863.[27] Did the people behind the lines win this battle against want and starvation? Despite the fact that soldiers went hungry, and civilians, too, in some places, there was food enough raised in the Confederacy to satisfy all. Its transportation and distribution to those who needed it created the problem which was never solved. By the fall of 1864 Lee's army was being provisioned over the rickety and attenuated railway lines leading to the faraway land of plenty in southwest Georgia and Alabama. But the freight cars still available were so scarce and dilapidated that some people advocated the use of passenger cars in hauling grain and even abandoning all passenger traffic until food could be more properly distributed.

The most important and immediate problem in dealing with food and subsistence was to see that these materials reached the armies. Two divisions of the War Department were charged with this duty, the Commissary or Subsistence Department and the Quartermaster Department. The one administered to the soldier's interior by providing him with food, the other was concerned with his exterior by affording him uniforms, shoes, blankets, tents, cooking utensils, and hospital supplies except medicines. The Quartermaster was also charged with army transportation by railway, steamboats, wagons, horses, mules, hospital wagons, with providing feed for all army horses, mules, and other livestock, and also with the payment of troops. These two departments from their very nature worked closely together. The Commissary Department collected food and feed throughout the Confederacy and the Quartermaster agents transported them to the armies wherever they were. The minute dealings of the officers and agents of these two departments with people everywhere, and their consequent control over commerce and transportation prompted strong temptations to en-

[26] *Southern Cultivator,* XXII (1864), 113; Macon *Daily Telegraph,* March 4, 1862; William M. Robinson, "Prohibition in the Confederacy," in *American Historical Review,* XXXVII (1931–1932), 50–58; Bell I. Wiley, *The Life of Johnny Reb, the Common Soldier of the Confederacy* (Indianapolis, 1943), 260.

[27] *Official Records,* Ser. I, Vol. XXIII, Pt. II, 771.

gage in private gain. A short time after the war began it became the custom to accuse these agents of widespread corruption. Congressman Foote in 1863 wanted to force all of them to tell how much property they had when the war began and how much they had when they were investigated, and Congressman George N. Lester of Georgia warned Congress to "save the country from the vampires, who are sucking up the very life of the nation." In 1864 a soldier in Virginia blamed all his woes on the Commissary agents, declaring that if anything was put in their hands the soldiers would "get but little by the time each commissary levies his tax on it," and adding, "Quartermaster and commissary are considered synonymous with scoundrel." [28] Wigfall charged that many men "utterly incompetent and dishonest got into the army as disbursing officers." [29]

The Commissary Department received the special maledictions of many, first because of the original Commissary General, and secondly because of its policy of impressment. The first Commissary General was Lucius B. Northrop, a native of South Carolina, a West Pointer, and a long-standing friend of President Davis. Very early he fell under the disapproval of Congressman Foote, who referred to him as "a pepper doctor from South Carolina" who believed in a vegetable diet and hoped to make the army into vegetarians like himself. Much was made of his attempt to conserve food by trying to induce the soldiers to eat the necks and hoofs of beeves. Beginning with the battle of First Manassas he was blamed for the army going hungry, despite his explanation that both before that battle and in subsequent times he had collected much food but was unable to secure transportation for it. He defended himself further against the charge that his food stores were actually depleted by showing that he had brought a great deal through the blockade, that he had tried to induce the higher authorities to allow him to trade cotton to the enemy for food, and that it was difficult to induce people at home to bring out of hiding or sell food when they had already gone long without payment for previous sales— all because the Confederate government had not supplied him with

[28] Richmond *Daily Examiner*, December 21, 1864; Athens *Southern Watchman*, January 25, 1865.
[29] *Southern Historical Society Papers*, XLV (1925), 145.

sufficient money.[30] Yet Northrop was described as an "inexorable, head-strong, ignorant & self-important" man,[31] and according to the Richmond *Whig,* South Carolinians even considered him crazy.[32] He was undoubtedly headstrong and contentious, however arduous and impossible was his task. He quarreled with General Joseph E. Johnston, with General Beauregard, and even with General Lee. His trouble with Lee was over his attempt to induce the general to feed his own army from supplies which he could secure in the vicinity of operations. Lee sternly refused to subsist his army off the regions through which it marched.[33]

The policy of impressing supplies as well as equipment, such as horses and wagons, began in 1861 and proceeded from military necessity and not by any legal right. So indefensible did this practice appear to even the most loyal Confederates that Congress in March, 1863, passed a highly complicated and involved law regulating in great detail the method of impressing supplies and fixing prices in the several states. The President of the Confederacy and the governor of the state should each appoint a commissioner to fix prices, and when these two could not agree they should appoint a third who would act as an umpire. At intervals of not more than two months they should establish and publish a scale of prices. An attempt was made to distinguish between the producer or owner of supplies for his own use and the middleman or speculator. It seemed to have been the intent of the law that the former class should have the additional protection of having the price of supplies impressed from them fixed, upon disagreement, by two loyal citizens of the vicinity, one appointed by the owner and one by the impressment agent and a third appointed by these two, if they could not agree; but it actually worked out that the schedules of prices periodically published related to prices irrespective of whether impressments were "on farms or elsewhere." Property and supplies needed by the owners for their support and for carrying on their ordinary operations were not subject to impressment.

Though the rates paid by impressment agents were notoriously

30 *Official Records,* Ser. I, Vol. XLVI, Pt. II, 1211, 1213.
31 Philip Clayton to Cobb, March 17, 1863, in Howell Cobb Papers.
32 Richmond *Daily Whig,* January 27, 1864.
33 *Official Records,* Ser. I, Vol. XXXIII, 1087; XXIX, Pt. II, 884.

under the market prices, often about half as much, by the summer of 1864 commissioners in some states offered prices entirely too high in order to facilitate collection of badly needed supplies. The practice led to such exclamations as this: "What on earth do the commissioners mean by their late schedule of prices? Wheat, $30 a bushel! A rise of $150 from $25 a barrel for flour!" [34] Hoping to remedy this situation and reduce prices, commissioners from six states east of the Mississippi River met in Montgomery in September, 1864, to consider a uniform scale of prices for their combined territory, but they came to no agreement.

The ubiquitous activities of the "pressmen," who conducted veritable raids on the private property of Confederate citizens, stirred up a storm of bitterness as they seized food, horses, wagons, and anything else they wanted, and too often left worthless promises to pay. It has been estimated that at the end of the war the Confederate government owed its citizens $500,000,000 for property it had impressed. [35] Occasionally impostors claiming to be impressment agents carried off much property and left in exchange worthless receipts. This interference with the normal rights of the individual struck a fatal blow at the morale of the people. "Let the laws of commerce alone—they are the result of daily compromise between man and man," declared a Richmond editor. "Let the people alone—let them enjoy the freedom they have ever been used to, and which does not conflict with the well being and safety of the States. Too much Government is almost as bad as no Government. Let us be able to turn around without feeling the pressure of a penal statute." [36] The government became the all-devourer, "so monopolising that private individuals are almost debarred the privilege of purchasing even for their families." [37]

States passed laws against illegal impressment agents; Toombs, Yancey, Stephens, Brown, Vance, and others thundered out their bitter disapproval of the whole impressment system; and the Supreme Court of Georgia declared the impressment law unconstitutional because it did not guarantee just compensation for property

34 *Ibid.*, Ser. IV, Vol. III, 538.
35 Frank L. Owsley, *State Rights in the Confederacy* (Chicago, 1925), 219 ff.
36 Richmond *Daily Whig*, January 31, 1863.
37 Easterby (ed.), *South Carolina Rice Plantation*, 204.

seized.[38] Northrop was accused of publishing many columns of "soporific twaddle, supposed to be intended as an attempt to justify" his agents' "robberies of the people"; but Davis defended the impressment system as the only method by which the armies could be supplied, and there can be no doubt that otherwise they would have been starved into submission long before Appomattox.

The accumulating attacks on Northrop mounted so high that finally in February, 1865, he resigned. To succeed him Davis appointed General Isaac M. St. John, who found the commissary situation so hopeless that he resorted to a most unusual plan to provision the armies. He induced a committee of Richmond citizens to send out a plea for every family in Virginia and North Carolina to adopt, in theory, a Confederate soldier, which would in practice amount to donating to the army enough food to sustain an additional member of the family—a burden not unusual with the growth of families or the coming and going of visitors. But it was now too late for this scheme or any other to succeed.

The Quartermaster Department, equally charged with supplying the army, was equally tarred with the brush of impressment activities and was equally unpopular. "Youans must be a d——d fool or a — quartermaster," reputed to a rustic, became a stock expression. Wild, unfounded charges were spread that one quartermaster officer had made $5,000,000 from his position, and the ubiquitous Foote agreed with the charge that a quartermaster " 'who was formerly a horse trader, and so poor that he could not get credit for a beefsteak,' had, since his connection with the Government, accumulated an immense fortune." [39] The quartermasters were in fact generally honest, and this defense of them by Bill Arp was something more than humorous: How consoling to hear the "eloquent remark from a trafficking Shylock of a French-German-Jew, 'I tot I could make some of de monish here 'mong dese officere, but by tam, dese quartermasters too tam hones; I do nothin' wid dem.' " [40]

---

[38] Though "just compensation" is mentioned in Section 5 of the Confederate Impressment law, the full working of the act as set forth in Sections 5 and 6 did not seem to the court to provide just compensation as guaranteed in Article I, Section 9, Paragraph 17 of the Confederate Constitution. The cases were Cox & Hill v. Cummings, and Cunningham v. Campbell et al.

[39] Southern Historical Society Papers, XLVIII (1941), 144.

[40] [Smith], Bill Arp, So Called, 71. Charges of irregularities were made in the Rich-

Unlike the Commissary Department, the Quartermaster Department was not weighed down by an unpopular head, and when in the summer of 1863 President Davis supplanted Abraham C. Myers with General Alexander R. Lawton he aroused bitter opposition in Congress.

The Negroes were a fundamental element in the agricultural economy of the Confederacy and an important factor in making possible the feeding of soldiers and civilians; and, indeed, the Negroes of the Confederacy, slave and free, constituted a great labor reservoir, which made it possible for the army to comb the white population much closer for its soldiers. In the eleven Confederate states there were in 1860 slightly more than 3,500,000 slaves, most of them in the Lower South, with Georgia having the largest number, 462,198.

Southerners were not entirely sure in their minds as to how their slaves would react toward the excitement brought on by secession and war. The wise Southerner never felt quite sure of what went on in the minds of his slaves, but he believed that eternal vigilance was the best policy. Of course time, place, treatment by the master, and the proximity of Federal troops all had their varying effects on the slaves; but in the beginning Southerners felt greater uncertainty than later when the effects of war had been observed. "How any sane man could ever expect the negro to 'rise' I cannot imagine," exclaimed an Englishman, who saw no possibility of their being organized; Russell, another English traveler in the Confederacy, said that none of the "Southern gentlemen" had "the smallest apprehension of a servile insurrection." [41] The stock answer of the Negro himself was supposed to be his own question as to whether when anyone saw two dogs fighting over a bone he ever saw the bone fight. But a Georgian warned slaveowners in 1861 to keep their slaves "at home very closely during the excitement which now agitates our country"; [42] another suggested that the patrol

---

mond *Daily Examiner,* October 20, 1862, but were successfully answered in an explanation in *General Orders, from Adjutant and Inspector-General's Office, Confederate States Army,* 1862–1863, Ser. 1862, pp. 148–49.

[41] *Two Months in the Confederate States . . . By an English Merchant,* 293; Russell, *My Diary North and South,* 233. The standard work on the Negro in the Civil War is Bell I. Wiley, *Southern Negroes, 1861–1865* (New Haven, 1938).

[42] Sandersville *Central Georgian,* May 15, 1861.

system be faithfully carried out; and people generally suspected in every stranger an abolitionist spy bent on plotting a slave insurrection.

Rumors of slave plots had been the customary order of the day in ante-bellum times, and it was not to be different in wartime; but the plots were all restricted in scope and highly flamboyant and impractical. No insurrection ever occurred during the war, but the customary conspiracies and plottings were unearthed and the participants executed or severely whipped. Most of the discoveries were during the excitement of the first year, when in Mississippi forty Negroes were hanged in the Natchez region. There were other hangings in Alabama and Arkansas. In Georgia a "quick spoken," long-haired stranger with "a down-East look" was caught tampering with slaves and warned to leave the state instantly; and in Atlanta a similar-looking stranger told a slave whom he was unsuccessfully trying to induce to run away, "You're a damn fool." [43] Governor Brown professed to believe there was danger of a slave uprising around Christmas time of 1862, but he was, in fact, using this rumor as an argument to convince the Secretary of War that he should return some powder lent the Confederate government. But in 1863 the Confederacy thought it had discovered a plot of gigantic proportions, supposedly promoted by the United States army, whereby all the slaves throughout the Confederacy were to rise up on the night of August 1 and with torch and hammer destroy bridges, telegraph wires, buildings—in fact, everything that would aid the South in carrying on the war—except they were not to take human life unless in self-defense. Confederates discovered evidences of it some months ahead and thereby prevented its fruition, if, indeed, it was ever seriously considered.[44] There were rumors of minor plots down to the end of the war, and additional hangings were recorded in Virginia, North Carolina, and Georgia. Negroes acted as spies for Federal armies and brought in valuable information; they aided Federals escaping from Con-

[43] Atlanta *Southern Confederacy*, May 28, 1861. See also, Des Arc (Ark.) *Semi Weekly Citizen*, May 10, 17, July 10, 1861; Montgomery *Weekly Mail*, January 10, 1861; Grove Hill (Ala.) *Clarke County Democrat*, June 13, 1861; Moore (ed.), *Rebellion Record*, I, 92 (diary); Bettersworth, *Confederate Mississippi*, 162 ff.

[44] New York *World*, August 26, 1864; Rowland (ed.), *Jefferson Davis, Constitutionalist*, V, 500; Johnston and Browne, *Alexander H. Stephens*, 444.

federate prisons; and they performed now and then unusual services, as in 1862 when a slave crew of the Confederate steamer *Planter* ran it out of Charleston Harbor and delivered it to the blockading fleet.

Against this background of suspicions there arose many shining examples of loyalty and affection on the part of slaves for their masters and their country. "Ninety five hundredths of those doomed children of inevitable destiny are our body guards," asserted a document written in 1861 for European eyes. "On our farms and plantations, with hundreds around us, we sleep with wooden latched doors, with open windows, and fear no evil." [45] Echoing their masters, slaves talked vengeance against the Yankees, went to war as body servants and probably on rare occasions actually fired on enemy soldiers, and frequently made contributions to Confederate funds. A South Carolina slave gave his total savings of $5.00 to help build a gunboat, "jist sich a boat as can whip ole Blunkum an de triflin no count Yankees"; the "Confederate Ethiopian Serenaders" of Charleston gave the proceeds of one of their concerts for a like purpose; a Virginia slave gave $10.00 to help outfit a regiment; and Yancey's slaves brought a load of their own watermelons, worth $60.00, to Montgomery to give to the soldiers. It became a custom for slaves to hold balls and concerts and give the money thereby obtained to aid soldiers' families and to other patriotic causes.[46]

In fact, some of the slaves begged their masters for permission to join the army as soldiers, and many did in the course of time serve as laborers to build fortifications and as cooks in the army. In 1861 a thousand slaves were busy around Charleston and "so far from inclining to insurrection, were grinning from ear to ear at the prospect of shooting the Yankees." Hundreds of slaves were marching through the streets of Memphis with picks, shovels, and axes, and according to a reporter "A merrier set were never seen. They were brimfull of patriotism, shouting for Jeff. Davis and

[45] Manuscript Address (in possession of the writer).

[46] The editor of the Atlanta *Southern Confederacy,* October 12, 1862, expressed opposition to slaves holding benefit balls and concerts: "The idea of a lot of buck negroes and saucy house gals meeting in a public hall, and dancing, fiddling, sweating and fuming to raise funds for our sick soldiers, is supremely ridiculous."

singing war songs." [47] Sometimes servants attached to soldiers in the army organized themselves in mock formations and followed dress parades of their units. They served as regimental musicians, and, by law, received the same pay as regularly enlisted musicians.

Taken as a whole, the slaves came through the period of the war with a greater feeling of happiness and well-being than the white people. An Alabama editor in recording his observations of Christmas time in 1862 wrote of the "fat sleek Dinahs and plump-jowled Sambos," who had paraded the streets of Selma, and he contrasted them with the "hollow-eyed, care-worn faces" of the whites, adding, "We seldom see a merry white man except when he is drunk." [48] Even the Federal soldiers were struck by the lightheartedness of slaves they met and by their lack of concern with freedom as attested in one instance by this song they sang in northern Virginia, having 139 stanzas, all alike:

> And it's Old John Brown don't you see
> It'll never do for you to try to set the darkies free
> For if you do the people will come from all around
> And take you down and hang you up in old Charlestown.

With the men absent from many Confederate homes, the slaves came to be more than ever before a closer part of the plantation organization. The remark of a Mississippi woman about her own slaves could well have been made by many others, "They were our greatest comfort during the war." [49] A soldier did not intend to be entirely facetious when he proposed loving commemoration of the fame of Confederate heroes by naming "Darkies of cast" for them, beginning with "Johnston Sir Beauregard Stonewall Jackson" for the "little Pickaninny" recently arrived.[50]

In fact, the effects of the war were to lighten the burdens and restrictions on slaves whether the people willed it so or not, for in the plantation regions especially most of the male population of military age had gone to war, leaving the women to exercise

[47] McPherson, *History of the . . . Rebellion*, 281.
[48] Selma *Daily Reporter*, December 30, 1862.
[49] Susan Dabney Smedes, *A Southern Planter* (4th ed., New York, 1890), 197.
[50] Lucien Barnsley, Richmond, Va., to Julia Barnsley, October 21, 1862, in Barnsley Papers (University of Georgia Library).

what control they could. In the cities, and notably in Richmond, the slaves led such carefree lives as to cause frequent complaints and demands for curbing them. The Richmond mayor's court was so cluttered with Negro cases as to lead to the observation that the city was at the mercy of its slave population, that the Negroes were the masters and the whites were the slaves, and that

> *The white man rule de day,*
> *De negro rule de night.*

Even so, there were voices raised, especially among churchmen and educators, calling for improvement in the status of slaves by legalizing their marriages, receiving their testimony in courts, and allowing them to be taught to read and write. Had the South gained its independence, slavery in the new nation undoubtedly would soon have developed into serfdom and eventual freedom.

Slaves were not only valuable in agriculture and in military service, as performed by teamsters, cooks, body servants, hospital attendants, and labor battalions, but distinctly so in a great many skilled occupations in civil life. When the gunboat fever seized the South in 1862, some leaders advocated that the government impress 15,000 or more slaves and set them to work building these engines of destruction; and by 1864 there was a great demand for them to work in armories, munition factories, and in other industries where they would serve as wheelwrights, blacksmiths, harness makers, shoemakers, and carpenters. The Macon Armory advertised for 100 for whom they would pay $25 a month in addition to upkeep; the Tredegar Iron Works wanted 1,000; the Naval Gun Foundry and Ordnance Works at Selma called for 200; the government shoe factory in Columbus, Georgia, wanted 200 cobblers; the saltworks in Clarke County, Alabama, advertised for 500—almost every industry was competing for Negro labor.

From the beginning of the war slaves were impressed by the military authorities for work on fortifications, but not until the passage of the Impressment Act of March 26, 1863, was this practice legalized. Duly regardful of state rights, Congress provided that impressment must conform to the laws and regulations of the state in which it was done, and in the absence of such, it must accord with rules set up by the Secretary of War. The Confederacy paid the owner for each slave $30 a month or some other agreed-upon wage, and in case of death, the full value of the slave. There was much opposition to Confederate impressment of slaves, both from the state governments and from the owners. Some of the state laws made it almost impossible for anyone except state agents to impress slaves. As time went on the need for slaves became so urgent that Congress passed an act in February, 1864, calling for as many as twenty thousand of them to be hired with the consent of their owners if possible, but otherwise to be impressed. Not more than one fifth of the slaves of any one planter might be taken, and they should be apportioned among the planters in equal ratio in the region visited. Only under the greatest urgency should any slaves be impressed from plantations producing grain exclusively.

The chief complaints of planters against impressment were that the Confederacy was slow in paying its bills and sometimes never paid them, that it kept slaves longer than agreed upon, that it took them at the busiest seasons, and that it returned them in poor condition and often without the implements which the planter had furnished. Toward the end waning patriotism played its part, too; and an ingrown tenacity to retain slave property actually led some to part with members of their own families as soldiers more gladly than to give up a few slave workmen. Senator Wigfall said he knew of a planter who had five sons in the army, but had not grieved half so much at parting with them as with one Negro slave. "The patriotic planters would willingly put their own flesh and blood into the army," he declared, "but when you asked them for a negro the matter approached the point of drawing an eye-tooth." [51]

There were many free Negroes in the Confederacy, ranging in numbers and locations from 58,042 in Virginia to 144 in Arkansas. In addition to Virginia, they were concentrated largely in North Carolina with 30,463 and Louisiana with 18,647. In the eleven Confederate states there were in 1860 about 132,000. Though their legal position in the South was not much better than that of slaves, there were many who had prospered and had held the respect of the whites, and it was only natural that there should have been stirrings of patriotism among them for the land of their birth.

[51] *American Annual Cyclopaedia . . . 1863*, p. 232.

War excitement led them to offer themselves as soldiers or as labor battalions and to make donations to the war efforts. Seventy in Lynchburg volunteered their services to Virginia in June, 1861; in the same year a regiment of 1,400 paraded with white troops in New Orleans; and an Alabama free Negro presented an Alabama regiment with 100 bushels of sweet potatoes. But, of course, the great majority continued passively in their lowly position, working as agricultural laborers, as hired help in the shops and factories of the cities, or in little businesses of their own. Demands were early made for impressing or conscripting free Negroes for war work and the clamor was intensified after the March, 1863, act impressing slaves. Finally, on February 17, 1864, Congress passed an act making all male free Negroes between eighteen and fifty liable to service in war manufactories, in erecting fortifications, and in military hospitals, and requiring that they should be taken in preference to the twenty thousand slaves impressed by the same act. They should receive the same pay and subsistence as soldiers. Though no free Negroes fought as soldiers, they performed many other war activities. Receiving the scanty pay of soldiers, they presented the Confederacy with the problem of taking care of their families—a problem some of the Negroes themselves solved by deserting.

In one way or another the Negroes were in the war and they were legitimate spoils for the enemy; conversely, Federal armies might be spoils of war for the Negroes to live upon. The first invading armies met the problem and solved it in various ways. General Butler, in Virginia, decided to keep as contraband of war the Negroes who came into his camps and use them as laborers; other commanders, refusing to be bothered, sent them back to their masters. In March, 1862, the Federal Congress passed a law forbidding the latter practice, for the Negroes could be made a valuable war weapon. Not only could they be converted into labor battalions and even into soldiers but also they could be worked on occupied plantations to raise cotton, so badly needed in the North.

As this program was highly detrimental to the Confederacy, Southerners made every possible effort to combat it. They told their slaves that the Yankees were veritable devils with hoofs and horns, who would slay outright or work to death any Negroes who came into their possession. As Sherman was marching through Georgia, reports were widely circulated that he left his trail littered with the corpses of Negro women and children. Planters in regions threatened with invasion hurried off to places of safety with as many of their slaves as possible, and after invading armies had passed through, masters set up special patrols to control the excited and bewildered masses who remained. But invasions were bound to upset the slaves and lead many of them to follow after the armies, and where military lines were relatively stationary as on the coasts of North Carolina and South Carolina, many slaves escaped into the occupied zones. A Confederate officer declared in August, 1862, that slaves worth a million dollars were fleeing through the Federal lines in eastern North Carolina, and Governor Brown declared in March, 1864, that fifty thousand Georgia slaves were in the hands of the Federals.

Invading Federal armies came in contact with large numbers of slaves first on the York Peninsula outside of Fortress Monroe in the summer of 1861; and in the following November, when they made a lodgment in South Carolina, around Beaufort, they ran into many more. During 1862 Federal forces occupied large plantation areas in the Mississippi Valley, and thereafter they spread out into many other parts of the Confederacy. These great masses of slaves became both a problem and an opportunity. Where their masters were loyal or took the oath and became so, and remained on their plantations, there was one problem; where masters fled, there was another. At the same time there was an opportunity for the United States to acquire considerable amounts of much-needed cotton. In the Beaufort region a social experiment attempted to build the Negroes into responsible citizens, but, despite abolition humanitarianism, there was little success; and elsewhere, even as around Beaufort, there was more zeal shown in exploiting the Negroes than in building them into responsible citizenship.[52]

Various schemes were used in managing Negroes in these occupied regions. Generally, the loyal planters were left in control of their slaves, but as the great majority of plantations were owned

[52] Elizabeth H. Botume, *First Days among the Contrabands* (Boston, 1893), *passim;* Guion G. Johnson, *A Social History of the Sea Islands, with Special Reference to St. Helena Island, South Carolina* (Chapel Hill, 1930), 154–89.

by the disloyal, their lands and slaves were taken over and managed in various ways. A frequent practice was to lease these plantations to Northerners, often shady speculators, who made contracts with the slaves to work for part of the crop or for a monthly wage ranging from $3.00 to $25.00 a month depending on what was furnished. In some cases the land was leased to Negroes. In the regions where the slaves were torn from their moorings and were drifting around in helpless masses, army commanders appointed superintendents to assemble, feed, and dole them out to plantation managers needing labor.

To add confusion to the picture, the War Department held oversight of the Negroes; but the Treasury Department, after March, 1863, was assigned the management of all abandoned and confiscable lands on which Negroes might be worked. Speculators made fortunes from cotton gathered up in this confusion of rules and permits for raising, buying, and removing it.[53] Not until a month before the end of the war was there promise of order with the establishment of the Freedmen's Bureau. The constant progress in Federal occupation of the Confederacy deprived it of its labor supply, its lands and food, its population, and its ability to raise taxes and sinews of war—it was a slowly creeping paralysis.

Marching armies were irresistible to many of the slaves. "Glory be to de Lord," shouted one Negro as he saw the troops coming, "bress de Lord, the day of jubilou is come; dis nigger is off to glory." [54] Another, on beholding Sherman's army, exclaimed, "Dar's millions of 'em, millions!" and asked, "Is dare anybody lef' up Norf?" [55] Many "willing wenches" submitted to Federal soldiers and thereby increased the mulatto population of the South. Some slaves became cooks, teamsters, and servants in the army, but most of them who followed the armies so cluttered up operations as to lead some commanders to turn them back. Sherman, as well as McClellan, was criticized by Northern Radicals for this attitude.

Many Negroes were enlisted as Federal troops, beginning with

[53] Thomas W. Knox, *Camp-Fire and Cotton-Field: Southern Adventure in Time of War. Life with the Union Armies, and Residence on a Louisiana Plantation* (New York, 1865), 227 ff. See also, Wiley, *Southern Negroes*, 198 ff.

[54] Capt. David P. Conyngham, *Sherman's March through the South . . .* (New York, 1865), 248.

[55] Lloyd Lewis, *Sherman, Fighting Prophet* (New York, 1932), 439.

General David Hunter's regiment organized in South Carolina in April, 1862, which, however, saw no service. Early the next year "The First Regiment of South Carolina Volunteers" was organized. It was led by Thomas W. Higginson of Massachusetts until a wound caused his retirement in 1864. It now became a practice for substitute brokers to provide Negroes to take the place of whites drafted in the North until the practice was stopped by law, but throughout the war the quotas of some Northern states were partly filled by Negroes recruited in the South. To carry out this work more than 1,400 agents scurried around in the occupied parts of the Confederacy looking for Negro recruits. Tricks, persuasion, and compulsion were used to bring them into the Federal armies, and even rumors such as this were spread: "They say they have got a colored general over in Tennessee, who rides a horse, and commands ten acres of men." [56] As to forcing Negroes into the service, one Federal soldier commented: "There may be a difference between stealing negroes from their homes on the Congo, in Africa, to hoe cotton and cane and stealing them from the Cumbahee in South Carolina, to compel them to perform an involuntary and disliked service, but many people are not able to see that difference." [57] About 93,000 Negro troops were gathered up in the Confederacy throughout the war.

Negro troops fought in the battles around Port Hudson, Fort Pillow, Petersburg, Milliken's Bend, Nashville in 1864, and at other places; but, being poorly trained, most of them were not conspicuous either for bravery or skillful fighting. An Englishman in a group observing a regiment marching through the streets of New Orleans declared that any "three white men in the crowd could have dispersed the whole regiment with a good cart-whip each, and a few yells." [58] After the war a Federal veteran stated that the Negro soldiers' fighting qualities had been greatly exaggerated and that "their most effective work during the war was done with the pick and spade." [59]

[56] Hadley, *Seven Months a Prisoner*, 125.

[57] W. W. H. Davis, *History of the 104th Pennsylvania Regiment, from August 22nd, 1861, to September 30th, 1864* (Philadelphia, 1866), 209.

[58] *Two Months in the Confederate States . . . By an English Merchant*, 40.

[59] James M. Nichols, *Perry's Saints; or, The Fighting Parson's Regiment in the War of the Rebellion* (Boston, 1886), 175.

Southerners resented with burning bitterness this attempt to use their slaves as soldiers against them. Feeling it a crowning indignity to be forced to oppose them in time-honored warfare, Confederate soldiers fought them with such ferocity that they were charged with refusal to take Negro soldiers prisoners, and General Nathan B. Forrest was unjustly accused of having massacred them at the engagement at Fort Pillow. A bill was introduced in the Confederate Congress, though not passed, providing that Negroes taken in battle should be hanged or shot if they were slaves and sold into slavery if they were free Negroes. The Confederate government refused to exchange slave prisoners of war but instead turned them over to their masters.

Though the stated purpose of the North in warring against the Confederacy was to save the Union and not to interfere in any way with slavery, it was soon evident to any intelligent person that the institution of slavery could never ride out the war. Some rash and impractical Federal commanders like John C. Frémont in Missouri, in 1861, and David Hunter in South Carolina, in 1862, on their own authority declared the slaves free within their respective jurisdictions; but President Lincoln, wisely knowing that the time was not yet ripe for such action, annulled their proclamations and rebuked them. Extremists forced through the Federal Congress in August, 1861, the First Confiscation Act, which deprived masters of their property in all slaves who had been used in war work against the United States, and in July of the following year they passed the Second Confiscation Act, granting freedom to slaves whether they were engaged in war work or not, provided their masters were aiding in the war. Lincoln held out tenaciously against issuing a proclamation freeing the slaves, and he did not act on the policy set up in the Confiscation Act until September, 1862, when he issued his preliminary Emancipation Proclamation, which became final on January 1, 1863, on the refusal of the Confederates to lay down their arms in the meantime. In fact, it freed no slaves, for it was made to apply only to those regions opposing at that time the authority of the United States, and, therefore, in effect, to regions where he had no power to enforce it.

But the effect of the Proclamation on the South was profound and electrical. It was at first ignored in the press but later published here and there "as a matter of history" under the appellation, "the wonderful proclamation of Abraham Lincoln," and declared to be as futile as the Pope's Bull against the Comet. It was as hopeless a task for Lincoln "to abolish the climate of the South—to stagnate its rivers, and to bow its mountain ranges to a level with the plains below, as to revolutionize and destroy its social institutions." [60]

Yet it was a deadly threat of servile insurrection—an "Insurrection Proclamation"—which Confederate officials immediately sensed; it was also an attempt to set nonslaveholders against slaveholders, as the war would now take on more the character of a defense of slave property. Hill of Georgia introduced in the Senate a resolution declaring that all soldiers hereafter captured should be presumed to have come "with intent to incite insurrection and abet murder," and unless proved otherwise should suffer death. Others advocated raising the black flag everywhere. Senator Phelan of Mississippi included this blistering attack in a resolution which he offered: "Infuriated by continual defeat, maddened by revengeful passion and exasperated by despair of effecting our subjugation through the modes of civilized warfare, our brutal foes at length seek to light in our land the baneful fires of servile war, by emancipating amongst us four million of negro slaves, with the design of effecting an indiscriminating slaughter, of all ages, sexes and conditions of our people. A scheme so atrocious and infernal is unparalleled in the blackest and bloodiest page of savage strife, surpasses in atrocious cruelty the most signal despotism that ever disgraced the earth, and reveals the design of our enemy to be, regardless of the laws of God or man, the subjugation or the annihilation of the people of these Confederate States." [61] Though Congress

[60] Augusta *Weekly Constitutionalist,* October 8, 1862.

[61] *Southern Historical Society Papers,* XLVII (1930), 29. A "Lincoln Epitaph" from the Bellefontaine (Ohio) *Logan County Gazette,* widely copied in the Confederacy ran:

> Beneath this stone, corrupt and stinking,
> Repose the bones of Abraham Lincoln.
> He freed the niggers, and for his pains
> His own old soul is now in chains.

The preliminary Emancipation Proclamation did not exclude Tennessee from its effects, and thereby raised a storm of opposition in loyal East Tennessee. The final proclamation did not apply to Tennessee. See *Official Records,* Ser. I, Vol. XVI, Pt. II, 909–11; XX, Pt. II, 171, 317.

passed no laws to implement these sentiments, President Davis informed that body that he would deliver to the states all commissioned officers captured, to be dealt with according to their laws "for the punishment of criminals engaged in exciting servile insurrection." [62]

A Richmond editor suggested that Lincoln should be informed that unless he withdrew the Proclamation the Confederacy would fill the seas with privateers to harry out of existence the last vestige of Federal commerce, and he advocated the formation of mobile groups of five hundred desperate men who should "dash into the enemy's country with orders to burn, blow up, and destroy everything destructible in their course—every city, town, hamlet and house, every barn, warehouse, workshop, mill and bridge." "We can no longer be held to the practice of civilized war," he asserted.[63]

The slaves soon heard of Lincoln's Proclamation; and all of the wild fears in the minds of some Confederates subsided, for the Negroes continued in their even course of life. The Proclamation "is causing some trouble by the bad ones," wrote a planter, "but there is no alarm." When Federal troops marched into a region there were isolated cases, as in Louisiana, where slaves broke into their masters' homes and appropriated what they pleased.[64] Slaves continued to work on the plantations and in the armories as usual, and people still bought them and sold them. "The contemptuous disregard by the people of the South of the emancipation 'bull' of Lincoln, and the utter abortiveness," declared a Virginian, "finds no truer nor stranger expression anywhere than in the auction marts of the 'peculiar institution.' " [65] The common prices of slaves during 1864 and 1865 were from $3,000 to $5,000 apiece, in inflated Confederate currency, of course.

But the strangest attitude toward slaves that the typical Southerner could ever in his liveliest fancies have imagined would have been to use them as soldiers, to help win his independence. Yet, in the very beginning there were some people who had thought

[62] Richardson (comp.), *Messages and Papers of the Confederacy*, I, 291.

[63] Richmond *Daily Whig*, October 22, 1862.

[64] John H. Ransdell to Thomas O. Moore, May 24, 26, 1863, in Thomas O. Moore Collection (Louisiana State University Archives, Baton Rouge).

[65] Richmond *Daily Examiner*, February 13, 1863.

not only of using the free Negroes but also of arming the slaves. There was not the faintest popular move in that direction, however, until 1863. By this time, when Confederate soldiers were becoming hard to get, a few voices were raised in the newspapers; and the Confederate propaganda newspaper in London, the *Index,* announced that 500,000 slaves might be armed to guarantee a speedy victory.[66] Early in 1864 General Pat Cleburne advocated this move before a meeting of the officers of the Army of Tennessee. A copy of his paper was sent to President Davis, who suppressed it for fear of the bad effect it would have on the people; but there was considerable sentiment for it among the officers, including General Joseph E. Johnston. In his message to Congress, in November, 1864, Davis threw out the hint that the Confederacy might ultimately be brought to a consideration of slaves as soldiers, now that they had been used so freely in various kinds of war work, and he threatened that he would advocate such a measure if he could not secure a sufficient number of white soldiers. Soon the governors of a few of the states began to lend their support, and a considerable number of newspapers fell into line. The Richmond *Enquirer* became a strong supporter and invited the opinions of the Confederate soldiers themselves.

The general argument in favor of Negro soldiers was that the North was enlisting them, and they should be made to fight for the South instead of against it. It was contended that slaves could be easily disciplined and would make good soldiers, that slave soldiers would ennoble still further the institution of slavery and lighten its rigors after the war, that without more soldiers the war might be lost, and that as slaves had fought for American independence during the Revolution they should now help gain Southern independence. Confederate soldiers themselves favored the plan. In an Alabama unit of 200 soldiers, 143 voted for it and 88 were willing to fight side by side with Negroes; some Mississippi soldiers likewise showed their agreement and asked Congress to pass the needed legislation.

But, naturally, opposition to making slaves into soldiers was deeply embedded in Southerners. It seemed bizarre and grotesque and wholly at variance with the very essence and character of

---

[66] London *Index,* September 10, 1863, pp. 312–13.

Southern civilization. How could white people ever look a Negro in the face again, knowing that they owed their very existence to their own slaves? It would be the end of slavery and the beginning of social equality and miscegenation. Senator Wigfall said he "wanted to live in no country in which the man who blacked his boots and curried his horse was his equal." [67] It would bring a blush to the cheeks of the old soldiers to have to tell their children and grandchildren that the Negroes had won independence for the Southerners. Once in his lifetime Howell Cobb was to find himself in agreement with Governor Brown on a public question, when both held that arming the slaves would be a negation of everything for which the South was fighting.

After almost continuous debate for months, Congress finally on March 13, 1865, passed a law, spurred into action more by the fact that General Lee had endorsed it than for any other reason. By this law the President was authorized to call on the owners of slaves for as many of their Negroes between the ages of eighteen and forty-five as he deemed expedient "to perform military service in whatever capacity he may direct," but not to the extent of more than a fourth of such slaves in any state. This law did not force the owner to volunteer his slaves nor did it give the slaves freedom, but it was generally understood that any slaves who should fight in the Confederate armies would be made free by state action. Congress was very careful not to tread on the rights of the states.

This law came too late to be of any value, and at the time it was so understood by most people. Yet efforts were immediately made to organize Negro troops and some were actually raised and trained. There was some little excitement among the slaves to go to war and many officers set about raising regiments, but the enthusiasm among planters to give up their slaves was not marked. Near the end of March an immense throng of spectators gathered around Capitol Square in Richmond to see a Negro unit parade. These black soldiers had been dressed in new uniforms and as they executed their maneuvers amidst the din of drum and fife corps, the crowd of onlookers showed great enthusiasm for the performance. A little more than a week later Richmond had fallen and with it the Confederacy. The day for soldiers, black or white, had passed.

[67] Richmond *Daily Enquirer*, February 3, 1865.

CHAPTER XIII

TRANSPORTATION AND COMMUNICATION

THE transportation of troops and commodities and the communication of ideas and intelligence were as important as the production of them; and it was in the struggle between the North and the South that railroads and telegraphs were first to play their parts in major warfare. In both, the Confederacy was far inferior to its enemy. There were about 22,000 miles of railroads in the North to 9,000 miles in the states that made up the Confederacy, and the former had many more miles of telegraph lines. Had both sections been deprived of these modern inventions, the Confederacy would have held the advantage, for its great territorial extent could not have been as readily penetrated by invading armies; though nature, having endowed the South with a widespread network of rivers and long coast line, made access to certain regions relatively easy even without railroads. Had secession taken place in 1850, when the railroads in both sections were more nearly equal strategically, the South might well have established its independence.

The most important lines of railroads in the Confederacy led to Richmond, its nerve center. The road extending northward to Fredericksburg was of much less importance than the two lines leading southward to the sources of supplies. One of these two, familiarly called the Weldon Road, reached the important blockade-running port of Wilmington, and from there lines continued to Charleston, Savannah, Columbia, Augusta, and Atlanta. The other ran from Richmond southwestward through Lynchburg, Knoxville, and Chattanooga, to Atlanta, and from that city a road continued to Montgomery and Mobile. Out of Chattanooga lines led to Nashville and Memphis, and from the Tennessee capital the Louisville and Nashville, completed in 1859, ran to Louisville. This was one of the two lines which connected with the Ohio River. The other was the Mobile and Ohio Railroad, which ran from Mobile to Columbus, Kentucky, on the Mississippi, finished in 1851, when the silver spike was driven at Corinth, Mississippi. A north-south road farther west, the New Orleans, Jackson, and Great Northern, ran from New Orleans through Jackson, Mississippi, to Grand Junction, Tennessee, with connections to Jackson, Tennessee, through which the Mobile and Ohio passed.

There were many shorter lines in Tennessee and in the Atlantic-seaboard and Gulf states. West of the Mississippi there were practically no railroads, only short lines running from the west bank at Memphis, Vicksburg, Baton Rouge, and New Orleans. Texas was unconnected with the rest of the Confederacy; though five roads radiated out of Houston, they reached no points of importance except Galveston on the Gulf and Orange on the Sabine River, the state's eastern border. Another state wholly unconnected by railroad with the remainder of the Confederacy was Florida, whose two railroads of any consequence ran from Fernandina across the state to Cedar Keys on the Gulf, and from Jacksonville, with a break or two, westward a short distance beyond Tallahassee, in the northern part of the state.

It was evident to Davis or Lee or any other Confederate strategist, as he looked at a railroad map of his country, that there were glaring gaps in the transportation lines which must be filled if possible. The one which attracted attention first and which appeared most dangerous was a forty-mile stretch between Danville, Virginia, and Greensboro, North Carolina. If a line were laid here, there would be a third railway from Richmond southward, lying safely between the exposed Weldon Road on the east and the line through the uncertain East Tennessee country on the west; for already there were railways from Richmond to Danville and from Greensboro to Salisbury, Charlotte, and Columbia. In November, 1861, President Davis strongly recommended to Congress that the government undertake the problem and not wait for private initiative, for the need was so pressing that constitutional scruples otherwise admissible should now be disregarded in favor of military necessity. Congress responded in the following February by appropriating $1,000,000 to be used by the President in aiding a private company "in the manner he may think will best promote the public interest." But some Confederate leaders had not yet learned their lesson and were never to learn it, that under some circumstances the Constitution must be liberally interpreted and the states must forgo some of their zealously guarded rights. Rhett, Toombs, Curry, and others signed a protest against this act, declaring that it established an executive tyranny and that it was a violation of the Constitution and of the rights of the states.[1] For purely selfish reasons North Carolina opposed the move, as it would take traffic from the Weldon Road and might cause the Confederacy to slacken its zeal in defending this eastern highway. Planters along the route refused to allow their slaves to work on the project, and Governor Vance declared that the road was "viewed with almost universal disfavor in the State." [2] As a result, instead of completing the road within six months, which could easily have been done, the contractors took more than two years. Not until the latter part of May, 1864, were trains running over this track. By this time the scarcity of railroad irons was so great that the track was taken up on the short York River line out of Richmond and used on the Danville-Greensboro link.[3] The wisdom of building this link became evident during the last year of the war; it was over this line that most of the supplies for Lee's armies were transported, for in August, 1864, the Weldon Road was permanently disrupted by Federal troops.

The only other gap in the Confederate railroad system to be bridged was between Selma, Alabama, and Meridian, Mississippi. The completion of this link would give an all-rail route from Richmond to Vicksburg, with the exceptions of the short Alabama River steamboat connection between Montgomery and Selma and a four-and-a-half-mile passage on the Tombigbee River near Demopolis. A few days after Congress had acted on the Danville-Greensboro line, it appropriated $150,000 on like terms for the Selma-Meridian link; and the next month it allowed the importation of railroad iron for this project, duty-free. Work on this road was rushed, and before the end of 1862 it was completed.

There were various other links calling for construction, and

---

[1] *Journal of the Congress of the Confederate States*, I, 781–82.
[2] *Official Records*, Ser. IV, Vol. II, 394; Richmond *Daily Whig*, April 6, 1864.
[3] Jones, *Rebel War Clerk's Diary*, I, 287.

much agitation was expended, but nothing practical resulted. It was of outstanding importance that Texas and Florida be connected by rail with the remainder of the Confederacy. While Congress was in the mood for appropriating money to aid in these railroad constructions, Davis prevailed on it to allot in April, 1862, the sum of $1,500,000 to aid in building a line from New Iberia (the point reached with a water connection from Brashear by the road westward out of New Orleans) to connect with the Texas system. This project was soon given up, for New Orleans fell to the Federal forces the next month. Floridians were anxious to have the Confederacy aid in connecting their roads with the Georgia system, but Congress refused to act. Not until 1864 did certain Confederate governmental agencies make the attempt, and it came too late.

Another less important link was between Columbia and Augusta. This line would obviate the roundabout route through Kingsville and Branchville. A company was chartered, and by January, 1864, five hundred Negroes with spades began grading; six months later a thousand were advertised for, but war conditions prevented the road's completion.[4] During the first year of the war a road was built from Little Rock eastward to the White River; however, Congress could not be induced to aid in completing it to the end of the line extending westward from Memphis.

In some cases the extension of railroads to strategic places was almost as important as bridging gaps. The last specific appropriation Congress made to aid in building a railroad was for such a project—a line to be run from Rome, Georgia, to the Blue Mountains coal fields in Alabama. The amount appropriated was $1,122,-480.92, but the shortage of materials prevented more than a beginning. Finally, a month before Lee's surrender, Congress in a spurt of desperation appropriated $21,000,000 "for the construction and repair of railroads for military purposes"; but, of course, nothing came out of this.

Another coal field in the Deep River region of Chatham County, North Carolina, invited more adequate railroad connections.

[4] Charleston *Daily Courier*, January 18, 1864; Augusta *Daily Constitutionalist*, July 15, 1864; Augusta *Daily Chronicle & Sentinel*, May 5, 1864; Jones, *Rebel War Clerk's Diary*, II, 370; Edwin B. Coddington, "A Social and Economic History of the Seaboard States of the Southern Confederacy" (Ph.D. dissertation, Clark University, 1939).

Much coal was being mined and taken out over a short line to Fayetteville and thence by the Cape Fear River to Wilmington. Cheraw, South Carolina, attempted to run a road to these deposits, and Raleigh on the north was likewise interested in extending its contemplated Chatham Railroad to the same place. Some grading was done, but it was impossible to get railroad equipment.[5]

Two ambitious long lines much talked about but not built until after the war were the Southern Pacific from Shreveport to El Paso and the Air Line from Atlanta to Charlotte. In early 1863 President Davis was anxious to have a short line built to Port Hudson, on the Mississippi, from the nearest point on the New Orleans, Jackson, and Great Northern, and he was equally anxious to have the road extended from Tallahassee to the Chattahoochee. Only the latter was constructed.

The greatest difficulty in developing new roads as well as in maintaining old ones was in equipping them. Though railroad irons could be rolled in the Confederacy and, contrary to contemporary assertions, some were, still there was a most serious shortage in this equipment. Whether a railroad should be allowed to remain in existence was predicated on how important it was, and soon railroad companies were fighting to keep their tracks from being seized or sequestered by the Confederate government or military authorities. Congress seized the Brunswick and Albany Railroad, in Georgia, on the ground that it was tainted with enemy ownership and took up its rails and distributed them to more needed routes. Other railroads dismantled were the Alabama and Florida, the Fort Gaines branch of the Southwestern Railroad, in Georgia, the York Railroad, as previously mentioned, and a few minor roads in North Carolina. The military authorities took up the rails of the Texas road from Beaumont to Orange and used them to ironclad the fort at Sabine Pass.[6]

A multiplicity of gauges added to the inadequacy of the railroad system and necessitated the transshipment of freight at many points.

[5] Charleston *Daily Courier*, February 7, December 2, 1862; Spencer, *Last Ninety Days of the War*, 240; William J. Battle (ed.), *Memories of an Old-Time Tar Heel, By Kemp Plummer Battle* (Chapel Hill, 1945), 173–78.

[6] St. Clair G. Reed, *A History of the Texas Railroads and of Transportation Conditions under Spain and Mexico and the Republic and the State* (Houston, 1941), 84–89; Virgil Powers to Howell Cobb, February 28, 1865, in Howell Cobb Papers.

The senseless rivalry of the many companies which ran Southern lines resulted in a variation of from three to six feet. The Weldon Road out of Richmond into eastern North Carolina was four inches narrower than the line running through Lynchburg into East Tennessee, and the third road southward out of Richmond by way of Danville changed gauges in a most exasperating fashion. One width prevailed from Richmond to Danville, a narrower gauge set in at Danville and continued through Greensboro to Charlotte, and then on to Columbia there was a change to a wider gauge.

Born of the same suspicions and distrust among railroad companies was the refusal to join their tracks at terminal points, whether the gauges were the same or not. Not only must cars be unloaded and reloaded at such points, but it was necessary to cart the freight across the city, a practice which greatly reduced the efficiency of the railroads. In a few instances the tracks of some of the roads were joined as a special concession to war needs as in Charleston and Savannah. In Richmond the tracks of the roads leading to Fredericksburg and to Petersburg were joined, but despite the pleadings of Lee and others the roads at the key point of Petersburg continued disconnected, thereby greatly slowing up the supplies for the armies of Virginia.[7]

More unfortunate for the Confederacy than its incomplete railway system was its inability to maintain properly what roads it had. The traditional dislike of Southerners for mechanical and industrial pursuits had left the railroads largely in the hands of Northern trainmen. When the war broke out, many returned to the North, and those who remained were looked upon with suspicion. Some of the Confederate troops on their way to the field of action at First Manassas were delayed by disloyal engineers. General Beauregard had one engineer court-martialed and shot for sabotaging his engine. "The truth is *all* of the engine runners on our roads are Yankees," charged Thomas R. R. Cobb, "and I hear in various quarters of the delay of troops attributed to them." [8] In East Tennessee

[7] Charles W. Ramsdell, "The Confederate Government and the Railroads," in *American Historical Review,* XXII (1916–1917), 794–810; Richmond *Daily Examiner,* July 27, September 21, 1861; Richmond *Daily Enquirer,* September 16, 1864; Richmond *Daily Whig,* August 5, 1861.

[8] Cobb, Richmond, to his wife, July 29, 1861, in Thomas R. R. Cobb Letters. The loss of much railway equipment on the fall of Huntsville, Alabama, was laid to the

an engineer deserted his engine rather than "haul rebels." Incompetent Southerners played havoc with the running of trains; and, with the scarcity of workmen incident to the exigencies of war, the railroads found it difficult to secure even slave labor. In 1862 the Virginia and Tennessee Railroad advertised for five hundred Negroes to act as trackmen, brakemen, firemen, depot hands, wood choppers, carpenters, and blacksmiths.[9]

At the outbreak of the war the equipment of Southern railroads was dismally inadequate in comparison with what Northern roads had. The Baltimore and Ohio Railroad alone had half as many passenger cars as the whole Confederacy, and the Pennsylvania and Erie roads had almost as many engines. Furthermore, in antebellum times the South had depended largely on the North for its railroad equipment, and now with this source cut off, the Confederacy was left to get along as best it could with what it had. True enough, there were a few factories already in existence in the South, as the Tredegar Iron Works, and others later developed, as the Macon and Western Machine Shops and the rolling mills in Atlanta, which could make railroad equipment, but their facilities were almost entirely monopolized by the requirements of the Confederate government. In 1863 one of Quartermaster General Lawton's officers informed him that there were at least fifty locomotives out of commission because of worn-out tires, which could be easily replaced at Richmond or Atlanta, "but the government absorbs the work of these shops and the material also; consequently, the railroads are impotent." By the same year a third of the locomotives and cars on the South Carolina Railroad were in disrepair. There was no possible relief "without machinists from the Army, iron from the mines, and permission for foundries and rolling-mills to work for railroads." The Confederacy had the materials and means for making needed supplies and equipment, but as long as it denied the railroads their use, there could be no relief.[10] About this time another officer informed Secretary of War Seddon that the railroads

---

treachery of Yankee trainmen. See J. W. Clay, Knoxville, to Clement C. Clay, May 15, 1862, in Clay Papers.

[9] Richmond *Daily Whig*, November 21, 1862.

[10] F. W. Sims to A. R. Lawton, October 23, 1863, in *Official Records*, Ser. IV, Vol. II, 882.

had made every effort to meet the requirements of the government for the past two years, but they could not continue to do so long unless there was "prompt action looking to a restoration of the principal roads in the country to the best possible condition." [11] Lawton complained in October, 1863, that the army in Virginia, the largest in the Confederacy, was drawing its subsistence from a distance of seven hundred miles, and yet the government did not regard the railroads as important enough to allow them the equipment necessary to keep them in operation.[12]

Railroad presidents in convention at Richmond in February, 1862, recommended to their respective roads the establishment of a number of rolling mills to make equipment or to contract with other capitalists to set up rolling mills. In another meeting the following September at Columbia they entreated the government to develop the iron mines in northern Alabama and in the Deep River country of central North Carolina. P. V. Daniel, Jr., president of the Richmond, Fredericksburg, and Potomac Railroad Company again called attention in 1863 to the great necessity of setting up four or five rolling mills, which could operate only if the Confederate government would allow them iron supplies; and he decried the practice of permitting freight cars to serve as storage warehouses, all because labor was not provided to unload them.[13] Some railroad equipment was brought in through the blockade from Europe, but not until May, 1864, did the Confederate government allow its entry duty-free. Confederate officials failed to realize that the upkeep of the railroads was as important as the upkeep of the army. At least, it was not realized until March, 1865, when Congress appropriated $21,000,000; but it was then too late to do any good either for the railroads or the armies, both of which were in a state of collapse.

From 1861 to 1865 railroad service grew progressively worse, with broken rails, flat wheels, rotten crossties, wheezy old powerless engines, and ramshackle cars. In 1862 it was estimated that there were 1,200 broken rails between Chattanooga and Nashville. The speed of trains slowed down to "a snail's pace." Trains which formerly

[11] William M. Wadley to Seddon, April 14, 1863, *ibid.*, 485.
[12] *Ibid.*, 883.
[13] *Ibid.*, 500, 501, 505, 512.

went from twenty to twenty-five miles an hour were making about ten miles by 1863, and by the end of the war six miles had come to be normal. The lack of fuel supplies at woodyards necessitated frequent stops while the crews gathered up wood wherever it could be found. In 1862 it took a soldier eight days to go from Manassas to Augusta, Georgia, and two years later the actor Harry Macarthy, probably stretching his humor a little, reported that it required seventeen days to go from Atlanta to Richmond, "travelling night and day." [14] In May, 1864, Vice-President Stephens decided to make one of his occasional visits to Richmond, from his Georgia home. He finally reached Danville after many mishaps and near escapes from death, but a wreck near that place persuaded him to return to Georgia. [15]

Passenger accommodations were miserable. The cars were generally crowded almost beyond imagination, the seats and floor alike filled with soldiers and civilians—sick soldiers, wounded soldiers, well soldiers, drunken and boisterous soldiers, meek, patriotic, and complaining civilians, men, women, and children. There was no water in the cars, except now and then a barrel with a tin dipper. The great numbers of soldiers moving by rail made it necessary to use freight cars, into which they were crowded on improvised plank seats or allowed to ride on the tops of the cars, which many seemed to prefer. In cold weather they made fires on the floors of the box-cars and sometimes carelessly left them blazing when they got off, resulting now and then in the destruction of cars and in at least one instance the burning of a railway station into which the cars had been shoved.

The lack of telegraphic dispatching of trains slowed down their movement from one end of a line to the other and occasionally led to wrecks, though wrecks were due more often to other causes. Such distressing accidents became more frequent as rails broke and wore out and equipment became dilapidated. A military officer declared that a trip from Montgomery to Richmond was "as hazardous as picket duty on the Potomac." [16] Two trains on the Mississippi Cen-

---

[14] Richmond *Daily Whig*, March 25, 1864.

[15] Johnston and Browne, *Alexander H. Stephens*, 462–67.

[16] Heros von Borcke, *Memoirs of the Confederate War for Independence* (Philadelphia, 1867), 10.

tral ran together, killing thirty-five soldiers and injuring about fifty; ten people and many horses were killed in a head-on collision on the Western and Atlantic; a troop train ran into a lumber train on the New Orleans, Jackson and Great Northern and killed twenty-five soldiers; in northern Virginia a train of soldiers moving south to meet McClellan's march up the Peninsula ran head on into an empty train, killing many, and only by good fortune did General John B. Gordon escape uninjured. Cattle on the track frequently caused wrecks. In Mississippi a large ox wrecked a train in which five soldiers were killed; and near Charlottesville, Virginia, a train ran into three sleeping oxen and was thrown down a seventy-foot embankment, killing nine soldiers and injuring forty-four. Other wrecks were caused by the collapse of bridges and trestles. A soldier-train broke through a bridge on the Chunkey River, in Mississippi, and killed at least nineteen. Now and then boilers exploded, causing wrecks and loss of life. Occasionally flying sparks from the wood-burning engines set cars afire and caused either wrecks or considerable property loss. A train from Danville to Richmond caught fire on a downgrade, and before it could be stopped a number of cars were consumed including the express car containing $25,000 in gold and silver, which was melted into a mass.

Enemy action also played havoc with railroad equipment and track. Invading armies tore up hundreds of miles of track, heating the rails and wrapping them corkscrew fashion around trees to prevent future use. Spies and Federal raiders accounted for other destructions. In the fall of 1861 disaffected East Tennesseans were paid $20,000 to burn five bridges in North Georgia and East Tennessee, and the next spring twenty-two disguised Federal soldiers, led by J. J. Andrews, attempted unsuccessfully to burn the bridges and blow up the tunnels on the Western and Atlantic Railroad.[17] Also, Federal troops captured much rolling stock. Cut off by a fallen bridge, General Joseph E. Johnston abandoned ninety locomotives and several hundred cars when he evacuated Jackson, Mississippi,

17 *Official Records*, Ser. I, Vol. XX, Pt. II, 70; Vol. X, Pt. I, 630–39; Atlanta *Southern Confederacy*, June 19, 1862; Coulter, *William G. Brownlow*, 168–74; William Pittenger, *Capturing a Locomotive: A History of Secret Service in the Late War* (Washington, 1885).

after the fall of Vicksburg and Port Hudson. President Davis declared that the Confederacy "never recovered from the injury to the transportation service occasioned by this failure on his part." [18]

Occasionally the Confederates made captures of Federal rolling stock. In the early part of the war, General Stonewall Jackson used trickery to capture thirty-six locomotives and three hundred cars from the Baltimore and Ohio, at Harpers Ferry; a little later the Confederates were able to run off to Nashville a great many Louisville and Nashville locomotives and cars. In 1864 they captured on the Chickahominy a locomotive which they renamed the "Jeff Davis," declaring that it was the finest in the Confederacy.[19] Federal armies constructed a few short military railroads in the Confederacy, the most important one being the City Point and Army Line in Virginia.[20]

"No corporations in the Confederacy have made such constant efforts to serve the Government as railroad corporations," affirmed an officer in the Quartermaster Department, adding, "The managers of them embraced the best business talent and exhibit as much patriotism as any class in the country." [21] On the outbreak of war railroads gave special rates to the government for carrying soldiers and war supplies, and a few in the flush of their initial enthusiasm offered to carry soldiers free. As late as the latter part of 1862, when inflation was skyrocketing the prices of everything, the railroads still adhered to their low rates to the government, but thereafter they were forced to revise their schedules. The higher rates, which had always prevailed for the public, were greatly increased with the coming of higher prices, leading some people to think that the railroads were thereby compensating themselves for their apparent patriotic regard for the government. In January, 1862, most of the Georgia roads announced a 20 per cent increase in their rates, and by 1863 it was announced that the Mobile and Ohio had run its

18 Rowland (ed.), *Jefferson Davis, Constitutionalist*, VI, 498.

19 Richmond *Daily Examiner*, April 29, 1864; Bradlee, *Blockade Running during the Civil War*, 194 ff.; Festus P. Summers, *The Baltimore and Ohio in the Civil War* (New York, 1939), 67; Alfred H. Bill, *The Beleaguered City, Richmond, 1861–1865* (New York, 1946), 63.

20 "Affairs of Southern Railroads," in *Reports of Committees of the House of Representatives*, 39 Cong., 2 Sess., No. 34, Serial No. 1306, p. 324.

21 *Official Records*, Ser. IV, Vol. II, 882.

freight rates up 300 per cent. About this time the Macon and Western was charging ten cents a mile for passengers and from two and a half to five cents for soldiers. In 1864 the Central of Virginia was charging twenty-five cents per mile for ordinary passengers. By this time the railroads had become exceedingly unpopular with the public and were being accused of outrageous profiteering. A Congressman advocated charging railroads $10,000 for each workman exempted from army service.[22] It was inevitable that the railroads would be forced to increase their rates or go out of business, for by 1863 clerical service of the South Carolina Railroad had advanced 100 per cent, unskilled labor 150 per cent, mechanical labor 200 per cent, and equipment about 2,000 per cent. Railroads as well as other corporations were apparently making a great deal of money: their dividend rates as well as their receipts increased, but as in the case of the South Carolina Railroad where the increase was from 7 per cent to 16 per cent by 1864, the gold value of money decreased at a greater ratio, being 38 to 1 by the end of 1864.[23]

Despite its appropriation of money to aid the construction of railroads, the Confederate government did not realize until too late its own responsibility in seeing that the railroads were properly maintained and operated efficiently. Very early it saw the desirability of co-ordinating the railroads by moving cars from one road to another, making contracts, joining tracks, and fixing time schedules; and to effect these ends it appointed William S. Ashe, president of the Wilmington and Weldon Railroad, to be superintendent and director of railroads. He was able to accomplish little, and in late 1862 he was succeeded by William M. Wadley, formerly superintendent of the New Orleans, Jackson and Great Northern Railroad, who was equally unsuccessful in getting practical results. In an attempt to remedy the situation, Congress passed a law May 1, 1863, which handed over to the Quartermaster General the management of all railroad equipment with the exception of one train on each line. Any railroad refusing to submit to this control might be seized and impressed under the provisions of the Impressment Act.

[22] Macon *Daily Telegraph*, January 24, 1862; October 9, 1863; Richmond *Daily Examiner*, September 3, 1864; Mobile *Daily Advertiser and Register*, November 20, 1863; *Southern Historical Society Papers*, XLVIII (1941), 36.

[23] Samuel M. Derrick, *Centennial History of South Carolina Railroad* (Columbia, 1930), 221, 222.

Lieutenant Colonel F. M. Sims of the Quartermaster Department was now placed in charge of railroads, and with this added authority he was able to improve the service, but it was impossible to bring much efficiency to a deteriorating system. In a final desperate effort to make all transportation more effective, Congress passed a law on February 28, 1865, placing all railroads, steamboats, canals, and telegraph lines under the control of the Secretary of War, and on March 9 it appropriated the previously mentioned $21,000,000 for the rehabilitation of the roads, but the Confederacy fell before anything practical resulted.

Indeed, the railroads had never played the part that could have been expected of them if the government had exercised proper foresight in the beginning. The food was in one place and the mouths in another, and transportation became scarcer than provisions. Lee said to Davis in the summer of 1864, "I think that it is clear that the railroads are not working energetically & unless some improvement is made, I do not know what will become of us." [24] He advocated the elimination of all pleasure travel and recommended that "everything be devoted to necessary wants," [25] and Commissary General Northrop at various times had advocated cessation of all civilian passenger traffic. No large, strategic troop movements were ever made by rail except the transfer of Longstreet's corps from Virginia to northern Georgia in the fall of 1863, which took seven and a half days by way of Wilmington and Atlanta. Had the railroads been efficient enough and had Lee possessed bold vision, part of his army in Virginia could have been sent to the relief of Vicksburg and the Gettysburg campaign would have been averted.

Part of railroad traffic, though not under the control of the railroads, was the express business. As soon as war broke out, the Adams Express Company, Northern-owned though operating also in the South, turned over its Southern business to Henry B. Plant, a Connecticut Yankee who since 1854 had managed its interests in the South. Plant organized the Southern Express Company, which in order to show its Confederate character and patriotism, carried soldiers' packages free if they did not weigh over one hundred pounds. It was so efficiently managed, with quick transfers of its

24 Freeman (ed.), *Lee's Dispatches*, 247.
25 Rowland (ed.), *Jefferson Davis, Constitutionalist*, VI, 224.

packages from one road to another, that the Confederate government sent all its money shipments by express rather than through the mails. But when inflation sent its rates up, people began to complain. They charged that it was a Yankee institution which ought to be suppressed and that the railroads should carry the express on their own accounts. The Pioneer Express Company handled most of the express business west of Montgomery. In 1864 its officials lent aid to those who were criticizing the Southern Express Company by declaring that their own rates were about one tenth as much as their rival's.[26]

Water transportation played little part in the life of the Confederacy, because the blockading fleet made it hazardous along the coast, and the Federal gunboats on the rivers disrupted traffic there. If the railroads be considered the arteries of the Confederacy, wagon routes were surely the veins. They ramified into every part of the inhabited land, gathering up subsistence and hauling it to the railroads and in turn hauling it away to the all-devouring armies. Yet there was an alarming shortage of these vehicles and of factories in which to make them, and as army recruiting combed the population, competent teamsters were difficult to find.

Quick transmission of intelligence could be as important in certain situations as the transportation of supplies, and at all times it was a vital necessity not only for armies but also for newspapers and civilians generally. In 1861 the principal cities of the Confederacy, with the exception of those in Texas, were connected by telegraph lines. Before secession the main lines in the Atlantic seaboard states were either owned or leased by the American Telegraph Company, a Northern enterprise; but on the organization of the Confederacy this company divested itself of its Southern interests and turned them over to the Southern Telegraph Company, headed by Dr. William S. Morris. The principal company in the Mississippi Valley east of the river, with lines running from Louisville to New Orleans, was the South-Western Telegraph Company, which had its headquarters in Nashville. The important

26 Montgomery *Daily Post*, August 10, 1861; Mobile *Daily Advertiser and Register*, August 12, 1861; Atlanta *Southern Confederacy*, August 24, 1861; January 18, 1863; Richmond *Daily Examiner*, December 9, 1862; Richmond *Daily Enquirer*, September 17, October 13, 1864; Brownlee, *Blockade Running during the Civil War*, 311–14.

lines west of the Mississippi were the Texas Telegraph Company and the Arkansas State Telegraph Company. There was a multiplicity of short lines radiating out to the smaller cities; yet there were many towns without telegraphic service, and Texas was isolated from the remainder of the Confederacy, though a line ran as far west as Shreveport.

Seeing the importance of controlling telegraphic business, Congress in May, 1861, gave President Davis the right to supervise all lines "to the end that no communications shall be conveyed of the military operations of the government to endanger the success of such operations, nor any communication calculated to injure the cause of the Confederate States, or give aid and comfort to their enemies." He might seize any lines refusing to co-operate. Davis appointed Postmaster-General Reagan superintendent of the telegraphs, and he in turn handed over direct supervision first to Morris and later to J. T. Caldwell. The control of telegraphs was never thoroughly co-ordinated because frequently military commanders took charge of the lines within their areas and appointed their own agents without regard to Reagan. Codes unknown to the supervisory agents at the principal points and news accounts detailing troop movements, the positions of particular units, or their strength were denied transmission.

As stringing up telegraph lines was much more easily done than building railroads, a great many new lines were constructed during the war. The only scarce material was wire, but a limited amount was obtained from a few factories set up in the Confederacy, captured from the enemy, or seized from little-used lines. President Davis was given power to authorize the construction of any new lines needed for military operations and to make connections between lines, and various private companies built or extended lines as investments. Supervisor Caldwell extended a military line fifty-seven miles in eleven days in the Gettysburg campaign and built a great many other lines, though he did not satisfy one North Carolinian who blamed the lack of telegraphic connections on "that skin-flint Reagan."

The Federals made much more use of the telegraph in their operations and constructed many more miles of military telegraph lines than did the Confederates: the former constructed about

15,000 miles of lines in war years; the latter, probably not more than 500. By the end of 1861 the gap separating Texas from the remainder of the Confederacy had been bridged, and now New Orleans had direct connections with Houston, though Austin, the capital of the state, did not receive its first telegraphic connections until the end of the war.

Apart from their military business, the telegraph lines served principally the newspapers, and they did not fail to come in for their share of condemnation for their high rates. Editors complained that they had kept down the price of their newspapers, even in the face of mounting prices for paper, but they were finally forced to give way in the face of exorbitant telegraphic rates. There were suspicions that the Southern Telegraph Company was really enemy-owned, and demands were unsuccessfully raised in Congress that it be sequestered.[27]

The railroads, as patriotic as they had seemed, were not equally efficient. Food in Georgia might as well not have existed as far as Lee's hungry armies in Virginia were concerned. It was not lack of food; it was lack of transportation. The railroads bore a heavy share of blame in the final collapse of the Confederacy.

[27] Sources of information on telegraph lines are: E. J. Hale, Fayetteville, N.C., to Vance, September 14, 1863, in Vance Papers; Greensboro (Ala.) *Beacon*, June 24, 1864; Austin *Texas State Gazette*, May 3, 1865; Little Rock *Daily State Journal*, November 17, 1861; Atlanta *Southern Confederacy*, May 4, 1861; August 8, 1862; Columbus *Weekly Enquirer*, October 7, 1862; Richmond *Daily Dispatch*, January 15, 1862; Richmond *Daily Examiner*, April 8, 1863; Richmond *Daily Whig*, September 22, 1862; April 30, 1864; *Official Records*, Ser. IV, Vol. I, 783, 1146–47; Vol. II, 149; *The Private Press Association of the Confederate States of America* (Griffin, Ga., 1863), 32; Plum, *Military Telegraph during the Civil War*, II, 120–21; Bradlee, *Blockade Running during the Civil War*, 291–306; Reagan, *Memoirs*, 159; Robert L. Thompson, *Wiring a Continent; The History of the Telegraph Industry in the United States, 1832–1866* (Princeton, 1947), 373–79, 394–95.

CHAPTER XIV

TRADE, BLOCKADE-RUNNING, AND THE NAVY

A S A new nation the South was free to adopt whatever tariff or free-trade policies it pleased. At its inception the Confederacy automatically succeeded to the tariff of 1857, then in force in the United States, but during the next few months various laws of the Confederate Congress greatly lowered the old rates.[1] Yet it did not adopt free trade, for it wanted to use the tariff to produce revenue and to promote Southern manufactories by the incidental protection afforded.

There was much discussion and conflicting opinion over this policy. To many people it seemed that now was the time for the South to adopt its long-sought direct trade with Europe, to cut loose forever from the middlemen of the North, and to develop its own importing houses. The blockade prompted the additional argument that free trade would likely lead European nations to intervene, and it would certainly encourage a great many individuals to enter into the blockade-running business and, thereby, help to supply the Confederacy with sinews of war. As tariff duties must be paid in specie, any rate so paid would greatly increase the cost of imports when translated into depreciated Confederate currency. For instance, a duty of 20 per cent in specie with the rate of exchange at 20 to 1 would advance the selling price of cloth from $5.00 to $25.00 a yard—the $20.00 increase a result of the tariff.

Either through considerations of national defense or of international policy, the Confederacy made important concessions to free trade and unobstructed entry into its waters by admitting railway materials without duty in certain special cases, and also all machinery necessary for making shoes and clothing for soldiers.

[1] See pp. 173-74.

Foreign nations were allowed to engage in coastwise traffic and use its rivers. To curry favor with the states of the interior Mississippi Valley and entice them into the Confederacy, the free and peaceable navigation of the Mississippi was opened to them during the secession period.

National policy forbade trading with enemies, but as the Confederacy assumed at the beginning that it had none, it looked for commercial intercourse with all nations. But firing on Fort Sumter made the United States an enemy, and the Confederacy in effect recognized a state of war when it authorized letters of marque to prey on Federal commerce following Lincoln's proclamation of a blockade. Knowing that cotton was a necessity in the North and realizing how easy it was to run it out across the land frontiers, Congress on May 21 forbade its exportation except across the Rio Grande and through ports which it could control. In the following August it extended these restrictions to tobacco, sugar, rice, molasses, syrup, and naval stores. When Federal armies invaded the Confederacy, Congress forbade taking such articles to any port or place in the hands of the enemy.

But with Federal troops overrunning the land, it was much more difficult to control trade, and from then until the fall of the Confederacy commercial intercourse with the enemy came to be a major activity of many people, winked at and even licensed by both the Confederate and Federal authorities, each hoping to reap the greater advantage in the traffic. During the first year of the war, vast amounts of war supplies came south through Kentucky, and thereafter Confederate armies in the Mississippi Valley were to a very considerable extent provisioned through commerce carried on with Federal agents and private traders.[2] When Memphis fell to the enemy, it came to be, according to a Federal officer, a greater outfitting point for Confederate armies than Nassau. General William T. Sherman charged that Cincinnati had "furnished more contraband goods than Charleston," and had "done more to prolong

[2] See E. Merton Coulter, "Effects of Secession upon the Commerce of the Mississippi Valley," in *Mississippi Valley Historical Review*, III (1916–1917), 275–300; E. Merton Coulter, "Commercial Intercourse with the Confederacy in the Mississippi Valley, 1861–1865," *ibid.*, V (1918–1919), 377–95.

the war than the State of South Carolina." [3] Efforts to stop unauthorized traffic were of no avail, for the profits to Yankee traders
made it possible for them to bribe their way through Federal
officers, and Southern need for Yankee goods and supplies overrode all considerations of aiding the enemy. An English lady
declared that to stop this traffic would require "a Chinese wall
from the Atlantic to the Pacific—and not even that—would prove
effectual, while diving-bells beneath the waves, and balloons above,
could be available." [4] Even women engaged in the traffic, bringing
in supplies of medicines and small articles hidden under their
ample skirts. Confederate state authorities got permission to run
cotton through the lines, the Quartermaster Department dealt with
the enemy, and near the end of the war General Lee strongly recommended to President Davis a widespread trade to secure additional
supplies for his army, which already had been subsisting considerably on New York bacon brought through the lines.

The Confederacy relied upon securing war materials abroad, in
supplying itself with war necessities, apart from essentials manufactured or captured, rather than depending upon trade with the
enemy. Blockade-running therefore came to be of outstanding
importance, with Wilmington, Charleston, Savannah, Mobile,
New Orleans, and Galveston serving as principal ports. There were
many smaller ports where vessels could land, and even inlets and
undeveloped parts of the coast were entered by small craft as such
landings were soon legalized. In 1862 the fall of New Orleans and
of Fort Pulaski, down the river from Savannah, prevented further
use of these ports; other coastal cities fell later, and in 1865 there
remained only Wilmington which had come to be the premier
blockade-running port of the Confederacy. Preparations were being
made to develop a port at the mouth of the Appalachicola River,
in Florida, when the Confederacy collapsed. As the Gulf ports
were farther from the European sources of supply, they were not
used as much as the Atlantic ports, but they were still valuable and
quite active during the first part of the war in running in materials
from Havana and the Mexican ports of Tampico and Vera Cruz.

---

[3] M. A. De Wolfe Howe (ed.), *Home Letters of General Sherman* (New York, 1909),
232.   [4] [Hopley], *Life in the South*, II, 39.

The blockade was most effectively run by dividing the trip from Europe into parts, or "legs" in the language of international law. Bermuda and Nassau were the most important dividing points. Here the cargoes were transshipped to smaller, fast-moving vessels, which underwent the dangers of breaking through the blockade. Applying its doctrine of continuous voyage, the United States attempted to break up this trade on the first leg between Liverpool and Nassau, two neutral ports; but despite prize-court decisions such as the *Springbok* and the *Bermuda,* allowing such seizures, Nassau and Bermuda developed a tremendous trade with the Confederacy.

The hazards of the blockade were open to anyone who cared to risk them. Foreigners, especially the British, the Confederate government, the states, and Confederate private interests engaged in blockade-running. The first vessel to fly the Confederate flag on entering a Southern port was British, and according to contemporary accounts many of the officers and crews of Confederate blockade-runners were British. More than half of the ships and cargoes brought into New York City to be tried in the prize court there were British.[5] Not only did many small craft run the blockade on their own account, but soon blockade-running companies were organized to develop small fleets and provide lucrative investments for their stockholders. Fraser, Trenholm & Company, the Liverpool branch of John Fraser & Company of Charleston, early entered the blockade-running business, and the Fraser Company itself was one of the largest. Gazaway B. Lamar headed a company owning four steamers; the Old Dominion Importing and Exporting Company, the Anglo-Confederate Trading Company, the Bee Company, Ravenel and Company, the Chicora Importing and Exporting Company, and many others soon sprang up. In England such companies as the British and American Southern Steamship Company and Alexander Collie and Company entered the trade. Some of the companies in the Confederacy were capitalized at more than $1,000,000 and their stocks were first offered at a price as high as $5,000 a share. Their steamers bore fantastic, romantic, and patri-

---

[5] Madeline R. Robinton, *An Introduction to the Papers of the New York Prize Court, 1861–1865* (New York, 1945), 150; Ella Lonn, *Foreigners in the Confederacy* (Chapel Hill, 1940), 299.

otic names such as *Let Her Be, Let Her Rip, Fox, Leopard, Lynx, Dream, Secret, Banshee, Kate, Hattie, Beauregard, Stonewall Jackson,* and *Jeff Davis.*

The profits of blockade-running were immense. If a ship made two trips the venture was a success, even if on the third it were captured. Companies paid from 500 per cent to 1,000 per cent on their stocks. In the spring of 1864 a South Carolinian bought a stock for $3,200 and sold it six months later for $6,000, having in the meantime received a dividend of $500. In the fall of 1864 a share of stock in the South Carolina Importing and Exporting Company was sold for $28,600.[6]

Such profits were irresistible not only to Southerners and foreigners but also to the canny Yankee traders, who had no more scruples against trading with the enemy by water than by land. It was easy enough to gain entrance to captured Southern ports such as Beaufort and New Orleans, and it was not too difficult to run the blockade after the fashion of Confederates and Europeans, especially if there was connivance with the Federal blockading fleets. Southerners early suspected that Northern goods, even though changed to bear English marks, were receiving special consideration, judging from the amount that successfully came through; and it was well known to Confederate forwarding agents in Nassau and Bermuda that many Northern products swelled the amount there. But this practice seemed to be pleasing enough to the Confederates; for Benjamin and Memminger smiled on it, and Gazaway B. Lamar even proposed to New York interests the organization of a blockade-running company.

Manifestly blockade-running was getting out of hand and actually becoming detrimental to the Confederate cause. What kinds of goods were being brought in and what was happening to prices? The biggest profits were in luxuries and other civilian goods—not in munitions of war whose price the Confederate government could hold down. To boost the price of their imports, blockade-running companies auctioned off their European silks and satins and mellow wines and liquors, their "Yankee gewgaws and notions" to the highest bidders. The Campbell Importing and Exporting Company in

6 Augusta *Weekly Chronicle & Sentinel,* October 19, 1864; *Burckmyer Letters, March, 1863–June, 1865,* p. 432.

February, 1864, sold at auction in Petersburg goods amounting to $4,000,000. The Confederate newspapers constantly carried advertisements of auctions of blockade goods to be held in the principal cities, seaports as well as inland towns. Confederate armies suffered a shortage of food and war supplies, while the blockade-running companies made it possible for rich Southerners to gorge themselves with exorbitantly priced luxuries. To pay for these foreign purchases, the blockade-runners drained the Confederacy of its specie and made serious inroads on the dwindling supplies of cotton. By 1863 Southerners were charging them with doing more to demoralize the people than all other factors combined.[7]

The Confederate government was not forced to depend entirely on privately owned blockade-runners, for it had enough vision in the very beginning to see that the government itself should own such vessels. James D. Bulloch, acting for the Navy Department, secured in Europe the *Fingal*, which in the fall of 1861 made its memorable trip into Savannah loaded with probably the most valuable cargo of military supplies ever run into the Confederacy—10,000 Enfield rifles, 1,000,000 cartridges, 2,000,000 percussion caps, 400 barrels of powder, and many cutlasses, swords, revolvers, and other materials. Later he secured other blockade-runners, and Josiah Gorgas of the Ordnance Department, with characteristic foresight, secured vessels for his own department's needs; but the government as a whole was woefully negligent in building up its own blockade-running fleet. The Confederate-owned blockade-runners which became most famous were the *Robert E. Lee, Columbia, Merrimac, Eugenia, Stag,* and *Lady Davis.*

Dependence on privately owned ships was not enough; such vessels brought in what they pleased—generally nonmilitary goods. The Secretary of War forced agreements with the owners of blockade-runners using the ports of Wilmington and Charleston, whereby they leased at least a third of their cargo space to the Confederate government at reasonable rates. As time went on it

[7] Richmond *Daily Examiner,* June 8, 24, August 5, 18, September 22, October 23, November 2, 1863; Richmond *Daily Whig,* February 20, 1864; Selma *Daily Reporter,* February 20, 1863; Austin *Tri-Weekly Gazette,* June 25, 1863; Columbus *Weekly Enquirer,* August 19, 1862; Jones, *Rebel War Clerk's Diary,* I, 299, 317; Robinton, *Papers of the New York Prize Court,* 180; Hill, *State Socialism in the Confederate States,* 8 ff.

became more and more difficult to enforce these agreements, especially in the face of the state governments, which were bidding for cargo space against the Confederate government. Soon the Confederate government's ability to pay for its foreign purchases became an additional problem. Secretary Seddon admitted early in 1864 that he could secure "as much freight room inward" as he desired; it was now the problem of securing "freight room outward" in which to send cotton on the account of the Confederate government. As an example, cited by Davis, of the heavy profits made by the private blockade-runners, the Confederate government paid them for imports in cotton at sixpence a pound which they took abroad and sold at twenty-four pence a pound. Allowing 11 per cent for captures on a shipment of 600 bales, the blockade-runners would make a profit of £15,360. Why should the Confederate government not make this profit? [8]

There were many others who began to ask this same question. Why should not the Confederate government take charge of all trade passing through the blockade, make the profits, and determine what articles should be imported and exported? In April, 1863, the Georgia legislature requested that Congress prohibit running the blockade "by any person whatever" except under the "direct control and for the exclusive benefit" of the Confederate government. [9] On February 6, 1864, the Confederate government took a step unprecedented in American history—the adoption of almost complete state socialism in foreign trade. Hereafter, without a permit granted by the president, no one might export cotton, tobacco, military and naval stores, sugar, molasses, or rice by land or water to a foreign country or to any part of the Confederacy occupied by the enemy, and only "articles of necessity and of common use shall be imported." Specifically listed as prohibited were most of the articles itemized in the Tariff Act of May, 1861, which included everything that might be considered luxuries and most articles which would be held as necessities except in the grimmest

[8] *Southern Historical Society Papers*, XII (1884), 79–80; *Official Records*, Ser. IV, Vol. III, 28; Bradlee, *Blockade Running during the Civil War*, 51; Thompson, *Confederate Purchasing Operations*, 24, 41, 86; Owsley, *King Cotton Diplomacy*, 386; Hill, *State Socialism in the Confederate States*, 8, 10–12, 16–18, 28–31.

[9] *Acts of the General Assembly of the State of Georgia . . . November and December, 1862; also Extra Session of 1863* (Milledgeville, 1863), 242.

times of war. As a Richmond news commentator remarked, "No more watered silks and satins; no more Yankee and European gewgaws; nothing but Confederate sackcloth!" Though people's costumes revert to the fig leaf, their food to roots, and beverages to water, "the battle of liberty must be fought out and won." [10] Indeed, had Southerners now become Spartans.

In a set of regulations published a month later, all privately owned blockade-runners must allot one half of their cargo space to the Confederate government at a fixed rate, and if they should agree to hand over two thirds of their space a slightly higher rate would be allowed. Those who refused should have neither Southern products to export nor clearance papers. These rules did not apply to state-owned vessels. This was a stunning blow to the blockade-runners, accustomed to their high profits. They furiously assailed the administration, enlisting the aid of Davis' enemies as well as states which had chartered space in blockade-runners. "It is no longer free trade we have," declared the editor of the Richmond *Examiner,* "it is not even restricted trade, it is trade by favour." [11] The blockade-runners threatened to tie up their vessels and abandon the business. The governors of North Carolina, South Carolina, and Georgia, especially, bitterly complained that they were being deprived of their noble and patriotic work of supplying their own troops, and to side-step the rules they attempted to lease the whole cargo space of blockade-runners, who willingly co-operated in the plot.

Some of the states had, in fact, long been engaged in an unseemly rivalry with the Confederacy both in securing space in blockade-runners and in purchases of materials in Europe. In March, 1862, Governor Pickens of South Carolina actually argued that the states should take charge of all blockade-running and reap its profits. North Carolina owned a blockade-runner, the *Ad-Vance,* but otherwise the states had merely chartered vessels or parts of them. Fuming against the new Confederate regulations, which required absolute ownership before the state could take the whole vessel but which allowed it to charter the other half not taken by the Confederacy, Governor Brown played with the idea of concocting a

[10] Richmond *Daily Examiner,* February 13, 1864.
[11] *Ibid.,* February 15, 1864.

dummy purchase of some of the blockade-runners after he was unable to get clearance papers for the *Little Ada,* a vessel which he had merely chartered. In April, 1864, Vance, Brown, Clark of Mississippi, and Watts of Alabama drew up a protest against the Confederate regulations. Aided by the private blockade-runners and the enemies of Davis in general, they were able to get Congress to pass a bill in June exempting ships owned in part or chartered by states. With irrefutable arguments Davis vetoed this bill, showing that there must be central control in supplying the armies of the Confederacy; for, unlike the Atlantic seaboard states, the others could not supply their troops through blockade-running. Brown still contended that states ought to be allowed to charter the full cargo space of blockade-runners. A Georgia editor likened his arguments to "the silly talk of an old woman, who wants a thing because she wants it." [12]

Though Davis' veto killed the bill, the governors were not yet through with the question. On October 17, 1864, the governors of Virginia, North Carolina, South Carolina, Georgia, Alabama, and Mississippi met in Augusta to discuss such serious problems confronting the Confederacy as the scarcity of soldiers, desertion, and relief of the poor; but very prominent in their minds was also the old problem of reviving the blockade-running business on their own terms. Although they resolved patriotically to support the Confederate administration in raising troops and otherwise strengthening the hand of the central government, they still insisted that Congress at its next session should pass laws allowing them to use any vessels "owned or chartered by them," which was a euphemistic way of asking for the repeal of the act of February 6.[13] Governor Milton of Florida refused to attend this meeting and answered Brown's invitation by boldly recommending to the

12 Augusta *Weekly Constitutionalist,* July 27, 1864; Athens *Southern Watchman,* July 6, 1864; Richardson (comp.), *Messages and Papers of the Confederacy,* I, 466–70; Rowland (ed.), *Jefferson Davis, Constitutionalist,* VI, 213; Owsley, *State Rights in the Confederacy,* 128–49; Hamilton, *Reconstruction in North Carolina,* 73; Schwab, *Confederate States of America,* 234. The state of Georgia bought during the war 6,432 bales of cotton and "safely exported" 1,556. Telamon Cuyler Collection (University of Georgia Library).

13 Vance, Raleigh, N.C., to Governor Charles Clark, September 23, 1864, Ser. E, Vol. LXVII, No. 66 (Mississippi State Archives, Jackson); *Journal of the Congress of the Confederate States,* VII, 257–58; Athens *Southern Watchman,* October 26, 1864.

Georgia governor that he mend his ways and support the Confederacy more loyally.[14]

As dictator of all foreign trade, the Confederate administration took charge of the collection of cotton and other products and licensed their exportation or carried them out on its own account. Thomas L. Bayne was appointed to take charge of all cotton purchases east of the Mississippi and Colin J. McRae was made sole fiscal agent of the Confederacy in Europe to handle the sale there and direct purchases of material for importation. By the end of 1864 Davis was able to report that this new trade policy had greatly increased supplies, had handsomely enhanced the Confederate financial position in Europe, and had put an end to the wasteful and ruinous system of contracting with private blockade-runners.[15] Had the Confederacy adopted this policy in 1861, its position would have been much stronger in these respects.

Without a doubt the blockade was one of the outstanding causes of the strangulation and ultimate collapse of the Confederacy; yet it was ineffective in the international-law sense until almost the last months. Had it been completely effective from the beginning, the Confederacy could never have lived four years. In the spring of 1861 the task of the half-dozen or fewer ships on hand for blockading the 3,549 miles of Confederate coast line and 189 inlets seemed almost unsurmountable; yet by the end of the war Secretary of the Navy Gideon Welles had got together about 600 vessels to serve in his blockading fleet. Effective as the fleet was to become with the passing of time, Davis estimated in 1864 that it caused the loss of only slightly more than a tenth of the cotton leaving the Confederacy; but the mortality of ships attempting to enter the Confederacy must have been much larger, and logically so, for a United States consul estimated this year that one out of three blockade-runners was being captured. Secretary Welles reported the number of prizes brought into port throughout the war to be 1,022, and counting those which were sunk, burned, or driven

[14] "Commissary Activities and War Correspondence 1863–1865" (Florida State Archives).

[15] Richardson (comp.), *Messages and Papers of the Confederacy*, I, 511; Hill, *State Socialism in the Confederate States*, 12–16.

ashore, the number of blockade-runners lost has been estimated at 1,500.[16]

In running the blockade the Confederates had many advantages in addition to the long coast line and the initially weak Federal fleet. The most daring and resourceful people, Confederate and foreign, entered the service. They took advantage of weather conditions and extinguished the lighthouses, and they secured specially constructed ships, lying low in the water, camouflaged in gray paint, equipped with strong boilers, and supplied with quick-steaming Welsh coal. The success of some steamers was phenomenal. The Scotch-built *Robert E. Lee*, shuttling between Wilmington and Nassau, made twenty-one trips, carrying out cotton worth $2,000,000 in gold; the *Antonica* ran the blockade twenty-eight times; the *Kate*, forty-four; and the *Hattie* won the pennant with sixty trips. One authority has estimated that the blockade was run 8,250 times. Wilmington and Charleston had more shipping while they were blockaded than before the war when they were free and unobstructed. In 1863 a foreign visitor saw twelve blockade-runners in the port of Wilmington at one time. The amount of cotton exported through the blockade or across the Rio Grande has been variously estimated from 500,000 to 1,000,000 bales.

The amount of materials which were brought into the Confederacy through the blockade can only be guessed at, but such estimates as these do not seem unreasonable: 600,000 small arms, 400,000 blankets, 550,000 pairs of shoes (from November, 1863 to December, 1864), and during November and December, 1864, 8,500,000 pounds of meat, 1,500,000 pounds of lead, 2,000,000 pounds of saltpeter, and 500,000 pounds of coffee.[17]

The Confederacy was too weak to institute a blockade against the North, but on April 17, 1861, even before Lincoln announced

---

[16] Richardson (comp.), *Messages and Papers of the Confederacy*, I, 349; George W. Dalzell, *The Flight from the Flag; The Continuing Effect of the Civil War upon the American Carrying Trade* (Chapel Hill, 1940), 238; Bradlee, *Blockade Running during the Civil War*, 125–26, 162; Robinton, *Papers of the New York Prize Court*, 40, 170; Owsley, *King Cotton Diplomacy*, 250, 284–85.

[17] William Diamond, "Imports of the Confederate Government from Europe and Mexico," in *Journal of Southern History*, VI (1940), 470–503; Owsley, *King Cotton Diplomacy*, 290; Schwab, *Confederate States of America*, 239.

his blockade, Davis called forth a weapon which had long been approved in American history—privateers, the "militia of the seas," designed to harry and scourge enemy commerce. Privateering had been outlawed by the Declaration of Paris of 1856; but the United States had refused to accede to that document, and the Confederacy honestly inherited this weapon. Now the United States wanted to sign the Declaration, and so did the Confederacy with the exception of the privateering clause, but the European nations considered it was too late to change the rules since war had begun. Nevertheless, in proclaiming the blockade on April 19, Lincoln declared that privateers would be considered pirates. The Confederate Congress on May 6, in a law as near a formal declaration of war as it was ever to make, set up rules to safeguard privateering and protect it against activities which might appear as actual piracy. Expanding further the regulations, Davis offered letters of marque to all who posted bonds to abide by the rules.[18]

Privateering appealed to the spirit of adventure and patriotism as well as of gain, for in addition to enjoying the excitement and the harm done the enemy, privateers received all except 5 per cent of the value of the sale of their prizes. The amount withheld was set apart as a fund designed to take care of the wounded and the widows and orphans of those slain. A wave of enthusiasm for this form of venture swept the South. Individuals fitted out their own ships, and companies promised riches to those who bought stock. The first vessel to receive a letter of marque was the *Triton,* a small thirty-ton schooner of Brunswick, Georgia. Soon privateers were sweeping out of many Southern ports, with Savannah and New Orleans as the chief centers, and capturing many prizes. The most spectacular and successful of the privateers was the *Jefferson Davis.* One of the most unfortunate was the *Savannah,* which was captured and taken to New York, where the crew were imprisoned and later tried for piracy. The jury did not convict, but the crew of another privateer, the *Enchantress,* which had been captured, were tried and convicted. All of these privateers were later exchanged as prisoners

---

[18] *Official Records of the Union and Confederate Navies,* Ser. II, Vol. I, 329 ff.; Richardson (comp.), *Messages and Papers of the Confederacy,* I, 60–61, 104–10. The standard work on Confederate privateering is William M. Robinson, Jr., *The Confederate Privateers* (New Haven, 1928).

of war, for President Davis had threatened retaliation to force an abandonment "of a practice unknown to the warfare of civilized man, and so barbarous as to disgrace the nation which shall be guilty of inaugurating it." [19] Two unusual types of privateering vessels were the *Manassas,* an ironclad, which was impressed into the Confederate naval service before it could embark on the high seas, and the *Pioneer,* a submarine which sank before it could begin a career.

Privateers created a great scare in the North and produced a real threat to United States shipping for the first few months of the war, but after the blockade was instituted they found it almost impossible to bring their prizes into Confederate ports. They could not operate in European waters after England, who set the pace in maritime law for Europe, refused to allow prizes to be brought into her ports.

Though it became customary in the North to designate as piracy all Confederate operations on the high seas, whether by privateers or cruisers, the nearest approach to this crime was in the remarkable exploits of John C. Braine, who as a passenger on the United States liner *Chesapeake* out of New York seized the ship with the aid of fifteen accomplices. He took it to Nova Scotia, where the British turned it over to its owners and freed the conspirators. Later Braine seized the *Roanoke* out of Havana and took it to Bermuda where he burned it.[20]

With the disappearance of privateering, the Confederate Congress passed a law in April, 1863, providing for a Volunteer Navy, an idea of a Louisiana planter, B. J. Sage. This proposed service approximated privateering, for the personnel were to provide their own ships and were to receive 90 per cent of the value of their captures and 25 per cent of the value of all United States armed vessels and transports destroyed, in addition to $25.00 for each prisoner taken. But it differed from privateering in that all officers and crew must be regularly enlisted in the Confederate navy and wear regular uniforms. It was contemplated that these vessels would not only

[19] Richardson (comp.), *Messages and Papers of the Confederacy,* I, 116; Robinson, *Confederate Privateers,* 30, 49–57, 59–78, 133–51.

[20] *Official Records of the Union and Confederate Navies,* Ser. I, Vol. II, 539–62; J. Thomas Scharf, *History of the Confederate States Navy from its Organization to the Surrender of its Last Vessel . . .* (New York, 1887), 812–14.

operate on the high seas but also raid the coast held by the United States and seize any property within the ebb and flow of the tide. The Virginia Volunteer Navy Company was organized to participate in this service and was soon offering its stocks to investors, but after various efforts it failed to put a vessel into operation. Incipient movements arose to organize two other companies, but they did not materialize.[21]

The activities of the regular Confederate navy were more spectacular than dangerous to American supremacy of the seas. Excepting the *Alabama-Kearsarge* duel, no naval battles were fought on the high seas, as the task of the Confederate cruisers was to destroy commerce and avoid engagements with warships of the enemy.

The gigantic task of assembling vessels and organizing a Confederate navy was never successfully accomplished, but Secretary of the Navy Mallory's achievements under adverse circumstances were nevertheless remarkable. Born in Trinidad, Mallory grew up in Key West, where he became a marine lawyer and collector of customs. Later a member of the American Congress, he became chairman of the Committee on Naval Affairs; thus he came, however reluctantly, to the naval post in Davis' cabinet, well versed in maritime matters. From the beginning he saw the impossibility of building up a navy which could compete on equal terms with the American navy; he, therefore, with vision and daring worked on the theory that only by unusual weapons could the Confederacy hope to perform its task on the seas. In his management of the Confederate navy he was subjected to carping criticism from the same element in Congress which consistently opposed everyone whom Davis supported. Mallory rode out this criticism, including an investigation of the Navy Department in 1862–1863 which cleared him of mismanagement, and he became one of two cabinet members to serve in the same position throughout the war.[22]

[21] Matthews (ed.), *Public Laws of the Confederate States*, 1 Cong., 3 Sess., 1863, pp. 111–13; Richmond *Semi-Weekly Enquirer*, June 26, 1863; Robinson, *Confederate Privateers*, 319–42; Scharf, *Confederate States Navy*, 91.

[22] *Southern Historical Society Papers*, XLV (1925), 257–59; Richmond *Semi-Weekly Enquirer*, February 19, 1864; Philip Melvin, "Stephen Russell Mallory, Southern Naval Statesman," in *Journal of Southern History*, X (1944), 137–60; Harrison A. Trexler, *The Confederate Ironclad "Virginia" ("Merrimac")* (Chicago, 1938), 10; Patrick, *Jefferson Davis and his Cabinet*, 244–71; *Official Records of the Union and*

The Confederacy was equally deficient in ships, in skill and the materials with which to construct them, and in the trained personnel needed to operate them. Southerners had never been a seafaring people nor even mildly enthusiastic for the sea. Of the Southerners in the American navy who resigned on the organization of the Confederacy, not one attempted to run his ship into a Southern port. In December of 1861 Congress called for the enlistment of not over two thousand seamen. The response was insufficient, and a bounty of $50 was offered for anyone enlisting for three years or the duration of the war. Still not enough came, and Congress then allowed anyone drafted into the army to choose the navy or later to transfer to that branch of the service. By 1864 the courts were trying to build it up by sentencing criminals to service in the navy. A lad of seventeen, who had swindled Mrs. Davis out of $50 was permitted to join the navy in lieu of punishment. Joseph W. Griffin, alias Tim Morris, a famous delineator of Negro character on the Richmond stage, dodged the draft and was sentenced to hard labor with ball and chain for the duration of the war, but later his sentence was commuted to service in the navy. Many foreigners entered the Confederate navy. At the end of the war those from England escaped the penalty of British laws by declaring that they had been Confederate citizens.

In March, 1861, Congress authorized a marine corps of six companies, but it was not organized until the next year when it developed around a nucleus of American marines who had resigned on the outbreak of war. This marine corps manned the guns on the James River, and later in small detachments performed sailor duty on ships and acted as gunners in the coastal forts.[23]

To train its naval personnel, the Confederacy established a naval academy, whose whole activities until near the end of the war were confined to the training ship *Patrick Henry,* anchored on the James below Richmond. Being a carefully selected group, under the same system of appointment by the President and Congressmen as in the United States, these naval cadets were highly trustworthy and efficient. When Richmond was on the point of falling, they were given the responsible duty of guarding the governmental archives

Confederate Navies, Ser. II, Vol. I, 431–809. Much of Mallory's correspondence is included *ibid.,* Vol. II. [23] Scharf, *Confederate States Navy,* 769–72.

and treasury as the Confederate government retreated southward.[24]

Secretary Mallory early turned to torpedoes in his program of developing secret and surprising weapons. Their novelty and hidden dangers were so devastating to enemy nerves and ships that their use called forth the bitterest condemnation. To promote this service the Confederacy set up a special Torpedo Bureau, in the development of which Gabriel J. Rains and Matthew F. Maury played important parts. Torpedoes strewn in the principal harbors and rivers of the Confederacy were so effective that Secretary Welles admitted after the war that more ships had been lost through torpedo action than by any other cause. After thoroughly mining the James River, Maury went to England to carry further the development of the torpedo.

Having little material suited for torpedo construction, the Confederates used remarkable ingenuity in devising these weapons. The floating torpedo was turned loose to drift with the current in rivers; a so-called "hunting torpedo," it was asserted, was magnetized and attracted by the metal in ships. Anchored torpedoes remained submerged with the ebb and flow of the tides. Some torpedoes were attached to the end of towlines and dragged against vessels; others fastened to the ends of poles attached to boats were rammed against enemy ships. Even infernal machines, made to look like lumps of coal, were secreted in the fuel bunkers of Federal vessels. Old barrels, kegs, demijohns, and cans were used in constructing torpedoes. As a protection to Charleston Harbor a large boiler, three feet in diameter and eighteen feet long, filled with three thousand pounds of powder, was sunk in the main ship channel, a mile off Fort Sumter. Torpedoes were exploded by contact fuses, by an electric spark controlled from the shore, and by clockwork arrangements.

To awaken the inventive genius of Southerners, Congress in April, 1862, offered as a reward 50 per cent of the value of ships destroyed by "any new machine or engine, or . . . new method for destroying the armed vessels of the enemy." Such promptings were unnecessary for those characters who bob up in all crises everywhere, whose vivid imaginations lead them into the most bizarre

[24] *Confederate Veteran* (Nashville), XII (1904), 170; XXIII (1915), 402; Scharf, *Confederate States Navy*, 773–81; Lonn, *Foreigners in the Confederacy*, 297–98.

schemes. A person appeared in Richmond in the summer of 1862 with plans for a machine to destroy the whole Federal navy, wooden as well as ironclad. Another in 1865 had a secret scheme to burn every vessel leaving a foreign port for the United States or a Northern port for the South and to destroy every gunboat and transport on the Mississippi. First to claim the reward under this act were two naval officers who planted in the Yazoo River two demijohns joined together and filled with powder, which they exploded by an electric current when the United States gunboat *Cairo* passed over the contraption. Despite destruction of the ship, the first of the many Federal vessels to meet a like fate, Davis objected to assigning them the reward on the ground that they had not qualified according to the regulations set up and furthermore because they were in the paid service of the government. The first Federal report of a Confederate effort to destroy a warship through the use of mines was on July 7, 1861, when the *Pawnee* saw a floating torpedo in the Potomac.[25]

The use of a torpedo on the end of a pole, or spar torpedo, as it was often called, led to the development of specially constructed torpedo boats. The best-known class of such boats was named the "Davids"; though small they were able to destroy the largest warships—a modern version of David against Goliath. They were small, cigar-shaped steamers almost submerged, but not intended as submarine boats, and carried on the bow a spar or pole holding on its end a torpedo. A David in 1863 with a spar torpedo attacked the Federal warship *New Ironsides* at Charleston and greatly damaged it, but the torpedo boat went down in the onset. The original *David* was so nearly submerged that it was only a step to the submarine, which the Confederates developed, and which later was to revolutionize naval warfare. In Mobile they built one called the

[25] Richardson (comp.), *Messages and Papers of the Confederacy*, I, 472–77; Matthews (ed.), *Public Laws of the Confederate States*, 1 Cong., 1 Sess., 1862, p. 51; *Official Records of the Union and Confederate Navies*, Ser. I, Vol. IV, 566–69; *Official Records*, Ser. I, Vol. XIV, 950; Ser. IV, Vol. III, 581, 1079; Milledgeville *Southern Recorder*, April 26, 1864; Richmond *Daily Examiner*, June 28, 1862; Augusta *Weekly Chronicle & Sentinel*, January 13, 1863; Macon *Daily Telegraph*, April 13, 1864; Charleston *Daily Courier*, May 14, 1864; Richmond *Daily Enquirer*, February 20, 1865; Scharf, *Confederate States Navy*, 750–53; *Confederate Veteran*, XVI (1908), 456–59.

H. L. Hunley, and took it by railway to Charleston, where it destroyed the United States warship *Housatonic* in the fall of 1864. It was propelled by cranks turned by the crew, and was designed to dive under the object of attack and drag against it a torpedo attached to the end of a towline. In the attack on the *Housatonic* the *H. L. Hunley* crashed its torpedo against the warship, but it sank with its victim, losing its whole crew of seven men. This submarine had sunk four times previously in its trial runs, each time carrying its crew to their death.[26]

In building or otherwise securing ships for the navy, Secretary Mallory had many difficulties. In ante-bellum times there were only two navy yards in the South, those at Norfolk and at Pensacola, and the Confederates soon lost both of them. Skilled workmen were scarce, and it was an almost impossible task to assemble seasoned timber, iron plates, engines, rope, and the many other materials which went into the construction of warships. Yet these materials were fabricated in many places, so-called navy yards such as those at Charlotte, Atlanta, Lynchburg, and Columbia, and were assembled and made into battleships in construction yards on the Mississippi River at New Orleans, the Alabama at Selma, the Chattahoochee below Columbus, and at other places. Before the end of 1861 a gunboat fever seized the Confederate authorities and the people generally; and in response Congress authorized the building of not more than a hundred. Many contracts let to private companies resulted in construction of gunboats, a few of which were converted into floating batteries, to be used largely in defending the mouths of rivers and harbors and to operate on the inland waters.

A type of vessel not unheard of before but, nevertheless, never tried in actual combat, was the ironclad ship. Mallory early saw great possibilities in this powerful craft, and, backed by the enthusiasm and drafting skill of John Mercer Brooke, he soon had plans afoot for powerful ironclads which might destroy the Federal fleet and break the blockade. He refloated the old *Merrimac,* which

[26] *Official Records of the Union and Confederate Navies,* Ser. I, Vol. XV, 10–21, 327–38; Richmond *Semi-Weekly Enquirer,* March 1, 1864; Richmond *Daily Examiner,* September 17, 1861; Charleston *Daily Courier,* March 3, 1863; Robinson, *Confederate Privateers,* 177–78; Scharf, *Confederate States Navy,* 759–60.

had been sunk by the Federals when they evacuated Norfolk in 1861, put iron plate on twenty-four inches of wood base, and renamed it the *Virginia*. Other ironclads were constructed in the Confederacy, but Mallory placed his greatest hopes in securing a powerful fleet of them in Europe.

Thus it was that the Confederacy early turned its attention to Europe with high hopes of procuring not only ironclads but also fast cruisers to be used as commerce destroyers. James D. Bulloch and James H. North were sent to Europe to obtain vessels in any way possible. They let contracts in both British and French ship-yards for powerful ironclads, rams, and fast cruisers. Companies in France agreed to build four corvettes and two rams, but the American minister in Paris was able to prevent their delivery to the Confederacy. However, one of them, a corvette later named the *Stonewall*, came into the possession of the Confederacy near the end of the war, and though it took to the high seas it was able to accomplish nothing before the war ended. It was finally run into Havana, where Spain turned it over to the United States. In England the Confederacy contracted with Laird and Company, shipbuilders in Birkenhead, to construct two powerful rams, which it was expected would be able to break the blockade and scatter or sink the Federal fleet. So great a danger did these ironclads become that the United States threatened war if the British permitted delivery to the Confederacy, while people in the Confederacy were expecting every day to hear of their appearance and the speedy ending of the war. The British government was frightened into forbidding their delivery and bought them for its own navy.

In the meantime, however, the Confederacy was able to secure some fast commerce raiders in England, and subsequently it secured more. The most famous were the *Alabama*, the *Georgia*, the *Florida*, and the *Shenandoah*. Another ship, the *Alexandria*, which was a gift to the Confederacy from Fraser, Trenholm and Company, was seized by the British government. As far as international law had crystallized on the delivery of warships by neutrals to belligerents, the Confederacy seemed to have had a right to these ships; it was the threat of war by the United States that made the British interpret their own law in special instances into withholding them. Now and then the Confederacy bought in its own ports

British-owned blockade-runners and converted them into commerce raiders, as for example the *Tallahassee* and the *Chickamauga;* and it seized a few vessels in its own ports when war broke out, such as the *Nashville*. Some ships seized on the high seas were converted into raiders.

The exploits of most of these cruisers were as stirring as any to be found in the annals of the sea. The first ship to begin its career as a raider of Federal commerce on the high seas was the *Sumter*, under the command of Raphael Semmes, the most famous naval officer of the Confederacy and to become one of its two admirals. It slipped out of New Orleans in June, 1861, and before it was finally blockaded in Gibraltar, in January, 1862, and later sold, it had accounted for eighteen vessels. Semmes later commanded the *Alabama*. The *Nashville* was not so successful as a commerce destroyer, but, leaving Charleston in the fall of 1861, it was the first warship to carry the Confederate flag into a British port. It was later renamed the *Rattlesnake* and was destroyed in 1863 off the coast of Georgia. The first of the cruisers built in England, the *Florida*, under the command of Captain John N. Maffit, had an eventful career. It raided in the West Indies, in the waters of the Gulf of Mexico, and in the South Atlantic. It made in the West Indies the most valuable capture of the war—the *Jacob Bell* which with its cargo was worth $1,500,000. A Federal warship seized the *Florida* in a Brazilian port and took it to Hampton Roads, where it was conveniently rammed and sunk before its promised restoration to Brazil could be completed.

Two cruisers which carried out devastating raids up the Atlantic Coast were the *Chickamauga* and the *Tallahassee*. The former took part in the defense of Wilmington near the end of the war, and on the fall of that city its crew burned and sank it; the latter, later changing its name to the *Chameleon* and finding all Confederate ports closed on its return from a cruise near the end of the war, sailed for Liverpool, where the British later handed it over to the United States.

The most famous and successful raider was the *Alabama*, commanded by Semmes, whom the Northern press called a "brigand of the seas" and a "vulgar freebooter." Escaping from Liverpool in 1862 through a ruse, it outfitted in the Azores and began a cruise which for the next two years took it from one end of the Atlantic Ocean to the other, into its adjoining waters, and around the Cape of Good Hope into the Indian Ocean. It was finally destroyed off Cherbourg, by the ironclad *Kearsarge*. It was charged by the United States government with having destroyed during its career fifty-eight vessels worth $6,547,000.

Taking the place of the *Alabama* and less renowned, though in some respects more spectacular in its exploits, was the *Shenandoah*. Glasgow-built, fast and rakish, it began its career in the fall of 1864. Outfitting in the Madeiras, under the command of Captain James I. Waddell, it sailed around the Cape of Good Hope into the Indian Ocean and thence south of Australia into the Pacific, where it carried on a devastating war against the whalers. Being far from sources of information, it did not learn of Lee's surrender until June 23; but not considering his capitulation to mean the end of the war, it continued until August 2, when it heard definitely that the Confederacy had ceased to exist. Dismounting its guns, closing its portholes, whitewashing its funnels, and otherwise disguising itself, it rounded the Horn, crossed the South Atlantic undetected, and sailed into Liverpool, where it gave itself up to the British, having circumnavigated the globe. In its career of less than a year it sailed 58,000 miles and captured 40 vessels, worth $6,488,000.[27]

At one time or another there were about eighteen of these Confederate commerce destroyers. They sailed every ocean and only occasionally did one attempt to slip into a home port. Most of them eluded the Federal warships which were hunting them and in the meantime were able to seriously disrupt Federal commerce. Though it was customary in the North to refer to all Confederate sea activity as piracy, when the war ended the Federal government accepted the surrender of the Confederate naval forces on the same terms which Grant had given Lee. Some commanders surrendered their ships, some destroyed them, and some sailed their vessels into foreign ports, where the United States eventually got possession of them. These cruisers had played well their part in the war; they had captured and destroyed much Federal shipping and driven much

[27] For a recent work on the career of the *Shenandoah*, see Stanley F. Horn, *Gallant Rebel; The Fabulous Cruise of the C.S.S. Shenandoah* (New Brunswick, 1947).

into British registry, and they had forced up marine insurance rates 900 per cent.

In addition to engaging in commerce-destroying activities on the high seas, the Confederacy entered into many conflicts along its coast line and on the rivers, though many of these operations were amphibian and were in fact more military than naval. The early onsets of the Federals against Southern ports were combinations of military and naval power—the capture of Roanoke Island, of the Beaufort–Port Royal region, of New Orleans, and of Mobile. In only the last two operations did the Confederates oppose with naval power of any force. The great number and strength of Federal gunboats on the rivers of the Confederacy soon gave them as great a supremacy as they had on the high seas, as far as Confederate naval power was concerned; their greatest hazards were Confederate torpedoes in the rivers and artillery attacks from the banks.

The only full-dress naval battle, excepting the *Alabama-Kearsarge* affair, was the *Virginia-Monitor* duel in Hampton Roads, in March of 1862. The ironclad *Virginia* sailed out into Hampton Roads to lay claim to the supremacy of Chesapeake Bay and disrupt McClellan's Peninsular campaign now about to begin. For a day the Confederacy gained potential control of the Bay and even theoretical control of the high seas, for the *Virginia,* impervious to the most terrific punishment the Federal wooden ships could inflict, proceeded to sink the U.S.S. *Cumberland,* burn the U.S.S. *Congress,* and scatter the rest of the Federal fleet. The next day the U.S.S. *Monitor* appeared and established at least parity in the Bay, for the fight was inconclusive. Later, when Norfolk was on the point of falling, Commodore Josiah Tattnall set fire to and sank the *Virginia* to prevent its capture, for the ship's great draught restricted its movements. The *Monitor* later went down in a storm off Cape Hatteras, leaving a numerous progeny, the Monitor-class vessels, so destructive on the Confederate rivers and along the coast.[28]

---

[28] The greatest collection of documents on the operations of the Confederate navy is *Official Records of the Union and Confederate Navies,* in 30 volumes. Scharf's *Confederate States Navy* contains a great deal of information not well arranged, and, of course, there are various memoirs of the participants and monographs on their careers.

The self-destruction of the *Virginia* was a bitter blow to Confederate hopes, which had pictured the war as all but won by this powerful ironclad. Commodore Tattnall passed before a court of inquiry and a general court-martial before he was finally cleared of the charges that he had unnecessarily sacrificed the Confederacy's outstanding asset. But for a brief season the people of the Confederacy had reveled in their powerful weapon, secret for a time, but evident enough thereafter. As the *Virginia* sat so deep in the water as to be almost a submersible, the poet of the day caught the idea, though not a very apt description, in this stanza of a poem called "The Turtle":

> *Caesar, afloat with his fortunes!*
> *And all the world agog*
> *Straining its eyes*
> *At a thing that lies*
> *In the water, like a log!*
> *It's a weasel! a whale!*
> *I see its tail!*
> *It's a porpoise! a pollywog!* [29]

And the contemporary commentator's enthusiasm over the exploit of the *Virginia* has been reaffirmed by the inexorable verdict of history: "The sinking of a splendid frigate in fifteen minutes settles one point; henceforth, wooden war-ships are obsolete, and Iron will rule the sea." [30]

[29] Charleston *Daily Mercury*, April 22, 1862.
[30] *Ibid.*, March 15, 1862.

RAISING TROOPS

WHETHER the future held war or peace for the Confederacy, it was the part of wisdom to make preparations quickly for raising armies—a Regular Army to which President Davis could immediately appoint officers who had resigned from the United States service and which would compose a small solid force if peace prevailed, and a Provisional or Volunteer Army into which the might of the Confederacy could be pumped if unhappily war should come. As hostilities soon broke out, the Regular Army never grew beyond a skeleton paper organization; it was the Provisional Army which fought the war.

An act of February 28, 1861, authorized the President to receive forts and munitions and all other war materials seized from the United States, to accept at his discretion state troops offered by the governors, and, in fact, to take control of the unified defense of all the states of the Confederacy. The law provided that state troops or militia should serve for not less than a year, but the next month an act stipulated that others might be received to serve for not over six months. According to the February law volunteers were to be received "by consent of their State," but the next month their number was limited to 100,000. After war broke out around Fort Sumter on April 12, the situation radically changed. On May 8 the President was given the right to receive any number of volunteers for the duration of the war, and three days later, to speed the reception of volunteers, he was given the right to accept them without the delay of state consent. Five days later Congress limited their number to 400,000 and the term of their service to three years or the duration of the war—but not over three years. By act of May 11 volunteers from the Upper South states, which had not seceded, might be received. To aid the recruit in getting to camp, a bounty of $10 was offered for each enlisted man. In August the President was given power to accept emergency volunteers, in any numbers desired and for as long a term of service as he pleased, to defend exposed places. Finally, in January, 1862, all state militia thereafter received should serve for three years or the duration of the war, putting them in the same class as volunteers in this respect.

Out of all these laws these facts emerged. A person might become a member of the Provisional Army either as a volunteer without passing through the hands of a governor or as a member of state militia offered by the governor, and his term of service might be for the duration of the war however long it might last, for the duration if not over three years, for three years, for twelve months, for six months, or possibly for any intermediate time. How much better it would have been for the Confederacy had it enlisted troops in the beginning for the duration of the war! It was the timidity of Congress that prevented it, for Davis and others wanted the first troops to serve for "a term of years," and it was only by compromising that the President was able to get as long as a year in the first law—"for any time not less than twelve months." [1]

Volunteers and state militias offered by governors were available immediately. A company of Georgians commanded by George Washington Lee were the first troops accepted by the Confederacy. After Fort Sumter an avalanche of troops descended upon the War Department, for many feared that the army might be filled before they could get there. It was considered a special favor to be accepted. The "Raccoon Roughs," led by John B. Gordon, came down to Atlanta from north Georgia, and on being informed by Governor Brown that he could receive no more troops, uncoupled the train and refused to return. [2] Eppa Hunton, later to gain fame as a soldier, wrote Governor Letcher, "I trust sir that you will not allow me an original advocate for secession to rust in inglorious ease." [3] In April, Davis declared that the "gravity of age and the

---

[1] Jefferson Davis, *A Short History of the Confederate States of America* (New York, 1890), 77; Reagan, *Memoirs*, 117. This expression was interpreted to mean not more than twelve months.

[2] John B. Gordon, *Reminiscences of the Civil War* (New York, 1904), 8 ff.

[3] Eppa Hunton to Governor Letcher, April 18, 1861, in Virginia Executive Papers, 1861 (Virginia State Archives).

zeal of youth rival each other in the desire to be foremost for the public defense." [4] A Georgian reported in November, 1861, that in his part of the state, the hill country, "only elderly men, disabled young ones, women and children" were left.[5] A poet described the general situation in this stanza:

> The wayside mill is still,
>   And the wheel drips all alone,
> For the miller's brother and son and sire,
>   And the miller's self have gone;
> And their wives and daughters tarrying still,
> With smiles and tears about the mill,
>   Wave, wave their heroes on! [6]

In the summer of 1861 Secretary of War Walker declared that he was forced to refuse 200,000 troops because of a lack of arms and that he had adopted the policy of accepting only those who volunteered for the duration of the war and the twelve-month men who came armed. In December, Secretary of War Benjamin, who had succeeded Walker, stated that he was firm in his "purpose not to give a musket to a man enlisted for less than the war." [7]

Governors looked with varying reactions on this building up of a great Confederate Provisional Army. It smacked of a concentration of power which might erect a tyranny as great as secession had sought to avert in the old government. As Governor John Milton of Florida wrote Davis in December, 1861, "the tendency of the assumption and exercise of such power by the Confederate Government is to sap the very foundation of the rights of the States and is to consolidation." [8] It deprived governors of strong state armies which they could use as they pleased to defend their own territories, and incidentally it deprived them of the glory of being commanders in chief of armies of their own. In fact, they were looking on the war in terms of each state rather than of the whole Confederacy, and were, therefore, working against a unified national strategy.

---

[4] Richardson (comp.), *Messages and Papers of the Confederacy*, I, 81.

[5] Barnsley, Woodlands, Ga., to J. M. Norman, November 25, 1861, in Barnsley Papers (University of Georgia Library).

[6] Charleston *Daily Mercury*, January 31, 1862.

[7] *Official Records*, Ser. I, Vol. VI, 340. See also, *ibid.*, Ser. IV, Vol. I, 497.

[8] *Ibid.*, Ser. I, Vol. VI, 342.

This was one of the logical results of the state-rights dogma on which the South had been fed for a generation and which had produced secession and the Confederacy. The states of the North, where state rights had not thrived, played a much more effective part than the Southern states in concentrating the national effort, and their governors never gave Lincoln the trouble which the Southern governors gave Davis. Governor Brown of Georgia became the first and most persistent critic of the development of Confederate power, military as well as civil.

Exhilaration over victory, war wastage, and the decline of enthusiasm for the conflict soon had their effects on raising further Confederate troops. The first great battle, at Manassas, a Confederate victory, had caused many people foolishly to believe the war had been won and that there was no need for more troops, and the following winter of inactivity in northern Virginia made the soldiers there discontented and further increased their desire to go home. A Georgian wrote his brother that there were already more troops in Virginia than were needed, adding this sour note: "If you dont want to lose your freedom, you had better stay where you are, for we are nothing better than slaves here, for we scarcely have any privileges whatever." [9] But early in 1862 the elation of victory was turned into despair by the quick succession of defeats at Fort Henry, Roanoke Island, Fort Donelson, and the capture of Nashville, the first Confederate state capital to fall—all from February 6 to 23.

The impact of victory, defeat, and the dislike of camp life dried up the enthusiasm to volunteer. In December, 1861, Lee, now in South Carolina, reported that volunteering was going on very slowly there, that none would enlist for the whole war, and that even for twelve months the recruiting was "very languid"; a little later he complained of Georgia that "neither the sentiment of the people nor the policy of the State seems to favor the organization of troops for Confederate service." [10] The editor of the *Southern Literary Messenger* tried to shame young men into volunteering with this sarcastic rebuke: "And you, ye despicable fops and popin-

[9] H. H. Freeman, Yorktown, Va., October 6, 1861, to his family (in possession of the writer).

[10] *Official Records,* Ser. I, Vol. VI, 335, 376.

jays, that dance pretty dances with flirts and fools in cozy parlours, quit, for a while, your monkey shows, and repair to the field of courage, there to be scared into a temporary sense of the value of life, and once, at least, to run fast enough to lay some claim to manhood." [11] To spur volunteering, Congress on January 27, 1862, passed a law allowing each company to send one commissioned officer and two privates back home to carry the news that all who would volunteer should receive a bounty of $50 and free transportation to camp. As a result many left armies, already too meager, to engage in this work. They paraded and ran glowing calls in the newspapers, with little success. Congress appropriated $2,000,000 to aid recruiting in Kentucky.

Also, governors became less enthusiastic in offering their state troops to the Confederacy. As the first law had given the President permission only to *accept* such troops, Congress, on January 24, 1862, authorized him to *call* on the governors for more militia. If the people would not volunteer, it was now the duty of the governors to get those troops in whatever fashion they could—or stand before the country as unpatriotic to the Confederacy. Already various states had passed draft laws, and Governor Brown devised on his own authority an informal draft to meet the President's requisition. He called on all able-bodied men between eighteen and forty-five years of age to parade in the county seats and other centers of population. This was to be a patriotic outburst before the assembled onlookers, where the enthusiasm of the moment would propel people into volunteering into the state troops to be turned over to Davis. Any county that did not provide its quota would be subject to Brown's draft. In one locality "a bevy of as beautiful and high souled women as ever made lovers' hearts beat quickly" stepped into line and so shamed the men that twice the number called for volunteered. By forcing the spotlight of public opinion on the men, Brown was able to raise 22,000 when Georgia's quota was only 12,000.[12]

Even with all the troops which Davis might now get through requisitions on the states, he might not be able to save Richmond

---

[11] *Southern Literary Messenger*, XXXIV (1862), 67.

[12] Macon *Daily Telegraph*, February 18, March 3, 5, 6, 10, 19, 1862; Sandersville *Central Georgian*, March 19, 1862.

from the onset of General McClellan's well-drilled Federal army, which was soon to march up the York Peninsula, for these new Confederate levies were raw troops. The veteran Confederate army was made up largely of twelve-month men, and as their term of service was about to expire, there was dire fear that most of them would not re-enlist. In fact, this danger had been realized long before the McClellan threat. In the hope of saving the army from disintegration, Congress, in December, 1861, had passed a furlough and bounty act, which allowed all twelve-month men who would re-enlist a bounty of $50 and a sixty-day furlough. As a further inducement, they might reorganize themselves from companies up through regiments and elect anew all their officers. The enemy could not have devised a more destructive law, for the army was now allowed to disintegrate for two months. When the soldiers returned they might disorganize every unit, turn out efficient officers, and elect charlatans and timeservers. Lee declared that disbanding and disorganizing troops was bad enough in peacetime and asked "what must it be in time of war, when it may occur at periods that might otherwise prove highly disastrous?" He added, "I tremble to think of the consequences that may befall us next spring when all our twelve-month's men may claim their discharge." [13] Officers from generals on down begged the men to re-enlist, but a majority of them did not chose to do so, and in many instances those who did elected lax disciplinarians and politicians instead of their efficient men. A Georgian, almost in despair, bitterly observed, "We shall need a million men in the spring. Turn out or perish, that history may not perpetuate the damning disgrace that ten millions of freemen, for the love of money, let themselves be subjugated by twenty millions whom they pronounced cowards." [14]

It was now time, if not past time, for the Confederacy to reorganize its whole system of raising troops and holding them. For some time there had been a sentiment growing among military officers, Congressmen, and newspaper editors that the Confederacy should conscript troops. Surprisingly enough among them were men who were later to be the most savage critics of conscription and of Davis for his enforcement of it: Yancey of Alabama, Rhett of

[13] *Official Records*, Ser. I, Vol. VI, 350.
[14] Macon *Daily Telegraph*, February 15, 1862.

the Charleston *Mercury,* Pollard of the Richmond *Examiner,* and Senator Wigfall of Texas. Pollard asserted that the *Examiner* had first suggested conscription, and his paper did, indeed, say that in war as well as in peace an apprenticeship in the army should be "a part of every man's education and training"; [15] and Wigfall, in defending the bill in Congress, declared in racy Texas language that if it were not constitutional anyone might "spit in his face and call him a horse." [16] Among the generals who pushed conscription were Joseph E. Johnston and Lee, who converted Davis to it. Senator Hill of Georgia favored it, as well as most other measures supported by Davis. In his message to Congress on March 28, 1862, Davis recommended conscription to Congress to bring order out of chaos and to make sure that the burden of fighting did not fall "exclusively on the most ardent and patriotic."

On the following April 16, Congress passed the first national law in American history providing for the conscription of troops. All male whites between the ages of eighteen and thirty-five, not legally exempt, were declared members of the Confederate army for a term of three years unless the war ended sooner, and all soldiers then in the army must continue for an equal term of service. These "conscripts" (though the term never appeared in the act) were to be used to fill up skeleton companies, but they must be assigned to units from their own states. Anyone who wished to volunteer before conscription reached him might do so and have the additional privilege of choosing his own company. Anyone who did not care to go to war was given permission to secure a substitute from "persons not liable for duty." Congress amended this act on September 27, 1862, to increase the age limit from thirty-five to forty-five and to give the President the right to suspend conscription "in any locality where he may find it impracticable to execute the same." The next month he suspended it in Kentucky and Missouri, which had been overrun by the enemy. Combing closer and closer for troops as the war wasted them away, Congress on February 17, 1864, changed the age limits to run from seventeen to fifty, but those under eighteen and over forty-five should con-

15 Richmond *Daily Examiner,* January 30, 1862.
16 *Ibid.,* May 6, 1864.

314

stitute a reserve for state defense and not be required to serve beyond their state's limits.

This program provided a selective service rather than a draft, for closely following these acts were others setting up elaborate exemptions not only for physical cause but also for professional and industrial reasons. The first exemption act (April 21, 1862) included Confederate and state civil officials, mail carriers, ferrymen, river and railway workers, telegraphic operators, miners and metal-workers, laborers in cotton and woolen factories, newspaper printers, one apothecary for each establishment, ministers of religion, professors in colleges and academies and teachers with as many as twenty pupils, teachers in deaf, dumb, and blind institutions, and nurses and attendants in hospitals. The act of October 11, 1862, following the second conscription law, greatly increased the exemptions to satisfy the clamor of those who had not been included in the first act and to conform more to the just needs of the industrial establishment of the Confederacy. Exemptions now included one editor for each newspaper, shoemakers, tanners, blacksmiths, millers, wheelwrights and other industrial workers (but the products of their labor must not be sold for more than 75 per cent increase on the cost of production), and all workers making munitions and other war materials. In agriculture the rule applied to one person for every 500 head of cattle or sheep or 250 head of horses or mules; one overseer for every plantation having as many as twenty slaves, or otherwise in conformity with any state law on the subject; and one overseer for any two plantations not more than five miles apart having as many as twenty slaves combined. For the first time people with religious scruples against war, such as Friends, Dunkards, Nazarenes, and Mennonites, were exempted if they provided a substitute or paid $500. This was largely a copy of the laws of Virginia and North Carolina on the subject.[17]

Immediately on the passing of the first exemption act a widespread stampede set in to qualify under some one of its clauses. Physical ailments were early seized upon. Boards of medical examiners appointed to weed out the physically unfit were instructed

[17] Edward N. Wright, *Conscientious Objectors in the Civil War* (Philadelphia, 1931), 91 ff.

to operate under the rule that "where a conscript is equal to all the active duties of the various occupations of civil life, he is able to discharge the duties of a soldier." Deafness was no disqualification "unless so excessive . . . as to incapacitate a man for the duties of a sentinel." Impediment of speech, nearsightedness, or the loss of an eye or of as many as two fingers did not constitute grounds for exemption, nor did dyspepsia or various other minor ailments. Examiners were warned to watch closely claims of rheumatism, deafness, epilepsy, and other diseases easily simulated.[18] It was equally important to watch dishonest medical examiners, who exempted for a price. A conscription inspector gave this experience: He approached an exempted person "to every appearance sound, and he thrusts into my face a certificate of disability. The disease is occult, the name scarcely known to me. He looks strong enough to brain an ox with his knuckle and eat him afterward." [19] According to a satire on the clamor of people to keep out of the army on physical grounds, "Rheumatism, which was once dreaded as a torturing fiend, has become as popular as a beautiful coquet, tormenting and yet enchanting her spellbound victims. . . . Gout is also much sought after; but in these hard times few families can get above rheumatism." Old age was simulated and to prove years beyond fifty many family Bibles were dusted off, records changed, and conniving witnesses produced. "Old age, once at an awful discount, has now become an object of universal respect. Men who once shuddered at the idea of becoming old, now look upon a grey beard with religious veneration." [20]

There was a rush to enter the exempted professions and occupations. New schools sprang up as teachers who had never taught before scurried around to obtain their twenty pupils, sometimes offering free tuition; people suddenly became apothecaries, collecting "a few empty jars, a cheap assortment of combs and brushes,

---

[18] General Orders from Adjutant and Inspector-General's Office, Confederate States Army, 1862–1863, Ser. 1863, pp. 17 ff.; J. Julian Chisolm, A Manual of Military Surgery, for the Use of Surgeons in the Confederate States Army . . . (2d ed., Richmond, 1862), 440.

[19] Official Records, Ser. IV, Vol. III, 977. See also, Albert B. Moore, Conscription and Conflict in the Confederacy (New York, 1924), 93 ff.

[20] Quoted from the Richmond Dispatch, in Ramsdell, Behind the Lines in the Southern Confederacy, 91–92.

a few bottles of 'hairdye' and 'wizard oil' and other Yankee nostrums"; [21] and people who had heretofore considered themselves citizens of the Confederacy now remembered that they owed allegiance to some foreign country. A favored few got themselves appointed on missions abroad and others who were wealthy enough to live in Europe slipped out of the country, while still others secured "bomb-proof positions" in the Confederacy. Senator Phelan, with considerable exaggeration, charged that "nine tenths of the youngsters of the land whose relatives are conspicuous in society, wealthy, or influential obtain some safe perch where they can doze with their heads under their wings." [22] Lawyers charged $500 to get people exempted or to secure their release from the army after they were conscripted, and counterfeiters sold fraudulent exemption papers as well as discharges and furloughs, ranging in price from $400 to $1,000 apiece. One person who was arrested confessed to having sold more than 4,000 such papers. Editors, who had not been exempted in the first act, loudly complained that the freedom of the press was destroyed; in the second exemption act they were included. Now there appeared such advertisements as these: "Military Exemption! Flourishing Daily Newspaper for Sale," and people who had never had ambitions to be editors bought newspapers and thereby exemptions.

One of the most prolific sources of exemptions was state offices. To clarify earlier laws on the subject and to satisfy complaining governors, Congress on May 1, 1863, allowed governors to exempt all state officials whom they considered necessary for "the due administration of the government." Under this authority governors, especially Brown and Vance, claimed as state officials almost any persons who suited their fancy—militia officers, justices of the peace, tax collectors, and even industrial workers. Contemporary estimates varied, and probably even the governors did not know how many they had exempted; but some reports stated that 25,000 had been exempted in North Carolina, 15,000 in Georgia, and smaller numbers in other states. These were no doubt exaggerations, but the Superintendent of Conscription stated in March, 1864, that

[21] Quoted from the Columbus *Weekly Sun*, September 2, 1862, in Moore, *Conscription and Conflict in the Confederacy*, 56.
[22] *Official Records*, Ser. I, Vol. XVII, Pt. II, 791–92.

from "one end of the Confederacy to the other every constituted authority, every officer, every man and woman is engaged in opposing the enrolling officer in the execution of his duties."[23] In November, 1864, the Richmond *Examiner* estimated that a total of 30,000 state officials had been exempted.

To get out of the army or keep from getting into it, hesitating patriots sought election to some office. In an election for five inferior court justices in Clarke County, Georgia, there were twenty candidates; in Greene County, to shame about two dozen men who were running for three offices, the women put out a ticket of old men who did not fall within the military age. Patriotic pressure frequently led candidates for office to explain that they were beyond the conscription age or had been wounded in the war and were incapacitated for further service. In biting invective an editor expressed his opinion of slackers in civil office who successfully avoided the combing by the Confederate officers: "There is one insect that no tooth or time will ever dislodge from its comfortable haunts on this well groomed carcass, and that is the patriotic parasites of the Government itself, and the respectable members of the Federal and Provincial Parliaments. *They* will survive every purification, and soap nor water, brush nor scraper, will ever carry them from the grateful pastures of the body politic to that unsavory arena where the sweepings of the stable are finally collected."[24]

Military service could also be avoided by securing a substitute, who, however, must not be subject to conscription. In its first conscription law Congress allowed this concession on the grounds that there might be important businessmen not included in stated exemptions, who could do more for their country in civilian life than in the army, but immediately anyone who did not care to go to war and who was able to secure a substitute took advantage of this clause. Advertisements for substitutes began to appear in the newspapers, offering a "competence at the end of a few months," "liberal wages," $20 a month and at the end of the war "a fine double-barrelled shot gun," $1,600 and a fine horse, $2,000, and even a small plantation. Soon dishonest substitute brokers arose to take advantage of both the principal and the substitute by charging

---

[23] *Ibid.*, Ser. IV, Vol. III, 225.

[24] Macon *Daily Telegraph and Confederate*, December 29, 1864.

exorbitant prices and giving the substitute only a small part of the price obtained. Prices exacted ran from $500 to $5,000. Even some medical examiners entered into this corruption by refusing to pass substitutes unless the broker divided the price with him; and the counterfeiter reaped his harvest by selling fraudulent substitute papers.

It is little wonder that under this system both the substitute and the principal were debauched. Many of the substitutes came from the scum of the Confederacy, deserted soon after they entered the army, and sold themselves again. One substitute sold himself twenty times in Richmond. Such men could not be made into soldiers. Military officers charged that nine tenths of the deserters came from this class, and some commanders refused to accept substitutes. No one knew how many substitutes had been sent to the army, but contemporary estimates ran from 25,000 to 150,000. There were probably about 50,000. All substitutes were not low characters, nor were all principals slackers. Howell Cobb came strongly to the defense of the latter, emphatically telling Secretary of War Seddon that "the wholesale denunciation of men who employed substitutes is wrong and unjust." [25] Nevertheless, so great was the evil, which did not stop with broker, principal, and substitute, but led to the cry of a rich man's war and a poor man's fight, that Congress abolished the system on December 28, 1863, and a few days later it declared that principals who had secured substitutes were no longer freed from military obligations. This law was denounced as a breach of contract, "an act of unparalleled infamy," and cases arose in the courts to have it declared unconstitutional; but no court of importance so held. [26]

Further opposition to the system of exemptions was revealed in

[25] *Official Records,* Ser. IV, Vol. III, 49.

[26] The Richmond *Daily Examiner,* January 6, 1864, published this bit of sarcasm: "And the man of little faith, who hired the substitute, opened a shop and sold cakes and calico, and waxed rich on his gains of fifteen hundred per cent. But it came to pass that the wise men of the nation arose, and debated among themselves whether the principal and the substitute should not keep company together.

"And the wise men passed a bill making the substitute[s] a nought, and sending their friends, the principals to greet them in the ranks, with a musket at the right shoulder shift. Then the principals waxed exceeding wrath, and straightway set about preparing to emigrate to another—yea a better—country, beyond the Potomac."

the outcry against the so-called "20-nigger law." Congress passed it because state laws required the presence of white men on slave plantations, and also because planters insisted that agricultural production could not be carried on without overseers. Some asserted that small farms with few slaves or none, rather than large plantations, were the chief source of food and that the law was really designed to save the rich planters' sons from the army. It was pointed out that no white laborers on small farms were exempted. Senator Phelan declared that never "did a law meet with more universal odium," in the army as well as at the home front.[27] Addressing the Mississippi legislature, Davis declared that it was designed to provide police protection and to increase production and that he would not think of signing a bill that favored the rich; and Senator Hill defended it with the remark, "As well turn a gang of monkeys in your fields as a gang of negroes without a supervisor to coerce and direct their labor." [28] To lessen the clamor of the opposition, Congress passed a law on May 1, 1863, providing that no person within military age should be exempted as an overseer unless he had served in that capacity before the enactment of the first conscription act, that no overseer could be exempted for a plantation that had been carved from a larger one since October 11, 1862 (the date of the second exemption act, which had first set up the 20-slave rule), and that the owner of a plantation should pay $500 for every overseer exempted.

To provide a source of future leadership for the Confederacy, educators sought exemption for college and university students who had been restrained from volunteering. Enrollment at the University of Virginia dropped from 600 in 1861 to 40 in January, 1863, but Secretary of War Seddon refused to exempt these students, though he did furlough them to the end of the scholastic year.

Although a North Carolina mountaineer could say near the end of 1862 that "seven families, living on adjoining lands" near by had only a ninety-year-old man among them,[29] yet conscription was

27 *Official Records,* Ser. I, Vol. XVII, Pt. II, 790.
28 *Southern Historical Society Papers,* XLVIII (1941), 105; Richmond *Daily Examiner,* January 5, 1863.
29 *Official Records,* Ser. I, Vol. XVIII, 773.

not yielding sufficient troops; and Lee could complain two months later that none of his victories had resulted in the destruction of enemy armies, because he lacked reserve troops to be used in following through. "More than once," he added, "have most promising opportunities been lost for want of men to take advantage of them, and victory itself has been made to put on the appearance of defeat, because our diminished and exhausted troops have been unable to renew a successful struggle against fresh numbers of the enemy." [30] There were too many exemptions, deserters, and conscription dodgers. Imperfect records showed that at least half of the men enrolled were exempted.[31] Deserters were proceeded against and dodgers were sought.[32] Conscription officials searched trains, investigated men emerging from theaters, and asked civilians wherever congregated to show their exemption papers. Even a Congressman in Tennessee was seized and temporarily held until identified because he could not show exemption papers. Increasing complaint was heard that too many in every occupation and profession were exempted. Congressman Charles M. Conrad of Louisiana insisted that many ministers could serve better on the battlefields than "in preaching to empty meeting houses or to old maids and grannies." [33] President Davis asked Congress in December, 1863, to enact legislation to bring in deserters, put a stop to substitutes, modify exemptions, and replace many able-bodied men in nonmilitary positions with the incapacitated, old men, and Negroes. Senator Albert G. Brown of Mississippi declared that the exemption laws "actually stunk in the nostrils of the people," [34] and a Georgia editor, with sound wisdom, advocated the abolition of all exemptions and the conscription of the total male population to serve industry, agriculture, the army, or the professions at a soldier's wages. The Confederacy "could thus obtain its workmen in factories and foundries, its army surgeons, clerks, etc., and this would be equal and exact justice to all men, for all owe to their Government the same measure

---

[30] *Ibid.*, Vol. XXI, 1086.

[31] For various estimates, see *ibid.*, Ser. IV, Vol. III, 1102–1103; Richmond *Daily Examiner*, December 25, 1863; Putnam County (Ga.) *Countryman*, March 14, 1865; Moore, *Conscription and Conflict in the Confederacy*, 99.

[32] For a discussion of desertion, see Chapter XIX.

[33] *Southern Historical Society Papers*, XLVII (1930), 175.

[34] *Ibid.*, XLVIII (1941), 182.

of service, and none should be allowed, more than others, to make its rendition a matter of pecuniary profit." [35]

The conscription act of February 17, 1864, radically changed the whole system of selection by abolishing all industrial exemptions but continued to exempt the physically unfit, ministers, editors and printers, apothecaries, physicians, hospital and asylum workers, indispensable railroad workers, mail carriers, and government officials—with governors retaining all the leeway they previously exercised. As a concession to the smaller plantations, one overseer should now be exempted for fifteen slaves, but the owner must promise to sell to the Confederate government bacon, beef, and other provisions at a price fixed by the impressment commissioners. Thereafter all necessary workmen in the industrial establishment of the Confederacy should be detailed on the authority of the President, either from the army or outside.

While the terms of this law were under consideration, newspaper editors became almost frantic in their opposition to any provision that would detail their own profession. They argued that it would end freedom of the press, for Davis would detail only editors who supported him, and thereby silence all criticism of his administration. It was an attempt to make the President an absolute dictator with the power of life or death over every citizen, and the measure would also give him the opportunity to place "his pets" in safe positions. Representative Waller R. Staples of Virginia declared that the bill would "clothe the President with the powers of an autocrat," and that it invested him "with prerogatives before which those of Napoleon sink into insignificance." [36] In theory, all exempted industrial workers were to be drafted into the army; but, in fact, there was little change brought about by the new system, for it was impossible to replace suddenly the many able-bodied skilled workers with the old, the wounded, and the ailing. Yet many eligible men who had heretofore held bombproof

35 Columbus *Weekly Enquirer*, September 2, 1862. A Texan wanted Congress to "conscript the entire Confederacy. While it takes one part to defend the country take the rest to support it & *make them work*. At the end of the war, we would all be on equality & our country out of debt. Another thing, I wish our Congress would set a price on every article & then pass a law to put every man in the army who violates that law." Thomas H. Compene (?), June 29, 1863, to H. Flanagin, in Oldham Papers.   36 Richmond *Daily Examiner*, January 9, 1864.

positions were acquired for the army. But petitions and other pressures were used to detail certain persons who were about to be conscripted. A land which had never been known for its skilled industrial workers suddenly became filled with them.

People still sought to take advantage of the exemptions. Magazine editors persuaded Congress to exempt them, but President Davis vetoed the bill; necessary railroad positions heretofore filled by Negroes were now taken by white men of military age, which led Congress to consider whether railroad workers should be taken out of the exempted class; and so many people turned to preaching that rules were adopted to deny exemption to "exhorters and local preachers." But when the military authorities attempted to detail to a bakery shop a man declared unfit for military service, a Georgia court refused to permit it on the grounds that President Davis had no control over civilians.

The draft act setting up the system of details also provided that seventeen-year-old boys and men from forty-five through fifty should compose a reserve for local defense under Confederate control, and later Adjutant and Inspector General Cooper ruled that all details were subject to training and might be called out for emergency duty. Earlier legislation had provided for local-defense troops and much bickering had ensued with governors, especially Governor Brown, over their control. Toward the end of the war local defense troops were frequently called out against a sudden foray of enemy cavalry. The most unusual of such forces was a group of old men, "the aged and infirm," organized in Athens, Georgia, who took on the name of "Mitchell's Thunderbolts," and in great seriousness were ready to beat off Sherman's raiders if they had come that way.

To administer the draft, a Bureau of Conscription was set up which used state officers as far as governors would permit. Some governors aided, but those like Brown refused to have any part in a program which they considered unconstitutional. A bureaucracy of enrolling officers, medical examiners, and other agents grew up to handle the immense task of enrolling or exempting every white male in the Confederacy from seventeen to fifty. In early 1864 President Davis reported that there were 2,813 officers engaged in this work. No wheel of fortune was necessary, as was the case in the North, for all were in the army, and it was merely a matter of reaching them and either exempting them or sending them on to camps of instruction, from which they would later be sent to the army. As the poet put it:

> *Oh weep not, conscript, weep not,*
> *Old Jeff has called for thee,*
> *A soldier Congress makes you,*
> *A soldier you must be.*
> *Make up your mind*
> *To stand in line,*
> *And quake not at the Yanks,*
> *To shoot your gun*
> *And call it fun,*
> *And for life return your thanks.*[37]

The Conscription Bureau had a checkered career of tribulation, contention, opposition, and futility. Brigadier General Gabriel J. Rains became superintendent and continued until May 25, 1863, when he was supplanted by Brigadier General Charles W. Field, who held the position until the following July 30. Field was followed by Colonel John S. Preston, who continued to the bitter end. General Bragg, who commanded the Army of Tennessee, finding that the Bureau sent him few recruits, appointed Gideon J. Pillow as a military recruiting officer for all of the region east of the Mississippi excepting the Atlantic seaboard. Pillow soon developed a little bureau of conscription of his own, and so thoroughly did he harrow and comb his territory, making it hard on the shirkers, dodgers, and deserters, that he secured surprising results. His thoroughness led Rains to complain that his civilian bureau was superseded by a military recruiter, and on being admonished by Davis, Pillow resigned. About the same time Rains was succeeded by Field and then by Preston, and Bragg was supplanted by Joseph E. Johnston as commander of the Army of Tennessee. At the urgent request of Johnston, Pillow was again placed in charge of recruiting in the regions west of the Atlantic seaboard as far as the Mississippi, and now Preston complained. Pillow remained in charge until January, 1864, and throughout his period of service under

37 Augusta *Weekly Constitutionalist*, January 20, 1864.

Bragg and Johnston he raised about 25,000 troops. The Bureau was undoubtedly very inefficient, since most of its officers were incompetent and worthless culls weeded out of the army, though some military commanders complained that the Bureau was being filled by able-bodied men who would make good soldiers.[38]

In some communities the country had been swept clean of men, however inefficient the Conscription Bureau was, as was pathetically described by a citizen of Egypt, Mississippi, who wrote to Governor Clark in September, 1864: "There are not men enough left to bury the dead. The people are subsisting on the ungathered crops, and nine families out of ten are without meat. I have myself within the last few days seen women driving oxcarts to Okolona for corn and salt." [39] Yet about the same time Lee was calling for more troops: "Our ranks are constantly diminishing by battle and disease, and few recruits are received; the consequences are inevitable." A little later he wrote Davis that Grant was opposing him with 150,000 men and unless "we can obtain a reasonable approximation to his force I fear great calamity will befall us." He added that a few days previously he had only three brigades to oppose six divisions of the enemy on one part of the battlefield.[40] To prevent even the smallest leaks, Congress, on February 3, 1865, declared that anyone of military age who should leave the Confederacy without permission would thereby make his property liable to sequestration and himself an alien enemy; and President Davis in March, 1865, advised legislation that would hold in the army those who had bad hearing and stiff joints, and even those who had lost an arm or a leg.

As the end of the Confederacy rapidly approached, the Conscription Bureau was abolished on March 7, 1865, and its duties were handed over to the generals in charge of the reserves in the several states.[41] A few days later Congress abolished practically

[38] Rowland (ed.), *Jefferson Davis, Constitutionalist,* VI, 374–79; Augusta *Weekly Chronicle & Sentinel,* May 3, 1865; Freeman (ed.), *Lee's Dispatches,* 294; Moore, *Conscription and Conflict in the Confederacy,* 191, 323.

[39] W. D. Holder, Egypt, Miss., to Governor Clark, September 15, 1864, in Ser. E, Vol. LXVII, No. 66 (Mississippi State Archives).

[40] Rowland (ed.), *Jefferson Davis, Constitutionalist,* VI, 328; Freeman (ed.), *Lee's Dispatches,* 305.

[41] This change was made because people generally flouted the authority of the

the whole power of the President to make details and partly restored industrial exemptions. It also abolished the exemption of
overseers for plantations. Howell Cobb and others wanted to abandon every vestige of conscription and depend entirely on volunteering.

The final and exact results of conscription can never be known
as the records were imperfectly kept, and no returns of the Bureau
included the regions west of the Mississippi River; but the system
brought in about as many volunteers as it did conscripts. According
to Preston's final, imperfect report there were 81,993 conscripts
and 76,206 volunteers. In some states the volunteers far outnumbered the conscripts, as in Virginia and Georgia where the numbers
were respectively 16,000 to 13,933 and 26,000 to 9,000. In North
Carolina, where Governor Vance vigorously supported conscription, there were 21,343 conscripts and 8,000 volunteers. This was
about 7,000 more conscripts than were got in any other state.[42]

Conscription was unpopular with a great many people. In
Georgia, where it was more unpopular and more resisted than in
any other state, one citizen said, "I do not wish my name ever to
be enrolled as a 'nigger' of Jeff Davis"; another declared that there
was "an amount of odium & disgrace attached to conscription which
we dislike to bear & hand down to our posterity"; and an editor
explained that the people considered it degrading and that "most
of our young men would just as soon be sent to the penitentiary
for a term of years as to be conscripted." [43] Congressman Reuben
Davis of Mississippi said that he "had rather be a 'naygur' than a

---

Bureau. An agent in Georgia declared in October, 1864, that of about 500 ordered to
report to a camp of instruction, only about 80 did so; and another reported that in
Florida, "there is scarcely any part of the state where a single officer can enforce
the attendance of conscripts when enrolled." J. H. Morgan to Browne, October 13,
1864 (manuscript in possession of the writer); S. S. Rogers to Cobb, March 12, 1863,
in Howell Cobb Papers.

42 *Official Records*, Ser. IV, Vol. III, 1101; Augusta *Daily Chronicle & Sentinel*,
March 31, 1865; Richmond *Daily Enquirer*, February 23, 1865; Richard E. Yates,
"Zebulon B. Vance as War Governor of North Carolina, 1862–1865," in *Journal of
Southern History*, III (1937), 43–75. These statistics are woefully incomplete and,
therefore, only indicative of a trend, for according to them the Confederacy received
from the region east of the Mississippi River during the period, 1862–1865, only 158,199
troops.

43 W. D. Grant to Cobb, April 26, 1862, in Howell Cobb Papers; J. C. Whitner
to Cobb, September 12, 1862, *ibid.*; Athens *Southern Watchman*, September 3, 1862.

victim of the Conscription Law." [44] Conscripts were looked upon with contempt by many army officers, despite the fact that there were many excellent soldiers who entered the army as conscripts for they were merely patriotically obeying the law and awaiting whatever disposition their government should make of them. Yet this was the experience of an instructor of conscripts at Camp Lee, near Richmond: "I soon found that . . . of all the mean filthy, ignorant, God-forsaken people it had ever been my lot to encounter, these conscripts exceeded all. You might drill them for hours without making the least impression, and when at last exhausted patience would draw forth language rather strong and unmilitary, you were sure to hear something like 'I don't know nuthin 'bout soldiern, nor darn ef I keer 'bout larnen, and jist say I might go home, mister, an' I'm off.' " [45]

Indeed, conscription had been a failure. As for producing troops, its chief value was to propel people into volunteering; as a selective service act, it sent into trades and industries no more or better workmen than would have found their way there otherwise, and doctors, teachers, preachers, and men of other professions could have been provided as well under another system. It was not conscription that saved the twelve-month veterans for the army in 1862 and Richmond from capture; the clause in the conscription act continuing these troops in the army was no part of the conscription system—it could have been provided for in an act of its own. National conscription was so foreign to all American thought and experience and so utterly at variance with the traditional state-rights dogma on which the South had long thrived that it came as a devastating shock to the people. State rights was a strong passion among Southerners; without it secession could hardly have taken place. Conscription destroyed the strongest weapon the Confederacy had, the co-operation of the state governments and their people. The question was not its constitutionality, but rather its workability. Those who promoted it could not read the future, but they must have recognized the gamble they were taking. They should have capitalized on state rights and made it a weapon for

[44] *Southern Historical Society Papers*, XLVII (1930), 205.

[45] William W. Goldsborough, *The Maryland Line in the Confederate States Army* (Baltimore, 1869), 103.

the Confederacy which they could easily have done. As disagreeable as conscription appeared, much of its sting was removed when used by the states, and state-rights argument could not be used against it. In the spring of 1862, when Davis called on the states for new troops, he received all he asked for; and Georgia, later the strongest opponent of national conscription, raised almost twice her quota. If raising troops had been left to the states, it is safe to say that they could have produced more than national conscription yielded. A modified system of national conscription, managed by the several states, would have recognized state pride and responsibility and have worked much more efficiently than the system that was adopted. In November, 1861, General Beauregard had suggested such a plan.[46] National conscription was not only a source of bitter contention but it prejudiced many Southerners against other measures the Confederate administration sought to promote.

Raising troops was no more important than providing officers to command them. The Confederacy had a considerable backlog of trained men, for the South had long looked upon an army career as an honorable profession. Of the many West Point graduates who remained in the army, about 90 per cent resigned to join the Confederacy, though only 70 per cent of the Virginians did so; and those who had entered civil life were now ready to join the Confederate forces. The Mexican War had been a nursery for future officers, and the military academies, such as the Virginia Military Institute, were to provide many more. A few Northerners accepted Confederate commissions. A number of Southerners who were to become important Confederate officers looked on secession with hesitation. Lee wrestled with his soul and conscience before resigning from the United States army; Jubal Early voted against secession in the Virginia Convention; George Pickett was saddened to see the old government broken up; and Braxton Bragg declared that secession had been engineered by a group of "political hacks and barroom bullies," who could "easily pull down a government," but who inspired no confidence in setting up another.[47]

[46] *Official Records,* Ser. IV, Vol. III, 168.
[47] Quoted in Lewis, *Sherman, Fighting Prophet,* 139.

A source of both strength and weakness in securing officers was their selection from men who had had no military training. There were such political appointees as Howell Cobb, Robert Toombs, Thomas R. R. Cobb, Henry A. Wise, and Roger A. Pryor; and there were others equally without military training who rose to high position through merit and who became adornments to the Confederacy. Outstanding among these were John B. Gordon, Nathan B. Forrest, James J. Pettigrew, John H. Morgan, Turner Ashby, and John S. Mosby. Before the army was reorganized under conscription, practically all officers excepting general officers were elected by the enlisted men or appointed by the governors; the field officers (colonels, lieutenant colonels, and majors) were generally appointed by the governors, while the company officers (captains, first lieutenants, and second lieutenants) were almost invariably elected by the men. It was a widespread practice for anyone who wanted to be an officer to raise the unit that he hoped to command; those joining it thereby recognized him as such. Once a person became an officer, however incompetent he might be, ordinarily the rules required his promotion as vacancies occurred.

There were both advantages and disadvantages in allowing the men to elect their officers. The Confederate soldier was an individualist, who believed in his personal rights, and among them he considered foremost the right to decide who should give him orders. He would fight better under an officer whom he knew and liked than under one whom he disliked. A Congressman declared that the Confederate army was composed of gentlemen, who knew best who could lead them and inspire their confidence. "They are not automatons," he insisted, "dancing to the turning of some official organ grinder. The best *mind* and the best *blood* in the country are in the army, and much of both are found in the ranks. They have not lost the identity of the citizen in the soldier." [48]

But the disadvantages far outweighed the advantages, for the person who could win election did not necessarily possess military skill; if he were a good handshaker, backslapper, fiddler, storyteller, or speechmaker he could generally win against the trained soldier. Candidates were always plentiful. "Authorize a squad of six

[48] Athens *Southern Watchman*, January 18, 1865.

men to elect a Lance Corporal," said one observer, "and five of the number will at once become candidates." [49] When the twelve-month men were continued in the service under conscription, as a concession to them they were allowed to reorganize from regiments on down and elect new officers. In many instances the results were most unfortunate, for those officers who had insisted on strict discipline were supplanted by privates and corporals who promised favors and lax discipline.

General Lee and many other high officers strongly opposed the system of election. In June, 1862, General Beauregard reported to a representative of the President that it had "nearly demoralized and disorganized his army"; [50] and a little later George W. Randolph, Secretary of War, insisted that the whole system of securing officers must be changed. "We cannot hope to rival the enemy in numbers," he said, "and unless we can surpass him in organization and discipline the odds against us will be fearfully great." [51] In October, Davis in a special message begged Congress to take up the matter, and asked that another method besides election and promotion be instituted to secure officers. As the system then stood, an officer must be promoted to a vacancy, however inefficient he might be, despite the fact that other units might have a surplus of officers, who, in some instances, exceeded the number of enlisted men. Davis would like to have the right to fill vacancies by appointing efficient officers from other units. Finally, in October, 1862, Congress enacted a law allowing commanders of departments to appoint boards to inquire into the efficiency of officers and to report their findings through the Secretary of War to the President, who might honorably demote them to privates or drop them from the army. Vacancies should be filled by promotion from the next lower grades, and if none promoted could meet the efficiency tests, then the President might appoint officers provided they came from the same state as the units they commanded. Through actual in-

49 *Ibid.*, July 29, 1863. An Alabama officer wrote to one of the Confederate senators from that state in 1862: "I have seen a company rendered inefficient for months because of the opportunity of exercising the elective franchise in the choice of a lieutenant." E. D. Tracy, Tuscumbia, Ala., to Clay, Richmond, February 22, 1862, in Clay Papers.

50 *Official Records*, Ser. I, Vol. X, Pt. I, 779; Vol. VI, 350.

51 *Ibid.*, Ser. IV, Vol. II, 98.

vestigations or the threat of them, the efficiency boards caused a rapid and widespread thinning out of incompetent officers. On June 4, 1864, Adjutant and Inspector General Samuel Cooper issued an order dropping 425 from the rolls of the army and a few days later he announced the "resignation" of about 1,300 others, from colonels through lieutenants. Not all of these were leaving on account of inefficiency, for many were displaced by combining skeleton regiments.

The Confederacy was fortunate in securing, with a few exceptions, excellent general officers; and the efficiency of the lower officers was greater than could have been reasonably expected, for the majority of them entered the service without previous military training. Most of their preliminary knowledge came from studying Hardee's *Tactics,* and thereafter they learned on the battlefields how to fight and command troops. The Confederacy never set up officers' training camps or a military academy, though, pending such an establishment, Congress provided for the appointment of cadets to be attached to companies as "supernumerary officers" while they got their training in actual combat. As for the private soldiers, there was little training for them before they went into battle, though they received some preliminary instruction in camps set up on fairgrounds, old camp-meeting sites, schoolyards, and in vacant lots and fields. As the war wore on, many groups in towns and rural communities, composed of workmen from factories and fields and from the mercantile houses and the professions, practiced the evolutions of soldiering; and some Southerners suggested that every able-bodied male in the Confederacy should drill a short time each day if he lived in town, and three times a week if in the country. For drilling enlisted troops, the cadets of the Virginia Military Institute and of other military schools were used, especially in the beginning.

The rank of general was the highest provided by the Confederacy, and there were eight who attained this grade. The Constitution made the President the commander in chief of the army and navy, but this was a form copied from the old Federal Constitution and was not intended to endow the President with field command. Congress passed a bill early in 1862 to provide the Confederate armies with an active commander in chief, but Davis vetoed it on the con-

331

stitutional ground that it did not subject such officer to the direction of the President. Finally, in January, 1865, during the last dying gasps of the Confederacy, Congress set up the rank of general in chief, to be endowed with command of all the military forces of the Confederacy. It was the Congressional understanding that Lee should be appointed to this office, and Davis would have considered no other; in fact, he might have vetoed the act had there been no Lee. It now made no difference in Confederate fortunes and would not have done so had the act come earlier, for Lee feared to try the grand strategy of commanding all the armies of the Confederacy. His mind and heart were attuned only to the Army of Northern Virginia, and he informed Davis that he would not attempt both.

Davis as constitutional commander in chief had his family of military advisers, but in March, 1862, he assigned Lee as "General to duty at the seat of Government." With the wounding of General Joseph E. Johnston at the battle of Seven Pines, Davis appointed Lee to take charge of the army around Richmond on June 1, and thereafter Lee gave his whole attention to this position. In February, 1864, Davis appointed his favorite, Braxton Bragg, to the position which Lee had held. There had long been a persistent movement to establish a general staff to plan major military strategy, and some of the Richmond papers published articles on the Prussian General Staff. Congress passed a bill setting up a general staff, but Davis vetoed it in May, 1864, on the sound constitutional grounds that it took the power of appointment of its members out of the hands of the President and vested it in the generals in the field.

With all their imperfections, Confederate officers led their troops with as much skill as was displayed by the enemy, and in top commands the Confederacy generally surpassed Federal generals.

CHAPTER XVI

MILITARY POLICY, CAMPAIGNS, AND THE AFTERMATH

"**T**HE race is not to the swift, nor the battle to the strong." There was consolation for the Southerners in these words of Holy Writ, for in military population the Confederacy was outnumbered by the North about four to one and in military equipment and the ability to obtain it far more. Their wagon trains, so necessary for keeping the armies supplied, were far inferior to those of the Federals; they had only half as many miles of railroads; their big guns were generally outranged by the enemy; and their small arms were less effective. If the Confederacy was to gain its independence, it must not only have the will to win, but it must take advantage of every possible weapon and stratagem, old and new.

The Confederates exploited every naval resource at their command; they also used every available land weapon. The first to employ marine mines or torpedoes, they also led the way in the use of land mines or "sub terra shells," as these weapons were generally called. General Gabriel J. Rains invented these mines and first used them extensively on the York Peninsula against McClellan in 1862, planting them in roadways and paths, near wells and springs, and, in fact, using them as "booby traps," made famous in later wars. They slowed down the advancing enemy and their hidden uncertainties struck him with consternation and terror. Before the enemy was in sight the positions of these mines were marked by little red flags, which were removed on his near approach. McClellan complained bitterly at this method of warfare and charged that Confederates were "guilty of the most murderous and barbarous conduct." He forced prisoners of war to risk their lives in locating and removing these torpedoes. The Confederates used them widely: Davis called on the troops in Georgia to mine the roads Sherman was likely to travel on his march to the sea.[1]

In ordinary weapons the Federals excelled; it was in the unusual, as the land mines, where the Confederates held the advantage— though as means of individual protection they never used the bullet-proof vests widely advertised in the North and worn by some Federal soldiers. The brains of many Southerners, more fertile than practical, worked away furiously on fearful weapons guaranteed to destroy the enemy. A double-barreled cannon shooting two balls tied together by a fifty-foot chain a distance of fifteen miles came from the unsettled brain of one Southerner, but another, reducing the effectiveness of his double-barreled monster, actually cast one, which did no damage to the enemy but remained to arouse the wonder of future generations.[2] An armored railroad car housing an immense cannon, a sort of land *Merrimac-Virginia*, was used in the defense of Richmond; and according to an ingratiating tale of a prisoner, one of its shells killed a hundred men and thirty horses. For a time masked batteries created as much consternation among the enemy as the "sub terra shells." Hand grenades, explosive and incendiary, were advocated but few were used. A Georgian believed a few fire engines supplied with nitric acid could keep a whole army at bay and strike troops with dismay "like Joshua's rams horns." Bizarre to the generation of 1861–1865 but commonplace three quarters of a century later, was an invention of a certain R. O. Davidson, which he called a "Bird of Art," "a machine for the aerial locomotion by man." A thousand of these flying machines, each loaded with fifty pounds of bombs, could be dropped on the enemy armies and navies and terminate the war immediately. He called on all patriotic citizens for $1.00 each with which to build them.[3]

A device which the Confederates used for spying upon enemy

[1] *Official Records*, Ser. I, Vol. XI, Pt. III, 509–11, 516; Vol. XLII, Pt. III, 1181–82; Rowland (ed.), *Jefferson Davis, Constitutionalist*, V, 504; Jones, *Rebel War Clerk's Diary*, I, 246; II, 8; M. A. De Wolfe Howe (ed.), *Marching with Sherman; Passages from the Letters and Campaign Diaries of Henry Hitchcock, Major and Assistant Adjutant General of Volunteers, November, 1864–May, 1865* (New Haven, 1927), 161–62; Henry N. Blake, *Three Years in the Army of the Potomac* (Boston, 1865), 67.

[2] It is now on the grounds of the city hall, Athens, Georgia.

[3] Moore (ed.), *Rebellion Record*, VIII, 323–24 (documents).

positions but which the Federals used much more widely and successfully was the balloon, already well known for more than half a century. Many were visible as McClellan marched up the York Peninsula. In fact, the Federals' use of the balloon, "skyscraping" as Richmond newspapermen called it, led the Confederates to attempt it. The Confederates were never able to approach enemy balloons close enough to shoot them down, but they did capture an inflater, which looked something like a street sprinkler. Colonel John B. Magruder, opposing McClellan, first attempted to use a balloon made of cotton bags and filled with hot air, but it soon came to grief. The first one to be successfully used was the so-called "silk dress balloon," erroneously supposed to have been made from the dresses of Southern ladies. It was moved about hitched to a railway car; later it was attached to the little steamer *Teaser* on the James River. Both the vessel and the balloon were captured by the Federals on July 4, 1862. It was soon replaced by another one, made similarly of many variously colored pieces of silk.[4]

Other ways, more orthodox, of gaining information about the enemy and quickly transmitting it were supplied by the Secret Service, Signal Corps, letters and documents captured on the battlefields, and by cavalry raids, telegraphs, couriers, spyglasses, and other adventitious means. In April, 1862, Congress authorized a Signal Corps, which functioned excellently, with its "flag floppers" perched on hills or in trees, using variously colored flags by day and colored lights by night. Stonewall Jackson made effective use of the Signal Corps in his attack on Harpers Ferry in September, 1862; at one time Lee carried on communications between Culpeper and Winchester through the use of about thirty-five stations. The messages sent by the Signal Corps might be seen by the enemy but presumably not understood. To make sure that important messages and orders sent by couriers, telegraph, or mail should likewise not be understood by the enemy, if perchance he should come into

[4] *Official Records of the Union and Confederate Navies*, Ser. I, Vol. VII, 543–44; Richmond *Daily Whig*, July 7, September 22, 1862; Charleston *Daily Courier*, July 8, 1862; Columbus *Weekly Enquirer*, September 30, 1862; Bradlee, *Blockade Running during the Civil War*, 298; J. Duane Squires, "Aeronautics in the Civil War," in *American Historical Review*, XLII (1936–1937), 663; F. Stansbury Haydon, *Aeronautics in the Union and Confederate Armies, with a Survey of Military Aeronautics prior to 1860* (Baltimore, 1941), I, *passim*.

possession of them, various secret codes were used. A convenient code consisted of words appearing in certain places in a dictionary or other book; figures were used to represent letters of the alphabet with the letter corresponding to the day of the month on which the message was written being equivalent to A (as, if it was the third of the month, C would represent A); and certain arbitrary values were given to letters.[5] To separate friend from foe, frequently changed countersigns or passwords were of course used. Confederates enjoyed using the names of girls, as Ophelia, Susan, Viola, Desdemona, or the names of battles, of places, or of generals. They set up an effective Secret Service, in which women often played an important role. Mrs. Rose Greenhow was given credit for warning the Confederates of the approach of the enemy before the First Battle of Manassas, and the incredible Belle Boyd undoubtedly gave Stonewall Jackson valuable military information. Some Secret Service agents conveyed information through the pictures they took.

Special squads of from twenty-five to fifty men were authorized to operate back of the enemy lines and on the rivers. They were awarded as much as 50 per cent of the value of enemy property destroyed.[6] Lee and other generals secured valuable information from Northern newspapers, which circulated freely in the Confederacy; but, conversely, the Federals made good use of the Confederate newspapers as well as other sources. Confederate authorities sensed the danger of writing and talking promiscuously about military affairs, and the War Department and some of the generals tried to control the newspapers; yet many careless leaks were al-

[5] *Official Records*, Ser. I, Vol. X, Pt. II, 310; Vol. XXX, Pt. II, 407; Rowland (ed.), *Jefferson Davis, Constitutionalist*, V, 225; Samuel P. Day, *Down South; or, An Englishman's Experience at the seat of the American War* (London, 1862), II, 47; Ross, *Visit to the Cities and Camps of the Confederate States*, 100; von Borcke, *Memoirs of the Confederate War for Independence*, 110 n.; Charles E. Taylor, "The Signal and Secret Service of the Confederate States," in *North Carolina Booklet* (Raleigh), II, No. 11 (March, 1903), *passim*; Douglas S. Freeman, *Lee's Lieutenants, A Study in Command* (New York, 1942–1944), II, 194.

[6] *Official Records*, Ser. IV, Vol. III, 202; Rowland (ed.), *Jefferson Davis, Constitutionalist*, VI, 245; Francis T. Miller (ed.), *The Photographic History of the Civil War* (New York, 1912), I, 25, 42; VIII, 290; Belle Boyd [Mrs. Sam W. Hardinge], *Belle Boyd in Camp and Prison* (New York, 1865), *passim*; Louis A. Sigaud, *Belle Boyd, Confederate Spy* (Richmond, 1944), *passim*; Margaret Leech, *Reveille in Washington, 1860–1865* (New York, 1941), *passim*.

lowed to develop. Soldiers in their uncensored letters home told everything they knew, and even President Davis in many of his earlier messages to Congress gave out information that should never have been made public. In April, 1861, he told of the disposition of Confederate troops and their number; in February, 1862, he informed the world that the Confederacy had four hundred regiments of infantry with proportional forces of artillery and cavalry; and in the following March he gave full information on the James River fortifications. Lee felt that "Negroes and traders" were always potential sources of information for the enemy. In March, 1865, Congress instituted the death penalty for any one guilty of thus assisting the Federals.

To aid in controlling certain disaffected or suspected people in the Confederacy and to prevent civil authorities from interfering with military activities, President Davis asked for and obtained from Congress the right to suspend the writ of habeas corpus. Three times Congress gave him permission to exercise this power for specified periods, with the result that the writ was suspended from February 27 to October 13, 1862; from October 13, 1862, to February 13, 1863; and from February 15 to August 1, 1864. The suspension was never made over all of the Confederacy but only in certain exposed regions. Some of the military commanders, assuming the power themselves, acted for districts under their control and thereby brought down upon themselves and upon the Confederate administration the ire of Congress and of the people. Widespread opposition to the whole system resulted in severe restrictions being applied. General Bragg in August, 1862, declared the Atlanta region under martial law and appointed a military governor. General Thomas C. Hindman applied the law in northwestern Arkansas; General Earl Van Dorn, in Mississippi; and other commanders, elsewhere. To put a stop to the irresponsible use of this dangerous power, Davis forbade it to all commanders without his permission. Under the exercise of this authority the sale of intoxicating liquors was forbidden, deserters were arrested and held, suspicious persons jailed, and the customary civil liberties of the people suspended.

Although the infantry was always the backbone of military power, the Confederacy early developed special services, but never to the extent, many strategists felt, that would have ensured victory. Picked sharpshooters existed from the beginning, but not until 1864 did Congress authorize for each brigade a battalion of sharpshooters, to be armed with long-range muskets and rifles. There was some sentiment favoring the authorization of guerrillas, but the Confederate authorities never countenanced such warfare; yet a service called the "partisan rangers" was set up and they were constantly charged by the Federals with being guerrillas. The rangers were authorized in April, 1862, to be "subject to the same regulations as other soldiers," but allowed to range widely as detached groups, especially back of the enemy lines, and to receive, in addition to the same pay as other soldiers, the full value of all munitions of war captured and brought back. The most famous of these soldiers was a band numbering no more than three hundred known as Mosby's Rangers, led by Colonel John S. Mosby. They operated in northern Virginia, back of the Federal lines, and so completely did they dominate Loudoun and Fauquier counties that this region came to be known as "Mosby's Confederacy." They scattered into smaller bands but quickly reassembled in Robin Hood fashion for important raids, willingly supplied by their sympathizers. Seizing sustenance from the Union element, capturing Federal supplies and even high officers, and threatening Federal communication lines and Washington itself, their presence helped to keep fifty thousand Federal troops in the vicinity of the national capital. On one occasion they wrecked a train and captured Sheridan's pay roll of $173,000. But partisan rangers became so troublesome to loyal Confederates that Congress abolished the service in February, 1864, except for those operating in the enemy country.

The Confederates developed the cavalry branch of the service earlier than the Federals, and for the first two years of the war maintained superiority. Yet the Confederacy never organized this service adequately before the Federals recognized its full value, and therefore lost opportunities to wreak such damage on the North as might possibly have brought the war to an end. When the Federals began to emphasize the use of cavalry under such leaders as Sheridan, armed with better equipment and supplied with better horses, the Confederates had waited too long ever to catch up again. In 1864 Lee complained of jaded horses, of having too few of any kind, and of a lack of feed for them, and warned that the outcome of the Virginia campaign rested on recruiting additional cavalry. By this time the Upper South and Texas were either occupied or cut off by the enemy, and the Confederacy was forced to depend on the dwindling supply in the rest of the country. To rehabilitate wounded, run-down, and diseased horses, in various parts of the South infirmaries were set up and succeeded in returning many animals to the service. But the mortality of cavalry and artillery horses, as well as of mules, was great; and Southerners, who loved horses, could agree with a correspondent of the Richmond *Examiner,* who wrote that tens of thousands "of them have fallen and died, and gone to the eternal pastures of the horse heaven that we trust is in reserve for all good loyal horses and mules that have discharged their burdens and duty in this world, neither neighing nor braying." [7]

Until near the end of the war all cavalrymen except commissioned officers were required to furnish their own horses, for the Confederate authorities knew that this service was the preferred branch and that the recruit would go to any length to provide himself a horse. But as the war wore on, the dashing cavalrymen came into disrepute with the infantrymen as well as with many civilians; for they were accused of neglecting their fighting to engage in love-making, marrying, gambling, horse stealing, and general marauding. An English observer declared that Confederate cavalrymen were "the most incorrigible horse-stealer[s] in the world"; [8] an army surgeon complained that they did "more stealing and less service than any other branch of the army" and were especially good at "flying around the young ladies"; [9] and Governor Vance observed that if God had a greater plague for the Confederacy than He had sent against Egypt, "I am sure it must have been a regiment or so of half armed, half disciplined Confederate cav-

---

[7] Richmond *Daily Examiner,* June 18, 1864. See also, *ibid.,* June 2, 1863; Athens *Southern Watchman,* February 17, 1864; Charles W. Ramsdell, "General Robert E. Lee's Horse Supply, 1862–1865," in *American Historical Review,* XXXV (1929–1930), 758–77; Lonn, *Salt as a Factor in the Confederacy,* 13.

[8] Fremantle, *Three Months in the Southern States,* 235.

[9] Edmund C. Burnett (ed.), "Letters of a Confederate Surgeon: Dr. Abner Embry McGarity, 1862–1865," in *Georgia Historical Quarterly,* XXX (1946), 39.

alry." [10] General Forrest offered a reward of $500 for the conviction of any of his men for horse stealing.[11]

The first Confederate company to become famous and strike terror into the enemy was the Warrenton "Black Horse Cavalrymen," who by their fierce charges at First Manassas led a prisoner in describing their performance to exclaim, "Heads and arms fell about in every direction like acorns from trees." [12] Actually, however, the most successful use of cavalry was not in cutting and slashing with sabers nor firing from the saddle, but in dismounting and fighting like infantry. An exponent of this method as well as one of the most resourceful Confederate cavalrymen was Nathan Bedford Forrest. Of powerful frame, with high cheekbones, light-gray eyes, and black hair, he was untrained in military affairs before the war, but soon learned how to get there first with the most men or make the enemy think he had. Fearless to the point of having been wounded four times and having twenty-nine horses shot from under him, he was reputed to have slain more men in battle with his own hand than any other Confederate. He won his fame in the West, operating mostly in Tennessee, Mississippi, and Alabama, turning up far in the enemy country to seize outposts, cut lines of communication, and even attack gunboats on the rivers. In the spring of 1864 he raided from Mississippi north to Paducah, Kentucky, and on his way back captured Fort Pillow on the Mississippi, killing 500 of the 700 in the garrison on their refusal to surrender, and capturing the remainder in addition to 200 horses. He lost 20 men killed and 60 wounded. If Forrest had been given permission to operate on Sherman's lines of communications before his invasion of Georgia in 1864, the March to the Sea might never have taken place. Forrest was never sufficiently recognized by the Confederate administration to be allowed to command over 4,000 men.

Equally successful as a cavalry raider but less fortunate in escaping enemy bullets was James Ewell Brown (Jeb) Stuart. He won fame for his love of the neighing of horses, the blare of bugles, and the good and bad performances of his musicians, for his high mili-

[10] Athens *Southern Watchman*, August 17, 1864.
[11] *Official Records*, Ser. I, Vol. XXXIX, Pt. II, 603.
[12] Richmond *Semi-Weekly Enquirer*, August 2, 1861.

tary boots, yellow sash, slouch hat topped with an ostrich plume, thick brown beard, and piercing blue eyes. But he was especially famous for his ride around McClellan's army on the York Peninsula in the spring of 1862, his raid to Chambersburg, Pennsylvania, after Antietam or Sharpsburg, his fruitless ride in the Gettysburg campaign, and his untimely death caused by a wound received at Yellow Tavern, in May, 1864—"amid the exciting scenes of this revolution, one of the bravest and most dashing cavaliers that the 'Old Dominion' has ever given birth to. Long will her sons recount the story of his achievements, and mourn his untimely departure." [13]

John Morgan was less stable and successful but equally as daring and resourceful, and as great a hero in the eyes of the people. He set the style for disruptive raids behind the enemy lines when he charged northward as far as Cave City, Kentucky, in the spring of 1862, following the battle of Shiloh. Later he carried the war across the Ohio River into Indiana and Ohio, where he was captured and imprisoned in the Ohio penitentiary until he made his escape. He was treacherously slain in East Tennessee in the fall of 1864.[14]

Joe Wheeler, less in physical build, was also less a hero to the people than Forrest, Stuart, or Morgan, his men having acquired the reputation of being the greatest horse thieves in the Confederacy. Wheeler performed his most celebrated services in raids in Tennessee and in Georgia in connection with Sherman's invasion of that state.[15] Minor in performance but unequaled in romantic appeal was black-bearded Turner Ashby. Astride his white horse, he played games with the enemy on the fields of northern Virginia but was shot down by enemy's bullets shortly before the engagement at Cross Keys in 1862. His death inspired John R. Thompson to write these lines:

[13] Richmond *Daily Examiner*, May 14, 1864. See also, John W. Thomason, Jr., *Jeb Stuart* (New York, 1930), *passim*.

[14] Two lives of Morgan are Cecil F. Holland, *Morgan and his Raiders, A Biography of the Confederate General* (New York, 1942); and Howard Swiggett, *The Rebel Raider; A Life of John Hunt Morgan* (Indianapolis, 1934).

[15] Joseph Wheeler to Cobb (telegram), December 27, 1864, in Howell Cobb Papers; Macon *Daily Telegraph and Confederate*, December 29, 1864; Charleston *Daily Courier*, January 12, 1865. See also, John P. Dyer, *"Fightin' Joe" Wheeler* (University, La., 1941).

> *To the brave all homage render,*
> *Weep, ye skies of June!*
> *With a radiance pure and tender*
> *Shine, oh saddened moon!*
> *'Dead upon the field of glory,'*
> *Hero fit for song and story,*
> *Lies our bold dragoon.*[16]

These and other cavalrymen showed the possibilities never fully realized in this branch of the service, and made it plain that Southerners could elevate cavalrymen to heroes despite the disrepute in which some of them were held.

The Confederacy was unfortunate in its failure to work out a general strategy for the whole war. From the beginning counsels were divided between an offensive concentration of forces and a dispersal to suit the whims of every local-minded governor and state-rights enthusiast. The philosophy which adventitiously controlled was a sort of combination of dispersal with a defensive concentration around Richmond. Eventually this was almost inevitable, for localism was so strongly embedded in the Southerners that little enthusiasm could have been developed for the war had important forces not been maintained in the states, and the dominant position of Virginia and Richmond in the minds of the people was such that the loss of Richmond would have seemed the loss of the war. If there could have been an equivalent concentration on the Mississippi and west of it, the back door of the Confederacy could not have been easily battered down and disintegration from the rear might not have set in. Northern strategy was planned to force a dispersal of Confederate forces by attacks at widely scattered points, and McClellan especially advised attacking Southern seaports as part of this plan.

Equally as disastrous and soul-killing as dispersal was the policy of considering the war solely defensive. This was part of the mass thinking promoted especially by Davis to show the world that the Confederacy did not want the war and that it would do nothing more than defend itself—a "simple demand that the people of the United States should cease to war upon us, and permit us to pursue

[16] Richmond *Daily Whig*, June 14, 1862. This is the first of five stanzas.

our own path to happiness, while they in peace pursue theirs." [17] This school of strategists thought that to invade the North would belie this position, stir up a hornet's nest, and promote an unwanted war. As one proponent of offensive action satirically remarked, "Cotton is fighting for us, tobacco is fighting for us, Yankee insolence is fighting for us, millions of famished Europeans are fighting for us," [18] and he might have added that many thought the Confederacy's feeling of righteousness would win the war. The defensive policy of holding positions, a West Point philosophy which so many came to hate, was derisively called the "digging and ditching policy," which if continued, one Southerner declared in 1862, would so lengthen the war that "our grand children will scarcely live to see the end." [19] Robert Toombs, who wanted quick offensive action, "swore he believed one engineer could find work for all the men that had been sent to Hell since Adam sinned." [20] The soldiers wanted to fight, not dig. The offensive strategists wanted to march on Washington immediately following Fort Sumter. In May a Southerner who lived west of the Mississippi declared that the Confederacy ought to seize the heights of the Rockies and cut off the Pacific states, and by making Missouri a center of operations seize the Old Northwest.[21] It was long a favorite topic with some strategists to make a thrust through West Virginia, cross the Ohio, march to Lake Erie, and thereby cut the North in two. Even such sound warriors as Stonewall Jackson and Beauregard considered such a plan feasible. When "Old Jack" had shown what mobile war could accomplish in the Shenandoah Valley, a Richmond editor in mock seriousness exclaimed, "This man Jackson must be suppressed, or else he will change the humane and Christian policy of the war, and demoralize the Government. Evidently he has lost his mind. Down with him, or he

---

[17] Davis to Lee, September 7, 1862, in *Official Records*, Ser. I, Vol. XIX, Pt. II, 599.

[18] From editorial in *Southern Literary Messenger*, XXXIV (1862), 66. Bemoaning the failure of the Confederates to follow up their victories and lamenting defeats, J. J. Ormond, Tuscaloosa, Ala., wrote Senator Clay, February 25, 1862, in Clay Papers: "So far the people have done everything, the Government little, and this little in the wrong direction; holding our hands, restraining our energies."

[19] From editorial in Athens *Southern Watchman*, June 11, 1862.

[20] Cobb to his wife, August 10, 1862, in Thomas R. R. Cobb Letters.

[21] *Official Records*, Ser. I, Vol. III, 578–79.

will establish the independence of the Southern Confederacy." [22]

The Confederate victory at First Manassas had two opposite effects. First, it drove the Confederate people insane with joy; they celebrated it from one end of the country to the other with speechmaking and popping guns; the Confederate Congress awarded all the credit to "the Most High God, the King of Kings and Lord of Lords," and then solemnly adjourned. With delightful derision, songs and stories and Bible paraphrases were used to describe the discomfited enemy. After the victory had been proclaimed from the Spotswood House in Richmond, amidst "the wildest and most tumultuous joy, through tickets for Washington, Philadelphia and New York were in high demand." [23] One strategist explained the victory as having been caused by news reaching the Federals that there were two vacancies in the New York customhouse, which caused a stampede in that direction. A poet paraphrasing Yankee Doodle advised:

> *Yankee Doodle, Oh! for shame,*
> *You're always intermeddling,*
> *Let guns alone, they're dangerous things,*
> *You'd better stick to peddling.*[24]

---

[22] Richmond *Daily Whig*, May 27, 1862.

[23] *Ibid.*, July 22, 1861. A song entitled, "Jonathan's Gallop, Performed at the Grand Rout Given in Honor of his Visit to Bull Run," was written and published in London. *Ibid.*, November 11, 1861. Following the tenth chapter of Joshua, a wit set to Biblical language a description of the rout of the Federals at Manassas:

"8. And the Lord discomfited them before the children of the South, and they were slain with a great slaughter at Manassa; and they were chased along the way that goeth up to Centreville, and smitten to Alexandria, and near unto Washington City.

"9. And it came to pass, as they fled from before the children of the South, that there were more that died from fear than were slain by the sword." Macon *Daily Telegraph*, quoted in Richmond *Daily Dispatch*, September 16, 1861.

Many poems were written about the battle. Following is a stanza of some doggerel, adapted to "Old Dan Tucker," appearing in the Athens *Southern Watchman*, October 23, 1861:

> Abraham Lincoln made a pledge,
> To save the Union with a *wedge!*
> Drove it in! but the more he hit
> The worse the glorious Union split.
> Yaw! yaw! ye bold Bull runners
> Wait a wee for the Terrell gunners.

[24] Atlanta *Southern Confederacy*, January 8, 1862.

According to rumor, it was the greatest and most sanguine battle ever fought on American soil; the number of guns captured was "unprecedented in the history of warfare"; Beauregard had seized Alexandria and Arlington Heights and the Yankees were fighting among themselves on the streets of Washington and the people in Baltimore had risen up and driven them out. And according to Thomas R. R. Cobb, *"It is one of the decisive battles of the world* and will be [so] estimated in History. . . . Some skirmishing may be had in other quarters but no battle will be fought. [It] *has* secured our Independence."* [25]

There were some who were not carried away by this senseless though understandable excitement and others were soon to regain their composure. Mrs. Braxton Bragg observed, "The overconfidence it has excited will I fear be disastrous"; [26] Mrs. Chesnut felt it sent "us off in a fool's paradise of conceit"; [27] and Benjamin H. Hill questioned whether the Confederate victories at Bethel and Manassas or the defeats at Roanoke and Donelson "were the greater blessings to us." [28]

The other major effect of Manassas was a demand that the Confederate armies immediately start a forward movement. It was the almost unanimous feeling of the press that Washington could be taken, and the editor of the Richmond *Whig* advocated annihilating the city. "There can be no peace," he said, "until that nest of Yankees and traitors is exterminated." [29] Although Confederate outposts for a time were pushed to a point where the pickets could see the spires of Washington, the main Confederate army remained stationary and went into winter quarters in northern Virginia. This policy soon led to bitter disputes and recriminations. President Davis, it was charged, prevented the army from following up its victory. But in the council of war held immediately after the

25 Cobb to his wife, July 24, 1861, in Thomas R. R. Cobb Letters.

26 Mrs. Braxton Bragg to her husband, August [day of month omitted and also year, but presumably 1861], in Braxton Bragg Papers (University of Texas Library).

27 Martin and Avary (eds.), *Diary from Dixie*, 196.

28 Benjamin H. Hill to J. W. Powell, March 1, 1862, in Sandersville *Central Georgian*, March 19, 1862.

29 Richmond *Daily Whig*, August 23, 1862. The editor of the Athens *Southern Watchman*, October 16, 1861, published this demand: "Devastate their fields, destroy their factories, burn their towns—carry desolation to their homes, as they have done in Virginia."

battle, Davis had not interposed his authority. Joseph E. Johnston did not want to make the attempt, for he realized that the Confederates were almost as demoralized by victory as the Federals were by defeat, and, too, there was a large Federal force to be met which had not been in the battle. In another council held the following October, the generals present wanted to strip the South for a force large enough to go forward, but Davis refused to allow the concentration.[30] The inactive camp life during the winter, with its diseases and homesickness, began the first important inroads on the war enthusiasm of the half-clad soldiers.

Closely related to the defensive plan of the Confederacy was Davis' stubborn policy of refusing actual retaliation on the enemy, both in the restricted meaning of the term and in "carrying the war into Africa." In numerous cases Davis threatened to enforce the laws of retaliation, but in no instance did he ever allow the execution of a person. For Butler's activities in New Orleans, Davis proclaimed him "an outlaw and common enemy of mankind" and ordered that if he were captured he should "be immediately executed by hanging." The President prepared to retaliate on prisoners taken at Manassas if the crews of the privateers *Savannah* and *Enchantress* were executed; he agreed with the policy of executing officers leading Negro troops after the Emancipation Proclamation; and in other instances he expressed himself in favor of retaliation. But Butler was never captured; the privateersmen were exchanged; Davis insisted that the states handle officers captured leading Negro troops and none were executed; and in the case of the Dahlgren raiders as well as in other instances, Davis resolutely refused to allow executions. He was bitterly condemned for this policy of leniency by a great many newspapers and by such constant critics as Pollard. The Richmond *Whig* thought that every newspaper in the Confederacy should, in every edition for six months, cry out for retaliation, but it concluded that it would have about as much effect on Davis as "the thinnest rill of lukewarm water ever squirted

[30] Rowland (ed.), *Jefferson Davis, Constitutionalist*, V, 128 ff.; Joseph E. Johnston, *Narrative of Military Operations, Directed, during the Late War Between the States* (New York, 1874), 59–68; Meade, *Judah P. Benjamin*, 184; Thomas C. De Leon, *Four Years in Rebel Capitals: An Inside View of Life in the Southern Confederacy, from Birth to Death. From Original Notes, Collected in the Years 1861 to 1865* (Mobile, 1890), 373–74.

from a quill would affect the rock of Gibraltar." [31] Lee agreed with Davis on retaliation, saying in 1863, "I am not in favor of retaliation excepting in very extreme cases, and I think it would be better for us to suffer, and be right in our own eyes and in the eyes of the world; we will gain more by it in the end." [32]

When it came to the general idea of retaliation through invasion of the North, the Confederacy made only two important attempts, the Antietam and the Gettysburg campaigns, and in both the Confederate officers were charged with exercising the strictest regard for private property. Commenting on the behavior of the Confederates in the Gettysburg campaign, Colonel Arthur J. L. Fremantle of the Coldstream Guards observed, "To any one who has seen *as I have* the ravages of the Northern troops in Southern towns, this forbearance seems most commendable and surprising." [33] The editor of the Richmond *Examiner* called Lee's invasion "a gigantic window shopping expedition." "Had General Lee's army struck terror into the Dutch farmers of Pennsylvania and laid waste their fruitful territory, Virginians could now with sterner fortitude contemplate the devastation of their beloved state." [34]

When the invasion of the Confederacy set in and the capture of its important cities seemed imminent, some people began to advocate a "scorched earth policy." A group of Georgia Congressmen, including the two Cobb brothers and Toombs, issued an address in February, 1862, declaring that dark days were ahead and that the approaching dangers could be met only by "desperate courage, unflinching daring and universal sacrifice." When the enemy arrived, nothing should be left for him to plunder. "Let every woman have a torch, every child a firebrand." Fire everything. "Let blackness and ruin mark your departing steps, if depart you must, and let a desert more terrible than the Sahara welcome the Vandals.

[31] Richmond *Daily Whig*, May 21, 1863.

[32] *Official Records*, Ser. I, Vol. XXVII, Pt. III, 931.

[33] Fremantle, *Three Months in the Southern States*, 245–46.

[34] Richmond *Daily Examiner*, August 6, 1863. Early in the war an advertisement ran in the Southern press, calling for from 5,000 to 10,000 volunteers, each mounted on horseback and armed with a sword, two five-shooters, and a carbine. They were to carry the war into the North in a most desperate fashion and none should expect to return. "They dedicate their lives to the destruction of their enemies!" Whether Davis killed this plan or men could not be found for such a "commando-like" venture, nothing came of it. See Athens *Southern Watchman*, September 18, 1861.

Let every city be levelled by the flame and every village be lost in ashes." [35] Governor Brown agreed and advocated the destruction of Savannah in the spring of 1862 rather than see it fall into the hands of the enemy, and the governor of South Carolina was willing to see Charleston reduced to ashes. But the "scorched earth policy" did not become popular, and, happily, was never applied. The mayor of Memphis forbade anyone setting fire to that city and declared he would "regardless of judge, jury, or the benefit of the clergy, hang him to the first lamp post, tree or awning." [36]

It soon became popular to argue that the loss of a city or of any given segment of Confederate territory would make little difference in determining ultimate victory. The vast size of the Confederacy would make its conquest impossible. The enemy could not hold the territory through which he marched, for a hostile people would close in behind him. Territory was not the Confederacy; wherever the Confederate army was, there was the Confederacy. In late 1864 Davis advocated a bold, correct strategy, which he seemed never willing to apply, when he argued that even if Richmond should fall, enemy victory would be as far away as ever, for the government could function in some other place just as well. "There are no vital points on the preservation of which the continued existence of the Confederacy depends," he declared. "There is no military success of the enemy which can accomplish its destruction. Not the fall of Richmond, nor Wilmington, nor Charleston, nor Savannah, nor Mobile, nor of all combined, can save the enemy from the constant and exhaustive drain of blood and treasure which must continue until he shall discover that no peace is attainable unless based on the recognition of our indefeasible rights." [37]

[35] Atlanta *Southern Confederacy*, February 20, 1862; Athens *Southern Watchman*, February 19, 1862. Cobb wrote his wife, January 23, 1862, in Howell Cobb Papers: "Let the North see in the hand of every Southern man woman & child a torch ready to be applied to their dwellings & property rather than see it fall into the hands of the vandal robbers & we shall soon have peace and independence."

[36] Charleston *Daily Mercury*, March 14, 1862; *Official Records*, Ser. I, Vol. VI, 377, 391, 396; Vol. XIV, 510; Augusta *Weekly Constitutionalist*, February 19, 1862; Macon *Daily Telegraph*, February 22, April 16, 1862.

[37] Richardson (comp.), *Messages and Papers of the Confederacy*, I, 485. See also, New York *World*, November 11, 1864; Charleston *Daily Mercury*, March 12, 1862.

In fighting the war the Confederacy had, in addition to its cavalry leaders, strength as well as weakness in its other military officers. Lee soon came to typify the Confederacy, though in the beginning his lack of success in western Virginia came near eliminating him. His shelving was prevented only by the stubborn determination of Davis, who read his character and ability correctly and sent him temporarily to strengthen the defenses of the South Atlantic coast. Now it was "Old Spade Lee," "King of Spades," and "Granny Lee"; [38] but when he took control of the Army of Northern Virginia in June, 1862, and held it thereafter, he grew into the man of the ages. A newspaper correspondent echoed the united voice of the Confederacy when he wrote in 1864: "Lee was grand around Richmond, on the hills of Fredericksburg, over the classic plains of Manassas, but on the day he uttered the inspiration, 'Tell them it is my fault,' after Gettysburg he rose above his race and communed with the angels of Heaven." [39] In 1861 he was youngish, wore a black mustache, and looked the part of the soldier; after a year of responsibility and concern for his men and his country his hair grew gray, he wore a white beard, and he looked more as if he should have been a bishop in his Episcopal Church. But his dark-brown eyes continued to shine with the luster of youth, his face appeared kindly and benevolent, his frame, strong and virile. He radiated confidence, though from 1864 he anticipated ultimate defeat. His reserve made familiarity with him unthinkable, and his gentility made him ever too considerate of those under him. His greatest military faults were a lack of stern-

[38] Ellsworth Eliot, Jr., *West Point in the Confederacy* (New York, 1941), 48. Alexander H. Stephens, in November, 1862, considered Lee "about as good a general as we have," but he did not think he was equal to "the great generals of the world." Johnston, *Autobiography*, 166. "Lee, foiled completely at Cheat Mountain and Big Sewell, has gone with his spade to sit down in South Carolina." Editorial in *Southern Literary Messenger*, XXXIII (1861), 465. Cobb, Winchester, Va., to his wife, October 29, 1862, in Thomas R. R. Cobb Letters, said that Lee reviewed the troops there yesterday: "The old fellow paid no attention to the officer's [sic] salutes but whenever a tattered battle flag, pierced with bullets passed by him, he uncovered his head."

[39] Macon *Daily Telegraph*, April 14, 1864. When the city council of Richmond was about to vote to Lee the gift of a house there, Lee heard of it and objected, saying that the money should be used for the relief of soldiers. Richmond *Daily Whig*, March 15, 1864; Richmond *Daily Examiner*, April 8, 1864.

ness and his inability or refusal to remove his attention from Virginia long enough to grasp the military problems of the whole Confederacy.[40]

Thomas Jonathan Jackson, "Stonewall" after the First Battle of Manassas, had piercing blue eyes, high broad forehead, small sharp nose, thin pallid lips, a dark rusty beard. He was not a supremely handsome man as was Lee, nor was he knightly as was Wade Hampton. He did not have the manly beauty of John C. Breckinridge nor the every-inch-a-soldier look of Joseph E. Johnston. He was taciturn, without vivacity or humor, sometimes rude and harsh and a stern disciplinarian, careless of personal appearance, severely religious by the strictest Presbyterian standards, loved by his men, and fearless. Pushing his "foot cavalry" on forced marches, he would ride along the lines and shout, "Close up, close up." On one occasion he marched them fifty-four miles in two days, "one of the greatest marches of history." [41] His quick movements and flanking attacks won him the acclaim of subsequent generations.[42]

Confederate officers generally wore beards, which made them look older than they were. Many of the outstanding officers were in their thirties and forties. Jackson, Stuart, and Pat Cleburne were killed in their thirties; Beauregard, Bragg, Longstreet, A. P. Hill, Forrest, Hardee, D. H. Hill, and Early were in their forties. Most officers became heroes to their fellow citizens during the war, and

---

[40] James C. Hunt to Massie, May 3, 1861, in Massie Papers; Jones, *Rebel War Clerk's Diary*, I, 179; Fremantle, *Three Months in the Southern States*, 248; Eliot, *West Point in the Confederacy*, 53–54; Freeman (ed.), *Lee's Dispatches*, xv. Joseph E. Johnston said that he would as gladly have served under Lee as his father had served under Lee's father. Johnston to Louis T. Wigfall, April 3, 1865, in Wigfall Papers (microfilms in University of Texas Library, originals in Division of Manuscripts, Library of Congress).

[41] Freeman, *Lee's Lieutenants*, II, 93. See also, Henry Kyd Douglas, *I Rode with Stonewall, Being Chiefly the War Experiences of the Youngest Member of Jackson's Staff* . . . (Chapel Hill, 1940), 234. The respect which the enemy had for Jackson was well shown when David Hunter's troops, passing by the cemetery in Lexington where Jackson was buried, halted, uncovered their heads, and marched slowly by. Mrs. Cornelia McDonald, *A Diary with Reminiscences of the War and Refugee Life in the Shenandoah Valley, 1860–1865* (Nashville, 1934), 221.

[42] The greatest haul of enemy stores made throughout the war fell to Jackson in his flank attack just before the Second Battle of Manassas. Freeman, *Lee's Lieutenants*, II, 100, 101.

their fame and respectability broadened thereafter: Beauregard, "Old Bory," a small, thin man, French in appearance, and anxious to be considered another Napoleon; John Bankhead Magruder, "Prince John," looking the part of a prince or duke, dashing, loving display and parades; Pat Cleburne, Irish, with tall, meager frame and an ugly scar across his gloomy face; Sterling Price, "Old Pap," hero of the Mexican War and former governor of Missouri; Joseph O. Shelby, who made his formal military reports in a most amazingly flamboyant style; [43] Richard S. Ewell, long a crusty old bachelor, picturesque, chivalrous, explosive. Then, there were Earl Van Dorn, nobody's hero but his sister's, killed by a fellow citizen who felt himself outraged; Bragg, called an old porcupine and the ugliest man in the army whom few, except Davis, regarded as a good soldier; and others, some of them brilliant and some mediocre.

The *esprit de corps* of Confederate officers was surprisingly low. There were rivalries, jealousies, and hatreds among them, which led to wordy conflicts, resignations, and even duels and threats of duels. Gideon J. Pillow quarreled bitterly with Leonidas Polk and ended by resigning; Jackson had Ambrose Powell Hill put under arrest twice and drew the ire of quarrelous Longstreet; William H. T. Walker resigned from the Confederate army because another received a higher rank; Roger A. Pryor resigned a brigadier generalship to become a private because Davis was slow in giving him a command; even Jackson wrote out his resignation because of interference by Secretary of War Benjamin, who was, in fact, merely carrying out an order of Davis. Almost every officer in the army disliked Bragg, and he reciprocated. Toombs was almost constantly in trouble with his superiors and fellow officers. Thomas R. R. Cobb, who hated him, remarked, "I have sergeants in my

---

[43] Examples of Joseph O. Shelby's flamboyancy are these excerpts from *Official Records*, Ser. I, Vol. XXII, Pt. I, 148, 150: "long before the full round moon had died in the lap of the dawn; long before the watching stars had grown dim with age," "driving the frightened Federals before them like chaff before the winds of heaven,"

> Tramp, tramp, along the land they ride,
> Splash, splash, along the lea;
> The scourge is red, the spur drops blood,
> The flashing pebbles flee!

legion in whose military capacity I have more confidence." [44] Toombs disliked Joseph E. Johnston and felt that Lee was "far below the occasion" in the Peninsular campaign. He challenged Daniel H. Hill to a duel, which the latter refused, and shortly before the Battle of Antietam he was put under arrest for disobedience of orders. Finally, he resigned early in 1863 because he was not given a promotion. Duels were fought and officers killed. A son of R. Barnwell Rhett killed W. Ransom Calhoun, a nephew of John C. Calhoun. So prevalent were duels that voices were raised against them. "If officers want to show their bravery, or imperil the lives of each other unnecessarily," pleaded an editor, "let them agree to charge a Yankee battery single-handed, without support of any kind. If they are not killed, probably a confinement of a few months in a Northern prison may cool their passions." [45]

Fort Sumter set off a war which began in earnest when, the next month, Federal troops crossed the border from the Chesapeake Bay to New Mexico, with the exception of the frontier of neutral Kentucky. The Federal strategy was destined to pierce and strangle the Confederacy by pushing southward to take Richmond in the East, cutting it in two in the West by gaining control of the Mississippi River, and seizing Confederate seaports from Norfolk to Brownsville, Texas. Confederate concentrations began in Virginia and Tennessee under Beauregard and Albert Sidney Johnston respectively. On June 10 came the first battle of the war, a Confederate victory at Big Bethel on the York Peninsula, followed the next month (July 21) by First Manassas, or Bull Run as the Federals liked to call it,[46] another Confederate victory. While the

44 Cobb to his wife, May 13, 1862, in Thomas R. R. Cobb Letters. In a letter to his wife, three days later, Cobb wrote: "Toombs is drinking like a fish and making an ass of himself. His disobedience of orders is notorious, and his disposition to shirk all positions of danger. His military career is a desperate failure." *Ibid.* J. D. Frierson wrote to Howell Cobb, July 31, 1861, in Howell Cobb Papers, "Ask Bob Toombs when he will be able to publish his new system of military tactics as the country will expect something of the sort from his rapid promotion."

45 Charleston *Daily Courier*, March 25, 1864. Mrs. Bragg to her husband, "Thursday 28th 1863," in Bragg Papers (University of Texas Library), "I cannot think much of the patriotism of men who would fight *duels* at such a time."

46 The frequency with which the Confederates and Federals did not agree on naming battles resulted in many engagements' receiving two names, some three, and a few even four. Two names for some of the battles have persisted with about equal popularity. In addition to Manassas or Bull Run, there were Sharpsburg or An-

Confederates rested on the glories of this victory, not too much disturbed by their setbacks in western Virginia, and the Federals began to train an army under General George B. McClellan around Washington, the frontier in Kentucky and Missouri flamed forth in battle. In August the Confederates won at Wilson's Creek, in the latter state, and the next month Kentucky neutrality was abandoned. The hordes of Grant and Don Carlos Buell poured across the Ohio River, gaining within the next six months disturbing Union victories, first at Mill Springs, or Fishing Creek, where Felix Zollicoffer was killed,[47] quickly followed by the fall of Forts Henry and Donelson [48] and the capitulation of Nashville on February 23, 1862. On April 6 and 7 a battle was fought at Shiloh, a short distance north of the Mississippi border, in which General Albert Sidney Johnston was killed. The next day Island Number 10 in the Mississippi fell to forces coming down the river; Fort Pillow, farther south on the river, fell June 4; and two days later Memphis was occupied by the enemy. In spilling over into northern Mississippi, the Federals had now cut the strategic Memphis and Charleston Railroad, which ran from Memphis to Chattanooga.

Meanwhile, an expedition by sea made a landing in early November, 1861, at Port Royal and Beaufort, South Carolina, and

---

tietam Creek, Seven Pines or Fair Oaks, Drury's Bluff or Fort Darling, Ball's Bluff or Leesburg, Mechanicsville or Ellerson's Mills, First Cold Harbor or Gaines' Mill, Chantilly or Ox Hill, Champion Hill or Baker's Creek, Olustee or Ocean Pond, Mansfield or Sabine Cross Roads, Brice's Cross Roads or Guntown, Pilot Knob or Ironton, Kennesaw Mountain or Kolb's Farm, Perryville or Chaplin Hill, Murfreesboro or Stone's River, Pea Ridge or Elkhorn Tavern, Arkansas Post or Fort Hindman. Some of the battles acquiring three names were Wilson's Creek or Oak Hills or Springfield, Cedar Run or Cedar Mountain or Slaughter Mountain, Prairie Grove or Fayetteville or Illinois Creek, Frayser's Farm or Glendale or Nelson's Farm. A four-name battle was Mill Springs or Fishing Creek or Logan's Cross Roads or Somerset.

47 Robert S. Garnett was the first Confederate general to be killed—at Carrick's Ford, July 13, 1861.

48 Many held the fall of Fort Donelson to be a disgrace to Confederate arms. Said a correspondent of the Atlanta Southern Confederacy, March 18, 1862: "The whole transaction is without a parallel in the history of the world." He claimed that the soldiers wanted to fight, but that the commanders forced them to surrender. "Congress ought to pass a law immediately, forbidding troops in the field to surrender and visiting upon such disgraceful and dangerous conduct the severest penalties," he demanded; "and it should be the sworn duty of every officer to put to death on the spot, any other who shall dare propose to disgrace, and endanger his country by capitulating on the field."

the next summer Charleston went under a siege which lasted until almost the end of the war. A force seized Roanoke Island in February, 1862, capturing a small Confederate army,[49] and the next month it seized New Bern and other North Carolina coastal cities and began raids farther into the interior. Also, in early March, a force seized Fernandina, Florida; and, a little later in the month, Jacksonville and Saint Augustine fell to the Federals. Around on the Gulf coast, Appalachicola, at the mouth of the river of the same name, fell on April 2; and on May 10, Pensacola was seized, never to be given up. On April 11, Fort Pulaski, guarding the mouth of the Savannah River, was captured, and in the same month Pass Christian and Biloxi, on the Mississippi coast, were occupied. The most soul-killing of all these calamities brought upon the Confederates by sea-borne troops was the fall of New Orleans in late April to the forces of Admiral David G. Farragut and the occupation of the city by General Benjamin F. Butler.[50] West of the river, in Arkansas, Confederates on March 7 and 8 lost the battle of Pea Ridge, or Elkhorn Tavern, where they were aided by Indians under Albert Pike and the Indian leader Stand Watie. Soon thereafter the main forces were transferred to Mississippi. After a few initial victories in New Mexico, the Confederates were defeated in late March at Glorieta Pass and pushed back into Texas.

The Confederacy had suffered reverses everywhere except in Virginia. By the spring of 1862 Federal forces had broken through the lines in the Mississippi Valley and pierced the Confederacy as far as northern Mississippi; they had cleared the river as far south as Vicksburg and as far north as Port Hudson; they had disrupted Confederate forces in Missouri and Arkansas; and they had made important lodgments on the coasts of every Confederate state except Alabama and Texas. With the waking of spring McClellan's forces embarked on transports and landed on the York Peninsula, thus averting the long land march on their way to Richmond. The Confederates, encamped in Northern Virginia, under the command of Joseph E. Johnston, were forced to make a sudden retreat,

---

[49] This defeat, soon followed by Fort Donelson, greatly shook the morale of the people. Davis called these defeats "deeply humiliating."

[50] On May 8 a Federal gunboat landed a small force at Baton Rouge, farther up the river.

A BANNER OF SECESSION. A reproduction of the banner suspended back of the president's chair in the South Carolina Secession Convention. From Benson J. Lossing, *Pictorial History of the Civil War in the United States* (Philadelphia, 1866–1868), I, 106.

SLAVE AND MASTER

UNCLE CLEM. "Say, Massa Jim, is I wan of them onfortunate Niggers as you was reading about?"
YOUNG GENTLEMAN. "Yes, Uncle Clem, you are one of them."
UNCLE CLEM. "Well, it's a great pity about me.—I'se berry badly off, I is."

From *Harper's Weekly* (New York), V (January 26, 1861), 64.

INAUGURATION OF JEFFERSON DAVIS AT MONTGOM-
ERY. From *Harper's Weekly*, V (March 9, 1861), 157.

THE FIRST CONFEDERATE CABINET. *Seated, left to right:* Judah P. Benjamin, *Attorney General;* Stephen R. Mallory, *Navy;* Alexander H. Stephens, *Vice-President;* Jefferson Davis, *President;* John H. Reagan, *Postmaster General;* Robert Toombs, *Secretary of State. Standing, left to right:* Christopher G. Memminger, *Treasury;* Leroy P. Walker, *War.* From Alfred H.

FORT SUMTER, SEEN FROM THE REAR, AT LOW WATER. From Guernsey and Alden, *Harper's Pictorial History of the Great Rebellion*, I, 26.

UNIONISTS OF EAST TENNESSEE SWEARING BY THE
[U.S.] FLAG.   From Guernsey and Alden, *Harper's Pictorial History of the
Great Rebellion*, I. 325.

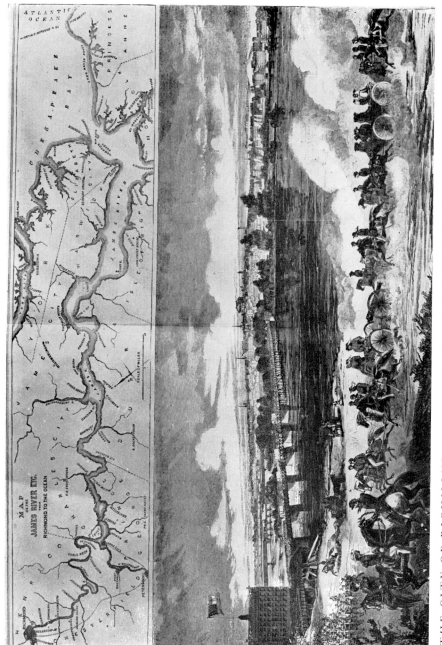

THE CITY OF RICHMOND, VIRGINIA. From *Harper's Weekly*, VI (January 18, 1862), 40–41.

MRS. JEFFERSON DAVIS, WIFE OF THE PRESIDENT
OF THE SO-CALLED "SOUTHERN CONFEDERACY."
From *Frank Leslie's Illustrated Newspaper* (New York), XIV (November 1, 1862),
88.

WILL ENGLAND RECOGNIZE THE CONFEDERACY?

LORD PUNCH. "That was Jeff Davis, Pam!
Don't you Recognise him?"

LORD PAM. "Hm! Well, not Exactly—
May have to do so some of
these days."

From *Punch, or the London Charivari* (London), XLVI (August 27, 1864), 85.

SALTPETER CAVE NEAR CHATTANOOGA. From *Harper's Weekly*, VIII (February 6, 1864), 85.

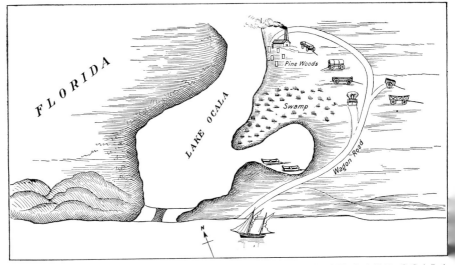

CONTEMPORARY CHART OF SALTWORKS AT LAKE OCALA NEAR ST. ANDREW, FLORIDA. From *Official Records of the Union and Confederate Navies in the War of the Rebellion* (Washington, 1894–1922), Ser. I, Vol. XVII, 595.

NEGROES AT WORK ON THE FORTIFICATIONS AT
SAVANNAH. From *Illustrated London News* (London), XLII (April 18,
1863), 433.

COTTONBURNERS IN THE NEIGHBORHOOD OF MEM-
PHIS SURPRISED BY FEDERAL SCOUTS. From *Illustrated
London News*, XLI (August 9, 1862), 149.

TRAIN WITH REINFORCEMENTS FOR GENERAL JOHNSTON RUNNING OFF THE TRACK IN THE FORESTS OF MISSISSIPPI. From *Illustrated London News*, XLIII (August 8, 1863), 128.

RE-OCCUPATION OF JACKSON, MISSISSIPPI, BY THE CONFEDERATES. From *Illustrated London News*, XLIII (August 8, 1863), 128.

CONFEDERATE WARSHIP *SUMTER* CAPTURING ENEMY MER-
CHANTMEN OFF GIBRALTAR. From *Illustrated London News*, XL (February 1,
1862), 114.

RECRUITING FOR THE CONFEDERATE ARMY AT WOODSTOCK, VIRGINIA. From *Harper's Weekly*, V (October 5, 1861), 632.

A BUMMER OF GENERAL SHERMAN'S ARMY. From George W. Nichols, *The Story of the Great March* (New York, 1866), 245.

TREASURE SEEKERS. From Nichols, *Story of the Great March*, 113.

THE BURNING OF COLUMBIA, SOUTH CAROLINA, FEBRUARY 17, 1865. From *Harper's Weekly* IX (April 8, 1865), 217.

A FEMALE REBEL IN BALTIMORE—AN EVERYDAY
SCENE. From *Harper's Weekly*, V (September 7, 1861), 561.

FEDERAL STEAMER, UNDER A FLAG OF TRUCE, UNLOADING REFUGEES FROM NEW ORLEANS WITHIN CONFEDERATE LINES ON LAKE PONTCHARTRAIN. From *Illustrated Lon-*

FRATERNIZING OF CONFEDERATE AND FEDERAL
PICKETS IN THE RAPPAHANNOCK. From *Harper's Weekly*,
VII (February 7, 1863), 93.

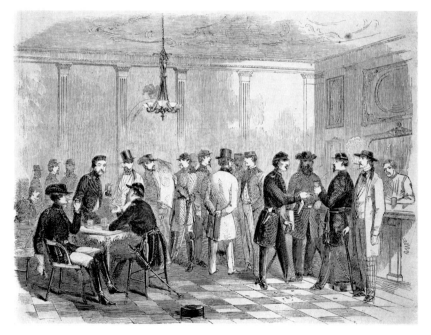

BAR OF THE SPOTSWOOD HOUSE, RICHMOND, VIR-
GINIA. From *Harper's Weekly*, V (September 7, 1861), 565.

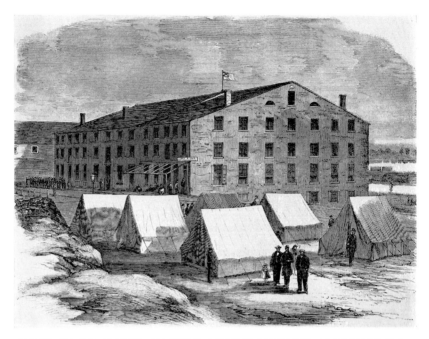

EXTERIOR VIEW OF THE LIBBY PRISON, RICHMOND, VIRGINIA. From *Harper's Weekly*, VII (October 17, 1863), 668.

ENCAMPMENT OF UNION PRISONERS AT BELLE ISLE, RICHMOND, VIRGINIA. From *Harper's Weekly*, VII (October 17, 1863), 668.

TITLE PAGE OF CONFEDERATE SHEET MUSIC. Courtesy of
Mr. Richard Barksdale Harwell of Emory University, owner of the original.

MR. JEFFERSON DAVIS SIGNING ACTS OF GOVERN-
MENT BY THE ROADSIDE. From *Illustrated London News*, XLVII
(July 22, 1865), 65.

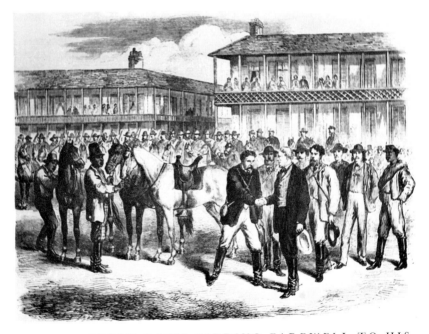

MR. JEFFERSON DAVIS BIDDING FAREWELL TO HIS
ESCORT TWO DAYS BEFORE HIS CAPTURE. From *Illustrated London News*, XLVII (July 22, 1865), 65.

amidst enough mud "to daub every negro cabin in the Southern Confederacy," to defend Richmond, needlessly burning their winter quarters and, what was much worse, a vast amount of supplies.[51] When McClellan finally worked his way up the Peninsula, pestered by skirmishing Confederates, he was greeted around Richmond between the last of May and the first of July with the battle of Seven Pines, or Fair Oaks, and the Seven Days' Battles—Mechanicsville, Cold Harbor, Golding's Farm, Savage Station, Frayser's Farm, and Malvern Hill. On June 1 Lee took charge of the Confederates after the wounding of Johnston, and he was joined by Jackson after his amazing Valley campaign in which he had defeated three armies. Lee ended the threat against Richmond, which at one time had almost led to its evacuation.[52] John Pope, having succeeded to McClellan's army, tried the land route to Richmond in August, but was badly defeated at the Second Battle of Manassas. Lee now took the offensive and made the first Confederate invasion of the North, crossing the Potomac into Maryland in September and meeting McClellan, who had succeeded Pope, at Sharpsburg, or Antietam Creek, on September 16 and 17. He was able to hold the battlefield only after the hurried return of Jackson's forces, which had gone to open up the Shenandoah Valley by the capture of Harpers Ferry.[53] Having made a strategic

[51] Davis later severely criticized Johnson's precipitate retreat and destruction of supplies: "The retreat was without molestation or even demonstration from the enemy; but was conducted with such precipitation as to involve a heavy loss of supplies. Some valuable artillery was abandoned; a large depot of provisions was burned; blankets, shoes and saddles were committed to the flames; and this great sacrifice of property was so wanting in apparent justification as to produce a painful impression on the public mind." Rowland (ed.), *Jefferson Davis, Constitutionalist*, VI, 494. "It was a sad necessity, and as the troops were guided on their way for many weary miles by the lurid flames from their burning buildings that seemed to lick the very heavens, all felt that the first battle of the war had proved more disastrous as a victory than would have been a defeat." Goldsborough, *Maryland Line in the Confederate States Army*, 41.

[52] Jackson's Valley campaign lifted the despondent Confederacy onto the pinnacle of exhilaration. The mobile Jackson army was pictured as likely to turn up next in Philadelphia, New York, or Portland.

[53] On September 8 Lee issued his proclamation of deliverance, expecting that the Marylanders would rise to his aid, but there was sad disappointment. The song "Maryland, My Maryland," which had been so popular with the army, was scarcely heard after that campaign. Cobb wrote his wife, October 27, 1862, in Thomas R. R. Cobb Letters: "I have not heard 'My Maryland' sung, whistled or played by a band,

failure, Lee returned to Virginia, and on December 13 he disastrously defeated General Ambrose Burnside at Fredericksburg.

By the time Lee was ready to go into winter quarters, Confederate prospects continued bright in Virginia and Benjamin H. Hill could say, "though it be early morning with us, every hour is brightening into day." [54] When northern Virginia thawed out with the coming of the spring of 1863, Lee fought the Federals, this time under General Joseph Hooker, at Chancellorsville from May 1–4. He won a resounding victory though he lost his incomparable lieutenant, General Jackson, the greatest flanking tactician of the war. Lee could not remain idle. Taking the offensive again for political and diplomatic as well as military reasons, he invaded the North and reached Gettysburg, in southern Pennsylvania, where, from July 1–3, he fought the most celebrated battle of the whole war, against General George Gordon Meade, the new commander of the Federals. Stopped again in his ultimate aim, despite Pickett's famous charge and other acts of valor, Lee retreated back to Virginia.[55] For the rest of the year, there were no great battles in Virginia.

But while Lee had been dealing with McClellan, Pope, Hooker, Burnside, and Meade, events had been happening in the region between the mountains and the Mississippi which afforded no one but the Federals joy. After Albert Sidney Johnston's death at

---

since I returned to the army. I hear that one band struck the tune not long since and the men groaned and hissed until they discontinued it." The famous Barbara Frietschie incident, whatever it was, took place on this campaign. See Dorothy M. and William R. Quynn, *Barbara Frietschie* (Baltimore, 1942).

[54] Hill, *Benjamin H. Hill*, 255.

[55] Many reasons have been given for the Gettysburg campaign—diplomatic, political, military; but Lee had especially in mind to force the Federals to concentrate their troops then scattered over the South and draw most of them out of Virginia. At the least, he thought he could embarrass "their plan of campaign in a measure," if he could "do nothing more and have to return." *Official Records*, Ser. I, Vol. XXVII, Pt. III, 931. After Gettysburg, Lee offered his resignation, but Davis answered, "To ask me to substitute you by some one in my judgment more fit to command, or who would possess more of the confidence of the army or of the reflecting men in the country is to demand for me an impossibility." Rowland (ed.), *Jefferson Davis, Constitutionalist*, V, 590. As to who won the victory, the Richmond *Daily Examiner*, July 13, 1863, remarked, "The Confederates did not gain a victory, neither did the enemy."

Shiloh and Beauregard's short tenure, Bragg, who had succeeded to the command, decided, about the time Lee was preparing to go into Maryland, to make a great thrust to the northward and regain the region to the banks of the Ohio. General E. Kirby Smith, with a force in East Tennessee, joined him in central Kentucky after Bragg had marched through central Tennessee; but so inept was Bragg's leadership that he was forced into a battle, October 8, 1862, at Perryville, Kentucky, against General Buell's forces, which had hurried northward and prevented Bragg from taking Louisville. He returned to Tennessee, having thrown away a pregnant opportunity for vast Confederate gains, and on December 31 to January 2, 1863, he fought the new Federal commander, William S. Rosecrans, in the indecisive battle of Murfreesboro, or Stone's River.

The main objective of the Federals in the West was now to clear the Mississippi River by the capture of Vicksburg and Port Hudson. Both Grant and Sherman were anxious to seize the Vicksburg prize, while Joseph E. Johnston, now in charge of all military operations in the West though in command of no army, had the duty of preventing it. John C. Pemberton commanded the army defending Vicksburg. After various Federal maneuvers in Mississippi in the spring of 1863, in which the state suffered not only the devastations of Benjamin H. Grierson's raid but also special treatment at the hands of Sherman, Grant surrounded Vicksburg. Following a memorable siege both by Grant's troops and by hunger, Pemberton surrendered his whole army, on July 4—purposely he made it the Glorious Fourth, hoping for better terms. Coming the day after the Battle of Gettysburg, this disaster was doubly shattering to Confederate morale everywhere. From this day many people saw the coming of the end. A few days later Port Hudson fell and Lincoln could now announce that the Father of Waters ran unvexed to the sea—but not quite so, for Confederate forces played havoc with river shipping to the end of the war.[56] Some Confederate strategists, Beauregard, Daniel H. Hill, Longstreet, and Post-

[56] As to the opening of the river, the Charleston *Daily Courier*, August 15, 1863, remarked, "Now, we assure the Admiral [David D. Porter] that proclamations don't open rivers any more than resolutions build rail-roads."

master General Reagan among them, advised that Lee should send the major part of his army to the West instead of going on his second invasion of the North.[57]

The Confederacy was now cut into two parts. A year before the fall of Vicksburg, Governor Frank R. Lubbock of Texas believed that the Trans-Mississippi region ought to be given a sort of autonomy within the Confederacy. In early 1863 the Trans-Mississippi Department was set up and placed under the command of General E. Kirby Smith, and after the fall of Vicksburg his powers both military and political were so greatly increased that he controlled this region almost as completely as Davis ran the Confederacy east of the Mississippi. He appointed officers and promoted them, provided for the exchange of prisoners of war, sent diplomatic agents to Mexico, controlled cotton exports, di-

[57] John C. Pemberton became extremely unpopular. The Augusta *Daily Constitutionalist,* July 26, 1864, said that Vicksburg "would never have been captured but for the errors of the most stupid ass that ever commanded a body of men." But one of Pemberton's soldiers replied, "We have many able generals, many redoubtable warriors, men who fight a battle every week and always conquer, but their battles are fought on street-corners and in bar-rooms, and are consequently bloodless." Mobile *Register and Advertiser,* quoted in *Official Records,* Ser. I, Vol. XXIV, Pt. III, 1063. Pemberton demanded a court of inquiry, which was set up but which never actually met. John C. Pemberton, *Pemberton, Defender of Vicksburg* (Chapel Hill, 1942), *passim.* See also, Rowland (ed.), *Jefferson Davis, Constitutionalist,* VI, 203; Reagan, *Memoirs,* 121. There were various stories of how near the garrison came to starvation, and especially as to whether the soldiers and civilians were reduced to eating mule meat and rats. A civilian stated that she spent $5.00 a day for a small piece of mule meat, and that she saw at the market dressed rats. Yet the reports of the number of rations surrendered would seem to disprove the story that anyone was near starvation. The editor of the Meridian *Clarion,* quoted in the Richmond *Daily Whig,* August 12, 1863, said, "We have yet to see or hear of the first private who ate the delectable flesh of the mule during the siege of Vicksburg, and we have seen, conversed with, and heard from, a great many hundreds of them." Undoubtedly, though, there was hunger among the soldiers, for on June 28, 1863, a communication from "Many Soldiers" was addressed to Pemberton, in which the men declared that they were hungry and could fight no longer: "Just think of one small biscuit and one or two mouthfulls of bacon per day." *Official Records,* Ser. I, Vol. XXIV, Pt. III, 983. See also, *ibid.,* 869; Edward A. Pollard, *The Third Year of the War* (New York, 1865), 68; Richmond *Daily Whig,* September 25, 1863; Ephraim M. Anderson, *Memoirs: Historical and Personal; Including the Campaigns of the First Missouri Confederate Brigade* (St. Louis, 1868), 337; George W. Cable (ed.), "War Diary of a Union Woman in the South," in *Famous Adventures and Prison Escapes of the Civil War* (New York, 1893), 68, 76. It seems that mule meat was eaten at Port Hudson. Henry S. Commager and Allan Nevins (eds.), *The Heritage of America* (Boston, 1939), 753.

rected conscription, called together in council the governors of the three states which made up his domain, issued proclamations for thanksgiving and prayers; in fact, in the words of Davis, "He has authority to execute the laws, and this is the only authority I have." Bureaus of the War, Treasury, and Post Office departments were set up. Indeed, this region was "Kirby-Smithdom," with its twin capitals at Shreveport, Louisiana, and Marshall, Texas.[58]

Smith was not only civil ruler but, of course, military commander. No major campaigns took place in his domain with the exception of General Nathaniel P. Banks's Red River expedition, which was turned back on April 8, 1864, at the battle of Mansfield, or Sabine Cross Roads.[59] The Federals made a few attacks on Texas, at Brownsville, Galveston, and Sabine Pass, but no permanent lodgments of any importance resulted. Davis could say on November 7, 1864, that no enemies were "known to remain except as prisoners of war." But in Arkansas and Missouri the Federals secured control and kept it. There were, however, two Confederate raids: Joseph O. Shelby's march in September and October of 1863, with less than a thousand cavalrymen, from southwestern Arkansas as far as the Missouri River; and Price's amazing raid a year later to the outskirts of St. Louis and as far west as the Kansas border where, at Westport, he was defeated and forced back into Arkansas.[60] When the war finally ended east of the Mississippi, Smith still had a formidable force of thirty thousand men which some Confederates hoped might have been the nucleus of a never-dying Confederacy to be transferred west of the river.

But the war could not be won west of the Mississippi; Richmond must be taken and the heart of the Confederacy (Georgia, South Carolina, and North Carolina), must be pierced. Soon after Vicks-

---

[58] Rowland (ed.), *Jefferson Davis, Constitutionalist*, V, 552; Florence E. Holladay, "The Powers of the Commander of the Confederate Trans-Mississippi Department, 1863–1865," in *Southwestern Historical Quarterly* (Austin), XXI (1917–1918), 279–82, 289; *Official Records*, Ser. I, Vol. LIII, 982.

[59] Nathaniel P. Banks's expedition up the Red River seems to have been more of an attempt to gather up cotton than to dispose of Confederate armies. Admiral Porter said that "it was an army of cotton speculators, commanded by General Greed, General Avarice, General Speculation, and General Breach of Trust, with all their attendant staff of harpies, who were using the army and navy for the vilest purposes." David D. Porter, *Incidents and Anecdotes of the Civil War* (New York, 1885), 227.   [60] Henry, *Story of the Confederacy*, 294.

burg, Rosecrans addressed himself to this task, marching his forces in Middle Tennessee against Chattanooga. In early September, 1863, he forced Bragg out of this stronghold and pursued him to Chickamauga, where the Federals were badly defeated on the nineteenth and twentieth. To aid Bragg, Lee sent Longstreet's corps on its long train ride from Virginia by way of Wilmington, Augusta, and Atlanta (the fall of Knoxville having cut the railway through East Tennessee). Arriving too late to be of effective service at Chickamauga, Longstreet led his forces in a fruitless attempt to recapture Knoxville, while Bragg suffered defeat at Lookout Mountain and Missionary Ridge and was forced to retreat into northern Georgia. Bragg, having lost completely the confidence of his officers, was replaced by Joseph E. Johnston; Rosecrans was retired and his army handed over to Sherman.[61]

The grand strategy of the Federals now sent Sherman to march south into Georgia, pierce the heart of the Confederacy, and ultimately come up from the south on Richmond, while Grant should campaign against it from northern Virginia. In the spring of 1864 Sherman set out for Atlanta, flanking Johnston successively out of every position he occupied except Kennesaw Mountain, where the Union general made the admitted mistake of a frontal attack and was badly cut up. An outcry against Johnston's retreating tactics led to his removal and the appointment of General John B. Hood.[62] After fierce fighting around Atlanta, Hood gave up the city on September 2 and marched northwestward into Tennessee, where his army was destroyed in the battle of Nashville in mid-December. Sherman, instead of following Hood, which would have been correct military strategy, burned Atlanta on November 15 and set out on his famous March to the Sea. Harrying Georgia through a swath of territory sixty miles wide, admittedly destroy-

[61] It was reported that the Confederates had been fraternizing with the Federal troops before the battles of Lookout Mountain and Missionary Ridge, and had decided not to fight their newly found "comrades." Richmond *Daily Examiner*, June 13, 1864. Davis declared the battles had been lost because certain Confederate troops had failed to do their duty—"the first defeat that has resulted from misconduct by the troops." Richardson (comp.), *Messages and Papers of the Confederacy*, I, 347.

[62] There was long a dispute over the relative merits of the defensive tactics of Johnston's and Hood's rash fighting. See Johnston, *Narrative of Military Operations*; John B. Hood, *Advance and Retreat. Personal Experiences in the United States and Confederate States Armies* (New Orleans, 1880).

ing $100,000,000 in property, Sherman captured Savannah on December 21. Intimating to his troops that they might treat South Carolina even worse than they did Georgia, Sherman marched northward and came to Columbia in mid-February, with his troops singing as they approached the South Carolina capital,

> Hail Columbia, happy land,
> If I don't burn you, I'll be damned.

The city was burned, by whom it is still disputed. Sherman did not order the burning, but he was no more perturbed by it than by the countless other destructions committed by his army. He continued his plundering march into North Carolina, where he found his old antagonist Joseph E. Johnston in his way again. Lee surrendered his army to Grant on April 9, 1865; seventeen days later, at Durham's Station, Johnston surrendered to Sherman on like terms. The war was over.

While Sherman had been marching through Georgia and the Carolinas, Grant, now military director of all Federal armies, was pounding his way toward Richmond. In early May he began his attacks against Lee at the Wilderness, near Chancellorsville, and for the next month and a half, using Sherman's flanking tactics, he fought his way to the James River, but he was still much farther away from Richmond than McClellan had been in 1862. During this time he had lost as many men as Lee had. At Spotsylvania Courthouse he would fight it out on that line if it took all summer, but he soon changed his mind and attempted to break through again farther south at Cold Harbor, where he suffered an amazing loss of men. In the meantime, Sheridan had threatened Richmond on a cavalry raid and at Yellow Tavern had mortally wounded Stuart, who was opposing him; [63] about the same time, Franz

[63] Shortly before this time, Ulric Dahlgren had made a raid against Richmond, which the Confederates claimed was intended to accomplish not only the freeing of the Federal prisoners in Libby Prison but also the assassination of Davis and his cabinet and the burning of Richmond. Dahlgren was killed. His body was brought to Richmond and viewed by throngs of people before it was disposed of; and according to the Richmond *Daily Examiner*, March 8, 1864, "It was a dog's burial, without coffin, winding sheet or service." Rear Admiral John A. Dahlgren indignantly denied the authenticity of the incriminating documents found on Ulric's body. He called them "a bare-faced, atrocious forgery." Moore (ed.), *Rebellion Rec-*

Sigel had been defeated at New Market in the Shenandoah Valley by a Confederate force made up partly of Virginia Military Institute cadets, and had been replaced by David Hunter, who marched southward up the Valley on a destructive raid to the gates of Lynchburg. To stop this movement, Lee sent Jubal Early against Hunter, and on June 18 the Confederates relieved Lynchburg and drove Hunter's forces into West Virginia. Early now turned northward on his remarkable raid that took him down the Valley into Maryland and to the very outskirts of Washington, which he might possibly have captured had he attacked immediately. Soon after his return to the Valley, Early sent John McCausland across the Potomac on a raid into Pennsylvania, which resulted in the burning of Chambersburg as retribution for Hunter's destructions and because the town refused to pay a contribution levied upon it.[64] Scared and embittered by these bold tactics, Grant sent Sheridan into the Valley with a large force of cavalry and infantry. He wrecked the region as thoroughly as Sherman was to do in Georgia and the Carolinas, and at the battle of Cedar Creek, in October, he defeated Early and then drove him out of the Valley.

Having failed to take Richmond from the north and the east, Grant moved his army across the James River in mid-June and attempted to take the Confederate capital from the south.[65] During the rest of the summer, much fighting, including the battle of the Crater, took place, and the war finally bogged down for the winter in the siege of Petersburg. The next spring, prospects for victory were dismal for Lee, whose army had fast been dwindling away through desertion brought on by hunger and despair. On April 1, Sheridan turned Lee's right flank at Five Forks and made impera-

ord, XI, 184–87. See also, Richmond *Daily Whig*, March 5, 8, 21, 26, 1864; *Official Records*, Ser. I, Vol. XXXIII, 168–225; Jones, *Rebel War Clerk's Diary*, II, 168.

[64] The citizens of Lynchburg presented John McCausland with a pair of silver spurs and a sword bearing on its scabbard "Retribution." Richmond *Daily Examiner*, September 6, 1864; Richmond *Daily Enquirer*, September 6, 1864.

[65] Lee was fully expecting Grant to move his troops south of the James, though it has been often stated that he was completely surprised by Grant's action. On June 14, 1864, Lee wrote Davis, "I think the enemy must be preparing to move South of James River." Freeman (ed.), *Lee's Dispatches*, 227. See also, Alfred H. Burne, *Lee, Grant and Sherman; A Study in Leadership in the 1864–65 Campaign* (New York, 1939), xi, 60.

tive the evacuation of Petersburg and Richmond, which the Confederates carried out the next day. Moving southwestward in the hope of joining Johnston in North Carolina, Lee reached Appomattox Courthouse, where on the ninth, finding all further progress cut off, he surrendered his army to Grant.

Wars are destructive both of life and of property, not only of soldiers and of military supplies, but also of civilian lives and private property in the territory invaded. As the war was fought almost entirely in the Confederacy, its people bore the brunt of hard realities. Some destructions such as ruining roads, demolishing fences, and cutting down and burning forests were inevitable; others depended on the attitudes of the officers. In the beginning the tendency among most Federal commanders was to deal as gently as possible with civilians as well as their property, the so-called "guarding-potato-patches policy." With some officers this policy never varied, but after a few months leniency gave way generally. Still, there were both officers and soldiers who condemned wanton destructions and pillaging almost as bitterly as did the suffering Southerners. General Thomas W. Sherman, who occupied the Port Royal region of South Carolina in November, 1861, issued a proclamation in which he referred to the "great sovereign State" and its "proud and hospitable people," and declared that he had "no desire to harm your citizens, destroy your property, or to interfere with any of your lawful rights or your social and local institutions." An officer in Virginia announced, "No thief shall be permitted to accompany this division on its march if it be in the power of the general commanding to prevent it"; and another warned, "Parties caught plundering the country will be treated as common robbers and shot upon the spot, whenever and wherever found by the patrols." A member of a Rhode Island regiment declared that their pillaging in northern Virginia "did not rise even to the dignity of burglary, for that requires a certain amount of courage"; [66] an officer in an Illinois regiment operating in Mississippi charged that there was more stealing there in one

[66] For the sources of quotations, respectively, see *Official Records*, Ser. I, Vol. VI, 5; Vol. XII, Pt. III, 55, 577; Augustus Woodbury, *A Narrative of the Campaign of the First Rhode Island Regiment, in the Spring and Summer of 1861* (Providence, 1862), 82.

day "than the whole United States suffered in a year before the war"; [67] and he added, "Rebels, though they are, 'tis shocking and enough to make one's blood boil to see the manner in which some of our folks have treated them. Trunks have been knocked to pieces with muskets when the women stood by, offering the keys, bureau drawers drawn out, the contents turned on the floor, and the drawer thrown through the window, bed clothing and ladies' clothing carried off and all manner of deviltry imaginable perpetrated." [68]

Hatred and contempt for the Confederates fanned into flame by certain elements in the North made it easy for a soldier to feel that it was part of his patriotic duty to mistreat civilians and pillage their property.[69] It was a common feeling in the North that Southerners, except the slaveholders so vividly portrayed by the abolitionists, were ignorant, illiterate, snuff-dipping, tobacco-chewing bumpkins, who knew no better than to say "we-uns" and "you-uns"; that they were barbarous in the conduct of the war, making drinking cups of the skulls of Federal soldiers and sawing their leg bones into finger rings, and constructing corduroy roads "to haul wounded Yankees over."

Pillaging and plundering, as well as major destructions such as burning cities, blowing up bridges, and tearing up railroads, were made into an "exact science." With few exceptions pillaging was not actually ordered and generally was forbidden, but most commanders winked at it. When an overzealous guard brought in a marauding soldier with a pig or sheep on his back, his humorous excuse that the brute tried to bite or kick him or refused to advance

[67] [Charles W. Wills], *Army Life of an Illinois Soldier, Including a Day by Day Record of Sherman's March to the Sea. Letters and Diary* . . . (Washington, 1906), 52.

[68] *Ibid.*, 135–36. A Federal officer after describing a raid up the Cumbahee River, in South Carolina, in which the Negroes were invited by their officers to pillage and burn, added, "What license to give to a parcel of half-civilized negroes! The operation was a disgrace to our arms." Davis, *History of the 104th Pennsylvania Regiment*, 210. Another Federal soldier declared that the burning of Jacksonville, Florida, was "a wanton act of vandalism." Charles W. Cadwell, *The Old Sixth Regiment* [Connecticut], *its War Record, 1861–5* (New Haven, 1875), 60–61.

[69] A Philadelphia preacher, in speculating on the possibility of the Emancipation Proclamation producing in the South a repetition of the San Domingo horror on a larger scale, said, "I affirm that it would be better that every woman and child in the South should perish, than that the principles of Confederate Statesmen should prevail." [Lawrence], *Border and Bastile*, 281.

and give the countersign was sufficient to secure his acquittal. No earthly belongings which Federal soldiers might want and were able to carry away were safe. They not only pillaged houses from cellar to garret and entered the smokehouses and granaries, but they carried off livestock both for food and locomotion, slaughtered it wantonly, and left the carcasses to rot. A captain of a Massachusetts regiment thus described the sacking of Fredericksburg: "Mirrors, pianos, and gorgeous furniture were destroyed; beautiful paintings and family portraits upon the walls were cut; busts were decapitated; and elegant silk dresses and garments were torn into shreds"; [70] and James K. Hosmer, a later historian of the war, described his experiences in Louisiana: "I have seen now what a scourge to a country an invading army is. We were turned loose. . . . All this marauding went on ruthlessly and wastefully. We left the road behind us foul with odor of decaying carcasses. Cattle were killed, a quarter or so taken out of them, and the remainder left to the buzzards. So with sheep and poultry. Pigs were bayoneted, sugar-houses plundered of sugar and molasses, private dwellings entered; and, if any resistance were offered by the owner, his arms were wrested from him, and he overmastered." Earrings and brooches were torn from women with children in their arms.[71]

Graves were robbed, skeletons piled in heaps, and vile epithets written on tombstones and in churches; [72] women were raped; [73] a sport was made of maltreating overseers and shooting dogs, which were popularly believed to be used in tracking down fugitive slaves and escaping prisoners of war; [74] and souvenirs relating to historic

[70] Blake, *Three Years in the Army of the Potomac*, 157.

[71] James K. Hosmer, *The Color-Guard: Being a Corporal's Notes of Military Service in the Nineteenth Army Corps* (Boston, 1864), 103. According to the editor of the Milledgeville *Southern Recorder*, March 3, 1863, "It is known that the wives of superior Yankee officers followed their husbands in Virginia and made it their special business to box up silver plate, fine china sets, pianos, and rich articles of furniture, which were shipped to their homes in the North."

[72] Conyngham, *Sherman's March through the South*, 321; [Wills], *Army Life of an Illinois Soldier*, 162; Parker, *History of the 51st Regiment of P.V. and V.V.*, 176–78; Anderson, *Memoirs; Historical and Personal*, 362, 412; Natchez *Weekly Courier*, May 27, 1863.

[73] Augusta *Daily Chronicle & Sentinel*, December 6, 1864; Richmond *Semi-Weekly Enquirer*, June 4, 1861.

[74] Howe (ed.), *Marching with Sherman; . . . Letters and Campaign Diaries of Henry Hitchcock*, 143; Joseph LeConte, *'Ware Sherman, A Journal of Three Months'*

places or persons were carried away. Not even "Wakefield," Washington's boyhood home, was spared.[75] There was, especially, wanton destruction of libraries, archives, and works of art. County courthouses and state capitols were entered and pillaged; many books were carried away from the Mississippi State Library; the Georgia capitol was ransacked and soldiers scattered books and documents, demolished minerals and fossils in the museum, and amidst the revelry of liquor drinking held a mock session of the legislature and "repealed" the secession ordinance. Soldiers pillaged the North Carolina capitol, poured a bottle of ink on the marble bust of Calhoun, and scribbled on the base, "Yes, father of Secession." Davis' Mississippi home, Jacob Thompson's home in Oxford, and in Virginia, the homes of Edmund Ruffin, John Tyler, and Henry A. Wise were gutted of their books and letters—burned, carried away, or trampled underfoot. William Gilmore Simms's library and that of another South Carolinian, the latter valued at $25,000, were destroyed. One of the greatest crimes in an enlightened age was the ransacking of the John Page Mansion in Virginia, where letters from Washington and Jefferson, records of the Continental Congress, files of the Virginia *Gazette,* and other priceless documents were stolen and scattered. Many lawbooks were carried away from law offices and shipped North, later to appear in some budding lawyer's library; even skeletons were stolen from physicians' offices. A New York major stole from Lewis Washington a painting of George Washington by Gilbert Stuart, and on later being captured he was ransomed from Libby Prison by the return of the portrait.[76]

Personal Experience in the Last Days of the Confederacy (Berkeley, 1937), 32; Nichols, *Story of the Great March,* 84.

[75] Blake, *Three Years in the Army of the Potomac,* 32; Edwin M. Haynes, *A History of the Tenth Regiment, Vermont Volunteers* . . . (Lewiston, Me., 1870), 104; Mrs. Sarah A. Palmer, *The Story of Aunt Beckey's Army Life* (New York, 1867), 51.

[76] "Librarian's Report, February 6, 1865," in Ser. E, Vol. LXVII, No. 68 (Mississippi State Archives); Richmond *Daily Examiner,* September 19, 1862; March 10, 1863; Milledgeville *Southern Recorder,* June 9, 1863; Charleston *Daily Courier,* August 15, 1863; John S. Wise, *The End of an Era* (Boston, 1901), 211; Conyngham, *Sherman's March through the South,* 254; Knox, *Camp-Fire and Cotton-Field,* 223; [Zenas T. Haines], *Letters from the Forty-Fourth Regiment, M.V.M.: A Record of the Experience of a Nine Months' Regiment in the Department of North Carolina in 1862-3* (Boston, 1863), 51; Richard Eddy, *History of the Sixtieth Regiment New*

Not only were houses ransacked, but many were burned. Some of them belonged to nameless men; others to prominent Southerners such as Governor John Letcher and George Pickett.[77] The torch was put to schools and colleges—the Virginia Military Institute, the University of Alabama, and so on. Cities, towns, and villages were given to the flames—Atlanta, Columbia, Jackson (Mississippi), Rome (Georgia), and many others. Cassville, Georgia, and Bellfontaine, Alabama, were completely destroyed and never rebuilt. Winton, North Carolina, claimed the unfortunate honor of being the first to be consumed by Federal flames, but Atlanta and Columbia came to be longest remembered.[78] Charleston, the

---

York State Volunteers . . . (Philadelphia, 1864), 110; James A. Mowris, *A History of the One Hundred and Seventeenth Regiment, N.Y. Volunteers* . . . (Hartford, 1866), 210-11; Oliver W. Norton, *Army Letters, 1861–1865* . . . (Chicago, 1903), 116; Edward H. Rogers, *Reminiscences of Military Service in the Forty-Third Regiment, Massachusetts Infantry . . . 1862–63* (Boston, 1883), 115; Robert Tilney, *Life in the Army. Three Years and a Half with the Fifth Army Corps, Army of the Potomac, 1862–1865* (Philadelphia, 1912), 164; Mason W. Tyler, *Recollections of the Civil War with many Original Diary Entries and Letters written from the Seat of War* . . . (New York, 1912), 217; Seth Eyland [Davis E. Cronin], *The Evolution of a Life, described in the Memoirs of Major Seth Eyland, late of the Mounted Rifles* (New York, 1884), 205-207. Before the war ended, every Confederate state capital except Austin and Tallahassee had fallen into the hands of the Federals.

[77] Arthur C. Inman (ed.), *Soldier of the South; General Pickett's War Letters to his Wife* (Boston, 1928), 104; McDonald, *Diary with Reminiscences of the War and Refugee Life*, 208; George S. Bradley, *The Star Corps; or, Notes of an Army Chaplain, during Sherman's Famous "March to the Sea"* (Milwaukee, 1865), 256.

[78] *Official Records*, Ser. I, Vol. IX, 196; Charleston *Daily Courier*, June 17, 1863; Richmond *Daily Examiner*, June 24, 1863; Fremantle, *Three Months in the Southern States*, 111; Conyngham, *Sherman's March through the South*, 323; Howe (ed.), *Marching with Sherman; . . . Letters and Campaign Diaries of Henry Hitchcock*, 43-44, 58; Moses D. Gage, *From Vicksburg to Raleigh; or, A Complete History of the Twelfth Regiment Indiana Volunteer Infantry, and the Campaigns of Grant and Sherman, with an Outline of the Great Rebellion* (Chicago, 1865), 93; Nichols, *Story of the Great March*, 41; *Diary of E[lijah] P. Burton, Surgeon 7th Reg. Ill., 3rd Brig., 2nd Div. 16 A.C.* (Des Moines, 1939), *passim*; J. H. E. Whitney, *The Hawkins Zouaves: (Ninth N.Y.V.) Their Battles and Marches* (New York, 1866), 89; Bettersworth, *Confederate Mississippi*, 279 ff. Concerning the burning of Marietta, Georgia, Sherman said that it made no difference how often the fires were put out, the soldiers would apply the torch again. "Set as many guards as you please, they will slip in and set fire. . . . [D]are say whole town will burn up, at least the business part. I never ordered burning of any dwelling—didn't order this, but can't be helped. I say *Jeff. Davis burned them.*" Howe (ed.), *Marching with Sherman; . . . Letters and Campaign Diaries of Henry Hitchcock*, 52-53. Much has been written on the responsibility for burning Columbia, but the following expressions by Fed-

cradle of secession, continued to exist, but not through the sufferance of the Federals, as they sought to destroy it by Greek fire and pound it to pieces with their famous gun, the "Swamp Angel," or close it as a port by the futile sinking of the "stone fleet" in its entrance.[79] Commanders arrested civilians as hostages and shot some of them, and ravaged the country in an effort to suppress so-called guerrilla activities.[80] Of all the Federal commanders who engaged in this unusual kind of warfare, General William T. Sherman was most successful and in subsequent generations came to be most bitterly hated for it. General Sheridan was equally as successful but he confined such activities largely to the Shenandoah Valley.[81] No other Federal commander was ever to be regarded with as loathing a contempt as General Benjamin F. Butler for his activities in New Orleans and no other commander was to be awarded the special title of "Beast"; but the wildest and most unrestrained barbarian wearing the American uniform was Ivan Vasilevitch Turchininoff, known under his American alias as Colonel John B. Turchin, a Don Cossack, who had learned his special type of warfare fighting against Hungarian independence in 1848–1849 and in the Crimean War. His rape of Athens, Alabama, in 1862 brought down

eral eyewitnesses might well be quoted here: "The result of all this was that partly by accident, from the burning cotton, partly by design by our escaped prisoners, and by our drunken men, fire was started in several places,—and once started, with the furious wind blowing, it was simply impossible to put it out." *Ibid.*, 269. "The boys, too, were spreading the conflagration by firing the city in a hundred places." Samuel H. M. Byers, *What I Saw in Dixie; or, Sixteen Months in Rebel Prisons* (Dansville, N.Y., 1868), 85. "The soldiers had a terrible drunk on liquor found in town, and they run riot all night. They not only fired houses but robbed and pillaged both houses & citizens almost indiscriminately." Burton, *Diary of E*[lijah] *P. Burton*, February 18, 1864. Conyngham, in his *Sherman's March through the South*, 335, declared that what he saw in Columbia "would have driven Alaric the Goth into frenzied ecstasies."

[79] Charleston *Daily Mercury*, February 3, 1862. Concerning the sinking of the stone fleet, Lee said in a letter to Benjamin, December 20, 1861, "This achievement, so unworthy any nation, is the abortive expression of the malice and revenge of a people which it wishes to perpetuate by rendering more memorable a day hateful in their calendar." *Official Records*, Ser. I, Vol. VI, 43.

[80] *Ibid.*, Vol. XXVII, Pt. II, 575; Ser. III, Vol. II, 944–45.

[81] Grant advised Sheridan: "Do all the damage to railroads and crops you can. Carry off stock of all descriptions and negroes, so as to prevent further planting. If the war is to last another year we want the Shenandoah Valley to remain a barren waste." Philip H. Sheridan, *Personal Memoirs of P. H. Sheridan* (New York, 1888), I, 486. See also, *ibid.*, II, 52.

upon him a court-martial trial and his dismissal from the army, but before the verdict was published he had been advanced to a brigadier-generalship of United States Volunteers. He accepted the post and continued in the army until 1864.[82] There were others of lesser fame, such as General William Sooy Smith, who could write Grant in 1862 that he had given "Colonel Hurst a roving commission with his regiment . . . , and directed him to 'grub up' West Tennessee." [83]

Sherman's own men described his path of destruction in as realistic terms as ever the Confederates or subsequent generations employed. David P. Conyngham, a New York *Herald* correspondent who accompanied Sherman's army, wrote of the march through South Carolina: "The middle of the finest day looked black and gloomy, for a dense smoke arose on all sides, clouding the very heavens. . . . As for the wholesale burnings, pillage, devastation . . . magnify all I have said of Georgia some fifty fold, and throw in an occasional murder, . . . and you have a pretty good idea of the whole thing." [84] Major George W. Nichols declared that what Alexander the Great or the Gauls did was almost forgotten, but "History, however, will be searched in vain for a parallel to the scathing and destructive effect of the Invasion of the Carolinas." [85]

---

[82] *Official Records,* Ser. I, Vol. XVI, Pt. II, 98, 273–78; John B. Turchin, *Chickamauga* (Chicago, 1888), 5, 10–11. A Federal soldier said, "Turchin's brigade has stolen a hundred thousand dollars' worth of watches, plate, and jewelry, in Northern Alabama." John Beatty, *The Citizen-Soldier; or, Memoirs of a Volunteer* (Cincinnati, 1879), 152.

[83] *Official Records,* Ser. I, Vol. XXXII, Pt. II, 124.

[84] Conyngham, *Sherman's March through the South,* 311, 344.

[85] Nichols, *Story of the Great March,* 277. "In the peaceful homes at the North there can be no conception how these people [Georgians] have suffered for their crimes." *Ibid.,* 38. Concerning Sherman's march through Georgia, the editor of the Augusta *Daily Chronicle & Sentinel,* December 10, 1864, said, "We doubt whether history records any story of wrong and outrage to surpass that of Sherman's present campaign through the State of Georgia. Its sickening and heart-rending details which reach our ears from day to day, shake our faith in humanity itself and lead us to believe that the actors in these scenes of violence and crime are transformed into fiends." An Illinois soldier wrote his wife, January 19, 1865, "I don't care how soon we get over into South Carolina, for I want to see the long chastisement begin. If we don't purify South Carolina it will be because we *can't get a light.*" "Major Connolly's Letters to his Wife, 1862–1865," in *Transactions of the Illinois State Historical Society for the Year 1928* (Springfield, 1928), 376. Of the South Carolinians, a Federal lieutenant colonel wrote, "Pity for these inhabitants, I have none. In the

General Butler with his cockeye, compressed lips, and livid complexion, issued his "Woman Order" on May 5, 1862, declaring that any woman who was contemptuous or insulting toward Federal soldiers should "be regarded and held liable to be treated as a woman of the town plying her avocation." Davis declared that the Northerners were "the only people on earth who do not blush to think he wears the human form." This acrostic represented the feeling of Southerners:

> *Brutal and vulgar, a coward and knave;*
> *Famed for no action, noble or brave;*
> *Beastly by instinct, a drunkard and sot;*
> *Ugly and venomous, on mankind a blot;*
> *Thief, liar and scoundrel in highest degree;*
> *Let Yankeedom boast of such hero[e]s as thee;*
> *Every woman and child shall for ages to come,*
> *Remember thee, monster, thou vilest of scum.*[86]

The Confederates, from the beginning and from Davis on down, made the most of the enemy's destructions and atrocities to steel

---

first place, they are rebels, and I am almost prepared to agree with Sherman that a rebel has no rights, not even the right to live except by our permission." [Charles F. Morse], *Letters written during the Civil War, 1861–1865* (Boston, 1898), 211. See also, William T. Sherman, *Memoirs of General William T. Sherman* (New York, 1875), II, 175; Hosmer, *Color-Guard*, 43, *passim*; Bradley, *Star Corps*, 274–76; Fenwick Y. Hedley, *Marching through Georgia. Pen-Pictures of Every-Day Life in General Sherman's Army* . . . (Chicago, 1890), 249, 381, *passim*; Gage, *From Vicksburg to Raleigh*, 274, 300–301, *passim*; Nichols, *Story of the Great March*, 96, 153, 188, 222, *passim*; Julian Street (ed.), *A Woman's Wartime Journal; An Account of the Passage over a Georgia Plantation of Sherman's Army on the March to the Sea, as Recorded in the Diary of Dolly Sumner Lunt* [Mrs. Thomas Burge] (Macon, 1927), *passim*; Augusta *Daily Chronicle & Sentinel*, December 8, 1864.

86 Charleston *Daily Courier*, February 9, 1863; Richmond *Semi-Weekly Enquirer*, January 9, 1863. The Darlington (S.C.) *Southerner*, for several issues, carried on its first page under the word NOTICE written in large letters, a copy of Butler's Woman Order. In 1863, when Butler visited the Federal prison camp at Point Lookout, the Confederate prisoners greeted him with such words as these: "What will you take for your head?" "You d—n lobster-eyed son of a b—h." "Pay me the money you robbed me of in New Orleans." "Why don't you fight men and not women?" "How much are you worth, you burglar?" Richmond *Daily Examiner*, December 30, 1863. See also, Richardson (comp.), *Messages and Papers of the Confederacy*, I, 269–74; *American Annual Cyclopaedia* . . . *1862*, pp. 645 ff.; *Two Months in the Confederate States*, 22; William Watson, *Life in the Confederate Army, Being the Observations and Experiences of an Alien in the South during the American Civil War* (London, 1887), 400 ff.

the people's hearts with grim determination to win the war. The Federals had the "fell purpose of subjugating both the bodies and souls of our people, or of exasperating and exterminating them"; their atrocities were "too incredible for narration"; they not only outraged civilians and pillaged, plundered, and destroyed private property, but it was charged that they used poisoned and explosive bullets and, at First Manassas, carried handcuffs to shackle their prisoners.[87] In fact, a dance of death had been planned and inaugurated by the authorities in Washington:

> *The night was heavy and mirk,*
>   *The moon shone dusky red,*
> *The air had an odor of sulphureous smoke*
>   *And of corpses newly dead.*
> *And I saw in fact, or dream,*
>   *Or both confused in one,*
> *A dance and a revel and a maniac rout*
>   *Too hideous for the sun;*
> *And out of it came a cry:*
>   Blood! blood! blood!
> *With a nation's tears for water!*
>   Blood! blood! blood!
> *Slabby and thick as mud,*
>   *To sprinkle the hungry soil*
> *For the carnival of slaughter!* [88]

Spurred on by this campaign of propagandic enlightenment, the people developed for their enemies a deep and bitter hatred which

[87] Richmond *Daily Examiner,* May 2, 1863; *Southern Historical Society Papers,* I (1876), 30; Richmond *Daily Whig,* July 5, 1861; Athens *Southern Watchman,* June 12, 1861; July 2, 1862; Whitney, *Hawkins Zouaves,* 33; Freeman, *Lee's Lieutenants,* I, 8; Augusta *Weekly Chronicle & Sentinel,* October 28, 1862; Macon *Daily Telegraph,* April 16, 1862; Richardson (comp.), *Messages and Papers of the Confederacy,* I, 120–21, 141, 233, 379–82. The handcuffs story was widely published and believed. Cobb wrote his wife, July 27, 1861, in Thomas R. R. Cobb Letters, that there had been displayed in Congress a "pair of iron hand-cuffs which the villains had prepared to put on the arms of the Congressmen they expected to arrest in Richmond. The indignation was very great." See also, Richmond *Daily Whig,* August 3, 1861; Richmond *Daily Dispatch,* July 25, 30, August 2, 1861; Athens *Southern Watchman,* August 7, 1861; Atlanta *Southern Confederacy,* August 7, 1861; Mobile *Advertiser and Register,* August 11, 1861; Easterby (ed.), *South Carolina Rice Plantation,* 183.

[88] Augusta *Daily Constitutionalist,* August 5, 1864.

a Richmond editor declared should be "undying eternal." One Southerner advised that "each one make it his own peculiar and holy mission to excite each other to hatred against the foe"; a soldier declared that he would "never take a prisoner, and never stop killing as long as he had strength to cut, stab or shoot"; and another wished "to see a wall built between us and the Yankees as high as Heaven and as low as Hell; for, if it were less deep, they would be sure to get under it!" A nine-year-old lad, after attending a flag raising at a church, said as he picked up his gun, "I only wish I could meet three Yankees in the woods as I go home," and added as he looked down his double-barreled gun, "two, any how." Someone wrote on a shingle at the head of the grave of a Federal soldier:

> *The Yankee host with blood-stained hand,*
> *Came Southward to divide our land,*
> *This narrow and contracted spot*
> *Is all that this poor Yankee got.*[89]

Hatred, indulged in equally by both Confederates and Federals, disintegrated that stolidity and grim composure which would have been a much better weapon to use. Some Confederates felt that Yankee baseness had been exaggerated, and some were generous enough to blame the worst atrocities on the foreign mercenaries, a large supply of whom the North was charged with having enlisted, and without whom "the invaders would ere this have been driven from our soil," said Davis in 1864.[90] As much as the Confederate

[89] Richmond *Semi-Weekly Enquirer*, July 8, 1862. Answering the threat of the Yankees confiscating Southern land, a Virginian said, "Yes, they shall have a farm in Virginia: it shall suit them exactly—a farm six feet by two, for each of them." [Hopley], *Life in the South*, II, 115. See also, *ibid.*, I, 288; Day, *Down South*, I, 219; Macon *Daily Telegraph*, March 27, 1862; Richmond *Daily Examiner*, March 23, 1863. The editor of the Richmond *Daily Examiner* wrote, "One would suppose that creatures so abounding in the stenches of moral decomposition would never be alluded to in decent society. But somehow the habit of expectorating upon the vermin that swarm in the Northern dunghill, has gotten the better of gentle natures, and the time drags heavily on the Southerner who refuses to indulge himself some twenty times a day in a volley of direful anathemas against the Yankees. . . . Cowards by nature, thieves upon principle, and assassins at heart it would be marvellous indeed if the people of the North refused to render homage to Benjamin Butler, the beastliest, bloodiest poltroon and pick pocket the world ever saw."

[90] Richardson (comp.), *Messages and Papers of the Confederacy*, I, 487. Said the editor of the Selma *Daily Reporter*, July 26, 1861, "The Northern people are not

civilians might hate the Yankees for their pillaging, these same Southerners found the temptation great when they themselves had the opportunity, especially when some city was about to fall to the enemy. Mobs of people pillaged Nashville when it was on the point of falling, and after Sherman had burned Atlanta, 250 wagons from the surrounding country came in to carry off the remains. Also, Confederate cavalrymen had a bad reputation in living off those parts of the South in which they operated. Never before had any part of the American people suffered to the extent the Southerners were forced to go in this war; generations of security from invasion had made it hard for them to understand the realities of war which had so frequently visited Europe and other parts of the world.

---

like us; we are made of different stuff; besides this, the rank and file of Lincoln's army is made up of Saur-kraut Dutch, red-mouthed Paddies from the fish markets of Ireland, and other specimens of the fag end of creation too tedious to mention." According to the editor of the Milledgeville *Southern Recorder*, May 19, 1863, "The Southern people have to contend not only against all Yankeedom, but against the scum of Europe, discharged from its jails and penitentiaries." See also, Martin A. Haynes, *History of the Second Regiment New Hampshire Volunteers* . . . (Manchester, 1865), vi; Jones, *Rebel War Clerk's Diary*, II, 34; Owsley, *King Cotton Diplomacy*, 518 ff.

CHAPTER XVII

INTERNAL DISSENSIONS

THE Confederacy was not blessed with a "one for all and all for one" patriotism with which future generations of sentimental romancers were to endow it. Had it been so, this new-born nation might well have established its independence. In the beginning the surface indications were that the Confederates did compose one great happy family, but beneath there were bitter rivalries and disappointments which were not long in showing themselves.

Both strength and weakness first asserted themselves around the personality of Jefferson Davis; he was first to be deified and first as well as last to be damned. William H. Russell, an Englishman traveling in the South for the London *Times,* found Davis in the first months of the Confederacy universally acclaimed; often this correspondent was asked the question, "Have you seen our President, sir? don't you think him a very able man?" [1] And yet less than a week after Davis' election, the critical Thomas R. R. Cobb was saying privately that many were already regretting it, and scarcely two weeks after that important event he judged that the President "acts for himself and receives no advice except from those who press their advice unasked." By the next year his feelings had developed into stinging hatred: "I am alarmed sometimes when I am conscious of the bitterness of my hatred toward him. The embodiment and concentration of cowardly littleness he garnishes over with pharisaical hypocrisy. How can God smile upon us while we have such a man [to] lead us." [2]

Before the end of 1861, a Virginian published the conviction that

[1] Russell, *My Diary North and South,* 260.

[2] For the two quotations, see Cobb to his wife, February 26, 1861, June 20, 1862, in Thomas R. R. Cobb Letters.

the Davis administration "is rotten and stinks," [3] and a Georgian declared, "Electing Jeff Davis, president is equalled by nothing except the election of Joe Brown Gov. by the people of Georgia." [4] By 1862, Rhett's Charleston *Mercury* was demanding "an entire change of men and policy in Richmond," and he agreed with a correspondent who declared, "The policy of the administration has been stupid at home and abroad; inefficiency has characterized their doings from the beginning until the present moment; and even with a change it will require the help of God to save us." [5] Mrs. Chesnut, the South Carolina diarist, wrote in March, 1862, "In Columbia I do not know a half-dozen men who would not gaily step into Jeff Davis's shoes with a firm conviction that they would do better in every respect than he does," and one person believed that Davis delighted "to spite public opinion." [6] William W. Boyce, a member of the Confederate Congress, in April, 1862, spoke of "the incredible incompetency of our Executive." [7] The next year James L. Alcorn, a Mississippian of questionable Confederate loyalty, called Davis a "miserable, stupid, one-eyed, dyspeptic, arrogant tyrant," and prayed that he might live to see Davis "damned! and sunk into the lowest hell." [8] A Georgian thought "Our President is our greatest misfortune & next to that is the fact that the people have so far lost their wits as not to know it." He feared that if Providence or the Yankees did not soon remove him, "the gig [*sic*] will be up with us before a great while." [9] Implacable Pollard of the Richmond *Examiner* called Davis "a literary dyspeptic who had more ink than blood in his veins, an intriguer, busy with private enmities." [10]

With such an estimate of Davis bandied around in the news-

[3] Richmond *Daily Whig*, September 6, 1861.

[4] John A. Cobb, Yorktown, Va., to "Uncle," December 16, 1861, in Howell Cobb Papers.

[5] Charleston *Daily Mercury*, March 8, 1862. See also, Du Bose, *Life and Times of William Lowndes Yancey*, 578.

[6] Martin and Avary (eds.), *Diary from Dixie*, 140, 149.

[7] Rosser H. Taylor (ed.), "Boyce-Hammond Correspondence," in *Journal of Southern History*, III (1937), 352.

[8] Percy L. Rainwater (ed.), "Letters of James Lusk Alcorn," *ibid.*, 204.

[9] M. C. Fulton, Athens, Ga., to Stephens, August 2, 1863, in Alexander H. Stephens Papers (microfilms in University of Texas Library, originals in Division of Manuscripts, Library of Congress).   [10] Pollard, *Jefferson Davis*, 168.

papers, mouthed in Congress, and scattered in private correspondence throughout the land, it was only natural that a great many people began to have a low estimate of their President and to despair of ultimate victory. An increasing number of Confederates determined to be satisfied with nothing which Davis might do and to hold him responsible not only for being himself and for having ulterior designs in all he did, but also for what he did not do or for what others did or for evils that developed in the natural course of events.

Early an outcry arose that Davis was favoring West Pointers and their method of fighting. "West Point sits down on enthusiasm, laughs it to scorn. It wants discipline," remarked Mrs. Chesnut.[11] A Virginian believed "Our greatest trouble has been too much *West Point Science & spade fighting.*" "We must *ditch less* and *fight more,*" this same Virginian argued.[12] West Point had taught stationary war with forts, fortifications, trenches, and mathematics, and made its graduates believe that war was "the greatest business of life." [13] Vice-President Stephens argued that West Point made a mechanism of a soldier, killed his spirit, enthusiasm, initiative, and native ability, and made him forget that he was a gentleman. It forced the war into an uneven contest of material force—thereby eliminating the only resource with which the South could ever hope to win—superior enthusiasm and spirit and morale.[14] A Congressman declared that "West Pointism had already done great injury to the country," [15] and Thomas R. R. Cobb, who was not a West Pointer, insisted that West Point graduates were guilty of self-sufficiency and self-aggrandizement and could see no merit in anyone who had not passed through the Academy. One of the most bitter attacks on West Pointers was made by John Tyler, Jr., son of the former President, who held that the Confederacy was overrun with them (and Yankee-Confederates): "one West Point fool as Commissary-General [Northrop]"; "another West Point fool and knave as Adjutant-General and senior general of the army [Samuel Cooper]"; "another West Pointer of known dishonorable origin

11 Martin and Avary (eds.), *Diary from Dixie*, 175.
12 Hunt & James, Richmond, Va., to Massie, May 7, 1862, in Massie Papers.
13 *Southern Historical Society Papers*, XLVI (1928), 34.
14 Johnston and Browne, *Alexander H. Stephens*, 414.
15 *Southern Historical Society Papers*, XLV (1925), 161.

and malignant heart and incompetent head [Bragg], who, by his stupendous military blunders, has done more than any and all others combined to place the country beneath the heel of the enemy"; and "another West Point pigmy [Pemberton]," who had given up Vicksburg. "The West Pointers have indeed counseled and generaled us to the verge of death itself"; and he added, "I am willing to perish, but the West Pointer must perish with me, since he has led me to the grave." [16] The total number of West Pointers who served in the Confederate armies was 304.[17]

Though some believed with Sam Houston that only God made generals and that all the West Points in the world could not make one if it were not in him to start with, much of the animus against West Pointers originated in the rivalry of political-civilian generals, who themselves came in for castigation. The editor of the *Southern Confederacy* declared that the latter were responsible for many of the Confederate reverses, which would continue "as long as broken down politicians and drunkards have command of our troops; so long as demagogues, place-hunters, and political favorites are appointed or elected Commanders, Quartermasters, Surgeons, &c." [18] Toombs, especially, was condemned for holding membership in Congress and a commission in the army at the same time. Only by resigning his secretaryship of state when he received his commission, had he kept himself from holding three positions. A Georgia editor remarked, "It was too much for even his modesty to hold three offices at the same time." [19]

Closely allied to the attacks on West Pointers was the ungracious onset against Northerners who chose to join the Confederate army, and against Davis for appointing them to commands. A Richmond editor charged in March, 1862, that "all the officials, who constitute the very pivot on which the whole war hinges are either Yankees, or foreigners, or Jews." [20] A few months later, becoming more specific, he pointed out that the Secretary of War (Benjamin) was "a

---

[16] John Tyler, Jr., Richmond, Va., to Sterling Price, June 11, 1864, in *Official Records*, Ser. I, Vol. LI, Pt. II, 1005–1006.

[17] Eliot, *West Point in the Confederacy*, xv; *Southern Historical Society Papers*, XXVII (1900), 297.

[18] Atlanta *Southern Confederacy*, March 22, 1862.

[19] Sandersville *Central Georgian*, August 21, 1861.

[20] Richmond *Daily Whig*, March 19, 1862.

foreigner and a Jew"; the Adjutant General (Cooper), "a New Yorker"; the Secretary of the Navy (Mallory), "born in the West Indies of Yankee parents, and educated in Connecticut"; the Quartermaster General (Abraham C. Myers), "a Pennsylvanian and a Jew"; the Commissary General (Northrop), "a native of Massachusetts or Connecticut [in fact a South Carolinian]"; and the Chief of Ordnance (Gorgas), "a Northern man of an unknown state." [21] The best-known Northerners who attained high rank in the Confederate army were Gorgas, Cooper, Mansfield Lovell, Pemberton, Daniel Ruggles, and Samuel G. French, though most of them had long been residents of the South. It was unfortunate that Lovell and Pemberton were in command of the defenses of the strategic cities of New Orleans and Vicksburg, respectively, which they surrendered to the Federals. Both became extremely unpopular. The onset against Jews and foreigners never reached sustained proportions; it was only incidental to expressions of dislike for Southernized Yankees.

Davis thought the attacks against these Confederate leaders of Northern birth were a great injustice. In defending Pemberton he declared that he could "imagine nothing more unjust and more ungenerous" in assailing him because of his Northern birth.[22] The editor of the Macon *Telegraph* reminded the people that there had "been as many traitors to our cause of Southern birth as of Northern birth." "Casting imputations of disloyalty upon those of Northern and Foreign birth," he added, "because of that fact alone is a poor way of displaying zeal in behalf of the Southern Confederacy." [23]

The criticism of Davis' appointment of Northerners to high positions was merely a part of the general onset against his whole use of the appointive power. There were few of his appointments, civil or military, which were not condemned by some petty faction, echoing the Richmond *Examiner's* dictum that the country stood "aghast at the President's appointments." [24] He was either playing

[21] *Ibid.*, September 1, 1862. See also, Jones, *Rebel War Clerk's Diary*, I, 245; II, 19, 26.

[22] Davis to William M. Brooks, April 2, 1863, in Rowland (ed.), *Jefferson Davis, Constitutionalist*, V, 465.

[23] Macon *Daily Telegraph*, January 31, 1862.

[24] Richmond *Daily Examiner*, March 25, 1862.

favorites to spite someone or he was making a place for some kinsman or rewarding some old crony. His critics never gave him credit for considerations of public service. John M. Daniel of the *Examiner* told Burton N. Harrison, Davis' secretary, that if he would "take the trouble to inform us which one of the President's family and of the late General Taylor's [Zachary, Davis' first father-in-law] *is not* holding any office anywhere, we shall not only print it with pleasure, but the public will receive his information with a gratification heightened by surprise." [25] In fact, in Davis' appointments nepotism was very slight; his stubbornness against criticism was perverted into favoritism.

An outstanding example of the President's refusal to be moved by public criticism from his support of an appointee was the case of General Bragg. Davis considered Bragg a steadfast friend but he also believed him to be especially fitted to command armies and direct military affairs. Though he was wrong in both suppositions, he could not be blamed for the first. Bragg had condemned Davis in 1861 for not appointing him to command at New Orleans, writing Governor Thomas Moore of Louisiana, "I am not surprised at the President, who, in his feeble condition is entirely under the control of a miserable *petticoat* government as tyrannical as Lincoln's despotism." [26] But this friendship and even the malicious falsehood that Davis and Bragg were brothers-in-law were used to explain Davis' support of Bragg. Taking note of his friendship for Bragg, Davis wrote him, "You have the misfortune of being regarded as my personal friend, and are pursued therefore with malignant censure by men regardless of truth." [27]

As to the supposition that Bragg was a military expert, Davis based his judgment on the same well-known facts which made most of Bragg's associates and the public in general regard him as a failure and an evil genius of the Confederacy. His failure in the invasion

[25] *Ibid.*, February 15, 1864.

[26] Bragg, Pensacola, Fla., to Moore, October 31, 1861, in Thomas O. Moore Collection.

[27] Davis to Bragg, August 5, 1862, in Rowland (ed.), *Jefferson Davis, Constitutionalist*, V, 312. Mrs. Bragg was an aggressive woman in promoting her husband's interests and ambitions. She wrote Bragg resenting the fact that Albert Sidney Johnston and others outranked him. She undoubtedly had considerable influence over her husband in matters which were not her concern. For instance, see Mrs. Bragg to General Bragg, March 3, 1862, in Bragg Papers (University of Texas Library).

of Kentucky in the late summer of 1862 was of poignant memory, and the collapse of Confederate morale around Chattanooga in the fall of 1863 forced Davis to remove Bragg from command. But when the President immediately transferred him to Richmond as military adviser "charged with the conduct of military operations in the armies of the Confederacy," the country could scarcely believe that this elevation had been made. Davis was widely condemned in bitter and sarcastic language for flying in the face of the army and the country by sticking to and elevating a played-out general who had made a failure of every military adventure in which he had engaged. This appointment came "like a bucket of water on a newly kindled grate." [28] "When a man fails in an inferior position," a Virginia editor sarcastically said, "it is natural and charitable to conclude that the failure is due to the inadequacy of the task to his capabilities, and wise to give him a larger sphere for the proper exertion of his abilities." [29]

The President was extremely sensitive to attempted inroads on his constitutional power of appointment, whether by public criticism or by the manipulations of Senators in exercising their right of confirmation. In 1863 Congress sought to increase the rank of Quartermaster General Myers by the trick of declaring that this position should carry the rank of brigadier general instead of colonel as provided in the original legislation. With sardonic cleverness, Davis took this to mean that Congress had vacated the office since Myers was only a colonel; and he thereupon appointed Alexander R. Lawton, who held the required rank of brigadier general. Thus, instead of getting Myers promoted, Congress succeeded in getting him dismissed. A bitter quarrel resulted. Seventy-six members of Congress signed a note to Davis recommending that Myers be retained, and the Senate by a vote of 15 to 9 declared that Myers was still the Quartermaster General. Davis replied that this resolution was unconstitutional; the Senate finally capitulated and the appointment of Lawton was confirmed.[30]

[28] Richmond *Daily Examiner*, February 25, 1864.

[29] Richmond *Whig*, quoted in Athens *Southern Watchman*, March 9, 1864. Linton Stephens, Sparta, Ga., writing to Mrs. Robert Toombs, Washington, Ga., March 3, 1864, in Robert Toombs Papers (University of Georgia Library), called Bragg "the most notorious military tyrant in the Confederacy."

[30] *Journal of the Congress of the Confederate States,* III, 604, 621, 622, 627, 628;

The most consistent and long-drawn-out attack on Davis' appointments centered about his cabinet members. Severally and collectively they were attacked. By June, 1861, Lawrence M. Keitt, South Carolina Congressman, was dubbing the cabinet "a farce"; Pollard called it "a ridiculous cypher"; and Rhett said in 1862 that no members were statesmen, though they might "be tolerably familiar and adroit in the local politics of their cities and neighborhoods." [31] Throughout the whole life of the Confederacy, Davis made thirteen changes, counting ad interim appointments, but seldom did he please his critics. The President took most interest in the War Department and held its secretaries closest under his thumb, but not even any secretary of war was the "cypher" charged by Pollard. The five changes in this department exceeded the number in any other. The ablest secretary of war was the gaunt and corpse-like James A. Seddon (November 21, 1862–February 6, 1865), appointed to succeed Thomas Jefferson's grandson George W. Randolph, who was forced out because he made a major military decision without consulting Davis. The President loyally supported Seddon, but early in 1865 when the Virginia Congressional delegation petitioned Davis to dismiss his whole cabinet, Seddon took umbrage and resigned. He had long been under attack from such scolds as Foote, who unjustly charged him with selling his wheat crop to the government for $40 a bushel while the wheat of others was being impressed at a small fraction of that price. Both Secretary of the Navy Mallory and Postmaster General Reagan were always under attack, but they held on until the flight from Richmond. Secretary of the Treasury Memminger, under constant bombardment from the beginning, finally quit in July, 1864.[32]

In the eyes of Davis' critics, the prince of villains was Benjamin, whether he be Attorney General, Secretary of War, or Secretary of State—all of which positions he held consecutively. This Sephardic Jew, born in the West Indies, early gained and never lost the ear and confidence of Davis by his ingratiating ways. Bland and suave

Richmond *Daily Examiner*, August 10, December 24, 1863; January 25, 27, 1864; Richmond *Daily Whig*, January 26, 1864.

[31] Sources of quotations, respectively: Martin and Avary (eds.), *Diary from Dixie*, 68; Pollard, *Second Year of the War*, 286; Charleston *Mercury*, February 27, 1862.

[32] Patrick, *Jefferson Davis and his Cabinet*, 60 ff.; Fremantle, *Three Months in the Southern States*, 215; Pollard, *Jefferson Davis*, 440–43.

and oleaginous like a well-fed shopkeeper, with his black hair and eyes, round face and red thick lips shining through his black re-treating beard and radiating an eternal smile—in fact not a smile, yet not unpleasant—this man, said John S. Wise, "had more brains and less heart than any other civic leader in the South," and when the war was over the South meant no more to him "than a last year's bird's-nest." [33] "A grander rascal than this Jew Benjamin does not exist in the Confederacy," declared Thomas R. R. Cobb.[34] He did not divorce himself from his Northern friends when the war came, nor from his wife whose infidelity was proved by the birth of her child, for Benjamin was "an eunuch," Cobb declared.[35] Others called for the "Christianizing" of the cabinet by removing Benjamin, who, they said, saw to it that Davis never mentioned Christ in his proclamations for supplication and prayer.[36]

Benjamin was extremely unpopular as Secretary of War, and, probably to prevent an uprising in Congress, Davis shifted him to the State Department. As War Secretary, Benjamin had borne the brunt of criticism for the Confederate defeats at Fort Henry, Fort Donelson, and Roanoke Island; and it was on account of his action, prompted by Davis, ordering troops of Stonewall Jackson from Romney, West Virginia, that led to that commander's temporary resignation. In February, 1865, a resolution in the Senate express-ing a lack of confidence in Benjamin was lost by a tie vote. A few days later Benjamin offered to resign, but Davis refused to coun-tenance it.

As Congress showed little confidence in any cabinet member, it is not surprising that that body never carried out its constitutional privilege and implied duty of granting to every cabinet member a seat "upon the floor of either House, with the privilege of discuss-ing any measures appertaining to his department." This question was frequently debated in both the House and the Senate, but was

[33] Wise, *End of an Era*, 176, 177, 402.

[34] *Southern Historical Society Papers*, XXVIII (1900), 290.

[35] Cobb, Richmond, Va., to his wife, January 15, 1862, in Thomas R. R. Cobb Letters.

[36] Jones, *Rebel War Clerk's Diary*, I, 89, 104; Athens *Southern Watchman*, October 19, 1864. Christ's name was mentioned in none of Davis' proclamations for fasting and prayer, and, of course, it was not because of Benjamin, for in the proclamations previously issued under Toombs, R. M. T. Hunter, and Browne, Christ's name was not mentioned.

never settled. In addition to the general dislike for cabinet members, there was the open argument that their sitting in Congress would give the executive branch too much authority. Those favoring it believed that it would lead to better cabinet appointments and would bring about a closer understanding between the legislative and executive branches of the government. Senator Benjamin H. Hill, remembering how this system had functioned in the Provisional Government, declared he "had seen information obtained then in fifteen minutes which could not be obtained in this Congress in a month." [37] The constant clamor in Congress to force Davis to reorganize his cabinet led to the consideration of a bill which would have limited cabinet appointments to two years (the life of the House), but honest convictions that such a measure would be unconstitutional and Davis' bloc of friends in Congress prevented its passage.

Nothing was too petty to lead to an attack on Davis by some critic. When retreating Confederate armies made it a patriotic duty to destroy all cotton in the path of the enemy and when planters were destroying hundreds of thousands of bales, the report was circulated that the cotton on Davis' Mississippi plantation had not been burned, implying that it had been bargained away to Yankee traders. On Davis' proof that it had been destroyed, a Mississippi editor wondered whether the destruction had not come after the criticism.[38]

The President had a knack for making enemies. A Richmond editor asserted that Davis was "ready for any quarrel with any and everybody, at any time and all times; and the suspicion goes that rather than not have a row on hand with an enemy, he would make one with the best friend he had on earth." [39] Such an explanation was given for enmities existing between Davis and Beauregard, Joseph E. Johnston, Wigfall, Yancey, Stephens, Toombs, Joseph E. Brown, Vance, old Sam Houston, and many others, great and small, military, political, and private. Of course, such an explanation was entirely too simple.

The grandiose and unpredictable Beauregard had advocated

---

[37] *Southern Historical Society Papers*, XLVIII (1941), 287–90.

[38] Richmond *Semi-Weekly Enquirer*, June 17, 1862; Raymond *Hinds County Gazette*, June 18, 1862.   [39] Richmond *Daily Whig*, January 27, 1864.

amazing military maneuvers which, he asserted, would have resulted in the capture of Washington before the First Battle of Manassas, but which did not appeal to Davis any more than his reports on that battle and his flighty plans to follow it up. Chafing over his dislike of subordination to Joseph E. Johnston, Beauregard was transferred to Albert Sidney Johnston's command in the West. Subsequently, relations between Davis and Beauregard did not improve.

The mutual dislike between Davis and Joseph E. Johnston was long-standing and was fed by various incidents. In addition to antebellum antipathies dating back to West Point, Johnston, a Virginian connected with many of the great Southern families, was seriously offended when he was outranked by three Confederate generals, though he had been senior to all of them in the old United States army. Basking in the smiles of the Richmond press, he did not always obey Davis' orders or take him very far into his confidence in his military aims around Richmond in the spring of 1862, which fact led Davis to write him this curt sentence: "While some have expressed surprise at my patience when orders to you were not observed, I have at least hoped that you would recognize the desire to aid and sustain you, and that it would produce the corresponding action on your part." [40] After Johnston had recovered from his wounds at Fair Oaks, Davis placed him in charge of all the armies of the West, but this "fourth ranking" general took charge personally of no one army and could not be induced to do so until he contributed to the fall of Vicksburg in July, 1863, by refusing to attack Grant on the ground that he must defend Jackson. But this town he soon gave up, with a vast supply of railroad equipment—reminiscent of his retreat from northern Virginia after the destruction and abandonment of immense supplies in the spring of 1862. In the fall of 1863 he took charge of Bragg's army, on his removal, and instead of taking the offensive, allowed himself to be driven to the gates of Atlanta, and, on refusing to divulge his plans to Davis, got himself removed at the behest of an almost universal demand. This and more too Davis charged against him in a communication to Congress, which he did not send. In this document

<hr />

[40] Davis to Johnston, May 10, 1862, in Rowland (ed.), *Jefferson Davis, Constitutionalist*, V, 243.

he said, "My opinion of Gen. Johnston's unfitness for command has ripened slowly and against my inclination into a conviction so settled, that it would be impossible for me again to feel confidence in him as the commander of an army in the field." [41] Yet near the end Davis was constrained by the exigencies of the times to place Johnston in command of an army, which he surrendered to Sherman at Durham's Station in April of 1865.

There were other military officers who did not like Davis, but the President found some of his worst enemies among political leaders. Wigfall of Texas was one of the earliest and continued so to the end. Characterized by a contemporary as a man with a coarse and grim mouth, square jaws, eyes of a wonderful depth and light as fierce as a Bengal tiger's, with beetling black eyebrows, a straight broad forehead from which his hair rose up like the vegetation on a river bank, Wigfall was the type which gave currency to the term "fire-eater." Thomas R. R. Cobb declared that he was "half drunk all the time and bullies and blusters about everywhere." [42] He fell out with Davis over some triviality and thereafter berated him relentlessly in the Senate. Yancey became hostile to Davis over some fancied slights relative to army promotions and the President's failure to consult him about the appointment of a postmaster in Montgomery. Davis was loath to have an open quarrel with him and in answer to Yancey's charges of presidential dislike, replied, "Will you have the goodness to inform me how you acquired that information? Not having made any declaration to that effect, I think I have a right to inquire." [43] Yancey, however, was not an implacable foe, for his will bequeathed to Davis a spyglass which George Washington had once owned.

The President had no desire to make an enemy of Toombs, or, indeed, of anyone else, but when this political brigadier general failed to get promoted to a major-generalship, he resigned from the army and thereafter held an undying hatred and contempt for Davis. He referred to the President as "that scoundrel Jeff Davis"

[41] Rowland (ed.), *Jefferson Davis, Constitutionalist*, VI, 491–503, for the whole communication; quotation on page 503. See also, *ibid.*, V, 434.

[42] Cobb, Montgomery, to his wife, April 30, 1861, in Thomas R. R. Cobb **Letters**. See also, Russell, *My Diary North and South*, 106–107; Reagan, *Memoirs*, 161.

[43] Davis to William L. Yancey, May 26, 1863, in Rowland (ed.), *Jefferson Davis, Constitutionalist*, V, 498. See also, *ibid.*, VI, 133.

and a "false and hypocritical . . . wretch." "We shall get our independence but it will be in spite of him," he declared, and then speaking of both Congress and Davis remarked, "I feel but little like fighting for a people base enough to submit to such despotism from such contemptible sources." He sought election to the Senate as a base from which to fight Davis, but he was defeated twice and won once under conditions which caused him to refuse the honor. But however much Toombs hated Davis, he always loved the Confederacy and insisted that any settlement short of independence "would be the consummation of all evils which even the power of God could inflict on us in this world." [44] And so, when the war got closer to Georgia in the fall of 1863, he offered his services to the state and was given command of a regiment which entrained for Savannah the following spring. As his troops were preparing to leave Augusta in their boxcars, they built small fires on the floors, protected by sand and bricks. On being told that the fires must be put out to avoid setting the train ablaze, the soldiers were about to obey, when Toombs came along and with great indignation and a flood of harsh expletives coupled with threats to cut the agent into small pieces and use him as fuel in the locomotive, ordered the train to proceed. Soon after reaching Savannah, Toombs made a highly incendiary speech to his troops. Bordering on treason, he said that liberty was dead and that the Confederate government was without honor, condemning it for all the controversial issues of the day —suspension of the writ of habeas corpus, impressment, conscription evils, and so on. He called upon the soldiers to defend their liberties against the President and Congress, but added, "I ask for no mutiny, unless it should be necessary in defense of Constitutional rights." Still smarting over the failure of his politico-military career, he declared, "Wherever we had victories, politicians were among the commanders." [45] Soon the Confederacy was filled with rumors that Toombs had been arrested by Beauregard because he refused to show a pass when he boarded a train in Savannah, but the consensus of the most reliable reports held that it was for his conduct in Augusta. According to another rumor, it might well

[44] For sources of Toombs quotations see Phillips (ed.), *Correspondence of Toombs, Stephens, and Cobb*, 608, 611, 592, 595, 626, respectively.
[45] Athens *Southern Watchman*, March 2, 1864.

have been for "treason, disloyalty &c." in his speech.[46] Toombs continued his course of vanity and futility to the end.

The most damaging enemies of Davis and of the Confederacy were some of the governors, whose power for mischief was enhanced by their position. They quarreled furiously about the control of troops and the appointment of officers, about conscription, the suspension of the writ of habeas corpus, impressment, a peace program, and various other questions and measures. In these contests Governor Brown was first, last, and most persistent. The Confederacy was not a month old before he began his opposition, lending the suspicion that he felt it was a mistake that he had not been elected President. In April, 1861, Thomas R. R. Cobb had found that "Davis holds Brown in great contempt, he says he is the only man in the seven states who has persistently thwarted him in every endeavor to carry out the policy of the government," [47] and the next month his brother Howell saw prospects of an open break in which he promised to help "put down the miserable demagogue who now disgraces the executive chair of Ga." [48] Brown found no opportunity for obstruction too petty or too important to ignore. Not recognizing Davis' proclamation for a fast day in 1862, Brown issued his own to come a week later; and when Sherman was on his way to Atlanta, Brown sought to direct Confederate operations and military policy. He glibly wrote Davis, "Your information as to the relative strength of the two armies in North Georgia cannot be from reliable sources." To this amazing effrontery Davis replied sarcastically: "I am surprised to learn from you that the basis of the comparison I made on official reports and estimates is incorrect. Until your better knowledge is communicated I shall have no means of correcting such errors, and your dicta cannot control the disposition of troops in different parts of the Confederate States. Most men in your position would not assume to decide on the value of the service to be

---

[46] Richmond *Daily Examiner*, February 3, 1864; Richmond *Semi-Weekly Enquirer*, February 5, 16, 1864; Athens *Southern Watchman*, February 17, 1864; Jones, *Rebel War Clerk's Diary*, II, 142. Mrs. Chesnut wrote in her diary for May 29, 1862: "Toombs is ready for another revolution, and curses freely everything Confederate from the President down to a horse boy." Martin and Avary (eds.), *Diary from Dixie*, 171.

[47] Cobb, Montgomery, to his wife, April 29, 1861, in Thomas R. R. Cobb Letters.

[48] Phillips (ed.), *Correspondence of Toombs, Stephens, and Cobb*, 568.

rendered by troops in distant positions. When you give me your reliable statement of the comparative strength of the armies, I will be glad also to know the source of your information as to what the whole country expects and posterity will judge." [49]

Davis and the Cobb brothers were not the only ones to pass hostile judgments on Brown. A Georgia editor declared that Brown had a hallucination which made him "imagine himself, alternately, the State of Georgia and the President of the Confederate States"; [50] a Virginia editor charged that Brown was "unquiet, self-assertive, wrong-headed, contentious and troublesome, to whom the plain beaten road of common sense, common feeling, and common duty, is odious, and always doing something that nobody else is doing"; [51] and the acid Pollard dubbed him a "coarse, obese prince of Southern demagogues," "an unmasked hypocrite and superfluous trifler on the stage of public life," raising "a false clamor with the ultimate design of weakening and betraying the Confederacy." [52] Even Toombs could condemn Brown at times and declare that some of his acts were "as unconstitutional and as foolish as anything that Davis or Lincoln have ever done." [53] A few weeks before the end of the war, an Augusta editor recorded this estimate of Brown: "We are satisfied, from what he says, that if he was the President and both Houses of Congress, and all the Generals, and the army, the Foreign Ministers and the collectors of the tax in kind, we should

[49] *Official Records*, Ser. I, Vol. XXXIX, Pt. II, 688. See also, Macon *Daily Telegraph*, March 7, 1862. Cobb, Richmond, to his wife, October 4, 1861, in Howell Cobb Papers: "We hear by telegraph to night that Joe Brown is elected. As a man, a Christian, a gentleman, and a Georgian I feel humiliated into the very dust. For my life I can never feel the same respect for any man that voted for him, that I have heretofore felt. Our state is disgraced and if you will consent I will arrange to bring my family out of the state and if the war should last for two years, I will not return there while the miserable scratch disgraces the executive chair. I cannot trust myself to write on the subject and I am glad that I do not have to meet with any person who by his vote and influence has contributed to this most humiliating event." John A. Cobb wrote from Macon to his wife, October 5, 1864, *ibid.*, that the best way to get along with Brown was to make "him think he is a great man," that it was "a smart trick . . . to first make a friend of Joseph I by soft soaping him a little."

[50] Sandersville *Central Georgian*, September 11, 1861.

[51] Richmond *Daily Examiner*, March 21, 1864.

[52] Pollard, *Jefferson Davis*, 212.

[53] Phillips (ed.), *Correspondence of Toombs, Stephens, and Cobb*, 609.

have a different state of things from what we have now, for great is Joseph the Governor of all the Georgias." [54]

Of the other outstanding governors, Vance stood next in tussles with Davis, but he was actuated by motives quite different from those of Brown. He was like Brown, however, in his passion to uphold and protect the good name of his state and to minister to the wants of its civilians and its soldiers. He asserted that Davis had not given proper recognition to North Carolinians in civil appointments and army promotions and that he preferred Democrats and secessionists over old Whigs and former Union-loving citizens. Davis replied that out of the thousands of appointments and promotions he had made, in North Carolina and elsewhere, there had not been one in which "an officer has ever been recommended on the ground of his party or political opinions or relations." Davis found Vance difficult and ungenerous: "Experience has taught me to expect of Governor Vance unjust constructions of my conduct, and I should hardly deem it worth my while to attempt any correction in the present instance, if he alone were concerned." [55] But Vance was a determined Confederate, and he never let differences with Davis obscure the ultimate purpose of all patriots.

Sam Houston of Texas never loved the Confederacy nor liked its President, whom he called "Jeffy Davis." Although he lost his governorship at the outbreak of the war, he never lost his ambition to recover it, and if he had succeeded there is reason to believe that he would have tried to withdraw Texas from the Confederacy and restore it as an independent republic.[56]

If liberty were not dead, contrary to Toombs's claims, it would soon disappear, the enemies of Davis shouted, for from the begin-

[54] Augusta *Weekly Constitutionalist*, March 1, 1865.

[55] Rowland (ed.), *Jefferson Davis, Constitutionalist*, VI, 194, 418. Davis ended a letter to Vance, March 31, 1864, answering his complaints about discriminations against North Carolina with this paragraph: "There are other passages of your letter in which you have so far infringed the proprieties of official intercourse as to preclude the possibility of reply. In order that I may not again be subjected to the necessity of making so unpleasant a remark, I must beg that a correspondence so unprofitable in its character, and which was not initiated by me, may here end, and that your future communications be restricted to such matters as may require official action." *Official Records*, Ser. I, Vol. LI, Pt. II, 845–46.

[56] Guy M. Bryan to Davis, March 9, 1863, in Rowland (ed.), *Jefferson Davis, Constitutionalist*, V, 443.

ning he had been attempting to set himself up as a military dictator. Governor Brown said in 1862 that the people had "much more to apprehend from military despotism than from subjugation by the enemy," and less than two months before Appomattox he was advocating an amendment to the Confederate Constitution which would take away the President's power as commander in chief.[57] Foote asserted in 1864 that Davis was seeking to erect a dictatorship through legislation then before Congress: "Others may vote to extend this man's power for mischief; I hold in contempt him and his whole tribe of servitors and minions." [58] As for Yancey, if he must have a dictator, he wanted it to be Lincoln—"not a Confederate dictator." [59] "Every step we have taken during the past four years," according to an Alabama editor, "has been in the direction of military despotism." "Half our laws are unconstitutional," he added.[60] Senator Williamson S. Oldham of Texas recalled that soon after conscription had been adopted in France, "Napoleon was enabled to put a diadem on his head." [61] On the contrary, Wigfall longed for a Napoleon, as a step toward peace, and he was seconded by a Richmond citizen who wrote to another Virginian, "We join you most heartily in wishing for a Washington or a Bonaparte." [62]

It was, indeed, conscription that jarred many a Southerner out of any complacency he may have had and led him to feel that the Confederacy had taken a fatal step. Before the bill had been passed in April, 1862, a Confederate soldier in Virginia said that if it became a law "all patriotism is dead, and the Confederacy will be dead sooner or later." [63] It was held widely that the law was unnecessary; it was unconstitutional; it was arbitrary, unrepublican, subversive of the doctrine of state rights; and was in fact an importation from

[57] Brown, Canton, Ga., to Alexander H. Stephens, September 1, 1862, in Phillips (ed.), Correspondence of Toombs, Stephens, and Cobb, 605.

[58] Athens Southern Watchman, November 30, 1864.

[59] Southern Historical Society Papers, XLVI (1928), 90.

[60] Quoted in Nathaniel W. Stephenson, The Day of the Confederacy (New Haven, 1919), 162.

[61] Southern Historical Society Papers, XLVI (1928), 77.

[62] Hunt & James, Richmond, Va., to Massie, March 5, 1862, in Massie Papers. See also, Journal of the Senate of . . . Georgia convened by Proclamation of the Governor, at Macon, February 15th, 1865 (Milledgeville, 1865), 7–29.

[63] Jesse W. Reid, History of the Fourth Regiment of S.C. Volunteers . . . (Greenville, 1892), 74.

degenerate Europe. It destroyed the proud, personal individualism and gentlemanly feeling of the soldier and made him a slave, a deserter, or a skulker or bushwhacker. When the age limits were amended and the old law continued as a permanent policy, one bewildered citizen asked, "Is it done to make the People hate the Government? They will hate it if this vile fungus shall be suffered to take root in our body politic." [64] Thomas R. R. Cobb called it "an infamous outrage," [65] and his brother Howell thought it should be abandoned; Stephens bitterly condemned it; Representative Caleb C. Herbert of Texas intimated that his state might secede from the Confederacy because of it; Sam Houston despised it; Toombs declared that there were no deserters before conscription; and Herschel V. Johnson and a host of other leaders with masses of their followers cried out against it.[66]

Most of the governors were either lukewarm or downright opposed to conscription. Governor John G. Shorter of Alabama declared that "if our liberties are to be won by *conscripts* or *Drafted-men,* the Contest is to become one much more dubious than I have ever, yet been inclined to admit"; [67] Governor Letcher of Virginia thought that more and better troops could be got through state action; Governor Vance of North Carolina disliked conscription; but it was left for Governor Brown of Georgia to lead all others in intemperate and obstructive opposition. Declaring that no "act of the Government of the United States prior to the secession of Georgia struck a blow at constitutional liberty so fell as has been stricken by the conscription acts," Brown devoted throughout the

[64] Athens *Southern Watchman,* September 3, 1862.

[65] Cobb, York Peninsula, to his wife, April 24, 1862, in Thomas R. R. Cobb Letters.

[66] Athens *Southern Watchman,* April 9, 16, September 10, 1862; July 8, 1863; Augusta *Weekly Constitutionalist,* January 27, 1864; February 22, 1865; Macon *Daily Telegraph,* April 4, 1862; Columbus *Weekly Enquirer,* September 2, 1862; *Southern Historical Society Papers,* XLVI (1928), 68–73; *Official Records,* Ser. IV, Vol. II, 34; Phillips (ed.), *Correspondence of Toombs, Stephens, and Cobb,* 629; Williams and Barker (eds.), *Writings of Sam Houston,* VIII, 325; Cleveland, *Alexander H. Stephens,* 766, 767; Stephens, *Constitutional View of the Late War Between the States,* II, 571–72; James D. Waddell (ed.), *Biographical Sketch of Linton Stephens,* 245–48; Flippin, *Herschel V. Johnson,* 236; Amanda McDowell and Lela M. Blankenship, *Fiddles in the Cumberlands* (New York, 1943), 129.

[67] Gov. J. G. Shorter to Col. John F. Morgan, February 14, 1862 (Alabama State Archives).

war his voice, his pen, and his physical strength to thwart its operation.[68] He carried on a long and bitter correspondence with Davis and Secretary of War Seddon, arguing the unconstitutionality of conscription. Permitting but not assisting the enforcement of the first act, he refused to allow Georgia to come under the force of the second until he could submit the question to his legislature.[69]

Though no state supreme court or Confederate district court declared conscription unconstitutional, Justice Richmond M. Pearson of the North Carolina Supreme Court, sitting in chambers, nullified the law by granting writs of habeas corpus; and Judge Thomas W. Thomas, a friend of Linton Stephens, declared the law unconstitutional in a Georgia superior court and ordered the arrest of an enrolling officer. So great was the opposition, official and unofficial, that John S. Preston, Superintendent of Conscription, declared in March, 1864, "From one end of the Confederacy to the other every constituted authority, every officer, every man and woman is engaged in opposing the enrolling officer in the execution of his duties." [70]

The suspension of the writ of habeas corpus was the most effective way to enforce conscription, maintain the integrity of the Confederate army, and put down potential traitors and spies. When in the summer of 1862 Bragg declared martial law for Atlanta and Van Dorn suspended the writ around Vicksburg and other commanders did likewise in other parts of the Confederacy, a flood of opposition swept over the country. These unauthorized acts were soon annulled by Davis, but an aroused country did not subside. Foote declared in the House that if another proclamation like Van Dorn's should be issued, he "would call upon the people to rise, sword in hand, and put down the domestic tyrant who thus sought

68 Brown to Davis, October 18, 1862, in *Official Records*, Ser. IV, Vol. II, 131.

69 Gov. Letcher, Richmond, Va., to Gov. Pickens, April 28, 1862, in "Correspondence, 1860–1865" (South Carolina State Archives); Athens *Southern Watchman*, July 2, 1862; Louise B. Hill, *Joseph E. Brown and the Confederacy* (Chapel Hill, 1939), 79 ff.; Moore, *Conscription and Conflict in the Confederacy*, 255.

70 *Official Records*, Ser. IV, Vol. III, 225. See also, Athens *Southern Watchman*, December 24, 1862; Columbus *Weekly Enquirer*, September 30, 1862; Gen. D. H. Hill, Petersburg, Va., to Vance, June 15, 1863, in Vance Papers (North Carolina State Archives); Robinson, *Justice in Grey*, 209; Jones, *Rebel War Clerk's Diary*, II, 163; Rowland (ed.), *Jefferson Davis, Constitutionalist*, V, 486.

to invade their rights." [71] Stephens, beginning his attack on the suspension of the writ in answering the question of what the powers of the military governor of Atlanta would be, continued to the end of the war to assail with intensifying fury this suppression of human liberties. At times his language became so irresponsible as to suggest that he had thrown to the winds all knowledge of American jurisprudence and constitutional law. He declared that Bragg had no more right to issue his proclamation than "any street-walker in your city," that as martial law was the absence of all law, the President, Congress, or anyone else had no such right.[72] During the discussion in Congress in early 1864 of a new suspension of the writ, Alexander H. Stephens declared if it were done, "constitutional liberty will go down, never to rise again on this continent." [73] But his most complete analysis of the meaning of the writ's suspension was given before the Georgia legislature on March 16, 1864, when a revolution appeared in the making in that state; and the most remarkable part of his conclusion was that in reality the suspension did not mean anything. But, of course, Davis was making it mean everything—the denial of every liberty guaranteed in the bill of rights. Stephens argued that the bill of rights stood above and qualified the effect of the suspension.[74] Only an unsettled mind could have believed in such sophistry. Toombs was equally as opposed and he dealt in the same kind of sophistry.

In the interim between the second and last suspension (February 13, 1863, to February 15, 1864), there developed the amazing spectacle of the Confederate District Court for Richmond, presided over by Judge Halyburton, devoting almost its whole time to issuing writs of habeas corpus whereby Confederate soldiers were being released on the grounds of being outside the draft age or on occupational exemptions or on various other pleas. It was charged that

[71] *Southern Historical Society Papers*, XLV (1925), 244.

[72] Cleveland, *Alexander H. Stephens*, 747.

[73] Johnston and Browne, *Alexander H. Stephens*, 453.

[74] James M. Calhoun, Atlanta, to Benjamin H. Hill, August 28, 1862 (in possession of the writer); Atlanta *Southern Confederacy*, September 28, November 12, 1862; Athens *Southern Watchman*, June 15, 1864; Augusta *Daily Chronicle & Sentinel*, June 4, 1864; Jones, *Rebel War Clerk's Diary*, I, 163; Cleveland, *Alexander H. Stephens*, 184–86, 767 ff.; Phillips (ed.), *Correspondence of Toombs, Stephens, and Cobb*, 639; Owsley, *State Rights in the Confederacy*, 155 ff., 171 ff.

a member of Congress served as an attorney for many of those gaining release. There were other judges equally as compliant. With spies, deserters, traitors, and malingering soldiers gaining freedom, Davis sent a message to Congress on February 3, 1864, urging the suspension of the writ. Meetings were being held widely, "in some of which a treasonable design" was "masked by a pretense of devotion to State sovereignty, and in others is openly avowed." "Desertion, already a frightful evil," he declared, would "become the order of the day." "Loyal citizens will not feel danger," he pleaded, "and the disloyal must be made to fear it." [75]

After long and acrimonious debate, Congress finally suspended the writ for the last time, for a period to run from February 15 to August 1, 1864. This suspension was greeted by an outburst of opposition. One editor wanted the names of those "who, in secret conclave [the law was enacted in secret session], obsequiously laid the liberties of this country at the feet of the President"; [76] and a Georgia editor, publishing the regulations in mourning borders, exclaimed, "Georgians, behold your chains!—Freemen of a once proud and happy country, contemplate the last act which rivets your bonds and binds you hand and foot, at the mercy of an unlimited military authority." [77] North Carolina passed a law nullifying it; Mississippi passed flaming resolutions against it; Louisiana bitterly opposed it; and the Georgia legislature, addressed by Stephens as previously indicated, planned a small revolution and passed resolutions against the suspension. The Richmond *Enquirer,* in defense of the suspension, said that "as soon as the inestimable privilege of deserters and traitors, skulkers and stragglers is trenched upon by seizing them for punishment the wail of expiring liberty is heard from every press inimical to the Government, and from some men whose official position was prostituted in the same service." [78]

The writ was restored on August 1, 1864, and the old conditions returned. The Davis supporters in Congress made a long fight to

[75] Richardson (comp.), *Messages and Papers of the Confederacy,* I, 396, 399, 400. See also, Pollard, *Jefferson Davis,* 327; Richmond *Daily Examiner,* September 4, 1863; November 23, 1864.

[76] Selma *Daily Reporter,* March 10, 1864.

[77] Athens *Southern Watchman,* April 6, 1864.

[78] Richmond *Enquirer,* quoted in Grove Hill (Ala.) *Clarke County Journal,* May 5, 1864.

have it suspended again, which nearly succeeded. The House passed the bill, and in the Senate the vote was a tie. Stephens, now in Richmond on one of those rare occasions, was presiding. Before exercising his right to cast the vote to break the tie, he started to address the Senate, but his right was challenged and by a vote of that body he was denied the floor. Considering himself grossly insulted, he told a Senator that he would resign, and was prevented from doing so only by a unanimous invitation to address the next meeting. His speech was a long indictment of the Davis administration for all of the controversial legislation that had been passed, including, of course, the suspension of the writ. He wanted it all repealed, and promised that enough enthusiasm would then arise in the Confederacy to win the war.[79]

Almost as galling as the suspension of the writ was the system of provost marshals. Originally employed to protect property and preserve order in the vicinity of armies, to arrest stragglers and deserters, and to guard armories, they exercised no authority over civilians, but their functions were soon greatly extended. They traveled on trains, loitered around railway stations, occupied seats on stage lines, and took positions anywhere they could intercept travelers—to catch spies and traitors. Anyone not able to show a passport was liable to be taken in charge and held until his identity could be established. Great numbers of able-bodied men were thus employed.

An outcry against them soon arose because of their interference with the customary liberties of travel and their harassment of "the loyal people of the Confederacy." The requirement that all travelers must secure passports led to great inconvenience, for passport offices were open only at certain hours of the day. Often soldiers on furlough lost days in reaching home on account of missing trains while awaiting passports. People did not like to be shouted at every time they got on a train, "Show your passport," and hear it repeated when they got off. Some of these provost marshals became little tyrants, and their conduct led to great bitterness in the communities where they operated. A lady in La Grange, Georgia, wrote Davis a letter bitterly complaining of the cruel treatment inflicted on her husband by a provost guard: "It seems that instead of these disgraceful, lawless, unfeeling and impolite *men* not Confederate soldiers in the strict sense, being at the front where patriots and good soldiers are needed, they with their provost marshals are seemingly ten times healthier than you are my dear President. They are running around over town and country insulting even weak unprotected women, who most assuredly expect better treatment." It was a common complaint that the provost guards should be put into the army, where their services were so badly needed.[80]

So ubiquitous and efficient were the provost guards that they arrested even Congressmen who happened to be traveling without passports. Congressman David W. Lewis of Georgia became highly incensed that he could not make a trip "without obtaining a pass like a negro." [81] To remedy this situation, Congress enacted a law in 1864 requiring the Secretary of State to issue special passports to Congressmen "for the gaze of the ten thousand provost marshals who line all the highways and byways of the country," allowing them to travel throughout the Confederacy without more identification or questioning except in military and naval areas. These documents were described as being about a foot square. Many held the whole passport system a farce "as any villain" might easily get one or "any fool" forge one.[82]

Faultfinding became a habit with a great many people, whether with Davis, the generals in the field, Congress, the cabinet, or the fact that a war was going on. Before the struggle was six months old, James H. Hammond, an outstanding ante-bellum South Carolina leader, remarked, "I am worn out with this abominable & tedious war." [83] A Georgian bemoaned the fact that no great leader had appeared in this new revolution, that the old political cliques whose ideas had long been worn threadbare were in charge, that no great speeches or oratory had come forth to supplant New England elo-

[80] Mrs. J. Y. Marble, La Grange, Ga., to Davis, December 17, 1864 (in possession of the writer). See also, Athens *Southern Watchman*, January 13, 1864; Richmond *Daily Examiner*, April 7, June 1, 1863; Fremantle, *Three Months in the Southern States*, 134; *Southern Historical Society Papers*, XLVI (1928), 80, 103–104; XLVIII (1941), 138.

[81] *Southern Historical Society Papers*, XLVII (1930), 46, 47.

[82] Richmond *Daily Whig*, May 28, 1864. See also, Richmond *Daily Examiner*, December 15, 1863; January 1, May 6, 1864.

[83] Hammond, Redcliffe, S.C., to William Gilmore Simms, November, 1861, in Hammond Papers, XXX.

quence which the schoolboys must still go on reciting. A Virginian regretted that the new government had been put into the hands "of a set of partisans, who had been mere politicians by trade." [84] In answer to those who took pleasure in criticizing generals and campaigns, Benjamin H. Hill sarcastically remarked, "Wonderful campaigns were planned, armies vanquished, States humbled, cities destroyed, and the enemy forced to sue for peace, by generals who remained at home, and by statesmen who wrote much, thought little, and knew less." [85]

The part played by state organizations—unlike the patriotic services of the Northern states in behalf of the Union—often became more of a hindrance than a help to the Confederacy. Frequently the states of the Confederacy not only opposed the central government, but sometimes engaged in recriminations among themselves. Both North Carolina and South Carolina embargoed foodstuffs. Most people singled out Virginia as the pet of the Confederate government. There the capital had been taken and there most of the troops were stationed. In 1862 Yancey resented the fact that Virginia had twenty-nine generals and Alabama only four. Virginia's great, historic past made her stand out, and Virginians did not forget to remind all of their superior citizenry. But an irate Southerner reminded them, "Their claim to this bastard heraldry will appear supremely ridiculous, when it is recollected that their great-great grand mothers were the refuse girls of Britain, gathered up, shipped over here and sold, each, for one hundred and fifty pounds of leaf tobacco." [86]

Yet this supposed favoritism made Virginia the battlefield of the Confederacy from Manassas to Appomattox and led to consequent fearful devastations. Her sacrifices were great and her loyalty to the Confederacy was probably greatest. Neither of her governors, John Letcher and William ("Extra Billy") Smith, became a problem for Davis.

Of North Carolina's war governors, John W. Ellis, Henry T. Clarke, and Zebulon B. Vance, the last-named, serving from Sep-

[84] Richmond *Daily Examiner,* January 14, 1864.

[85] Hill, *Benjamin H. Hill,* 258. See also, Athens *Southern Watchman,* May 14, 1862.

[86] Athens *Southern Watchman,* February 8, 1865. See also, *Southern Historical Society Papers,* XLVI (1928), 60.

tember, 1862, to the end, was the state's great war leader, who rallied his people against the attempted disruptions of William W. Holden. In his excessive desires to see that his state was first served, he tended to lose sight of the paramount needs of the Confederacy. Yet, in his own way, he was as determined as Davis on securing independence for the Confederacy, and when in 1864 it appeared that Holden might win the governorship and make peace, Vance declared that if he could not prevent such a calamity, which would steep the name of his state "in infamy, and make her memory a reproach among the nations, it is my determination quietly to retire to the army and find a death which will enable my children to say that their father was not consenting to their degradation." [87]

South Carolina had three war governors, Francis W. Pickens, Milledge L. Bonham, and Andrew G. Magrath. No one became an outstanding leader either in good or bad works. On March 22, 1862, Pickens circularized all the Confederate governors on a proposal to hold a conference to discuss their common problems, especially the raising of troops. His inference was that there should be built up a great reservoir of soldiers, 100,000 at least, controlled by the governors and collected in one camp. This seemed to have been an attempt to take charge of important military strategy in the Confederacy—probably to decentralize the Virginia area.[88]

John Milton was Florida's war governor. The resources of his state were not great, either in soldiers or provisions—though after the fall of Vicksburg when Texas cattle could no longer be easily secured, Florida herds became of first importance. Milton was a good Confederate, conscientious and loyal to the general interests. In 1863 Davis highly complimented him: "It is gratifying to me to be able to say to you that in this time of our great trouble when so many are disposed to withhold from the Confederate Government the means of success, you should occupy the high standpoint of strengthening its hands by all the means in your power and of nobly disregarding all considerations except the common weal." [89]

Georgia was important both for weal and woe, and to both her

[87] Spencer, *Last Ninety Days of the War,* 125.

[88] A copy of this circular is in loose gubernatorial papers (Texas State Library). See also, Charleston *Daily Mercury,* February 26, 1862.

[89] Rowland (ed.), *Jefferson Davis, Constitutionalist,* VI, 39.

war governor, Brown, contributed. Bitterly hated or warmly defended by most of his contemporaries, to some he was an enigma, a puzzle which future generations have not wholly solved. Able, energetic, and ambitious, with the aid of Stephens and Toombs he ruled Georgia as an empire of his own, easily defeating all opponents in his two wartime elections. Taking cognizance of the special interests of his state and appealing to the common people through personal and governmental charities, he placed state rights and old-time personal liberties ahead of Confederate independence. Brown's conception of his position logically led him to attach great importance to a state army of which he would be ex-officio commander in chief: hence, his early and never-ending contest with the Confederacy over maintaining such an army, leading to the bitter quarrels over the appointment of officers, over conscription, and all the other controversial issues of the times. He himself was guilty of instituting for Georgia many of the policies which he stoutly condemned the Confederacy for using—for instance, impressment, conscription, and placing military power above the civil—but he never seemed abashed by these inconsistencies. And despite his unmeasured condemnation of Confederate practices and officials, he eventually organized Georgia for war efficiently and effectively. He early gained the reputation of having armed Georgia more completely than was the case in any other state.

Alabama entered the secession movement under Andrew B. Moore, but soon John G. Shorter organized the state for war. He desired to have the governors of all the Confederate states act in unison in support of the Confederate administration. He was succeeded in 1863 by Thomas W. Watts, who served for the remainder of the war. Alabama became less excited over the controversial issues of the war than did some of her sister states.

Mississippi under her two war governors, John J. Pettus and Charles Clark, behaved more like Georgia than her next-door neighbor Alabama, and over much the same issues as Georgia. Though Governor Thomas Moore chaperoned Louisiana into the Confederacy, it was Henry W. Allen who showed the rest of the Confederate governors how good a Confederate a state governor could be. With his capital in Shreveport, Allen governed that part of the state which was not occupied by Federals and controlled by a rival government, and made an excellent record, though with all his ability and good sense he could contribute little to the Confederacy east of the Mississippi. In the secession movement in Texas, Sam Houston was forced to vacate the governorship; Edward Clark held the position until the end of the year, when Frank R. Lubbock assumed the office. Lubbock was a good Confederate, and after he gave way in 1863 to Pendleton Murrah he became a member of Davis' staff and remained with him to the end. Before the fall of Vicksburg, Texas contributed much to the Confederacy; but thereafter Louisiana, Arkansas, and Texas became a sort of Little Confederacy, known as the Trans-Mississippi Department, continuing more than a month after Appomattox as a last hope of Davis. Arkansas and Tennessee suffered early invasion which upset their governments and led to rival enemy administrations. Thereafter neither was organized well enough to offer much aid or hindrance to Confederate success.

Davis realized the importance of using the states and their governors in carrying out Confederate policies, but he seems never to have realized the greater advantage in using them to help establish Confederate policy. If he could have made an advisory council or second cabinet of the governors (functioning by frequent confidential correspondence and occasional meetings), he might have prevented the blighting quarrels which sapped the Confederacy of its morale. Now and then he sent identical letters to the governors asking their aid in enforcing conscription, returning deserters, collecting provisions, rounding up slave labor for military use, and curbing extortion. One governors' conference, held in Augusta in October, 1864, but not at the instance of Davis, was likely designed for subversive purposes by some who attended. The conference planned by Governor Pickens in 1862 never met. Davis keenly felt the lack of support the states might have given. Complaining that his own troubles were sufficient, he wrote when the war was drawing to a close, "but these difficulties have been materially increased by the persistent interference by some of the State Authorities, Legislative, Executive, and Judicial, hindering the action of this Government, obstructing the execution of its laws, denouncing its necessary policy, impairing its hold upon the confidence of the people, and dealing with it rather as if it were the public enemy than the Government which they themselves had established for the common defense, and which was their only hope of safety from the untold horrors of Yankee despotism." [90]

State rights was the Southerner's deepest political passion. It had provoked secession; might it not have brought victory? If the Confederacy was to win at all it could not be through greater military resources; it must be through superior morale. Whatever destroyed this morale would make victory impossible, irrespective of how logical it was to place power in the central government. If the Confederate administration had recognized the rights of the states by taking the governors into its counsel, the states might have been satisfied with such theoretical recognition, and have more willingly allowed in practice Confederate direction of affairs. The editor of the Richmond *Examiner* simplified the whole purpose of the war in these few words: "The principle now in contest between North and South is simply that of State sovereignty"; [91] and another Virginian declared that there were now "no 'people of the South,'" but only "States of the South." [92] Calhoun had long ago implanted in the Southern mind the doctrine that there was no consolidated people of the United States. How could there now be a consolidated Confederate people? It mattered not that this time-honored defensive weapon of state rights might no longer be needed, now that all Southerners were embraced in a government of their own; the scars it had made were too deep to be brushed away even by irrefutable logic. According to a modern scholar, "Mistaking the means for the end and being unable to see that because of homogeneity of population and similarity of climate and occupation no reason existed for their use in the Confederacy, [Southerners] transformed a weapon into an abstract principle and themselves into doctrinaires." [93] But what more could be expected from a people who named their streets and towns and children "State Rights" and of whom it could be said with much truth that there was a "not inconsiderable class of men in the South who would draw the sword at the behest of their States as readily against the government of Jeffer-

90 Davis to S. J. Person, December 15, 1864, *ibid.*, 421.
91 Richmond *Daily Examiner*, September 11, 1862.
92 Athens *Southern Watchman*, July 20, 1864.
93 Hill, *Joseph E. Brown*, 257.

son Davis as against that of Abraham Lincoln"? [94] There were too few who agreed with Mrs. Davis when she said at the end of the war, "I am disheartened with popular sovereignty, still more with State sovereignty, and fear both are fallacies." [95]

Not only had state rights seized the minds of the people but what this dogma was supposed to secure and protect, "our liberties," was deified. A strange fatuity seized Stephens, Brown, Toombs, and many others. Some of them, if not all, argued themselves into an impractical, unreal world. They placed their accustomed peacetime rights ahead of all else or at least equal to any other thing. They were fighting for their rights, forgetting that independence must come before those rights could be permanently established. A Georgia Congressman exclaimed, "Why, sir, this is a war for the *constitution,* it is a *constitutional war.*" [96] Stephens argued that "we quit the Union, but we rescued the constitution." "Away with the idea of getting independence first, and looking after liberty afterwards. Our liberties once lost, may be lost forever," he warned.[97] Even Governor Milton could say, "Infractions of the Constitution during the war are more dangerous than in peace." [98] Brown declared that even "the Lincoln government, despotic as it [was, had] not dared to attempt any such encroachment upon the liberties of the people of the United States" as the Confederacy was suffering; and as proof that independence and liberty did not necessarily go together, he cited the Turks and Russians as being independent but without liberty.[99] Constitutionalists professed to believe that

[94] Prince de Joinville, *The Army of the Potomac* . . . (New York, 1862), 111.

[95] Gamaliel Bradford, *Wives* (New York, 1925), 192. "I have the honor to request that you will inform me so soon as my obligations to the Federal Government may conflict with the natural allegiance I owe to Virginia." Dabney H. Maury, Santa Fe, N. Mex., to Adjutant General Richardson, January 21, 1861, in Executive Papers (Virginia State Archives). The following, signed "T. Southron," is a fanciful sentimental play on state rights, from the Richmond *Whig,* quoted in the Atlanta *Southern Confederacy,* September 14, 1862: "$100,000 Reward. Lost, Strayed or Stolen, My Valuable Horse 'State Rights.' " He had been raised by Thomas Jefferson, tended and groomed by John Randolph of Roanoke and more recently cared for in some of the Gulf States. He may have made his way to Joe Brown of Milledgeville, Georgia "by whom he was always kindly and humanely treated."

[96] Joseph E. Echols, in Athens *Southern Watchman,* February 8, 1865.

[97] Cleveland, *Alexander H. Stephens,* 760.

[98] *Official Records,* Ser. IV, Vol. II, 488.

[99] Augusta *Daily Chronicle & Sentinel,* November 30, 1864.

liberties suspended during the war would not be restored at the end —forgetting that the great danger to their liberties had come from being tied to a government run by the North and that if the South got its independence the same common interests that brought on secession would bring whatever liberties they pleased to have. Former governor David L. Swain of North Carolina said in 1864 that terror had seized the people, that they spoke "sparingly, cautiously, warily"; [100] and a Virginian said that when the rights of states ended in consolidation, "it would be a kind boon in an overruling Providence to sweep from the earth the soil, along with the people. Better to be a wilderness of waste, than a lasting monument of lost liberty." [101]

The many attacks against Davis and the Confederacy did not go unanswered. There were always defenders in Congress, in the press, in the army, and in private life. Outstanding were Benjamin H. Hill and Lucius Q. C. Lamar. Meetings in support of Davis were held in some places and even a few Northern papers had a kind word for him, as did the New York *World* when it remarked, "The Richmond papers abuse Jeff. Davis without stint, and declare that he is the occasion of all their woes. All this is very shabby, for Davis has done wonders in a bad cause." [102] The New York *Times* believed that no one else in the Confederacy could have done half as well as Davis in continuing the struggle with such limited resources. And, of course, some of the Southern press could be even much more cordial as was the *Eastern Clarion*, a Mississippi paper, when it said, "Jeff. Davis is the special gift of Providence to this people struggling for safety and life, for independence and liberty." [103] Davis himself was not averse to self-defense. He wrote an Alabama judge in 1862 in answer to the charge that the President had scarcely a friend left and no defender in Congress, "I must hope it is falsely so said, as otherwise our fate must be confided to a multitude of hypocrites." He also informed the judge that he had no political ambitions: "If we can achieve our independence, the office seekers are welcome to the one I hold, and for which possession has

100 David L. Swain, Chapel Hill, N.C., to Vance, September 28, 1864, in Vance Papers (North Carolina State Archives).
101 John H. Gilmer, in Athens *Southern Watchman*, July 20, 1864.
102 New York *World*, December 27, 1864.
103 Paulding (Miss.) *Eastern Clarion*, November 1, 1861.

brought no additional value to me than that set upon it when before going to Montgomery I announced my preference for the commission of a General in the army." [104] Later Davis confided to Lee that "there has been nothing which I have found to require a greater effort of patience than to bear the criticisms of the ignorant, who pronounce everything a failure which does not equal their expectations or desires, and can see no good result which is not in the line of their own imaginings." [105]

Many asked what all those people attacking the President meant by it and what their ultimate purpose was. Did they expect to drive Davis from office and start a revolution within a revolution? An Alabama editor remarked that "To force our President to resign, would be virtually the giving up of our Republic to anarchy and destruction." [106] In an address to Congress, Davis warned that he who sowed "the seeds of discontent and distrust [prepared] for the harvest of slaughter and defeat." [107] But, nevertheless, the seeds of discontent were sown in plentiful supply, and the harvest was defeat and Reconstruction.

[104] Davis to Brooks, March 13, 1862, in Rowland (ed.), *Jefferson Davis, Constitutionalist*, V, 218–19.

[105] Davis to Lee, August 11, 1863, in *Official Records*, Ser. I, Vol. XXIX, Pt. II, 639. See also, Cate, *Lucius Q. C. Lamar*, 108 ff.; *Speech of Hon. L. Q. C. Lamar, of Miss., on the State of the Country. Delivered in the Atheneum, Atlanta, Ga., Thursday Evening, April 14, 1864* (Atlanta, 1864), 30 pp.; Richmond *Semi-Weekly Enquirer*, April 11, 1862; Athens *Southern Watchman*, September 9, 1863.

[106] Selma *Daily Reporter*, August 14, 1863.

[107] Richardson (comp.), *Messages and Papers of the Confederacy*, I, 336–37.

CHAPTER XVIII

PROGRESS AND DECAY—WOMEN, HOSPITALS, AND RELIEF

THE war was too much with the people, but they were help-less. What it did not consume it changed, hard though they tried to live their lives as usual. True enough, they continued to love and hate, to be born and to die, but the first they did more intensely and the latter, more speedily. This war, like all wars, hurried up marriages, and in 1862 a Richmond editor, after recording the fact that marriages in his city had increased 90 per cent over peacetime, remarked that the people were "evidently pre-paring for a long war, and taking wise precautions against any serious decrease of population." [1] They still popped their firecrack-ers at Christmas time and served their eggnog and apple toddy. On Christmas of 1863 a special occasion was made of the day in Rich-mond as "Honest John" Letcher turned over the Virginia gover-norship to "Extra Billy" Smith amidst the scenes of a great apple toddy party, accompanied by oratory and music and attended by high state and Confederate officials. And though the red curtain of war had fallen, separating the Confederacy from the rest of the world, the children were told that Santa Claus, like the true Con-federate that he was, "had slipped across the ice-bound blockade of the Potomac" with his reindeer team or had "run the gauntlet of the Wilmington blockaders in his gossamer ship." [2]

Other days were celebrated, such as the Fourth of July and Hal-loween. The celebration of Washington's Birthday was reinforced by the fact that the Permanent Government had been inaugurated that day; but sending Valentine greetings was largely abandoned

---

[1] Richmond *Daily Whig*, October 10, 1862.

[2] Richmond *Daily Examiner*, December 21, 1864. See also, Richmond *Daily Whig*, December 24, 1862; December 30, 1863; [McGuire], *Diary of a Southern Refugee*, 329.

because the times were "too stern, the mails too uncertain, and gilt-edged, flowered and embossed stationery, too expensive in these blockade days, to admit of such indulgencies." [3]

Social activities were continued out of the exuberance of youth as well as purposely to maintain and build up morale. Towns and community centers organized musicales, minstrels, *tableaux vivants*, and plays, generally to raise money for relief; and private parties, enlivened sometimes by nothing more than a three-stringed fiddle, danced "the double-shuffle," "the Virginia reel, and the Virginia back-step," "the Georgia turn-down," "chicken-in-the-bread-tray-peck-peck-peck," and cut "the pigeon-wing." In the larger cities society took on a more refined tone, and in Richmond it reached its zenith. Here the Confederacy centered, not only governmentally and militarily, but also socially. Statesmen and military officers added a special brilliance to the society of the capital; Lee might appear at some party and claim the right to kiss a pretty girl or two; Benjamin was often present displaying his enticing conversational ability and his love for wine and cigars; companionable Benjamin H. Hill, chivalrous Yancey, and even occasionally Stephens attended social gatherings; and, of course, other Congressmen, cabinet members, and military officers and their wives were there. The President and his wife were too busy with their own official receptions to venture widely into Richmond society. There were charades, music, dancing, and conversation. Since during those bleak times toward the end of the war all refreshments were omitted, these gatherings were called "starvation parties." As times became more serious, the easy informality of unannounced calls in Richmond homes was abandoned for certain set times for receptions—to save the expense of having the house always heated and prepared for visitors. Some old Richmonders opposed this new departure as too cold and formal and, in addition, as being a Yankee invention.[4] Excursion parties on the James down to Drewry's Bluff were

---

[3] Richmond *Daily Examiner*, February 14, 1863.

[4] George Barnsley, Richmond, Va., to Julia Barnsley, November 10, 1863; January 24, 1864, in Barnsley Papers (University of Georgia Library); Richmond *Daily Examiner*, September 19, 1862; May 30, 1863; Richmond *Semi-Weekly Enquirer*, February 16, 1864; Richmond *Daily Enquirer*, July 15, 1864; [McGuire], *Diary of a Southern Refugee*, 328; Edward M. Alfriend, "Social Life in Richmond during the War," in *Cosmopolitan* (New York), XII (1891), 229–33.

frequent, with music and dancing on deck; occasionally social groups visited the old battlefields to see the results of war and to bring back relics; and groups often went to Ashland to enjoy good food, dancing, and a breath of the country. Now and then army units staged tournaments, especially for the entertainment of the ladies.

War played havoc with women's styles. The blockade served one useful purpose, many men thought, in making it difficult for women to secure hoop skirts, those Yankee-made contraptions which encircled "their forms like the rings of Saturn." [5] But skirts with long trains were still worn, and it was "quite common to see an ornament of several inches of dirt, ashes, cigar stumps, and tobacco quids, dragging their slow lengths along as the ladies gracefully(?)" promenaded the streets.[6] Most women were forced to content themselves with their old fineries or improvise their new clothing from Confederate resources; and those who might be able to secure Paris styles soon found that they were too conspicuous to feel comfortable. A Confederate soldier wrote home from Richmond that he had been studying "the arrangement of the ladies dresses." "The more I try to clear up all the mass of flounces etc the more I become confused," he said. "Some ladies seem to have left off wearing hoops and present an old fashioned look. The dresses are hung all round with flounces in some cases; in others there are two or three at the skirt usually a different color from the main body of the dress." As for the bonnets, they looked "exactly like coal scuttles filled with flowers, quills and fixings generally." At first he thought the bonnets were "hideous." It was hard to get accustomed to "the slim lamp-post appearances of the fashionable dresses," but he later came to like them, particularly those "trimmed with narrow borders of white," and even the "coal scuttle mantilla shaped bonnets" came to look very well.[7] A movement was started against the wearing of black mourning by women; why could not a bit of black crepe worn on the sleeve be enough?

Men's styles were not affected by the war nor were many of their

[5] Richmond *Daily Whig*, August 19, 1863.

[6] *Southern Cultivator*, XXII (1864), 71.

[7] George Barnsley, Lynchburg, Va., to Julia Barnsley, May 8, September 29, November 12, 1862, in Barnsley Papers (University of Georgia Library). See also, Athens *Southern Watchman*, August 20, 1862; Pollard, *Jefferson Davis*, 233.

pastimes and sports. An English visitor observed that everyone seemed to be chewing tobacco. "Why won't the Southerners be content to blow the cloud without spitting the offensive juice?" he asked.[8] Yet there were some new developments in the use of tobacco, for after the first year of the war fewer smoked cigars, now scarce and expensive, and many more took to the pipe. By 1864 nearly all smokers used pipes and carried little red cambric bags of tobacco. Gentlemen still fought duels, for fighting the Yankees did not settle private affairs. Duels were fought in civilian life as well as in the army. In 1861 a duel was fought on the Richmond race track and one of the participants was killed. A baffling duel was an encounter with pistols near Richmond in 1864 between Edward C. Elmore of the Confederate Treasury Department and either H. Rives Pollard or John M. Daniel, both newspaper editors. A witness was jailed for refusing to testify as to who fought or where. After the war, Pollard, who was a brother of Edward A., was assassinated on the streets of Richmond. Hunting continued as a sport as well as a gainful venture, but so many occasional hunters were in the army that unmolested small game greatly increased. Those who found time to hunt were likely to be as successful as sixteen gentlemen in Albemarle County, Virginia, who in November, 1863, brought back thirty-two deer, three wild turkeys, twenty-two pheasants, a fox, a coon, a wildcat, and two rattlesnakes. Horse racing continued as a sport until cavalry service made steeds scarce. Prize fights were held infrequently. One that took place near New Orleans indicated the nature of the sport: Edward Burnett fought James Fitzgerald through 252 rounds, requiring more than three hours—"one of the most obstinate, desperate and prolonged fistic encounters on record." [9]

War breeds both heroism and decadence. Gambling, drunkenness, thieving, demagogism, faultfinding, carping criticism, and general moral disintegration suggest the darker side. A Georgian described his neighborhood in late 1862: "The character of the population here was never very good, but it is growing worse—

[8] Malet, *Errand to the South,* 285.

[9] Richmond *Daily Examiner,* January 6, 1862. See also, Charleston *Daily Courier,* December 10, 1864; Richmond *Semi-Weekly Enquirer,* December 10, 1861; October 21, 1862; Richmond *Daily Examiner,* August 18, 29, 1864; Richmond *Daily Whig,* December 9, 1861; December 16, 1862; November 2, 14, 1863; January 15, 1864.

lying and cheating seem to be the rule—and latterly thieving—they are stealing all my chattels they can lay their hands upon in no small way." [10] After Sherman passed through and burned much of Atlanta, an estimated 1,500 people came in their wagons as far as 100 miles to haul away whatever they could load. Some classes of people, especially clerks in stores and other tradespeople, forgot customary politeness. An observer ruefully remarked of Richmond clerks: "There is no rushing forward of two or three assistants, all anxious to serve you. No pleasant, bland, 'what will you have, sir?' No, sir. The shopkeeper hardly turns upon his heel at your entrance. You ask the price of an article, and he names it, with a tone that says, as plain as words, 'you can buy or not, just as you please; rather you wouldn't; it will fetch a higher figure tomorrow." [11]

The pestilences of the times showed themselves most vividly in the cities. Out of the 102 cities of 10,000 population or more in the United States in 1860, only ten were in the states later to compose the Confederacy, with North Carolina, Florida, Mississippi, Arkansas, and Texas having none. Augusta was the smallest of this class, having 12,493, and New Orleans with her 168,675 was the largest, being more than four times as populous as any other Southern city. Charleston and Richmond were almost the same size, having 40,522 and 37,910, respectively. Of course, there were many small towns, but even so the Confederacy was overwhelmingly rural. The villainies as well as the good works were naturally more apparent in the cities. Practically all were unpaved; at least two, New Orleans and Richmond, had horse-drawn streetcars, but in 1863 the Confederate Government took both the horses and the rails of the latter for war use, and the previous year the former city had been captured. Fires were frequent. A disastrous conflagration visited Charleston in December, 1861; three years later all of Wilmington west of the Cape Fear River burned; and Richmond had a siege of fires throughout the war. Gambling dens and saloons were breeding places for crime. In an Atlanta dive at least $20,000 might change hands in one night. Stores were broken into and

10 Barnsley, Woodlands, Ga., to T. C. Gilmour, December 31, 1862, in Barnsley Papers (University of Georgia Library).
11 Richmond *Daily Examiner,* December 16, 1862.

pedestrians waylaid and robbed. Thieves carried away carpets and other furnishings from the Baptist church in Charleston. The spirit and necessities of the times led people to towns and cities, jamming practically every facility and leading easily to crime. Most hotels at best were bad, and now they became frightfully overcrowded. Guests were packed two to a bed and a half dozen or more were put in a room. One guest who slept with his clothes and boots on remarked that "they were a d——d sight cleaner than the bed." [12]

Every characteristic of Southern cities, good or bad, was exaggerated in Richmond. Being the governmental and military center of the Confederacy, it soon became deluged with people of every character and from every direction: petty politicians, statesmen, soldiers, military officers, anxious visitors looking for sick soldiers or seeking their bodies to be returned to their homes, government workers, blockade-runners, deserters, spies, traitors, gamblers, vice peddlers, extortioners, thieves, lewd women, "plug-uglies," "dead-rabbits," "shoulder-hitters," "and a hundred other classes of villains for whom the hangman had sighed for many a long year." [13] The cultured Richmond of the past no longer existed; its population's outward appearance had been assaulted and captured by strangers. A new city had been erected "after the model of Sodom and New York and Washington." [14] Old inhabitants retired behind closed doors in shame. According to Pollard, it grew into a city of 140,000 people, "the most corrupt and licentious city south of the Potomac." [15] To supplement the city government's efforts to preserve law and order, the Confederate Government erected the city

[12] Fremantle, *Three Months in the Southern States*, 78. See also, Athens *Southern Watchman*, December 18, 1861; Atlanta *Southern Confederacy*, August 3, 1862; Augusta *Daily Chronicle & Sentinel*, May 3, 1864; Charleston *Daily Courier*, January 3, April 28, 1864; Macon *Daily Telegraph*, April 14, 1862; New Orleans *Daily Picayune*, May 9, 1861; Richmond *Daily Examiner*, July 5, 1861; June 3, 1863; Richmond *Daily Whig*, July 15, 1863.

[13] *Two Months in the Confederate States*, 153.

[14] Charleston *Daily Courier*, April 2, 1864.

[15] Pollard, *Jefferson Davis*, 132. A Richmond editor moaned the decline of Richmond: "With the Confederate Government came the rag, tag and bobtail which ever pursue political establishments. The pure society of Richmond became woefully adulterated. Its peace was destroyed, its good name was defiled: it became a den of thieves, extortioners, substitutes, deserters, blacklegs and cyprians. The glory and the shame of a great city was [sic] its heritage." Richmond *Daily Whig*, April 30, 1863.

and environs into a military district and placed it under the rule of General John H. Winder of Baltimore. He brought in a sort of secret police who came to be berated and hated almost as much as the criminals they sought to apprehend.

In a city suddenly grown to three times its normal size of population, housing conditions became almost unbearable. Rooms in its principal hotels, the Spotswood House, American, and Ballard House, were crowded with strangers, some of whom upon awakening found themselves robbed and their roommates gone. Conditions in the smaller hotels and boardinghouses were worse. Hotel rates mounted until Congressmen clamored for removal of the capital to a less expensive city. When Congress convened in November, 1864, rates advanced to $40 a day, which seemed outrageous to many guests even though Confederacy currency had been steadily declining, for by this time the European plan had been adopted by some of the Richmond hotels.[16]

Robberies, thefts, and other petty and serious crimes were the order of the day and the happening by night. Vandals broke into the hall of the House of Representatives, smashed the clock, and removed various furnishings; a thief took one of Davis' highly prized horses, and his coachman stole himself by running away to the North, where he became a lionized hero; and even the recorder's courtroom was broken into one day between sessions. "This robbery, in broad daylight, and under the very nose of justice, as it were," remarked a Richmond editor, "surpasses in audacity any performance lately recorded." [17] Jones, the war-clerk diarist, stayed at home on Sundays to prevent robbery while his family was at church. During the ten months preceding February, 1864, there were 11,494 arrests for crime, 1,784 of them for felonies. Gambling houses were raided, saloons closed, and cockfighting stopped. One attendant at a cockfight remarked, "We trust the season will never return. Bull fighting is more manly than cock fighting." [18] After raiding a gambling den and making arrests,

---

16 Richmond *Daily Examiner*, November 9, 1864; Richmond *Daily Whig*, December 30, 1863; April 5, 1864; Richmond *Whig and Public Advertiser*, November 8, 1861.

17 Richmond *Daily Whig*, November 1, 1862.

18 Richmond *Daily Examiner*, December 31, 1864. See also, Jones, *Rebel War Clerk's Diary*, I, 285; II, 120; Augusta *Weekly Constitutionalist*, June 18, 1862; Rich-

police gathered up elaborately finished faro tables, ivory chips, playing cards, "shove-it-up-the-spout" machines, and other equipment and made a bonfire of all in front of the City Hall on Broad Street.

Time and again fires broke out, many of them supposedly of incendiary origin. Among the buildings and businesses wholly or partly consumed were the Tredegar Iron Works, the Crenshaw Mills, Congress Hall (a restaurant), the Government Bakery, the Shot and Shell Works, and warehouses near the Petersburg depot. An effort was made to fire the Presidential Mansion.

Other peeps into Richmond happenings show that the city was not its usual self. The slave population lived its life more boldly, constantly engaging in petty crimes, unrestrained by their masters or hirers, and none too well controlled by the police and recorder's court. Negro teamsters were reckless and noisy as they made their steeds "whirl through the streets at a rapid rate, and produce by their empty wagons a din equal to the noise of a hundred triphammers." [19] A live tadpole was drawn from the city hydrant by a servant in filling her pail, and a farmer brought a live cat to the city market, a fact which was declared to be unique in Richmond's history, though previously cats might often "have been sold here dead, under the spacious guise of sausage." [20] The large supply of wild game at the markets, such as deer, wild turkey, ducks, and partridges took the place of the conventional fowls and meats of better days. Richmond's illuminating gas came to be "as odiferous as a 'skunk' in early spring." [21] According to the *Daily Examiner*, "Never to our knowledge, was swearing more universal, or more persistently followed." [22] Yet to offset some of these more horrid innovations, there was this small compensation among others, that Capitol Square had come to be the scene of many band concerts and maneuvers by military units.

---

mond *Daily Examiner*, August 25, 1862; April 2, 1863; February 6, 1864; Richmond *Daily Whig*, November 11, December 28, 1861.

[19] Richmond *Daily Whig*, December 9, 1861.

[20] *Ibid.*, April 5, 1864.

[21] Richmond *Daily Examiner*, December 19, 1863.

[22] *Ibid.*, May 21, 1863. See also, Jones, *Rebel War Clerk's Diary*, II, 135; Richmond *Daily Examiner*, February 17, 1863; August 24, September 8, 1864; Richmond *Daily Whig*, May 25, September 18, 1863; January 22, March 21, 25, 1864.

Richmond was transformed both for good and bad because of the constant visits of officers and enlisted men on leave or passing through the city. Sometimes dozens of generals in addition to many officers of lesser rank were present at one time, and Richmond became the destination for short visits, partaking of a triumphal entry, of Confederate heroes such as John Morgan and even William Clarke Quantrill, Missouri guerrilla, "a mild and modest looking man of thirty," who boasted that he had killed with his own hand eighty-five people. It was also the scene of state funerals of heroes who had passed on, as Stonewall Jackson and O. Jennings Wise. But there was a common feeling that too many officers spent too much time enjoying Richmond,

> Standing on the corner,
>   Decked in braid and lace,
> Scarcely room to pass them,
>   Staring in your face;
> Staring at the ladies,
>   Decked in lace and braid,
> Braid-courageous soldiers,
>   They are not afraid.[23]

To entertain them and all other comers, there were many cafes, some of outstanding excellence, and drinking saloons not to be numbered even by the city authorities who tried to make them pay a license fee—some evading it by claiming to be confectionary stores, keeping in the front "a few pounds of fly-specked mint-stick, a dozen or so indigestible horse-cakes, and a considerable show of superannuated peanuts." [24] They bore such names as Manassas Hall, Chickahominy Saloon and Cafe, Brandy Station, Bragg Saloon, and Congress Hall, monopolizing "the most rapidly lucrative business carried on in Richmond." [25] On Christmas Day of 1863, having taken in "more money than they wanted," they closed in the evening, leaving the drunken men to go to bed and the merry ones to brawl "through the streets until midnight came

---

[23] Richmond *Daily Whig*, November 20, 1863. See also, Richmond *Daily Examiner*, March 14, 1863; Jones, *Rebel War Clerk's Diary*, II, 170–71.

[24] Richmond *Daily Examiner*, July 11, 1861.

[25] *Ibid.*, November 16, 1863.

down, and threw her mantle of silence over the exhausted city." [26]
The most famous of these cafe-saloons, until it burned, was Congress
Hall, made so largely by its slave *chef de cuisine,* the celebrated Jim
Cook, "the immortal, magnificent, prince-royal, high, grand, and
mighty potentate of juleps and monarch of turtle soup and turtle
steaks." [27] The mint juleps pleased General Morgan and other con-
noisseurs, and his fine foods and exotic viands delighted the highest
statesmen of the Confederacy.

The hope of every soldier was to visit Richmond as often as
possible, there to get drunk, attend the theater, or enjoy his furlough as his mother back home would have him do. Soldiers drank
and fought one another and others on the streets, broke open
saloons on Sundays, visited the markets and slashed watermelons
with bowie knives or tossed them into the air and caught them on
their bayonets. In order to win a bet, a soldier smashed a thick
plate glass window in the American Hotel with his fist; and now
and then, thinking of nothing better to do, one would march
down Broad Street furiously playing on a kettledrum but attracting no attention. They sometimes carried on their bayonets loaves
of bread or flower wreaths which admiring women gave them. Frequently drunken soldiers were arrested and placed in jail or handed
over to General Winder. Two drunken Georgia soldiers were arrested and brought before the recorder for shooting two Italian
shopkeepers. One declared that he did not know and did not care
anything about it, that he felt "confident he would not, no matter
how drunk, assault any man without sufficient provocation. And
as for the matter of dying, if he [were] hung in Richmond he
[would] not live to be killed at Fredericksburg." [28] At times there
was a whisky shortage, and it was facetiously asserted that men were
"cutting off their mustachios to keep from losing a tenth part of
every drink by capillary attraction." [29] Finally in 1864 it was made

26 *Ibid.,* December 26, 1863.

27 Richmond *Daily Whig,* June 25, 1863. See also, Richmond *Daily Examiner,*
April 18, 1863; January 15, 1864; Richmond *Daily Whig,* June 11, August 13, 1863.

28 Richmond *Daily Examiner,* March 20, 1863.

29 Charleston *Daily Mercury,* April 24, 1862. See also, Jones, *Rebel War Clerk's
Diary,* I, 276; Pollard, *Jefferson Davis,* 133; Richmond *Daily Whig,* July 13, August
2, 6, 1861; May 23, 1864.

illegal to sell liquor by the drink, but half-pint bottles made their appearance and people continued to get drunk.

Soldiers whether drunk or sober liked to go to the theaters, where they frequently engaged in boisterousness or were overcome by pathos. At the Varieties Theatre, on one occasion a beautiful woman was singing a song in which the line "Who'll have me" was repeated a few times. A prankish soldier shouted, "I'll take you," and thereby produced such hilarity that the song could not be continued.[30] At the same theater Mlle Boisvert sang "Home Sweet Home" so touchingly that she brought tears and sobs to a Mississippi soldier, who offered her five dollars to repeat it, and when she did, adding the "Marseillaise," the soldier shouted, "I was a child just now, but now I am a man—hurrah for Jeff Davis and the Southern Confederacy!"[31] To administer to the wants of the more serious and reflective soldiers Richmond, as well as other cities of the Confederacy, supplied them with writing paper, and set up reading rooms which kept on file a wide variety of newspapers and magazines.

The war made soldiers out of the men and thereby it affected little less the lives of the women. The restricted confines of the home over which Southern women had traditionally presided heretofore were now extended to include the whole Confederacy and to lead them into almost every activity which could aid in winning the war. Their services were so useful and their support so powerful that all people, friends and enemies alike, soon came to recognize this fact. The newspapers recounted women's deeds, Congress and state legislatures passed resolutions of thanks and praise, and in 1863 H. W. R. Jackson wrote a book entitled *The Southern Women of the Second American Revolution*. A Southerner wrote in 1861 that never "in any age or country, was there ever witnessed such an intense war spirit as that now prevailing among the women of the Confederate States";[32] and a Federal

[30] Richmond *Daily Examiner*, June 1, 1863.

[31] Natchez *Weekly Courier*, March 26, 1862. See also, Augusta *Weekly Chronicle & Sentinel*, June 22, 1864; Mobile *Advertiser and Register*, November 8, 1863; Richmond *Daily Examiner*, September 19, 1861; May 15, July 1, 1863; Richmond *Daily Whig*, July 3, October 23, 1861.

[32] *Southern Literary Messenger*, XXXIII (1861), 316.

soldier expressed his conviction in 1864 "that the South stands today quite as much indebted for a successful prolongation of this struggle to her women, as to her generals and soldiers in the field," and added, "Fully, fiercely, terribly, malignantly, have they entered into this conflict." [33] "It is the part that woman is acting in this great cause that fires the heart and nerves the arm of our soldiery," declared a Confederate captain.[34] It was, indeed, a strenuous life Southern women led, and Mrs. Chesnut with some exaggeration declared, "Grief and constant anxiety kill nearly as many women at home as men are killed on the battle-field." [35]

Early in the war they began making flags and presenting them in special ceremonies to military units; they shamed laggards into volunteering by offering themselves as soldiers in mock seriousness; they did men's work to release those fit to be soldiers; girls refused to marry civilians, following the advice of one who counseled sulking and pouting until their sweethearts fell into line; they made Confederate flags into aprons and wore Confederate badges; they decorated Confederate graves as early as 1862; they even carried out the rites of burial services for at least one Confederate soldier, William Latané, which inspired the famous painting depicting this pathetic scene. They entertained Confederate soldiers by playing pianos for them, and in invaded regions they played "Dixie" when Federal soldiers asked for music or refused to play anything at all. One irate girl hacked the piano to pieces rather than let a Federal soldier perform. In the Spotswood House in Richmond a woman, vigorous and enthusiastic in her patriotism and wearing "Turkish pantaloons," played on the piano and sang war songs and was followed about by admiring soldiers and urchins.[36]

To promote their efforts more effectively, women early organized

33 Alexander M. Stewart, *Camp, March and Battle-Field; or, Three Years and a Half with the Army of the Potomac* (Philadelphia, 1865), 403.

34 Macon *Daily Telegraph*, February 3, 1862.

35 Martin and Avary (eds.), *Diary from Dixie*, 178. See also, Matthews (ed.), *Public Laws of the Confederate States*, 1 Cong., 1 Sess., 1862, p. 54; Augusta *Daily Chronicle & Sentinel*, February 14, 1863.

36 Martin and Avary (eds.), *Diary from Dixie*, 82–83; Francis B. Simkins and James W. Patton, *The Women of the Confederacy* (Richmond, 1936), 37; Jones, *Rebel War Clerk's Diary*, I, 33; "Major [James Austin] Connolly's Diary," in *Transactions of the Illinois State Historical Society for the Year 1928*, p. 402; Richmond *Daily Whig*, March 27, July 26, 1862; Selma *Daily Reporter*, November 30, 1861.

themselves into clubs and societies, especially to provide soldiers with warm clothing and other home supplies. As early as July, 1861, Ladies' Aid Associations were in operation in Greenville, South Carolina, and in Montgomery; soon groups were organized throughout the Confederacy bearing such names as Ladies' Knitting Clubs, Soldiers' Aid Societies, Humane Societies, and Clothing Societies. Typical was the work of the Society of Centre Ridge, Alabama, which in November, 1862, forwarded 422 shirts, 551 pairs of drawers, 80 pairs of socks, 3 pairs of gloves, 6 boxes and a bale of hospital stores, 128 pounds of tapioca, and $18 for hospital use. During the first year of the war the women practically took over the work of clothing the Confederate armies, and as a contemporary put it, "Heaven only knows what the soldiers of the South would have done without the exertions of the women in their behalf." [37] To provide special services for soldiers going back and forth to the armies, there grew up in many parts of the Confederacy, Wayside Inns, oases in the deserts traveled by forlorn and needy soldiers. Soldiers were given beds, food, hospital services, and entertainment in buildings taken over for the purpose. The Wayside Inn at Millen, Georgia, assisted over 3,000 soldiers in one month of 1864. These institutions were credited with accomplishing more than conscription officers in maintaining morale and leading soldiers to return to the army. The aged Joseph Henry Lumpkin in 1862 paid this tribute to the women engaged in this work: "One of the regrets of my declining years is, that in the course of nature so short a time remains to me to love and honor these legitimate successors of the Apostolic women—the Mary's and Martha's of the New Testament. Their charities shall be remembered as a sweet memorial of them to the end of time." [38]

Nothing seemed too difficult or ambitious for women to attempt. The gunboat soon captured the popular imagination as a weapon so important that it might well win the war for either side. The Federals made effective use of it in their campaigns, especially in

37 [Hopley], Life in the South, I, 413.

38 Athens Southern Watchman, November 5, 1862. See also, Simkins and Patton, Women of the Confederacy, 95; James W. Patton (ed.), Minutes of the Proceedings of the Greenville Ladies' Association in Aid of the Volunteers of the Confederate Army (Durham, 1937), passim; Augusta Daily Constitutionalist, July 15, 1864; Montgomery Daily Post, July 23, 1861; Selma Daily Reporter, November 20, 1862.

the West, and the Confederates demonstrated its vast possibilities when it became an ironclad like the *Virginia (Merrimac)*. In early 1862 a wave of enthusiasm for building gunboats and presenting them to the Confederacy swept over the women of the South. In state after state they set out to raise money to build at least one gunboat. Subscriptions were started through the newspapers; fairs, bazaars, raffles, and concerts were held; collections were taken at prayer meetings and Sunday schools; no respectable and legitimate way for raising money was neglected. Day after day the newspapers published lists of contributions: five cents from a little girl; forty cents from "2 little Negroes"; $5.00 from a Selma, Alabama, girl who had a seventeen-year-old brother in the army, determined to win or emigrate to South America; and larger amounts from adults. People who did not give money sent objects to be sold at bazaars or raffled off: jewelry, china sets, silverware, watches, vases, Audubon's *Quadrupeds of America* in two volumes bound in red morocco, almost anything in the household which could be spared. At Charleston a doll labeled "Daughter of the Confederacy" was sold. A patriotic family in Rome, Georgia, agreed to give enough money to buy a cannon for the Georgia gunboat.[39]

Out of all this effort and enthusiasm came tangible results. The Georgia ladies decided to change their plans for a gunboat and instead construct a floating battery with propellers. This craft was built at Savannah, finished by midsummer of 1862, and christened the *Georgia*. Instead of following the original plan of painting on its ten cannon the names of the ladies most instrumental in its consummation, it was decided to honor the ten towns which had raised the most money. The South Carolina women had a gunboat constructed which they named the *Palmetto*, though *Nemesis*,

[39] For the gunboat movement, see Charleston *Daily Courier*, March 3, 4, April 18, May 7, 1862; Charleston *Daily Mercury*, March 12, 26, 1862; Macon *Daily Telegraph*, March 24, 31, April 7, 10, 1862; Mobile *Advertiser and Register*, April 6, 1862; Natchez *Weekly Courier*, March 26, 1862; Richmond *Daily Dispatch*, May 6, 1862; Richmond *Semi-Weekly Enquirer*, March 28, 1862; Richmond *Daily Examiner*, March 25, 28, April 5, 9, 12, 1862; Selma *Daily Reporter*, April 10, 1862. Ridiculing the gunboat craze, some disaffected person in Richmond scribbled on the walls of buildings there, "Something new under the sun, to wit: 'Petticoat gunboats.'" Richmond *Daily Examiner*, April 21, 1862. For starting the gunboat idea, some people gave credit to the Mobile ladies, but others claimed it was due the New Orleans ladies.

Avenger, or *Rebel Rover* had been suggested. It was launched in October, 1862, amidst prayers and speechmaking, with General Beauregard, Governor Gist, and many other people in attendance. Miss Sue L. Gelzer, who started the gunboat movement in South Carolina by contributing $5.00 and the idea, broke a bottle of champagne on its prow. Virginia built a gunboat which was named the *Virginia* and launched late in June of 1863. After the fall of a few of North Carolina's seaports, the ladies in that state gave up the idea of a gunboat and decided to devote their collections to soldiers' relief.[40]

With many men at the military front, the women were left to make a living as well as to take up many occupations primarily to aid the Confederacy. They managed farms and plantations; they made wine, pickles, catsup, and hats of straw, shucks, and palmetto leaves. Some manufactured cartridges and percussion caps in armories; many worked in government clothing factories; and others served as clerks in the War and Treasury departments.[41]

Some, sniffing the martial atmosphere, could be content with nothing less than the smoke of battle. Wives of officers followed their husbands to war to be with them and nurse them when sick or wounded; other women, mostly of uncertain character, were drummed out of camp. When the war broke out, women in various parts of the Confederacy asked for arms with which to defend themselves and their communities. An Alabama group, calling themselves the "Gainesville Unconquerables," informed the governor in March, 1861, that they had organized immediately on news of Lincoln's election, that they were ready to go wherever

[40] James H. Peebles, Goldsboro, N.C., to Vance, October 31, 1862, in Vance Papers; Athens *Southern Watchman*, July 16, 1862; Charleston *Daily Courier*, October 3, 13, 1862; Charleston *Mercury*, March 15, April 21, 1862; Richmond *Daily Examiner*, June 30, 1863; Sandersville *Central Georgian*, July 16, 1862.

[41] *Official Records*, Ser. I, Vol. XXIII, Pt. II, 767; Russell, *My Diary North and South*, 231; Jones, *Rebel War Clerk's Diary*, II, 140, 338, 357; [McGuire], *Diary of a Southern Refugee*, 107, 196; *Two Months in the Confederate States*, 278; Macon *Daily Confederate*, August 9, 1864; New Orleans *Daily Picayune*, May 11, 1861. M. C. Wootton, Belle Vue, Va., in a letter to Virginia C. Clay (Mrs. Clement C. Clay, Jr.), March 6, 1862, in Clay Papers, said that one of the wealthiest and most refined ladies of that region had been supervising a gang of Negroes in repairing the turnpike and reconstructing bridges. All the men, except the old and infirm, had gone to war.

ordered, and that "We can leave the Old Women and children in charge of the *gallant* gentlemen." [42] There were frequent rumors that women disguised as men were fighting in the Confederate armies, and a few were actually apprehended and expelled from the army when their sex was discovered. The most persistent will-o'-the-wisp was the mythical Lieutenant Harry T. Buford, who was arrested in Richmond and thrown into Castle Thunder, but who, after the war, claimed to be Madame Loreta Janeta Velasquez and the heroine of a thousand military adventures. And, perhaps varying the name a little, there was a Lieutenant Henry Benford, who, according to wartime stories, was Mrs. Laura J. Williams of Arkansas, who raised and commanded a company of Texans and fought at Shiloh and elsewhere in the West.[43]

Women acted as spies, some to be known later only locally, others over the entire Confederacy. Among them were Ellie M. S. Poole of West Virginia, Norah McCartney of Missouri, Diana Smith of Virginia, and Anne and Julia Lomax of Maryland. Some gained enough fame to be arrested by the Federals and imprisoned, but the two most famous Confederate spies were Belle Boyd and Mrs. Rose O'Neal Greenhow. Belle was supposed to have made her debut in the war by killing a Federal soldier who entered the Boyd home in Martinsburg, West Virginia, and maltreated her mother. Thereafter she had an almost incredible career of spy

[42] "Gainesville Unconquerables" to Gov. Andrew B. Moore, March 30, 1861 (Alabama State Archives). Jennie L. McCormick, Auburn, Va., to General Beauregard, December 17, 1861, in Beauregard Papers, informed the General that she had been practicing target shooting guided by some of his soldiers and that they said she was "progressing finely." As she had no firearms, she wanted him to send her a revolver, promising him "Should the opportunity ever present itself I will prove to you that your gift is in no Cowards hand—and should the services of our Southern Girls be needed to resist their Countrys foes, Fauquier's daughters will be the first to answer to the call."

[43] Ladies of Ingleside (near Warrenton, Fauquier County, Va.), to Gov. Letcher, April 25, 1861, in Executive Papers (Virginia State Archives); Matthew P. Andrews (comp.), *The Women of the South in War Times* (rev. ed., Baltimore, 1927), 112 ff.; Fremantle, *Three Months in the Southern States*, 173; Jones, *Rebel War Clerk's Diary*, II, 343; C. J. Worthington, *The Woman in Battle; A Narrative of the Exploits, Adventures, and Travels of Madame Loreta Janeta Velasquez, Otherwise known as Lieutenant Harry T. Buford, Confederate States Army* . . . (Richmond, 1876), *passim;* Atlanta *Southern Confederacy*, May 30, 1862; Richmond *Daily Examiner*, July 2, September 16, 1863; November 25, 1864; Richmond *Daily Whig*, June 19, 1863; Selma *Daily Reporter*, March 3, 1862.

service, arrests, imprisonments, and sentences to be shot. In the meantime, she captivated a Federal officer, married him, and lived for thirty-five years after the war. Mrs. Greenhow, of high social standing in Washington, was credited with sending news of the Federal approach before the First Battle of Manassas, for which Mrs. Chesnut said the Confederacy owed her a debt which it could never pay. She was imprisoned, but was released to go to Richmond, where she was received with high honors. She was drowned near the end of the war while attempting to run the blockade.[44]

There were unnamed women throughout the Confederacy who were as belligerently inclined as if they had worn the uniform, but probably none as ferocious as to "wear rings and ornaments made of our soldiers' bones," as charged in the North.[45] Yet there were Louisiana women who, after reading Butler's "Woman Order," could write such sentiments as these: "Oh! how I hate the Yankees! I could trample on their dead bodies and spit on them," [46] and "Come to my bosom, O my discarded carving-knife, laid aside under the impression that these men were gentlemen. We will be close friends once more. And if you must have a sheath, perhaps I may find one for you in the heart of the first man who attempts to Butlerize me." [47] A Richmond editor admitted that the enmity of the Confederate women was "more deadly than all the engines of war ever invented by man," [48] and a Federal soldier remarked that if the Southern girls could love as they hate, "it would be well worth one's trying to get one of them." [49]

---

[44] Boyd, *Belle Boyd in Camp and Prison, passim*; Sigaud, *Belle Boyd, Confederate Spy, passim*; Simkins and Patton, *Women of the Confederacy, passim*; James J. Williamson, *Prison Life in the Old Capitol and Reminiscences of the Civil War* (West Orange, N.J., 1911), 51–52; Martin and Avary (eds.), *Diary from Dixie*, 176; *Southern Illustrated News*, I (1862), 5; Richmond *Daily Dispatch*, January 24, 1862; Richmond *Daily Whig*, October 16, 1862.

[45] Edmonds, *Nurse and Spy in the Union Army*, 299.

[46] *Two Months in the Confederate States*, 30.

[47] Dawson, *Confederate Girl's Diary*, 36.

[48] Richmond *Daily Whig*, August 30, 1861.

[49] Kate Mason Rowland and Mrs. Morris L. Croxall (eds.), *The Journal of Julia LeGrand, New Orleans, 1862–1863* (Richmond, 1911), 86. A Richmond editor declared that the women of New Orleans were solely responsible for defeating the Federals, that no Yankee "ever gained entrance into a decent family, except when he went officially to insult a lady or steal something." Richmond *Semi-Weekly Enquirer*, January 22, 1864. A Virginia girl told Federal soldiers that only "niggers and

But not all women were consumed by patriotic emotions or hatred of the enemy, and as the rigors of war increased their numbers grew. Many of them wanted their sons, husbands, and sweethearts back at any price. More girls were willing to marry slackers and deserters and flirt with Federal soldiers and entertain them, and some women, becoming tired of "Dixie silk" (homespun), traded cotton to the Federals for luxuries. Near the end of the war a Confederate soldier declared that he had seen plenty of women who by their complaints had caused "numberless desertions from the army." [50]

Many women, more tired of the war and high prices than hungry, engaged in "bread riots" and acts of banditry. The most serious of these riots occurred in Richmond in early April of 1863. The riot was instigated by Mrs. Mary Jackson, a huckster possessed of "straight, strong features, and a vixenish eye" and armed with a "six-shooter" and a bowie knife. She harangued a meeting of women in the Oregon Hill Baptist church, telling them that they must demand goods at government prices or forcibly take them. Soon thereafter about three hundred women and children gathered in Capitol Square, demanded bread, and then marched into the business section where they wrecked shops and carried out anything they wanted, more jewelry, clothing, and other goods than bread. Governor Letcher called out the City Battalion and threatened to fire on them if they did not disperse, and President Davis rushed out into the mob, mounted a drayman's cart, and begged the mob

---

trash come to see you" march by. Blake, *Three Years in the Army of the Potomac*, 33. Federal soldiers marching through eastern North Carolina came upon "a spunky secesh female, who, with a heavy wooden rake, stood guard over her winter's store of sweet potatoes. Her eyes flashed defiance, but so long as she stood upon the defensive no molestation was offered her," but when she became emboldened and slapped an officer's face, the soldiers raided her potatoes and soon none were left. [Haines], *Letters from the Forty-Fourth Regiment*, 55. Southern women, presuming too often on the general regard for their sex, berated Federal soldiers in unbecoming manner. One Louisiana Confederate woman could say, "Thank Heaven, I have never yet made my appearance as a Billingsgate orator on these occasions." Dawson, *Confederate Girl's Diary*, 72. Another Southern woman declared that an acquaintance talked "nothing but blood and thunder, yet . . . fainted at the sight of a worm." Cable (ed.), "War Diary of a Union Woman in the South," in *Famous Adventures and Prison Escapes of the Civil War*, 6.

[50] Joseph T. Durkin (ed.), *John Dooley, Confederate Soldier, His War Journal* (Washington, 1945), 198–99.

to go home. The police arrested many participants, and for the next year trials were held. Some of the women were sentenced to jail for thirty days or more.[51]

About this time an epidemic of riots and forcible seizures of food and goods broke out in various places. A group of fifteen or twenty well-dressed women, wearing golden earrings and breastpins, entered a store on Whitehall Street, Atlanta, and asked the price of bacon. On being informed that it was $1.10 a pound, a tall woman, a shoemaker's wife and leader of the group, "on whose countenance rested care and determination," whipped out a navy revolver and told the women to take what they wanted. They went to other shops and paid their own prices or nothing. Similar raids took place in Macon, Columbus, Augusta, Salisbury, Bladenboro (North Carolina), Mobile, and other places. Countrywomen, taking lessons from their city sisters, soon began attacking wagon trains and occasionally raided towns. Fourteen women, armed with "guns, pistols, knives and tongues," made an attack on a mill near Lafayette, Alabama, and seized a supply of flour. Near Thomasville, Georgia, a half-dozen women, armed with rifles, stopped a wagon and grabbed three sacks of corn; determined women stopped a Negro driver near Marietta, Georgia, and robbed him of his load of yarn; and, about the same time, twenty-eight armed women took a wagonload of cloth en route from the Seven Island Factory to Forsyth. About a dozen women, carrying pistols and knives, came down out of the hills to Abingdon, Virginia, and intimidated merchants into giving them cotton yarn and cloth, and this success led another mob of women from the hinterland to rob the merchants of further supplies.[52] These manifestations of lawlessness

51 [McGuire], *Diary of a Southern Refugee*, 203–204; Jones, *Rebel War Clerk's Diary*, I, 284–85; Richmond *Semi-Weekly Enquirer*, March 1, 1864; Richmond *Daily Examiner*, April 6, 14, 24, 1863.

52 R. P. Hallett, Thomasville, Ga., to Capt. I. N. Williams, February 20, 1865 (in possession of the writer); Simkins and Patton, *Women of the Confederacy*, 127; *The Grayjackets: And How They Lived, Fought and Died, for Dixie. With Incidents & Sketches of Life in the Confederacy. . . . By a Confederate* (Richmond, 1867), 247–49; *American Annual Cyclopaedia . . . 1863*, p. 6; Athens *Southern Watchman*, April 8, 1863; Atlanta *Southern Confederacy*, March 19, April 16, 24, 1863; Augusta *Daily Chronicle & Sentinel*, April 5, 1865; Jackson *Daily Mississippian*, April 7, 1863; Jackson *Daily Southern Crisis*, March 24, 1863; Montgomery *Weekly Mail*, April 1, 1863; Richmond *Daily Whig*, March 25, 1864; Savannah *Republican*, April 13, 1863.

were unmistakable signs of the Confederacy's disintegration, brought on not so much by hunger as by war weariness and resentment at high prices.

Among the best evidences of the people's deep desire for independence was their early wholehearted support of relief measures for the needy and especially for the families of soldiers. With the accepted doctrine of the restricted rights and duties of government, state as well as Confederate, providing relief immediately fell upon the people as private citizens; and although later state and local governments aided relief, the Confederate government never dared to venture into that field. The first widespread appeal which inspired Confederate sympathy was for aid to the widow and children of the hotelkeeper James W. Jackson in Alexandria, Virginia, who, in May, 1861, killed Elmer E. Ellsworth for removing the Confederate flag from the Marshall House and who himself was immediately pierced with bullets and bayonet. A year later a Confederacy-wide collection was being taken up for the family of William B. Mumford, whom Butler hanged for removing a United States flag from the New Orleans Mint.

But taking care of soldiers' families was the greatest and most persistent claim on the charity of everyone, for the Confederate conscription laws, allowing no exemptions for dependents, placed this great burden of relief on the states or the people. In rallying the people of Georgia to this task, Governor Brown, in May, 1861, sent out an appeal, promising a gold cup to the woman who should send in the most valuable contribution, a gold medal to the man, and a Confederate flag to the county giving the most money according to its ability. The names of all contributors of money or material were to be inscribed in books kept by the state government as a memorial to their patriotism. Brown himself was a heavy contributor throughout the war. The people of the Confederacy needed little prodding, for it seemed that all who were able, business concerns and individuals, vied with one another in making contributions of every nature. Five Georgia cotton-spinning mills offered an eighth of their output to the state at one half of the market price, to be distributed to the families of indigent soldiers; William Gregg, factory master of Graniteville, South Carolina, distributed $7,000 in relief to the people of his town and vicinity, uniformed two companies of troops, and gave the state free of cost 5,000 yards of cloth a week for an unspecified time. The Augusta Manufacturing Company gave the mayor $40,000 for distribution among soldiers' families; the Macon and Western Railroad, in May, 1861, gave $500; the Central of Georgia donated $1,000 and promised $100 a month for soldiers' families living in Savannah; the Montgomery and West Point and the Alabama and Florida railroads in July, 1861, agreed to carry free all sick and wounded soldiers as well as all materials for soldiers' hospitals, and charge half fares for soldiers on furlough. To aid further soldiers' families, a Florida tanner offered to tan free one cowhide a year and take toll of one-half the leather thereafter; a Georgia doctor gave free medical service; a Richmond miller greatly reduced the price of his flour; and various people offered houses rent free. A Sandersville, Georgia, merchant in June of 1861 invited all members of the local company of soldiers to come to his store and select free "such articles as they [needed]." [53]

Various people agreed to support a soldier's family; a Georgian gave the yield of corn on fifty acres of bottom land; a North Carolinian sold 1,800 bushels of corn to his neighbors at one fourth the market price; an Alabama planter used his slaves to work the lands of soldiers' families; a Mississippian offered a bushel of salt to the needy widow of any soldier; a Georgian offered a bushel of meal to the wife or widow of any poor soldier. In June, 1861, a woman's organization in New Orleans raffled a portrait of Davis, by E. Wood Perry, for $275 for soldiers' relief; a Richmond lady auctioned her Hudson's Bay sable furs for soldiers' benefits; and people almost everywhere gave money and supplies. A Georgian, who had prospered during the war, gave $100,000 in 1864 for the benefit of orphans, and a little girl six years old gave a pair of socks knitted "all by herself" to a Confederate general.[54]

[53] William Gregg, Graniteville, S.C., to Gov. Milledge L. Bonham, October 27, 1863, in "Correspondence 1860–1865" (South Carolina State Archives); Jones, *Rebel War Clerk's Diary*, II, 7; Athens *Southern Watchman*, May 29, 1861; March 4, May 27, November 4, 1863; Atlanta *Southern Confederacy*, May 4, 28, 1861; Macon *Daily Telegraph*, May 31, 1861; Montgomery *Daily Post*, July 23, 1861; Quincy (Fla.) *Semi-Weekly Dispatch*, October 14, 1863; Richmond *Daily Whig*, October 14, 1862; November 2, 1863; Sandersville *Central Georgian*, May 29, June 5, 1861; May 27, 1863.
[54] *Southern Cultivator*, XIX (1861), 211; Garner, *Reconstruction in Mississippi*, 8;

Individual efforts soon came to be supplemented by associations, some state-wide and others confined to a county or town. In Richmond the Union Benevolent Society, helped by the city government, was, near the end of the war, feeding about 4,500 people. In some cities these associations operated free markets, as in New Orleans, Mobile, Charleston, Richmond, and elsewhere, where ticket holders might receive supplies free; in other places, such as Macon, Atlanta, Savannah, and Shreveport, stores were maintained to sell to the needy at cost and operating expenses.[55]

Inevitably state and local governments were forced to take a hand in providing for the needy at home, as indeed they had from the beginning been making outstanding contributions to the clothing and comforts of their own soldiers. This aid came in the form of large appropriations, estimated at $26,000,000 state and local in North Carolina, and in the passing of stay laws by most of the states, which prevented the collections of debts until the end of the war. Money was raised by increasing the old tax rates, as much as 150 per cent in Mississippi, and by levying new taxes. This relief was administered by the local authorities, sometimes in the form of money allotments and toward the end of the war, when money meant little, in supplies. Louisiana had for a time a pension system

---

Athens *Southern Watchman*, March 4, July 22, 1863; April 13, 1864; January 25, April 19, 1865; Jackson *Daily Southern Crisis*, March 7, 1863; New Orleans *Daily Picayune*, June 2, 1861 (afternoon edition); Richmond *Semi-Weekly Enquirer*, July 5, 1864; Richmond *Daily Whig*, February 3, September 26, 1863; Sandersville *Central Georgian*, April 9, 1862. A Mississippian as relief commissioner fed seventy families and on being conscripted objected: "Have calls every day from some family for assistants [*sic*] they say if they are not fed they will wright [*sic*] for their husbands to come home. Therefore I have taken a greadeal [*sic*] of pains to keep them supplied." W. A. Wade, Gallatin, Miss., to Gov. Clark, July 18, 1862, Ser. E, Vol. LXVII, No. 66 (Mississippi State Archives).

[55] Athens *Southern Watchman*, November 4, 1863; Charleston *Daily Courier*, November 19, 1862; Charleston *Mercury*, March 20, April 23, 1862; Macon *Daily Telegraph*, February 9, 1864; Macon *Daily Telegraph and Confederate*, January 2, 1865; Richmond *Daily Enquirer*, August 20, November 24, 1864; February 1, 1865; Richmond *Daily Examiner*, April 8, 1863; Richmond *Daily Whig*, April 15, 1863; Sandersville *Central Georgian*, November 20, 1861; Bragg, *Louisiana in the Confederacy*, 89, 193–94. John Fraser and Company, a large Charleston trading house, gave to the free market $500 a week for four weeks. Charleston *Daily Courier*, November 22, 1862.

for soldiers' dependents whereby wives, widows, and children received a fixed amount each month.[56]

During the early years of the war, relief was adequate, but with the coming of invasion and the turmoil of internal dissensions, there were undoubtedly many soldiers' families and others who found themselves near the edge of constant hunger and nakedness. The responsible people of the Confederacy, the protectors of the old social and economic orders, might well have been actuated by other considerations than humanitarianism in the care of the poor; for the expression, "a rich man's war and a poor man's fight," came to be heard more and more. It pointed to the possibilities of a new order when the war should be over and won. An ominous petition came up from two Mississippi counties, asking Congress to pass a law aiding their poor people. These people knew slavery had caused the war, and they were "ready and willing to protect that Class of property at the perrel of our lives but not willing to sacry fize our wives and childron and leave them to starve for bread and clothing." [57]

Refugees were another class of people who held a claim on the sympathy and support of more fortunate Confederates. They were those civilians who had fled before the approach of the enemy, electing to fly to unknown ills rather than remain and suffer the insults and injuries incident to an occupied land. The first invaded regions, northern Virginia, middle Tennessee and Mississippi, Louisiana, and the coastal regions, started the refugee hegira. Richmond, Atlanta, and many other towns and cities of the up-country and of the central South, resorts in the mountains, and Texas became places of refuge. At first, wherever refugees drifted,

[56] Bettersworth, *Confederate Mississippi*, 24, 114; Garner, *Reconstruction in Mississippi*, 40; Hamilton, *Reconstruction in North Carolina*, 79; Ella Lonn, *Desertion during the Civil War* (New York, 1928), 115; Martin, *Desertion of Alabama Troops*, 160 ff.; Ramsdell, *Behind the Lines in the Southern Confederacy*, 62 ff.; Schwab, *Confederate States of America*, 107; Atlanta *Southern Confederacy*, December 3, 1862; Augusta *Daily Chronicle & Sentinel*, February 14, 1863; Columbus *Weekly Enquirer*, September 9, 1862; Greensboro (Ga.) *Planters' Weekly*, May 1, 1861; Richmond *Daily Examiner*, June 13, August 23, 1864; Richmond *Daily Whig*, September 24, 1861.

[57] Citizens of Smith and Scott counties, Miss., to Stephens, May 5, 1862, in Alexander H. Stephens Papers (microfilms in University of Texas Library, originals in Division of Manuscripts, Library of Congress).

residents turned over their parlors and other spare rooms to them, but gradually welcomes wore out, sometimes because of an attitude of superiority (since most of these displaced people were of the higher classes) and sometimes because of the frayed nerves of wartime. Toward the end of the war, some people looked on refugees as a scourge and showed them slight attention, which led Richard Malcolm Johnston to observe, "Our people are infinitely more covetous and far less charitable than they were before the war." [58] By 1864 some refugees concluded that there was no safe place to go. Better to "try by our presence to save something," remarked a lowland South Carolinian, "instead of going on the rampage refugeeing *where?* that's the question, shew me a safe point and I'll go tomorrow, but no such happy Valley exists in the Confederacy." [59] Bill Arp, the Confederate humorist, remarked that Job had suffered much, that he "stood the test of all the severe afflictions his Maker visited upon him; but from a careful examination of his sacred record, I do not find that he was ever a refugee." [60]

The people in the greatest need of help were the sick and wounded soldiers. The real heroes were not those who had been killed in battle and knew nothing thereafter, nor the wounded and diseased who suffered the terrors of the damned and speedily died, but those who suffered the tortures of living through their wounds and diseases. Dr. Joseph Jones, a Confederate medical authority, estimated that three times as many soldiers died of disease as were killed in battle; and Dr. John Julian Chisolm of the Confederate medical service summed up the causes of soldiers' diseases thus: "Continued exposure and fatigue, bad and insuf-

---

[58] Richard M. Johnston to Stephens, May 24, 1863, *ibid.*

[59] Easterby (ed.), *South Carolina Rice Plantation*, 206.

[60] [Smith], *Bill Arp, So Called*, 112. See also, Mary E. Massey, "Southern Refugee Life during the Civil War," in *North Carolina Historical Review*, XX (1943), 132–56. Quoting the Mobile *Advertiser*, the *Southern Cultivator*, XXII (1864), 131, said of the refugees: "You may see them on the highways jogging along in a hopeless sort of manner, in search for a hiding place, or at the little stations along the railroad huddled together in box cars—negroes, dogs, and household goods indiscriminate. Here a handsome mirror, there a pot or kettle, a divan, a milk-pail, a family picture, a coop of chickens, a watch-dog lying upon a Brussels rug, a cat on an ottoman, a crock of butter and a basket of eggs amid a profusion of broken china, parlor curiosities and pantry niceties, nice no longer. Doleful, inexpressibly doleful. Let the grim picture pass on."

ficient food, salt meat, indifferent clothing, want of cleanliness, poor shelter, exposure at night to sudden changes of temperature, infected tents and camps, form a combination of causes which explains the fatality of an army in the field." [61] An Englishman correctly held that the Southern army had "sustained greater loss by the monotony and *ennui* of camp than by the various encounters" it had with the enemy.[62] Soldiers were too reckless of their own health. On the march they might throw away their blankets and be forced to bivouac on the bare ground until they could get others; they might leap into a cold stream when they were hot and fatigued; they slipped away from hospitals before they were well; and when thirsty they drank any water they could get. The more discriminating longed for the spring back home. A Georgia soldier wrote: "The water is enough to kill a man. I would give $5 this minute to have a drink of our spring water." [63] President Davis deplored the fact that the lack of soap was producing sickness among the soldiers, besides affecting "their self respect & morale." [64] Lice, called "graybacks," were a terrible scourge and were a greater cause of disease than people then knew. It was generally held that, strangely enough, soldiers from cities remained freer from disease than those from the country; but this was explained by the fact that urban soldiers had had children's diseases— promoted by density of population—before they became adults, and also by the fact that people in cities knew and practiced better hygiene than countrymen. Southerners illogically claimed that their soldiers were healthier than the Federals.

The most common diseases were diarrhea, dysentery, typhoid fever, erysipelas, pneumonia, and measles. The last seldom proved fatal, but by weakening the system it led to the ravages of more serious ailments. Not infrequently soldiers had smallpox, malaria, tuberculosis, and sometimes scurvy and itch. There was surprisingly little venereal disease. Wilmington was visited in 1862 by an epidemic of yellow fever, but few soldiers ever contracted it.

[61] Chisolm, *Manual of Military Surgery*, 2.

[62] Day, *Down South*, I, 133.

[63] Lucien Barnsley, at camp in northern Virginia, to George Barnsley, February 7, 1862, in Barnsley Papers (University of Georgia Library).

[64] Freeman (ed.), *Lee's Dispatches*, 288. See also, Bell I. Wiley, *The Plain People of the Confederacy* (Baton Rouge, 1943), 12; Wiley, *Life of Johnny Reb*, 244.

With the Federals blockading the South and declaring medicines contraband of war, doctors were hard pressed to secure supplies. Some medical supplies were run through the blockade and some were smuggled in under women's spacious hoop skirts, in doll heads, and by other unsuspected methods. The Confederacy early set up medical laboratories at Lincolnton (North Carolina), Charlotte, Columbia, Atlanta, Macon, Montgomery, and Mobile. The one at Columbia, under the direct supervision of Dr. Chisolm, Medical Purveyor, was outstanding. These laboratories manufactured drugs from known formulas and devised many substitutes from roots and herbs growing in the Southern fields and forests. The Medical Department also made thousands of gallons of blackberry wine, needed especially for the hospitals. As Dr. Chisolm recommended a gill of whisky for extreme fatigue and exposure, and as it was also needed in hospitals and in drug manufactories, the Medical Department, after getting unsatisfactory results from contracts with private businesses, set up distilleries of its own at Salisbury and Columbia.[65]

To aid in the collection of herbs and to acquaint the people with the helpful properties of plant life in the South, Surgeon General Samuel P. Moore detailed Francis P. Porcher to prepare a work on the subject. The result was the well-known book, *Resources of the Southern Fields and Forests,* containing 601 pages of valuable information. Porcher listed the medicinal properties of many plants which could be used as substitutes for drugs then scarce or no longer obtainable: dogwood, boneset, tulip poplar, sweet gum, and holly (taking the place of quinine), for fevers; sugar from watermelon juice, for colds and diarrhea and useful as a purgative; and sundry other substitute medicines for many other diseases. The Medical Department urged people to gather such herbs and barks as snakeroot, wild-cherry bark, Indian turnips,

[65] *Official Records,* Ser. IV, Vol. II, 1072; Vol. III, 116, 1074; Chisolm, *Manual of Military Surgery,* 43; *Journal of the Congress of the Confederate States,* I, 724–25; Charleston *Daily Courier,* February 29, March 18, 1864; Macon *Daily Confederate,* August 9, 1864. In 1862, from earth obtained in a cave in the Great Smoky Mountains, 300 pounds of Epsom salts and 400 pounds of alum were being made daily. Augusta *Weekly Chronicle & Sentinel,* June 17, 1862. To promote the manufacture of drugs and to raise the professional standing of druggists, a convention of druggists was held in Augusta in May, 1863. Charleston *Daily Courier,* May 1, 8, 1863; Augusta *Weekly Chronicle & Sentinel,* May 12, 1863.

pokeroots, skunk cabbage, Jimson weeds, sassafras, white-oak bark, persimmon bark, dandelions, henbane, and fleabane. Every neighborhood was asked to garner its valuable herbs; army purveyors were instructed to assemble scurvy-preventing greenstuffs around the camps or along the line of march, such as wild mustard, water cress, wild garlic, sassafras, lamb's quarter, sorrel, pepper grass, wild yams, pokeweeds, and dandelions; and the women were especially advised to plant poppies from which to obtain opium and to gather rose leaves for making blue pills. In this enthusiasm to find substitutes, many foolish remedies were announced as sure cures. Although vaccination for smallpox was practiced, someone discovered that the inhalation of burnt leather aroma was also a preventative; that the best way to relieve the pains of gunshot wounds was to hold them over the fumes made by lard poured on live coals; that spirits of turpentine was a cure for typhoid fever; that the roots of Indian hemp and tea made of red pepper flavored with salt were good substitutes for quinine.[66]

Apart from army field hospitals, the first care of the sick, wounded, and convalescent soldiers was given in the homes of people near the battlefields, and as hospitals later became overcrowded home nursing was continued through the war far from the fields of operations. Shortly after the First Battle of Manassas the women of the Natural Bridge district of Rockbridge County invited all invalid and convalescent soldiers to their homes, there to enjoy good food and to behold the beauties of the country; and following the Battle of Chickamauga the people of Marshallville, Georgia, and the surrounding country asked for a hundred sick and wounded soldiers.[67]

The medical service was set up as a division in the War Department and placed in charge of Dr. Samuel Preston Moore, a South Carolinian who had for many years been in the United States army. As Surgeon General, it was his duty to organize personnel, estab-

[66] *Official Records*, Ser. IV, Vol. II, 13, 442, 467; *Southern Literary Messenger*, XXXVII (1863), 365–69; Atlanta *Southern Confederacy*, August 18, 1861; Augusta *Weekly Chronicle & Sentinel*, July 13, 1864; Macon *Daily Telegraph*, September 9, 1863; Richmond *Daily Examiner*, September 26, 1861; January 24, April 2, 1863; Richmond *Daily Whig*, August 12, 1863; Selma *Daily Reporter*, October 1, 1862.

[67] *Official Records*, Ser. I, Vol. X, Pt. I, 782; Macon *Daily Telegraph*, October 9, 12, 1863; Richmond *Daily Whig*, September 28, 1861.

lish hospitals, secure medical supplies and equipment, and administer to the general health of the soldiers. He was given the rank of brigadier general of cavalry, and his surgeons and assistant surgeons were commissioned respectively majors and captains. Black facings for collars and cuffs and black stripes down the trousers distinguished medical officers from those in the other services. During the course of the war, the Surgeon General used about 3,400 medical men. In the haste of organization, many doctors crept in through favoritism and without proper investigation of their qualifications, but later medical examination boards were appointed to weed out quacks and incompetents. To improve the service General Moore organized in August, 1863, "The Association of Army and Navy Surgeons of the Confederate States," and began in the following January the publication of *The Confederate States Medical and Surgical Journal*, which continued through February, 1865. One of the most eminent surgeons in the service was Hunter Holmes McGuire, who was medical director of Jackson's Corps and served later with other commanders. Two other eminent men were David Y. Yandell, Medical Director of the Department of the West, and Edward Warren, with Lee's army for a time and then Surgeon General of North Carolina.[68]

As Virginia was the scene of the greatest and most persistent military operations of the war, Richmond soon came to be the hospital center of the Confederacy. Here at first every home, warehouse, or other available building was called into use as a hospital, but by 1862 most of the hospital service was concentrated into two great compounds, Winder and Chimborazo. The latter, consisting of 150 buildings, was often said to be the largest hospital in the world. Patients at Chimborazo were assigned to buildings according to their respective states. This plan eliminated confusion in directing visitors to patients, recognized state pride, and encouraged state participation in hospital maintenance. Georgia, with four buildings to her credit, was the most active. Immediately following the

[68] *Confederate Veteran*, XXXIII (1925), 406–407; XXXIV (1926), 140–43, 172–73, 254–56; Miller (ed.), *Photographic History of the Civil War*, VII, 349–50; George W. Adams, "Confederate Medicine," in *Journal of Southern History*, VI (1940), 151–66. There is much less known about the operations of the Confederate Medical Department than of other departments, on account of the destruction of most of the records in the Richmond fire at the end of the war.

First Battle of Manassas, Georgians organized the Georgia Relief and Hospital Association, with locals and auxiliaries scattered throughout the state, designed to collect money and supplies, not only for the Richmond hospitals but for home relief also. The state government aided it with appropriations at various times, $200,000 in December, 1861, $400,000 a year later, and so on.[69]

And, of course, there were hospitals scattered throughout the Confederacy, some under the control of the Surgeon General and some privately maintained. The Florence Nightingale of Georgia was Madame M. C. Cazier, who in the fall of 1861 organized and largely supported through her own efforts a hospital in Savannah, using the old Oglethorpe Medical College building, and taking care of an average of a hundred patients daily. Churches, school buildings, dwelling houses, and almost any structure with a roof were pressed into use, both by private and governmental agencies. The summer-resort hotels in the Virginia springs region made excellent hospital buildings, and as long as that region remained in the hands of the Confederates, thousands of soldiers were accommodated there. As hospitals in regions subject to invasions must be frequently moved to keep out of the enemy's path, such buildings were often temporary and flimsy, with canvas walls if not entirely of canvas. A field hospital might be only a tent or the bare ground or a jolting ambulance. A yellow flag always marked a Confederate hospital, just as a white flag indicated a smallpox pesthouse. After a battle the surgeons and assistants, and sometimes women of the neighborhood, swarmed over the field locating the wounded and bearing them off to improvised hospitals. Among these workers of mercy there were no enemies; Confederates and Federals met on friendly terms, and when a wounded soldier was found he received the same treatment in hospitals irrespective of his nationality.[70]

[69] *Two Months in the Confederate States*, 166; *Confederate Veteran*, XXXVI (1928), 184; Matthews (ed.), *Public Laws of the Confederate States*, 1 Cong., 2 Sess., 1862, pp. 63–65; Athens *Southern Watchman*, October 29, 1862; Richmond *Daily Whig*, October 30, 1861.

[70] Cumming, *Journal of Hospital Life*, 93, 150; [Hopley], *Life in the South*, II, 264; "An Appeal in Behalf of the 'Bartow Hospital'" (handbill in possession of the writer); Macon *Daily Telegraph*, October 9, 1863; Richmond *Daily Whig*, October 24, 1861.

Once inside a hospital the soldier had entered another world, and over his door there might appropriately have been inscribed the old motto, "Abandon hope, all ye who enter here." It was not so because of the lack of devoted nursing, for many brave women offered themselves for this service; and although at first there was a strong prejudice against women attempting such trying tasks, the hospital authorities in the end came to value them highly. Sally L. Tompkins' work in heading a hospital in Richmond during the first days of the war had been so valuable that when the hospital service was more thoroughly organized, making it necessary that all persons in charge of hospitals be regularly in the Medical Department, President Davis commissioned her captain of cavalry. Mrs. Arthur Francis Hopkins was largely responsible for organizing the Alabama unit of the Chimborazo Hospital. She became a nurse and was wounded on the battlefield of Seven Pines, and she and her husband gave $200,000 for hospital work and relief. Mrs. Phoebe Yates Pember was a valuable assistant in the same hospital, and Mrs. Ella King Newsom, a rich Arkansas widow, devoted her life and fortune to hospital work in the Department of the West. There were many other devoted women nurses, among whom was Miss Kate Cumming, who left a vivid account of her hospital experiences. In many hospitals the Sisters of Mercy, Sisters of Charity, and other Catholic sisterhoods performed outstanding work. Stephens was much interested in the wounded, and he could often be seen visiting the Richmond hospitals, carrying out some act of mercy either for a patient or for some fond parent who had sought the aid of the Vice-President.[71]

[71] Anderson, *Memoirs: Historical and Personal*, 341; *Confederate Veteran*, VI (1898), 162; Kate Cumming, *Gleanings from Southland; Sketches of Life and Manners of the People of the South before, during and after the War of Secession* . . . (Birmingham, 1895), 37, 271–75; Cumming, *Journal of Hospital Life*, 11, 12; Douglas S. Freeman, *The South to Posterity; An Introduction to the Writings of Confederate History* (New York, 1939), 113–15; [McGuire], *Diary of a Southern Refugee*, 169; J. Fraise Richard, *The Florence Nightingale of the Southern Army; Experiences of Mrs. Ella K. Newsom, Confederate Nurse in the Great War of 1861–65* (New York, 1914), *passim*; Simkins and Patton, *Women of the Confederacy*, 86, 94. A petition from Limestone County, Ala., July 31, 1861, to Stephens, in Alexander H. Stephens Papers (microfilms in University of Texas Library, originals in Division of Manuscripts, Library of Congress), asked that Congress make it possible for poor men to go to see their sons in hospitals: "I need not say our sons are as dear to us poor men, as the sons of the rich is [*sic*] to them."

In addition to the constant need for better scientific equipment and drugs, hospitals were always ready to receive dishes, spoons, bottles, straw for beds, and especially milk and other fresh foods; and the people were quick in their response with a little or nearly all of what they had. One announcement of gifts to the Macon Hospital in October, 1863, filled a whole column of a newspaper and included such items as these: two gallons of syrup, six chickens, six bushels of potatoes, a basket of dried fruit, a dozen eggs, a bag of sage and pepper, a turkey, a bucket of butter, a beef, two hams, a sack of meal, a bushel of peas, a sheep, a shoat, a sack of flour, a bottle of wine, a gallon of vinegar, a loaf of bread, a lot of teacakes, fifteen pounds of lard, a fourth of a bushel of grits, fifteen pounds of rice, a bag of biscuits, two sacks of onions, a basket of cooked provisions, a mattress, etc. Many who did not give provisions gave money; Roger A. Pryor donated his Congressional salary to hospitals. The churches of Richmond banded together in December, 1863, to provide a New Year's Day dinner for all the patients in the Richmond hospitals.[72]

But with all the devotion and liberality that people both in and out of hospitals could offer, conditions were generally bad, sometimes fearful, mostly for reasons which no one in the Confederacy could help, just as was true in Confederate prisons. Dr. Josiah C. Nott said in 1861 that the hospitals presented "a horrible picture," and there was a widespread feeling among soldiers that the greatest calamity that could happen to them was to be taken to a hospital.[73] Especially during the earlier period, many people blamed the doctors, whom Senator William E. Simms of Kentucky charged in 1862 with having "slain more of our troops than all of Lincoln's minions." [74] An Englishman in the Confederate army declared that in "every regiment there were not less than a dozen doctors, from whom, for the most part, our men had as much to fear as from their Northern enemies." [75] A Richmond editor characterized the

---

[72] Cumming, *Journal of Hospital Life*, 49, 131; [Hopley], *Life in the South*, II, 43; Atlanta *Southern Confederacy*, August 28, 1862; Macon *Daily Confederate*, July 24, 1864; Macon *Daily Telegraph*, October 9, 1863; Richmond *Daily Whig*, November 9, 1861; December 28, 1863; Selma *Daily Reporter*, November 8, 1861.

[73] Mobile *Advertiser and Register*, August 8, 1861.

[74] *Southern Historical Society Papers*, XLV (1925), 223.

[75] *Battle-Fields of the South, from Bull Run to Fredericksburg* (London, 1863), I, 276.

Medical Department as "unfeeling, shameful and brutal." [76] Senator Albert Gallatin Brown of Mississippi said he had heard that a sick soldier had been allowed to lie on the station platform at Lynchburg for three days "without one mouthful, except what he could beg from the boys who were peddling cakes and apples about the depot," and that a doctor, on being reproached for it, had said it was not his business—the whole a most improbable if not impossible story, yet dignified by being recounted in a Congressional debate.[77] Doctors and hospital stewards were accused of partiality to officers, of drinking up the whisky and wine sent for patients and eating the best food, even of selling supplies presented to hospitals and being impolite to visitors. Critics maintained that wounded soldiers had been jolted to death on rough field ambulances, and half-frozen in unheated trains.

But the most harrowing descriptions of hospital scenes related to amputations, and here the truth was too evident. To give the doctors some information on surgery which they had little practiced in their profession in the South, Dr. Chisolm wrote his book *A Manual of Military Surgery, for the Use of Surgeons in the Confederate States Army.* Doctors were too prone to chop off a limb rather than probe for a bullet, pretty much of a meat-ax, hack-saw performance. In fact, the common name for a surgeon was "saw-bones." Despite the fact that Crawford W. Long, a Georgia doctor, had used an anesthetic in major operations almost twenty years before the war, anesthesia had not come to be generally practiced; and, according to Dr. Chisolm, "Some of the older surgeons characterize the cries of the patient as music to the ear, and speak of it as an advantage to be courted, and not to be surpressed." A prejudice had grown up against anesthesia, largely because it had not been properly administered. To induce surgeons to use anesthetics, which Dr. Chisolm recommended "should be given to every patient requiring a serious or

[76] Richmond *Whig*, quoted in Charleston *Daily Courier*, November 3, 1862.

[77] *Southern Historical Society Papers*, XLV (1925), 233. See also, *Journal of the Congress of the Confederate States*, I, 726; *Southern Historical Society Papers*, XLV (1925), 185–86, 188; Cumming, *Journal of Hospital Life*, 151–52; Raymond *Hinds County Gazette*, September 17, 1862; Richmond *Daily Examiner*, December 1, 1863. The Medical Department provided some dental work for soldiers both in active service and in hospitals. *Ibid.*, August 27, 1864.

painful operation," he invented a chloroform inhaler, which fitted over the nose and conserved the valuable fumes.[78] Opium and whisky were also used for deadening pain. But it seems that most soldiers suffered amputations writhing in indescribable agony. One nurse described hospital scenes in terms of tubs of blood and piles of amputated limbs. Having passed through even such a horrible experience, a soldier might laugh and joke about his new appearance; but if the all-too-common gangrene set in, he turned pale as death and lost all hope. An English merchant traveling in the Confederacy concluded "that bungling surgery and incompetent physicians killed as many men as the sword, bullet, or disease." [79] Added to the charge of incompetency was the accusation that half-drunken surgeons sometimes operated on soldiers. A correspondent to a newspaper declared in 1864: "I have seen surgeons so stupefied by liquor that they could not distinguish between a man's arm and the spoke of a wagon wheel, and who would just as soon have sawed off one as the other." [80]

Deaths in Richmond hospitals and burials, generally in Oakwood and Hollywood cemeteries, became so common that the gruesome sight of hearses and pine coffins drawn through the streets no longer frightened the children or caused their elders to take notice—their passing having "become as frequent as the vehicles of merchandise, and death . . . [drove] the brisker business, and the fastest nag." [81] Relatives, when able, insisted on transporting the remains of their dead ones back to their homes. Embalmers advertised their uncertain art, but their skill was too weak to overcome the summer heat, and often it was necessary to bury the corpse by the roadside before the earthly home had been reached. When remains were sent by railway they were generally stored in the front of mail cars, where stenches sometimes drove out the clerks

---

[78] Chisolm, *Manual of Military Surgery*, 433, 434.

[79] *Two Months in the Confederate States*, 98.

[80] Athens *Southern Watchman*, December 14, 1864. See also, *Manual of Military Surgery. Prepared for the Use of the Confederate States Army* (Richmond, 1863), 71; Chisolm, *Manual of Military Surgery*, iii; *American Annual Cyclopaedia . . . 1864*, pp. 13 ff.; Bradlee, *Blockade Running during the Civil War*, 48; Cumming, *Journal of Hospital Life*, 17, *passim;* Wiley, *Life of Johnny Reb*, 268 ff.; Charleston *Mercury*, March 15, 1862.

[81] Richmond *Daily Examiner*, October 17, 1862.

and afforded another reason for poor postal service. An Englishman noted in the countenances of relatives accompanying coffins back south how "patience, resignation, and resolve had conquered mourning!" [82]

The hospital situation aroused strong Congressional criticism, both as to alleged incompetence of doctors and the system of dismissing soldiers. Relatives of soldiers convalescing in hospitals applied pressure to have them furloughed to their homes, thereby affording them better treatment and relieving congested conditions in hospitals, making possible the better care of the more seriously sick and wounded. As the furloughing of a soldier from a hospital had to pass through the same military channels as if he were present in the army, there was naturally great delay and inconvenience. Congress became excited over this condition and passed a bill in December, 1861, allowing not only surgeons in the Medical Department to grant furloughs, but even doctors in private practice to pass on the physical condition of soldiers absent from the army and grant furloughs or permanent dismissal. Davis vetoed this bill on the grounds that it would place the disposal of soldiers in the hands of authorities not in the military establishment and might lead to the disintegration of the army. Congress repeated this bill in a different form two months later, and Davis vetoed it again. The final dismissal later granted to soldiers by surgeons of the Military Department afforded another problem, which seems never to have been satisfactorily solved. Too often the soldier did not return to the army but went home or elsewhere and helped to swell the tide of deserters. From September, 1862, to December, 1863, 4,446 soldiers thus deserted from the Virginia hospitals alone. One suggested remedy was to notify the soldier's military unit when he was about to be discharged and also to publish his name in the newspapers.[83]

The picture of life back of the lines had two sides. There were examples of devotion and self-sacrifice almost unparalleled and

[82] Mallet, *Errand to the South*, 107. See also, Charleston *Daily Courier*, July 2, 1862; Richmond *Daily Enquirer*, May 11, 1863; Richmond *Daily Whig*, September 10, 1861.

[83] Richardson (comp.), *Messages and Papers of the Confederacy*, I, 156–58, 162–65; *Journal of the Congress of the Confederate States*, V, 288–89; Johnston, *Autobiography*, 163; Richmond *Daily Examiner*, March 31, 1863; January 28, 1864.

there were instances of sordidness and decay which Southerners later sought to forget. With Shakespeare's epigram reversed, the good that they did lived after them, the evil was interred with the Confederacy.

CHAPTER XIX

SOLDIERS AS FIGHTERS, DESERTERS, AND PRISONERS OF WAR

IT IS an exercise in utter futility to attempt to arrive at the exact number of Confederate soldiers, either throughout the whole war or at any specific time. Only an approximation can be determined, and that, after all, is sufficient for any historical purpose. And it is equally impossible to determine the exact number of troops the Southerners fought against. But it is significant first to note that the population of the United States in 1860 was 31,443,000. In the eleven states seceding there were 9,103,000, of whom 5,449,000 were white; 3,521,000, slaves; and 133,000, free Negroes. There was, therefore, in the remainder of the country a total of 22,340,000. Of these, 355,000 were free Negroes; 433,000, slaves; and the rest, whites and civilized Indians. Practically all of the slaves and 118,000 free Negroes lived in the four Border slave states, Delaware, Maryland, Kentucky, and Missouri, which did not secede. In these four states there were 2,590,000 whites.

Although the Border slave states did not give as fully of their resources to the Union as did the Northern states, there can be little doubt that they afforded many more troops to the North than to the South; for, in addition to the whites, free Negroes and slaves were soon enlisted by the North wherever its authority extended. And even in the Confederacy there were large disaffected areas, such as East Tennessee and West Virginia, from which exaggerated estimates have placed the number of soldiers serving in the Federal armies as high as 300,000. There were probably 1,550,000 men who wore the Federal uniform at one time or another; half that number would be a liberal estimate of the number of Confederate soldiers. The problem is greatly complicated by the fact that available statistics record enlistments, which means that a soldier was counted each time he enlisted. Many enlisted more than once, and some, such as bounty jumpers and substitutes, enlisted many times. A significant basis of comparison is afforded by the number of veterans surviving in 1890, when there were 432,020 Confederates and 1,034,073 Federals.[1]

From the standpoint of fighting the war, the most important and practical consideration was how many men were actually present and under arms. Probably the largest number of men ever on the Confederate rolls at one time was about 500,000, in the summer of 1863, when there were actually present for duty slightly more than 300,000. And this number the editor of the Richmond *Whig* asserted, no doubt correctly, was all that the Confederacy could maintain. Confederate armies in the field hardly ever ran beyond 60,000.[2] It has been estimated that 94,000 Confederates were killed in battle or mortally wounded and that 164,000 died of disease, as compared with a total of Federal deaths amounting to 360,000.[3]

Every class of Southerners and almost every nationality entered the Confederate army. The mass of armies has always been composed of members of the poor and middle classes, as there are more of them, but there were many rich Southerners who prided themselves on becoming private soldiers. In 1861 William H. Russell, traveling through the South for the London *Times,* was impressed with the number of rich men who had joined the army. From the Natchez region a party of sixty cavalrymen each worth from $100,-000 to $250,000 had recently gone to Richmond, he declared. It was often true that soldiers were far wealthier than their officers. The uniforms of one New Orleans company were said to have been

[1] For population statistics, see *Population of the United States in 1860; Compiled from the Original Returns of the Eighth Census* (Washington, 1864), x, xvii, 595–99; *American Annual Cyclopaedia . . . 1862,* p. 235. Thomas L. Livermore, *Numbers and Losses in the Civil War in America, 1861–1865* (Boston, 1900), though inaccurate, is the standard work on its subject. For a scholarly appraisal of the numbers of soldiers, see Edward Channing, *A History of the United States* (New York, 1905–1925), VI, 431–36.

[2] *Official Records,* Ser. IV, Vol. II, 380, 530, 1073; Vol. III, 520, 989, 1182; Columbus *Times,* December 30, 1864; Richmond *Daily Whig,* December 29, 1863; Burne, *Lee, Grant and Sherman,* 1; Carl Russell Fish, *The American Civil War; An Interpretation* (New York, 1937), 249.

[3] James Ford Rhodes, *History of the United States from the Compromise of 1850* (New York, 1902–1920), V, 187.

worth $20,000, and the flag it carried had cost $750. The Georgia Hussars left Savannah in uniforms costing $25,000. Occasionally a rich soldier would treat his whole company to a sumptuous feast.[4]

Young and old as well as rich and poor hurried off to war. For a time it was a major problem for parents to control their children. New Orleans urchins dressed as Zouaves with their swords and baggy trousers and engaged in "all sorts of pseudo-military tom-foolery," and the "Davis Life Guards" of Athens, Georgia, paraded with their colored playmates as drummers and fifers. But young-sters not only played war games; some of them seriously set out to join the army. In 1863 an anxious mother wrote General Howell Cobb that her twelve-year-old son had run away to join his com-mand and begged him to send her boy back; and a Georgian ad-vertised in the newspapers for his eight-year-old son who had set out with his little Negro retainer to find the army. They were discovered twenty miles away and were returned much against their will. About the time Sherman was well on his way to Atlanta, four Augusta boys, ranging in ages from nine to fourteen, mounted on a mule, a pony, and two horses, set out to stop him. After a forced march of twenty miles the first day, they were overtaken at their first encampment and arrested by their worried parents, who were able to get by the nine-year-old picket. The boys in Macon, Georgia, organizing for serious work, complained to military authorities that they had no weapons: "If we are boys that is nothing; we can fight as well as men, and a great sight better than some we know of."[5] At least one boy in Mobile got himself properly armed; he was "buttoned up to the throat in a military jacket and a bowie knife girded to his waist as long as his own leg."[6] In some regularly organized companies there were large numbers of boys who fought

[4] Russell, *Civil War in America*, 35; Russell, *My Diary North and South*, 105, 292; [Napier Bartlett], *A Soldier's Story of the War; Including the Marches and Battles of the Washington Artillery, and of other Louisiana Troops* (New Orleans, 1874), 28–29; New York *World*, November 11, 1864.

[5] Macon *Daily Telegraph*, April 26, 1862.

[6] *Ibid.*, January 24, 1862. Emeli Ramouin, Bayou Goula, La., wrote General Beaure-gard, July 16, 1861, in Beauregard Papers, that she was a widow and that all of her sons were in the army, including Numa, who was "but a mere boy and but *sixteen* years of age, who in a moment of patriotic enthusiasm and fired by the example of his older brothers and cousins left me without my knowledge or consent." She wanted him released.

442

like veterans, for as the war continued, the age of youngsters was winked at, and boys from sixteen to eighteen were actually called for home defense. More than 250 Virginia Military Institute cadets, some as young as fifteen, bravely helped defeat General Franz Sigel at New Market on May 15, 1864, and their exploits became a classic in Confederate military history. Men who had reached their second childhood, like the doddering and headstrong "Mitchell's Thunderbolts" of Athens, Georgia, paraded and drilled in seriousness but never smelled burning powder; others in their fifties and even sixties actually bore the hardships of fighting. Some, sensing that defeat was inevitable, sought the enemy's bullet and found it, while others failed to receive this boon. Few rivaled Edmund Ruffin, who after Appomattox provided the bullet himself.[7]

Fighting for the Confederacy were many foreigners; some fought for the adventure and others were propelled into the service through residence in the South. There were Irish, Germans, English, Scotsmen, Welsh, Polish, Italians, French, Spaniards, and Mexicans—with such names as Augustini, Avenado, Bahr, Bohled, Brummenstadt, Bustilla, Cognavich, De Vaugh, Forsbert, Gonzales, Jackalanwiski, Kaminski, Lloyd, McGregor, Moroso, Noquet, O'Bannon, Santini, Szynanski, and von Scheliha. Some foreign names were difficult for ordinary Southerners to spell or pronounce; Lieutenant Colonel H. Oladowski, in closing a communication added, "Please order your clerk to spell my name properly." [8] The Irish came first in numbers of soldiers, with the Germans and English following respectively. In hyperbolic language an Irishman shouted to his "Brother Exiles," "If we would overflow history with glory, and be worthy our name and nation, in the name of liberty we will tear the eagles from the invaders' standard, and sow its stars to the waves and winds." [9] Germans formed several companies and the British organized a Foreign Legion. Some foreigners were already well known and others were to gain distinction. John

---

[7] Athens *Southern Watchman*, May 29, June 12, 1861; Macon *Daily Telegraph*, April 23, 1861; March 19, 20, April 18, 1862; October 9, 1863; February 9, April 14, 1864; Mrs. S. A. Noble, Columbus Ga., to Cobb, May 4, 1863, in Howell Cobb Papers; William Couper, *One Hundred Years at V.M.I.* (Richmond, 1939), II, 266–345; Cumming, *Journal of Hospital Life*, 23; Russell, *My Diary North and South*, 253.

[8] *Official Records*, Ser. I, Vol. XVI, Pt. II, 752.

[9] Atlanta *Southern Confederacy*, May 9, 1861.

Mitchel, Jr., son of the famous Irish exile, became captain of the Irish Volunteers of Charleston; the six-foot, four-inch Heros von Borcke, a dashing blond Prussian with blue eyes and curling mustache and beard, joined Jeb Stuart's staff and received for his services the thanks of Congress; St. George Grenfel, an Englishman and a veteran of wars in Turkey, India, Morocco, and South America, became a member of John Morgan's staff. Prince de Polignac, of royal French blood, a veteran of the Crimean War, was the only foreigner to reach the rank of brigadier general. The Pole, Gaspard Tochman, unsuccessfully sought to organize a Polish brigade and thereby failed to receive a brigadier generalship, whereupon he bitterly complained of Confederate ingratitude.[10]

Justus Scheibert, a Prussian engineer who came as an observer and unofficially joined the Gettysburg campaign, did no actual fighting but viewed much of the battle from a tall tree. William H. Russell of the London *Times* and Francis G. Lawley of the *Illustrated London News* were newspapermen; Arthur Fremantle and Garnet Wolseley (afterward Lord Wolseley) were officers in the British army who came to observe military activities and not to fight; and coming as sight-seers were the Marquis of Hartington, Lord Talbot, Sir James Ferguson, and William Leslie, who were members of Parliament, and Prince Napoleon Joseph Charles Paul Bonaparte, a son of Jerome Bonaparte.[11]

After the first year of the war, foreigners residing in the Confederacy lost most of their enthusiasm for fighting and most of them tried to avoid conscription. Confederate authorities insisted that a foreigner domiciled in the Confederacy was subject to the draft, but it was difficult to prove domicile. A Richmond judge, however, held that a Scotsman who had come to America as an infant and now claimed to be a subject of Queen Victoria was

[10] Charleston *Daily Courier*, July 2, August 23, 1861; Richmond *Semi-Weekly Enquirer*, July 3, 1863; Richmond *Daily Examiner*, August 5, 1863; Richmond *Daily Whig*, August 8, 1862; Ross, *Visit to the Cities and Camps of the Confederate States*, 212. The Athens *Southern Watchman*, October 2, 1861, said of the Irish, "Everywhere in the Confederate States, they have been among the foremost to volunteer, and among the most liberal in contributing to the comfort of the brave soldiers in the field." Lonn, *Foreigners in the Confederacy*, is the standard work on this subject.

[11] Von Borcke, *Memoirs of the Confederate War*, 333; [Justus Scheibert], *Sieben Monate in den Rebellen-Staaten während des Nordamerikanischen Krieges, 1863* (Stettin, Germany, 1868), *passim;* Richmond *Daily Whig*, January 30, 1863.

domiciled in the Confederacy and must become a soldier.[12]

Soldiers adopted fierce names for their units in addition to their official designations. They became Invincibles, Avengers, Irrepressibles, Killers, Hunters, Desperadoes, Terrors, Fire Eaters, Rebels, Gideonites, Minutemen, Yankee Catchers, Wild Cats, Bull Dogs, Lions, Tigers, Scorpions, Eagles, and Hornets. Their tents were the Lions' Den, the Tigers' Lair, the Eagles' Nest, Mars' Delight, and so on. The most famous of the Tiger class were the Louisiana Tigers, a daredevil, reckless bunch of roustabouts and "plug-uglies" recruited from the New Orleans levees. They were led by the filibuster Bob Wheat.

Soldiers' equipment was as varied as the names of their units. It was a misnomer throughout the war to refer to a Confederate uniform, for soldiers' dress was uniform in neither cut nor color. Despite the fact that gray became official in June, 1861, and traditional thereafter, as often as not the color was butternut brown (made from copperas or walnut hulls), "the ugliest snuff-colored stuff imaginable," [13] causing the enemy to call Confederates butternuts. In the early part of the war, blue was sometimes worn, obliging one Louisiana battalion in the Battle of Shiloh to turn their coats inside out to prevent mistaken identity. During the first year and a half of the war soldiers provided their own clothing in exchange for government commutation, which resulted in the variegated dress of Confederates. Even after October, 1862, when commutation was ended, they continued to receive clothing from home. An editor remarked that never before in history had an army been clothed "by direct private contribution." [14] A Mississippi soldier wearing a bearskin jacket attracted much attention in Virginia. According to Fremantle, soldiers in Texas were "dressed in every variety of costume, and armed with every variety of weapon." [15] Soldiers robbed the dead of considerable clothing on the battlefields. They appropriated shoes and overcoats especially, and later dyed the blue coats. It was estimated that the Confederates acquired 60,000 overcoats in McClellan's Peninsular campaign. In

---

[12] Richmond *Semi-Weekly Enquirer*, August 28, 1863.

[13] Martha Derby Perry (ed.), *Letters from a Surgeon of the Civil War* [John Gardner Perry] (Boston, 1906), 5.

[14] Milledgeville *Southern Recorder*, January 28, 1862.

[15] Fremantle, *Three Months in the Southern States*, 74.

at least one instance a Confederate dressed in "Yankee blue" was himself captured by a compatriot.[16]

Soldiers had definite prejudices about various articles of clothing. They disliked caps; they wanted felt hats. Many agreed with a Tarheel that "he had rather go Barefooted than Bare Headed," [17] and, indeed, in the summertime soldiers frequently carried their shoes thrown over their shoulders. In the early days of the war, soldiers felt that they were not properly clothed unless they wore boots; but this prejudice against shoes soon wore away, and from the first winter to the end of the war soldiers were glad to get anything to protect their feet from the cold ground. One of the quartermasters' biggest problems was to keep the soldiers shod, and one of the persistent criticisms against the government was its failure to provide shoes. There were frequent denials that soldiers marched and fought in bare feet, but the proof was overwhelming that they did. In the fall of 1863 Lee declared that thousands of his men were barefooted, "a greater number partially shod, and nearly all without overcoats, blankets, or warm clothing." [18] The following January he wrote the Quartermaster General that in one regiment only fifty men were properly shod. A soldier informed his sister in November, 1862, from Lynchburg, "I heard today that many of our troops are unshod, and that they had to march recently barefooted in the snow"; [19] and another wrote, "I have seen so much suffering of late, that I am growing careless of every thing. Every day I see men walking barefooted thru' the snow and in my nightly rounds see men sleeping on the bare ground without even a blanket." [20]

[16] Matthews (ed.), *Statutes at Large of the Provisional Government of the Confederate States, 1861–1862*, p. 195; Matthews (ed.), *Public Laws of the Confederate States*, 1 Cong., 2 Sess., 1862, p. 69; *Regulations for the Army of the Confederate States, and for the Quartermaster's and Pay Departments. The Uniform and Dress of the Army. The Articles of War, as Amended by Act of Congress. Also all the Laws Appertaining to the Army* (rev. ed., New Orleans, 1861), 255–56; Richmond *Daily Examiner*, July 7, 1862; von Borcke, *Memoirs of the Confederate War*, 43. The standard work on Confederate soldiers is Wiley, *Life of Johnny Reb*.

[17] Hamilton (ed.), *Correspondence of Jonathan Worth*, I, 214.

[18] Robert E. Lee, Jr., *Recollections and Letters of General Robert E. Lee* (Garden City, 1904), 104.

[19] George Barnsley, Lynchburg, Va., to Julia Barnsley, November 12, 1862, in Barnsley Papers (University of Georgia Library).

[20] Thomas G. Jackson, in Virginia, to his sister "Puss," undated (in possession of the writer). See also, *Two Months in the Confederate States*, 217.

In the early winter of 1862 a report that barefooted soldiers had marched through the streets of Richmond led to a great outburst of indignation and sympathy, enthusiastically promoted by the critical Richmond newspaper editors, who saw here additional ammunition for their attacks on the Davis administration. A campaign was immediately started to provide shoes for Lee's army through private contributions. By the middle of November $40,000 had been raised, with Davis and other high Confederate officials making contributions; and soon 6,000 pairs of shoes were on their way to Lee's troops. But still soldiers marched through Richmond with bleeding feet, and the *Examiner,* in December, with considerable satisfaction confronted the doubters with this news item: "The painful proof was furnished by the brigade of General Evans last Thursday, when many of the men marched through the city in a snow storm on bare feet and in tattered garments." A Georgian tried to start a movement for every man in the South not in the army to send a pair of shoes to a soldier. Some army units set up shoemaking departments which operated in quiescent periods. During the winter of 1864, General William Mahone's brigade turned out 2,000 pairs of shoes from leather received in exchange for hides which the army butchers had thrown away. Despite strenuous efforts to provide shoes, many soldiers went barefooted to the bitter end.[21]

The problem of providing soldiers with blankets was fully as persistent. The soldiers themselves were somewhat to blame for their lack of blankets as well as shoes. On marches in warm weather they were notorious for throwing away anything they did not want to carry, even ammunition. At any time they were prone to sell almost anything for money, especially if they anticipated a furlough in Richmond or were already there. Governor Edward Clark begged Texan families to contribute blankets for the state's soldiers. Many families throughout the Confederacy cut their carpets into blankets, and soldiers on the march often used them poncho-style as overcoats. Yet many soldiers had no blankets, and some of the coverings they improvised were "hardly large enough to envelop a cat." Knowing the cold-resistant qualities of paper, soldiers reinforced scanty

---

21 For quotation, see Richmond *Daily Examiner,* December 13, 1862. See also, Athens *Southern Watchman,* October 22, 1862; Richmond *Semi-Weekly Enquirer,* April 12, 1864; Richmond *Daily Examiner,* November 12, 13, 15, 1862.

447

blankets with newspapers and a few wore papers under their shirts. A Georgia soldier wrote home and asked that sheepskins with the wool on be sewed together and that two such blankets be sent to him so that he and his brother might lie on one and cover up with the other.[22]

As for shelter, soldiers on the march, more often than not, bivouacked, and when they were in winter quarters they built huts, in many instances digging a pit half the height of the inside and finishing it off above the ground with logs. Available canvas tents were of such poor quality that they tore easily after a short time, and soldiers often complained that they were too small for the number of men designed to be accommodated. Five soldiers were supposed to sleep in a tent covering six feet square. A newspaper correspondent queried, should "men who have left their homes to fight for their liberties, be forced to sleep like wild hogs, with barely enough space to turn over in?" [23]

At the beginning of the war the adjutant general of Georgia recommended that soldiers provide themselves with the following equipment: one coat or jacket, two pairs of trousers, a black necktie, a fatigue cap, a comb, two flannel shirts, two pairs of drawers, three pairs of socks, two pairs of boots, a pocketknife, a small tin cup, a knife and fork, and an iron spoon. Apparently he did not think a blanket necessary. The government would try to furnish fighting equipment except bowie knives, which most soldiers felt were as necessary as other items. Those who were able to acquire this "Arkansas toothpick" often wore it attached to their right boot top, if they had boots. A beard was also desirable, both for looks and protection against the winter cold, and soldiers who could not normally grow one were reminded by advertisements in the newspapers that Bellingham's Stimulating Unguent never failed to grow a thick stand.[24]

A Confederate soldier generally presented "a rough and ragged appearance," as much from desire as necessity. Frequently with a

[22] For quotation, see [Bartlett], *Soldier's Story of the War,* 32. See also, *Official Records,* Ser. I, Vol. IV, 102; Richmond *Semi-Weekly Enquirer,* January 5, 1864; Richmond *Daily Examiner,* March 27, 1865.

[23] Charleston *Mercury,* March 18, 1862.

[24] Athens *Southern Watchman,* May 29, 1861; Macon *Daily Telegraph,* April 23, 1861.

grimy face, made so with black smudge from using his teeth to open paper cartridges to release powder for his muzzleloading rifle, he presented a fierce appearance to the enemy. A newspaper correspondent, after viewing the ragged Army of Northern Virginia in the fall of 1862, became indignant with righteous anger, and exclaimed that "if this army of veterans, thus clad and shod, with tattered uniforms and banners, could march from Richmond to the Mississippi, it would produce a sensation that has no parallel in history since Peter the Hermit led his swelling hosts across Europe to the rescue of the Holy Sepulchre." [25]

The pay promised infantrymen and artillerymen was $11.00 a month ($12.00 for cavalrymen), but the government was so inefficient in distributing this pittance that many soldiers fought with almost no pay. After the rapid decline in value of Confederate currency, there arose a movement to raise soldiers' pay, which culminated in June, 1864, in an increase of $7.00 a month. Some critics argued that there should be no distinction between the pay of a soldier and of an officer, while others averred that soldiers were not fighting for "pay or plunder, but for patriotism."

Just what the Confederate soldier was fighting for stood out little more clearly in his mind than what most soldiers fight for in any war. In the beginning the enthusiasm of the moment and the propulsion of mass feeling put him into the army. Later the force of the conscription laws and finally the fear of being conquered and losing his dignity as a citizen and his property kept him going. Of course, all understood that they were fighting for independence and all it implied, but toward the end many soldiers felt no great urge to continue when they compared this hazy ideal with the personal sacrifices they were making. "No use to give a reason—," said one cryptically, "a fellow could not stay away from the fight—not

---

[25] "P.W.A.," in Augusta *Weekly Constitutionalist*, October 8, 1862. This is a description of one of Jubal A. Early's soldiers, found dead on the outskirts of Washington, after the famous raid of 1864: "His feet, wrapped in rags, had coarse shoes upon them, so worn and full of holes that they were only held together by many pieces of thick twine. Ragged trousers, a jacket, and a shirt of what used to be called 'tow cloth', a straw hat, which had lost a large portion of both crown and rim, completed his attire. . . . A haversack hung from his shoulder. Its contents were a jack-knife, a plug of twisted tobacco, a tin cup, and about two quarts of coarsely cracked corn, with, perhaps, an ounce of salt, tied in a rag." Lucius E. Chittenden, *Recollections of President Lincoln and his Administration* (New York, 1891), 420.

well." [26] A North Carolina woman could not understand what her husband was fighting for and concluded that "i don't think that he is fighting for anything only for his family to starve." [27] Yet there were soldiers who had such a burning sense of patriotism that they felt all in life worth while would be lost if defeat came. When Lee surrendered at Appomattox one cried out in anguish, "Blow, Gabriel! Blow! My God, let him blow, I am ready to die." [28] Another anxiously asked, "Is it true?" and on being told that it was so, exclaimed, "My God! . . . That I should have lived to see this! . . . I did not think I should live to this day. I hoped I should die before this day!" [29]

The government attempted to take care of disabled veterans by setting up the Invalid Corps. Members were promised their pay throughout the war, though they must submit every six months to an examination to determine their continuing disability. Some disabled veterans found employment as clerks in government departments. In 1864 Congress passed a bill to establish a home for disabled veterans, but Davis vetoed it on constitutional grounds. The War Department distributed some crutches, and in 1864 citizens of Richmond formed an Association for the Relief of Maimed Soldiers to provide artificial limbs, and soon raised $20,000. They hoped it would become Confederacy-wide. There were slight signs that soldiers were contemplating a "Confederate Legion" which would work for the promotion of veterans in politics. "Cast your votes for no candidate for office but those who have served their country in the *Ditches*," advised one.[30]

To reward "courage and good conduct" and to meet a demand that a Legion of Honor be established in which private soldiers as well as officers be recognized, Congress in October, 1862, authorized medals for officers and badges of distinction for soldiers. After a signal victory every participating company should elect the

26 Martin and Avary (eds.), *Diary from Dixie*, 163.

27 Wiley, *Plain People of the Confederacy*, 66.

28 Wiley, *Life of Johnny Reb*, 148–49.

29 James F. J. Caldwell, *The History of a Brigade of South Carolinians, Known first as "Gregg's" and subsequently as "McGowan's Brigade"* (Philadelphia, 1866), 237.

30 For quotation, see Macon *Daily Telegraph and Confederate*, December 29, 1864. See also, Richmond *Semi-Weekly Enquirer*, January 26, 1864; Richmond *Daily Whig*, January 20, 27, 1864.

private in its own ranks "best entitled" to receive the badge. The difficulties in obtaining these insignia prevented distribution. But a year later Adjutant General Cooper ordered that the names of all such soldiers should be entered on a Roll of Honor to be kept in his office and that the names of all chosen thus far should be read to every regiment in the Confederacy. This list contained about eight hundred names of heroes of the battles of Murfrees-boro, Chancellorsville, and Gettysburg. Thereafter such battles at Chickamauga, Wilderness, Spotsylvania Courthouse, Battery Wagner, and Drewry's Bluff yielded a great many more names of veterans. One critic considered the method of company selections an absurdity. He thought it was bad enough for soldiers to elect their own officers, but to elect their heroes was unthinkable. Some-time after the defense of Sabine Pass, in Texas, admirers of the brave participants had medals made from Mexican silver dollars and presented to them. Years after the war the New Market Cross of Honor was struck for the Virginia Military cadets and the Southern Cross of Honor for Confederate soldiers generally.[31]

Soldiers' food was little better than their clothing, except when they got packages from home, made rich captures from the enemy, received invitations to meals in countryside homes, or made trips by rail. When soldiers were in winter quarters or otherwise sta-tionary over long periods of time, they might receive their food through an army cooking establishment. On other occasions they formed mess groups of four to eight, with possibly a Negro cook in the earlier days of the war, but thereafter with members of the group cooking in rotation. Their prescribed rations were corn bread, beef or bacon, and coffee when obtainable, and in the sum-mer they consumed various vegetables (called "small rations"). They liked especially green corn and raw onions. Peanuts and molasses were also favorites with them. Sometimes stationary groups

[31] Beauman L. Belden, *War Medals of the Confederacy* (New York, 1915), 1–12; Matthews (ed.), *Public Laws of the Confederate States*, 1 Cong., 2 Sess., 1862, p. 89; *General Orders from Adjutant and Inspector-General's Office, Confederate States Army*, 1862–1863, Ser. 1863, pp. 157–81; *Official Records*, Ser. I, Vol. XVIII, Pt. I, 580; Vol. XXX, Pt. II, 533; Vol. XXXVI, Pt. I, 1099–1101; Vol. XL, Pt. I, 810; Charleston *Daily Courier*, September 14, 1864; Richmond *Semi-Weekly Enquirer*, May 9, 1862; Richmond *Daily Whig*, May 5, 1864; James S. Harris, *Historical Sketches, Seventh Regiment, North Carolina Troops* (n.p., 1893?), 31–32; Robert Stiles, *Four Years Under Marse Robert* (New York, 1910), 341.

planted vegetable gardens, but on the march they were likely to engage in considerable foraging (sometimes called "jayhawking" and "jerking"), despite strict army regulations against it. In one instance Bragg, on his invasion of Kentucky, had a soldier shot for crossing a fence to get apples. The army called upon the people of the Confederacy to make special efforts to provide soldiers with fresh vegetables, and farm experts advised the people to dry for the army's winter consumption not only fruit but also various vegetables such as okra, squash, carrots, and pumpkins. Troop trains were met by the people at the way stations and the soldiers were given many tasty victuals. Many packages from home helped to feed the Confederate army.[32]

Yet the army was seldom properly fed. Often soldiers were forced to subsist on half or quarter rations. Lee wrote Davis in the spring of 1864, "I cannot see how we can operate with our present supplies," and more than once he was prevented from assuming the offensive or following up a battle because of lack of food supplies. One veteran remarked that his most vivid memory of the war was his constant gnawing hunger. To give Lee's army one good meal at least, and to show continued thankfulness for his starving, ragged army's resistance to hunger as well as to the enemy, the people of Virginia, assisted somewhat by other Confederate states, provided an amazing performance as the year 1864 drew to a close. They

[32] *General Orders from Adjutant and Inspector-General's Office, Confederate States Army, 1862–1863,* Ser. 1862, p. 146; *Official Records,* Ser. I, Vol. VII, 891; *Southern Cultivator,* XXII (1864), 110; Richmond *Daily Whig,* April 12, 1864; Don C. Seitz, *Braxton Bragg, General of the Confederacy* (Columbia, 1924), 174; Wiley, *Life of Johnny Reb,* 90 ff. A captured Federal bake oven on wheels attracted much attention in Richmond. Plans were made to send it to Lee's army for use. Richmond *Daily Examiner,* February 29, 1864. Soldiers often let their home folk know what kind of food they desired. A Tarheel wrote his mother: "I wish you would send me a big cake and some dried apple pies or 'slapjacks', I believe they call them, some molasses, dried fruit, lard, vegetables &c any thing you choose. Please send me a bottle of brandy and some sugar and I will make an eggnog for Christmas if I can manage to get some eggs. Please send me a pound or two of butter for we very seldom get any up in these diggings." Henry M. Wagstaff (ed.), *The James A. Graham Papers, 1861–1884* (Chapel Hill, 1928), 167. The next Christmas (1864) this same Tar Heel and two other officers got up a Christmas dinner for about a dozen of their friends which consisted of "bacon & cabbage, turnips, potatoes fried & boiled, ham, chicken, turkeys, geese, beef &c with cake for dessert." *Ibid.,* 205. It was reported that one North Carolina regiment received from home for Christmas 200 turkeys. Ross, *Visit to the Cities and Camps of the Confederate States,* 208.

decided to give the whole army a Christmas Dinner, later changed to New Year's. There was a great outpouring of money and provisions in a land that seemed devoid of both. Secretary of the Treasury Trenholm gave $2,000, members of the Virginia legislature voted a day's pay, and clerks in the War Department did likewise. Mrs. James A. Seddon and her neighbors gave a keg of cakes, seven turkeys, a duck, a piece of mutton, a piece of pork, and several bushels of vegetables; the Richmond Theatre raised about $15,000 by a benefit performance; one of Richmond's bakeries gave 36,000 loaves of bread; the Southern Express Company carried all provisions free. Day after day the Richmond papers published lists of contributions. Cooking was done and other preparations were made in the vacant Ballard House (formerly a principal hotel), from which operations flowed 900 pounds of grease, later sold to the Central Railroad for $7.50 a pound. This was "the biggest barbecue ever gotten up on this continent." The food was packed in boxes and barrels and served to the troops on a twenty mile front—"a table twenty miles long." [33]

Northern participants took due note of the hardships which Confederate soldiers endured and were thankful that their own troops were never called upon to pass similar tests. Admiral David D. Porter observed that in point "of endurance they set us an example it would have been hard to follow. I do not know whether we could have endured the hardships as well as they, as we were never called upon to try it." [34] A Federal chaplain doubted that his own soldiers would have continued to fight if they had been fed no better than the Confederates, whom he considered to be "dreadfully in earnest, ready for any sacrifice." [35]

An Englishwoman called the Confederate soldiers an "army of 'sovereigns,' " [36] a thought which Lee expressed in these words, "invincible if . . . [they] could be properly organized and officered." He added, "There never were such men in an Army before. They will go anywhere and do anything if properly led." [37]

[33] For Lee quotation, see Rowland (ed.), *Jefferson Davis, Constitutionalist*, VI, 224. See also, Richmond *Daily Examiner*, December 20–22, 24, 28, 29, 31, 1864; January 2, 4, 1865.

[34] Porter, *Incidents and Anecdotes of the Civil War*, 180.

[35] Stewart, *Camp, March and Battle-Field*, 389.

[36] [Hopley], *Life in the South*, I, 402.   [37] Freeman, *Lee's Lieutenants*, I, xvii.

The material of which his army was composed was "the best in the world." [38] Wise old Sam Houston said of them, "Equal them in point of discipline, and there will be no danger." [39] When the war had about run its course, a Richmond editor observed, "There never has been discipline in the armies of the Confederacy, but instead thereof a kind of universal suffrage, which fights when it chooses and straggles when it feels like it." [40] Herein lay both strength and weakness. Confederate soldiers were brave, patriotic, and resourceful; they had boundless confidence in their favorite leaders and above all in themselves. That is why they were undisciplined. "Everything favors us," said one, "the star of promise beckons us on,—and we follow it. Providence says to us, arise and conquer. We have generals equal to Moses and Joshua, and greater than Caesar." [41] A soldier declared after Gettysburg that Confederates would fight until hell froze over and then they would fight on the ice; and a Kentucky Confederate boasted, "If they beat us in the field, we'll take to the woods, and shoot them down like squirrels." [42] Texans, who came from a land where it was considered nothing to attack and slay a bear with a pocketknife, were held to be recklessly courageous. In the early days, soldiers were made to feel "that to be taken alive by the enemy . . . [was] a disgrace more terrible than death itself." [43] They disliked digging trenches and working around camps. "I dont mind the fighting one bit," said a Georgia soldier, "but I tell you it tries one's patriotism to go through this routine, most of which duty is perfectly useless." [44] They disliked showing deference to officers, and often associated with some of them on equal terms. One soldier who felt that he had been slighted by his captain said, "I have nothing to say to or about him till my 12 months service is out—then he and I living I want his company for five minutes—then he can go the way he has

[38] *Ibid.*, II, 282.

[39] Williams and Barker (eds.), *Writings of Sam Houston*, VIII, 304.

[40] Richmond *Daily Enquirer*, February 18, 1865.

[41] James J. Marks, *The Peninsular Campaign in Virginia; or, Incidents and Scenes on the Battle-Fields and in Richmond* (Philadelphia, 1864), 366.

[42] *Blackwood's Edinburgh Magazine* (Edinburgh, London), XC (1861), 757.

[43] Macon *Daily Telegraph*, February 27, 1862.

[44] George Barnsley, Manassas, Va., to Julia Barnsley, August 30, 1861, in Barnsley Papers (University of Georgia Library).

chosen I mine." [45] When in 1864 there was an incipient movement to re-establish the Society of the Cincinnati, Lee opposed this attempt to draw a sharp and invidious distinction between officers and soldiers.

A characteristic peculiar to Confederate soldiers was the so-called Rebel Yell, variously described as a shout "more overpowering than the cannon's roar," [46] "a mingling of Indian whoop and wolf-howl," [47] "the scariest sound that ever split a human ear," [48] "a soul-harrowing sound to hear." [49] It was said to have originated spon-

[45] Thomas G. Jackson, Yorktown, Va., to his sister, June, 1861 (in possession of the writer). See also, [Hopley], *Life in the South*, II, 274; Freeman (ed.), *Lee's Dispatches*, 160. In a letter addressed by a Texas soldier to Mrs. Davis and others, in September, 1861, he gives this remarkable apotheosis of the Confederate army: "But his [Davis'] Army! Never has mortal man reviewed such an army of troops as he can look upon, when the morning Sun causes the hill-tops to blush. Xerxes, nor Cyrus, Hannibal, nor Scipio, Caesar, nor Pompey, Napoleon, nor Wellington, with all their serried phalanxes of free-born men and slaves, could not; nor does the history of armies afford any thing like a parallel to the forces of this Confederacy compared in the scale of moral and intellectual worth.

"I speak not in the language of hyperbole: an examination will substantiate the assertion without pursuing the idea further. Our men are brave; they are virtuous; they are patriotic; they are *invincible*. They have entered the service, and *gone into the ranks*, from places as proud as any feudal baron ever boasted: opulent and proud fathers and sons of the Republic—who could stand up on a mound by the 'Father of water,' and looking over possessions which the eye cannot span, say, 'I am monarch of all I survey,' whose fatted cattle fleck the thousand hills, and whose bondsmen dot the distant fields, you find as privates in the ranks. The intellect and talent of the country, the Bench and Bar, the Church and College, the Laboratory and the Press, are here represented. Scorning office or place, seeking no reward, careless of losses, mindful of obligations to loved ones around the domestic hearth, it is true—but stifling the calls of affection and love in a sterner feeling and more heroic sentiment—you find them in the ranks, *willing to die for Jefferson Davis and the South*." Richmond *Daily Whig*, September 30, 1861. In 1864 Dr. Julian Chisolm said, "To have 'been to the wars' and acted honorably and bravely is a life-long honor, increasing with advancing years; to have received wounds in defense of our Country is as good title to nobility as an American citizen should wish to attain." *De Bow's Review*, XXXIV (1864), 47.

[46] [Hopley], *Life in the South*, II, 21–22.

[47] Augustine J. H. Duganne, *Camps and Prisons. Twenty Months in the Department of the Gulf* (3d ed., New York, 1865), 148.

[48] William M. Dame, *From the Rapidan to Richmond and the Spotsylvania Campaign. A Sketch in Personal Narration of the Scenes a Soldier Saw* (Baltimore, 1920), 77.

[49] Cable (ed.), "War Diary of a Union Woman in the South," in *Famous Adventures and Prison Escapes of the Civil War*, 58. See also, Ross, *Visit to the Cities and Camps of the Confederate States*, 40; William H. Morgan, *Personal Reminiscences of the War of 1861–5; In Camp—en Bivouac—on the March—on Picket—on the Skirmish*

taneously at the First Battle of Manassas, and seems to have been born of a spirit of triumph mixed with a feeling of release from fright on going into battle. Federals asserted that they heard Stonewall Jackson's troops give the yell a mile away.

As the morale of some soldiers began to deteriorate and Southerners became loath to join the army, Augustus B. Longstreet, a preacher and college president, sought to reassure the timid. A veteran had told him, he declared, that "he had been in six battles and he had never seen a man killed by a cannon or bomb in his life," that if a soldier would stand his ground with his bayonet he would never have to use it, and that he had never heard of an actual bayonet fight, for the soldiers with the greater determination would always put the others to flight.[50]

To instill discipline, courts-martial were held, and, after October, 1862, standing special military courts came into existence to deal with frequent infractions of rules. Punishments were severe and at times seemingly barbarous, but they were spasmodic, and in the end critics declared that the army was allowed to disintegrate for lack of firmness in enforcing discipline. A soldier convicted of sleeping at his post was sentenced to "Hard labor with ball and chain for two weeks and, then, to solitary confinement on Bread and water for two weeks." General Beauregard was so outraged by the leniency of this sentence that he released the soldier and restored him to duty. In addition to these punishments, "bucking" and "gaging" were resorted to, as well as branding with the letter C for coward; whipping with thirty-nine lashes; wearing a barrel shirt (a barrel with both ends knocked out) bearing such placards as "I am a thief" and "I am a shirker from battle"; confinement in the guardhouse; carrying a log; receiving a public reprimand; or shooting. Bragg was accused, probably unjustly, of having a soldier "shot down like a dog in his tracks," because on being refused a

---

Line—on the Battlefield—and in Prison (Lynchburg, 1911), 70; Wiley, *Life of Johnny Reb*, 71; *Confederate Veteran*, XIX (1911), 521–22.

50 Moore (ed.), *Rebellion Record*, VIII, 433–37 (documents). The editor of the Richmond *Daily Examiner*, August 7, 1863, gave this description of the true soldier: "he who remains at his post; he who asks few furloughs, and is never absent without leave; who never straggles on the march; who does not skulk from the fire; who is seen in the ranks of the army or in the hospital, but never at home, never in the wayside house, never in the cities, unless with a broken limb."

furlough he had left without one to visit his wife on her death-bed.[51]

As actual fighting took up very little of soldiers' time, they must do something to relieve the boredom of camp life and racking homesickness. Thus arose many of their amusements and pastimes. They played baseball, football, and quoits, but more important than these games were foot races, cockfighting, gambling with cards and dice, singing, and reading. One regiment at least actually went to school. Frequently *tableaux vivants* were staged. In the Upper South soldiers engaged in great snow battles carried out with military precision; in the Lower South they threw flaming pine knots; they made rabbit hunts into important events; and occasionally they played menagerie with each participant assuming the guise of some animal. Civilians visited soldiers, and now and then a politician, perhaps a governor, would make speeches to his constituency, as did Vance in 1864 when he spoke to about 5,000 soldiers, including Jubal Early, Jeb Stuart, and other officers.[52]

Some soldiers set out to keep diaries, most of which soon lapsed, as paper was hard to get and it was difficult to preserve journals on the march. But letter writing occupied much time, and many soldiers who had written few or no letters previously now tried their hands at it. Never before had there been so much letter writing in the South, for never before had there been so many members of families absent from home. They wrote about army strength and military plans, and these uncensored letters were often captured by the enemy or talked about by people at home. Toward the end of the war there was some interception of defeatist letters from the homefolk to the soldiers. Next to a letter from home, soldiers enjoyed newspapers, and to aid their distribution Congress passed a bill allowing papers directed to soldiers to go postage free; but Davis vetoed it on constitutional grounds, though his enemies

[51] Court-martial record, June 28, 1861, in Milledge L. Bonham Papers (South Caroliniana Collection, University of South Carolina Library); Raymond *Hinds County Gazette*, September 24, 1862; Richmond *Daily Examiner*, October 30, 1862; June 4, 1863; Durkin (ed.), *John Dooley, Confederate Soldier*, 73; Spencer G. Welch, *A Confederate Surgeon's Letters to his Wife* (New York, 1911), 45.

[52] J. W. Blackshear's journal, in Baber-Blackshear Papers (University of Georgia Library); Macon *Daily Telegraph*, April 7, 14, 1864; Richmond *Semi-Weekly Enquirer*, April 5, 1864; Richmond *Daily Whig*, August 20, 1861; von Borcke, *Memoirs of the Confederate War*, 340, 341–42; Wagstaff (ed.), *Graham Papers*, 184, 205, 208.

said his action was in spite against the editors who criticized his administration. But the most soul-killing and pathetic experience a soldier could have was to receive neither letter nor newspaper. The men constantly complained that they got no letters from home and many became haunted with the feeling that no one cared about the tattered and hungry soldiers. But it was difficult for the postal authorities to keep up with soldiers who were moving around and often changing their military units, and to deliver improperly addressed letters. An Army Intelligence Office was set up in Richmond as a clearinghouse for soldiers' mail, but it never functioned well.[53]

Profanity was common in a soldier's conversation and drunkenness became a serious problem. Whisky flowed in almost every town and hamlet of the Confederacy and it easily found its way into the army. Most of it was a terrible concoction whose effects were often described in humorously exaggerated language. A drop of it falling on the cobblestones would sound like a peal of thunder as it rent

[53] Richmond *Daily Whig*, November 25, 1862; April 14, 1863; February 29, 1864; Ramsdell (ed.), *Laws and Joint Resolutions*, 28; Richardson (comp.), *Messages and Papers of the Confederacy*, I, 556–58; Stiles, *Four Years under Marse Robert*, 350; Wiley, *Life of Johnny Reb*, 192 ff. The editor of the Augusta *Chronicle & Sentinel*, quoted in the *Southern Cultivator*, XX (1862), 199, advised the home folk never to write bad news or air their own troubles in letters to a soldier: "If the cows get in the cotton patch, or if his favorite dog dies some fine morning, there is not much occasion to mention it; and if his sweetheart has got married during his absence, tell him all the gossip of the neighborhood, but above all things don't *that*—lest in his rage he takes his revenge out of [sic] the newly-made husband's 'substitute,' and thus get himself in the guard house." Probably this letter (in possession of the writer) is among the first its author ever attempted: "Ronoke I lant [Island] December the 3 1861   Deer sir   I take the prason opertunity to rite you a few lines to in form you of my helth   I am Wel at the present time hoping these few lins may find you en-going the saime Blessing . . . We hant bin enterrupted by the ennimy bot We expect it evry day now   if they com We Will give them the best We have   i Wil tel you I have sean a heap Sins i left home   We caim to this plase cold [called] Ronoke ilunt a bout 2 monts a go and it is the Worst thicket you ever Sead   We com her[e] by steam bote and We cant git a Way only by a steam bote   the boys ant sad is fide [satisfied] like they was at Ports mouth   I ant ny as Wel sad is fide as i Was at Potys mouth   We Was thar at town Whar We cod git eny thing We Wanted and at the postofis and now We ar Won hundred mile from town and Postoffs and We cant git nothing to drink   We got nouse that We had to go back to Ports mouthe   if We do i Wil be glad but i dont think We Wil for We have got our winter quarts most don . . .   I dont think of eny thing els to rite now   you must excuse me for not paing no postage for i hant got a sent in the World and so remains your effeshonate freind until dethe."

asunder the earth's surface for a quarter of a mile around. Spying a bottle of it through a microscope, the eye could see "a dozen fights, six shootings and five stabs." [54] A Macon editor reached the heights of absurdity in this description: it "would conglomerate the vesicles of the aorta, phlogistify the phylacter maximus, hemstitch up the hepatic ducts, insulate the asperifollus gland, deflagrate the dudonian process, and wilt the buttons off the waistcoat, besides doing a good many other things which it might be too tedious to specify." [55] Brawls, disease, and death resulted. Bragg declared that it was the "cause of nearly every evil from which we suffer" and prohibited it in his army except for medicinal purposes.[56] On January 9, 1862, Adjutant General Cooper extended Bragg's order to all Confederate armies, but later he permitted troops to have whisky "in cases of extraordinary fatigue and exposure." [57] Not only soldiers but also many officers drank, and it was frequently charged that battles were lost because of drunken officers. Yancey declared in April, 1862, that he had heard that during a battle in North Carolina "an officer was drunk in bed with his boots on." [58] That same month Congress passed a law providing trial and dishonorable dismissal from the army of any officer found drunk on duty or off. By the end of 1864, 151 had been charged with drunkenness and 80 had been found guilty.

The use of tobacco was a much less reprehensible habit than drinking, and soldiers took full advantage of it. As cigars were too expensive and cigarettes had not yet been invented, soldiers chewed tobacco or smoked a pipe, and some did both. A North Carolina soldier, trying to obey his mother's injunction against the use of tobacco, wrote her, "I have quit chewing and will try to quit smoking also." [59] Pipe smoking seems to have won out over chewing in most cases. A Richmond editor asserted that soldiers burned more tobacco than powder, and another sug-

---

[54] Macon *Daily Telegraph*, April 7, 1862.   [55] *Ibid.*, April 3, 1862.

[56] *General Orders from Adjutant and Inspector-General's Office, Confederate States Army,* 1862–1863, Ser. 1862, pp. 5–6.   [57] *Ibid.*, Ser. 1863, p. 43.

[58] *Southern Historical Society Papers,* XLV (1925), 127. See also, Thomas E. Dabney, *One Hundred Great Years; The Story of the Times-Picayune from its Founding to 1940* (Baton Rouge, 1944), 177; Richmond *Daily Examiner,* December 23, 1864. A Richmond editor declared, "Whiskey is to be master of this Confederacy, not the Yankees." *Ibid.,* January 22, 1863.   [59] Wagstaff (ed.), *Graham Papers,* 124.

THE CONFEDERATE STATES OF AMERICA

gested that the emblem of the Confederacy should be a soldier walking down the street with a pipe in his mouth and a loaf of bread under his arm. But tobacco was hard to get, and one soldier complained, "if ever anything causes a mutiny in the army, it will be the want of tobacco." [60] Beginning in 1864 the government furnished each soldier three quarters of a pound a month, but the grade was little better than that of the whisky. A Virginian declared that "nothing under heaven, unless it might be a billy-goat could keep any portion of . . . [rationed tobacco] in the mouth five minutes and not vomit. The tobacco is not funky but absolutely *rotten*. It isn't worth one cent a pound in Confederate money." [61]

Undoubtedly one reason why fraternization thrived between Confederate and Federal soldiers was because the former generally had a supply of some sort of tobacco on hand and the latter had plenty of coffee. Certainly trading in these two articles, and others too, especially newspapers, became a common occurrence wherever armies were encamped near each other. Probably the most famous "siege of fraternization" followed the Battle of Fredericksburg, when the armies were encamped with only the Rappahannock River between them. This river became an artery of commerce in which tiny boats and rafts were used, and occasionally parties of Federals were invited over to the Confederate side to spend the day. When the day was over, the Federal band would play "Dixie" and the Confederate, "Yankee Doodle." Now and then friendly bantering would go on across the lines, as when the Federals would shout out to the besieged defenders of Vicksburg that they were merely prisoners feeding themselves, or when on the York Peninsula a Federal asked a Confederate what his regiment was and received the reply, "the ten thousandth Georgia, what is yours," and got the answer, "the eighty seventh thousand six hundredth and seventy fifth Vermont." [62] There was a sort of unwritten code between the pickets that they must not fire on

60 Richmond *Daily Examiner*, August 26, 1864.

61 Richmond *Daily Whig*, May 31, 1864. See also, *General Orders from the Adjutant and Inspector-General's Office, Confederate States Army, From January 1, 1864, to July 1, 1864*, p. 84; Richmond *Daily Examiner*, December 1, 1862; Richmond *Daily Whig*, January 21, 1863.

62 Cobb, Lee's Mill, Va., to his wife, April 16, 1862, in Thomas R. R. Cobb Letters.

one another, and when operations were about to begin, a Confederate might shout out, "Look out, Yanks, we've been ordered to fire." [63] When news reached the Federal troops that a son had been born to General George Pickett, they lit bonfires to celebrate the arrival of the "little general." Now and then Confederates and Federals would fraternize over a bottle of bourbon. Officers frowned on these good-natured manifestations of affection and claimed that battles had been lost on account of fraternization. A Richmond editor warned fraternizing Confederates that there was time enough to give the Federals "a friendly call, partake of their pure coffee and good whiskey, when the war is over and commercial relations with them are resumed, if they ever are to be." [64] A variation from ordinary fraternization was to trick the enemy whenever possible; for instance, more than once Confederates in the confusion of battle cried out to a squad of Federals, "For God's sake, stop firing! You are killing your own men!" [65]

Confederates were not only playful with the enemy; they were uncommonly full of tricks, banter, buffoonery, and foibles among themselves. Caught foraging "with the goods on him," a soldier might offer the defense that the sheep had tried to bite him, or the pig to kick him, or the fowl to peck him. A person with a spyglass might be greeted with the exclamation, "Look at that man with the Parrot gun on his back"; [66] or a person in high boots, "come

[63] [Morse], *Letters Written during the Civil War*, 177.

[64] Richmond *Daily Examiner*, June 13, 1864.

[65] A. P. Smith, *History of the Seventy-Sixth Regiment New York Volunteers . . .* (Cortland, N.Y., 1867), 154. See also, Gordon, *Reminiscences of the Civil War*, 107, *passim;* Inman (ed.), *Soldier of the South*, 111; Jones, *Rebel War Clerk's Diary*, I, 290–91; Richard W. Surby, *Grierson Raids, and Hatch's Sixty-Four Days March, with Biographical Sketches, and the Life and Adventures of Chickasaw, the Scout* (Chicago, 1865), 206–207; Oscar O. Winther (ed.), *With Sherman to the Sea; The Civil War Letters, Diaries & Reminiscences of Theodore F. Upson* (Baton Rouge, 1943), 62, 92. Deep down, there was a friendly regard officers on each side had for one another. George Pickett said of McClellan, at the time he was on his Peninsular campaign, "He was, he is and he will always be, even were his pistol pointed at my heart, my dear, loved friend," and of General Phil Kearney, killed at the Battle of Chantilly or Ox Hill, "I wish we had taken him prisoner instead of shooting him. I hate to have such a man as Kearney killed. Marse Robert, who was his old friend, sent his body to Pope under a flag of truce. I am glad he did that—poor old Kearney!" Inman (ed.), *Soldier of the South*, 15, 19.

[66] Ross, *Visit to the Cities and Camps of the Confederate States*, 95.

461

forth from *them boots,* 'taint no use hiding"; or a person with twisted and greased mustache, "take them mice out of . . . [your] mouth; 'taint no use saying they ain't thar—see their tails a waggin'." [67] They tied captured United States flags to the tails of horses and cows; they enjoyed Bill Arp's humorous stories; they liked to pick up souvenirs; they gave their military buttons to their sweethearts; they had their bywords and senseless expressions. "Here's your mule," an expression that swept the Confederacy, was used as the title for a song. It meant nothing except a nonsensical greeting or sometimes an indication that "I'm the real thing." The mythical Confederate soldier was "Bolivar Ward," similar to "Kilroy" of a later time, except that Bolivar Ward's fame grew up and died during the war. A recruit would be sent with a message to Bolivar Ward, and often a soldier would shout "Bolivar Ward" for no reason at all. Soldiers advertised for wives in language which generally indicated that it was a humorous outburst or a hoax. An Alabama soldier wanted a wife

> *To calm his sorrows*
> *And soothe his woes,*
> *Cook his victuals*
> *And wash his clothes.* [68]

She must be under fifty, have a full set of teeth and no artificial hair, not wear larger than number eleven shoes, use no snuff nor

[67] Durkin (ed.), *John Dooley, Confederate Soldier,* 61.

[68] Greensboro *Alabama Beacon,* April 8, 1864. The expression "Here's your mule" is said to have originated in Tennessee, when some soldiers secretly unhitched a huckster's mule and hid it in a tent. When he began looking for it, he heard cries on all sides "Here's your mule." Poems were written and songs were parodied with the cry in it, as this stanza on "Maryland, My Maryland":

> The Yankee tread is on your streets,
> Here's your mule, O here's your mule!
> I hear the tread of the vandal's feet,
> Here's your mule, O here's your mule!
> Hark! I hear a rooster squall;
> The vandal takes it, hen and all,
> And makes the boys and women bawl,
> Here's your mule, O here's your mule!

Bromfield L. Ridley, *Battles and Sketches of the Army of Tennessee* (Mexico, Mo., 1906), 632–35. See also, Augusta *Weekly Constitutionalist,* August 13, 1862.

tobacco, and have a sweet disposition. A Virginia gentleman of the Confederate infantry, "unfortunately not handsome, but wealthy, intelligent, and very gallant," wanted a wife—and only Virginia ladies need apply.[69] A Louisiana soldier seemed to offer most: "the comforts and luxuries of a lovely home on the banks of the majestic Mississippi, deeply embowered midst clustering roses and creeping clematis, where the breezes come laden with the sweet perfume of orange blossoms and myrtle groves." [70]

Unfortunately for both armies, soldiers did not want to remain soldiers all of the time; they wanted to go home on furloughs and some of them wanted to stay. It was never possible to determine absolutely in all cases who were deserters, either individually or in the aggregate. According to the Confederate definition, a deserter was a soldier who left the army with no intention of returning; but establishing intention was difficult. Length of absence was not always a sure test; hence the impossibility of distinguishing deserters from absentees or stragglers—those absent without leave. Absenteeism became an "evil of enormous magnitude," "a most extraordinary phenomenon," to use contemporary expressions. It began with the war itself and continued to grow until, just before the end, the armies had practically melted away. It first became marked in the spring of 1862, and after that time scarcely more than half of the Confederate troops on the rolls were ever present for duty, with sickness and furloughs supplementing desertion and straggling. After the retreat from Shiloh almost four thousand soldiers absented themselves, and a few months later, in June, 1862, the Secretary of War asserted that desertion had so weakened the armies that they could no longer reap the fruits of victory or invade the enemy's territory. A little later when Lee invaded Maryland on his Sharpsburg campaign, desertion became frightening and it was asserted that the Confederates could have won a resounding victory there if the deserters and stragglers had been present. In one company only six turned up for the fight. In the summer of 1863 Lee wrote Davis, "The number of desertions from the army is so great and still continues to such an extent that unless some cessation of them can be caused I fear success in the field

[69] Richmond *Daily Examiner,* March 19, 1863. [70] *Ibid.,* March 24, 1863.

will be seriously endangered." [71] After Sherman's capture of Atlanta in the fall of the next year, Davis boldly stated in a speech at Macon that "two-thirds of our men are absent—some sick, some wounded, but most of them without leave." [72] He promised that if half of those absent without leave would return, Sherman could be driven from the state. According to incomplete records, almost twice as many soldiers from North Carolina deserted as those from any other state.

Reasons for deserting were many. Lee thought "that the insufficiency of food and non-payment of the troops . . . [had] more to do with the dissatisfaction among the troops than anything else." [73] To these Governor Vance added dislike of the conscription laws, the refusal to grant furloughs, and homesickness; and another North Carolinian believed that Davis' alleged preferment of Democrats for office was a potent cause for discontent in his state—"a belief that we are fighting to perpetuate Democratic rule and ascendency, . . . a Democratic war and a Whig fight." [74]

[71] Freeman (ed.), *Lee's Dispatches*, 123.

[72] Athens *Southern Watchman*, September 28, 1864. See also, *Official Records*, Ser. IV, Vol. II, 7; *Southern Historical Society Papers*, XLII (1917), 53–56; Richmond *Semi-Weekly Enquirer*, October 14, 21, 1862; Richmond *Daily Examiner*, January 15, 1864; Bettersworth, *Confederate Mississippi*, 202; Lonn, *Desertion during the Civil War*. Straggling was a special type of absenteeism taking place on the line of march or in battle. Major General Gustavus W. Smith, commanding at Goldsboro, North Carolina, issued on January 15, 1863, a general order against straggling, in which he said, "Our victories have with few exceptions been rendered fruitless, the war prolonged and thousands of lives sacrificed by the disgraceful and cowardly habit of straggling, and the straggler has become a traitor, an enemy to his country more deadly and despicable than the vilest among the hordes of the invader." To prevent straggling he ordered that no one be allowed to fall out on the march or in battle except for physical ailment, which must be attended to and certified by a surgeon, and for "the demands of nature." In both cases he should be placed in the hands of a noncommissioned officer, who in the first case should report him, and in the second should see that the soldier returned to his ranks promptly. Each brigade should have a provost guard of a hundred men to follow the army to pick up stragglers, and in battle to post themselves in the rear to return to the battle line all soldiers not wounded, except the ambulance corps. No one except members of the ambulance corps should be allowed to accompany a wounded soldier to the rear. Copy in Thomas Lanier Clingman Papers (University of North Carolina Library).

[73] *Official Records*, Ser. I, Vol. XLVI, Pt. II, 1143.

[74] Calvin J. Cowles, Wilkesboro, N.C., to Governor Vance, October 19, 1863, in Vance Papers, III (North Carolina State Archives).

There was also the conviction that the poor man was fighting the rich man's battle. Soldiers were especially bitter because they believed that the government was guilty of bad faith in granting furloughs. Dislike of certain generals, such as Pemberton and Bragg, caused many desertions. And the continuous attacks against the Confederate administration by various newspapers and other critics had a tremendous effect in producing a spirit of defeatism and consequent desertion. One soldier gave as his reason for deserting the fact that he had been reading the Raleigh *Standard* and had become convinced that Davis was a tyrant and the Confederate cause wrong.[75]

But a greater source of discontent than any other was what might be called the home front, which gave rise to a cluster of reasons for desertion, including the furlough problem. The gnawing feeling that their families were suffering and that speculators were taking the bread from their mouths caused soldiers to set out for home. This situation was the most prolific cause for desertions, said the Tuskegee Baptist Association, and it cautioned, "Let our soldiers realize that the danger from the rear is greater than the danger in front, and can we expect any other result but that our armies will melt away like the morning dew?"[76] But how could soldiers get that impression except through letters from home and from newspaper editorials? An Alabamian warned, "Wives! Mothers! beware what you write to your husbands and sons in the army.—A thoughtless and imprudent letter may lead to discontent, desertion and death."[77] Yet such letters as this went to the soldiers at the front: "[Our] son is lying at death's door . . . he cannot live long in the fix he is in   he is raving distracted   his earnest calls for Pa allmost breaks my heart. John come if you can if they will not let you off I dont know the reason."[78] A soldier on furlough wanting an extension of his leave wrote to Governor Clark of Mississippi: "i want a little chance to prepare for my

---

[75] Rowland (ed.), *Jefferson Davis, Constitutionalist*, V, 487; Welch, *Confederate Surgeon's Letters*, 79; Richmond *Daily Whig*, November 13, 1863.

[76] Tuskegee *South Western Baptist*, October 1, 1863.

[77] Selma *Reporter*, quoted in Grove Hill (Ala.) *Clarke County Journal*, February 19, 1863.

[78] Louisa to John, no place and undated (in possession of the writer).

family to live and not suffer. if you will be so kind as to let me stay at home this time Just write me a few lines." [79] This typical situation prompted a feeling that there was nothing wrong in deserting; it led others to desert, and diminished the possibility of getting them back into the army. Early in 1864, Congress passed a law providing punishment for anyone who counseled desertion or aided a deserter.

Simple homesickness unassisted by any feeling of distress at home was a powerful force, often resulting in desertion or even death. The lack of letters from home played an important part in the development of this disease. Soldiers thought of home; they often dreamed of home; delirious in hospitals they talked only of home. "It seems strange that [of] almost all the sick I have seen at the Hospital the larger number when asleep talk of home," wrote a Georgia soldier to his sister. "Who can blame them? No one knows the hardship a soldier has to go through without he has tried it." [80] A Congressional committee reported that a furlough home would often cure a sick soldier suffering from the "low, depressing diseases of the camp, preying as much on the mind and the spirit of the sufferer as on his body." [81]

But it was the home front that gave way first, and many brave soldiers sensed it. "Letters from home cause almost all the desertion in our army," said one. "It pains me greatly to see the letters some of our boys receive, counselling them to desert their posts in this the time of our country's need; and I feel grateful that my own parents and friends never write me any such letters." [82] Some soldiers did not want to go home because of the low morale there, and army units held meetings begging the people at home to hold out, to remember that the soldiers at the front were much worse off than they were. One newspaper editor commented, "It is enough to make a soldier hate his home, his kindred and his neighbors to hear them complaining and groaning on beds of ease, while he has been sleeping on the cold, wet ground, eating hard bread,

[79] Michael Tearman (?) to Governor Clark, no date except "the 21st," Ser. E, Vol. LXVII, Nos. 66, 68, 69 (Mississippi State Archives).

[80] Lucien Barnsley, Culpeper Courthouse, to Julia Barnsley, September 14, 1861, in Barnsley Papers (University of Georgia Library).

[81] *Journal of the Congress of the Confederate States*, I, 726.

[82] Athens *Southern Watchman*, October 21, 1863.

marching, and fighting, and fighting for three long years." [83] Another observed, "If we are defeated, it will be by the people at home." [84]

The Confederacy pursued the wrong policy in punishing deserters. Instead of dealing sternly with them in the beginning and setting an example to others, military authorities published their names on a Black Roll, called them Tories and Vampires, and advertised a $30 reward for the return of each one. But other punishments were resorted to, such as branding them with the letter D, applying fifty lashes, assigning hard labor with ball and chain for varying periods of time, confinement on bread and water for fifteen days, bucking and gaging, and death either by shooting or hanging. Unfortunately there was always lacking the certainty of punishment or of the degree of its severity. Officers were merely reduced to the rank of privates. In April, 1863, Congress abolished whipping and decreed that punishment might be death or imprisonment with or without hard labor for a period from one to five years. Frequently when death was decreed, Davis pardoned the offender or commuted his sentence; and Lee often recommended clemency on account of extreme youth, previous good record, or some other sentimental reason. Jackson and Forrest were the most stern. The editor of the Richmond *Examiner* attacked Davis' leniency and declared his "snivelling compound of selfish vanity and nervous sensibility, which the weak mistake for mercy . . . [had] usurped the place of the monarch of the soul, justice." [85] But the death sentence was carried out now and then, sufficiently often to create a profound impression on those who saw an execution or read a newspaper account of it. A North Carolina soldier who had been present at the execution of three deserters wrote his mother, "It was the saddest sight I ever witnessed and I hope I may never see the like again. I heard that they were caused to desert by letters from home." [86]

[83] Milledgeville *Confederate Union*, February 9, 1864.

[84] Atlanta *Southern Confederacy*, October 25, 1862. See also, Richmond *Daily Enquirer*, February 23, 1865; Richmond *Whig*, September 5, 1863; Wagstaff (ed.), *Graham Papers*, 177. A soldier wrote in 1864 that it was "a great contrast between the spirit of the army and that which every veteran brings concerning those at home." Macon *Daily Telegraph*, April 14, 1864.

[85] Richmond *Daily Examiner*, December 16, 1863.

[86] Wagstaff (ed.), *Graham Papers*, 178. See also, Richardson (comp.), *Messages and*

Desertion steadily increased despite punishment; its futility soon caused a resort to begging and coaxing. On August 1, 1863, Davis issued a proclamation pardoning those under punishment for desertion as well as all soldiers absent from the army if they would return within twenty days, provided in both cases they were not second offenders. Various commanders thereafter offered pardon to deserters who would return, and in an effort to prevent desertion, Congress, in February, 1864, attempted to bribe soldiers by offering a $100 bond to all who should not absent themselves without leave during the six months following April 1. Davis begged the people back home, and especially the women, to shame deserters into returning to the army. Governors, including even the obstructionist Joseph E. Brown, used their best efforts to return deserters. Detachments of regular troops were sent out to intercept deserters, the Conscription Bureau accepted as a principal duty rounding them up, and after September, 1864, commanders of the reserves in the various states lent their efforts.

Deserters banded together with bushwhackers and outlaws and infested and controlled extensive areas of the Confederacy, especially mountainous regions in Virginia, North Carolina, Tennessee, South Carolina, and Alabama, swamps in Florida, and iso-

---

Papers of the Confederacy, I, 329–31; Augusta Daily Chronicle & Sentinel, May 11, 1864; Richmond Daily Dispatch, August 27, 1862; Richmond Daily Examiner, October 6, 1862; January 31, June 23, November 16, 1863; March 22, 1864. This estimate of the times appeared in the Richmond Daily Examiner, September 4, 1863: "Patriotism, chivalry; heroism, the warlike spirit, eloquent speeches and proclamations, answered their end in the early days of this struggle. But the volunteer system is now effete, worn out, good for nothing but mischief. The hey-day of glory is past.—Duty now is the only sentiment except the fear of death, which can operate on the mind of the soldier. The class which is controlled by the sense of duty is limited." A soldier who went home without a furlough soon repented when "The old man broke into tears and told me that I could not stay with him, that I must go back to my regiment." Athens Southern Watchman, July 22, 1863. Governor Vance's stinging proclamation of May 11, 1863, against deserters told them that after the war, "the land will be full of veteran soldiers, before whose honest faces you will not have the courage to raise your eyes from the earth. If permitted to live in the State at all, you will be infamous. You will be hustled from the polls, insulted in the streets, a jury of your countrymen will not believe you on oath, and honest men everywhere will shun you as a pestilence; for he who lacks courage and patriotism can have no other good quality or redeeming virtue." Official Records, Ser. I, Vol. LI, Pt. II, 707. Vance's prediction did not come true; for after the war the record of deserters was speedily forgotten publicly. Only privately if at all was the deserter remembered.

lated piney-woods sections in other parts of the Confederacy. They robbed and intimidated throughout their little kingdoms, controlling towns and burning courthouses. A mob of deserters forced a jail delivery in Cherokee County, Alabama; Florida deserters who controlled some of the coastal counties captured an incoming blockade-runner and robbed it of 10,000 blankets and 6,000 pairs of shoes; and twenty-five North Carolina deserters broke into a tannery in Louisa County, Virginia, and stole $3,000 worth of leather, leaving this note: "Don't think that it was niggers that robbed you. It was twenty-five North Carolina deserters, and we are going home. We are well armed and hell can't take us." [87] When deserters in their own habitat were asked for their furloughs, "they just pat their guns and defiantly say, 'This is my furlough.' " [88]

Some Confederate deserters did not return to their homes but went over to the enemy, propelled by their desire not to "stay in this one horse barefooted naked famine stricken Southern Confederacy" [89] or enticed by the flattering invitations of Northern commanders sometimes extended by handbills and by Lincoln's amnesty proclamation of December 8, 1863. They were required to take the oath of allegiance to the United States. They might be imprisoned for a time, given work in the North, or enlisted in the Federal armies to fight either against their erstwhile compatriots or against the Indians in Minnesota or elsewhere. Near the end of the war hundreds of them in Virginia crossed the lines into the Federal army. And conversely many Federal soldiers deserted to the Confederacy, took the oath of loyalty, and received promise of friendly treatment. Some of them were employed in factories and in other skilled occupations; others were aided to return home as paroled prisoners of war with the assurance that the laws of war prevented them from taking further part in the struggle. In 1864, Adjutant General Cooper issued a proclamation in English,

[87] Richmond *Daily Examiner*, October 23, 1863.

[88] *Official Records*, Ser. IV, Vol. II, 721. See also, Gov. Milton to Mallory, May 23, 1864, in "Commissary Activities and War Correspondence, 1863–1865," pp. 72–74 (Florida State Archives); Milton to Seddon, June 30, 1864, pp. 104–105, *ibid.;* Duncan L. Clinch to Cobb, April 4, 1865, in Howell Cobb Papers; Grove Hill (Ala.) *Clarke County Journal*, April 14, May 19, 1864; Richmond *Daily Examiner*, January 11, 1862; Albert D. Richardson, *The Secret Service, the Field, the Dungeon, and the Escape* (Hartford, 1865), 463–66.   [89] Wiley, *Plain People of the Confederacy*, 66.

French, and German inviting all discontented Federal soldiers, especially foreigners, to cross into the Confederate lines, where they would be treated with friendship. There was always the danger, however, that the deserter might in fact be a spy.[90]

But the vast number of soldiers reaching the enemy were prisoners of war, taken against their will on the field of battle. The exact number can never be determined with absolute certainty. Various estimates have been made, but these statistics are within reason: The Confederates took nearly 212,000 Federal prisoners and paroled almost 17,000, leaving about 195,000 in their hands to be imprisoned; the Federals took more than 463,000 Confederates and paroled about 248,000, leaving slightly less than 215,000 to be imprisoned. The large number of Confederate prisoners included the surrendered armies of the Confederacy at the end of the war, and does not give an accurate impression of the prisoners taken in actual combat.[91]

The Confederacy fell heir to its first prisoners in April and May of 1861 when General David E. Twiggs, who commanded United States troops in Texas, surrendered them and then joined the Confederacy. Thereafter Confederate armies took prisoners in every battle, and detention of these unwilling visitors became a problem. Richmond became a clearinghouse and dispersed prisoners to the four corners of the country; and the city's available buildings, principally tobacco warehouses, were converted into prisons. Libby, facetiously called Hotel de Libby, a ship-chandlers' warehouse, became the parent prison of the Confederacy and one of the most famous of all Civil War prisons. Soon Belle Isle, on an island in the James River, took care of the overflow. According to a Richmond news item in 1864, "Belle Isle, in the ancient and historical James, has at present over three thousand visitors, mostly from the dis-United States, but with representatives among them

[90] Richmond *Daily Enquirer*, November 2, 1864; Martin, *Desertion of Alabama Troops*, 241; Tyler, *Recollections of the Civil War*, 321, 332–33.

[91] For statistics on prisoners of war, see Rhodes, *History of the United States*, V, 507–508. The standard work on prisoners of war is William B. Hesseltine, *Civil War Prisons. A Study in War Psychology* (Columbus, Ohio, 1930). A scholarly, concise, and clear discussion is in Randall, *Civil War and Reconstruction*, 436–43. All of the *Official Records*, Ser. II, 8 vols., and much of Miller (ed.), *Photographic History of the Civil War*, VII, are devoted to the subject of prisoners of war.

from all the countries of Europe, Asia, and Africa and Patagonia. It is uncertain when the season will close at this favorite Yankee resort." [92] Other Virginia prisons were located at Danville, Lynchburg, and Petersburg. An old cotton factory at Salisbury, North Carolina, housed political prisoners, deserters, and prisoners of war. Among other Confederate prisons were "Camp Sorghum" at Columbia; the Florence Prison, the jail, fair grounds, and Castle Pinckney at Charleston; prisons at Millen, Macon (Camp Oglethorpe), Atlanta, Savannah, Blackshear, and Andersonville in Georgia; Cahaba (Castle Morgan), Tuscaloosa, and Mobile in Alabama; New Orleans; and Camp Groce and Camp Ford in Texas. The best known of these prisons were Andersonville, Libby, Belle Isle, and Salisbury.

Richmond was always congested with prisoners, but the situation became so critical that by 1863 it was determined to set up a great prison compound in Georgia where the climate was more salubrious and the food more plentiful. At Andersonville was chosen a tract of twenty-six acres, sloping up on both sides from a small stream, and it was enclosed with a palisade. Prisoners were first sent there in the spring of 1864; by August 8 the number had reached a peak of 33,114; and by the close of the war a total of 45,613 had passed through this prison. Like Andersonville, the prisons at Millen, Columbia, and Florence were large tracts of land with only such buildings as the prisoners constructed. Millen, covering forty-two acres, was the most extensive in the Confederacy. Almost uniformly the other prisons were centered around large buildings.

Prisoners were moved frequently as prisons became crowded or were threatened by the invaders. Sometimes it seemed they were needlessly transferred unless, indeed, evidence of Confederate victories served to build up the morale of the people. Prisoners almost invariably asserted that the boxcars into which they were crowded were uncleaned cattle cars; in reality they were the same cars in which many Confederate soldiers rode. As they passed through the small towns, they were variously greeted—sometimes by an expression which the prisoners made into these words, "What did you'ens come down here to fight we'uns for?" And they sometimes

[92] Richmond *Daily Examiner,* August 26, 1864.

snapped back, "We can whip you like Irish potatoes. Damn you, you will see us again." [93] A prisoner on his way through Richmond passed a compliment on "a mulatto wench" who tartly replied, "Go long, you nasty Abolition Yankee." [94] At Atlanta people came out to see a trainload of prisoners, having heard the facetious description, "That they were naked and hairy all over, and had horns, hoofs and tails, and all were chained like so many oxen in a stock car." [95] There was much trading with them at the stations, and frequently they were given refreshments, though one prisoner claimed that a woman in a little Georgia town spat upon him. As the trains traveled only from six to twelve miles an hour, many prisoners made their escape, 150 jumping off the train on a trip from Charleston to Columbia.

Most Confederate prison walls were so weak, if there were walls at all, that escapes were constant, despite guards and cannon. At Libby on one occasion a charge of gunpowder was planted to be set off against an expected mass break. Tunneling was a favorite method of engineering attempted escapes, but these operations were generally discovered. The most famous resort to this means was at Libby, where Colonel Thomas E. Rose directed the escape of 109 prisoners. Other prisoners gained freedom by breaking paroles, simulating sickness to escape from hospitals, forging passes, or simply walking away undetected. When once out, the prisoner usually made his way to the mountains or other disaffected regions where Federal prisoners were welcomed by deserters and bushwhackers, and especially to East Tennessee where the Federals were in control after the autumn of 1863. On their way they were assisted by slaves and Unionist whites. Subsisting on corn and sweet potatoes, in season, they traveled mostly by night, dodging their pursuers. Almost invariably, fleeing prisoners told of being followed by fierce bloodhounds. Nero and Spot were the names of two of these mythical brutes, vicious as the imagination of absent artists could make them. In fact, there were few bloodhounds in the Confederacy; any mongrel which would "track a rabbit" was used.

[93] Richmond *Daily Whig*, October 25, 1861.
[94] Jones, *Rebel War Clerk's Diary*, I, 318.
[95] Atlanta *Southern Confederacy*, September 25, 1861. See also, Alonzo Cooper, *In and out of Rebel Prisons* (Oswego, N.Y., 1888), 122–23.

A sprinkling of prisoners chose to take the oath of allegiance to the Confederacy and left prison walls to work in factories and other skilled trades, and some joined the Confederate army. Now and then a prisoner was paroled to live outside the prison and work at some skilled trade. In early 1863, 200 prisoners in Richmond took the oath and began working at $2.00 a day, 60 of them at the Tredegar Iron Works. At Florence, 1,000 were reported to have taken the oath by November, 1864. A Federal prisoner asserted, undoubtedly with great exaggeration, that 2,000 at Belle Isle joined the Confederate army; and another said that 300 left Millen for Confederate military service. Undoubtedly many of these "galvanized Yankees" were foreigners who cared little for either belligerent, and others took the oath as a means of securing freedom and escaping to the North. A Virginian remarked, "The man who is fool enough to fight in this crusade against the South will always prove knave enough to violate his oath." [96] About a thousand captured Catholic Irishmen took the oath of loyalty and joined the Confederate army, and at their first opportunity all deserted. A Confederate Catholic suggested that the oath could be made to hold if such prisoners swore it before a Catholic priest.

Prison life had no attractions and few amusements, though many soldiers in self-defense disciplined their minds to the situation as far as possible. Filth, vermin, disease, exposure to weather, bad water, and poorly cooked food desolated the souls of prisoners with disappointment and homesickness and racked their bodies with pain; yet there were many who accepted the situation with some success. Prison life had its varying experiences, some merry and some sad. Prisoners greeted newcomers with the expression "Fresh fish"; they referred to captives taken at the battle of Plymouth, North Carolina, as "Plymouth Pilgrims." They played card games and gambled with what little they had to lose; they read books and newspapers; inveterate traders, they "dickered" not only among

[96] Richmond *Daily Examiner*, January 7, 1864. See also, Morgan E. Dowling, *Southern Prisons* . . . (Detroit, 1870), 62; Henry M. Davidson, *Fourteen Months in Southern Prisons* . . . (Milwaukee, 1865), 335; Dabney H. Maury, *Recollections of a Virginian in the Mexican, Indian, and Civil Wars* (New York, 1894), 191–92; *Official Records*, Ser. II, Vol. III, 711; Vol. V, 816; Charleston *Daily Courier*, November 5, 1864; Richmond *Daily Examiner*, September 15, 1864; Richmond *Daily Whig*, January 12, November 18, 1863.

themselves but with their prison guards and the adjacent population; they whittled sticks and made trinkets. Some became vicious thugs and robbers, carrying on their "mugging" operations even to the point of murder. An Andersonville prison gang was apprehended and hanged by a committee of prisoners. Captives spent much time "skirmishing" for vermin, and they ostracized anyone who became disgustingly infested: a Belle Isle prisoner was pushed out of the tent one cold night and he froze to death. Prisoners were allowed to write and receive letters, but all incoming and outgoing mail was censored in Richmond, where it was dispatched both ways by a flag-of-truce boat on the James. They were also permitted to receive packages from home, but this privilege was briefly suspended at Richmond when it was reported that packages to Confederate prisoners in the North were not delivered and that Confederate prison authorities were charged with confiscating packages. Thereafter prison keepers searched all Federal packages to secure enclosed money, which might be used to bribe guards. In one or two instances prisoners found boxes of tobacco left in their warehouse prisons. To humor prisoners the authorities at most of the prisons allowed them to cast straw votes in the Presidential election of 1864, using beans, black and white, for Lincoln and McClellan respectively.

If prisons were to serve their purpose, keepers and guards had to be determined, fearless, and alert; yet they gave some of the prisoners paroles to go outside for wood and water, to cook, and to visit the countryside, and in some instances loaned them money. Preachers visited some of the prisons, distributing religious publications and delivering sermons. Moses D. Hoge and J. D. McCabe often preached in Libby, and almost every prison was ministered to by kindhearted women of the neighborhood: Elizabeth Van Lew at Richmond, Mrs. Amelia Feaster at Columbia, Mrs. Amanda Gardner at Cahaba, a Mrs. Allen at Camp Ford, and the South Carolina Soldiers Relief Society at Florence.

Yet the most bitter accusation ever leveled by Northerners against the Confederacy was its treatment of prisoners of war. During the struggle prison horrors were exaggerated in order to prevent Federals from going across the lines, to make them fight harder, and to stimulate recruiting; after the war charges of atrocities became part of the "waving of the bloody shirt" for political purposes and pensions. A Northerner in 1863 declared that the Confederate prison question was "the most effective war-cry" that had yet been raised. Secretary of War Stanton charged that the Confederacy appeared to have set up "a deliberate system of savage and barbarous treatment and starvation" for the purpose of incapacitating the prisoners for further military service.[97]

As a matter of fact, the Confederacy suddenly found itself in possession of a great mass of prisoners for whom it had made no preparations, and throughout the war its bungling efforts never solved the problem. But it took care of its prisoners almost as well as its own soldiers, for broken-down railroads and inefficient supply organizations served both alike. Not until almost the end of 1864 was a prison system evolved and placed under General John H. Winder, as commissary general of prisoners, but the situation was not really improved. As soon as there were prisoners to feed, Congress declared that rations should "be the same in quantity and quality as those furnished to enlisted men in the army of the Confederacy," and this policy was adhered to surprisingly well throughout the war. Even if humanitarian feelings had not dictated it, policy, some Confederates declared, would require the new government to keep the good opinion of the world by treating its prisoners fairly. Conditions were not uniformly bad in the Confederate prisons. By February, 1865, more than 20,000 prisoners had passed through Belle Isle; yet, according to a Congressional committee report, the number of deaths there had been only 164. Most prisoners commended Camp Groce, Camp Ford, and the prison at Savannah; it was Andersonville and Libby which colored the thinking of Northerners on the prison question, and at the former conditions were extremely bad. Out of a total of 45,613 prisoners received, 12,912 died. Here as well as elsewhere starvation was not the cause of the deaths, but rather a combination of

97 W. A. Croffut (ed.), *Fifty Years in Camp and Field. Diary of Major-General Ethan Allen Hitchcock, U.S.A.* (New York, 1909), 457; R. Randolph Stevenson, *The Southern Side; or, Andersonville Prison* (Baltimore, 1876), 243; Davidson, *Fourteen Months in Southern Prisons*, 57; Homer B. Sprague, *Lights and Shadows in Confederate Prisons. A Personal Experience, 1864–5* (New York, 1915), 121–22. An immense amount of prisoner-of-war literature appeared during and especially after the war. For an estimate of many items, see Coulter, *Travels in the Confederate States.*

conditions and circumstances over which the Confederacy had little control. Homesickness, a change in food, water, and climate, and lack of medicines and doctors were conditions no different from elsewhere in the Confederacy. To a proposition that each side be allowed to send surgeons and distribute food and medical supplies among their own prisoners, General Ethan Allen Hitchcock, the Federal Commissioner of Exchange, never made reply. The diseases most prevalent in the prison camps were diarrhea, scurvy, dysentery, and gangrene.[98]

Though it was good policy for Federal prisoners of war to exaggerate the horrors and cruelties of prison life and make monsters of such prison officials as Major Henry Wirz at Andersonville, there were some who took it more philosophically. A prisoner who had been held only a few days said, "I was used first-rate by the rebels, better than their men are used by ours, I think." Another who had an extended prison life wrote of Camp Ford, "There were cases of personal ill-treatment which came under my notice, but they were the great exceptions, and, as a rule, the rebels of my acquaintance did for their prisoners all that was possible with the means in their power, and treated them as well as prisoners could expect to be treated." [99]

Confederate soldiers likewise became prisoners of war and were taken to prison camps scattered over the North. The best known were Camp Douglas at Chicago, the Elmira prison in New York

[98] Matthews (ed.), *Statutes at Large of the Provisional Government of the Confederate States, 1861–1862*, p. 154; Richardson (comp.), *Messages and Papers of the Confederacy*, I, 376; *Official Records*, Ser. II, Vol. VIII, 122–23; Stevenson, *Southern Side; or, Andersonville Prison*, 28, 41, 240, 404, *passim*; Jefferson Davis, *The Rise and Fall of the Confederate Government* (New York, 1881), II, 598; Richmond *Daily Examiner*, July 8, 1862. Some prisoners asserted that the Confederate authorities through malignancy raised hopes of exchange and then dashed those hopes by not going through with it; but many of the prisoners learned that it was their own government that was refusing to exchange, and they became embittered, especially against Secretary of War Stanton, for this "atrocious inhumanity." In some of the prisons they held protest meetings and prepared resolutions to be sent to Washington. See Richardson, *Secret Service*, 457; James M. Page, *The True Story of Andersonville Prison: A Defense of Major Henry Wirz* (New York, 1908), 43, 126; Stevenson, *Southern Side; or, Andersonville Prison*, 43.

[99] *Letters from Two Brothers* [Warren H. and Eugene H. Freeman] *serving in the War for the Union to their Family at Home in West Cambridge, Mass.* (Cambridge, 1871), 78; S. A. Swiggett, *The Bright Side of Prison Life. Experiences in Prison and out, of an Involuntary Sojourner in Rebeldom* (Baltimore, 1897), 228.

state, Point Lookout in Maryland on the tip of the peninsula made by the Potomac River and Chesapeake Bay, Johnson's Island in Lake Erie off Sandusky (for officers), and Fort Delaware on Pea Patch Island in the Delaware River. Among the others were Camp Chase at Columbus; Camp Morton at Indianapolis; Camp Butler at Springfield, Illinois; Rock Island, on an island in the Mississippi River; and Camp Randall at Madison, Wisconsin. Confederates were soon taking note of the ill-treatment of their prisoners, alleging many of the same evils charged against themselves. A Richmond newspaper in 1863 compared the atrocities at Camp Chase "with the Black Hole of Calcutta," [100] and a committee of Congress in defending the Confederacy's record called attention to the cruelties practiced by the North. A Richmond paper in 1864 advised the Confederacy to publish the facts, adding that thousands "of Confederates may freeze in shanties on bleak prairies, or by the shores of frozen lakes; starve in the midst of plenty; rot in their vile dungeons, and nothing is known of it to the outside world." [101] Conditions at Point Lookout and Elmira were held to be especially bad. It was charged that prisoners were scantily clad in the cold Northern winters and that food was insufficient and bad. But Europeans and Southerners knew that Confederate prisoners were woefully in need, for Englishmen raised £3,000 for relief, and in 1864 the Federal government allowed the Confederacy to ship to New York City 1,000 bales of cotton which were sold for $348,622. From the net proceeds ($331,789), a paroled prisoner in charge bought for his fellow prisoners 17,000 blankets, 16,000 jackets and coats, 19,888 pairs of pants, 19,000 shirts, 5,900 pairs of drawers, 10,000 pairs of socks, and 17,000 pairs of shoes. Some of the Confederate state governments sought to aid their prisoners by asking permission to send cotton, tobacco, and sterling exchange to the North. The Confederacy asked authorization to send an additional 1,500 bales of cotton, but the war was now drawing to a close and the United States refused to grant further permission.[102]

[100] Richmond *Daily Examiner,* May 15, 1863.

[101] Richmond *Semi-Weekly Enquirer,* February 5, 1864.

[102] *Official Records,* Ser. II, Vol. VII, 1063–1299, *passim;* Vol. VIII, 2–661, *passim;* London *Index,* September 10, 1863, p. 304; Richmond *Daily Whig,* December 20, 1861. In retaliation against the Confederate practice of placing prisoners of war in Charleston while it was undergoing bombardment, the Federal authorities selected

One of the great tragedies of the war was that there were any prison camps at all, for if the cartel of July 22, 1862, had been carried out, all prisoners of war would have been exchanged or paroled within ten days of their capture. Prior to this cartel, commanders on their own authority exchanged prisoners, but the Federal government was loath to enter into a written agreement for fear it might appear to be a recognition of the Confederacy. After long negotiations the cartel was agreed to. All prisoners should be exchanged man for man and rank for rank except that an officer might be exchanged for an equivalent of soldiers, as a general for sixty enlisted men, and the excess of prisoners should be paroled and returned home not to engage in further military activities until exchanged. Famous Article IX of this cartel provided that any misunderstandings as to the meaning of the document should "not interrupt the release of prisoners on parole." But almost immediately many misunderstandings arose, and by the summer of 1863, exchanges had almost ceased. They were resumed spasmodically in driblets, especially for the sick, until April, 1864, when General Grant with understandable realism forbade further exchange. In August he explained, "It is hard on our men held in Southern prisons not to exchange them, but it is humanity to those left in the ranks to fight our battles. Every man we hold, when released on parole or otherwise, becomes an active soldier against us at once

six hundred Confederate officers and men in Fort Delaware and placed them on Morris Island, near batteries being fired at by the Confederates. Fritz Fuzzlebug [John J. Dunkle], *Prison Life during the Rebellion; Being a Brief Narrative of the Miseries and Sufferings of Six Hundred Confederate Prisoners sent from Fort Delaware to Morris' Island to be Punished* (Singer's Glen, Va., 1869). Few Confederate prisoners of war wrote accounts of their experiences in Northern prisons, as there was nothing to be gained by it, either financially or politically. For harrowing accounts of prison life at Point Lookout and Fort Delaware, published many years after the war, see J. G. de Roulhac Hamilton (ed.), *The Papers of Randolph Abbott Shotwell* (Raleigh, 1929–1937), II, 100–211. This inscription on a plaque in the Students' Union Building on the campus of Indiana University attests the esteem in which the Confederates held at least one prison keeper:

COLONEL RICHARD OWEN
COMMANDANT
CAMP MORTON PRISON 1862
TRIBUTE BY CONFEDERATE PRISONERS
OF WAR AND THEIR FRIENDS
FOR HIS COURTESY AND KINDNESS

either directly or indirectly." In February, 1865, there was a general resumption of exchange, with the sick being sent out first.[103]

The blame for raising misunderstandings was about equally divided, but the North in cutting off exchanges and paroles, which the South was always willing to continue slightly less than fully, was clearly violating Article IX. The first difficulty arose over paroled soldiers whom the North, in violation of the cartel, wanted to use to guard camps or fight Indians. The policy of exchange, the North soon realized, was an invitation to Federal soldiers to get captured and paroled, an easy way for soldiers to get out of the war and go home. Manifestly the cartel was becoming irksome to the North, and when the Confederacy began violating its terms, it gave the Federal government an excuse to stop exchanging, though in contravention of Article IX. This opportunity came with Davis' unwise proclamation of December 24, 1862, in which he pronounced General Benjamin F. Butler a felon and outlaw, and ordered him hanged by the officer of the force that captured him. The proclamation declared that all commissioned officers serving under Butler should be considered "robbers and criminals deserving death," and if captured should be "reserved for execu-

[103] For the cartel, see *Official Records*, Ser. II, Vol. IV, 266–68; for Grant's refusal, *ibid.*, Vol. VII, 62–63, 607. In his message to Congress, May 2, 1864, Davis said, "I confess my inability to comprehend their [Federal authorities'] policy or purpose. The prisoners held by us, in spite of humane care, are perishing from the inevitable effects of imprisonment and the homesickness produced by the hopelessness of release from confinement. The spectacle of their suffering augments our longing desire to relieve from similar trials our own brave men who have spent so many weary months in a cruel and useless imprisonment, endured with heroic constancy." Richardson (comp.), *Messages and Papers of the Confederacy*, I, 445–46. Exchange of prisoners was carried out by a flag-of-truce boat plying the James River, between Richmond and City Point. Gala occasions were made of the return of prisoners, as in March, 1864, when 1,100 prisoners were welcomed in Capitol Square with a speech by Davis, much flag-waving by the populace, and the distribution of cakes and coffee. Richmond *Daily Whig*, March 21, 1864. Many of the prisoners were forlorn, dried up and shrunken, with "a strange look in their eyes . . . placidly vacant, as if they had been dead to the world for years." Martin and Avary (eds.), *Diary from Dixie*, 301. One prisoner, on landing at City Point, expressed so vociferously his exuberance at being upon Southern soil again that he insulted a Federal guard, who then spat in his face, whereupon the soldier "drew a bowie knife and carved the guard in a terrible manner." Richmond *Daily Examiner*, March 19, 1863. To keep from losing track of returning paroled prisoners the Confederacy set up camps for parolees, but as the soldiers greatly objected to them and many slipped away, this system never worked successfully.

479

tion"; furthermore, no captured commissioned officers should be paroled until Butler should have met with his "due punishment." This blood-and-thunder proclamation contained an additional stumbling block, which became the cornerstone of Federal opposition to continued exchanges, namely that all Negro slaves captured in arms against the Confederacy be turned over to their respective states to be dealt with as the laws thereof required.

Here the South was threatening to violate the cartel by refusing to parole or exchange all prisoners, but the proclamation soon fell into disuse and all the points raised became academic. By the end of 1863, Colonel Robert Ould, the Confederate Commissioner of Exchange, was holding communication with General Butler himself, who had got himself appointed as an agent to work out exchanges. The Confederacy continued to exchange Federal officers as long as any exchanging went on; and, as for retaining Negro prisoners, Ould said in May, 1864, that the Federals could not point to "any well-authenticated case." As long as the Confederates held the excess of prisoners, the Federals had continued the exchanging, but after the summer of Gettysburg and Vicksburg, when the Federals held the excess, they used every obstacle to prevent a resumption of the cartel.[104]

The bitter years of Reconstruction which followed the war delayed a dispassionate view of the prison question. Statistics vary widely as to the deaths of prisoners. In 1866 Hitchcock, the Commissary General of Prisoners, placed the deaths of Confederate and Federal prisoners at 26,436 and 22,576, respectively, but as his Confederate records were incomplete he did not know that there was a larger number of Federal deaths. In 1903 the Chief of the

[104] For Davis' proclamation, see Richardson (comp.), *Messages and Papers of the Confederacy*, I, 269–74; for Robert Ould on Negro prisoners, *Official Records*, Ser. II, Vol. VII, 105. Ould's denial did not mean that the Confederacy did not hold Negro prisoners but that it was refusing to exchange them, for anyone could have read in the Richmond *Daily Examiner*, March 8, 1864, a news item stating that Negro prisoners had been received at Libby, "ranging in colour from gingerbread brown to tobacco black, greasy and loud smelling; encased in blue uniforms, close buttoned up to the chin." None of these may have been a slave, but in May a slave prisoner, anxious to return to his master, was brought to Libby, "in the hateful Yankee blue, which is enough to make a Southerner slay a negro at sight, no matter how harmless he may be." *Ibid.*, May 28, 1864.

Record and Pension Office reported 25,976 Confederate deaths and 30,218 Federal deaths. The absolute numbers will always remain a riddle, but in the words of an eminent historian who studied thoroughly the question of prisoners of war, "All things considered the statistics show no reason why the North should reproach the South. If we add to one side of the account the refusal to exchange the prisoners and the greater resources, and to the other the distress of the Confederacy the balance struck will not be far from even. Certain it is that no deliberate intention existed either in Richmond or Washington to inflict suffering on captives more than inevitably accompanied their confinement." [105]

[105] Rhodes, *History of the United States,* V, 508 (quotation used by permission of The Macmillan Company, publishers). For Hitchcock's statistics, see *Official Records,* Ser. II, Vol. VIII, 946.

CHAPTER XX

THE FINE ARTS AND THE PRESS

THE war was all-pervading. No aspect of life was left untouched. Not only were political and economic conditions attuned to the new day, but also music, the drama, painting, sculpture, newspapers, books, pamphlets, schools, and churches were awakened into greater activity or became casualties of war.

The South had always done a great deal of singing, but little publishing of music or composing of either the ballad or the air; but with the coming of secession and war the singing South leaped into pronounced activity in all these respects. There was hardly anyone who was so inhibited as not to feel that he could write a song, either the words or music, and frequently both. Illiterate soldiers concocted songs or added a verse to "McClellan's Retreat" until it became as long as "Mademoiselle from Armentieres" of a later time. In 1861 there appeared a 16-page booklet of *Original Songs of the Atlanta Amateurs, Containing more Truth than Poetry* and Hopkins' 18-page *New-Orleans 5 Cent Song-Book,* and the next year a work of 210 pages, entitled *War Songs of the South,* was published. Thereafter, almost until the end of the war, many songbooks such as *Rebel Songster, Jack Morgan Songster, General Lee Songster,* and *Southern Soldiers' Prize Songster* made their appearance, and in 1864 a Charleston publishing house got out monthly a little pocket-sized booklet called *Taylor's Southern Songster.* In addition to these compilations there were hundreds of songs published as sheet music by such companies as P. P. Werlein & Halsey in New Orleans, J. H. Snow in Mobile, John C. Schreiner & Son in Macon and Savannah, Schreiner & Hewitt and Blackmar and Brother in Augusta, and George Dunn & Company in Richmond. "If all the music manufactured in the South found a market," said a Richmond editor, "we should certainly be a very musical people," but a Macon publisher correctly declared that a great deal of it was trash.[1]

There were polkas, waltzes, schottisches, marches, and simply songs to be sung or played on instruments, and many of the old songs were given greater currency. They were sentimental, especially about mother, home, sweetheart, and death; they were warlike, patriotic, and defiant; they honored favorite generals and moaned their loss (it is said that there were no fewer than forty-seven monodies and dirges on the death of Jackson alone); [2] they were humorous; they celebrated the Confederate flag. Out of more than half a thousand songs published in the Confederacy, but not all written by Southerners, these are illustrative: Sentimental— "The Dearest Spot of Earth to Me Is Home," "Who Will Care For Mother Now?" "Dear Mother, I'll Come Home Again," "Mother, Oh! Sing Me to Rest," "Dear Mother, I've Come Home to Die," "Her Bright Smile Haunts Me Still," "I Cannot Forget Thee," "How Can I Leave Thee," "Wait Till the War, Love, Is Over," "The Soldier's Grave," "The Vacant Chair: or, We Shall Meet, but We Shall Miss Him," "When This Cruel War Is Over"; warlike and patriotic—"On Guard," "Soldier's Suit of Grey," "Boys, Keep Your Powder Dry," "The Murmur of the Shell," "Fort Sumter Quickstep," "Our Triumph at Manassas," "Pickett's Charge March," "We Conquer or Die," "Song of the South," "Grand March of the Southern Confederacy," "Virginian Marseillaise," "Richmond on the 'James', and Bingen on the Rhine," "Palmetto Schottische," "Empire State Grand March," "Jeff Davis Inaugural March," Jefferson Davis Grand March"; defiant—"Southrons' Chaunt of Defiance," "Adieu to the Star Spangled Banner Forever," "No Surrender"; celebrating the fame of generals—"Stonewall Jackson's Way," "Stonewall Jackson's Grand March," "Riding

---

[1] For quotation, see Richmond *Daily Examiner*, December 2, 1863. See also, *ibid.*, August 31, 1864; Charleston *Daily Courier*, April 2, 1864; London *Index*, May 21, 1863, p. 61; Macon *Daily Telegraph*, January 24, 1862; Charles N. Baxter and James M. Dearborn (comps.), *Confederate Literature; A List of Books and Newspapers, Maps, Music and Miscellaneous Matter Printed in the South during the Confederacy, now in the Boston Athenaeum* (Boston, 1917), 80; Freeman, *South to Posterity*, 13; Wiley, *Life of Johnny Reb*, 152 ff.

[2] De Leon, *Four Years in Rebel Capitals*, 296.

a Raid" (for Jeb Stuart), "Beauregard's Manassas Quickstep," "Gen'l Beauregard's Grande Polka Militaire," "Gen'l Morgan's Grand March"; humorous—"You Are Going to the Wars, Willie Boy!" "Nobody Hurt Grand March," "Short Rations," "The Captain with his Whiskers."

Southerners honored their flag as they played or sang "Confederate Flag," "Flag of the Free Eleven," "The Southern Cross," and "The Stars and Bars"; but they enjoyed most "The Bonnie Blue Flag." This piece, set to the Irish air "The Jaunting Car," was written by the self-styled "Arkansas comedian" Harry Macarthy (actually born in England) and was first sung by him in a Jackson theater when Mississippi was on the point of seceding. Macarthy wrote other songs, among them "Missouri! or a Voice from the South" and "The Volunteer! or, It is my Country's Call."

James Ryder Randall, a Marylander, wrote "Maryland! My Maryland!" while serving as a professor at Poydras College in Pointe Coupee Parish, Louisiana, and Jennie, one of the beautiful Baltimore Cary sisters, set it to the old tune "Lauriger Horatius," later adapted to "O Tannenbaum." It was one of Beauregard's favorite songs. Probably the most eminent composer in the Confederacy was the English-born Frederick W. N. Crouch, a bugler in the Richmond Howitzers and formerly connected with the choir of St. Paul's Church, Richmond, and musical editor of *Godey's Lady's Book*. He wrote hundreds of songs during his lifetime, but his air to "Kathleen Mavourneen" is best known, a song which the soldiers sang and liked. The long life of Blind Tom spanned the Civil War years. He was taken by his master to the chief towns of the Confederacy to entertain audiences with his remarkable piano playing. This slave, "The Inspired Musician! The Wonder of the World! The Greatest Marvel on Earth! A Living Miracle!" not only played the music of others but also his own compositions. "Battle of Manassas" and "Rain Storm" were considered his best pieces.[3]

[3] Atlanta *Southern Confederacy*, December 18, 1861; Charleston *Daily Mercury*, April 18, 1862; Greensboro *Alabama Beacon*, March 27, 1863; Macon *Daily Telegraph*, February 3, 11, 1862; Richmond *Daily Examiner*, January 29, 1862; Richmond *Daily Whig*, October 26, November 6, 1861; January 30, 1862; *Confederate Veteran*, IV (1896), 295; Dame, *From the Rapidan to Richmond*, 21; Mrs. Burton Harrison, *Recollections Grave and Gay* (New York, 1912), 57.

The song which came to personify the South during the war as well as afterwards was "Dixie," written in 1859 by Dan Emmett of Ohio, who though a Federal veteran was adopted after the war by the South as its special hero. This tune was immediately seized by the Confederate soldiers, though Federals used it for a short time, and after the latter gave it up, Emmett wrote them one called "Dixie for the Union." Herman Arnold, a German who had immigrated to America in 1852, added a few notes, changed the structure of the melody somewhat, scored the music for rendition by his band, and played it at the first inauguration of Davis, in Montgomery. It was Arnold's version which became the stirring song heard thereafter. It was sung by the soldiers, it was sung by everybody; even steamers on the rivers played it on their calliopes before pulling up to landings. It was a song of defiance—children lined up on roadsides to sing it as Federal soldiers passed by. There were various sets of words; it was parodied; and other songs including the title word were written, such as "Southern Dixie," "Dixie War Song," "Dixie Variations," and even "Dixie Doodle." "Dixie" was the nearest the Confederacy came to having a national anthem, though Ernest Halphin [George H. Miles] and C. T. De Coëniél produced "Our National Confederate Anthem" or "God Save the South," the ballad by the former and the air by the latter. It never succeeded as it was too labored and artificial, being a potpourri of the "Star Spangled Banner," "Marseillaise," and "God Save the Queen" (Victoria being England's ruler at that time).[4]

Having seized "Dixie," Southerners abandoned and spurned "Yankee Doodle." They hissed it in theaters and used it instead

[4] New Orleans *Daily Picayune*, June 2, 1861; Richmond *Daily Examiner*, November 11, 1863; Richmond *Daily Whig*, November 11, 1863; Willard O. Waters, "Confederate Imprints in the Henry E. Huntington Library Unrecorded in Previously Published Bibliographies of Such Material," in *The Papers of the Bibliographical Society of America* (New York, Chicago), XXIII (1929), 82; Russell, *My Diary North and South*, 176. The explanation of the origin of "Dixie Land," given at this time in the South, was that it meant the land south of Mason and Dixon's line, and did not refer to a plantation on Manhattan Island owned by a man named Dixie. The tune was said to be that applied to an old boat and corn song which the slaves sang. Athens *Southern Watchman*, July 17, 1861; Mobile *Advertiser and Register*, June 15, 1861. For a critical discussion of the origin of "Dixie," see David Rankin Barbee, "Who Wrote Dixie?" in *Musical Digest* (New York), XXX (1948), 6–9, and the editorial on page 4. The lyric which became the standard version was written by William Shakespeare Harp, according to this account.

of the "Rogue's March" to drum soldiers out of camp, though they did sing to that tune a song called "Southern Yankee Doodle." Hundreds of songs written during the war the soldiers never sang, but in addition to the favorites previously mentioned they liked "Lorena," "When This Cruel War Is Over," "Pop Goes the Weasel," "The Southern Wagon," and "Listen to the Mocking Bird." Apart from soldiers' choruses, church choirs, operas, theatrical troupes, and brass bands, there was no organized music in the Confederacy, though there was set up in Richmond late in 1861 the Richmond Philharmonic Association, which seems never to have accomplished anything.

The theater flourished during the war years. After the fall of New Orleans, Richmond had no rival in the Confederacy as a theatrical center; yet all the principal towns kept up their interest in the theater, especially Charleston (using Hibernian Hall after the destruction of the Charleston Theater in the fire of 1861), Nashville (until its fall in the spring of 1862), Columbia, Augusta, Savannah, Atlanta, Mobile, Montgomery, and Jackson. Almost all of the principal stars and companies traveled from town to town, but they spent most of their time in Richmond and some never left it. The most famous group was the W. H. Crisp Company, all male members having been in the army and honorably dismissed. Various so-called amateur companies sprang up to entertain soldiers and the home folk and to provide soldiers' relief. Soon they took to the road and in reality became professionals. During 1863–1864 a Richmond theater manager spent $60,000 attempting to bring an English company there. Some of the players got as far as the North but were unable to cross the lines into the Confederacy. The best known and most popular actresses were Jennie Powell, Mary Partington, Ida Vernon, and Ella Wren, the "accomplished Tragedienne and Prima Donna." Among the actors were E. R. Dalton, Walter Keeble, D'Orsay Ogden, Harry Macarthy, and Charles Morton, the "most versatile and popular Comedian and Vocalist in the Confederacy," according to a playbill.[5]

[5] Atlanta *Daily Commonwealth,* September 6, 1862; Augusta *Daily Chronicle & Sentinel,* August 20, 1862; Charleston *Daily Courier,* July 23, 1862; April 30, 1863; Richmond *Semi-Weekly Enquirer,* October 11, 1861; Richmond *Daily Whig,* October 12, 18, 1862; April 12, 1864.

Macarthy made much of singing his own songs, especially the "Bonnie Blue Flag," when he would have a young lady on the stage wave the flag. Being a comedian, he seldom attempted serious parts, but, according to one critic, he was "equally at home" in "high or low comedy, fine drama, songs, comic or sentimental." [6] Another had no desire to hear him "tune his throat and stamp his feet in the rendition of vulgar songs and vulgar dances and vulgar jokes, to small audiences of questionable character." [7]

Ogden, an Englishman who had come to America at the age of eight, was a versatile actor and an outstanding theatrical manager. He assisted John Hill Hewitt, the manager of the old Richmond Theatre, before it burned early in 1862, and after the New Richmond Theatre was opened a year later Ogden assumed full management. At the first performance, a gala occasion, Ogden awarded a prize to the "Inaugural Ode" by a recognized South Carolina poet, Henry Timrod, "a small, melancholy-looking man, [with] black moustache, grey eyes and sallow complexion," who apparently was not present.[8] Ogden was "the best abused theatrical manager we have ever had among us," thought one critic, referring to the Richmond *Examiner*'s continual hounding. The manager answered his enemies by producing a skit entitled "Ogden at Home; or, Life among the Critics." But the critics came near having the last word when in 1864 the Confederacy, in dire need of soldiers, began a drive on the male personnel of the theatrical world. It conscripted Ogden and others in Richmond and sent them to near-by Camp Lee, but Ogden seems to have gained his release, for almost immediately he was rehearsing a skit, "Ogden's Adventures." When he produced it the *Examiner*'s critic declared, "Any half dozen drunken men picked up from the street, and set before the foot lights without text or previous rehearsal, but with an injunction to do their worst, could have done better than Mr. D'Ogden [a sarcastic mix-up of his name constantly used in this paper] and his friends did in these 'Adventures' of his." [9] A few weeks later he was again in the hands of the conscript officers. Claiming to be a

---

[6] Richmond *Daily Whig*, April 13, 1864.

[7] Richmond *Daily Examiner*, December 5, 1862.

[8] Armistead C. Gordon, *Memories and Memorials of William Gordon McCabe* (Richmond, 1925), I, 132.   [9] Richmond *Daily Examiner*, June 27, 1864.

subject of Queen Victoria, he now obtained a writ of habeas corpus, but his petition was denied on the ground that he was domiciled in the Confederacy. He was allowed the freedom of Richmond, however, and continued as the manager of the theater until in October he mysteriously disappeared and it was reported that he had escaped to the North. In October he was captured in northern Virginia, brought back and lodged in Castle Thunder, where some of his theatrical friends serenaded him. In December he was court-martialed and sentenced to three months at hard labor; but the next month he was out again managing the New Richmond Theatre, a rigid physical examination having shown him unfit for military service.[10]

Richmond's chief theaters were the New Richmond, the Varieties, and the Metropolitan. Undoubtedly they degenerated in their audiences and in the esteem of the cultured Richmonders, who quit attending; but with the conglomerate population of the wartime capital and the many soldiers on furlough or passing through seeking release from the hard realities of war in drinking and theater-going, it could hardly have been otherwise. Performances were sometimes broken up by the rowdyism of drunken riffraff, who occupied the cheap third tier and sometimes fired their pistols. Street urchins who congregated on the outside and sometimes got in often created pandemonium. When the New Richmond Theatre was being built, there was an outcry against putting in a third tier. In 1864 the editor of the Richmond *Whig* said, "We have long since despaired of that 'elevation of the drama,' of which we have heard and read so much in our day," and he would continue to despair "until its exponents everywhere are better exemplars of morality in their habits and associations; until bars and 'third tiers' are closed, or prevented from being used as the rendezvous for the dissolute— until short skirts and *nigger* dancing, ribaldry, blasphemous mock-

---

[10] Charleston *Daily Courier*, February 20, 1863; Richmond *Daily Enquirer*, October 3, 13, 24, 1864; January 27, 1865; Richmond *Daily Examiner*, January 3, 1862; January 6, December 22, 1863; July 26, August 12, 16, September 13, 17, October 4, 6, 15, 22, 25, November 7, 22, December 21, 30, 1864; January 17, 1865; Richmond *Daily Whig*, February 7, November 16, 18, 20, 1863; May 23, 1864. For interesting facts on Hewitt and incidentally Ogden, see Richard B. Harwell, "A Reputation by Reflection: John Hill Hewitt and Edgar Allan Poe," in *Emory University Quarterly* (Emory University), III (1947), 104–15.

piety, gross buffoonery, and other 'piquant' and profane attractions for the carnal-minded and illiterate, are excluded from the stage." [11]

Minstrels were a great attraction for the lower classes, and Tim Morris [Joseph W. Griffin], "the renowned negro delineator" with his Iron-Clad Ethiopian Troupe, was their hero. The popularity of minstrels tended to pull down the tone of the better performances. Morris and his troupe were among those conscripted in 1864.

But the theater performers tried to be as patriotic as any other group. After the bread riot in Richmond, Lee Mallory, manager of the Metropolitan, distributed monthly 1,200 loaves of bread, and on other occasions he donated 1,000 tickets each to the ladies' gunboat fund and to a fund being raised to erect a statue of Stonewall Jackson. Macarthy gave the proceeds of an evening's performance to the sufferers of the Confederate Laboratory explosion; and Ogden offered boxes to Davis and his staff any evening they wanted to attend the New Richmond. These actors believed they were making entertainment which would build up the morale of soldiers and prevent them from getting drunk and becoming involved in crimes.[12]

Many of the productions were written for the times and related to the war or to some aspect of Southern civilization, as *The Ticket-of-Leave-Man, The Roll of the Drum; or, The Battle of Manassas, The Maiden's Vow; or, the Capture of Courtland, Alabama, The Guerillas; or, The War in Virginia, The Battle of Chickamauga, Love's Ambuscade; or, The Sergeant's Strategem, The Virginia Cavalier, Parlor and Cabin; or, The Master and Slave,* and *Miscegenation; or, A Virginia Negro in Washington.* Prizes were offered for the best war play, but the results were not flattering. Now and then companies departed from war themes and presented operas, as *Il Trovatore* and *Guy Mannering;* such Shakespearean plays as *Hamlet* and *Richard III;* and special favorites like *The Corsican Brothers, The Marble Heart,* and *East Lynne.* The New Richmond Theatre arranged some clever mechanical contrivances

11 Richmond *Daily Whig,* January 14, 1864. Rev. J. L. Burrows of the First Baptist Church, Richmond, delivered a strong sermon against the local theaters and published it in a pamphlet. *Ibid.,* April 25, 1863.

12 R. D. Ogden to Jefferson Davis, April 7, 1864, in Davis Papers (microfilms in the University of Texas Library, originals in Duke University Library); Richmond *Daily Examiner,* April 7, 1863; Richmond *Daily Whig,* March 16, June 8, 1863.

which made realistic representations of ghosts to be used in a play written especially for this purpose, *The Ghost of Dismal Swamp; or, Marteau, the Guerilla*. The play was described as "the great Spectral wonder of the nineteenth century," and the Richmond *Whig* critic declared that the "illusion of the ghost . . . [was] worth seeing," [13] but he was surfeited with horrors after seeing *Duchess of Malfi*, in which within twenty minutes he was treated to enough murders and terrors to last a lifetime. He added, "People who go to the theatre now want something cheerful and amusing. In all conscience, there are horrors enough in the daily walks of life without people going to a theatre to see them." [14] Now and then light burlesque extravaganzas were offered, as *Family Jars* and *Po-Ca-Hon-Tas*.

Using an entirely different technique, the *tableau vivant* idea which had been prevalent in America for about forty years, Lee Mallory worked out his famous "War Illustrations—Pantechnoptomon," a "Magnificent Scenic and Automatic Spectacle" consisting of "Five Hundred Thousand Life-like Figures" of soldier life, battles, pyrotechnic displays, and also natural scenes such as swamps, prairies, and forests. He was constantly adding to them as the war continued. He accompanied this animated display of these "miniaature moving, like life figures" with an explanatory lecture. Somewhat different from Mallory's display was Burton's "Southern Moving Dioramic Panorama," a canvas seventy-five feet long and eight feet high, on which he had painted a conglomeration of scenes from the Bosporus to the First Battle of Manassas. In Mallory's and Burton's contraptions were the germ of the moving pictures of a subsequent generation. For those who did not care to see animated pictures at the theater, there were stereopticon views which they could buy and look at in their own homes.[15]

Quite a number of artists were active with their painting during the war. They almost invariably depicted war scenes or painted portraits of officers. By the middle of 1862, Louis M. Montgomery

---

13 Richmond *Daily Whig*, May 23, 1864. See also, *ibid.*, May 20, 1864.

14 *Ibid.*, May 7, 1864.

15 *De Bow's Review*, XXXI (1861), advertisement; Charleston *Daily Courier*, April 24, May 22, 1862; Richmond *Semi-Weekly Enquirer*, April 15, May 16, 1862; Richmond *Daily Examiner*, March 28, 1862; March 18, 25, 1863; January 26, 1864; Richmond *Daily Whig*, March 27, April 26, 1862.

of the Washington Artillery of New Orleans had done in water colors 180 sketches of battles, troops, bivouacs, military works, and other points of interest; Adalbert J. Volck (pseudonym V. Blada) of Baltimore made many war etchings, especially of life back of the lines, such as "Making Clothes for the Boys in the Army" and "Offering of Bells to be Cast into Cannon"; John A. Elder of Virginia did several landscapes with war backgrounds including the Petersburg Crater; John R. Key, of the Francis Scott Key family, painted many landscapes, water scenes, Drewry's Bluff on the James being one of them; and William D. Washington of Virginia put on canvas not only the bombardment of the Federal camp on the Gauley, but he also made one of the most famous paintings of the war, "The Burial of Latané." This picture represented women and slaves burying one of Stuart's cavalrymen, Captain William Latané, the only man lost on the celebrated ride around McClellan's army in the Peninsular campaign. The painting was photographed and many copies were sold. Elder painted a portrait of Lee; William Shephard, another Virginian, painted one of Jeb Stuart; and an oil portrait of Stonewall Jackson, done "by one of the best artists of the South [unnamed]," brought $320 in Richmond in November, 1863. J. B. Irving, Jr., a talented young South Carolinian, painted a portrait of Governor Francis W. Pickens. Although there were no outstanding artists in the Confederacy, the spirit of the artist was there.[16]

To honor living heroes, memorialize the dead, or signalize the new star in the firmament of nations, sculptors and amateur architects set their chisels and imaginations to work. In 1862 someone signing the name "Daughter of the Confederacy" suggested that when peace came this new nation erect a great memorial to itself, "a gigantic circular marble 'Memorabilia' on the Acropolis of Vicksburg," in perfect proportions with frieze and architrave portraying in chiseled lines the great events of the war, with cotton leaves wreathing the capitals, and statues of the leading generals occupying appropriate niches. The names of fallen heroes were to

16 De Leon, *Four Years in Rebel Capitals*, 300; Spencer, *Last Ninety Days of the War*, advertisement; Charleston *Daily Courier*, July 1, 1861; December 20, 1862; Richmond *Daily Enquirer*, July 22, October 25, 1864; Richmond *Daily Examiner*, November 11, 12, 1863; August 26, 1864; Richmond *Daily Whig*, August 7, 1862; September 1, 1863.

be inscribed on the marble walls and their sacred ashes deposited under the great dome, painted in blue and lighted by southern constellations. A mighty bronze image of Liberty cast from captured cannon should occupy the center of the floor.[17] A less ambitious undertaking which was later to be carried out in a modified form was advocated by Bishop Stephen Elliott, who said, "Truly, the first monument which our Confederacy rears, when our independence shall have been won, should be a lofty shaft, pure and spotless, bearing this inscription: *'To the Unknown and Unrecorded Dead.'* "[18] Another suggestion which was often made and which was carried out in great profusion years after the war was the erection of a monument to Confederate soldiers in every county of the Confederacy.

The death of Jackson led immediately to the organization of a monumental association to raise money for casting a bronze statue of him to be placed on Capitol Square in Richmond. It was to be cast by the same Munich firm which had produced the equestrian statue of Washington, then gracing the Capitol lawn. Soon $8,000 was raised in Richmond, much was given by soldiers, and contributions were received from England and France. In December, 1863, the artist Frederick Volck ran the blockade with fifteen bales of cotton to be sold in Europe for the Jackson fund. But the war ended before the statue could be erected, and not until 1875 did Jackson take his place on Capitol Square. A white marble shaft placed in September, 1861, on the battlefield of First Manassas to the memory of Colonel Francis Bartow, killed there, was undoubtedly the first monument to be raised in the Confederacy.[19]

The greatest sculptor in the Confederacy was William R. Barbee, who had studied in Italy, and whose "Coquette" was sold at auction in 1863 for $7,000. At one time he planned to chisel busts

[17] Augusta *Daily Chronicle & Sentinel*, August 11, 1862.

[18] *Southern Literary Messenger*, XXXVII (1863), 61. See also, Richmond *Daily Whig*, December 9, 1862; Tuskegee *South Western Baptist*, March 31, 1864.

[19] Atlanta *Daily Commonwealth*, September 6, 1862; Atlanta *Southern Confederacy*, August 23, 1861; Augusta *Weekly Chronicle & Sentinel*, May 26, 1863; Augusta *Weekly Constitutionalist*, August 28, 1861; Mobile *Advertiser and Register*, September 15, 1861; Richmond *Semi-Weekly Enquirer*, July 3, 1863; Richmond *Daily Examiner*, May 19, November 21, 1863; Richmond *Daily Whig*, May 20, June 11, December 19, 1863; May 2, 1864.

of all Congressmen who would give him their orders. Volck executed a bust of Jackson, plaster casts of which were being sold in Richmond in 1863 for $10 apiece. He also made one of Davis, and five hundred duplicates were offered for sale in England to aid the Confederate prisoner-of-war fund being raised there. Alexander Galt, a Virginian trained in Italy, died in the midst of the war at the age of thirty-five, before he had had time to chisel war heroes. His most pretentious work was a statue of Jefferson, done for the University of Virginia and placed in the Rotunda, where it still stands.[20]

The war profoundly affected Confederate journalism. Newspapers greatly decreased in number and size and their newsprint deteriorated in quality, because of the volunteering of editors, the lack of paper, the falling off of advertisements, the age-old difficulty of nonpayment of subscriptions, poor postal service, the high cost of everything going into the making of a newspaper, and the invasion of the enemy. The impact of war came quickly. Before a year had passed forty newspapers had suspended in Virginia and by the end of 1862 only about 14 per cent were left; in North Carolina twenty-six of the fifty-seven ceased during the war; in Florida only seventeen of the twenty-six remained by the end of 1861; in Mississippi, hard hit by invasion, only nine of the seventy-five continued publication by the end of 1863; and in Texas only ten of sixty were left before the war was a year old. "Another Gone" was the sad refrain of the remaining newspapers as they recorded the passing of their contemporaries. Yancey declared early in 1863 that he had heard that only fifty newspapers still remained in the Confederacy—undoubtedly a great understatement.[21]

20 London *Index*, December 24, 1863, p. 559; Montgomery *Weekly Mail*, March 29, 1861; Richmond *Daily Whig*, January 21, April 2, September 1, 1863.

21 Charleston *Daily Mercury*, January 8, 1862; Jackson *Weekly Mississippian*, December 25, 1861; *Southern Historical Society Papers*, XLVIII (1941), 181. The *Tenth Census of the United States, 1880*, VIII, *Newspaper and Periodical Press* (Washington, 1884), 186–87, 359–423, gives the number of newspapers and periodicals in the Confederate states, in 1860, as follows: Alabama, 96; Arkansas, 37; Florida, 22; Georgia, 105; Louisiana, 81; Mississippi, 73; North Carolina, 74; South Carolina, 45; Tennessee, 83; Texas, 89; Virginia (including, of course, West Virginia), 139. There were few periodicals to be included in these statistics. The numbers of newspapers alone, at the outbreak of the war, given in other sources for some of the states follow: Florida, 26 (Charleston *Daily Mercury*, January 28, 1862); Mississippi, 75 (Rich-

During the first year of the war two thirds of the newspaper-men in Mississippi volunteered, and eleven went from one newspaper office in Georgia. Soon practically all of the dailies and many of the weeklies were issuing only half sheets, but a few reduced their sizes and continued with double sheets. "Half sheets and all the colors of the rainbow, are rapidly growing epidemic," declared the editor of the Charleston *Mercury* early in 1862.[22] To provide newsprint, much of which had heretofore been bought in the North, Southerners set up paper mills; but these turned out a low grade paper, and some were accidentally burned and others destroyed by the invaders. Because of the scarcity of paper and the high prices resulting from inflated currency, newspapers frequently found it necessary to increase their subscription rates, until near the end of the war some were charging $120 a year. By 1864 subscriptions were taken for only three months at a time, and in March, 1865, the Augusta *Daily Chronicle & Sentinel* receded to a day by day sale, announcing that it was *"only fifty cents per copy"* and that anyone forced by newsboys to pay more should report it.[23] At the end of the war newspapers returned to their old rates, one announcing in May, 1865, that its rate was $2.00 a year "when paid in produce at old prices, or in currency on the old basis." [24] To avoid the psychological effect of high rates, many papers quoted them in terms of barter: "any kind of country produce—corn, wheat, flour, oats, rye, butter, hay, shucks, fodder, chickens, eggs—

---

mond *Daily Examiner*, February 4, 1864); North Carolina, 75 (Spencer, *Last Ninety Days of the War*, 245); Texas, 60 (Charleston *Daily Mercury*, February 12, 1862); Virginia, about 121 (Lester J. Cappon, *Virginia Newspapers, 1821–1935; A Bibliography with Historical Introduction and Notes* [New York, 1936], 18.) The considerable variation in Florida, Mississippi, North Carolina, and Texas can be attributed to an increase in the newspapers after the 1860 census had been taken and to unreliable information as well as to the fact of the variable number of periodicals. See also, Rabun Lee Brantley, *Georgia Journalism of the Civil War Period* (Nashville, 1929), *passim;* James Melvin Lee, *History of American Journalism* (Boston, 1917), 285–316; James G. Randall, "The Newspaper Problem in its Bearing upon Military Secrecy during the Civil War," in *American Historical Review*, XXIII (1917–1918), 303–23.

[22] Charleston *Daily Mercury*, January 18, 1862.

[23] Augusta *Daily Chronicle & Sentinel*, March 30, 1865.

[24] Athens *Southern Watchman*, May 3, 1865.

any thing that can be eaten or worn, or that will answer for fuel." [25]

In the larger towns papers were delivered by newsboys, white and colored, who usually received a dollar recompense at the end of the year out of the voluntary contributions of the recipients— hence the newsboys' Christmas poetry which the papers published for them to pass around. Sometimes the boys engaged in sharp practice on street sales and charged more per issue than was allowed. According to a Federal prisoner of war this was the cry of one Negro newsboy in Richmond: "Great tallyraphic news in de papers! Mighty news from de Army of Northern Virginny! Great fightin' in de Souf-west!" Some enterprising Richmond newsboys boarded trains in search of customers and carried their newspapers to the soldiers in the vicinity. After Stuart's famous ride around McClellan's army, a few were induced by jubilant Richmonders to carry a bundle of papers detailing this feat to the Federal troops, and some newspapers made a practice of crossing into the Federal lines to sell papers.[26]

A few newspapers were published in German, especially in Texas, and the *Taglicher Anzeiger* was a well-known Richmond paper. Some French as well as bilingual papers continued publication in Louisiana. To escape the invading enemy some became peregrinating presses as they moved from town to town on wheels. These continued to publish under their original titles, as the Memphis *Appeal,* issued in Montgomery in 1864. It became famous for its wanderings, being facetiously referred to as the *Moving Appeal.* It was asserted seriously though erroneously in 1880 that this paper kept in its title the name of each town it had visited and

---

[25] *Ibid.,* October 16, 1861. See also, Grove Hill (Ala.), *Clarke County Journal,* February 23, 1865; Macon *Daily Telegraph,* May 31, 1861; Paulding (Miss.) *Eastern Clarion,* March 28, 1862; Richmond *Daily Sentinel,* March 27, 1865; Sandersville *Central Georgian,* August 21, 1861; Bettersworth, *Confederate Mississippi,* 330. Some newspapers for a time were printed on wallpaper. The one to become best known was the Vicksburg *Daily Citizen,* on account of its seizure when Grant captured the city and because of the many spurious copies later got out on wallpaper.

[26] For quotation, see Willard W. Glazier, *The Capture, the Prison Pen, and the Escape* . . . (New York, 1870), 57. See also, Richmond *Daily Whig,* November 27, 1862; November 11, 1863; Joel Cook, *The Siege of Richmond: A Narrative of the Military Operations of Major-General George B. McClellan during the Months of May and June, 1862* (Philadelphia, 1862), 268; Sheridan, *Personal Memoirs,* I, 385.

that when last heard of it was the Memphis-Hernando-Grenada-Vicksburg-Jackson-Atlanta-Griffin *Appeal*. It was finally overtaken in Columbus, Georgia, at the end of the war. Some papers in the occupied regions, if not destroyed, were taken over by Northern editors and conducted in the interest of the Union. Two newspaper correspondents, Thomas W. Knox and Alfred D. Richardson of the rival New York *Herald* and *Tribune*, respectively, edited the Memphis *Argus* for a time. When Sherman captured Savannah he allowed the editors of two newspapers to continue but forbade them to publish any mischievous matter, premature news, exaggerated statements, "or any comment whatever upon the acts of the constituted authorities." There is at least one instance of a fugitive Unionist Southerner, the fiery William G. Brownlow, returning with the Federal invaders and re-establishing his abandoned newspaper under the defiant title of the Knoxville *Whig and Rebel Ventilator*. The journalistic spirit did not die in the Confederate army, for soldiers in camp now and then issued newspapers. The best known was the *Vidette*, published by John Morgan's men. There were also the *Free Speech Advocate*, the *Daily Rebel Banner*, and the *Missouri Army Argus*. In the absence of printing presses, some soldiers issued papers in manuscript form, as the "Rapid Ann [the old name for Rapidan]," the "Mule," and the "Woodchuck." Besides serious news there was some humor, insipid or risqué jokes, and ribaldry. The newspaper best edited and of most distinguished format was the Confederate propaganda publication, the *Index*, published in London under the supervision of Henry Hotze, aided somewhat by John R. Thompson.[27]

Cut off from their customary news service in the North, the Confederate papers were forced to devise various means for obtaining their information. Three agencies for collecting news were soon

---

[27] For quotation, see Savannah *Daily Republican*, January 4, 1865. See also, Charleston *Daily Courier*, December 1, 1862; Chattanooga (Marietta, Ga.) *Daily Rebel* April 1, 1865; Richmond *Daily Enquirer*, December 14, 1864; Richmond *Daily Examiner*, January 12, 1863; Cappon, *Virginia Newspapers*, 18, 164; Henry, *Story of the Confederacy*, 300–301; Holland, *Morgan and his Raiders*, 139; Knox, *Camp-Fire and Cotton-Field*, 189 ff.; *Tenth Census*, 1880, VIII, *Newspaper and Periodical Press*, 155; Bell I. Wiley, "Camp Newspapers of the Confederacy," in *North Carolina Historical Review*, XX (1943), 327–35. There was published in Mobile a newspaper called the *Army Argus and Critic*, devoted to news of casualties, hospital happenings, and other military interests.

in operation, located in New Orleans, Nashville, and Montgomery. The last-named followed the government to Richmond and soon came to be the principal agency. It was controlled by William H. Pritchard, a South Carolinian who was editor of the Augusta *Constitutionalist* and, before the war, the Southern representative of the "New York Associated Press." There soon developed among the newspapers a feeling that they should organize an associated press which should be mutual and, therefore, not enrich Pritchard. In March, 1862, an attempt was made to organize such an association in Atlanta, which would not only provide news but also arrange to supply members with newsprint and seek lower postal rates, but the meeting was so little attended that it resulted in failure. Another futile attempt was made in Macon the following January, but the next month a successful meeting was held in Augusta and the "Press Association of the Confederate States" was organized of all dailies east of the Mississippi River and a few triweeklies. Dr. R. W. Gibbs of Columbia was elected president and J. S. Thrasher of Atlanta general manager.

Meanwhile, Pritchard had died, and his agency was now crowded out by the new mutual association, which scattered its reporters over the Confederacy but depended upon members to send news to the nearest agent from communities not served by reporters. News was copyrighted to prevent its use by nonmembers. The association made contracts with the telegraph lines to handle its news at half the rates to private individuals. Its work became so efficient that an Atlanta editor remarked with pleasure on receiving news from Port Hudson within a day that it was "a thing unprecedented in the history of our Western telegraph." [28] To save costs and time, a sort of code was worked out whereby all easily inferred words were omitted, leading some editors to complain that they could not make sense out of the dispatches. In reply an Atlanta editor curtly said, "The Superintendent of the Press Association was not employed to *educate* editors or supply them with brains," but to send dispatches "in a shape that would be intelligible to men who are *capable* of conducting a daily paper." [29] But there were other complaints, especially from the Richmond papers, that

[28] Atlanta *Southern Confederacy*, April 23, 1863.
[29] *Ibid.*, May 7, 1863.

trivialities were sent out, such as that the gas went off at Wilmington at midnight, which led Pollard of the *Examiner* to remark that reporters should exercise some "reason and common sense." [30] Dissatisfaction led four of the Richmond dailies (all except the *Whig*) to form the Mutual Benefit Press Association in the fall of 1862 with J. W. Lewellen as president, and to invite all newspapers to join. Members were obligated to pay $5.00 a month and to forward significant local news, and they received all news originating in Richmond including Congressional proceedings. There would be no expense for reporters, as each member would act in that capacity. This association was formed so late that it seems never to have amounted to much. In April, 1863, the Weekly Press Association of Georgia was organized principally to set scales of prices for subscriptions, advertisements, and legal notices.[31] After June 1, 1861, when the mails and telegraphs were severed with the North, the Confederate papers depended largely on Northern newspapers for their reports on happenings in the rest of the world. These papers were easy to obtain, either from across the lines or by exchange on the flag-of-truce boats.

Reporters were stationed at the principal news centers and especially, when permitted, in the area of military operations. As they were ordinarily paid only $25 a week, they found it difficult to subsist in army camps. Thrasher made unsuccessful efforts to get subsistence for them and their horses from army supplies. Some papers had special correspondents and reporters of their own. "Personne" (Felix Gregory Fontaine), who was directly associated

[30] Richmond *Daily Examiner*, April 19, 1864.

[31] Athens *Southern Watchman*, April 15, 1863; Atlanta *Southern Confederacy*, January 15, March 5, 15, 22, 29, 1862; March 14, April 14, 16, 1863; Augusta *Weekly Constitutionalist*, April 2, 1862; October 19, 1864; Charleston *Daily Courier*, March 29, June 30, 1862; New Orleans *Daily Picayune*, May 16, 1861; Richmond *Semi-Weekly Enquirer*, November 28, 1862; October 21, 1864; Richmond *Daily Examiner*, December 7, 1863; May 28, September 29, 1864; Richmond *Daily Whig*, September 26, 1862; Sandersville *Central Georgian*, April 22, 1863; *Private Press Association of the Confederate States*, 5–7, 9, 24–26, 45–50, 56. The press association published a monthly pamphlet of current news, called the *News Reports of the Press Association*. Richmond *Daily Whig*, August 13, 1863. For a time there was an attempt to operate in Atlanta the European and Confederate States Advertising Agency, designed to promote an exchange of advertisements with European newspapers. Charleston *Daily Courier*, January 7, 1862.

with the Charleston *Courier* and one of the editors of the Columbia *Carolinian*, served also the Richmond *Whig* and a few other papers. At least one paper had a correspondent in occupied New Orleans. The Richmond *Enquirer* sent a special reporter to cover Governor Vance's celebrated speech at Wilkesboro on February 22, 1864. Newspaper reporters covering Congressional debates sometimes ran into trouble because of their alleged failure to report speeches properly. A reporter for the *Enquirer* was excluded from the Senate on the grounds that he had garbled a Senator's speech. Brown of Mississippi remarked that a Senator "hardly knew his own speech when he read it in the Enquirer." [32]

As these newsgathering agencies served only the daily newspapers, the small country press found great difficulty in obtaining news and especially timely news. Many papers and, indeed, all of the Texas newspapers had no telegraphic connections and the mails were notoriously inefficient. They resorted to copying much from their exchanges.

Richmond was the news and newspaper center of the Confederacy. Here were five dailies, the *Examiner*, the *Enquirer*, the *Dispatch*, the *Whig*, and the *Sentinel*, all of which exercised much influence over the Confederate press, especially through their editorials. John Mitchel, the Irish patriot, was for a time on the staff of the *Enquirer*, but the best-known newspapermen in Richmond were John Moncure Daniel and Edward A. Pollard of the *Examiner*. The *Examiner* soon became the bellwether of the Richmond press in its vitriolic attacks on Davis and his whole administration, to be followed next by the *Whig* and later by the *Enquirer*, and to a lesser extent by the *Dispatch* and the *Sentinel*. So bitterly did the *Examiner* hate Davis that in 1863 it gave a bad summary of Davis' message to Congress but published in full Lincoln's message to the United States Congress. It ultimately came to hate almost everything which bore the name Confederate. Both the *Enquirer* and the *Sentinel* were accused of being Davis organs, the former because in August, 1862, Adjutant General Cooper announced

[32] *Private Press Association of the Confederate States*, 10; Richmond *Semi-Weekly Enquirer*, March 8, 1864; Richmond *Daily Whig*, October 14, 1863; May 5, 24, 1864; *Southern Historical Society Papers*, XLVIII (1941), 182, 292–94.

that thereafter all orders published in that paper would be considered official, and the latter because it sometimes came to the defense of Davis.[33]

Other papers throughout the Confederacy at one time or another took up the chorus of opposition—the Lynchburg *Virginian,* the Memphis *Appeal,* the Atlanta [and Macon] *Southern Confederacy,* the Macon *Intelligencer,* the Macon *Telegraph,* the Columbus *Sun,* the Augusta *Chronicle & Sentinel,* the Savannah *Republican,* and pre-eminently R. Barnwell Rhett's Charleston *Mercury,* which antedated and outdid the Richmond *Examiner.* The paper which came nearest to downright treason to the Confederacy was the Raleigh *Standard,* edited by William W. Holden. A soldier later shot for desertion declared that he had left the army because he had become convinced after reading the *Standard* that Davis was a tyrant and that the cause of the Confederacy was wrong. The editor of the Richmond *Enquirer* averred that he "would as soon undertake to follow the girations of a bat as it whirls to and fro through the twilight" as to follow the *Standard* in its twists and turns to escape exposure for its treason, and that "to execute justice upon the traitor of the North Carolina 'Standard' would no more be a party movement or a political struggle than the stringing up of a highwayman." [34] In September, 1863, Henry L. Benning's Georgia Brigade on passing through Raleigh sought Holden and on failing to find him sacked the office of the *Standard* and threw the type into the street. In retaliation Holden's supporters utterly destroyed the type, paper, presses, and machinery of the Raleigh *State Journal,* a Davis supporter.[35]

In the summer of 1864 there were strange things said and done in the secret correspondence and conversations among Governor Brown, Vice-President Stephens, and Henry Cleveland, subsequently the biographer of Stephens, as they sought either to buy a Georgia newspaper or to set up one in order better to sabotage the

33 *General Orders from Adjutant and Inspector-General's Office, Confederate States Army,* 1862–1863, Ser. 1862, pp. 74 ff.; Richmond *Semi-Weekly Enquirer,* March 13, 1863.

34 Richmond *Semi-Weekly Enquirer,* January 16, August 18, 1863.

35 Welch, *Confederate Surgeon's Letters,* 79; Hamilton, *Reconstruction in North Carolina,* 54–55; Athens *Southern Watchman,* November 11, 1863; Richmond *Semi-Weekly Enquirer,* September 15, 1863.

Davis administration. After failing in their efforts to buy the Augusta *Constitutionalist*, for which Brown had raised the money, and giving up the idea of starting a paper in Savannah, they saw their scheme succeed in the purchase of the Augusta *Chronicle & Sentinel* for $80,000. The ostensible purchaser was N. S. Morse, a round-faced, boyish-looking Northerner with a stiffly protruding mustache, who affected a Wild Bill Western swagger with his huge revolver and shining bowie knife. Having left the North to escape the Lincoln tyrannies, he was now ready to do battle against the Davis tyrannies. Professing love for the Confederacy, this editor outdid Pollard of the *Examiner* and Rhett of the *Mercury* in his spleen against the Richmond administration.[36]

Added to the malignancy of the anti-Davis newspapers was an overzealous feeling for the freedom of the press—the right to publish anything the editor chose—and a lack of understanding of what might give aid and comfort to the enemy. Editors published plans of campaigns and battles, the numbers of troops and names of regiments and their movements, the arrival and departures of blockade-runners; they invited raids by describing factories, munitions works, and their location; they criticized not only Davis but the generals; they fought and planned campaigns in the safety of their offices. The North needed no spies, declared Mrs. Chesnut, "Our newspapers tell every word there is to be told, by friend or foe." [37] "They keep old Scott as well posted about the strength of our forces at every point where we have any forces at all as if he were present at every dress parade and heard the morning orders read," declared a newspaper correspondent a few days before the the First Battle of Manassas.[38] It was charged that the battles around Chattanooga in the fall of 1863 were lost because of newspaper indiscretions. Colonel Fremantle reported that he constantly saw

---

[36] Henry Cleveland, Augusta, Ga., to Stephens, June 28, July 15, 1864; Brown, Atlanta, Ga., to "Dear Sir [Richard M. Johnston?]," July 15, 1864; Cleveland, Augusta, Ga., to Stephens, July 16, 1864, in Stephens Papers (microfilms in University of Texas Library, originals in Division of Manuscripts, Library of Congress); Charles C. Jones, Jr., and Salem Dutcher, *Memorial History of Augusta, Georgia* . . . (Syracuse, 1890), 280–81; Augusta *Weekly Chronicle & Sentinel*, April 20, June 22, 1864; *ibid.* (daily), April 6, 1865.

[37] Martin and Avary (eds.), *Diary from Dixie*, 50.

[38] Charleston *Daily Courier*, July 18, 1861.

in the Confederate press "the most violent attacks upon the President—upon the different generals and their measures," and that the liberty of the press was "carried to its fullest extent." [39] According to Benjamin H. Hill, Lee allowed himself to become involved enough in the controversy to utter this striking epigram: "We put all our worst generals to commanding our armies, and all our best generals to editing newspapers! . . . If some of these better generals will come and take my place, I am willing to do my best to serve my country editing a newspaper." [40] Northern generals customarily retailed among themselves information got from the Confederate press.

Not all newspapers were guilty of malignancy or indiscretions. The Charleston *Courier* was an example of a prominent paper remaining true to the Davis administration, and many of the smaller weeklies were content to support Davis and the Confederacy. The *Courier* declared that the freedom of the press was "really threatened more by the reckless abuse and excessive license practiced by some of its advocates and expounders" than by anything Davis could do.[41] Also the Richmond *Enquirer* decried the course of the anti-Davis newspapers: "Our armies have been discouraged, our citizens disquieted, our harmony imperiled, our energies weakened, by the dissensions and distrust which have been diligently and unsparingly propagated by a few misguided citizens." [42]

President Davis had more reason than any other person to react

---

[39] Fremantle, *Three Months in the Southern States*, 154, 220.

[40] Hill, *Benjamin H. Hill*, 289. See also, Richmond *Semi-Weekly Enquirer*, December 1, 1863; *Official Records*, Ser. I, Vol. XLV, Pt. II, 212, 284; Vol. XLVI, Pt. II, 783. The Richmond *Enquirer*, quoted in Grove Hill (Ala.) *Clarke County Journal*, May 5, 1864, said, "The grossest injustice, the foulest abuse, the vilest aspersions, have been indulged in, and never once has such 'freedom' been questioned." Regarding the effect these criticisms in Southern newspapers had on the North, the Richmond *Semi-Weekly Enquirer*, November 14, 1862, quoted this from the New York *Times:* "Every one knows with *what keen interest* any indication of hostility to the Confederate administration, whether coming from a rebel Congressman or from a rebel newspaper, is received in the North. It is generally accounted a token of dissatisfaction with the war itself, and is used here as an inducement for perseverance."

[41] Charleston *Daily Courier*, November 23, 1864.

[42] Richmond *Semi-Weekly Enquirer*, March 28, 1862. The Charleston *Daily Courier*, April 22, 1864, inquired, "Is it the best way to aid and support a Government of elected and responsible rulers to be ringing into the ears of the citizens and electors at all times that they have elected fools or knaves?"

violently against the unbridled license of the press; yet when Mrs. Greenhow asked him why he did not suppress the *Examiner,* he replied that there would be nothing gained to win independence by losing liberties. But he could not praise the press for its course. He wrote Lee in 1863, "I wish I could feel that the public journals were not generally partisan nor venal." There were others who would not deal so gently with the "termagant sheets." Speaker Bocock of the Confederate House, who was another target of the *Examiner,* thought that that paper ought to be destroyed and its editors hanged. George Fitzhugh, a Virginia fascist before his day, believed that newspapers should not be privately run, but that each state and the Confederacy should have their official press and that no other newspapers should be allowed to exist. Congress debated curbing the press but never acted.[43]

No newspaper was ever suppressed by state or Confederate authority throughout the war, and thereby Secretary of War Randolph's ardent wish expressed in 1862 was realized: that "this revolution may be successfully closed without suppression of one single newspaper in the Confederate States, and that our experience may be able to challenge comparison with our enemy." [44] This was, indeed, one victory of the Confederacy over the enemy, for within the United States there were no less than two dozen papers suppressed (temporarily or permanently) or destroyed by the Federal government, military commanders, or mobs. The only interference with Confederate newspapers came from the War Department, commanders in the field, and the Postmaster General. In the beginning Secretary of War Walker allowed reporters to go to the army camps but begged them not to write anything about the strength and movement of troops, and later the only attempt to enforce these injunctions was the requirement that all dispatches sent by telegraph be submitted to military authorities, who would not pass information considered improper even if it had been got from Northern newspapers. Mail dispatches escaped censorship. As has appeared, censorship was ineffective, for the papers often

[43] For quotation, see Rowland (ed.), *Jefferson Davis, Constitutionalist,* V, 589. See also, Richmond *Semi-Weekly Enquirer,* January 22, 1864; Richmond *Daily Examiner,* May 20, September 10, November 23, 1864.

[44] *Official Records,* Ser. I, Vol. XI, Pt. III, 636.

published information valuable to the enemy. In 1862 Lee complained after reading in the Richmond *Daily Dispatch* the number of troops he had at a certain point, "I thought it was understood that our papers were to be silent on all matters appertaining to the movements of the army." [45] Some commanders, especially Joseph E. Johnston, Bragg, Beauregard, and Jackson, refused to allow reporters in their camps.

Some of the newspapers complained bitterly at this interference. It was the people's war and they had a right to know all about it, just as much as they had the right to govern themselves. With justifiable indignation newspapers asked why the government could not issue a bulletin which would give the military news it wanted printed. Had the Confederacy done so, it would have built up the morale of the press and of the people; for then the country would not have been flooded by false rumors of great victories, and Toombs might not have said that newspapers were "such liars I can not rely on them." [46] Often editors first learned of important military happenings from Northern papers. The Richmond *Examiner* did not know of Lee's advance into Maryland and Pennsylvania in 1863 until it saw the news in New York papers, and an Augusta paper got its first knowledge of the fall of Island No. 10 by seeing it in the New York *Herald*. Also, the delay of news was devastating to editorial morale. The Richmond papers did not know until four days after the fall of Vicksburg that the Confederacy had suffered disaster there, and it was five days after Gettysburg before they knew that Lee had not captured forty thousand prisoners. This situation led papers to wax sarcastic. A Richmond paper reported that when McClellan had retreated from the Peninsula, one half of his forces went by balloon and the other half by a subterranean passage cut under Richmond; and a Macon paper knew as everyone on the streets knew that Price had captured St. Louis and the Confederates had occupied Louisville, but that news was too good to be sold for two cents. Yet newspapers

45 *Ibid.* See also *Tenth Census, 1880*, VIII, *Newspaper and Periodical Press*, 153–54; Atlanta *Southern Confederacy*, June 7, 1861; Richmond *Daily Examiner*, July 2, 1861; Richmond *Daily Whig*, October 15, 1862.

46 Phillips (ed.), *Correspondence of Toombs, Stephens, and Cobb*, 576.

were realistic. They published the bold facts when they could get them. They published column after column of casualty lists—sometimes they filled the whole front page. A Macon paper at the end of 1864 declared that "the people have been deluded and hoodwinked long enough, and it is the duty of the press to no longer indulge in such inglorious experiments but enter immediately upon the task of opening the eyes of the people to the true state of affairs." [47]

The Confederate press had an immense responsibility, which it variously met. It had almost within its keeping the very destiny of the Confederacy, and it was a shortcoming of the government that it did not recognize this fact by using it in such a way as to maintain better morale among the people. Southerners who could not read listened to others recite what the newspapers had to say. James A. Bayard of Delaware asserted early in the war that the newspapers by a cordial support of the administration had it within their power to bring the war to a successful end within six months. Their criticisms of the government were published in Northern papers and thereby retailed to Europe to make infinitely more difficult the efforts of Confederate agents abroad. Congressman Charles M. Conrad of Louisiana declared that the newspapers were doing greater harm than good, for despite the loyal service of some papers, the evil done by others traveled faster and farther. The power of the newspapers was the greatest factor in bringing on secession. As Congressman Ethelbert Barksdale of Mississippi said, "It had literally heated the boiler and generated the steam which had set in motion the mighty train which is moving onward, freighted with the destiny of this great people." [48] That destiny

[47] Atlanta *Southern Confederacy*, December 30, 1864. See also, Atlanta *Daily Southern Confederacy*, March 1, 1862; Augusta *Weekly Chronicle & Sentinel*, April 29, 1862; Macon *Daily Telegraph*, February 3, 1862; Richmond *Daily Examiner*, July 7, 1862; June 22, July 9, 1863; Richmond *Daily Whig*, May 3, 1863.

[48] For quotation, see *Southern Historical Society Papers*, XLV (1925), 246. See also, Mallet, *Errand to the South*, 214; *Official Records*, Ser. IV, Vol. III, 6; Athens *Southern Watchman*, February 25, 1863. Yet shutting their eyes to the plain facts, Southerners sang this senseless praise of the press: "It has been left to our young Confederation, to exhibit to the world the first instance of the entire Press of a people combining in one body to prosecute the labors of its high Mission." J. S. Thrasher, May 13, 1863, in *Private Press Association of the Confederate States*, 41. "[No] Government was

rested in no small degree on its continuing support of the movement it had started.

---

ever more nobly and patriotically sustained by the press than ours." Postmaster General Reagan, in Atlanta *Daily Southern Confederacy*, March 14, 1863. "History has no instance where such unanimity existed among so large a number [of the press]." Correspondent, in Macon *Daily Telegraph*, April 14, 1864.

CHAPTER XXI

LITERARY ACTIVITIES, EDUCATION, AND RELIGION

THE prospect of independence acted as a spur on literary activities, but the war itself profoundly affected their trends and dimmed ambitious expectations. The talking South, having at last cut itself loose from its dependence on Northern books as well as European, should now become a reading and especially a producing South. It would have an opportunity to develop a literature uncontaminated by outside influences. Sweet were the uses of adversity; Southerners would now find "honey in the jaws of the lion." As a New Orleans newspaper put it, the South "now stands upon the threshold of a mysterious and wonderful future. Beneath the rainbow's arch that spans the dreadful cloud of war, her gateway lies and her path extends." [1] But war, seeping into and corroding everything, soon captured the souls of writing Southerners and made them turn their literary efforts to the promotion of the struggle. By 1863 it was realized by a Richmond editor that everything must be subordinated to war—that now only the seedbeds could be sown for a mighty Southern literature which would flower in peacetime. As for the present, "It is a literature which has the ring of steel; its color is not rose-pink, but blood-red, and its perfume is that of sulphur and nitre." [2]

Only now and then could the Southern soul rise above its travail. In 1864 there was an incipient movement to celebrate the Shakespeare Tercentenary, and actor Crisp, who was born in Shakespeare's county, was called upon to help. Lawrence S. Benson of

[1] New Orleans *Delta,* quoted in *Southern Literary Messenger,* XXXIII (1861), 318.

[2] Richmond *Semi-Weekly Enquirer,* February 18, 1863. See also, *De Bow's Review,* XXXI (1861), 347–61; *Southern Literary Messenger,* XXXVII (1863), 620–27; XXXVIII (1864), 315; Augusta *Weekly Constitutionalist,* November 6, 1861; Charleston *Daily Courier,* July 2, 1861; Richmond *Daily Whig,* December 20, 1861.

Aiken, South Carolina, carried on a heated mathematical dispute with all who would take issue on such propositions as these: that the true relation of the diameter to the circumference of a circle is not 3.1416 plus but 3.4641016150 plus, that the circle can be squared ("the Quadrature of the Circle"), that things which are equal to the same things are not necessarily equal to each other, and that the whole is not necessarily greater than a part. These controversies were carried on in the columns of the newspapers and in at least one book, and lasted almost as long as the war.[3]

The Confederate government immediately made arrangements to protect literary works through copyrights to run twenty-eight years, and under certain circumstances an additional fourteen years; to transfer to loyal Confederates all their ante-bellum United States copyrights; and as a distinct advance over the old piratical activities in the United States, to set up international copyrights with European countries. As no nation recognized the independence of the Confederacy, no copyright treaties were ever negotiated despite the efforts of Confederate agents to do so. But to call attention to the pirating that went on in the North, S. H. Goetzel & Company, Mobile publishers, in bringing out a reprint of Edward Bulwer-Lytton's *Strange Story*, set aside as author's royalties ten cents a copy, which soon amounted to over $1,000. The best-known publishing houses were West & Johnston and Ayres & Wade in Richmond, Evans & Cogswell first in Charleston and then in Columbia, Burke, Boykin & Company in Macon, S. H. Goetzel & Company in Mobile, and H. C. Clarke in Vicksburg and elsewhere after the fall of that city.[4]

[3] Charleston *Daily Courier*, November 29, December 9, 17, 1862; February 14, 20, 23, March 3, 18, 21, October 26, November 9, 1863; March 30, 1864; Gainesville (Ala.) *Independent*, April 9, 1864. Lawrence S. Benson wrote at least nineteen books and pamphlets on mathematical subjects. One of them was *Scientific Disquisitions Concerning the Circle and the Ellipse. A Discourse of the Properties of the Straight Line and the Curve* . . . (Augusta, 1862).

[4] Matthews (ed.), *Statutes at Large of the Provisional Government of the Confederate States, 1861–1862*, pp. 93, 157–61; Matthews (ed.), *Public Laws of the Confederate States*, 1 Cong., 3 Sess., 1863, pp. 113–14; *Southern Literary Messenger*, XXXVII (1863), 185; Richard B. Harwell, *Confederate Belles-Lettres, a Bibliography and a Finding List* . . . (Hattiesburg, Miss., 1941), 17–20; Robinson, *Justice in Grey*, 31; Atlanta *Southern Confederacy*, March 18, 1861; Richmond *Daily Whig*, March 6, 1863. Evans and Cogswell, in Charleston, were at the outbreak of the war the largest publishing house in the South with the exception of the Methodist Publishing

Poetry, always prolific among Southerners, thrived with uncommon vigor under the influence of war. Editors fought off the poets in their columns almost as consistently as they did the Yankees. In 1863 the *Southern Illustrated News* said that it had received "not less than a flour barrel full of poems"; [5] an Atlanta editor announced that he would consider it "a particular favor if nobody would send us any more shabby attempts"; [6] and in July, 1863, the *Southern Literary Messenger* said: "We are receiving too much trash in rhyme. . . . Fires are not accessible at this time of the year, and it is too much trouble to tear up poetry. If it is thrown out of the window, the vexatious wind always blows it back." [7] Of course, war themes and sentiments provoked by the war were always uppermost, and some people who reveled in these effusions early began the compiling of anthologies. When the Federals besieged Charleston in the second year of hostilities, there began a stream of poetry about it almost as continuous as the enemy shells bursting over the city. The Richmond *Examiner* observed, "The city of Charleston is a great epic in herself, daily and nightly repeated in the lines of fire streaming and streaking from her deep-mouthed guns," and it begged the poets to let her "tell her own story of honour and glory." [8] Some papers quit publishing poetry, good or bad; and one paper dried up the stream by charging ten cents a line, the same rate as for obituaries.

There were a few recognized poets whose names were to live after them. Paul Hamilton Hayne wrote poetry of merit; Francis O. Ticknor's "Little Giffen," published after the war, became a favorite with many people; and Henry Timrod's war songs such as "A Cry to Arms" and "Carolina" were among his best. Less famous as poets, yet authors of poems which live, were James R. Randall

---

House at Nashville. In 1864 they removed to Columbia, where they set up 76 printing presses and many binding machines. At this time they employed 344 hands, of whom 74 were artists and printers brought from Europe. In June of this year this publishing house had in the course of manufacture 20 books in addition to the large amount of printing it was doing for the army and for the Treasury Department. Augusta *Weekly Constitutionalist*, June 29, 1864.

[5] *Southern Illustrated News*, I (1862–1863), 8.

[6] Atlanta *Southern Confederacy*, March 17, 1863.

[7] *Southern Literary Messenger*, XXXVII (1863), 447.

[8] Richmond *Daily Examiner*, April 13, 1864. See also, Greensboro (Ala.) *Beacon*, April 3, 1863; Richmond *Semi-Weekly Enquirer*, March 13, 1863.

with his "Maryland, My Maryland" and "John Pelham" and John R. Thompson with his "Ashby." George W. McKnight, formerly on the staff of the New Orleans *Delta,* joined the Confederate army and under the name "Asa Hartz" wrote witty poetry, even after he was taken prisoner and sent to Johnson's Island, as shown in his " 'Asa Hartz's' Appeal for an Exchange." The poem which occasioned greatest controversy as to authorship was "All Quiet Along the Potomac To-night," tenaciously claimed by Lamar Fontaine and generally attributed to Mrs. Ethelinda [Ethel Lynn] Beers of New York. The sentiment in the poem cannot identify it either as Northern or Southern. It was set to music by John Hill Hewitt, with Fontaine given credit for the words, and published in Columbia in February, 1863; though it is said to have been published in an unnamed Northern newspaper on October 21, 1861, and certainly it did appear in *Harper's Weekly* on November 30, 1861, under the title "The Picket-Guard" and signed "E. B." Fontaine insisted both during the war and afterwards that he wrote it in August, 1861, gave various copies to his comrades, and sent President Davis a copy for which he received a reply of thanks, and explained that a Federal soldier likely found a copy on a dead Confederate and sent it to Mrs. Beers. In 1863 Fontaine's father, an Episcopal rector, claimed authorship for his son. Fontaine's own testimony is somewhat weakened by the improbable career he claimed for himself: a native of Texas, he was soon captured and held for four years by the Comanches; he was a hero of the Crimean War; and he was wounded sixty-seven times in the Civil War, having fought in twenty-seven battles and fifty-seven skirmishes. Certainly wartime newspapers presented him as a hero little less renowned than John Morgan but more remarkable in his exploits.[9]

[9] Edwin A. Alderman, Joel Chandler Harris, and Charles W. Kent (eds.), *Library of Southern Literature* (Atlanta, 1907–1923), XV, 150; Baxter and Dearborn (comps.), *List of Books and Newspapers printed in the South,* 148; Waters, "Confederate Imprints in the Henry E. Huntington Library," in *Papers of the Bibliographical Society of America,* XXIII (1929), 81; Lamar Fontaine, *My Life and my Lectures* (New York, 1908), 80–82; Miller (ed.), *Photographic History of the Civil War,* IX, 142; Mildred Lewis Rutherford, *The South in History and Literature* . . . (Athens, 1907), 261–62; *Southern Field and Fireside* (Augusta), May 9, July 4, 1863; Charleston *Daily Courier,* November 14, 1863; Grove Hill (Ala.) *Clarke County Journal,* March 5, 1863; Jackson *Daily Southern Crisis,* January 19, 1863; Selma *Daily Reporter,* September 16, 1863; Richmond *Daily Whig,* August 1, 1863. The first appearance of the

Many diaries were written during the war by soldiers and particularly by women, but few if any were published contemporaneously. The best known and cleverest of all the women diarists was Mrs. Mary Boykin Chesnut, the wife of James Chesnut, Jr., former United States Senator, a member of Jefferson Davis' staff, and a brigadier general in the Confederate army. Her diary was not published until 1905. In 1867 "A Virginia Lady," Mrs. Judith B. McGuire, published anonymously *Diary of a Southern Refugee, during the War;* and among those which appeared years later were *A Confederate Girl's Diary* by Sarah Fowler Morgan (Dawson) and *The Journal of Julia LeGrand, New Orleans, 1862–1863.*

Southerners were quite conscious of the history they were making, and they were determined to write as much of it as they could during the making and to collect and preserve its records for later use. The critical Edward A. Pollard of the Richmond *Examiner* wrote the first and most pretentious history of the war, in four volumes, bringing out the first volume in 1862 under the title, *The First Year of the War* and the others year by year, varying the title by *Second, Third,* and *Fourth.* At the end of the war he combined them under the title, *Southern History of the War* (New York, 1866), and rehashed it into another volume called *The Lost Cause; a New Southern History of the War of the Confederates* (New York, 1866). This history was highly hostile to Davis and was in other respects undependable. It was bought and read widely, five thousand copies of the first volume having been sold by the end of 1862. In the midst of the war H. C. Clarke of Vicksburg brought out his *Diary of the War for Separation.* Various other accounts appeared, usually as pamphlets. John Esten Cooke, a Virginia novelist and a member of Jeb Stuart's staff, wrote immediately after Stonewall Jackson's death the first biography of him, which was first published in 1863. Various other biographies, in pamphlet form, soon appeared—of Jackson and of others. Previously there had been pub-

"All Quiet" poem in a Southern publication noted by this writer was in the Richmond *Daily Whig,* June 25, 1862, with this explanation, "The following poetical gem we copy from a Western paper. The original was found in the pocket of a volunteer who died in camp on the Potomac." The authorship was attributed to no one. The *Whig* reprinted it January 10, 1863, and claimed that Fontaine had written it. For a further discussion of the authorship, see James Wood Davidson, *The Living Writers of the South* (New York, 1869), 194–201.

lished a pamphlet *Life of* [James W.] *Jackson, the Martyr,* of Alexandria hotel fame. There were, of course, writings on the questions and issues of the times. Alexander St. Clair-Abrams wrote *President Davis and his Administration,* a defense of Davis against Pollard's attacks.

T. W. MacMahon of Richmond, well known for his best seller *Cause and Contrast,* was busily preparing in 1862 a history of the war, which never saw the light; and even as early as May, 1861, James D. McCabe, Jr., another Virginian, began collecting documents, which at the end of the war amounted to more than 15,000 pieces, and yielded tangible results in his life of Lee in 1866 and in many other works thereafter. Documentary materials published during the war were the monthly *Telegraphic Reports of the Press Association,* and, of course, governmental works such as the statutes of Congress and of the various states and other state documents, military orders, some reports of Congressional committees, but never the proceedings or journals of the Congress, except as they appeared in the newspapers. Many people considered newspapers one of the best sources for a history of the times, and one historically-minded person deplored the fact that many journals were being thrown away or used as wrapping paper "which in a few years will command a dollar a page or more in gold"; [10] yet in 1863 the Natchez *Courier* was offering for sale "A few thousand old papers, for wrapping paper. Old files of many years past—fit only to be used for that purpose." [11]

Virginia provided by law in 1862 for the collection and preservation of the records of all her soldiers, a work that seems not to have been done, and later North Carolina and South Carolina began making such collections. In 1862 Andrew H. H. Dawson set out with good intentions to write a short biography of every Alabama soldier, but manifestly he was never able to carry out his task. Some of the historical societies continued active, especially the one in Georgia; but none seems to have made any large collection of war material, despite the fact that some people begged them to do so. A soldier thought that the officers of the army should form historical societies to write the accounts of their battles, and in Virginia

10 Charleston *Daily Courier,* December 13, 1864.
11 Natchez *Semi-Weekly Courier,* September 15, 1863.

there was an incipient movement in 1864 to form a Confederacy-wide historical society to be called "The Historical Art Association of the Confederate States" and to have Jefferson Davis as its president. Its purpose was to collect information and documents about all the soldiers and battles of the war, photographs and artistic drawings of battlefields, copies of military reports, and comments by the newspapers of the Confederacy, of the North, and of Europe. It would begin by planning first for the Army of Northern Virginia two books, "The Battle-Roll of the Army of Northern Virginia," containing soldiers' records, and "The Battle-Book of the Army of Northern Virginia," which was made up mostly of illustrations and sketches. This interesting movement, though well conceived, was never born.[12]

Southerners had the urge but little time to produce, and since they were so much a part of the war and their minds so attuned to it, most of what they did produce had a war tinge. A few works of fiction got away from eternal war, but most of them soon succumbed to oblivion. Augusta Jane Evans (Wilson) of Mobile, whose novels *Inez* and *Beulah* had already made her famous in the South and whose life was almost consumed in the anxieties, prayers, and tears of war, wrote in 1863 the widely read *Macaria: or, Altars of Sacrifice*. It got people away from the war despite the fact that it was not a cheerful story. There was such war fiction as Alexander St. Clair-Abrams' *The Trials of the Soldier's Wife* and Mrs. Sally Rochester Ford's *Raids and Romance of Morgan and his Men*. The Reverend E. W .Warren, a Macon minister, wrote in 1864 a moral and social novel which he called *Nellie Norton; or Southern Slavery and the Bible—A Scriptural Refutation of the Principal Arguments upon which the Abolitionists Rely—A Vindication of Southern Slavery from the Old and New Testament*. Constance Cary, afterwards Mrs. Burton Harrison, had finished a novel, "Skirmishing," to be published by West & Johnston, but it was destroyed in the fire which burned Richmond at the end of the war. There were reprints of various works, both domestic and foreign. Of the former there were *Wild Western Scenes: or, The White Spirit of the Wilderness*, by John B. Jones, the "rebel clerk" who kept a war diary; the ever

[12] Charleston *Daily Courier*, April 20, 1864; Montgomery *Weekly Mail*, July 25, December 3, 1862; Richmond *Daily Whig*, March 31, April 5, 11, 1864.

513

popular "Crusoic book for boys," *Robert and Harold, or the Young Marooners on the Florida Coast,* by Francis R. Goulding; and *Master William Mitten,* by Augustus Baldwin Longstreet, now made into book form from the files of the *Southern Field and Fireside.* Victor Hugo's *Les Misérables,* republished in the Confederacy soon after it first appeared in France in 1862, was the most famous of the foreign works. It was widely read and its title soon became corrupted into a standard joke of the times, arising from a supposed occasion when a lady went into West & Johnston's bookstore and asked for "a copy of that book about Gen. Lee's poor miserable soldiers faintin'." After some puzzlement the clerk asked her if she wanted *Les Misérables. Fantine* (this title being Part I), but she insisted that was not the book and refused to buy it.[13]

That saving grace of humor, which Southerners possessed in abundance, was not lost during the war. Much that appeared in newspapers and periodicals was not collected and published in book form. Some appeared in pamphlets, and some in books. The letters of Bill Arp to "Mr. Linkhorn" began in the newspapers in 1861, continuing until they were collected and published after the war. *The Letters of Mozis Addums to Billy Ivvins,* written to newspapers in the 1850's by George William Bagby, a famous Virginia humorist and from 1860 to 1864 editor of the *Southern Literary Messenger,* were collected and published in 1862. Richard Malcolm Johnston, under the pseudonym "Philemon Perch," brought out his *Georgia Sketches,* recommended for all who wanted to laugh. These were humorous camp pamphlets: *Fun for the Camp. A Comic Medley; The Camp Jester; or, Amusement for the Mess; The Camp Follower;* and *Ups and Downs of Wife Hunting, or Merry Jokes for Camp Perusal.* A few humorous periodicals made their appearance, as the *Confederate Spirit and Knapsack of Fun* in Mobile and the *Bugle Horn of Liberty* in Griffin, Georgia. *Hard Tack* was promised in Atlanta. The most pretentious humorous periodical was *Southern Punch,* begun in Richmond in 1863 and patterned after the English publication.

---

[13] Richmond *Daily Whig,* June 12, 1863. See also, Douglas S. Freeman, *Calendar of Confederate Papers* . . . (Richmond, 1908), *passim;* J. W. West, Richmond, to Miss Constance Cary, April 12, 1865, in Burton Harrison Collection (Division of Manuscripts, Library of Congress).

Up to 1861 there had existed in the Southern slave states excepting Missouri, for varying periods of time, at least 757 periodicals of all kinds, literary, agricultural, religious, medical, and so on. When the war began there were a hundred; during the struggle many ceased publication and a few were started. The *Southern Literary Messenger* had long been the most scholarly of the literary magazines, and in the words of its editor in 1861 "the oldest and most neglected literary journal in the South." [14] Realizing that people were now more interested in war than anything else, this journal sadly fell from its high estate of scholarly detachment and became almost billingsgate in the language it used against the enemy. Lincoln was called the "Springfield Gorilla." Finally it ceased publication in 1864. The only agricultural journal to ride out the war was the *Southern Cultivator*. Consciously imitating the London *Illustrated News* and somewhat like *Harper's Weekly* without wanting to be, the *Southern Illustrated News* began its career in Richmond in September, 1862, "the only enterprise of the kind ever undertaken in the South," [15] and it thrived uncommonly for a time. As poor as its cuts, paper, and ink were, it became so popular that it could not accept all the subscriptions offered, though it was issuing twenty thousand copies each week. Beginning in 1862 and continuing through the war, *The Countryman*, published by Joseph Addison Turner on his plantation in Putnam County, Georgia, announced that it was continuing the tradition of *Niles' Register* as well as of Joseph Addison's *Spectator*, Richard Steele's *Tatler*, Samuel Johnson's *Rambler and Adventurer*, and Oliver Goldsmith's *Bee*. It would publish nothing "dull, didactic, or prosy," and it would get people's minds away from the "engrossing topics of war news." [16] It need not be added that this was too ambitious a program to achieve. An editor in Lynchburg began in 1864 a publication, patterned after *Niles' Weekly Register*, which he called

---

[14] *Southern Literary Messenger*, XXXIII (1861), 395.

[15] *Southern Illustrated News*, I (1862–1863), 4.

[16] Macon *Daily Telegraph*, April 29, 1862. See also, Bertram H. Flanders, *Early Georgia Magazines; Literary Periodicals to 1865* (Athens, 1944), *passim*; Gertrude C. Gilmer, *Checklist of Southern Periodicals to 1861* (Boston, 1934), *passim*; Richmond *Semi-Weekly Enquirer*, January 5, 1864; Richmond *Daily Whig*, March 25, 1863; January 9, 1864. It was reported in the *Southern Literary Messenger*, XXXIV (1862), 689, that the *Southern Illustrated News* was making money at the rate of $50,000 a year.

the *Weekly Register*. Two eclectic magazines, both begun in Richmond, were called *The Age* and *The Record*. To add further to Richmond's importance as a publication center, the *Confederate States Medical and Surgical Journal* was begun there early in 1864. *Smith & Barrow's Monthly Magazine,* a literary publication, was set up in Augusta, and *The Children's Guide* was published in Macon. The *Southern Field and Fireside,* a literary magazine of considerable merit, began publication in 1859 in Augusta and continued to almost the end of the war. Almanacs were periodicals in the sense that they were published yearly. As was usual with almanacs, they contained much useful information in addition to the calendar and weather information. H. C. Clarke published his *Confederate States Almanac, and Respository of Useful Knowledge* in Vicksburg and then in Mobile; of long standing was *Grier's Almanac for the State of Georgia, South Carolina, Alabama, and Tennessee,* changing with the years both title and publishers; and there were others such as the *Constitutionalist Commercial Almanac* for Georgia, *Miller's Planters' & Mechanics' State Rights Almanac* published at Charleston, and *Turner's North Carolina Almanac.*

Education and educational institutions immediately felt the effects of secession and war. As education in all times and places has been made to conform more or less to national policy, it was unthinkable to Southerners in 1861 that teachers who did not support the Confederacy could remain in their positions and poison the minds of the new generation against the work of their elders. J. A. Brown, elected president of Newberry College in 1860, was induced to resign the next year in the face of a projected investigation of his Unionism, and Edward C. Boynton was dismissed at the University of Mississippi for his supposed disloyalty to the Confederacy. "He certainly met with mild treatment in being allowed to depart in peace," remarked a Mississippi newspaper editor.[17] Southerners realized that they were a distinctive people, and they demanded that educators support their point of view. Education should be made to administer to the war, but it should not be allowed to wither away in the stress of the times. Although common-school education had never permeated the South, the meager be-

17 Paulding (Miss.) *Eastern Clarion,* September 27, 1861.

ginnings must not be sacrificed. What good was liberty if the people must grow up in ignorance and illiteracy? "Sad, sad, indeed will be this war to us if it results in the utter neglect of our educational interests," mused a South Carolina woman.[18] Women should fill the gaps made by men teachers going to war, the Sunday School should be called into use, the children should be taught the three R's in their homes, and they should be made to detest "not simply the Yankees who are making war upon us, but the whole Yankee character." [19] Edward A. Pollard preferred no common schools at all to the New England variety. He believed that common-school education was so administered in the Northeast that it became dangerous and bore "no better fruits than presumption, disrespect to superiors, a vain passion for reform, infidelity, and the agitations of revolution." [20]

The need for textbooks soon arose, for the South had heretofore depended on the North for them, filled though some of them were with sentiments hostile to Southern institutions. The war might produce a hidden benefit if Southerners should be forced to write and publish their own textbooks and thereby properly mold the minds of the children. In 1861 Sigmund H. Goetzel, the Mobile publisher, suggested that the teachers of the Confederacy should hold a convention to discuss the subject of textbooks, but it was April 28, 1863, before some seventy delegates from six states convened in Columbia. They met in response to a call sent out by Calvin H. Wiley and other members of the Educational Association of North Carolina. Professor Edward S. Joynes, writing in the *Southern Literary Messenger,* hoped that this convention would formulate a broad program of education both for war and peace. The utilitarian idea should not dominate it, for in the past "it was impossible to induce students, generally to look beyond *immediate practical results,* as the end of education, or to restrain long enough their impatient desire to enter upon the arena of 'practical' life." [21] The few subjects "that are more purely intellectual and moral, and therefore better fitted for purposes of discipline and

[18] Charleston *Daily Courier,* March 22, 1862.
[19] Athens *Southern Watchman,* May 20, 1863.
[20] *Southern Literary Messenger,* XXXII (1861), 310. See also, Charles W. Heathcote, *The Lutheran Church and the Civil War* (New York, 1919), 119 ff.
[21] *Southern Literary Messenger,* XXXVII (1863), 487.

culture," should be learned well.[22] Joynes hoped that there might be set up "a National Institution for the encouragement of Education and Letters in the South" which would set standards and act as a sort of accrediting agency. This convention recommended the writing and publishing of textbooks, the organization of an educational association in each state, the establishment of state school systems with superintendents of education, and education of incapacitated soldiers for the teaching profession.

Noah Webster's *American Spelling-book* ("blue-back speller"), as old as the republic, had long been the standard and often the only book in the hands of Southern pupils, and it had become as dear to them as the Stars and Stripes. Though they abandoned the flag in 1861, they were determined not to give up Webster. No longer able to import it, Confederate publishers laid plans to reprint it. Taking advantage of the situation a Mr. Fleming "improved" on Webster by adding some "Bible readings in defense of slavery," but this tampering with the text of a book almost as sacred as the Bible led some critics to declare it an abomination and to call for its suppression. Departing from Webster, some authors compiled books of their own, as W. R. Watson's *Home Spelling Book, or Mothers' Assistant* and a *Confederate Speller*, first and second. In addition to spellers, authors wrote readers, arithmetics, grammars, geographies, and other texts, frequently inserting examples and problems designed to popularize the Confederacy and belittle the North. As an example, an arithmetic posed the problem, "If one Confederate soldier can whip 7 Yankees, how many soldiers can whip 49 Yankees?" In addition to Webster's speller, publishers brought out new editions of Latin works such as *Caesar's Gallic Wars* and some original French and German grammars. William Bingham wrote his well-known Latin grammar at this time. Mrs. S. A. Poindexter and Mrs. A. D. Chaudron each compiled a series of readers. The chief publication centers were Richmond, Raleigh, Greensboro, Charleston, Augusta, Macon, and

22 *Ibid.*, 491. See also, Athens *Southern Watchman*, May 6, 1863; Atlanta *Southern Confederacy*, May 5, 1863; Charleston *Daily Courier*, May 15, 1863; Mobile *Daily Advertiser and Register*, September 12, 1861; Richmond *Semi-Weekly Enquirer*, March 13, 1863.

Mobile—and Nashville before its fall in the early days of the war.[23]

Prominent educational casualties of war were the orphans of soldiers, for whom a sentimental concern soon sprang up. Enoch Steadman, a Georgia cotton manufacturer, contributed $100,000 for the education of such orphans despite heavy losses in the destruction of his factories by Federal soldiers. By the middle of 1864 North Carolina had raised $500,000 and Alabama $175,000 for this purpose. The Episcopal Church set up in Livingston, Alabama, a school for orphans and promised all contributors giving as much as $2,000 the right to name a soldier's orphan to be educated. The disabled soldier was an object of almost equal educational attention. Steadman provided for educating fifty disabled soldiers at Mercer University; Congressman Ely M. Bruce of Kentucky promised to contribute to the education of disabled Kentucky soldiers; and Newberry College offered scholarships to the sons of deceased veterans.[24]

Educational institutions were hard pressed by war. The common schools receded to almost nothing and many of the colleges ceased their activities. The enthusiasm of secession times carried many of the college students into the army, causing the suspension of the University of Mississippi in 1861 and the University of Georgia and South Carolina College (University of South Carolina) in 1863. Many denominational colleges closed their doors. In Mississippi only Mississippi College, a Baptist institution, remained open. Most students whom initial enthusiasm did not propel into the army were later taken by conscription. Some universities sought exemption of their students, and some slight concessions were made,

---

23 Baxter and Dearborn (comps.), *List of Books and Newspapers printed in the South*, 85; Bettersworth, *Confederate Mississippi*, 326; Putnam County (Ga.) *Countryman*, November 3, 1862; *De Bow's Review*, XXXII (1862), 164; Stephen B. Weeks, "Confederate Text-Books (1861–1865): A Preliminary Bibliography," in *Report of the [United States] Commissioner of Education for the Year 1898–99* (Washington, 1900), I, 1139–55; Athens *Southern Watchman*, November 5, 1862; August 5, 1863; Austin *Weekly State Gazette*, August 24, 1864; Charleston *Daily Courier*, November 1, 1862; August 5, 1863; Sandersville *Central Georgian*, October 9, 1861; Richmond *Daily Whig*, July 25, 1863; January 16, 1864.

24 Athens *Southern Watchman*, April 22, July 29, 1863; Charleston *Daily Courier*, March 14, 1863; Richmond *Semi-Weekly Enquirer*, June 4, July 5, 1864; Richmond *Daily Enquirer*, February 7, 1865; Richmond *Daily Whig*, April 4, 1864.

but there was no general exemption of college students. As South Carolina College was about to close its doors, a Charleston paper bemoaned the fact that for the sake of getting a hundred youths into the army the proud history of the college must be brought to an end. Some schools of the Confederacy suffered destruction at the hands of Federal soldiers; the most conspicuous examples were the University of Alabama and the Virginia Military Institute. Students from both of these institutions had been useful in training Confederate recruits, and as cadets they had participated in some fighting, leading John C. Breckinridge to observe, "But we cannot afford to 'grind seed corn' in this style." [25]

The higher education of women, in which the South had pioneered, suffered least during the war. The many female colleges and collegiate institutes, as they were generally called, most of which granted no degrees, continued to thrive in the uninvaded parts of the Confederacy and continued to advertise for students. The college at Huntsville, Alabama, announced in its call for students a few months before the town was occupied by Federal troops, that it was out of the way of military operations and that its president had "been well known, *for months past,* as an open advocate, with tongue and pen, for Southern rights and Southern independence." [26] Some efforts were made to have the states support education for women to the same extent as for men, to show that they too had minds, but to avoid the Northern example of making women "horrible abortions, nondescripts, utter perversions of human nature." [27] The wisdom of government interference at all in education might

[25] For quotation, see Richmond *Daily Whig,* May 18, 1864. See also, Rufus C. Burleson, Waco, Tex., to Gov. P. Murrah, July 24, 1864, in Governors' Letters (Texas State Archives); *Official Records,* Ser. IV, Vol. III, 1093; Bettersworth, *Confederate Mississippi,* 296, 308 ff.; E. Merton Coulter, *College Life in the Old South* (New York, 1928), 312; Walter L. Fleming, *Civil War and Reconstruction in Alabama* (Cleveland, 1911), 212; Albert B. Moore, *History of Alabama and her People* (Chicago, 1927), I, 535–36; Spencer, *Last Ninety Days of the War,* 257; Charleston *Daily Courier,* May 3, 1862; Charleston *Daily Mercury,* March 14, 1862; Richmond *Daily Whig,* May 25, 1864. Excitement among the students at the University of Virginia was so intense that before Virginia had seceded, a group raised the Confederate flag on the rotunda. After a tactful speech by Albert T. Bledsoe they removed it. Randolph H. McKim, *A Soldier's Recollections; Leaves from the Diary of a Young Confederate . . .* (New York, 1910), 1–3.

[26] Printed circular (in possession of the writer).

[27] *De Bow's Review,* XXXI (1861), 388.

be questioned, but if it did exercise control, it was "but just that the female sex should share, to some extent, in its bounty," [28] thought a writer in *De Bow's Review*. Jeff. Davis Female Academy at Shubuta, Mississippi, was one of the few schools for girls set up during the war.

Although churches may be of divine origin, they have always been managed by human beings and in modern times none has survived long which opposed the government under which it found itself. Members of Southern churches took the South out of the Union, and it was only logical that they should take the churches out of the Union too. Political dissensions were discouraged, and so were sectarian animosities—with much more success. Any preacher continuing the dispute over the forms of baptism or any other doctrinal matter would likely find himself frowned down by the united opinion of the community. Methodists and Baptists had separated from their Northern brethren in the 1840's, and their Southernism was intensified by secession and war; even so, some observers felt that the Methodists should drop the word South from their designation after the establishment of the Confederacy. Both Methodists and Baptists were militantly Confederate, believing that the Old Testament doctrines of an eye for an eye and a tooth for a tooth should be applied to the enemy, and the Southern Baptist Convention meeting in Savannah in May, 1861, called on all Baptist churches throughout the Confederacy to observe June 1 as a day of humiliation, fasting, and prayer.[29]

Catholics, whose world-wide system of government was attuned to support any secular establishment under which they were living, naturally found themselves loyally supporting the Confederacy, and acknowledging Northerners "no longer as our countrymen." [30] Their clergy blessed the flags of Confederate regiments, and their opposition to the Federal regime in New Orleans was more uncompromising than that of any other group. Augustin Verot, Bishop of Savannah, declared that the South was fighting for liberty and justice and that slavery was "not reproved by the law of nature or

[28] *Ibid.*, 384. See also, *Southern Christian Advocate,* October 2, 1862 (advertisements); Paulding (Miss.) *Eastern Clarion,* September 6, 1861.

[29] *Journal of the Congress of the Confederate States,* I, 237–38; Charleston *Daily Courier,* March 29, 1864; Richmond *Daily Whig,* September 22, 1863.

[30] McPherson, *History of the . . . Rebellion,* 516–17.

by the law of the Gospel." [31] *The Pacificator,* a Catholic newspaper in the Confederacy, believed that if a convention of all American Catholics could be held, the Southern members could readily convince their Northern brethren of the righteousness of the Confederate cause and thereby lead the Pope to induce the countries of Europe to recognize Southern independence. And a Richmond editor appreciatingly said that the "Catholic Hierarchy of the South . . . [were] warm supporters of the Southern cause, and zealous advocates of the justice upon which this war of defense . . . [was] conducted." [32]

In ante-bellum times the Episcopal Church had always refrained in its triennial meetings from entering into discussions of the controversial political and social questions of the day, and as a consequence its organization had weathered the storms which wrecked the Methodists and Baptists. As the first General Conference after the secession of the South would not take place until 1862, the Southern Episcopalians for reasons purely of expediency and convenience separated themselves from the national organization— "a Church with whose doctrine, discipline and worship . . . [they were] in entire harmony, and with whose action, up to the time of that separation, . . . [they were] abundantly satisfied." In July, 1861, delegates from five states met in Montgomery and made preliminary plans for another meeting, which was held the following October in Columbia. Here they formed the Protestant Episcopal Church in the Confederate States of America. Imbued with strong conservatism, some delegates wanted to leave out the word Protestant, which reminded them too much of the Protestantism of Emerson, who held that the leaves of the forests were God; they would call the new church organization "The American Catholic Church" or the "Reformed Catholic Church." But as either one of these designations would have been confused with Roman Catholicism, both were rejected—though the bishops voted for the latter 8 to 6. The Northern Episcopalian convention, the next year, took no note of the Southern separation and called the names of the Southern dioceses as usual. This absence of animosity between Northern

[31] Richmond *Daily Whig,* January 2, 1864.
[32] *Ibid.* See also, Rowland and Croxall (eds.), *Journal of Julia LeGrand,* 269; Augusta *Pacificator,* January 28, 1865.

and Southern Episcopalians made it easy for the two divisions to coalesce after the war without any formal action.[33]

In May, 1861, while the firing on Fort Sumter was still fresh in mind, the General Assembly of the Presbyterian Church convened in Philadelphia, with most of the Southern synods unrepresented. Departing from the old Presbyterian custom of avoiding a stand on political issues, this Assembly adopted the famous Spring Resolution, which committed the Church to the support of the Union; and, thereby, it hastened a realization of the logical expectation that the Southern Presbyterians would set up a Confederate church. Presbyteries all over the South now began dissolving their connections with the national organization. In August, Southern Presbyterians assembled in Atlanta and called a convention to meet the following December in Augusta, where they established the Presbyterian Church in the Confederate States of America, consisting of ten synods. Back in 1837 the Presbyterian Church had split into Old School and New School organizations but not on strictly sectional questions, and it was the Old School which continued as the dominant group and which had here broken again. In 1864 at Lynchburg the less important New School Presbyterian faction united with the Confederate church and brought an end to this old schism in the South.[34]

The Lutherans were the last of the churches to break up into Northern and Southern branches. Their chief strength in the South lay in Virginia and the Carolinas. Despite the attempt of the General Synod, which represented two thirds of the Lutherans of the United States, to avoid a schism by postponing its 1861 meeting to the next year, Virginia in 1861, followed by North Carolina and South Carolina in 1862, voted separation. These states held a

[33] For quotation, see Moore (ed.), *Rebellion Record*, Supplement I, 253. See also, William W. Sweet, *The Story of Religions in America* (New York, 1930), 452; Charles C. Tiffany, *A History of the Protestant Episcopal Church in the United States of America* (3d ed., New York, 1907), 496; Richmond *Daily Whig*, October 24, 26, 1861. All of the *Historical Magazine of the Protestant Episcopal Church* (New Brunswick, etc.), XVII (December, 1948) is devoted to a history of that Church in the Confederacy.

[34] Benjamin M. Palmer, *The Life and Letters of James Henley Thornwell . . .* (Richmond, 1875), 501, 503; Sweet, *Story of Religions in America*, 449, 452; Lewis G. Vander Velde, *The Presbyterian Churches and the Federal Union, 1861–1869* (Cambridge, 1932), 43, 75, 102; Charleston *Daily Courier*, September 3, 1864.

meeting in Salisbury in May, 1862, looking toward the formation of a Southern church, and a year later at Concord they organized the General Synod of the Evangelical Lutheran Church in the Confederate States of America. The *Southern Lutheran,* which South Carolina Lutherans had set up in 1861 as their organ, was now adopted by the General Synod. The other denominations in the Confederacy were of too little importance to create problems for anyone except themselves and these led to no schisms. They supported the Confederacy as did the other denominations, but the pastor of the Universalist Church in Richmond gave aid and comfort to the enemy until he was arrested and imprisoned and his place filled by one who prayed for the success of the Confederacy. Other national organizations, fraternal and moral—the Sons of Temperance, the Improved Order of Red Men, the Independent Order of Odd Men, and so on—soon severed their ties with their Northern brethren.[35]

The churches suffered much from the incidence of war, with their preachers scattered, their congregations disrupted, their periodicals suspended; but especially did they pay for their support of the Confederacy when they fell under the heavy hand of Federal military occupation. Episcopal rectors who solved their dilemma of whom to pray for in civil authority by omitting that part of the prayer got various treatments. In Arkansas a Federal officer shouted in the midst of the service, "Stop, sir!" and read the prayer himself; in Alexandria, Virginia, soldiers violently interrupted the services and arrested and imprisoned the rector; in Natchez and Vicksburg women of the congregation were banished for leaving the services while an unwilling rector read the prayer for the President of the United States.

The Methodist Church was the object of special oppression because it was outstanding in the Confederacy and also because the other Methodists, who were a powerful influence in the North, had never forgiven the Southern Methodists for breaking away in 1845. The War Department gave Bishop Edward R. Ames of the North-

[35] *American Annual Cyclopaedia . . . 1863,* p. 597; Heathcote, *Lutheran Church and the Civil War,* 9, 65, 68, 99 ff.; Austin *Weekly Texas State Gazette,* February 15, 1862; Charleston *Daily Courier,* February 1, 1862; November 21, 1864; Macon *Daily Telegraph,* March 24, 1862; Richmond *Daily Examiner,* March 18, 1862; Richmond *Semi-Weekly Enquirer,* April 18, 1862; Richmond *Daily Whig,* June 8, 1863.

ern church the right to lay violent hands on any Confederate Methodist minister he could reach and to seize the Church property. Lincoln insisted that the army should keep hands off Southern churches and interfere with ministers only where they were preaching treason, but much damage was done before he interposed his authority, and there were clever ways invented to circumvent his order. And, of course, little could be done to restrain soldiers who wished to demolish churches and desecrate their walls and pews with nauseating and obscene writings. In describing what happened to Pohick Church, where Washington had worshiped, a Federal chaplain in shame admitted, "Our troops took possession of this church, and the walls were blackened with a thousand names. The seats were cut to pieces and borne away as memorials of the church of Washington." [36] At Hardeeville, South Carolina, Sherman's troops tore down a church for lumber with which to construct huts for a few days stay, and when the church had become a pile of rubbish, a soldier shouted "There goes your d—d old gospel shop." [37] Federal soldiers removed the Catholic cemetery in Savannah and erected breastworks on the site, while Bishop Augustin Verot stingingly protested to Secretary of War Stanton.

Preachers had played an effective part in bringing on secession, and they were more loyal than many of the politicians to a movement which both had started. Benjamin M. Palmer's support did not end with his famous New Orleans Thanksgiving Day sermon of 1860, of which thirty thousand copies were distributed by the New Orleans *Delta;* he continued to pour forth his pulpit oratory to the end. In Columbia Mrs. Chesnut heard him preach: "What a sermon! The preacher stirred my blood. My very flesh crept and tingled. A red-hot glow of patriotism passed through me. Such a sermon must strengthen the hearts and hands of many people." In

[36] Marks, *Peninsula Campaign in Virginia,* 84.

[37] Stephen F. Fleharty, *Our Regiment. A History of the 102d Illinois Infantry Volunteers* . . . (Chicago, 1865), 132. See also, *American Annual Cyclopaedia* . . . *1862,* p. 580; *ibid., 1863,* pp. 629–30; Joseph B. Cheshire, *The Church in the Confederate States; A History of the Protestant Episcopal Church in the Confederate States* (New York, 1912), 169; Day, *Down South,* II, 69; Garner, *Reconstruction in Mississippi,* 37 ff.; *Official Records,* Ser. I, Vol. XLVII, Pt. II, 967; Pt. III, 202, 203, 205, 220, 566; Sweet, *Story of Religions in America,* 460 ff.; Richmond *Daily Whig,* January 14, 1864. For an example of the Federals breaking up a church and arresting the preacher, see *Official Records,* Ser. I, Vol. XVII, Pt. II, 731.

Savannah he bolstered up the people by telling them that the Confederacy must win, for it was against divine plans to allow great consolidated governments. Had not God sent the flood to destroy an antediluvian consolidation, and on the Plains of Shinar had he not confounded the builders of the Tower of Babel and shattered their growing power? And, indeed, in modern Europe was there not a present example of a dispersal of the nations? Early in 1863 a group of ministers met in Richmond and sent out to the world a plea that this senseless and cruel war be stopped, for the Confederacy stood as a unit unalterably determined on independence, which undoubtedly would come sooner or later. As the sky darkened, Bishop George F. Pierce of Georgia took to the road in 1864 to awaken the lagging spirits of the people and preach a veritable crusade against the enemy. Andrew Johnson charged that preachers had done more than any other force to make fanatical Confederate fiends out of the women.[38]

Many preachers became chaplains in the army; others became active officers, among them Brigadier General William N. Pendleton, chief of artillery of the Army of Northern Virginia, and Major General Leonidas Polk of the Army of Tennessee, previously Bishop of Louisiana. What the former said on one occasion before ordering the artillery to fire became a standing bit of conversation in the Confederacy. It was variously reported, this being one of the versions: "While we kill their bodies, may the Lord have mercy on their sinful souls—FIRE!" [39] The great preachers of the Confederacy, Palmer, Bishop Stephen Elliott, Charles Todd Quintard, and many lesser ones, visited the Confederate armies, especially the armies in the West, and, aided by the army chaplains, converted and baptized probably as many as 150,000 soldiers and a half-dozen or more generals including Joseph E. Johnston, John B. Hood, and William J. Hardee. For a time vice among the soldiers was routed, and the Confederate army took on the nature of Cromwell's

[38] For quotation, see Martin and Avary (eds.), *Diary from Dixie*, 334. See also, Meade, *Judah P. Benjamin*, 144; James W. Silver, "Propaganda in the Confederacy," in *Journal of Southern History*, XI (1945), 493; Athens *Southern Watchman*, February 3, 1864; Jackson *Daily Southern Crisis*, March 20, 1863; Macon *Daily Telegraph*, February 9, 1864. For a copy of the address, see London *Index*, June 11, 1863, pp. 108–10; McPherson, *History of the . . . Rebellion*, 517–21.

[39] Atlanta *Southern Confederacy*, March 29, 1862.

Ironsides. The greatest of the revivals broke out in the winter of 1863–1864. A North Carolina soldier in March, 1864, wrote from Orange Courthouse, Virginia, "We have preaching almost every night. Our Brigade has constructed a very neat and very comfortable log house as a Chapel and we have preaching in it almost every day." [40] "Let the voice of prayer mingle with the din of arms," exclaimed an Alabama Baptist.[41] Many Confederate commanders needed no conversion, for religion was so much a part of their lives that they could have claimed the right to convert others. Such were Robert E. Lee and Stonewall Jackson, Episcopalian and Presbyterian respectively, both of whom constantly gave the Lord credit for their victories.

The churches and other religious groups provided for the soldiers a vast amount of religious reading material, small pamphlets (tracts), religious periodicals, and Bibles. The Evangelical Tract Society of Petersburg was the principal organization of its kind in the Confederacy, though the South Carolina Tract Society was very active. Tract societies published and distributed great numbers of booklets ranging generally from four to sixteen pages in length. One of the most popular was J. B. Jeter's *A Mother's Parting Words to her Soldier Boy.* There was some opposition to such activities from hard-bitten warriors and realists, who declared that the sickly sentimentalism of these publications, such as *Are You Ready to Die* and *Sinner, You are Soon to be Damned,* unnerved the soldiers. Some people maintained that the profanity of officers had won battles and that drinking was the mark of a virile soldier. Yet, it was reported by the middle of 1863 that agents of the Society of

[40] Wagstaff (ed.), *Graham Papers,* 182.

[41] Tuskegee *South Western Baptist,* June 7, 1864. See also, Cheshire, *Protestant Episcopal Church in the Confederate States,* 47–48; Jabez L. M. Curry, *Civil History of the Government of the Confederate States with Some Personal Reminiscences* (Richmond, 1901), 178; Fremantle, *Three Months in the Southern States,* 154, 162; Mary A. H. Gay, *Life in Dixie during the War . . .* (Atlanta, 1897), 81; Gordon, *Reminiscences of the Civil War,* 230; Jones, *Christ in the Camp, passim;* Jones, *Rebel War Clerk's Diary,* I, 70, 316; [McGuire], *Diary of a Southern Refugee,* 34; Arthur H. Noll (ed.), *Doctor Quintard, Chaplain C.S.A. and Second Bishop of Tennessee; Being his Story of the War (1861–1865)* (Sewanee, 1905), 1, 80, 96; Athens *Southern Watchman,* July 1, 1863; Richmond *Daily Examiner,* September 3, 1863; Richmond *Daily Whig,* February 16, April 27, 1864. The Missionary Society of the Methodist Church in Richmond elected to life membership Stonewall Jackson and "Circuit Rider" Jeb Stuart. Richmond *Daily Examiner,* November 11, 1862.

Army Colportage had distributed 35,000,000 pages of tracts. The principal religious periodicals, which the soldiers probably enjoyed more than tracts, were the *Army and Navy Messenger*, published by the Evangelical Tract Society; the *Soldier's Paper*, by the Methodists; the *Soldier's Visitor*, by the Presbyterians; and the *Soldier's Friend*, by the Baptists.

Prized highest by soldiers was the Bible, especially the New Testament and the Psalms.[42] In ante-bellum times the South had depended on Northern and European publishers for its Bibles. In war, cut off from both, the Confederacy used various means to secure supplies of Holy Writ. In December, 1862, the Reverend Moses D. Hoge, pastor of the Second Presbyterian Church in Richmond, slipped through the blockade to England and was soon rewarded by a gift from the British and Foreign Bible Society of 310,000 Bibles, Testaments, and Psalms. Fraser, Trenholm & Company shipped them to Nassau free of charge. A little later the London Bible Society made a gift of thirteen large cases of Bibles, which successfully ran the blockade in the summer of 1864. Most agencies in the North considered Bibles contraband and refused to assist in sending them to the Confederacy, though the American Bible Society was able to get through the lines to the Confederate distributing agencies an estimated 300,000 Bibles and parts of the Bible.

But the Confederacy was not forced to depend entirely on foreign supplies; perhaps for the first time in the history of the South, Southerners began printing this work and before the end of the war they had turned out hundreds of thousands of Bibles, New Testaments, and Psalms. To promote the printing of Bibles as well as their distribution, Bible societies sprang up in several of the states. The South Carolina Bible Society was the most active. To co-ordinate this work members of various denominations, mostly from Georgia and South Carolina, met in Augusta in March, 1862, and organized the Confederate States Bible Society, which promoted the print-

[42] William W. Bennett, *A Narrative of the Great Revival which Prevailed in the Southern Armies during the Late Civil War Between the States of the Federal Union* (Philadelphia, 1877), 74, 76; Wiley, *Life of Johnny Reb*, 174 ff.; Atlanta *Southern Confederacy*, April 23, 1863; Charleston *Daily Mercury*, January 8, February 16, 1862; Charleston *Daily Courier*, May 8, 1863; April 22, 1864; Richmond *Daily Enquirer*, May 11, 1863.

ing and distribution of many Bibles. This Society brought out its first edition in 1862 and a second the following year. Both were printed in Atlanta. In 1864 the well-known Columbia publishing house of Evans & Cogswell announced that it had in press for the Society 100,000 copies of the New Testament and the Psalms. In 1861 a Nashville firm printed the first Bibles produced in the Confederacy, from stereotype plates smuggled across the lines from the North. Of course, most of the Bibles were printed for the soldiers, and before a supply could thus be obtained, many people presented their home Bibles to the army.[43]

The Young Men's Christian Association, notably the Richmond branch of it, carried on a remarkable work of relief, both spiritual and material. It was especially effective in the latter kind of service. It sent out appeals for food and clothing for sick and wounded soldiers as well as for the robust; it acted as a sort of unofficial agency to distribute packages sent from home; it was of great aid in distributing the food in the celebrated 1865 New Year's Dinner to Lee's army; it sponsored lectures on religious subjects and maintained a reading room for soldiers in Richmond; and its committees worked with various brigades in active service. Before the war was half over, it had spent for soldier relief more than $500,000.[44]

In fact, religion was almost as ever-present with the people as was the war itself, and there were a few whispers that a national church should be established. If the war was to be won it should be through the aid of the Lord, and when victories came He should be given the credit—not Lee or Jackson. Many considered prayer an irresistible power. At the very time the First Battle of Manassas was being fought a congregation in Oglethorpe County, Georgia,

[43] Bennett, *Great Revival which Prevailed in the Southern Armies,* 49; *General Orders from Adjutant and Inspector-General's Office, Confederate States Army,* 1862–1863, advertisement on back cover; Sweet, *Story of Religions in America,* 458; Charleston *Daily Courier,* March 21, June 28, 1862; Macon *Daily Telegraph,* March 4, April 14, 1862; Selma *Daily Reporter,* June 28, 1862; *Southern Christian Advocate,* October 2, 1862; Richmond *Daily Dispatch,* September 12, 1861; Richmond *Semi-Weekly Enquirer,* January 1, 1864; Richmond *Daily Examiner,* June 18, 1864; Richmond *Daily Whig,* September 8, 1862. See also, Harold R. Willoughby, *Soldiers' Bibles through Three Centuries* (Chicago, 1944), 25–32.

[44] Richmond *Daily Dispatch,* April 17, 1862; Richmond *Semi-Weekly Enquirer,* August 16, 1861; September 18, 1863; Richmond *Daily Whig,* February 25, 1862; September 11, 1863.

was praying for the safety of the Oglethorpe Rifles, and it was reverentially announced that not a member of that unit was killed though it had been in the thick of the fight. To give the proper credit for that victory Congress resolved, "That we recognize the hand of the Most High God, the King of Kings and Lord of Lords, in the glorious victory with which He hath crowned our arms at Manassas." [45] There was widespread praying over the Confederacy, singly and in mass. The Reverend Henry H. Tucker of Mercer University in Georgia started a movement whereby all people, military and civilian, whether on land or sea, should fall upon their knees every day at one o'clock and pray for the success of the Confederacy. They were to be reminded of this duty by the ringing of church bells and firing of signal guns. The mass psychological power of such a movement had it materialized might easily have brought permanent victory through a sustained morale. A modification of this plan was a widely heeded call to all the women of the Confederacy to pray on December 1, 1862, for peace and victory. It was suggested that the prayer be repeated every month until victory came. Many of the churches opened their doors for daily prayer meetings, and in some places these meetings rotated among the churches to emphasize the nonsectarian nature of the movement. A Richmond editor affirmed in November, 1861, that the cause of the South appeared "to have hitherto been under the special protection of Providence." "Our arms have been crowned with success," he continued, "and many times the influences of an agency greater than that of man could be seen too plainly to be mistaken." [46]

The government itself took ample note of the God of War and of Victory—and of Peace, too. Both Davis and Congress and the governors of states and mayors of cities frequently set apart days for fasting, humility, and prayer. According to typical proclamations, as "sorrow sits at the hearthstones of our countrymen," "[we pray] that we may be saved from our enemies, and from the hand

[45] *Journal of the Congress of the Confederate States*, I, 276.

[46] Richmond *Daily Whig*, November 14, 1861. See also, Athens *Southern Watchman*, June 26, 1861; Charleston *Daily Courier*, March 3, 1862; September 1, 1864; Richmond *Daily Examiner*, July 29, 1861; Richmond *Daily Whig*, August 20, 1861; November 26, December 1, 24, 1862. Before the people of Macon had become accustomed to the ringing of church bells to summon the people to prayer, on one occasion, hearing the bells, they ran out into the streets in great commotion, thinking the city was on fire. Macon *Daily Telegraph*, February 17, 1862.

of all that hate us," "[that He] will scatter our enemies, set at naught their evil designs," and restore peace. Occasionally days of thanksgiving were set apart when the people need not come "in the garb of fasting and prayer, but with joy and gladness," to praise the Lord for the victories He had given.[47] In calling on the people not to forget to observe the day of fasting and prayer set apart for March 27, 1863, a Mississippi paper showed the confidence it placed in prayer when it warned, "To-morrow may decide the fate of our country!"[48] After three weary years of war and many proclamations for prayer, President Davis set aside April 8, 1864, for an extraordinary effort, as it was about this time that Grant was making ready his campaign against Richmond. This prayer day was probably more widely observed than any others, unless it were those in 1861 while the experience was still new. In Richmond it was estimated that five thousand people crowded into the New Richmond Theatre to pray, sing, and hear a sermon by J. L. Burrows, a local Baptist minister, in which he seemed to have visualized the age of atomic power when he exclaimed, "If some patriotic genius could only invent some enginery of war which would render our success certain—if he could gather the electricity of Heaven and hold it back until the favorable moment should arrive, and then let it fall with destructive violence upon the serried host of the enemy, how glad we all would be—how rejoiced by the certainty of a speedy peace."[49] And on the military front soldiers observed the day with impressive solemnity and little of the customary noises around camp. A North Carolina soldier near Orange Courthouse reported that most of the regiments in his brigade "stayed in their tents and kept very quiet."[50]

Of course there were Southerners who were unimpressed by these calls on God, and there were some who scoffed at them and more especially so because most of them were issued by Davis. Of the nonreligious element, a Georgia paper said that they "no more

[47] Richardson (comp.), *Messages and Papers of the Confederacy*, I, 228, 218, 325, 268, respectively.

[48] Jackson *Daily Southern Crisis*, March 26, 1863.

[49] Richmond *Daily Whig*, April 11, 1864.

[50] Wagstaff (ed.), *Graham Papers*, 185. See also, Richardson (comp.), *Messages and Papers of the Confederacy*, I, 103–104, 135, 328, 412–14, 567–68; Charleston *Daily Mercury*, February 20, 1862; Greensboro *Alabama Beacon*, November 22, 1861; Richmond *Semi-Weekly Enquirer*, April 12, 1864.

endeavor to gain the divine favor, than if there was no God, no war, no danger." [51] When Davis joined St. Paul's Episcopal congregation in June, 1862, his enemies sneered at him for being scared into the church by McClellan's near capture of Richmond at that time. War-clerk Jones hoped that membership in a Christian church might develop a gulf between the President and that "descendant of those who crucified the Saviour [referring to Benjamin]," [52] and a Baptist in Alabama quarreled with Davis because none of his proclamations referred to the Son or Holy Spirit—further evidence of Benjamin's influence over him or an indication that the President was a Deist. Wigfall sarcastically answered a question as to how a certain military difficulty could be overcome by saying that Davis would set the women and children to praying over it at six in the morning. But the most blistering irreverence employed in attacking Davis' calls for prayer came from John M. Daniel of the *Examiner*. Before the war was a year old he was saying that the country had had enough of Davis' prayer proclamations. Religion was "the sentiment of individuals, not a matter of military order or formal injunction." "In truth, these devotional proclamations of Mr. Davis," said Daniel, "have lost all good effect upon their repetition, are regarded by the people as either cant or evidences [of] mental weakness, and have become the topic of unpleasant reflection with intelligent men." But when Daniel wrote the following he reached the height of his spleen: "When we find the President standing in a corner telling his beads, and relying on a miracle to save the country, instead of mounting his horse and putting forth every power of the Government to defeat the enemy, the effect is depressing in the extreme." [53]

The Confederacy attempted to make as thorough a use of its religious resources as of any others, but as with the others it could not command enough. As laboriously as the Confederacy sought to make it so, religion was not a vital interest to the mass of the people, but if a morale or fanaticism could have been captured and held in the name of religion it might well have been the determining factor in winning Confederate independence.

[51] Macon *Daily Telegraph*, March 19, 1862.
[52] Jones, *Rebel War Clerk's Diary*, I, 120.
[53] Richmond *Daily Examiner*, March 19, 1862. See also, Jones, *Rebel War Clerk's Diary*, II, 231; Tuskegee *South Western Baptist*, January 7, 1864.

CHAPTER XXII

LONGINGS FOR PEACE—
AND THE END

SOUTHERN movements for peace began as early as the war itself; they had a variety of origins, differences in intensity, diversities of purpose. All Southerners had hoped to avoid war, and original Union men who had not been overcome by the war spirit, after fighting started advocated a negotiated peace leading to reconstruction of the Union. But as the struggle continued, accompanied by military defeats and internal dissensions over conscription, impressments of property, suspensions of the writ of habeas corpus, tax laws, the inflation of the currency, and many petty rivalries and personal dislikes, there arose the disturbing cry of the "Rich man's war and the poor man's fight," the profiteer against the simple patriot, and even the slaveholder against the non-slaveholder. By 1864 a Virginian reached the conclusion that the situation resolved itself into "the *higher* class staying home and making money, the *lower* class thrust into the trenches," [1] and the well-to-do, doubtful of ultimate victory, sending their gains to Europe for investment. A Georgia office seeker promised if elected "to give the rich fits in the way of taxes," [2] and an Alabamian, complaining of the wealth-proud aristocracy, could say, "If a man is poor—no matter how virtuous or intelligent he may be—his poverty as effectually excludes him from the presence of the *aristocracy* as if he were afflicted with the leprosy or the small pox." [3] And widespread and intense was the feeling against the so-called twenty-Negro law, which made the ownership of twenty or more slaves ground for exemption.

It mattered little to discontented people to be told what they al-

[1] Jones, *Rebel War Clerk's Diary*, II, 281.
[2] Macon *Daily Telegraph and Confederate*, December 29, 1864.
[3] Selma *Daily Reporter*, January 15, 1863.

ready knew, that if slaves were to be used at all they must be controlled by overseers; the fact was that they still thought this was a loophole to let rich men out of the war. And though the nonslaveholders, who made up two thirds of the Southerners, knew they were fighting as much for themselves as for the slaveholders, in that slavery solved the problem of the races living together, many still continued to think in terms of rich man against poor man. To close the gap between slaveowner and nonslaveowner, a North Carolinian suggested in early 1865 that all soldiers who owned no slaves and land be given fifty acres and a slave at the end of the war.[4]

The movement for peace made by the original and persisting Unionists grew from small beginnings (as in North Carolina in early 1862 when fifty men raised a white flag and marched around it praying for peace) to the development of many disloyal secret societies scattered throughout the Confederacy. The best known of these was the Heroes of America, sometimes called Sons of America and also Red Strings from symbols worn on their coat lapels, which had secret connections with the enemy and was said to have numbered among its members Lincoln and Grant. Membership in this society was thought to guarantee protection against molestation by Federal soldiers. Another group was called simply the Peace Society.[5]

This defeatist and disloyal movement having peace as its object early developed strength in Alabama and Arkansas, but it first came out dangerously into the open with only thin disguise in North Carolina. There it was expressed in the Congressional election of 1863 and mounted to a dangerous outburst in the gubernatorial campaign the next year. At the head of it was William W. Holden, able politician and editor of the Raleigh *Standard,* who bordered on treason. He whipped many Carolinians into a furor by crying "Peace! When shall we have peace?" [6] and called upon them to assemble and shout for peace. He asserted that more than a hundred meetings responded. His plan advocated a state convention which

---

[4] *Official Records,* Ser. IV, Vol. III, 1041–42.

[5] *Ibid.,* 393–98, 802–16; J. G. de R. Hamilton, "The Heroes of America," in *Publications of the Southern History Association,* XI (1907), 10–19; Hamilton, *Reconstruction in North Carolina,* 64; Hamilton (ed.), *Correspondence of Jonathan Worth,* I, 164; Richardson, *Secret Service,* 429; Tatum, *Disloyalty in the Confederacy,* 24 ff., 67.

[6] Quoted by Hamilton, *Reconstruction in North Carolina,* 50.

should offer to rejoin the Union, maintaining that North Carolina would be received back with old rights guaranteed. Governor Vance became alarmed, and to silence the disaffected he decided another attempt should be made to negotiate a peace, admitting that it would probably be futile. He demanded of President Davis, in a letter of December 30, 1863, that the Confederacy reopen negotiations. "The *effort* to obtain peace is the principal matter," he insisted.[7] Davis answered that three attempts had already been made without result, and asked, "Have we not been apprised by that despot [Lincoln] that we can only expect his gracious pardon by emancipating all our slaves, swearing allegiance and obedience to him and his proclamations, and becoming in point of fact the slaves of our own negroes?" [8] Davis was here referring to Lincoln's proclamation of December 8, 1863, granting amnesty to those swearing allegiance and providing for readmission of any state after a tenth of its voters of 1860 did so and organized a loyal government. This proclamation played into Holden's hands but seems to have had little effect elsewhere, despite the fact that it was widely scattered by invading Federal soldiers. Still unsatisfied, Vance on February 9, 1864, wrote Davis a stinging letter chiding him with partyism in failing to recognize in his government old Whigs and antisecessionists.

But Vance was no defeatist, and in the gubernatorial election of 1864 he ran against Holden, who roused up another wave of peace meetings. Probably a less superb campaigner than Vance might have gone down in defeat. This Buncombe County man did not deal in buncombe in two telling speeches he made, one in Fayetteville in the eastern section of the state and the other in Wilkesboro in the western part, in the very midst of the most disaffected region. The second speech was considered so crucial for the Confederacy that the Richmond *Enquirer* sent a special correspondent to report it. Vance branded Holden as a traitor who knew that peace could not be made with Lincoln without rejoining the Union on terms which no true Confederate could accept. In trying to take North Carolina out of the Confederacy he was adding civil war to civil war, for if the state joined the Union it would be surrounded by

[7] Richmond *Daily Whig*, May 31, 1864.
[8] Rowland (ed.), *Jefferson Davis, Constitutionalist*, VI, 145.

the Confederacy and would be promptly propelled into another war. Vance won the election and thereafter, though critical of some Confederate policies, he heroically supported the war to the end.[9]

From the beginning there had been various efforts of the Confederate administration to make peace, but only with independence recognized. In answer to those who cloaked their designs of re-entering the Union under the term "honorable peace men," Davis declared in 1861 that "separation is final, and for the independence we have asserted we will accept no alternative." [10] Time and again he reiterated this sentiment in terms growing stronger, saying in 1863, "With union and energy, the rallying of every man able to bear arms to the defense of his country, we shall succeed, and if we leave our children poor we shall leave them a better heritage than wealth." [11]

Both by direct and indirect methods Davis sought to win peace with independence. The Confederacy considered the Northwestern states to be the weakest spot in the Northern armor, and from the very beginning sought to pierce it. This region was linked to the Confederacy by the great highway of the Mississippi River which had in times past bound the two sections together economically. The southern parts of Ohio, Indiana, and Illinois had been largely populated by Southerners, who had not forgotten their sentimental connection. Politically the Old Northwest seemed fruitful ground, for there was a strong Democratic peace party there which

[9] For the text of Vance's Wilkesboro speech, see Richmond *Semi-Weekly Enquirer,* March 8, 1864; for his Fayetteville speech, see Augusta *Daily Chronicle & Sentinel,* May 1, 1864. For a discussion of Vance and peace, see the two articles by Richard E. Yates, "Governor Vance and the Peace Movement," in *North Carolina Historical Review,* XVII (1940), 1–25, 89–113; "Governor Vance and the End of the War in North Carolina," *ibid.,* XVIII (1941), 315–38.

[10] Richardson (comp.), *Messages and Papers of the Confederacy,* I, 141.

[11] Rowland (ed.), *Jefferson Davis, Constitutionalist,* V, 550. The early uncompromising attitude was expressed thus in the Richmond *Daily Examiner,* July 4, 1861: "Again we would be flooded with Yankee goods, Yankee manufactures, Yankee teachers, preachers, pedlars and drummers. Again their vile literature—their books, newspapers, reviews and magazines would infest us, thick and noxious as the plagues of Egypt, inoculate our people with their shallow thought, tawdry fashions, mischievous theories and gross immoralities. . . . If disunion does not build up centres of trade and centres of thought, and centres of fashion in the South, disunion will have effected little good."

was to win important victories in the fall elections of 1862. So when Bragg invaded Kentucky in the autumn he issued from Bardstown an appeal to the Northwestern states. In this proclamation, directing attention to the domination of the government by the East, always hostile to Western interests, he advised these states to force Lincoln to make peace. He got no direct response, but he helped to plant in that region the seeds of discontent which were to sprout forth during the next two years in the growth of a secret society known as the Knights of the Golden Circle, in the organization of the Order of American Knights or Sons of Liberty, and in the promotion of the Copperhead movement.[12]

Many Southerners helped to promote Bragg's efforts. Beauregard became actively interested and wrote to various Southern governors and to Congressman William Porcher Miles suggesting the calling of a conference at Memphis with the Northwestern governors. Governor Pickens of South Carolina fell in with the idea. Foote became fanatical over promoting peace with the Northwest and frequently brought up the subject in Congress. The Confederate peacemakers had varying ideas as to what might come out of the movement. Some hoped that it would result at least in disrupting the United States further by the erection of a Northwestern Confederacy and the removal from the war of the Western soldiers, who were generally regarded as the best Federal fighters; others thought these states might be induced to join the Confederacy. There were still others who felt that these efforts were futile of good and actually dangerous if the Northwestern states were admitted, for free members might endanger the nature and policies of the Confederacy and actually lead to the restoration of the South to the Union through the back door. In fact, they could be a whole herd of Trojan horses. Senator John B. Clark of Missouri declared there was "no such feeling among them [people of the Northwest] as many here were pleased to fancy." [13] And when in the summer of 1863 Clement L. Vallandigham, the Ohio Democratic leader, was banished to the Confederacy, he was treated with scant attention as being no dependable friend, though Davis ordered that he be con-

12 For the text of Bragg's appeal, see Seitz, *Braxton Bragg*, 181–84. See also, George Fort Milton, *Abraham Lincoln and the Fifth Column* (New York, 1942), *passim*.
13 *Southern Historical Society Papers*, XLVIII (1941), 271.

ducted with "all the courtesy and kindness due to his condition" [14] to Wilmington, whence he was to sail for Canada.

Apart from the frustrated attempt of Stephens to explore peace possibilities in 1863, the greatest peace offensives of the North and of the South spent themselves in futility as part of the Presidential election campaign of 1864 and finally faded into nothingness at the Hampton Roads Conference in February of 1865. In June, 1863, Stephens wrote to Davis from Georgia (where he spent most of the war years) suggesting that he would like to go on a mission to Washington to see if he could alleviate the suffering of prisoners and humanize the conduct of the war, but that when once there he might drive in an entering wedge for peace. He would like to negotiate for peace, he said rather cryptically, on the basis of "the recognition of the sovereignty of the States and the right of each in its sovereign capacity to determine its own destiny." "The full recognition of this principle covers all that is really involved in the present issue," he added. Recognition of this doctrine might well have been as great a threat to the integrity of the Confederacy as to that of the old Union, for, as Stephens undoubtedly thought then and later made plain, he had never become reconciled to the permanency of this new government. With the barbarities of the war preying as much on Davis' mind as on Stephens', the President fell in with the idea; but he may have tricked Stephens on the peace-mission part of the trip by withholding the information that Lee was preparing to invade the North and that he had the highest hopes that Lee would administer a knockout blow which would make it convenient to have a negotiator in Washington at the time. When Stephens heard of the Lee expedition he felt that all chances of peace negotiations would be killed by Northern infuriation at military invasion. Nevertheless, armed with two letters from Davis to Lincoln, identical except as to the form of address, one being from Commander in Chief Davis to Commander in Chief Lincoln and the other from President to President, the one to be presented which was acceptable, Stephens set out on a flag-of-truce boat down

[14] Rowland (ed.), *Jefferson Davis, Constitutionalist*, V, 508. See also, *Journal of the Congress of the Confederate States*, V, 404–407; *Official Records*, Ser. IV, Vol. II, 137; Athens *Southern Watchman*, September 10, 1862; March 4, April 1, 1863; Richmond *Daily Enquirer*, February 19, March 3, May 4, 1863; Richmond *Daily Examiner*, February 14, 1863; Richmond *Daily Whig*, January 17, 1863.

the James. He got no farther than Newport News, for by the time he arrived there news of Gettysburg had been received; and the Federal authorities, believing this to be a much greater victory for them than it really was, refused to receive him.[15]

Stephens' statement that the only issue in the war was state sovereignty, as simple as it was, seemed to be his true view and that of other defeatists and peacemongers from 1863 on to inevitable defeat. But it appeared to them that this fact would never be recognized through military means; only through negotiations could it ever be arrived at. If the war continued, both sides would become exhausted without a real victory on the part of either, and when an armed peace should be arrived at through this method the liberties of both South and North would be lost in the erection of military dictatorships in both sections. Hence peace must be got as soon as possible through negotiations by "statesmen," not through Davis and Lincoln, who were imbued with the military spirit. As Governor Brown put it, "In a crisis like the present Statesmanship is even more important than Generalship. Generals can never stop a war, though it may last twenty years till one has been able to conquer the other. Statesmen terminate wars by negotiation." These negotiations should be conducted through the convention method, and how this could be done was variously argued. It might be by a convention of all the Confederate states approaching a convention of the Northern states or the legislatures of willing Northern states; the two conventions might meet in the same city, as Baltimore or even Montreal, as Foote suggested, or all the delegates might meet in one convention; and if no general conventions could be got together, then separate states might hold their own conventions and hope that this would in some way lead to peace. Some "Confederate statesmen" even suggested that a few Northern and Southern governors might meet at Memphis or in the Bermuda Islands and start the movement.[16]

15 For quotation, see Rowland (ed.), *Jefferson Davis, Constitutionalist*, V, 514. See also, Richardson (comp.), *Messages and Papers of the Confederacy*, I, 339–43; Stephens, *Constitutional View of the Late War between the States*, II, 565 ff.; Pollard, *Lost Cause*, 414; Johnston and Browne, *Alexander H. Stephens*, 445.

16 For quotation, see *Journal of the House of Representatives of . . . Georgia . . . November 3rd, 1864* (Milledgeville, 1864), 16. See also, Athens *Southern Watchman*, November 11, 1863; Richmond *Daily Enquirer*, September 17, 1864.

Looking forward to the Federal Presidential election of November, 1864, Stephens, Brown, and others initiated a peace conspiracy in Georgia, which worked in with the furor being whipped up in North Carolina by Holden and with the defeatism of Congressman William W. Boyce in South Carolina, who had the boldness to ask Davis, "Indeed, if you were appointed Military Dictator, what greater powers could you exercise than you now do?" [17] In March, 1864, Brown and Stephens developed their scheme through a special session of the legislature, which Brown addressed in his message and Stephens in an almost interminable speech. Stephens condemned in strong terms the chief measures of the government whose vice-president he was, playing on the sentiments of his audience by saying, "I do not know that I shall ever address you again, or see you again," and at the conclusion cumbersomely paraphrasing the heroics of Patrick Henry, "As for myself, give me liberty as secured in the constitution with all its guaranties, amongst which is the sovereignty of Georgia, or give me death." [18] Brown talked about re-establishing the principles of the Declaration of Independence—"the *right of all self-government and the sovereignty of the States*," [19] by which he meant, as he later said, that each state, Northern and Southern, should "determine for herself what shall be her future connection, and who her future allies." [20] Thus he would have a disintegration of the Confederacy, and of the North too, into sovereignties which could rearrange themselves as they pleased or remain independent of all. He was quick to say that, of course, no Southern state would join the North. If Lincoln would not hear to this procedure, the Confederacy should continually drum it into his ears, and after each victory offer the plan again. The legislature adopted a set of resolutions embracing these "principles of 1776."

The defeatists loudly praised Stephens and Brown, one writing the former that he had rather have made that speech than "to wear the crown the Bourbon lost"; [21] and Henry Cleveland, a close as-

[17] Athens *Southern Watchman*, October 19, 1864.

[18] Cleveland, *Alexander H. Stephens*, 785, 786.

[19] Georgia *House Journal*, November 3, 1864, p. 42.

[20] Athens *Southern Watchman*, October 5, 1864. See also, Augusta *Weekly Constitutionalist*, October 26, 1864. For the text of Stephens' speech, see Cleveland, *Alexander H. Stephens*, 761–86.

[21] J. D. Waddell to Stephens, April 11, 1864, in Stephens Papers (microfilms in University of Texas Library, originals in Division of Manuscripts, Library of Congress).

sociate and later biographer of Stephens, wrote him, "I am satisfied that the immediate secession of the State of Georgia from the Confederate States would be the best thing we could do." [22] But in addition to the praise of doubtful patriots, Stephens received widespread denunciation. A Virginia editor cautioned: "But beware of rhetoric: it is a dangerous Pegasus: ought not to be mounted without a strong snaffle—and has a vicious propensity to get the bit between its teeth and bolt." [23] A fellow Georgian charged that Stephens chose "to mingle in a factious conspiracy, as a volunteer, and to lend his official influence and his spotless reputation to cripple his own Government." [24] If critics might have considered Stephens a little sacrosanct, they had no such feeling toward Brown. A Georgian writing to the Macon *Telegraph* and veiling himself under the pseudonym "Troup," appraised the situation thus, "Wherever you meet a growling, complaining, sore-headed man, hostile to the government and denunciatory of its measures and policy, or a croaking desponding dyspeptic who sees no hope for the country, but, whipped, himself, is trying to make everybody else feel as badly as himself, you will invariably find a friend, admirer and defender of Gov. Brown." [25] The humorist Bill Arp, charging Brown with wanting to replace Davis in the presidency, said, "It aint everybody that kan git to be President—my kandid opinyun is, that you will make a mity good Governor if you will stik to it a few more terms." [26] An Alabamian thought that "Brown's Legislature had better be at home planting corn and sorghum cane," and that Brown himself, if other governors should follow him, would "prevent us from having any rights at all." [27] Various Georgia regiments at the battlefront passed resolutions in bitter terms against his disruptive tactics and near-treason, which Brown answered by charging that no soldier voted for the resolutions "whose official promotion and self-importance . . . [did] not depend upon a continuance of the war." [28]

22 Cleveland to Stephens, June 8, 1864, *ibid.*
23 Richmond *Daily Examiner,* April 19, 1864.
24 Milledgeville *Southern Recorder,* May 17, 1864.
25 Macon *Daily Telegraph,* April 13, 1864.
26 Milledgeville *Southern Recorder,* April 26, 1864.
27 Montgomery *Weekly Mail,* March 22, 1864.
28 *Official Records,* Ser. IV, Vol. III, 374. See also, Cumming, *Journal of Hospital Life,* 131–32; Mayes, *Lucius Q. C. Lamar,* 651; Athens *Southern Watchman,* April 20,

The effect of the Georgia disruptive movement was marked on the North. Newspapers published Brown's messages in full and copied from Confederate papers such condemnations of Brown as this, "While other states and other governors were *arming against the Yankees,* Governor Brown was arming *against the confederacy.*" [29] Northern people saw general disruption of the Confederacy in this peace movement, whether in Georgia or elsewhere. Edward Everett exclaimed in his Gettysburg speech, "In North Carolina the fatal chain at length is broken. At Raleigh the lips of honest and brave men are unsealed, and an independent press is unlimbering its artillery." [30] There was little wonder, then, that after Sherman had marched into Georgia and seized Atlanta he should have correctly guessed that Brown was ready to make the peace he had talked so much about, now that he had removed the Georgia militia from Hood's army and disbanded them. The General, believing that "it would be a magnificent stroke of policy if we could, without surrendering principle or a foot of ground, arouse the latent enmity of Georgia against Davis"; [31] and, having reason to believe that Brown and Stephens wanted to see him, Sherman sent them an invitation to come to Atlanta. He was prepared to offer Georgia, in return for her withdrawal from the war, the keeping of his troops to the roads in his further invasion and the payment for what he consumed. Fearing they might be caught in this web of intrigue, both refused to go—Stephens basing his refusal on the grounds that neither Sherman nor himself had the right to treat, and Brown, though believing that Georgia had the right to make peace, thinking that it would not be honorable for her to do so at that time.

Peace maneuvers in 1864 were not confined to a few regions of the South. Ramifying out of the Presidential campaign, they embraced Washington, Niagara Falls, Chicago, the whole Northwest, and Richmond, and they involved Lincoln, Horace Greeley, Davis, and many lesser *dramatis personae.* The Southern peace movement

---

1864; Macon *Daily Telegraph,* April 7, 1864; Richmond *Semi-Weekly Enquirer,* April 8, 22, May 6, 1864; Richmond *Daily Examiner,* April 20, 1864.

29 New York *World,* December 10, 1864.

30 Quoted by Hamilton, *Reconstruction in North Carolina,* 53.

31 Sherman, *Memoirs,* II, 139. See also, Cleveland, *Alexander H. Stephens,* 197; Athens *Southern Watchman,* October 5, 1864; February 1, 1865; Augusta *Weekly Constitutionalist,* October 19, 1864.

owed much of its strength to the rumblings for peace that had long been heard in the North, reaching loud peals by 1864 and mounting their crescendo in the Democratic National Convention in Chicago in August. Vallandigham, now back from exile in Canada during which in 1863 he had run for governor of Ohio, was directing Democratic peace activities; the Republicans were badly split with their radical wing in open revolt under the banner of the flighty Frémont; the regular Republicans had renominated Lincoln at their convention in Baltimore. Now the Democrats, also torn into war and peace factions, came out strongly for peace in their platform, but nominated General McClellan, so warlike as to have nearly taken Richmond in 1862. This pronouncement in the platform greatly heartened the peace men of the South: It was the sense of the American people "that after four years of failure to restore the Union by the experiment of war, . . . justice, humanity, liberty and the public welfare demand that immediate efforts be made for a cessation of hostilities, with a view to an ultimate convention of the States, or other peaceable means, to the end that at the earliest practicable moment peace may be restored on the basis of the Federal Union of the States." [32] This in reality was no less than what Stephens and Brown wanted; and though McClellan was considered more determined than his party in his resolve to preserve the Union, he seemed little more emphatic than the platform when he said in his letter of acceptance, "The Union is the one condition of peace—we ask no more." The nominee played mightily into the hands of Brown when he said in the same letter that "when any one State is willing to return to the Union, it should be received at once, with a full guaranty of all its constitutional rights." [33] Lincoln himself was offering these terms, in fact, assuming that his Emancipation Proclamation would ultimately be translated into a constitutional amendment.

Sentiment varied in the South as to the desirability of McClellan's election, for the Northern peace program might eventuate in the destruction of the Confederacy through re-entry of Southern states into the Union; but no one came out openly in favor of Lincoln over McClellan. All open expressions favored the Democrats, and

[32] McPherson, *History of the . . . Rebellion*, 419.
[33] *Ibid.*, 421.

many people placed fervent hope in McClellan's success—all because they believed it would end the war. Some felt that the result would restore the Union with proper safeguards and complete oblivion of the past; others sensed that once fighting stopped it could never be resumed and that the South would be left independent with probably a close alliance with the North. Lincoln was convinced that the success of the Democrats would ultimately mean Southern independence.

Stephens looked with joy on the Democratic performance in Chicago and declared that the Chicago platform was "the first ray of light I have seen from the North since the war began," [34] and a Confederate soldier in Virginia believed that if McClellan were elected "the war is over," adding that "The thought is indescribable. May we not be disappointed." [35] Benjamin H. Hill fervently hoped for Lincoln's defeat, and he believed the best way to secure it was to demoralize Northerners by military defeats before the election and make them turn to McClellan and peace. "McClellan will never be elected," he said, "unless Sherman is defeated." [36] Many agreed with him, and Confederate commanders directed their war policies to this end in the summer of 1864. For a time it looked like they might hold off Federal victories until after the election, as Grant suffered terrible losses above Richmond and Sherman floundered in the mountains of north Georgia. At one time even Lincoln lost hope of his election, but the fall of Atlanta and the occupation of Mobile Bay heartened the North and saved the day for Lincoln.

The re-election of Lincoln probably did not greatly perturb Davis, for there is good reason to believe that he had never looked kindly on the enthusiasm in the South for McClellan. This was so because Davis was utterly uncompromising on Confederate independence, and he feared McClellan's election would result in the reconstruction of the Union. Though it was not politic or becoming the President of the Confederacy to express views openly on a

[34] Athens *Southern Watchman*, October 12, 1864.

[35] Edmund C. Burnett (ed.), "Letters of a Confederate Surgeon: Dr. Abner Embry McGarity, 1862–1865," *loc. cit.*, 36.

[36] Athens *Southern Watchman*, October 5, 1864. See also, Hill, *Benjamin H. Hill*, 88; Richmond *Daily Enquirer*, November 16, 1864; Richmond *Daily Examiner*, September 6, 1864.

foreign presidential contest, Stephens truly sensed Davis' feelings and boldly stated that the chief executive preferred Lincoln— "Judging from his acts I should think that he did." [37] And on another occasion he asked the rhetorical question, "Can you trust the President?" [38] Cut to the quick by this charge, Davis demanded of Stephens an explanation: "I am quite at a loss to imagine the basis for your conclusion, and have therefore to ask to what acts of mine you refer." [39] It turned out that the main point Stephens had in mind was Davis' refusal to release David F. Cable, an insignificant prisoner of war in Andersonville Prison, who had tricked Stephens into making him believe that if he were released he would go North and work for peace. Davis put a stop to the correspondence with the remark that it did not appear to be useful or becoming for "the two highest Executive officers of the Government, especially when the country is engaged in a foreign war" [40] to be so employed. Davis would not have been writing him then did he not believe that Stephens "intended quite plainly to disparage me and to inspire distrust of me among the people . . . and to do public injury." He closed his letter, "I assure you that it would be to me a source of the sincerest pleasure to see you devoting your great and admitted ability *exclusively* to upholding the confidence and animating the spirit of the people to unconquerable resistance against their foes." [41]

But the idea of a convention or even two conventions, bruited about so much in the South and advocated by the Democratic Convention in Chicago, played a controlling part in the thinking of many people during the campaign. Stephens, Hill, and especially Brown put great faith in it as the ultimate solution of the trouble. On November 3, five days before the election, the Georgia legislature met, and Brown's message called for the Confederate states to

---

[37] Rowland (ed.), *Jefferson Davis, Constitutionalist*, VI, 409.

[38] Athens *Southern Watchman*, April 20, 1864.

[39] Rowland (ed.), *Jefferson Davis, Constitutionalist*, VI, 409.

[40] *Ibid.*, 439.

[41] *Ibid.*, 444, 445. For Cable's letter to Stephens, see communication dated June 21, 1864, in Stephens Papers (microfilms in University of Texas Library, originals in Division of Manuscripts, Library of Congress). See also, New York *World*, September 17, 1864; Robert McElroy, *Jefferson Davis; The Unreal and the Real* (New York, 1937), II, 423, 440.

join in a convention with the Northern states which the Democratic party in that region would call, and there peace should be made, with each state acting in its sovereign capacity and separately ratifying the treaty or not as it pleased. Brown was so hypnotized by his state-sovereignty ideas that he would have both Northern and Southern states ignore their national constitutions in the treaty-making process. Few who had the convention method in mind thought of going Brown's length; the idea generally held was that the convention would negotiate proposals which would be included in a treaty regularly arrived at. Davis declared on November 17 that the proposal was utterly chimerical and unworkable and that Lincoln's election would make it impossible for the North to participate in a peace convention. "It seems much more prompt and simple," he said, "to negotiate for peace at once than to negotiate for the appointment of negotiators, who are to meet without power to do anything but make proposals." [42]

In 1864 the air was surcharged with rumors of peace commissioners about to make peace, in Richmond, in Washington, in Niagara Falls, in Bermuda. On one occasion crowds of people in Richmond flocked to the railway station expecting to see Northern commissioners alight, and in August there was a sharp decline on the New York stock market on the rumor that peace agents from Georgia and North Carolina were in Washington. The rumor of the Georgia mission may have had some relationship to one C. C. Baylor, who, claiming to be Brown's agent, turned up in New York City and wrote the Georgia governor that he was giving him an "opportunity of interposing your power between the folly and ambition of the Richmond leaders and a further and useless and wicked destruction of human life." But peace expectations and unofficial efforts were not new, for as early as 1861 the Masons of Ohio, Indiana, and Kentucky had tried unsuccessfully to start negotiations with Southern Masons. And in 1863 James Jaquess, a former Methodist-college president now in William S. Rosecrans' army in Tennessee, made a peace trip to Richmond through the efforts of James R. Gilmore, also known under his pen name as "Edmund

[42] Rowland (ed.), *Jefferson Davis, Constitutionalist*, VI, 405. See also, Georgia *House Journal*, November 3, 1864, pp. 6–16; Johnston and Browne, *Alexander H. Stephens*, 469 ff.; Athens *Southern Watchman*, April 27, October 12, November 30, 1864.

Kirke." Jaquess believed that by working through the Northern and Southern Methodists he could unite the country again. Davis refused to see him, but in the summer of 1864, accompanied by Gilmore, he made another trip to Richmond, saw Davis, and learned that there could be no peace without independence for the Confederacy.[43]

But the most important play in the peace game in 1864 took place in Niagara Falls, Canada. It was part of the clever contest between Davis and Lincoln in which each was trying to pin on the other the blame for the continuation of the war. The Confederate President wanted to make it plain to all his people that there was no possibility of the Confederacy making peace with Lincoln without giving up its independence, while the Federal President would show Northerners that a negotiated peace was impossible without allowing the South to go free. In the spring Davis dispatched to Canada as his secret agents James P. Holcombe, former Congressman from Virginia, Clement C. Clay, Jr., former Senator from Alabama, and Jacob Thompson, formerly a member of Buchanan's cabinet, well supplied with money and orally instructed as to their duties. They were to use every means within the limits of civilized warfare to build up opposition in the rear of the Federal armies and especially to use the services of John B. Castleman and Thomas H. Hines, who had also been sent there, for any military adventures that might be entered into. Their most important duty was to develop a conspiracy with the disaffected people in the Northwestern states whereby at a given signal, acting through their secret societies of the Order of American Knights or Sons of Liberty, they

[43] Augusta *Daily Chronicle & Sentinel,* November 6, 1864. See also, Davis, *Rise and Fall of the Confederate Government,* II, 610–11; Kirke (pseud.), *Down in Tennessee,* 266–82; Edward C. Kirkland, *The Peacemakers of 1864* (New York, 1927), 85–96; New York *World,* August 25, 1864; Richmond *Daily Dispatch,* September 12, 1861; Richmond *Daily Examiner,* August 23, 1864. A strange peace mission in 1863 involving a Jewish merchant, I. Zacharie, is described by Fred H. Harrington in "A Peace Mission of 1863," in *American Historical Review,* XLVI (1940–1941), 76–86. L. P. O'Connell, a Catholic chaplain in the Confederate army, thought that if the Catholics in the North would agitate for peace and refuse to join the army, the war might be ended. He also thought that if six priests from each side were to be appointed to negotiate, peace might be had. O'Connell, Columbia, to Davis, December 30, 1864, "Correspondence, C.S.A.," Case VI (University of Texas Library); Charleston *Daily Courier,* January 11, 1865.

should rise up and release the Confederate prisoners of war in the various camps in that region. All of this was timed to take place when the Democratic National Convention should meet in Chicago, and Vallandigham, who was soon to return from Canada, was to be the chief instrument in bringing on the uprising. The Federal armies would thus be scattered from the rear, a Northwestern Confederacy would be set up and allied with the Southern Confederacy, and the war would be ended. The plot was never sprung, though there were activities on Lake Erie by John Y. Beall; St. Albans was raided by Bennet Young; and hotel fires were set in New York City, as previously detailed.[44]

It was in July, before the final collapse of the Northwest conspiracy, that the Niagara Falls conference took place. Horace Greeley had become convinced that the Confederate agents in Canada were ready to enter into a peace conference with Federal agents, and so sure was he that peace could be made and the Union saved that he belabored Lincoln to try, until the President consented by appointing Greeley himself to treat with them. The New York editor saw Holcombe and found that he had no authority to negotiate, and the whole adventure blew up in a fiasco, with the Confederate agents claiming they had been made the victim of a "double cross" by Lincoln. Thereby they left "Old Abe" in a somewhat disadvantageous position before the peace men of the North. But Lincoln was able to capitalize on the Jaquess mission which showed plainly that Davis would make no peace short of independence.

If peace could have been made in 1864, whether with McClellan had he been elected, or with Lincoln, the South and the whole country would have been spared the unfortunate chapter of Reconstruction which came with the defeat of the Confederacy the next year. Certainly if McClellan could have made peace and saved the Union the South would have fared well; had the South made peace with Lincoln in 1864 or even later, it would have fared almost as well, for Lincoln insisted on no points additional to McClellan's terms of

44 "The Northwestern Conspiracy," in *Southern Bivouac* (Louisville), II, 437–45, 500–10, 567–74, 699–704; Miller (ed.), *Photographic History of the Civil War*, VIII, 296; John B. Castleman, *Active Service* (Louisville, 1917), 129–88; Wood Gray, *The Hidden Civil War* . . . (New York, 1942), 148–88; Pollard, *Lost Cause*, 508.

Union except freedom for the slaves, and this would have come anyway.

Lincoln's election lifted none of the gloom which had begun to settle over the South and which had long been resting on some Southerners. As early as the middle of June, 1862, Stephens had thought "we are ruined irretrievably," [45] and the next year a Mississippian who before the war had been worth $1,250,000 but now had nothing left begged Davis to make peace on the best terms possible. By 1864 even the stalwart Vance had lost heart: Davis displayed "his obstinacy in defying public sentiment," Brown was "a *hum bug* & can do nothing but get in the way . . . the great *popular heart* is not now & never has been in the war. It was a case of revolution of the *politicians* not *the people;* was fought at first by the natural enthusiasm of our young men, and has been kept going by state & sectional pride assisted by that bitterness of feeling produced by the cruelties & brutalities of the enemy." But Vance was no defeatist; he had had no part in starting the war, yet he would fight to the bitter end. "They never shall shake their gory locks at me & say that I did it." [46] Sherman's march had had a terrifying effect on the people and humbled them to the dust. One thought that it had done more to demoralize both soldiers and citizens than what all the other Federal generals combined had done. After the fall of Atlanta a Georgia editor reported that "a kind of gloom overshadows the face of many, their minds have lost buoyancy, and hope seems to linger around them, instead of being a part and parcel of them." [47] South Carolinians had lost heart even more than Georgians; some of them on Sherman's approach suspended white sheets or tablecloths on which they had written "Have mercy on me!" [48] The effect Sherman's march had on a North Carolina soldier he expressed thus, "i hev konkludud that the dam fulishness uv tryin to lick shurmin Had better be stoped. we hav bin gettin nuthin but hell & lots uv it ever sinse we saw the dam yankys & i

---

[45] Johnston, *Autobiography*, 160.

[46] Vance to Swain, September 22, 1864, in Vance Papers, V (North Carolina State Archives).

[47] Milledgeville *Southern Recorder*, September 27, 1864.

[48] Conyngham, *Sherman's March through the South*, 346.

am tirde uv it. . . . Thair thicker an lise on a hen and a dam site ornraier." [49]

In Congress there had long been loud peace men, especially James T. Leach of North Carolina and Foote of Tennessee. Congress as a body, however, was standing true to Confederate independence. It published in June, 1864, its manly peace manifesto to the world; the House passed unanimously thirteen days after Lincoln's second election a resolution declaring that the Confederacy would never give up the fight short of independence; and on the following December 29, Congress passed a law making conspiracy against the Confederacy or holding secret intercourse with the enemy punishable by a fine of $5,000 and five years in prison. The Texas legislature on November 12 declared that it would never treat with the North on any terms and that it would be satisfied with nothing less than independence.[50]

But the peace movement did not die in the South with Lincoln's re-election. It was a simple guileless desire on the part of many people that peace should be negotiated either with independence or the restoration of the Union, and with Davis and the irreconcilables peace negotiations still could be used as an important military weapon—to show the people time and again that any peace not made through Confederate victory on the battlefield would be worse than war. It was still a game in which Davis played for independence, and Lincoln for the Union—with each trying to bolster his war by showing his people the impossibility without a military decision of getting their desire, independence in the South

---

[49] Welch, *Confederate Surgeon's Letters,* 121. See also, Howe (ed.), *Marching with Sherman; . . . Letters and Campaign Diaries of Henry Hitchcock,* 289–90, *passim;* Nichols, *Story of the Great March,* 99; Jones, *Rebel War Clerk's Diary,* II, 16. A soldier declared that Sherman had done more to demoralize the people of the Confederacy, both civil and military, than all of Lincoln's other generals combined. Burnett (ed.), "Letters of a Confederate Surgeon: Dr. Abner Embry McGarity, 1862–1865," *loc. cit.,* 65. A Virginia woman wrote in her diary, "I trust that the doctrines of Brown, Stephens, and such like, are not now bearing their bitter fruits!" [McGuire], *Diary of a Southern Refugee,* 317–18. The Richmond *Daily Enquirer,* December 30, 1864, said, "A season of gloom has rested upon our people for now nearly thirty days—quite long enough for one people!"

[50] The text of the manifesto may be found in Matthews (ed.), *Public Laws of the Confederate States,* 2 Cong., 1 Sess., 1864, pp. 286–88. The Texas resolutions were issued as a broadside. See also, Ramsdell (ed.), *Laws and Joint Resolutions,* 11–12; Richmond *Daily Examiner,* June 13, November 22, 1864.

and Union in the North. Again Foote was introducing in the House his resolutions for a convention, and when he got nowhere with them he fled Congress and made his escape to the North where he hoped to have more success. Josiah Turner, Jr., a North Carolina Congressman, introduced resolutions calling for the appointment of thirteen commissioners (one from each state) to attempt to negotiate with the North. And John A. Campbell, the inveterate peacemaker from Fort Sumter to the very fall of Richmond, wrote his former associate on the United States Supreme Court, Justice Nelson, seeking to institute peace parleys. All these moves took place in December, 1864, and then on the thirieth of the month Davis received a letter from aged Francis P. Blair, Sr.[51]

Blair, who had been a power in national politics from Jackson to Lincoln, with intermittent eclipses, was now only dimly shining. Eager to recoup his importance and genuinely desirous of bringing the war to an end to save his own Southern people from further horrors, he got permission from Lincoln to visit Davis. He made two trips to the Confederate capital during January, 1865, and though not an accredited representative, he was able to prepare the road for the famous Hampton Roads Conference in early February. His plan was to end the war through an armistice incident to an agreement or alliance between North and South looking toward driving the French out of Mexico. United on the Monroe Doctrine in this new venture, the two governments would forget the bitterness of the present war as Davis turned the Confederate armies around to attack the French with the Federals in reserve. Thus would Davis' name be linked with Washington and Jackson in the galaxy of great Americans. If when this venture had been successfully concluded, it did not result in an almost unconscious coalition of the two countries into one again, at least they would be closely allied. Though Davis could not help feeling that this was an old

[51] Connor, *John Archibald Campbell*, 160 ff.; Kirkland, *Peacemakers of 1864*, p. 229; Memphis *Daily Appeal*, December 27, 1864. Fayette McMullen, Virginia member of the House, said that he understood that Grant would allow Confederate commissioners to pass through his lines. Richmond *Daily Examiner*, December 17, 1864. James W. Singleton, Virginia-born resident of Illinois, made several visits to Richmond, which led to the belief that he was in someway concerned with peace missions. Spencer, *Last Ninety Days of the War*, 114; Richmond *Daily Examiner*, January 16, March 10, 1865.

man's dream, he thought it was worth trying to the extent of entering into negotiations with the North, and if an armistice materialized he could immediately forget the Mexican venture, for an armistice meant Confederate independence. And if nothing should come of the negotiations, Davis would have in that fact a mighty propaganda weapon in continuing the war. Stephens, who was now on speaking terms with the President, fell in with the idea, believing that if the conference failed it would "unite our people and divide the North." Lincoln never considered the Mexican venture as sensible or practical.[52]

After some fencing between Davis and Lincoln as to whether the negotiations were to secure peace "to the two countries" or "to the people of our one common country," and after the Confederate commissioners had had some complications in getting through the Federal lines, Stephens, Campbell, and Hunter, whom Davis had appointed to negotiate, reached Fortress Monroe. There on February 3 they met Lincoln and Seward on the *River Queen* and carried on their negotiations without the presence of anyone else except a Negro servant who occasionally brought in refreshments. No minutes were kept, and as a result there have been endless versions of the actual conversations. The upshot was what doubtless both Lincoln and Davis expected—no agreement, for though Lincoln was liberal in all else he would hear to nothing less than Union, Emancipation, and no armistice; and Davis would be satisfied with nothing less than independence. This ended all further attempts at peace negotiations unless Davis' move to secure an armistice through a military convention between Lee and Grant should be so considered. Lee wrote Grant on March 2 for a meeting, which Grant refused on the ground that his authority did not extend to anything beyond purely military matters.[53]

[52] For quotation, see Johnston and Browne, *Alexander H. Stephens*, 486. See also, *Official Records*, Ser. I, Vol. XLVI, Pt. II, 1037–39; Rowland (ed.), *Jefferson Davis, Constitutionalist*, VI, 432; Davis, *Rise and Fall of the Confederate Government*, II, 612–16; Stephens, *Constitutional View of the Late War between the States*, II, 587–89; Kirkland, *Peacemakers of 1864*, pp. 198, 202.

[53] Richardson (comp.), *Messages and Papers of the Confederacy*, I, 520–30, 550; Rowland (ed.), *Jefferson Davis, Constitutionalist*, VI, 465; *Southern Historical Society Papers*, III (1877), 168–76; XLII (1917), 45–52; John A. Campbell, *Reminiscences and*

In the light of the future and even of contemporary times, how much better Davis would have served his people had he accepted peace at Hampton Roads and led the South back into the Union under the humane plans of Lincoln rather than face inevitable defeat and the terrors and humiliations of Radical Reconstruction. Lincoln said enough at Hampton Roads to show that if the Union were re-established and the slaves freed with compensation as far as he was able to promote it, the South would be guaranteed its rights and protection against confiscations and punishments, to the full extent of Lincoln's powers and influence.

But Davis was determined to suffer the evils he knew rather than fly to others which he thought he saw too clearly—war was less an evil than the reconstruction he sensed. Thinking too much of the pronouncements and speeches of Northern Radicals—Thaddeus Stevens, Henry Winter Davis, Charles Sumner—Davis was envisioning their type of reconstruction, which all too truly justified his fears. But who would be so rash as to say that Lincoln would have had his Booth, had peace come at Hampton Roads?

When the Confederate commissioners returned and made their report, Davis steeled his heart even more than ever before. He decided to set off a crusade for Southern independence by reviving Confederate war effort and spirit which should lead on to certain victory or Götterdämmerung if it must be. There were immediately held in Richmond a series of meetings which Davis led off on February 6 in the African Church with a speech so dramatic and compelling that his bitterest enemy, Pollard, declared that he did "not recollect ever to have been so much moved by the power of words spoken for the same space of time." Davis argued that the Hampton Roads Conference showed that the South must fight on to victory, and it could be had if the people willed it with all their might. If half the men absent from Lee's army would return, Grant could be defeated. Even the Confederate armies in the field at that time were greater than Napoleon ever had. Ten thousand people attempted to hear this speech. Three days later another great gathering at the

---

Documents Relating to the Civil War during the Year 1865 (Baltimore, 1887), 11 ff.; Connor, *John Archibald Campbell*, 164 ff.; Stephens, *Constitutional View of the Late War between the States*, II, 588 ff.; Kirkland, *Peacemakers of 1864*, pp. 206–58.

African Church heard speeches by Hunter, Benjamin, and various other orators, lasting most of the day and continuing on into the evening.[54]

The contagion of these fervent messages of resistance was carried to the four corners of the Confederacy by speakers who set out from Richmond or by irreconcilables already there. Faithful Ben Hill departed to carry the enthusiasm to his own disaffected state of Georgia, speaking in Columbus, Macon, Forsyth, and making one of the proudest speeches of his life at Lagrange. He declared that the Confederacy had enough of everything except fighting spirit to win the war; it had 500,000 men of military age and enough material resources of food and munitions to supply them. Its spiritual resources had fallen low and must be revived; the old Union was gone forever, perverted by the Radicals, and it was courting death to re-enter it. "And if we are conquered, subjugated, disgraced, ruined," he said, "it will all be the work of those enemies among us; and they will accomplish that work by destroying the faith of our people in their own government." [55] With Brown still in mind, he dreaded "the subtle power of the serpent that coils within the garden, far more than I do a million of bayonets bristling without the walls!" [56] Cobb in Macon called on the people to unite behind their government. The Confederacy could never be conquered if it would fight with its full resources; every year 50,000 men reached military age; and if the absent soldiers would return, the Confederate armies would have more soldiers than Lincoln. "Put me in my grave," he exclaimed, *"but never put on me the garment of a Submissionist!"* [57] Sulking Toombs was aroused to make a flaming speech at Augusta, in which he declared that all the people needed was the will to win. "We have resources enough to whip forty Yankee nations," he declared with characteristic emphasis, "if we could call back the spirit of our departed heroes." [58] Zebulon Vance, North Carolina's governor, assuming that Lincoln's terms were abject submission, issued on February 14 an eloquent proclamation in which he recommended that the people all over the state as-

[54] Athens *Southern Watchman,* March 8, 1865; Richmond *Daily Enquirer,* February 7, 10, 1865; Pollard, *Jefferson Davis,* 468–70; Pollard, *Lost Cause,* 684–86.

[55] Hill, *Benjamin H. Hill,* 283. [56] *Ibid.,* 290.

[57] Augusta *Weekly Constitutionalist,* February 22, 1865.

[58] Athens *Southern Watchman,* February 22, 1865.

semble "and let the whole world, and especially our enemies, see how a free people can meet a proposition for their absolute submission to the will of their conquerors. . . . Great God! Is there a man in all this honorable, high spirited, and noble Commonwealth so steeped in every conceivable meanness, so blackened with all the guilt of treason, or so damned with all the leprosy of cowardice as to say: Yes, we will submit to all this; and whilst there yet remains half a million men amongst us able to resist. . . . Should we willfully throw down an organized government, disband our still powerful armies, and invite all these fearful consequences upon our country, we would live to have our children curse our gray hairs for fastening our dishonor upon them." [59] Congress in a set of resolutions recited how the Confederacy from the beginning had sought to make peace and how its efforts had been resisted, and now called on the people to put forth their full effort for independence.

Newspapers which had been highly critical of Davis secretly admitted what their criticisms had now helped to bring down upon the country, and turned to the defense of the Confederate administration—even Pollard and the Richmond *Examiner*. Letters to the press called on the people to take heart and resist. "Nil Desperandum" declared that now there was less of the Confederacy occupied by the enemy than in 1862, that the enemy had marched through it but had not garrisoned or held it, or as Bill Arp had said, that even if Sherman did march through Georgia, he did not whip anybody. "Didn't the rebellyun just klose rite up behind him, like shettin a pair of waful irons?" he queried. [60]

Army units began passing resolutions expressing confidence in victory and calling on the people back home to support the war, and clergymen of the various denominations offered their services to the government, to preach a new crusade in their churches and to take to the road. A group of a hundred citizens in Mobile organized the League of Loyal Confederates to promote independence

---

[59] *Official Records*, Ser. I, Vol. XLVII, Pt. II, 1192, 1190, 1191 (pages given in the order of quotations). See also, Ramsdell (ed.), *Laws and Joint Resolutions*, 134–35; Haywood J. Pearce, Jr., *Benjamin H. Hill, Secession and Reconstruction* (Chicago, 1928), 106–107; Spencer, *Last Ninety Days of the War*, 116; Athens *Southern Watchman*, March 8, 1865; Greensboro *Alabama Beacon*, March 3, 1865.

[60] For quotation, see [Charles H. Smith], *Bill Arp's Peace Papers* (New York, 1873), 105; for "Nil Desperandum," Richmond *Daily Enquirer*, February 8, 1865.

and to spread their society to every county and city in the Confederacy. In Richmond a group of citizens set up the Patriotic Publishing Association to print and broadcast over the country leaflets, pamphlets, and booklets to develop and sustain the morale of the people. Here in the last days a propaganda campaign had been started which, had it existed in the first years, might have played an outstanding part in promoting Confederate morale; but now it was too late.[61]

Of the Confederate commissioners who had gone to Hampton Roads, only Hunter offered his services to this campaign. Campbell refused to participate, and Stephens, thoroughly whipped by the outcome of the conference, went back to Georgia to sulk and lend secret aid to Brown. Hampton Roads, said Hill, had *"silenced his* pernicious tongue." [62] Stephens, however, had said after the conference, "We don't want a counterrevolution—we only desire to keep the present one *on the right track."* [63] But this was more than could be said of Governor Brown, who was promoting and taking full advantage of the deepening gloom in Georgia following Lincoln's election and Sherman's march. Deserters and men of military age who had never been soldiers held peace meetings in many parts of the state, threatened anyone who attempted to put them into the army, and refused to pay Confederate taxes. A thousand such characters were reported to be in the vicinity of Athens. In Irwin County a meeting was held "at which incendiary Sentiments were promulgated in fact it was a regular Lincoln demonstration, denouncing the Confederacy and its Authority & shouting for Lincoln. Fifty Six Deserters marched up to the Court House four deep in a line well armed. They beat severely every man who expressed loyal sentiments and it was with difficulty their lives were saved." [64] No wonder John A. Campbell could say that Georgia was in a state

[61] *Official Records,* Ser. IV, Vol. III, 1118; Rowland (ed.), *Jefferson Davis, Constitutionalist,* VI, 490; Augusta *Weekly Constitutionalist,* March 29, 1865; Greensboro *Alabama Beacon,* March 24, 1865; Richmond *Daily Enquirer,* February 8, 1865; Richmond *Daily Examiner,* March 18, 1865.

[62] "Georgia and the Confederacy, 1865," in *American Historical Review,* I (1895–1896), 101.

[63] Athens *Southern Watchman,* March 22, 1865.

[64] William A. Harris, Isabella, Ga., to Cobb, January 16, 1865, in Howell Cobb Papers.

of insurrection and that her leaders "have cast reproach upon the laws of the Confederacy" and made their enforcement almost impossible.[65] And again it was no wonder that Governor Brown called the legislature into special session on February 15, and in his message excoriated Davis, recommended a constitutional amendment removing his powers as commander in chief, and asked the legislature to authorize a state convention. The previous month Governor Vance had begged Brown not to call a state convention as it would amount to open rebellion against the Confederacy. "Nothing that we have seen, or heard of, since the war commenced, has caused us more despondency, than the late message of Gov. Brown," said a fellow Georgian; [66] and a Virginia editor declared that "no pure patriot can read Brown's message without the liveliest emotions of indignation and disgust" and that Brown "is as noisy as a fishwoman; and carries grievances about with him as some animals their perfume, and one is . . . equally as offensive as the other." [67]

The patriotic outburst after Hampton Roads was the dying gasp of the Confederacy; it was fast disintegrating. Georgia was now effectively out of the war; South Carolina had practically succumbed. Only in North Carolina and Virginia was there still organized strength that could count in the struggle. Addressing a secret session of the Senate before Hampton Roads, Stephens had called for a complete change in Confederate policy, the abandonment of conscription, impressment, and acts suspending the writ of habeas corpus, and the development of a new military policy in which Richmond might be abandoned. Agreeing with much of this program, Cobb, always a pro-Davis man, argued that Joseph E. Johnston should be restored to his old command. About this time (January, 1865) a "palace revolt" seemed in the making. Davis was the constitutional commander in chief and he had been making the most of his authority. By this time many people had lost confidence in him as a civil ruler as well as military director. Strange as a coup might seem in an Anglo-Saxon country, there were now great pos-

[65] *Southern Historical Society Papers,* XLII (1917), 55.

[66] Putnam County (Ga.) *Countryman,* March 14, 1865.

[67] Richmond *Daily Enquirer,* March 1, 1865. See also, *Official Records,* Ser. I, Vol. XLVI, Pt. II, 1093; Georgia *Senate Journal,* February 15, 1865, pp. 17–29; Stephens, *Constitutional View of the Late War between the States,* II, 625.

sibilities for a "man on horseback"; but the only such person who could have unseated Davis was the shrinking Lee, who had already declined to assume command over more than his Virginia army. Nevertheless, with Lee in mind, Congress passed an act on January 23 to set up a general in chief who should "have command of the military forces of the Confederate States." Davis immediately appointed Lee, but the situation remained unchanged, for the law took no powers away from the President, and Lee would not have assumed them anyway. But Lee in his new position at least relieved Davis of the unpleasant task of placing Johnston at the head of an army.[68]

Governmentally as well as militarily the Confederacy was sick unto death. The gulf between the Congress and the President was wide and there was little co-operation between the two. Congress debated interminably the President's recommendations but did not act upon them, and by early March, Davis heard rumors that it was about to adjourn sine die. In a rather sharp but dignified message on the thirteenth, he chided Congress for having done nothing to meet the terrible situation which confronted the country. The Senate took umbrage at what it considered a lecture and in a sharp retort, adopted in secret session on March 16, reminded the President that nothing was "more desirable than concord and cordial coöperation between all departments of Government," accused him of unjust criticism of the legislative branch, and expressed regret "that the Executive deemed it necessary to transmit to Congress a message so well calculated to excite discord and dissension." Davis was greatly surprised at this reaction. In a private communication to Mrs. Howell Cobb he explained, "My style was not intended to provoke controversy and does not seem to me to have been wanting in decorum and deference," yet a few days later the Senate's answer was published in the newspapers, "and if not intended to destroy the confidence of the people in me, is certainly calculated to have that effect." On March 18, two days after the Senate's reply, the Confederate Congress with its work still undone went silent forever, the House in open session, the Senate secretly. The executive

[68] *Official Records*, Ser. I, Vol. LIII, 393–94; Freeman (ed.), *Lee's Dispatches*, 323–26; Jones, *Rebel War Clerk's Diary*, II, 372; Pollard, *Jefferson Davis*, 416–38.

department alone was left in Richmond to see the structure collapse.[69]

Swift now was the descent to Avernus. Grant was moving to run an iron ring around Richmond and Petersburg and Sherman had swept across South Carolina into North Carolina and would soon be on his way to join Grant. Lee's army was fast melting away by desertion, and he informed Davis on Sunday, April 2, that it would be impossible to hold his lines and advised the government to evacuate Richmond. Davis' family had already left, and now trains were got ready to carry away what specie remained, the most important government archives, and the principal officials. Government property, consisting of tobacco warehouses, armories, magazines, and storehouses were ordered fired. The flames spread to many business houses and even residences, and soon an important part of Richmond lay in ashes, long to be referred to as the "burnt district." Consternation reigned as the retreating soldiers marched through the city taking away as much food as they could carry and turning over the rest to the populace. The gutters ran with whisky from the staved barrels, and worthless Confederate money and bonds (and even some of the priceless archives) were scattered over the streets or burned. The defeated and dispirited people were stunned. The Richmond *Whig* declared, "If there lingered in the hearts of our people one spark of affection for the Davis dynasty, this ruthless, useless, wanton handing over to the flames their fair city, their homes and altars, has extinguished it forever." [70]

The fall of Richmond was just an episode to Davis in his fight for Confederate independence. Daring not to desert Virginia until forced to do so, he moved his capital to Danville, and there on April 4 he issued an address to the people, breathing courage and defiance. Giving up Richmond, the President declared, freed Lee for a "promising enterprise," and nothing was "now needed to render our triumph certain but the exhibition of our unquenchable

[69] Davis' message, in Richardson (comp.), *Messages and Papers of the Confederacy,* I, 544–51; the Senate's reply, *Journal of the Congress of the Confederate States,* IV, 726–31; Davis to Mrs. Cobb, Rowland (ed.), *Jefferson Davis, Constitutionalist,* VI, 525.

[70] For quotation, see Athens *Southern Watchman,* May 3, 1865; for other descriptions of the burning of Richmond, see Jones, *Rebel War Clerk's Diary,* II, 467–71; [Putnam], *Richmond during the War,* 362–71.

559

resolve." The Confederacy had now "entered upon a new phase of a struggle" the memory of which would endure through the ages. "Let us but will it," he pleaded, "and we are free; and who, in the light of the past, dare doubt your purpose in the future?" [71] Mrs. Davis wrote him at this time "that your strength when stirred up is great, and that you can do with a few what others have failed to do with many." [72] Despite the utter hopelessness of the situation, there were many who, refusing to be realistic, were as heroic as Davis. A South Carolinian held that the loss of Richmond was nothing; many other towns had fallen without fatal effect; and now Grant was being drawn away from his water communications. A soldier wrote that Richmond, Selma, and many other towns might fall, "But if all that and more be true I am not whipped but feel like holding on as long as a man is left." [73] Bill Arp had his solution in the cavalry: "The truth is, that the Konfederit cavilry can fite on, and dog em, and dodge em, and bush-whack em, and bedevil em for a thousan years, and that is as long as the most sangwinery hav kalkulated this war to last. The Konfederit cavilry is ubikuitous and everlastin." [74] With the collection of taxes now completely disrupted, a call went out for gifts and some were volunteered. At Jefferson, Georgia, a mass meeting was held at which donations from $10 to $5,000 were made. It was argued that one should give what one had to the Confederacy rather than have it seized by the enemy if the war were lost.

But Confederate fortunes went quickly from bad to worse. On April 9 Lee was cut off and forced to surrender at Appomattox Courthouse. The plan had been for him to retreat to Danville and somewhere in that vicinity join the forces of General Joseph E. Johnston, then operating in North Carolina, but Grant was too quick for him. Lee's army during the past month had been without meat frequently for as long as three days, and some of his soldiers had been retained in the line of battle for two days and nights in succession. In Lee's words, "all were suffering from reduced rations

[71] Richardson (comp.), *Messages and Papers of the Confederacy*, I, 568, 569.

[72] Rowland (ed.), *Jefferson Davis, Constitutionalist*, VI, 538.

[73] C. S. Newton to Frank Pope, April 7, 1865 (in possession of the writer).

[74] [Smith], *Bill Arp's Peace Papers*, 106. See also, Athens *Southern Watchman*, April 19, 26, 1865; Augusta *Weekly Constitutionalist*, April 11, 1865; Chester *Daily South Carolinian*, April 6, 1865.

and scant clothing, exposed to battle, cold, hail, and sleet." [75] The march from Five Forks on through Amelia Courthouse and Sayler's Creek to Appomattox beggared description—the soldiers with a handful of parched corn in their pockets, weary, starving, despairing. Lee surrendered the pitiful remnant of about 8,000 men in arms, all that remained of his 28,000—the others stragglers, deserters, sick. But for some, adversity had only increased their spirit to resist. A Virginian with a small band of associates declared, "We refused to take part in the funeral at Appomattox C. H. & cut or crept our way out. . . . I am off for Miss—No notion of laying down my arms—Probably make Texas during the Summer. . . . I did not leave till firing ceased and preparations began for general surrender— . . . I cant stay here—Twould kill me—by inches." He later contemplated a trip to "regions where the Great Bear is no longer seen & men walk on their heads." [76]

Communications went completely to pieces. After Davis left Richmond, he lost touch with Lee and did not know for some days that he had surrendered. Not until eleven days later did the news reach South Carolina; about a week thereafter the newspapers in Georgia learned it; and in early May people in Alabama knew it with certainty. Meanwhile, wild rumors were afloat; Lee had whipped Grant and Johnston had cut Sherman to pieces. Lee's surrender was a great blow to Davis; now for the first time he began to lose heart. Later he said that if Lee's army had held together, the plans determined upon would have been successful and the Confederacy "would have been today on the high road to independence." [77]

Giving up the last place which could be called the capital of the Confederacy, Davis and his cabinet retreated to Greensboro, where he saw General Johnston and gave him permission to negotiate

[75] *Official Records,* Ser. I, Vol. XLVI, Pt. II, 1210.

[76] C. G. Chamberlayne (ed.), *Ham Chamberlayne—Virginian; Letters and Papers of an Artillery Officer in the War for Southern Independence, 1861–1865* (Richmond, 1932), 320, 322, 330. See also, Davis, *Rise and Fall of the Confederate Government,* II, 676; Freeman, *R. E. Lee; A Biography,* IV, 156; Gordon, *Reminiscences of the Civil War,* 429 ff.; Lee, *Recollections and Letters of General Robert E. Lee,* 155; James Longstreet, *From Manassas to Appomattox. Memoirs of the Civil War in America* (Philadelphia, 1896), 631.

[77] Rowland (ed.), *Jefferson Davis, Constitutionalist,* VI, 559.

with Sherman for an armistice and to request him to induce Grant to "take like action in regard to other armies," to the end that the civil authorities should negotiate a treaty "to terminate the existing war." On the eighteenth Johnston and Sherman arrived at the extremely liberal terms which had been suggested in late March in a conference which Sherman had had with Lincoln on the *River Queen,* anchored in the James at City Point. These terms Lincoln himself had planned to carry out for Virginia on the fall of Richmond, but had abandoned them on account of Radical opposition in Washington. They were: the disbanding of all Confederate armies after their arms had been deposited in their state capitals; recognition of the Confederate state governments as soon as their officials swore allegiance to the United States; the re-establishment of the Federal courts and giving the guarantee, as far as the President's powers extended, of their political and civil rights; and freedom from molestation for all the people as long as they abstained from armed hostility. These terms were sent to Davis, who had by this time arrived in Charlotte. After polling members of his cabinet and on their recommendation he agreed to accept them. But the same forces in Washington which had led Lincoln (already dead by the hand of an assassin) to abandon his Virginia plans now violently reacted against Sherman and forced him to negotiate new terms which were signed on the twenty-sixth and were similar to the terms Grant had allowed Lee: that is, the paroling of the soldiers and their retention of side arms, horses, and baggage. When Davis heard of the rejection of the first set of terms, he ordered Johnston to march westward with all the men he could mount and direct his infantry to meet him at an appointed place. Johnston refused and accepted on April 26 the final terms of surrender without Davis' permission, which greatly upset the President.

As the Confederate Constitution, like that of every other country, did not provide for its own dissolution, Davis worked out a way for the Confederacy to fold its robes and march off the stage, a method which would have worked logically and smoothly had Sherman's first terms been carried out. Legalistic and constitutionally-minded to the last, the President as commander in chief had the right to end hostilities; but, since Lincoln would not treat with him as the head of a government, he could resign the presidency and leave it to the states to dissolve the Confederacy, even as they had made it. Then each state could separately accept the Sherman terms and find itself functioning again in the old Union. Benjamin suggested this solution, but undoubtedly it had already been a part of Davis' thinking on the problem. Thus would the President finally accept state sovereignty, so long clamored for by Brown and others in their peace movement. As long as the Confederacy had a chance to win, Davis considered the movement treason, but he now embraced it as the legal way by which the Confederacy could terminate its existence. As for Davis himself, he mused, "it may be that our enemy will prefer to banish me. Or it may be that a devoted band of cavalry will cling to me, and that I can force my way across the Mississippi, and if nothing can be done there which it will be proper to do, then I can go to Mexico and have the world from which to choose a location." [78]

Johnston surrendered all troops in North Carolina, South Carolina, Georgia, and Florida, and soon thereafter General Richard Taylor surrendered the land and naval forces in Alabama and Mississippi. The war was now over except for the Trans-Mississippi Department, and there, after waiting in vain for a change in fortune and the arrival of Davis, E. Kirby Smith surrendered his army on May 26, thirteen days after the last engagement of the war had taken place at Palmetto Ranch near Brownsville, Texas. But the final surrender of the war did not come until the gallant *Shenandoah* made her way from the far Pacific to Liverpool and gave herself up to the British authorities on November 6—almost seven months after Appomattox.

In the meanwhile, Sherman's final terms having changed Davis' method of securing peace, he was now more than ever adrift both in mind and body—what could he do, where could he go? He

[78] Eron Rowland, *Varina Howell, Wife of Jefferson Davis* (New York, 1927–1931), II, 409. For the situation leading up to Johnston's surrender, see *Official Records,* Ser. I, Vol. XLVII, Pt. III, 821 ff.; Davis, *Rise and Fall of the Confederate Government,* II, 681 ff.; Johnston, *Narrative of Military Operations,* 396–420; McElroy, *Jefferson Davis,* II, 498 ff.; Patrick, *Jefferson Davis and his Cabinet,* 349 ff.; Pollard, *Jefferson Davis,* 512 ff.; Robinson, *Justice in Grey,* 536–38; Rowland (ed.), *Jefferson Davis, Constitutionalist,* VI, 563; Sherman, *Memoirs,* II, 322–80. For Lincoln's terms allowing Virginia's re-entry into the Union, see *Official Records,* Ser. I, Vol. XLVI, Pt. III, 656–57. See also, J. G. Randall, *Lincoln and the South* (Baton Rouge, 1946), 117–61.

would still try to make his way to the great trans-Mississippi region, where General Smith was still in charge of an army. Who could say that in this unsettled world the Confederacy might not still maintain itself under the protection of the French and Maximilian on the southern border? Davis left Charlotte, passing southward through South Carolina and on into Georgia to the little town of Washington. Being more concerned for the safety of Mrs. Davis than with any plans of his own, he set out in early May to join her party, which was making its way toward Florida. He soon overtook her, but early on the morning of the tenth he was surrounded by Federal cavalry near Irwinsville and captured. It was sixteen days later that General Smith surrendered in Texas—the Confederacy was now to become a memory sentimentalized into the "Lost Cause." [79]

In the twilight times of the breakup of the Confederacy, the people were as much adrift as Davis. A Georgian expressed himself as "silenced—stunned—paralyzed—by rapidly occurring events"; [80] a Virginia lady felt that she had "no country, no government, no future"; [81] but the day after Johnston's surrender a soldier wrote, "The smiling faces and light hearted remarks of our people and I am sorry to say of many of our army would seem that we had attained the wished for consummation of our hopes. The prospect of an early peace carries away the reason and joy usurps the hearts where sorrow should sit most heavily." As for him, he would be off for South America or Europe.[82] More rumors filled the air: the Confederacy had been recognized by a secret league of France, Spain, and Austria with the blessings of the Pope; recog-

---

[79] Davis, *Rise and Fall of the Confederate Government*, II, 701; Davis, *Short History of the Confederate States*, 488 ff.; Alfred J. Hanna, *Flight into Oblivion* (Richmond, 1938), *passim;* Henry, *Story of the Confederacy*, 461 ff.; James E. Walmsley, "The Last Meeting of the Confederate Cabinet," in *Mississippi Valley Historical Review*, VI (1919–1920), 336–49; *Official Records*, Ser. I, Vol. XLIX, Pt. I, 515–57. The last instance of resistance took place in Texas near Brownsville, on May 13, a Confederate victory, which led Davis to observe the anomalous situation wherein the war opened with a Confederate victory and closed with one. Davis, *Rise and Fall of the Confederate Government*, II, 698.

[80] Athens *Southern Watchman*, May 3, 1865.

[81] [McGuire], *Diary of a Southern Refugee*, 357.

[82] Philip Vacaro to Barnsley, April 25, 1865, in Barnsley Papers (University of Georgia Library).

nition had been granted by England; a French fleet had annihilated the Federal navy at the mouth of the Mississippi and had appeared off New Orleans and demanded its surrender; Sherman had been captured and Smith had been reinforced in Texas by 200,000 men; a new government had been set up with Lee as president and Grant as vice-president; there might be two governments with two presidents, two congresses, and two sets of courts but one foreign policy; Lincoln had been assassinated by a man named Smith. An Alabama newspaper carried these headlines:

GLORIOUS NEWS
LINCOLN AND SEWARD ASSASSINATED!
LEE DEFEATS GRANT
ANDY JOHNSON INAUGURATED
PRESIDENT

but thinking better of it in a subsequent issue it ran these headlines:

DEATH OF LINCOLN
GREAT TRAGEDY IN WASHINGTON

It was the latter sentiment that expressed the feeling of the intelligent, thoughtful Southerners, so well put by General Richard S. Ewell in a letter to General Grant: "No language can adequately express the shock. . . . Of all the misfortunes which could befall the Southern people, or any Southern man, by far the greatest, in my judgment, would be the prevalence of the idea that they could entertain any other than feelings of unqualified abhorrence and indignation for the assassination of the President of the United States, and the attempt to assassinate the Secretary of State." [83]

In the last dying days of the Confederacy some of the states sought to act on Davis' abortive plan and make terms individually with the adversary. Vance in North Carolina sought to get in touch with Sherman to negotiate for his state's return; Brown tried unsuccessfully to convene his legislature again; in Mississippi the legislature actually met for a short time but was soon dispersed; and the trans-Mississippi governors or their representatives met in Marshall,

[83] *Official Records*, Ser. I, Vol. XLVI, Pt. III, 787. See also, Cumming, *Journal of Hospital Life*, 174, 177; Athens *Southern Watchman*, May 3, 1865; Augusta *Daily Chronicle & Sentinel*, April 9, 1865; Augusta *Weekly Chronicle & Sentinel*, April 26, 1865; Austin *Weekly State Gazette*, March 1, 1865; Greensboro *Alabama Beacon*, April 21, May 12, 1865; Grove Hill (Ala.) *Clarke County Journal*, February 16, 1865.

Texas, on May 13 in an effort to resolve the question of their political status. Whether these movements were or were not consciously following in a fashion Lincoln's 10 per cent plan as announced in his Amnesty Proclamation of December 8, 1863, which might easily coincide with Davis' first plan of dissolving the Confederacy, it was evident to all that a new day had dawned with the end of the war. The new President, Andrew Johnson, soon adopted a general plan which was much the same as that which Lincoln had in mind.

Why did the Confederacy fail? The forces leading to defeat were many but they may be summed up in this one fact: The people did not will hard enough and long enough to win. Wars in those times were not inevitably won by the side strongest in material resources and numbers of soldiers; otherwise the South would have been foolhardy to enter the struggle. It was not the last dollar or the last soldier but the last ounce of will power or morale. In this realm the Confederacy started out with boundless enthusiasm which began sadly to deteriorate as early as 1862. Why? Because of conscription; the progressive decline in the worth of money brought on chiefly by delay in adopting a system of taxation, or to express the same fact in other words, the ever increasing price of all things for sale; the exasperations incident to poor postal service; dissension and factionalism brought on by leaders congenitally touched with state-rightism, who stirred up the people into believing that a military despotism was forming in the Confederate government to deprive them of their ancient liberties; the raising of false hopes of foreign recognition only to have them dashed in despair; the battering-ram of rumored victories with the subsequent truth of defeats pounding bright visions into dust; the absence of a concerted effort to maintain morale by spreading among the people proper information; the lack of personable inspiring leadership in Davis, however sound his policies might have been; and during the latter period, the false feeling that the old Union might be reentered with all rights guaranteed, which might have come true had Lincoln lived. These factors were fundamental and most of them could have been avoided. As important as were the blockade and the Federal navy, the breakdown of transportation, short-term enlistments and the election of officers by the soldiers, the failure to send cotton to Europe during the first part of the war, and other

566

forces, the fact remains that the Confederacy never fully utilized the human and material resources it had. It never succeeded in developing an *esprit de corps,* either in its civil or military organization, and in that sense it did not deserve to win. But, of course, if enemy morale always exceeded what the Confederates could have mustered, then defeat was always inevitable; but there are reasons to believe that the Confederacy had within its being the potentialities of a stronger and more persistent will to win independence than the Federals had to save the Union. It is easy to argue in circles as to why the Confederacy did not win. It must be remembered that there were the seeds of destruction, state rights, which were implanted at its birth, destined to sprout and flourish, tended and watered by such expert gardeners as Governor Brown, Vice-President Stephens, and others.[84] And it must also be remembered that it was the Federal armies, aided by these forces, which actually destroyed the Confederacy.

The life of the Confederacy presented a picture of contrasts. It seized the souls of many with an ardor and a devotion to an ideal which have seldom been equaled. With these there was a feeling of a loyalty and self-sacrifice for the common good, which, if instilled into more Confederates, would have made success inevitable. As a contemporary put it, "If this Revolution has produced some of the meanest and most groveling of mankind, it has held an even balance by the example of some of the most exalted and aspiring souls—the true lords of the creation." [85] The ideal of the Confederacy was to

[84] In assessing blame a Texas soldier said, "OUR OWN PEOPLE AT HOME, they should and MUST blame themselves." William W. Heartsill, *Fourteen Hundred and 91 Days in the Confederate Army* . . . (Marshall, Tex., 1876), 245. Secretary Mallory told an acquaintance at the end of the war "that his greatest regret was that he had spent four years of his life in working for a people unfit for independence." Noll (ed.), *Doctor Quintard,* 143–44. As early as April, 1862, Mrs. Chesnut wrote in her diary, "The Confederacy has been done to death by the politicians." Martin and Avary (eds.), *Diary from Dixie,* 159. A few years after the war, Davis' verdict was, "We were more cheated than conquered into surrender." Quoted in Hill, *Joseph E. Brown,* 255.

[85] Augusta *Weekly Constitutionalist,* April 19, 1865. The per capita expenditures of the Confederacy were three times what they were in the North. James L. Sellers, "The Economic Incidence of the Civil War in the South," in *Mississippi Valley Historical Review,* XIV (1927–1928), 179–91; James L. Sellers, "An Interpretation of Civil War Finance," in *American Historical Review,* XXX (1924–1925), 282–97. See also, Smith, *History of the Confederate Treasury,* 112; Fish, *American Civil War,* 443.

preserve life and civilization as her people knew it; it was fundamental with them; it was what made slaveholders and nonslaveholders stand together; it caused soldiers to fight with a bravery and devotion which became so much a part of their very souls as to make their ideal more dear to them than life itself; and it instilled into them and into many who remained at home a feeling for the Confederacy akin to that of a parent for a child. Such people deserved a better fate than awaited them.

There was nothing immoral or evil in secession and in the attempt of the South to establish its independence. Neither nature nor God had decreed that a region of the earth's surface as diversified as the United States in geography, economic interests, and political theories should be one nation. Whether there should be one or two nations or even more was a question of political expediency and self-interest. The fall of the Confederacy was an example of might making right; but in the light of subsequent history, including even the Reconstruction of the Union, who is there today to argue that in this instance might was not ultimately to prove right in the preservation of one country?

CRITICAL ESSAY ON AUTHORITIES

PHYSICAL REMAINS

CERTAIN periods of history are especially prolific in physical remains, and none are more so than war years. True enough, these remains, relating mostly to military activities, do not portray the whole life of the people, but they serve to restore remarkably well the atmosphere which pervaded the times. The most evident and enduring of such survivals are battlefield sites with their significant natural terrain, their earthen embankments, and the monuments and markers erected by subsequent generations to commemorate the deeds of heroes and to explain the progress of the fighting. Most of the principal battle sites have been marked and some of them have been set apart as national parks. Especially notable are overmarked Gettysburg, Chickamauga, Sharpsburg, or Antietam, Murfreesboro, or Stone's River, and Fredericksburg and many other Virginia battlefields. One of the most satisfying and easily understood battlefields is Shiloh. Fort Mc-Allister at the mouth of the Ogeechee River in Georgia is as clearly marked today by its earthen embankments as it was in wartime.

To keep alive the memories of the times, apart from any particular battle, many statues and monuments have been erected to individuals, and there is scarcely a courthouse square in any Southern county which does not have a monument to its Confederate soldiers. Here and there a marker points out the site of some historic incident.

The ruins made by invading armies were soon cleared away, and few survivals of them remain beyond the pockmarks of bullets or bayonet jabs on buildings. A few lone chimneys in Georgia are still referred to as "Sherman's sentinels." Cannon balls embedded in the walls of Fort Pulaski (near Savannah) and the scars on the statehouse in Columbia, made by Sherman's bombardment, are still pointed out.

The sites of the several Confederate prison camps have for the most part gone unmarked and unkept. Andersonville Prison Park and the nearby Andersonville National Cemetery mark the site of the largest Confederate prison. The famous Libby Prison building was carried away from Richmond to be exhibited at the World's Columbian Exposition at Chicago. In the North there may be seen today the well-kept cemeteries of Confederate soldiers, marking the near-by sites of Federal prisons, such as Camp Chase (Columbus, Ohio), Elmira, and Rock Island.

Most buildings still standing from wartime are of equal significance for the ante-bellum period, as there was little permanent construction during the struggle; but a few of these houses are of special interest. The first White House of the Confederacy is preserved in Montgomery and cherished, though it is not located on its original site. The White House in Richmond was rescued from destruction by the Confederate Memorial Literary Society and is an object of interest. As examples of other notable houses, there are the Green-Meldrim mansion in Savannah, where General William T. Sherman made his headquarters, and the Barbara Frietschie dwelling in Frederick, Maryland. The Bennett House near Durham, North Carolina, where General Joseph E. Johnston surrendered to General Sherman was standing until recently. The two locomotives associated with the famous Andrews Raid have been preserved. The *Texas* is in Grant Park, Atlanta, and the *General* is displayed in the Union Station, Chattanooga. Indispensable in locating historical sites and objects are the volumes in the American Guide Series, written by the Federal Writers' Project of the several states, published and republished at various times and places during the 1930's and 1940's.

Indoors, one may find a great many objects of interest, especially in museums, the more important and formal of which are listed by the American Association of Museums in its *Handbook of American Museums* (Washington, 1932). The most extensive collection of objects of Confederate war interest is in the White House of the Confederacy in Richmond, generally called the Confederate Museum. The White House in Montgomery contains furniture and other objects associated with President Jefferson Davis and his family. The Confederate Memorial Institute, or Battle Abbey, in Richmond contains many portraits of Southern heroes. Every Southern state has in its capitol and in various other public buildings objects of war interest; and museums of battlefields which have been erected into national parks or monuments contain objects relating especially to the battles.

It should not be inappropriate to mention here several sources of contemporary illustrations—pen and pencil sketches and photographs. Most of these are not of Southern origin, as the Confederates busied themselves little along these lines, though the *Southern Illustrated News*

(Richmond, 1862–1865) made the attempt in its crude sketches. The publications which the *News* was trying to imitate produced a great many war illustrations, a considerable number relating to the Confederacy, but some of them were little better than those in the *News*. These publications were *Frank Leslie's Illustrated Newspaper* (New York, 1855–1922), *Harper's Weekly, A Journal of Civilization* (New York, 1857–1916), and the *Illustrated London News* (London, 1842–). All of these publications had artists in the field. *Punch, or the London Charivari* (London, 1841–), as well as *Harper's Weekly,* carried significant cartoons. A collection of war cartoons is *American Caricatures Pertaining to the Civil War . . .* (New York, 1918). Many of the illustrations appearing in *Harper's Weekly* were reproduced in Alfred H. Guernsey and Henry M. Alden, *Harper's Pictorial History of the Great Rebellion,* 2 vols. (New York, 1866–1868); and some of the sketches in *Harper's Weekly* and in *Leslie's* helped to make up the large number of excellent illustrations in Benson J. Lossing, *Pictorial History of the Civil War in the United States of America,* 3 vols. (Philadelphia, 1866–1868). Many war illustrations were reproduced in Volume VII (1928) of Ralph H. Gabriel (ed.), *The Pageant of America,* 15 vols. (New Haven, 1925–1929). The greatest of the war photographers was Matthew B. Brady, who made thousands of pictures. Many of these were reproduced in Francis T. Miller (ed.), *The Photographic History of the Civil War,* 10 vols. (New York, 1912). A recent work by Roy Meredith, *The Face of Robert E. Lee in Life and in Legend* (New York, 1947), contains all the known likenesses of that great commander.

Maps also should be mentioned here. Apart from contemporary maps appearing in *Harper's Weekly, Leslie's,* and other publications of the war years, is the outstanding collection by Calvin D. Cowles (comp.), *Atlas to Accompany the Official Records of the Union and Confederate Armies,* 2 vols. (Washington, 1891–1895). This work also contains many views of forts, other military works, buildings, ships, trains, uniforms, flags, etc. Mention should be made of maps in railway guides, such as *Appletons' Railway and Steam Navigation Guide* (New York), and [W. Alvin] *Lloyd's Southern Railroad Guide with New Railroad Map; Containing Time Tables, Stations, Connections and Distances on all the Railroads throughout the Southern States . . .* (Mobile, Atlanta), which were issued periodically. Though not seen by the present writer, there appeared early in 1862 "Wadsworth's Railroad Map of the Confederate States," by George Wadsworth, a civil engineer of Dalton, Georgia. Among the several atlases of American history, these are notable: Charles O. Paullin and John K. Wright, *Atlas of the Historical*

Geography of the United States (Washington, 1932); James Truslow Adams and R. V. Coleman, *Atlas of American History* (New York, 1943); and Clifford L. Lord and Elizabeth H. Lord, *Historical Atlas of the United States* (New York, 1944). For a guide to the large map collection in the Library of Congress, see P. Lee Phillips, *A List of Maps of America in the Library of Congress, Preceded by a List of Works Relating to Cartography* (Washington, 1901).

MANUSCRIPTS

The manuscripts for the war years, as they are for any other period, are widely scattered, and many of them are still in private hands and largely unknown and unavailable. Many collections, however, have been gathered into public depositories. The story of the Confederate States archives, like the Confederacy itself, is tragic. What happened to these archives is well told by Dallas D. Irvine, "The Fate of Confederate Archives," in the *American Historical Review* (New York, 1895–), XLIV (1938–1939), 823–41. Many records were destroyed on the burning of Richmond and others which were taken southward with the fleeing government were captured, scattered, or destroyed. Some which survived and were captured were taken to Washington where they now repose in the National Archives and in the Division of Manuscripts, Library of Congress. Among these are many of the records of the War, Treasury, and Post Office departments. A great mass of State Department records, after a checkered history, were finally bought by the United States government and are now kept in the Division of Manuscripts, Library of Congress, under the title "John T. Pickett Papers." Various folders of these records, mentioned specifically in the footnotes of this work, were used. Fragments of the Confederate States archives have found their way into the libraries of educational institutions, among them Duke University, which has eighty-nine acts and resolutions of the Confederate Congress, the "Register of Acts, C. S. A.," and many other items; the University of Georgia, which has the Permanent Constitution; and the University of Texas, which has the "Official Correspondence of Confederate Collector of Customs, New Orleans, 1861–1862," and other papers. *A Calendar of the Ryder Collection of Confederate Archives at Tufts College* (Boston, 1940), describes a fragmentary mass of military papers, which William H. Ryder found in Richmond at the close of the war. Some of the records just mentioned, especially those of the Confederate Secretary of War, have been published in various works.

The state archives of all of the Confederate states have varying amounts of official and unofficial manuscripts. Those states richest in this material are Virginia, North Carolina, South Carolina, Alabama, Mississippi, and Texas. In Virginia, the "Executive Papers" are voluminous, and here, also, are the governors' letter books; in North Carolina, the "Governors' Papers" contain correspondence relating to all the war governors, but especially rich are the Zebulon B. Vance Papers; in South Carolina, the papers are arranged under such titles as "Military Affairs," "Confederate Relations," "Correspondence, 1860–1865," etc.; in Georgia, the letter books of Governor Joseph E. Brown are copied in a ledger book of 758 pages, there are a few hundred loose letters to him, and in the Telamon Cuyler Collection in the University of Georgia Library are many official and semiofficial papers. Florida has "Commissary Activities and War Correspondence, 1863–1865" copied in a ledger book, and some other correspondence as well as handbills and clippings; Alabama has a mass of letters to its governors as well as many military records in its war archives; Mississippi has "Correspondence" to governors, 1861–1865, "Petitions for Pardon etc.," "Military Telegrams," and various other records, mostly listed in *12th Annual Report of the Director of the Department of Archives and History* (Jackson, 1913), Appendix, 59–60. There are no official state archives in Louisiana, but there are a few papers in the Thomas O. Moore Collection, in the Department of Archives of the Louisiana State University. In Arkansas, most of the extant official archives are in a collection listed as Kie Oldham Papers; Texas has a mass of loose letters to the war governors, labeled "Governors' Letters"; and the Tennessee archives contain some of the adjutant generals' letter books, some copies of letters to and from Governor Isham G. Harris, some records of the Military and Financial Board, and other miscellaneous papers. All of the state archives are located in the state capitals, and are housed in specially constructed buildings except in Florida, Arkansas, Texas, and Tennessee, where they are in the capitols.

The greatest collections of unofficial manuscripts of the war years are in the libraries of the University of North Carolina, Duke University, and the University of Texas; but there are smaller collections in many other places. Space limitations here prevent more than a mention of the different collections examined. They relate to the great, to the near great, and to the most lowly citizen. The collections in the first two institutions mentioned are described in their respective guides: *Guide to the Manuscripts in the Southern Historical Collection of the University of North Carolina* (Chapel Hill, 1941), and Nannie M. Tilley and Noma Lee Goodwin, *Guide to the Manuscript Collections in the Duke University Library* (Durham, 1947).

These collections, relating to the better-known figures, yielded a wide variety of information: at the University of North Carolina, the Thomas Lanier Clingman Papers, William Alexander Graham Papers, now being edited for publication by J. G. de Roulhac Hamilton, Edmund Kirby-Smith Papers, William Porcher Miles Papers, Josiah Turner Papers, and the James Lusk Alcorn Papers, a selection of which was published by Percy L. Rainwater, "Letters of James Lusk Alcorn," in *Journal of Southern History* (Baton Rouge, 1935–), III (1937), 196–209; at Duke University, Pierre Gustave Toutant Beauregard Papers, Clement Claiborne Clay Papers, Jefferson Davis Papers (microfilms at the University of Texas), Thomas Jonathan Jackson Papers, Thomas Jenkins Semmes Papers, and William Henry Talbot Walker Papers; in private possession, the Howell Cobb Papers; at the University of Georgia, the Thomas R. R. Cobb Letters (transcripts of letters from Cobb, location of originals unknown), some of which have been published as "Thomas R. R. Cobb," in *Southern Historical Society Papers* (Richmond, 1876–), XXVIII (1900), 280–301; at the Library of Congress, James H. Hammond Papers, Francis W. Pickens Papers (microfilms at the University of Texas), and Louis T. Wigfall Papers (microfilms and typed copies at the University of Texas); at the University of Texas, "Memoirs of Williamson Simpson Oldham, Confederate Senator, 1861–1865" (typescript, location of original unknown); at the Texas State Archives, John H. Reagan Papers.

In several instances papers relating to one person are assembled in two or more depositories: the Milledge L. Bonham Papers and the George Alfred Trenholm Papers at the Library of Congress and the University of South Carolina; the Braxton Bragg Papers at Duke University and the University of Texas; the Christopher Gustavus Memminger Papers at the Library of Congress and the University of North Carolina (microfilms of the latter collection at the University of Texas); the Alexander H. Stephens Papers at the Library of Congress (microfilms at the University of Texas), and at Manhattanville College of the Sacred Heart, New York, many of which have been published in James D. Waddell (ed.), *Biographical Sketch of Linton Stephens . . . Containing a Selection of his Letters, Speeches, State Papers, etc.* (Atlanta, 1877), and scattered Stephens letters in various collections and in private possession; the Robert Toombs Papers at Duke University, the University of Georgia, and the University of South Carolina (copies of letters to Toombs, 1861).

574

Quite frequently some of the most significant information necessary for an understanding of the times comes from collections relating to people who held no position of leadership or prominence; and, of course, it should be borne in mind that the collections of outstanding leaders are generally composed not of letters written by them, but letters to them from people of every walk in life. Collections of less well-known figures are: Alexander-Hillhouse Papers, Campbell-Colson Papers, Stephen Elliott Letter Book, and Peter Mallett Papers at the University of North Carolina; Godfrey Barnsley Papers at Duke University, Emory University, and the University of Georgia; "Letters to and from Mrs. [Rose O'Neil] Greenhow" at the National Archives (microfilms at the University of Texas); "Letters of Mrs. Jestin Collins Hampton, 1862–1865," typed copies at the University of Texas (location of originals not stated); "Letters of Thomas B. Hampton, 1862–1865," typed copies at the University of Texas (location of originals not stated); Burton Harrison Collection at the Library of Congress; Ellison Keitt Papers at the University of South Carolina; and the William Massie Papers at the University of Texas.

Soldiers' letters are the most widely scattered manuscripts relating to the war years; having a personal and sentimental value, many of them are still treasured in the families of descendants, and others are interspersed in various collections. Among the collections of soldiers' letters used are: Baber-Blackshear Collection at the University of Georgia; "Samuel W. Farrow Correspondence, 1862–1865" and the "Thomas S. Gullett Letterbook, 1862–1864" at the University of Texas; and the Frank Pope Collection, in possession of the writer.

Among the collections consulted, difficult to classify, are "Collection. Autograph Letters, Documents, Manuscripts, etc. Relating to the Confederacy, 1861–1865" (5,080 pieces) at the University of Texas; and Miscellaneous Manuscripts in possession of the writer. Tapering out into scrapbook material, the John Hill Hewitt Collection at Emory University and the Jefferson Davis Scrapbooks at the University of Texas were examined.

GOVERNMENT DOCUMENTS

The Confederate States government never set up a printing office nor, indeed, found time or money for the publication of many of its records. Much that was published did not issue through its orders, but as will appear below, came out through the United States government. Most of President Davis' messages were compiled and published almost a half century later by James D. Richardson in *A Compilation of the Messages and Papers of the Confederacy, Including the Diplomatic Correspondence, 1861–1865*, 2 vols. (Nashville, 1906). Various reports of executive departments appeared contemporaneously, as *Regulations for the Army of the Confederate States, and for the Quartermaster's and Pay Departments. The Uniform and Dress of the Army. The Articles of War, as Amended by Act of Congress. Also all the Laws Appertaining to the Army* (rev. ed., New Orleans, 1861); *General Orders from Adjutant and Inspector-General's Office, Confederate States Army, from January, 1862, to December, 1863, (Both Inclusive)* (Columbia, 1864); *ibid., from January 1, 1864, to July 1, 1864, Inclusive* (Columbia, 1864); *Report of the Postmaster General, Post Office Department, Richmond, Va., Nov. 27th, 1861* (Richmond, 1861). The reports of the Secretary of the Treasury are available in the Appendix of Henry D. Capers, *The Life and Times of C. G. Memminger* (Richmond, 1893). A vast number of official war dispatches, reports, and other Confederate documents were published by the United States government in the monumental compilation, *The War of the Rebellion: A Compilation of the Official Records of the Union and Confederate Armies*, 127 books and index (Washington, 1880–1901); and the naval dispatches as well as Confederate diplomatic documents are included in *Official Records of the Union and Confederate Navies in the War of the Rebellion*, 30 vols. and index (1894–1927).

All of the Confederate statutes were published contemporaneously, except those for the last session of Congress and certain secret acts, under these titles: James M. Matthews (ed.), *The Statutes at Large of the Provisional Government of the Confederate States of America, from . . . February 8, 1861, to . . . February 18, 1862 . . . and the Treaties Concluded by the Confederate States with Indian Tribes* (Richmond, 1864); Matthews (ed.), *Public Laws* [and *Private Laws*] *of the Confederate States of America . . . First Session of the First Congress; 1862* (Richmond, 1862); Matthews (ed.), *Public Laws* [and *Private Laws*] *of the Confederate States of America . . . Second Session of the First Congress; 1862* (Richmond, 1862); Matthews (ed.), *Public Laws* [and *Private Laws*] *of the Confederate States of America . . . Third Session of the First Congress; 1863* (Richmond, 1863); Matthews (ed.), *Public Laws* [and *Private Laws*] *of the Confederate States of America . . . Fourth Session of the First Congress; 1863–4* (Richmond, 1864); Matthews (ed.), *Public Laws* [and *Private Laws*] *of the Confederate States of America . . . First Session of the Second Congress; 1864* (Richmond, 1864). The completion of the publication of the Confederate States laws was made by Charles W. Ramsdell (ed.), *Laws and Joint Resolutions of the Last Session of the Confederate Congress (November 7, 1864–March 18, 1865) Together with the Secret Acts of Previous Congresses* (Durham, 1941).

The debates of Congress were never published, and, indeed, no stenographic records were made; but copious reports were published in the Richmond newspapers. Beginning with the First Congress, these reports are now being reprinted in the *Southern Historical Society Papers* (Richmond, 1876–), the first installment appearing in Volume XLIV (1923). The United States government published the *Journal of the Congress of the Confederate States of America, 1861–1865,* 7 vols. (Washington, 1904–1905), as *Senate Documents,* 58 Cong., 2 Sess., No. 234, Serial Nos. 4610–16.

Besides authorizing the publication of the laws, the Confederate Congress published several reports of its committees, as *Report of the Special committee, on the Recent Military Disasters of Forts Henry and Donelson, and the Evacuation of Nashville* (Richmond, 1862); *Report of Evidence Taken before a Joint Special Committee of both Houses of the Confederate Congress, to Investigate the Affairs of the Navy Department* (Richmond, 1863); and *Minority Report of the Special Committee to Investigate the Affairs of the Navy Department* (Richmond, 1863).

All of the Confederate states published their laws and journals as well as other documents; but the limitations of space and the ease with which they may be located preclude a listing here.

As Federal documents, apart from those already mentioned, are only incidental to this study, and as the relevance of the *Congressional Globe* and such documents is self-evident, they need not be listed here. Reference should be made, however, to *The Eighth Census,* 1860 (Washington, 1864–1866), which appeared in its final form in four volumes, providing population, agriculture, manufactures, and mortality and miscellaneous statistics.

YEARBOOKS, STATISTICAL WORKS, AND DOCUMENTARY COLLECTIONS

Convenient for various documents, statistics, and a wide variety of information for the successive war years are *The American Annual Cyclopaedia and Register of Important Events of the Year 1861. Embracing Political, Civil, Military, and Social Affairs; Public Documents; Biography, Statistics, Commerce, Finance, Literature, Science,*

Agriculture and Mechanical Industry, and the volumes for the following four years, 15 vols., Ser. I (New York, 1862–1876). A somewhat similar work is Frank Moore (ed.), *The Rebellion Record: A Diary of American Events, with Documents, Narratives, Illustrative Incidents, Poetry, etc.,* 11 vols. and Supplement (New York, 1861–1868). Made up almost entirely of governmental documents, Confederate and Federal, is Edward McPherson, *The Political History of the United States of America, during the Great Rebellion, . . .* (2d ed., Washington, 1865). Ben La Bree (ed.), *The Confederate Soldier in the Civil War, 1861–1865* (Louisville, 1897), is a collection of documents and miscellaneous information under a misleading title; Henry Steele Commager (ed.), *Documents of American History* (New York, 1934), is a handy collection of official documents; and Henry Steele Commager and Allan Nevins (eds.), *The Heritage of America* (Boston, 1939), contains documents of a social and cultural nature. Convenient collections of editorials on secession are Dwight L. Dumond (ed.), *Southern Editorials on Secession* (New York, 1931), and Howard C. Perkins (ed.), *Northern Editorials on Secession,* 2 vols. (New York, 1942). Almanacs were useful for certain statistical information. Of these, there should be noted: *The Confederate States Almanac . . . ,* title varies, 4 vols. (Vicksburg, Mobile, 1861–1864). There are few collections of the speeches of the Confederate participants in American history; but one, especially, needs to be mentioned here: Benjamin H. Hill, Jr., *Senator Benjamin H. Hill of Georgia. His Life, Speeches and Writings* (Atlanta, 1893). Some of these speeches are not verbatim, as Hill wrote them from memory after he had delivered them.

PRINTED CORRESPONDENCE, MEMOIRS AND AUTOBIOGRAPHIES

The two most valuable collections of letters for this work are Ulrich B. Phillips (ed.), *The Correspondence of Robert Toombs, Alexander H. Stephens, and Howell Cobb,* in American Historical Association, *Annual Report,* 1911, II (Washington, 1913); and Dunbar Rowland (ed.), *Jefferson Davis, Constitutionalist, His Letters, Papers and Speeches,* 10 vols. (Jackson, Miss., 1923). Waddell (ed.), *Biographical Sketch of Linton Stephens,* already mentioned, is also valuable. The small part Sam Houston played is completely set forth in Amelia W. Williams and Eugene C. Barker (eds.), *The Writings of Sam Houston, 1813–1863,* 8 vols. (Austin 1938–1943), VIII. Special periods and aspects of Confederate history are illuminated by the following collections of letters: J. G. de Roulhac Hamilton (ed.), *The Correspondence of Jonathan Worth,* 2 vols. (Raleigh, 1909), only the first volume being concerned with the war years; *The Burckmyer Letters, March, 1863–June, 1865* (Columbia, 1926), relating to a South Carolina family with some members in Europe; J. Harold Easterby (ed.), *The South Carolina Rice Plantation as Revealed in the Papers of Robert F. W. Allston* (Chicago, 1945); Richard H. Shryock (ed.), *Letters of Richard D. Arnold, M.D., 1808–1876, Mayor of Savannah, Georgia, First Secretary of the American Medical Association* (Durham, 1929); and Edward E. Dale and Gaston Litton, *Cherokee Cavaliers; Forty Years of Cherokee History as told in the Correspondence of the Ridge-Watie-Boudinot Family* (Norman, 1939). Various letters and other documentary materials are available in Armistead C. Gordon, *Memories and Memorials of William Gordon McCabe,* 2 vols. (Richmond, 1925), a work on a distinguished Virginia educator. A bit of correspondence relating to a quarrel involving Postmaster General Reagan is published in *Correspondence of the President of the Virginia Central Rail Road Company and the Postmaster General, in Relation to Postal Service* (Richmond, 1864), 25 pp. Letters included incidentally in biographies will be noted in another section of this bibliography.

Small groups of letters published in historical magazines often give interesting glimpses into Confederate history. Among the many which have appeared, these should be mentioned: Albert B. Hart (ed.), "Letters to Secretary Chase from the South, 1861," in *American Historical Review,* IV (1898–1899), 331–47; Rosser H. Taylor (ed.), "Boyce-Hammond Correspondence," in *Journal of Southern History,* III (1937), 348–54; and Arthur E. Bestor, Jr., "Letters from a Southern Opponent of Sectionalism, September, 1860, to June, 1861," *ibid.,* XII (1946), 106–22, the writer being a Baptist preacher in Alabama.

Reminiscences, though affording valuable information, must be used with caution, depending always, of course, on the character of the author and the time at which he wrote. Disappointing in that it gets little below the surface is John H. Reagan, *Memoirs, with Special Reference to Secession and the Civil War,* ed. by Walter F. McCaleb (New York, 1906). Two brief works by other Confederate officials are John A. Campbell, *Reminiscences and Documents Relating to the Civil War during the Year 1865* (Baltimore, 1887), 68 pp.; and Caleb Huse, *The Supplies of the Confederate Army, How they were Obtained in Europe and how Paid for. Personal Reminiscences and Unpublished History* (Boston, 1904), 36 pp. A well-written account is John S. Wise, *The End of an Era* (Boston, 1901).

Valuable especially for its comments on Alexander H. Stephens is the *Autobiography of Col. Richard Malcolm Johnston* (2d ed., Washington, 1901); William J. Battle (ed.), *Memories of an Old-Time Tar Heel, by Kemp Plummer Battle* (Chapel Hill, 1945), is delightful for its homespun comments and philosophies. Thomas Cooper De Leon, *Four Years in Rebel Capitals: An Inside View of Life in the Southern Confederacy, from Birth to Death. From Original Notes, Collected in the Years 1861 to 1865* (Mobile, 1890), deals with a variety of subjects and is inaccurate in some details. Critical of President Davis and of the "tyrannies" of the Confederate government, George Cary Eggleston wrote an interesting narrative in *A Rebel's Recollections* (3d ed., New York, 1897). The home front is set forth in H. S. Fulkerson, *A Civilian's Recollections of the War Between the States*, ed. by Percy L. Rainwater (Baton Rouge, 1939). A few interesting glimpses into Confederate affairs are afforded by the highly unreliable reminiscences by the United States Register of the Treasury Lucius E. Chittenden, *Recollections of President Lincoln and his Administration* (New York, 1891).

The writings on the war years by women are of outstanding value; the following are reminiscent in nature: Myrta Lockett Avary (ed.), *A Virginia Girl* [not identified] *in the Civil War, 1861–1865; Being a Record of the Actual Experiences of the Wife of a Confederate Officer* (New York, 1903); Mary A. H. Gay, *Life in Dixie during the War 1861–1862– 1863–1864–1865* (3d ed., Atlanta, 1897); Mrs. Parthenia Antoinette (Vardaman) Hague, *A Blockaded Family: Life in Southern Alabama during the Civil War* (Boston, 1888); Mrs. Burton (Constance Cary) Harrison, *Recollections Grave and Gay* (New York, 1912); Mrs. Sara Agnes (Rice) Pryor, *Reminiscences of Peace and War* (New York, 1924); "A Virginia Lady" [Mrs. Sallie A. (Brock) Putnam], *Richmond during the War; Four Years of Personal Observation* (New York, 1867); Susan Dabney Smedes, *A Southern Planter* (4th ed., New York, 1890); Mrs. Cornelia (Phillips) Spencer, *The Last Ninety Days of the War in North Carolina* (New York, 1866); and Mrs. Louise (Wigfall) Wright, *A Southern Girl in '61. The War-Time Memories of a Confederate Senator's Daughter* (New York, 1905).

DIARIES, JOURNALS, AND TRAVEL ACCOUNTS

Women with all their wartime cares found time to keep diaries and they excelled in this activity as they did in their later reminiscences. The most penetrating and sprightly diarist of the war was Mrs. Chesnut, whose diary was published years later under the title, Isabella D. Martin and Myrta Lockett Avary (eds.), *A Diary from Dixie, as Written by Mary Boykin Chesnut, Wife of James Chesnut, Jr., United States Senator from South Carolina, 1859–1861, and Afterward an Aide to Jefferson Davis and a Brigadier-General in the Confederate Army* (New York, 1905). Other outstanding diaries by women are Judith White (Brockenbrough) McGuire, *Diary of a Southern Refugee, during the War. By a Lady of Virginia* (New York, 1867); Sarah Morgan Dawson, *A Confederate Girl's Diary* (Boston, 1913); and Mrs. Cornelia McDonald, *A Diary with Reminiscences of the War and Refugee Life in the Shenandoah Valley, 1860–1865* (Nashville, 1934). Less valuable are Amanda McDowell and Lela McDowell Blankenship, *Fiddles in the Cumberlands* (New York, 1943); and Lindsay Lomax Wood (ed.), *Leaves from an Old Washington Diary, 1854–1863, Written by Elizabeth Lindsay Lomax* (New York, 1943). As famous as Mrs. Chesnut's diary but written with an eye to publication and probably amended somewhat after the events described is John B. Jones, *A Rebel War Clerk's Diary at the Confederate States Capital*, 2 vols. (Philadelphia, 1866; reprinted New York, 1935). The most valuable diary by a foreigner is William H. Russell, *My Diary North and South* (Boston, 1863). In more excursive form the contents of this diary appeared in letters Russell wrote to the London *Times*, which he collected and brought out under the title *The Civil War in America* (Boston, 1861). Alexander H. Stephens' diary, interspersed with reminiscences while he was a prisoner after the war, was edited by Myrta Lockett Avary under the title *Recollections of Alexander H. Stephens; His Diary Kept when a Prisoner at Fort Warren, Boston Harbour, 1865; Giving Incidents and Reflections of his Prison Life and Some Letters and Reminiscences* (New York, 1910). The well-edited diary of the Chief of the Ordnance Bureau, Frank E. Vandiver (ed.), *The Civil War Diary of General Josiah Gorgas* (University, Ala., 1947), is disappointing in content. Interesting as the diary of an unnamed Southern Unionist woman is George W. Cable (ed.), "War Diary of a Union Woman in the South," in *Famous Adventures and Prison Escapes of the Civil War* (New York, 1893), 1–82. Two short diaries appearing in a historical magazine are Edgar L. Erickson (ed.), "Hunting for Cotton in Dixie: From the Civil War Diary of Captain Charles E. Wilcox," in the *Journal of Southern History*, IV (1938), 493–513; and Jay B. Hubbell (ed.), "The War Diary of John Esten Cooke," *ibid.*, VII (1941), 526–40.

Scarcely distinguishable at times from diaries, and of about equal reliability, are journals. Again women almost pre-empt the field in this form of writing. Two well-known ones are Eliza Frances Andrews, *The*

War-Time Journal of a Georgia Girl, 1864–1865 (New York, 1908); and Kate Mason Rowland and Mrs. Morris L. Croxall (eds.), *The Journal of Julia LeGrand, New Orleans, 1862–1863* (Richmond, 1911). Julian Street edited a valuable little journal under the title *A Woman's War-time Journal; An Account of the Passage over a Georgia Plantation of Sherman's Army on the March to the Sea, as Recorded in the Diary of Dolly Sumner Lunt (Mrs. Thomas Burge)* (Macon, 1927). Essentially a journal, although not always in that form, is the valuable work by Catherine C. Hopley, a British subject, entitled *Life in the South; from the Commencement of the War. By a Blockaded British Subject. Being a Social History of those who took Part in the Battles, from a Personal Acquaintance with them in their own Homes. From the Spring of 1860 to August, 1862*, 2 vols. in one (London, 1863).

A journal may be essentially a travel account, as, indeed, may also a diary, a memoir, or even a series of letters. Including these categories the writer has described and evaluated 492 titles of books of travel in the Confederacy under the title *Travels in the Confederate States: A Bibliography* (Norman, 1948). Only a few travel accounts will be mentioned here, the first group by foreigners, who were the keenest observers. Foremost of these was Lieutenant Colonel Arthur James Lyon Fremantle of the Coldstream Guards, who left an account of *Three Months in the Southern States: April–June, 1863* (New York, 1864). Other accounts by foreigners are: [George A. Lawrence], *Border and Bastile* (New York, 1863); Samuel Phillips Day, *Down South; or, An Englishman's Experience at the Seat of the American War*, 2 vols. (London, 1862); Edward [James Stephen] Dicey, *Six Months in the Federal States*, 2 vols. (London, 1863); Rev. William W. Malet, *An Errand to the South in the Summer of 1862* (London, 1863); Fitzgerald Ross, *A Visit to the Cities and Camps of the Confederate States* (Edinburgh, 1865); [Justus Scheibert], *Sieben Monate in den Rebellen-Staaten während des Nordamerikanischen Krieges, 1863* (Stettin, Germany, 1868); and "An English Merchant" [name unknown], *Two Months in the Confederate States, Including a Visit to New Orleans under the Domination of General Butler* (London, 1863). The adventures and observations of a Northern newspaper correspondent are set forth in Thomas W. Knox, *Camp-Fire and Cotton-Field: Southern Adventure in Time of War. Life with the Union Armies, and Residence on a Louisiana Plantation* (New York, 1865). The work of another Northerner should be noted, Edmund Kirke [James R. Gilmore], *Down in Tennessee, and Back by Way of Richmond* (New York, 1864). The wanderings of a Southerner are told by Joseph LeConte, *'Ware Sher-*

man, *A Journal of Three Months' Personal Experience in the Last Days of the Confederacy* (Berkeley, 1937). The writer has grouped in a subsequent section entitled MILITARY ACCOUNTS all diaries, journals, and travel accounts which deal principally with military affairs.

CONTEMPORARY PAMPHLETS AND LEAFLETS

Pamphlets and leaflets not subsequently classified under their subject matter are: *Letter of Hon. Howell Cobb to the People of Georgia, on the Present Condition of the Country* [December 6, 1860] (Washington, 1860), 16 pp.; *Substance of Remarks Made by Thomas R. R. Cobb, Esq., in the Hall of the House of Representatives, Monday Evening, November 12, 1860* (Atlanta, 1860), 16 pp.; "Cincinnatus," *Address of the Atlanta Register to the People of the Confederate States* (Atlanta, 1864), 16 pp.; Lucius Q. C. Lamar, *Speech of Hon. L. Q. C. Lamar, of Miss., on the State of the Country. Delivered in the Atheneum, Atlanta, Ga., Thursday Evening, April 14, 1864.* Reported by A. E. Marshall (Atlanta, 1864), 30 pp.; *Speech of Hon. Robert Toombs, Delivered in Milledgeville, on Tuesday Evening, November 13, 1860, before the Legislature of Georgia* [Milledgeville, 1860], 8 pp.; *Speech of Hon. Robert Toombs, on the Crisis. Delivered before the Georgia Legislature, December 7, 1860* (Washington, 1860), 15 pp.; *The Capital of the Confederate States*, by James H. Smith, May 23, 1861 (n.p., 1861), 1 p.; *Circular. An Appeal in Behalf of the "Bartow Hospital"* (n.p., 1861), 1 p.; *Copperhead Conspiracy in the Northwest. An Expose of the Treasonable Order of the "Sons of Liberty", Vallandigham, Supreme Commander* ([Washington], 1864), 8 pp.; *Huntsville Female College. Circircular Letter, April 27, 1861, J. G. Wilson, President* (n.p., 1861), 1 p.; *Mass Commercial and Financial Convention. To the Merchants, Bankers and Others of the Confederate States of America, July 29th, 1861* (n.p., 1861), 1 p.; *Opelika Ala. In Nomination for the Capitol* (n.p., n.d.), 1 p.

NEWSPAPERS

As newspapers played an important part in the war, they have constituted an outstanding source of a vast amount of varied information for this study. Except as a source of editorial opinion, newspapers must be used with certain well-known cautions. Occasionally a news story will be found corrected in a subsequent issue. The histories of most newspapers yet remain to be written. Thomas Ewing Dabney, *One*

Hundred Great Years; The Story of the Times-Picayune from its Founding to 1940 (Baton Rouge, 1944), is the story of New Orleans' most famous newspaper. James Melvin Lee has written a *History of American Journalism* (Boston, 1917); and Rabun Lee Brantley has produced a study on *Georgia Journalism of the Civil War Period* (Nashville, 1929). A collection of editorials in a famous newspaper is Frederick S. Daniel, *The Richmond Examiner during the War; or, The Writings of John M. Daniel. With a Memoir of his Life* (New York, 1868); and the editorials on secession collected by Dumond and Perkins should be recalled here. *The Private Press Association of the Confederate States of America* (Griffin, Ga., 1863), is a rare and interesting item. Short special studies of the press are John P. Jones, "The Confederate Press and the Government," in *Americana* (New York, 1906–), XXXVII (1943), 7–27; James G. Randall, "The Newspaper Problem in its Bearing upon Military Secrecy during the Civil War," in *American Historical Review*, XXIII (1917–1918), 303–23; and Bell I. Wiley, "Camp Newspapers of the Confederacy," in *North Carolina Historical Review* (Raleigh, 1924–), XX (1943), 327–35.

There were probably eight hundred or more newspapers in the Confederacy at the outbreak of war, but the number greatly dwindled as the struggle continued. Statistics for 1860 may be found in S.N.D. North, "The Newspaper and Periodical Press," in the *Tenth Census, 1880*, 22 vols. (Washington, 1883–1888), VIII, 3–446. Lester J. Cappon, *Virginia Newspapers, 1821–1935; A Bibliography with Historical Introduction and Notes* (New York, 1936), is a handy guide for Virginia newspapers. For the location of newspaper files as well as for data on newspapers relating to changes in title, place of publication, and periodicity, Winifred Gregory (comp.), *American Newspapers, 1821–1936: A Union List of Files Available in the United States and Canada* (New York, 1937), is invaluable. This work, is however, far from complete in listing the locations of files.

As Richmond was the capital, it is not surprising that the outstanding newspapers of the Confederacy should have centered there. Five great dailies (all with weekly editions) tended to set the pace for the rest of the Confederacy, both in support and in condemnation of the Confederate administration. The bitterest scold of all the papers which attacked President Davis was the Richmond *Examiner* (1859–1867), edited by John M. Daniel and Edward A. Pollard. The *Enquirer* (1804–1877) and the *Whig* (1824–1888) were more restrained in the earlier days, while the *Dispatch* (1850–1903) and the *Sentinel* (1863–1866) were generally friendly. The last-named was charged with being a Davis organ.

Charleston, Augusta, Macon, Montgomery, Mobile, and New Orleans had powerful and influential daily newspapers. In Charleston, the Robert Barnwell Rhett organ, the *Mercury* (1822–1868), was fiercely anti-Davis; the *Courier* (1803–) defended the Confederate administration. Augusta's two important dailies were the *Constitutionalist* (1823–1877) and the *Chronicle & Sentinel* (1785–). In the later period of the war, when the *Chronicle & Sentinel* came under the editorship of N. S. Morse, it was probably at times the most rabid anti-Davis paper in the Confederacy. There were two papers in Macon which should be mentioned, the *Telegraph* (1826–), which became the *Telegraph and Confederate* in September, 1864, by combining with the *Daily Confederate* (1863–1864), and the *Journal and Messenger* (1847–1869). The *Southern Confederacy* (1859–1865), an Atlanta newspaper, fleeing Sherman, stopped in Macon long enough to use that city in its date line before going out of existence in Columbus. The *Advertiser* (1850–), the *Mail* (1854–1871), and the *Post* (1860–1861) were the three principal papers in Montgomery, the first capital; the *Advertiser and Register* (1833–1910) and the *Evening News* (1850–1869) were the important papers in Mobile. In New Orleans, the *Picayune* (1837–) and the *Delta* (1845–1863) held sway.

Other papers used in this study, many of which were of more than local significance, were: VIRGINIA, the Lynchburg *Daily Republican* (1840–1875), the Winchester *Republican* (1810–1862), and the Lynchburg *Virginian* (1855–1887?); SOUTH CAROLINA, the Manning *Clarendon Banner* (1859?–?), the Lancaster *Ledger* (1852–1907), the Chester *Daily South Carolinian* (1850?–1867?), and the Darlington *Southerner* (1860–1883?); GEORGIA, the Sandersville *Central Georgian* (1841–1879), the Atlanta *Commonwealth* (1861–1862?), the Milledgeville *Confederate Union* (1862–1865), the Columbus *Enquirer* (1828–1873), the Darien *Gazette* (1818–?), the Atlanta *Gate City Guardian* (1861), the Greensboro *Planters' Weekly* (? – ?), the Savannah *Republican* (1802–1873), the Milledgeville *Southern Recorder* (1819–1873), the Athens *Southern Watchman* (1854–1882), and the Columbus *Times* (1841–1870?); FLORIDA, the Quincy *Semi-Weekly Dispatch* (1859?–); ALABAMA, the Greensboro *Beacon* (1835–1911), the Grove Hill *Clarke County Journal*, called the *Democrat* earlier (1862–1866), the Florence *Gazette* (1820–1863?), the Gainesville *Independent* (1854–1868?), the Selma *Morning Reporter* (1859–1865?), the Jacksonville *Republican* (1837–1894), and the Huntsville *Southern Advocate* (1825–?): MISSISSIPPI, the Jackson (afterwards Meridian) *Daily Clarion* (1863?–1867?), the Paulding *Eastern Clarion* (1837–1862), the Raymond *Hinds County Gazette* (1844–), the Natchez *Daily Courier* (1852–1871), the Natchez *Mississippi Free Trader,* sometimes called the *Daily Free Trader* (1835–1861?), the Jackson (sometimes Meridian) *Daily Mississippian* (1862–1867), the Jackson *Daily Southern Crisis* (1862–1863), merged March 30, 1863, with the *Daily Mississippian,* and the Columbus *Southern Republic* (? – ?); ARKANSAS, the Little Rock *Arkansas Patriot* (1862?–1863?), the Fayetteville *Arkansian* (1859–1861), the Des Arc *Weekly Citizen* (1854–1890), the Des Arc *Constitutional Union* (? – ?), the Little Rock *Daily State Journal* (1861–?), the Washington *Telegraph* (1840–1876), and the Fort Smith *Daily Times and Herald* (? – ?); TEXAS, the Galveston (at times Houston) *Tri-Weekly News* (1842–1873) and the Austin *Texas State Gazette* (1849–1879?) (sometimes *State Gazette);* and TENNESSEE, the Memphis (Montgomery and elsewhere) *Daily Appeal* (1840–1890) and the Chattanooga (Marietta, Ga., and elsewhere) *Daily Rebel* (1862–?).

The Fort Smith *New Era* (1863–1885) was a Union paper. Near the end of the war, on the occupation of much of the Confederacy by Federal troops, many newspapers were seized and continued under the same name with Union editors. No valid purpose within practical accomplishment could be served in this study by a wide use of Northern newspapers, though the writer is well acquainted with many of them. For certain special purposes the following were examined: the Cincinnati *Daily Commercial* (1843–1883), the Fulton (N.Y.) *Patriot and Gazette* (1858–1891?), and the New York *World* (1860–1931).

The religious press became quite vocal for Southern independence, and although the following church papers are classified in Winifred Gregory, *Union List of Serials in Libraries of the United States and Canada* (2d ed., New York, 1943) as periodicals they are for the war period more like newspapers. Some use was made of the following: the Atlanta (at times Augusta) *Baptist Banner* (1860–1865), the Roman Catholic Augusta *Pacificator* (1864–1865?), the Marion (at times Montgomery and Tuskegee) *South Western Baptist* (1851–1865), and the Methodist Augusta *Southern Christian Advocate* (1836–). A moral and literary newspaper combined is the Atlanta *Georgia Literary and Temperance Crusader.* A few camp or soldiers' newspapers have survived. The writer possesses a copy of the "Buzzard's Roost" (Macon?) *Free Speech Advocate.* A weekly publication combining characteristics of both a newspaper and a magazine is the well-known Putnam County (near Eatonton, Ga.) *Countryman* (1862–1866), edited on a plantation, by Joseph A. Turner. The only foreign newspapers examined were the London *Times* and the well-got-up Confederate propaganda publication, *The London Index* (1862–1865), subtitled *A Weekly Journal of Politics, Literature, and News; Devoted to the Exposition of the Mutual Interests, Political and Commercial, of Great Britain and the Confederate States of America.* It should be stated that most daily newspapers had weekly editions and a few semiweekly, and that they occasionally made minor changes in their titles.

PERIODICALS

A valuable guide to periodicals, giving pertinent information on the publication and the location of holdings, is Winifred Gregory, *Union List of Serials in Libraries of the United States and Canada* (New York, 1943), and *Supplement, January 1941–December 1943* (New York, 1945). More restricted helps are Gertrude C. Gilmer, *Checklist of Southern Periodicals to 1861* (Boston, 1934), Bertram Holland Flanders, *Early Georgia Magazines; Literary Periodicals to 1865* (Athens, 1944), and William S. Hoole, *A Check-list and Finding-list of Charleston Periodicals, 1732–1864* (Durham, 1936). Outstanding among the contemporary publications used are *De Bow's Review,* subtitle varies (New Orleans, Washington, Charleston, Columbia, Nashville, New York, 1846–1864, 1866–1870, 1879–1880), and the *Southern Literary Messenger* (Richmond, 1834–1864). Another, less valuable, is the *Record of News, History and Literature* (Richmond, 1863). This publication was merged with the *Richmond Age, A Southern Monthly Eclectic Magazine* (Richmond, 1864–1865). The *Southern Field and Fireside* (Augusta, 1859–1865), contains some news but is mostly literary. Patterned after a famous London publication was *Southern Punch* (Richmond, 1863–1865). The *Southern Illustrated News* (Richmond, 1862–1865), has been previously noted. The most valuable agricultural magazine, and the only one to last through the war, is the *Southern Cultivator, A Monthly Journal, Devoted to the Interests of Southern Agriculture, and Designed to Improve both the Soil and the Mind; to Elevate the Character of the Tillers of the Soil, and to Introduce a more Enlightened System of Agriculture* (Augusta, Athens, Atlanta, 1843–1935). Periodicals devoted to the Confederate tradition but published after the war are the *Bivouac,* after the first number entitled the *Southern Bivouac: A Monthly Literary and Historical Magazine* (Louisville, 1882–1887), the *Confederate Veteran* (Nashville, 1893–1932), and *Southern Historical Society Papers* (Richmond, 1876–).

Many articles of value appear in the current historical journals, some of which are noted in this bibliography. Those used most often are the

Journal of Southern History (Baton Rouge, 1935–), the *Mississippi Valley Historical Review* (Cedar Rapids, 1914–), the *American Historical Review* (New York, 1895–), the *Southwestern Historical Quarterly* (Austin, 1897–), the *North Carolina Historical Review* (Raleigh, 1924–), and the *Georgia Historical Quarterly* (Savannah, 1917–). A few foreign periodicals were examined for special purposes. The *Illustrated London News* (London, 1842–), and *Punch, or the London Charivari* (London, 1841–), have already been mentioned. *Blackwood's Edinburgh Magazine,* entitled *Blackwood's Magazine* after 1905 (Edinburgh, London, 1817–), took some notice of the Confederacy.

BIOGRAPHY

Biographies of the leaders in the Confederate period of American history are few, apart from those dealing with military and naval officers, which will be noted under another division. Jefferson Davis, the chief actor, has, of course, attracted most attention, but an adequate biography of him has not yet appeared. His latest biography, and probably the best, is Robert [M.] McElroy, *Jefferson Davis; The Unreal and the Real,* 2 vols. (New York, 1937), though a more sprightly work is Robert W. Winston, *High Stakes and Hair Trigger; The Life of Jefferson Davis* (New York, 1930). William E. Dodd, *Jefferson Davis* (Philadelphia, 1907), is a scholarly study, and H. J. Eckenrode, *Jefferson Davis, President of the South* (New York, 1923), offers a special interpretation. Not surprising are the bias and bitterness in Edward A. Pollard, *Life of Jefferson Davis, with a Secret History of the Southern Confederacy, Gathered "Behind the Scenes in Richmond"* . . . (Philadelphia, 1869). Sympathetic, naturally, is *Jefferson Davis, Ex-President of the Confederate States of America. A Memoir by his Wife,* 2 vols. (New York, 1890). Studies of Davis, including other Confederate leaders, are Burton J. Hendrick, *Statesmen of the Lost Cause; Jefferson Davis and his Cabinet* (Boston, 1939); Rembert W. Patrick, *Jefferson Davis and his Cabinet* (Baton Rouge, 1944); and Gamaliel Bradford, *Confederate Portraits* (Boston, 1914). Throwing some light on Davis during war times is John J. Craven, *Prison Life of Jefferson Davis* . . . (New York, 1866). A good understanding of Mrs. Jefferson Davis may be had from Eron Rowland—Mrs. Dunbar Rowland, *Varina Howell, Wife of Jefferson Davis,* 2 vols. (New York, 1927–1931); and Gamaliel Bradford, *Wives* (New York, 1925).

The latest life of the Vice-President is Rudolph von Abele, *Alexander H. Stephens, A Biography* (New York, 1946), which gives a penetrating

588

insight into his character. Other lives of Stephens which were consulted with profit are Henry Cleveland, *Alexander H. Stephens in Public and Private. With Letters and Speeches, before, during, and since the War* (Philadelphia, 1866), and Richard M. Johnston and William H. Browne, *Life of Alexander H. Stephens* (Philadelphia, 1878).

There are biographies of several of the other civilian Confederate leaders. A recent work on Benjamin, and the best, is Robert D. Meade, *Judah P. Benjamin, Confederate Statesman* (New York, 1943). As yet there is no adequate biography of Toombs; the best is Ulrich B. Phillips, *The Life of Robert Toombs* (New York, 1913). The best study of Lamar is Wirt A. Cate, *Lucius Q. C. Lamar, Secession and Reunion* (Chapel Hill, 1935), though valuable for documentary material is Edward Mayes, *Lucius Q. C. Lamar: His Life, Times, and Speeches, 1825–1893* (Nashville, 1896). Percy S. Flippin, *Herschel V. Johnson of Georgia, State Rights Unionist* (Richmond, 1931), is largely made up of letters and other documents. Some other biographies found useful are James B. Ranck, *Albert Gallatin Brown, Radical Southern Nationalist* (New York, 1937); Henry G. Connor, *John Archibald Campbell, Associate Justice of the United States Supreme Court, 1853–1861* (Boston, 1920); Edwin A. Alderman and Armistead C. Gordon, *J. L. M. Curry. A Biography* (New York, 1911); Haywood J. Pearce, Jr., *Benjamin H. Hill, Secession and Reconstruction* (Chicago, 1928); Henry D. Capers, *The Life and Times of C. G. Memminger* (Richmond, 1893); Barton H. Wise, *The Life of Henry A. Wise of Virginia, 1806–1876* (New York, 1899); and John W. Du Bose, *The Life and Times of William Lowndes Yancey. A History of Political Parties in the United States, from 1834 to 1864; Especially as to the Origin of the Confederate States* (Birmingham, 1892). A scholarly study of an old Virginian is Avery Craven, *Edmund Ruffin, Southerner; A Study in Secession* (New York, 1932). An article rehabilitating the reputation of the Secretary of the Navy is Philip Melvin, "Stephen Russell Mallory, Southern Naval Statesman," in *Journal of Southern History*, X (1944), 137–60; and an appreciation of North Carolina's principal war governor is Richard E. Yates, "Zebulon B. Vance as War Governor of North Carolina, 1862–1865," *ibid.*, III (1937), 43–75. E. Merton Coulter, *William G. Brownlow, Fighting Parson of the Southern Highlands* (Chapel Hill, 1937), is a biography of the well-known Tennessee Radical, with five chapters on the war years.

The lives of two bitter critics of the Confederate administration are Louise B. Hill, *Joseph E. Brown and the Confederacy* (Chapel Hill, 1939), and Laura White, *Robert Barnwell Rhett; Father of Secession*

(New York, 1931). A small part of the gap in the business history of the Confederacy is filled by Broadus Mitchell, *William Gregg, Factory Master of the Old South* (Chapel Hill, 1928), and Edwin B. Coddington, "The Activities and Attitudes of a Confederate Business Man: Gazaway B. Lamar," in *Journal of Southern History*, IX (1943), 3–36. The lives of two outstanding clergymen are Thomas Cary Johnson, *The Life and Letters of Benjamin Morgan Palmer* (Richmond, 1906), and Benjamin M. Palmer, *The Life and Letters of James Henley Thornwell, D.D., LL.D., Ex-President of the South Carolina College, Late Professor of Theology in the Theological Seminary at Columbia, South Carolina* (Richmond, 1875). Of the myriad biographies and studies of Abraham Lincoln, these two scholarly works should be noted: James G. Randall, *Lincoln, the President; Springfield to Gettysburg*, 2 vols. (New York, 1945), and James G. Randall, *Lincoln and the South* (Baton Rouge, 1946).

GENERAL AMERICAN HISTORY

Works of this nature are so well known that it seems unnecessary to note more than a few here. With some exceptions they are of little value in a study such as this, save for perspective. The most ambitious study of the Civil War period was made by James Ford Rhodes, *History of the United States from the Compromise of 1850*, 8 vols. (reprint, New York, 1902–1920), of which Volumes III (1904, c. 1895), IV (1904, c. 1899), and V (1904) deal with the war years. Largely military is his *History of the Civil War, 1861–1865* (New York, 1917). Dealing with the Civil War period is Edward Channing, *A History of the United States*, 6 vols. (New York, 1905–1925), VI. The volume attuned to the best modern scholarship is James G. Randall, *The Civil War and Reconstruction* (Boston, 1937). Another scholarly volume is Carl Russell Fish, *The American Civil War; An Interpretation* (New York, 1937), published posthumously. John B. McMaster, after having finished *A History of the People of the United States, from the Revolution to the Civil War*, 8 vols. (New York, 1883–1913), added to his work *A History of the People of the United States during Lincoln's Administration* (New York, 1927). Three series collaborated in by several authors include volumes on the war years, which are as follows: In Albert B. Hart (ed.), *The American Nation: A History*, 28 vols. (New York, 1904–1918), are French E. Chadwick, *Causes of the Civil War, 1859–1861*, Volume XIX (1906); James K. Hosmer, *The Appeal to Arms, 1861–1863*, Volume XX (1907); and James K. Hosmer, *Outcome of the Civil War, 1863–1865*,

Volume XXI (1907); in Allen Johnson (ed.), *The Chronicles of America Series*, 50 vols. (New Haven, 1918–1921), are Nathaniel W. Stephenson, *Abraham Lincoln and the Union*, Volume XXIX (1918); Nathaniel W. Stephenson, *The Day of the Confederacy*, Volume XXX (1919); and William Wood, *Captains of the Civil War*, Volume XXXI (1921); and in Arthur M. Schlesinger and Dixon R. Fox (eds.), *A History of American Life*, 13 vols. (New York, 1927–1948), is Arthur C. Cole, *The Irrepressible Conflict, 1850–1865*, Volume VII (1934).

HISTORIES OF THE CONFEDERACY AND OF STATES AND CITIES

The first and most ambitious attempt to write a history of the Confederacy, not primarily military, was made by the prolific writer Edward A. Pollard. He set to work immediately and produced, under the general title *Southern History of the War*, the following volumes: *The First Year of the War* (New York, 1863, c. 1862); *The Second Year of the War* (New York, 1863); *The Third Year of the War* (New York, 1865, c. 1864); and *The Last Year of the War* (New York, 1866). These volumes were reprinted under the title *Southern History of the War*, 2 vols. (New York, 1866). Leaving out many of the details of his previous works, Pollard wrote *The Lost Cause; A New Southern History of the War. Comprising a Full and Authentic Account of the Rise and Progress of the Late Southern Confederacy . . .* (New York, 1866). Immediately after the war the disaffected John Minor Botts wrote *The Great Rebellion: Its Secret History, Rise, Progress, and Disastrous Failure. The Political Life of the Author Vindicated* (New York, 1866); and the noisy Henry S. Foote wrote *War of the Rebellion; or, Scylla and Charybdis. Consisting of Observations upon the Causes, Course, and Consequences of the Late Civil War in the United States* (New York, 1866). Most of the well-known actors in the drama were in the army and navy and those who became authors wrote military and naval histories; but the two highest civil officials attempted general accounts of the Confederacy and neither produced a remotely well-balanced history. These works are Jefferson Davis, *The Rise and Fall of the Confederate Government*, 2 vols. (New York, 1881); a second attempt by him called *A Short History of the Confederate States of America* (New York, 1890); and Alexander H. Stephens, *A Constitutional View of the Late War Between the States; its Causes, Character, Conduct and Results. Presented in a Series of Colloquies at Liberty Hall*, 2 vols. (Philadelphia, 1868–1870). Stephens came to the defense of his work in *The Reviewers Reviewed; A*

Supplement to the "War Between the States," etc., with an Appendix in Review of "Reconstruction," So Called (New York, 1872).

Recent scholarship has produced better balanced works. Charles W. Ramsdell surveyed some of the difficulties in "Some Problems Involved in Writing the History of the Confederacy," in *Journal of Southern History*, II (1936), 133–47; and "The Changing Interpretation of the Civil War," *ibid.*, III (1937), 3–27. Robert S. Henry, *The Story of the Confederacy* (Indianapolis, 1931), is popular and reliable. Clifford Dowdey has popularized the story still more and has largely centered his account around Richmond in *Experiment in Rebellion* (Garden City, 1946). William B. Hesseltine gives to the Confederacy six chapters in his *The South in American History* (New York, 1943); and in Francis Butler Simkins, *The South, Old and New: A History, 1820–1947* (New York, 1947), there are two. The upper fringe of the South is dealt with in Edward C. Smith, *The Borderland in the Civil War* (New York, 1927).

The war period of a few of the states has appeared in separate books. Reconstruction studies of most of the Southern states give substantial attention to this period. Under the former classification are John K. Bettersworth, *Confederate Mississippi, The People and Policies of a Cotton State in Wartime* (Baton Rouge, 1943), and Jefferson Davis Bragg, *Louisiana in the Confederacy* (Baton Rouge, 1941). Of the latter kind, these were found helpful: E. Merton Coulter, *The Civil War and Readjustment in Kentucky* (Chapel Hill, 1926); William W. Davis, *The Civil War and Reconstruction in Florida* (New York, 1913); Walter L. Fleming, *Civil War and Reconstruction in Alabama* (Cleveland, 1911); James W. Garner, *Reconstruction in Mississippi* (New York, 1901); J. G. de Roulhac Hamilton, *Reconstruction in North Carolina* (New York, 1914); James W. Patton, *Unionism and Reconstruction in Tennessee, 1860–1869* (Chapel Hill, 1934); Charles W. Ramsdell, *Reconstruction in Texas* (New York, 1910); and Thomas Staples, *Reconstruction in Arkansas, 1862–1874* (New York, 1923). A study of a city during the war years is Alfred Hoyt Bill, *The Beleaguered City, Richmond, 1861–1865* (New York, 1946). Charles C. Jones, Jr., and Salem Dutcher, *Memorial History of Augusta, Georgia* . . . (Syracuse, 1890), was found useful. A general history of the South, in which the Confederate period is, of course, given its place, is Julian A. C. Chandler *et al.* (eds.), *The South in the Building of the Nation* . . . , 13 vols. (Richmond, 1909–1913).

CONFEDERATE GOVERNMENTAL DEVELOPMENTS

No adequate study of the Confederate government in principle and in operation has ever been made. Jabez L. M. Curry, *Civil History of the Government of the Confederate States with Some Personal Reminiscences* (Richmond, 1901), is superficial and disappointing. A short study by a competent authority is William M. Robinson, Jr., "A New Deal in Constitutions," in *Journal of Southern History*, IV (1938), 449–61. A valuable study of Confederate finances is John C. Schwab, *The Confederate States of America, 1861–1865. A Financial and Industrial History of the South during the Civil War* (New Haven, 1913, c. 1901). Other works on this subject are: William W. Bradbeer, *Confederate and Southern State Currency* (Mt. Vernon, N.Y., 1915); James L. Sellers, "An Interpretation of Civil War Finance," in *American Historical Review*, XXX (1924–1925), 282–97; and Ernest A. Smith, *The History of the Confederate Treasury* (Harrisburg, Pa., 1901).

The judiciary has in recent times attracted considerable study. William M. Robinson, Jr., *Justice in Grey; A History of the Judicial System of the Confederate States of America* (Cambridge, Mass., 1941), is an outstanding work, scholarly and remarkably complete. An article by the same author is "Admiralty in 1861: The Confederate States District Court for the Division of Pamlico of the District of North Carolina," in *North Carolina Historical Review*, XVII (1940), 132–38. Another article on a district court is Warren Grice, "The Confederate States Court for Georgia," in *Georgia Historical Quarterly*, IX (1925), 131–58. Relating to state courts are Joseph G. de Roulhac Hamilton, "The State Courts and the Confederate Constitution," in *Journal of Southern History*, IV (1938), 425–48, and his article, "The North Carolina Courts and the Confederacy," in *North Carolina Historical Review*, IV (1927), 366–403.

A remarkable work on Confederate postage stamps is August Dietz, *The Postal Service of the Confederate States of America* (Richmond, 1929). Too much in praise of the postal service is Walter F. McCaleb, "The Organization of the Post-Office Department of the Confederacy," in *American Historical Review*, XII (1906–1907), 66–74. Two pertinent items are Mrs. Lucile L. Dufner, "The Flags of the Confederate States of America" (M. A. thesis, University of Texas, 1944), and Louise B. Hill, *State Socialism in the Confederate States of America*, in *Southern Sketches*, Ser. I, No. 9 (Charlottesville, 1936), 31 pp.

593

AGRICULTURE, COMMERCE, TRANSPORTATION AND INDUSTRY

The changes in Southern agriculture necessary to make it conform to war conditions are set forth in E. Merton Coulter, "The Movement for Agricultural Reorganization in the Cotton South during the Civil War," in *Agricultural History* (Chicago, Baltimore, 1927–), I, 3–17. By the same author is a short article, "Planters' Wants in the Days of the Confederacy," in *Georgia Historical Quarterly*, XII (1928), 38–52. Charles W. Ramsdell, "Materials for Research in the Agricultural History of the Confederacy," in *Agricultural History*, IV (1930), 18–22, and Harrison A. Trexler, "The Opposition of Planters to the Employment of Slaves as Laborers by the Confederacy," in *Mississippi Valley Historical Review*, XXVII (1940–1941), 211–24, were found useful in this study. Also valuable for background is Herbert Weaver, *Mississippi Farmers, 1850–1860* (Nashville, 1945), and Lewis C. Gray, *History of Agriculture in the Southern United States to 1860*, 2 vols. (Washington, 1933). Easterby (ed.), *The South Carolina Rice Plantation as Revealed in the Papers of Robert F. W. Allston*, previously noted in another division of this bibliography, is useful for agriculture as well as for other subjects. Largely an agricultural study is Guion G. Johnson, *A Social History of the Sea Islands, with Special Reference to St. Helena Island, South Carolina* (Chapel Hill, 1930).

The most striking aspects of Confederate commerce related to blockade-running and trade across the frontiers. No mention need be made here of the several accounts detailing the experiences of blockade-runners, but attention should be called to these studies in the field: Francis B. C. Bradlee, *Blockade Running during the Civil War and the Effect of Land and Water Transportation on the Confederacy* (Salem, Mass., 1925); George W. Dalzell, *The Flight from the Flag; The Continuing Effect of the Civil War upon the American Carrying Trade* (Chapel Hill, 1940); William Diamond, "Imports of the Confederate Government from Europe and Mexico," in *Journal of Southern History*, VI (1940), 470–503; Samuel B. Thompson, *Confederate Purchasing Operations Abroad* (Chapel Hill, 1935); and Frank E. Vandiver (ed.), *Confederate Blockade Running through Bermuda, 1861–1865; Letters and Cargo Manifests* (Austin, 1947). The last work has a long introduction on blockade-running.

Special items dealing with trade across national boundaries and military frontiers are: *Cotton Sold to the Confederate States* (Washington, 1913), in *Senate Documents*, 62 Cong., 3 Sess., No. 987, Serial No. 6348;

E. Merton Coulter, "Commercial Intercourse with the Confederacy in the Mississippi Valley, 1861–1865," in *Mississippi Valley Historical Review,* V (1918–1919), 377–95; E. Merton Coulter, "Effect of Secession upon the Commerce of the Mississippi Valley," *ibid.,* III (1916–1917), 275–300; Joseph H. Parks, "A Confederate Trade Center under Federal Occupation: Memphis, 1862 to 1865," in *Journal of Southern History,* VII (1941), 289–314; and A. Sellew Roberts, "The Federal Government and Confederate Cotton," in *American Historical Review,* XXXII (1926–1927), 262–75.

There is need for a full history of the railroads of the Confederacy. There are some special studies of individual railroads and of railroad problems, among which these should be noted: Festus P. Summers, *The Baltimore and Ohio in the Civil War* (New York, 1939); Robert S. Cotterill, "The Louisville and Nashville Railroad, 1861–1865," in *American Historical Review,* XXIX (1923–1924), 700–15; Samuel M. Derrick, *Centennial History of South Carolina Railroad* (Columbia, 1930); St. Clair G. Reed, *A History of the Texas Railroads and of Transportation Conditions under Spain and Mexico and the Republic and the State* (Houston, 1941); Charles W. Ramsdell, "The Confederate Government and the Railroads," in *American Historical Review,* XXII (1916–1917), 794–810; Robert E. Riegel, "Federal Operation of Southern Railroads during the Civil War," in *Mississippi Valley Historical Review,* IX (1922–1923), 126–38; "Affairs of Southern Railroads," in *Reports of the Committees of the House of Representatives,* 39 Cong., 2 Sess., No. 34, Serial No. 1306. The schedules of trains may be found in many of the Confederate newspapers. Published periodically at Griffin, Georgia, was *H. P. Hill & Co.'s Confederate States Rail-Road Guide, Containing the Time-Tables, Fares, Connections and Distances on all the Rail-Roads of the Confederate States* . . . , followed by *Hill & Swayze's Confederate States Rail-Road & Steam-Boat Guide* . . . , and at Mobile and Atlanta, [W. Alvin], *Lloyd's Southern Railroad Guide.* . . . These three items on the telegraph were found useful; William R. Plum, *The Military Telegraph during the Civil War in the United States, with an Exposition of Ancient and Modern Means of Communication, and of the Federal and Confederate Cypher Systems; also a Running Account of the War Between the States,* 2 vols. (Chicago, 1882); Robert L. Thompson, *Wiring a Continent; The History of the Telegraph Industry in the United States, 1832–1866* (Princeton, 1947); and C. P. Culver, *The Southern Telegraph* (n.p., 1863).

Confederate manufactories were developed largely for war purposes and most of what has been written about them relates to munitions of war. Claud E. Fuller and Richard D. Steuart, *Firearms of the Confederacy; the Shoulder Arms, Pistols and Revolvers of the Confederate Soldier, including the Regular United States Models, the Imported Arms and those Manufactured within the Confederacy* (Huntington, W. Va., 1944), is more a list of arms than a discussion of their manufacture. The great powder works at Augusta are described in George W. Rains, *History of the Confederate Powder Works* (Augusta, Ga., 1882). Kathleen Bruce in her *Virginia Iron Manufacture in the Slave Era* (New York, 1931), has a valuable chapter on the Tredegar Iron Works in Richmond. A badly organized and garrulous work is Ethel M. Armes, *The Story of Coal and Iron in Alabama* (Birmingham, 1910). Other items dealing with the economic picture are Edwin B. Coddington, "A Social and Economic History of the Seaboard States of the Southern Confederacy" (Ph.D. dissertation, Clark University, 1939); Charles W. Ramsdell, "The Control of Manufacturing by the Confederate Government," in *Mississippi Valley Historical Review*, VIII (1921–1922), 231–49; James L. Sellers, "The Economic Incidence of the Civil War in the South," *ibid.*, XIV (1927–1928), 179–91; Elizabeth Y. Webb, "Cotton Manufacturing and State Regulation in North Carolina, 1861–'65," in *North Carolina Historical Review*, IX (1932), 117–37; and Gordon Wright, "Economic Conditions in the Confederacy as seen by the French Consuls," in *Journal of Southern History*, VII (1941), 195–214. Two broadly social and economic studies, by competent scholars, are Charles W. Ramsdell, *Behind the Lines in the Southern Confederacy* (Baton Rouge, 1944), and Bell I. Wiley, *The Plain People of the Confederacy* (Baton Rouge, 1943). A glimpse into wartime Richmond society is given by Edward M. Alfriend, "Social Life in Richmond during the War," in the *Cosmopolitan. A Monthly Illustrated Magazine* (New York, 1886–1925), XII (1891), 229–33.

CULTURAL HISTORY

Valuable for listing and locating Confederate publications along cultural lines as well as all other kinds of contemporary publications (and in some instances also manuscripts) are Charles N. Baxter and James M. Dearborn (comps.), *Confederate Literature; A List of Books and Newspapers, Maps, Music and Miscellaneous Matter Printed in the South during the Confederacy, now in the Boston Athenaeum* (Boston, 1917); Douglas S. Freeman, *A Calendar of Confederate Papers, with a Bibliography of Some Confederate Publications* ["now in the Confederate Museum"] . . . (Richmond, 1908); Richard B. Harwell, *Confederate*

Belles-Lettres, A Bibliography and A Finding List . . . (Hattiesburg, Miss., 1941); Hugh Alexander Morrison, *The Leiter Library. A Catalogue of the Books, Manuscripts and Maps relating principally to America, Collected by the Late Levi Ziegler Leiter. With Collations and Bibliographical Notes* (Washington, 1907), Confederate items, pages 241–341; and Willard O. Waters, "Confederate Imprints in the Henry E. Huntington Library Unrecorded in Previously Published Bibliographies of such Material," in *The Papers of the Bibliographical Society of America* (New York, Chicago, 1904–), XXIII (1929), 18–109. A popular discussion of many items is Douglas S. Freeman, *The South to Posterity; An Introduction to the Writing of Confederate History* (New York, 1939).

For the biographies of writers and samples of their work, Edwin A. Alderman, Joel Chandler Harris, and Charles W. Kent (eds.), *Library of Southern Literature,* 17 vols. (Atlanta, 1907–1923), may be consulted with profit. Somewhat similar but less critical works are James Wood Davidson, *The Living Writers of the South* (New York, 1869); Mary Forrest [Mrs. Julia Deane Freeman], *Women of the South Distinguished in Literature* (New York, 1866); and Mildred Lewis Rutherford, *The South in History and Literature; A Hand-Book of Southern Authors, from the Settlement of Jamestown, 1607, to Living Writers* (Athens, 1907). A collection of humorous writings of Charles H. Smith ("Bill Arp"), many of which originally appeared in newspapers, is *Bill Arp, So Called. A Side Show of the Southern Side of the War* (New York, 1866), with the original dialect somewhat tampered with but restored in a republication of some of these writings under the title *Bill Arp's Peace Papers* (New York, 1873).

Titles of songs appeared frequently in the newspapers, and there are collections of Confederate sheet music in various depositories, one of the largest being in the Duke University Library. Among several compilations of lyrics, Frank Moore (ed.), *Songs and Ballads of the Southern People, 1861–1865* (New York, 1886), should be noted. A recent article on the ever interesting "Dixie" is David Rankin Barbee, "Who Wrote Dixie?" in *Musical Digest* (New York, 1920–), XXX (1948), 6–9. More dependable works on "Dixie" are Charles Burleigh Galbreath, *Daniel Decatur Emmett, Author of "Dixie"* (Columbus, Ohio, 1904); and John Tasker Howard, *Our American Music; Three Hundred Years of It* (New York, 1931). Also of interest is Carl Frederick Wittke, *Tambo and Bones; A History of the American Minstrel Stage* (Durham, 1930). The John Hill Hewitt Collection in the Emory University Library, previously mentioned, contains a great deal of material

597

THE CONFEDERATE STATES OF AMERICA

relating to the theater during the Confederacy. A recent exploitation of some of this material is Richard Barksdale Harwell, "A Reputation by Reflection: John Hill Hewitt and Edgar Allan Poe," in *Emory University Quarterly* (Emory University, 1945–), III (1947), 104–15. Theater programs may be found in the Confederate newspapers of the larger cities. On the Charleston theater, W. Stanley Hoole has written an article, "Charleston Theatricals during the Tragic Decade, 1860–1869," in *Journal of Southern History,* XI (1945), 538–47.

Several of the college and university histories give more than perfunctory attention to the war years, among which should be mentioned Colonel Oliver J. Bond, *The Story of the Citadel* (Richmond, 1936); E. Merton Coulter, *College Life in the Old South* (New York, 1928); William Couper, *One Hundred Years at V.M.I.,* 2 vols. (Richmond, 1939); and Walter L. Fleming, *Louisiana State University, 1860–1896* (Baton Rouge, 1936). An interesting educational item is Stephen B. Weeks, "Confederate Text-Books (1861–1865); A Preliminary Bibliography," in *Report of the* [United States] *Commissioner of Education for the Year 1898–99,* 2 vols. (Washington, 1900), I, 1139–55.

The war years made religion a greater reality to many Southerners than it had ever been to them, both in the army and at home. William Warren Sweet, *The Story of Religions in America* (New York, 1930), is serviceable for background; and good for special studies for the war are Joseph Blount Cheshire, *The Church in the Confederate States; A History of the Protestant Episcopal Church in the Confederate States* (New York, 1912); Charles W. Heathcote, *The Lutheran Church and the Civil War* (New York, 1919); and Lewis G. Vander Velde, *The Presbyterian Churches and the Federal Union, 1861–1869* (Cambridge, 1932). Charles C. Tiffany, *A History of the Protestant Episcopal Church in the United States of America* (3d ed., New York, 1917), is valuable in this study for its discussion of the separation of the Southern church. Religion in the army is set forth in two badly organized and integrated accounts: William W. Bennett, *A Narrative of the Great Revival which Prevailed in the Southern Armies during the Late Civil War Between the States of the Federal Union* (Philadelphia, 1877), and Rev. J. William Jones, *Christ in the Camp; or, Religion in Lee's Army. Supplemented by a Sketch of the Work in the Other Confederate Armies* (Richmond, 1888). All of the *Historical Magazine of the Protestant Episcopal Church* (Garrison, N.Y., New Brunswick, N.J., 1932–), XVII (December, 1948), is devoted to a history of that Church in the Confederate States. A recent short study is John Shepard, Jr., "Religion in the Army of Northern Virginia," in *North Carolina Historical Review,* XXV

(1948), 341–76. An interesting item on Bibles is Harold R. Willoughby, *Soldiers' Bibles through Three Centuries* (Chicago, 1944). Among the many sermons printed and circulated, these should be noted: [Stephen Elliott?], *Gideon's Water-Lappers. A Sermon Preached in Christ Church, Savannah, on Friday, the 8th Day of April, 1864, the Day Set apart by the Congress of the Confederate States, as a Day of Humiliation, Fasting and Prayer* (Macon, Ga., 1864), 22 pp.; Rev. Benjamin M. Palmer, *Thanksgiving Sermon Delivered in the First Presbyterian Church, (New Orleans,) on Thursday, Nov. 29th, 1860* (Milledgeville, 1860), 16 pp.; and Rev. Joseph C. Stiles, *National Rectitude the only True Basis of National Prosperity: An Appeal to the Confederate States* (Petersburg, 1863), 45 pp. Lives of the famous clergymen Benjamin M. Palmer and James H. Thornwell, previously mentioned under the division of BIOGRAPHY, should be recalled here.

MILITARY ACCOUNTS

The numerous listings under this heading are not out of proportion to their value for this study, for although all deal principally with military or naval activities, they touch incidentally every aspect of Confederate history. For convenience they are grouped with relation to their major significance, in the same general order used in the foregoing part of this bibliography.

In the field of general accounts no effort is made here to list the many histories of the campaigns of the war. Edited by Clement A. Evans and written by various Southerners is *Confederate Military History*, 12 vols. (Atlanta, 1899). Another collaborative work edited by Robert U. Johnson and C. C. Buell and written by both Northerners and Southerners is the well-known *Battles and Leaders of the Civil War . . . ,* 4 vols. (New York, 1887–1888). More than a half century ago, Charles Scribner's Sons published thirteen volumes by different authors and titles under the general series *Campaigns of the Civil War* (New York, 1881–1883). Previously mentioned are the monumental collections of military and naval documents published by the United States government, the *Official Records of the Union and Confederate Armies*, 127 books, and the *Official Records of the Union and Confederate Navies*, 30 vols.

For locating the many special accounts on the war, *Bibliography of State Participation in the Civil War, 1861–1866* (Washington, 1913), is valuable. A recent scholarly study on the war in Virginia is Douglas S. Freeman, *Lee's Lieutenants, A Study in Command*, 3 vols. (New York, 1942–1944); and an incisive study of three great commanders is Alfred

H. Burne, *Lee, Grant and Sherman; A Study in Leadership in the 1864–65 Campaign* (New York, 1939). Of the many writings on special topics, the following are listed because they made some definite contribution to this study: E. Merton Coulter, "Sherman and the South," in *North Carolina Historical Review*, VIII (1931), 41–54; John P. Dyer, "Some Aspects of Cavalry Operations in the Army of Tennessee," in *Journal of Southern History*, VIII (1942), 210–25; Frank Freidel, "General Orders 100 and Military Government," in *Mississippi Valley Historical Review*, XXXII (1945–1946), 541–56; Thomas R. Hay, "Confederate Leadership at Vicksburg," *ibid.*, XI (1924–1925), 543–60; Thomas R. Hay, "The Davis-Hood-Johnston Controversy of 1864," *ibid.*, 54–84; Florence E. Holladay, "The Powers of the Commander of the Confederate Trans-Mississippi Department, 1863–1865," in *Southwestern Historical Quarterly*, XXI (1917–1918), 279–98, 333–59; Stanley F. Horn, *The Army of Tennessee; A Military History* (Indianapolis, 1941); Alfred P. James, "General Joseph Eggleston Johnston, Storm Center of the Confederate Army," in *Mississippi Valley Historical Review*, XIV (1927–1928), 342–59; Alfred P. James, "The Strategy of Concentration, as Used by the Confederate Forces in the Mississippi Valley in the Spring of 1862," in *Proceedings of the Mississippi Valley Historical Association* (Cedar Rapids, 1909–1924), X, Pt. II (1919–1920), 363–72; Charles W. Ramsdell, "General Robert E. Lee's Horse Supply, 1862–1865," in *American Historical Review*, XXXV (1929–1930), 758–77; Bromfield L. Ridley, *Battles and Sketches of the Army of Tennessee* (Mexico, Mo., 1906); John B. Turchin, *Chickamauga* (Chicago, 1888).

An excellent modern study of the character of the Confederate soldier is Bell I. Wiley, *The Life of Johnny Reb, the Common Soldier of the Confederacy* (Indianapolis, 1943). Susan R. Hull, *Boy Soldiers of the Confederacy* (New York, 1905), is an uncritical study. *The Grayjackets: And How they Lived, Fought and Died, for Dixie. With Incidents & Sketches of Life in the Confederacy. . . . By a Confederate* (Richmond, 1867), is a miscellany. Breaking into an unworked field is F. Stansbury Haydon, *Aeronautics in the Union and Confederate Armies, with a Survey of Military Aeronautics prior to 1860*, 1 vol. and another promised (Baltimore, 1941). On the same subject is J. Duane Squires, "Aeronautics in the Civil War," in *American Historical Review*, XLII (1936–1937), 652–69. Works on other special topics are Bauman L. Belden, *War Medals of the Confederacy* (New York, 1915), reprinted from *American Journal of Numismatics* (New York, 1866–1924), XLVIII (1913–1914), 12 pp.; Ellsworth Eliot, Jr., *West Point in the Confederacy* (New York, 1941); Thomas L. Livermore, *Numbers and Losses in the*

Civil War in America, 1861–65 (Boston, 1900); and Jennings C. Wise, *The Long Arm of Lee; or, The History of the Artillery of the Army of Northern Virginia; With a Brief Account of the Confederate Bureau of Ordnance,* 2 vols. (Lynchburg, 1915).

As most of the important diaries, journals, and collections of letters have been evaluated in Coulter, *Travels in the Confederate States,* some will be simply listed here. The following were by Confederates: Joseph T. Durkin (ed.), *John Dooley, Confederate Soldier, His War Journal* (Washington, 1945); James S. Harris, *Historical Sketches, Seventh Regiment, North Carolina Troops* (n.p., 1893?), really a diary; Randolph H. McKim, *A Soldier's Recollections; Leaves from the Diary of a Young Confederate, with an Oration on the Motives and Aims of the Soldiers of the South* (New York, 1910); William S. White, "A Diary of the War, or What I saw of It," in *Contributions to a History of the Richmond Howitzer Battalion* (Richmond, 1883), No. 2; and William Watson, *Life in the Confederate Army, Being the Observations and Experiences of an Alien in the South during the American Civil War* (London, 1887). These are by Federals: John Beatty, *The Citizen-Soldier; or, Memoirs of a Volunteer* (Cincinnati, 1879), really a diary; "Major [James Austin] Connolly's Letters to his Wife, 1862–1865" and "Major Connolly's Diary," in *Transactions of the Illinois State Historical Society for the Year 1928* (Springfield, 1928), 215–438; W. A. Croffut (ed.), *Fifty Years in Camp and Field. Diary of Major-General Ethan Allen Hitchcock, U.S.A.* (New York, 1909); Clement Eaton (ed.), "Diary of an Officer in Sherman's Army Marching through the Carolinas," in *Journal of Southern History,* IX (1943), 238–54; M. A. De Wolfe Howe (ed.), *Marching with Sherman; Passages from the Letters and Campaign Diaries of Henry Hitchcock, Major and Assistant Adjutant General of Volunteers, November 1864–May 1865* (New Haven, 1927); Charles W. Wills, *Army Life of an Illinois Soldier, Including a Day by Day Record of Sherman's March to the Sea. Letters and Diary . . .* (Washington, 1906); and Oscar O. Winther (ed.), *With Sherman to the Sea; The Civil War Letters, Diaries & Reminiscences of Theodore F. Upson* (Baton Rouge, 1943).

Of first importance are Robert E. Lee, Jr., *Recollections and Letters of General Robert E. Lee* (Garden City, 1904); and Douglas S. Freeman (ed.), *Lee's Dispatches; Unpublished Letters of General Robert E. Lee, C.S.A., to Jefferson Davis and the War Department of the Confederate States of America, 1862–65* (New York, 1915). Other collections of letters by Confederates are: Edmund Cody Burnett (ed.), "Letters of Barnett Hardeman Cody and Others, 1861–1864," in *Georgia Historical*

Quarterly, XXIII (1939), 265–99, 362–80; Edmund Cody Burnett (ed.), "Letters of Three Lightfoot Brothers, 1861–1864," *ibid.,* XXV (1941), 371–400; XXVI (1942), 65–90; John A. Cawthon (ed.), "Letters of a North Louisiana Private to his Wife, 1862–1865," in *Mississippi Valley Historical Review,* XXX (1943–1944), 533–50; C. G. Chamberlayne (ed.), *Ham Chamberlayne—Virginian; Letters and Papers of an Artillery Officer in the War for Southern Independence, 1861–1865* (Richmond, 1932); George D. Harmon (ed.), "Letters of Luther Rice Mills—A Confederate Soldier," in *North Carolina Historical Review,* IV (1927), 285–310; Arthur C. Inman (ed.), *Soldier of the South; General Pickett's War Letters to his Wife* (Boston, 1928); "Thomas R. R. Cobb," in *Southern Historical Society Papers,* XXVIII (1900), 280–301; Henry M. Wagstaff (ed.), *The James A. Graham Papers, 1861–1884* (Chapel Hill, 1928); and Henry M. Wagstaff (ed.), "Letters of Thomas Jackson Strayhorn," in *North Carolina Historical Review,* XIII (1936), 311–34.

Some collections of letters by Federals are: [Warren H. Freeman and Eugene H. Freeman], *Letters from Two Brothers Serving in the War for the Union to their Family at Home in West Cambridge, Mass.* (Cambridge, 1871); [Zenas T. Haines], *Letters from the Forty-Fourth Regiment, M.V.M.: A Record of the Experience of a Nine Months' Regiment in the Department of North Carolina in 1862–3* (Boston, 1863); M. A. De Wolfe Howe (ed.), *Home Letters of General Sherman* (New York, 1909); [Charles F. Morse], *Letters Written during the Civil War, 1861–1865* (Boston, 1898); and Oliver W. Norton, *Army Letters, 1861–1865* . . . (Chicago, 1903).

Many works which appear in their titles as regimental histories are in fact reminiscences and autobiographies. The following were written by Confederates: John H. Alexander, *Mosby's Men* (New York, 1907); Ephraim M. Anderson, *Memoirs: Historical and Personal; Including the Campaigns of the First Missouri Confederate Brigade* (St. Louis, 1868); [Napier Bartlett], *A Soldier's Story of the War; Including the Marches and Battles of the Washington Artillery, and of other Louisiana Troops* (New Orleans, 1874); *Battle-Fields of the South, from Bull Run to Fredericksburg; with Sketches of Confederate Commanders, and Gossip of the Camps,* 2 vols. (London, 1863); Heros von Borcke, *Memoirs of the Confederate War for Independence* (Philadelphia, 1867); James F. J. Caldwell, *The History of a Brigade of South Carolinians, Known first as "Greggs'" and Subsequently as "McGowan's Brigade"* (Philadelphia, 1866); John B. Castleman, *Active Service* (Louisville, 1917); William M. Dame, *From the Rapidan to Richmond and the Spotsylvania Campaign. A Sketch in Personal Narration of the Scenes a Soldier Saw*

(Baltimore, 1920); Henry Kyd Douglas, *I Rode with Stonewall, Being Chiefly the War Experiences of the Youngest Member of Jackson's Staff from the John Brown Raid to the Hanging of Mrs. Surratt* (Chapel Hill, 1940); Basil W. Duke, *Reminiscences of General Basil W. Duke, C.S.A.* (Garden City, 1911); Bela Estvàn, *War Pictures from the South* (New York, 1863); Lamar Fontaine, *My Life and My Lectures* (New York, 1908); William W. Goldsborough, *The Maryland Line in the Confederate States Army* (Baltimore, 1869); General John B. Gordon, *Reminiscences of the Civil War* (New York, 1904); Joseph G. de Roulhac Hamilton (ed.), *The Papers of Randolph Abbott Shotwell*, 3 vols. (Raleigh, 1929–1937); William W. Heartsill, *Fourteen Hundred and 91 Days in the Confederate Army* . . . (Marshall, Texas, 1876); John B. Hood, *Advance and Retreat. Personal Experiences in the United States and Confederate Armies* (New Orleans, 1880); Joseph E. Johnston, *Narrative of Military Operations, Directed, during the Late War Between the States* (New York, 1874); James Longstreet, *From Manassas to Appomattox; Memoirs of the Civil War in America* (Philadelphia, 1896); Dabney H. Maury, *Recollections of a Virginian in the Mexican, Indian, and Civil Wars* (New York, 1894); John W. Munson, *Reminiscences of a Mosby Guerrilla* (New York, 1906); Arthur Howard Noll (ed.), *Doctor [Charles T.] Quintard, Chaplain C.S.A. and Second Bishop of Tennessee; Being his Story of the War (1861–1865)* (Sewanee, 1905); Jesse W. Reid, *History of the Fourth Regiment of S.C. Volunteers, from the Commencement of the War until Lee's Surrender* . . . (Greenville, S.C., 1892); and Robert Stiles, *Four Years under Marse Robert* (New York, 1910).

These are some of the accounts by Federals: Henry N. Blake, *Three Years in the Army of the Potomac* (Boston, 1865); Rev. George S. Bradley, *The Star Corps; or, Notes of an Army Chaplain, during Sherman's Famous "March to the Sea"* (Milwaukee, 1865); Charles K. Cadwell, *The Old Sixth Regiment [Connecticut], its War Record, 1861–5* (New Haven, 1875); Capt. Davis P. Conyngham, *Sherman's March through the South* . . . (New York, 1865); Joel Cook, *The Siege of Richmond: A Narrative of the Military Operations of Major-General George B. McClellan during the Months of May and June, 1862* (Philadelphia, 1862); [Davis E. Cronin], *The Evolution of a Life, Described in the Memoirs of Major Seth Eyland [pseud.]* (New York, 1884); W. W. H. Davis, *History of the 104th Pennsylvania Regiment, from August 22nd, 1861, to September 30th, 1864* (Philadelphia, 1866); Richard Eddy, *History of the Sixtieth Regiment New York State Volunteers, . . . 1861, to . . . 1864* (Philadelphia, 1864); Stephen F. Fleharty, *Our Regiment.*

A History of the 102d Illinois Infantry Volunteers, with Sketches of the Atlanta Campaign, the Georgia Raid, and the Campaign of the Carolinas (Chicago, 1865); Moses D. Gage, *From Vicksburg to Raleigh; or, A Complete History of the Twelfth Regiment Indiana Volunteer Infantry, and the Campaigns of Grant and Sherman, with an Outline of the Great Rebellion* (Chicago, 1865); Willard W. Glazier, *Three Years in the Federal Cavalry* (New York, 1870); Edwin M. Haynes, *A History of the Tenth Regiment, Vermont Volunteers . . .* (Lewiston, Me., 1870); Martin A. Haynes, *History of the Second Regiment New Hampshire Volunteers . . .* (Manchester, 1865); Fenwick Y. Hedley, *Marching through Georgia. Pen-Pictures of Every-Day Life in General Sherman's Army . . .* (Chicago, 1890); Thomas Wentworth Higginson, *Army Life in a Black Regiment* (Boston, 1870); James K. Hosmer, *The Color-Guard: Being a Corporal's Notes of Military Service in the Nineteenth Army Corps* (Boston, 1864); Prince de Joinville ["Translated from the French with Notes by William Henry Hurlbert"], *The Army of the Potomac: Its Organization, its Commander, and its Campaign* (New York, 1862).

Also in this group of writings used in this study are: James J. Marks, *The Peninsular Campaign in Virginia; or, Incidents and Scenes on the Battle-Fields and in Richmond* (Philadelphia, 1864); *Memoirs of General William T. Sherman*, 2 vols. (New York, 1875); James A. Mowris, *A History of the One Hundred and Seventeenth Regiment, N.Y. Volunteers, . . . from . . . 1862, till . . . 1865* (Hartford, 1866); George W. Nichols, *The Story of the Great March . . .* (26th ed., New York, 1866); James M. Nichols, *Perry's Saints; or, The Fighting Parson's Regiment in the War of the Rebellion* (Boston, 1886); Mrs. Sarah A. Palmer, *The Story of Aunt Beckey's Army Life* (New York, 1867); Thomas H. Parker, *History of the 51st Regiment of P.V. and V.V., from . . . 1861, to . . . 1865* (Philadelphia, 1869); *Personal Memoirs of U.S. Grant*, 2 vols. (New York, 1885–1886); *Personal Memoirs of P. H. Sheridan*, 2 vols. (New York, 1888); Admiral David D. Porter, *Incidents and Anecdotes of the Civil War* (New York, 1885); Edward H. Rogers, *Reminiscences of Military Service in the Forty-Third Regiment, Massachusetts Infantry . . . 1862–63* (Boston, 1883); Louis A. Simmons, *The History of the 84th Reg't Ill. Vols.* (Macomb, Ill., 1866); A. P. Smith, *History of the Seventy-Sixth Regiment New York Volunteers . . .* (Cortland, N.Y., 1867); Alexander M. Stewart, *Camp, March and Battle-Field; or, Three Years and a Half with the Army of the Potomac* (Philadelphia, 1865); Richard W. Surby, *Grierson Raids, and Hatch's Sixty-Four Days March, with Biographical Sketches, and the Life and Adventures of*

Chickasaw, the Scout (Chicago, 1865); Robert Tilney, *Life in the Army. Three Years and a Half with the Fifth Army Corps, Army of the Potomac, 1862–1865* (Philadelphia, 1912); H. Clay Trumbull, *The Knightly Soldier: A Biography of Major Henry Ward Camp, Tenth Conn. Vols.* (6th ed., Boston, 1871); Mason W. Tyler, *Recollections of the Civil War with Many Original Diary Entries and Letters Written from the Seat of War* . . . (New York, 1912); J. H. E. Whitney, *The Hawkins Zouaves: (Ninth N.Y.V.) Their Battles and Marches* (New York, 1866); Augustus Woodbury, *A Narrative of the Campaign of the First Rhode Island Regiment, in the Spring and Summer of 1861* (Providence, 1862); and Henry H. Wright, *A History of the Sixth Iowa Infantry* (Iowa City, 1923).

The greatest biography of any of the military leaders, Confederate or Federal, is Douglas S. Freeman, *R. E. Lee; A Biography*, 4 vols. (New York, 1934–1935). Also George F. R. Henderson, *Stonewall Jackson and the American Civil War*, 2 vols. (London, 1898), is outstanding. Of the many biographies of other Confederate leaders, these should be mentioned: Gamaliel Bradford, Jr., *Lee the American* (Boston, 1912); John P. Dyer, *"Fightin' Joe" Wheeler* (University, La., 1941); Cecil F. Holland, *Morgan and his Raiders, A Biography of the Confederate General* (New York, 1943); Howard Swiggett, *The Rebel Raider; A Life of John Hunt Morgan* (Indianapolis, 1934); William Preston Johnston, *The Life of Gen. Albert Sidney Johnston, Embracing his Services in the Armies of the United States, the Republic of Texas, and the Confederate States* (New York, 1878); John C. Pemberton, *Pemberton, Defender of Vicksburg* (Chapel Hill, 1942); Don C. Seitz, *Braxton Bragg, General of the Confederacy* (Columbia, 1924); Arthur M. Shaw, *William Preston Johnston, A Transitional Figure of the Confederacy* (Baton Rouge, 1943); and John W. Thomason, Jr., *Jeb Stuart* (New York, 1930). A strange and improbable account of the exploits of a woman is C. J. Worthington, *The Woman in Battle: A Narrative of the Exploits, Adventures, and Travels of Madam Loreta Janeta Velasquez, Otherwise Known as Lieutenant Harry T. Buford, Confederate States Army* . . . (Richmond, 1876). Of the more numerous lives of Federal commanders and of the several biographies of General Sherman, this one should be noted: Lloyd Lewis, *Sherman, Fighting Prophet* (New York, 1932).

Many works relating to hospitals and medicine were consulted. Prepared and published by order of the Confederate Surgeon General is the remarkable work, illustrative of the ingeniousness of a blockaded people at war, Francis P. Porcher, *Resources of the Southern Fields and*

Forests, Medical, Economical, and Agricultural. Being also a Medical Botany of the Confederate States; with Practical Information on the Useful Properties of the Trees, Plants, and Shrubs (Richmond, 1863). Two articles on medical conditions in the Confederacy are George W. Adams, "Confederate Medicine," in *Journal of Southern History*, VI (1940), 151–66; and Joseph Jacobs, "Some of the Drug Conditions during the War Between the States, 1861–1865," in *Georgia Historical Quarterly*, X (1926), 200–22. Interesting descriptions of hospital life are in Kate Cumming, *A Journal of Hospital Life in the Confederate Army of Tennessee, from the Battle of Shiloh to the End of the War: with Sketches of Life and Character, and Brief Notices of Current Events during that Period* (Louisville, 1866). Largely the same work was republished under the title, Kate Cumming, *Gleanings from Southland; Sketches of Life and Manners of the People of the South before, during and after the War of Secession* . . . (Birmingham, 1895). Describing the career of another woman in the Confederate hospitals is Jacob F. Richard, *The Florence Nightingale of the Southern Army; Experiences of Mrs. Ella K. Newsom, Confederate Nurse in the Great War of 1861–65* (New York, 1914). Letters and accounts of surgeons in the war are surprisingly devoid of details of their own work; but these should be noted: Edmund Cody Burnett (ed.), "Letters of a Confederate Surgeon: Dr. Abner Embry McGarity, 1862–1865," in *Georgia Historical Quarterly*, XXIX (1945), 76–114, 159–90, 222–53; XXX (1946), 35–70; and Spencer G. Welch, *A Confederate Surgeon's Letters to his Wife* (New York, 1911). These Federal accounts, used incidentally, are just as disappointing: *Diary of E[lijah] P. Burton, Surgeon 7th Reg. Ill., 3rd Brig., 2nd Div. 16 A. C.* (Des Moines, 1939), a mimeographed work by The Historical Records Survey; Thomas T. Ellis, *Leaves from the Diary of an Army Surgeon; or, Incidents of Field, Camp, and Hospital Life* (New York, 1863); and Martha Derby Perry (ed.), *Letters from a Surgeon of the Civil War* [John Gardner Perry] (Boston, 1906). The outstanding work on the medical history of the war is *The Medical and Surgical History of the War of the Rebellion (1861–1865), Medical History*, 3 vols., *Surgical History*, 3 vols. (Washington, 1870–1888). Two contemporary works on Confederate surgery are J. Julian Chisolm, *A Manual of Military Surgery, for the Use of Surgeons in the Confederate States Army; with an Appendix of the Rules and Regulations of the Medical Department of the Confederate States Army* (2d ed., Richmond, 1862), and *Manual of Military Surgery. Prepared for the Use of the Confederate States Army* (Richmond, 1863).

A tremendous number of detailed facts about the Confederate navy, generally trustworthy but badly organized and presented, is J. Thomas Scharf, *History of the Confederate Navy from its Organization to the Surrender of its Last Vessel. Its Stupendous Struggle with the Great Navy of the United States; the Engagements Fought in the Rivers and Harbors of the South, and upon the High Seas; Blockade-Running, First Use of Iron-Clads and Torpedoes, and Privateer History* (New York, 1887). William M. Robinson, Jr., *The Confederate Privateers* (New Haven, 1928), is an excellent study. Of the many other accounts of naval activities, these should be mentioned: John Bigelow, *France and the Confederate Navy, 1862–1868* (New York, 1888); Stanley F. Horn, *Gallant Rebel; The Fabulous Cruise of the C.S.S. Shenandoah* (New Brunswick, 1947); and Harrison A. Trexler, *The Confederate Ironclad "Virginia" ("Merrimac")* (Chicago, 1938). Of course, there is the great compilation previously mentioned, *Official Records of the Union and Confederate Navies in the War of the Rebellion.* As interesting as any sea tale is Raphael Semmes, *Memoirs of Service Afloat, during the War Between the States* (Baltimore, 1869).

The question of the treatment of prisoners of war provoked a great many accounts of prison experiences and a few studies of the subject by scholars. In the *Official Records of the Union and Confederate Armies,* Series II, consisting of eight volumes, is devoted to both Confederate and Federal records relating to prisoners of war. The best treatment is William B. Hesseltine, *Civil War Prisons. A Study in War Psychology* (Columbus, Ohio, 1930). Two defenses of the South against charges of prison cruelties are J. William Jones, *Confederate View of the Treatment of Prisoners, Comp. from Official Records and Other Documents* (Richmond, 1876), and R. Randolph Stevenson, *The Southern Side; or, Andersonville Prison . . .* (Baltimore, 1876). Most prison accounts were by inmates, and by far the larger number of writings were by Federals. Most of the following accounts have been appraised by Coulter, *Travels in the Confederate States.* Accounts by Confederates are: Fritz Fuzzlebug [pseud. for John J. Dunkle], *Prison Life during the Rebellion; Being a Brief Narrative of the Miseries and Sufferings of Six Hundred Confederate Prisoners Sent from Fort Delaware to Morris' Island to be Punished* (Singer's Glen, Va., 1869); Mrs. Rose Greenhow, *My Imprisonment and the First Year of Abolition Rule in Washington* (London, 1863); William H. Morgan, *Personal Reminiscences of the War of 1861–5; In Camp—en Bivouac—on the March—on Picket —on the Skirmish Line—on the Battlefield—and in Prison* (Lynchburg, 1911); Edward A. Pollard, *Observations in the North; Eight Months in Prison and on Parole* (Richmond, 1865); W. A. Wash, *Camp,*

Field and Prison Life; Containing Sketches of Service in the South, and the Experience, Incidents and Observations Connected with almost Two Years' Imprisonment at Johnson's Island, Ohio, where 3,000 Confederate Officers were Confined. With an Introduction by Gen. L. M. Lewis, and a Medical History of Johnson's Island by Col. I. G. W. Steedman, M. D. (St. Louis, 1870); and James J. Williamson, *Prison Life in the Old Capitol and Reminiscences of the Civil War* (West Orange, N. J., 1911).

A few of the many Federal accounts are: Junius H. Browne, *Four Years in Secessia: . . . the Author's Capture at Vicksburg . . . his Imprisonment . . . his Escape . . .* (Hartford, 1865); Samuel H. M. Byers, *What I saw in Dixie; or, Sixteen Months in Rebel Prisons* (Dansville, N. Y., 1868); *Famous Adventures and Prison Escapes of the Civil War* (New York, 1893); Lieut. Alonzo Cooper, *In and out of Rebel Prisons* (Oswego, N.Y., 1888); William J. Crossley, *Extracts from my Diary, and from my Experiences while Boarding with Jefferson Davis, in Three of his Notorious Hotels, in Richmond, Va., Tuscaloosa, Ala., and Salisbury, N.C., from July, 1861, to June, 1862* (Providence, 1903); Henry M. Davidson, *Fourteen Months in Southern Prisons . . .* (Milwaukee, 1865); Morgan E. Dowling, *Southern Prisons; or, Josie the Heroine of Florence . . .* (Detroit, 1870); Augustine J. H. Duganne, *Camps and Prisons. Twenty Months in the Department of the Gulf* (3d ed., New York, 1865); Charles Fosdick, *Five Hundred Days in Rebel Prisons* (Chicago, 1887); Willard W. Glazier, *The Capture, the Prison Pen, and the Escape . . .* (New York, 1870); Warren L. Goss, *The Soldier's Story of his Captivity at Andersonville, Belle Isle, and Other Rebel Prisons* (Boston, 1875); John V. Hadley, *Seven Months a Prisoner* (New York, 1898); Solon Hyde, *A Captive of War* (New York, 1900); Robert H. Kellogg, *Life and Death in Rebel Prisons . . .* (Hartford, 1865); Charles Lanman (ed.), *Journal of Alfred Ely, a Prisoner of War in Richmond* (New York, 1862); Lessel Long, *Twelve Months in Andersonville . . .* (Huntington, Ind., 1886); John McElroy, *Andersonville: A Story of Rebel Military Prisons . . .* (Toledo, 1879); William H. Merrell, *Five Months in Rebeldom . . .* (Rochester, 1862); James M. Page, *The True Story of Andersonville Prison: A Defense of Major Henry Wirz* (New York, 1908); Christian M. Prutsman, *A Soldier's Experience in Southern Prisons . . .* (New York, 1901); Homer B. Sprague, *Lights and Shadows in Confederate Prisons* (New York, 1915); and S. A. Swiggett, *The Bright Side of Prison Life . . .* (Baltimore, 1897).

Accounts by or about secret service agents and spies are often clothed with uncertainties and improbabilities, and in this field there are few means of verification. A well-known account of the Confederate secret service abroad is James D. Bulloch, *The Secret Service of the Confederate States in Europe: or, How the Confederate Cruisers were Equipped,* 2 vols. (New York, 1884). J. Franklin Jameson (ed.), "The London Expenditures of the Confederate Secret Service," in *American Historical Review,* XXXV (1929–1930), 811–24, also should be mentioned. Other items relating to the Confederate secret service are: John W. Headley, *Confederate Operations in Canada and New York* (New York, 1906); Milo M. Quaife (ed.), *Absalom Grimes, Confederate Mail Runner* (New Haven, 1926); and Charles E. Taylor, "The Signal and Secret Service of the Confederate States," in *North Carolina Booklet* (Raleigh, 1901–1926), II, No. 11 (March, 1903), 24 pp. The celebrated Confederate spy Belle Boyd (Mrs. Sam W. Hardinge) wrote of her experiences in *Belle Boyd in Camp and Prison* (New York, 1865). A recent biography of her is Louis A. Sigaud, *Belle Boyd, Confederate Spy* (Richmond, 1944). Two Federal women spies are discussed in S. Emma E. Edmonds, *Nurse and Spy in the Union Army* . . . (Hartford, 1865); and Ferdinand L. Sarmiento, *Life of Pauline Cushman. The Celebrated Union Spy and Scout* . . . (Philadelphia, 1865). A none too reliable account of the Federal secret service is Lafayette C. Baker, *History of the United States Secret Service* (Philadelphia, 1867). Two other Federal accounts are William Pittenger, *Capturing a Locomotive: A History of Secret Service in the Late War* (Washington, 1885, c. 1881), and Albert D. Richardson, *The Secret Service, the Field, the Dungeon, and the Escape* (Hartford, 1865). A copy of a code is given in John G. Westover (ed.), "A Civil War Secret Service Code," in *Journal of Southern History,* VIII (1942), 556–57.

MISCELLANEOUS TOPICS

It seems desirable to isolate for special treatment in this bibliography a few topics that do not fit well into the previous divisions. Some of the attempts made to explain the cause and course of the disintegration of the Confederacy follow: "Georgia and the Confederacy, 1865," in *American Historical Review,* I (1895–1896), 97–102; Lawrence H. Gipson, "The Collapse of the Confederacy," in *Mississippi Valley Historical Review,* IV (1917–1918), 437–58; Alfred J. Hanna, *Flight into Oblivion* (Richmond, 1938); Frank L. Owsley, "Local Defense and the Overthrow of the Confederacy: A Study in State Rights," in *Mississippi Valley Historical Review,* XI (1924–1925), 490–525; Frank L. Owsley, *State Rights in the Confederacy* (Chicago, 1925); Col. Robert Tansill, *A Free and Impartial Exposition of the Causes which Led to the Failure of the Con-*

federate States to Establish their Independence (Washington, 1865); Charles H. Wesley, *The Collapse of the Confederacy* (Washington, 1937); James E. Walmsley, "The Last Meeting of the Confederate Cabinet," in *Mississippi Valley Historical Review,* VI (1919–1920), 336–49; and Richard E. Yates, "Governor Vance and the End of the War in North Carolina," in *North Carolina Historical Review,* XVIII (1941), 315–38.

A scholarly and comprehensive account of the Negroes during the war is Bell I. Wiley, *Southern Negroes, 1861–1865* (New Haven, 1938). Other works are: Elizabeth H. Botume, *First Days amongst the Contrabands* (Boston, 1893); John Eaton, *Grant, Lincoln and the Freedmen; Reminiscences of the Civil War with Special Reference to the Work for the Contrabands and Freedmen of the Mississippi Valley* (New York, 1907); Thomas R. Hay, "The South and the Arming of the Slaves," in *Mississippi Valley Historical Review,* VI (1919–1920), 34–73; and Nathaniel W. Stephenson, "The Question of Arming the Slaves," in *American Historical Review,* XVIII (1912–1913), 295–308.

The best account of the main peace movement is Edward C. Kirkland, *The Peacemakers of 1864* (New York, 1927). More limited studies are: Fred H. Harrington, "A Peace Mission of 1863," in *American Historical Review,* XLVI (1940–1941), 76–86; A. Sellew Roberts, "The Peace Movement in North Carolina," in *Mississippi Valley Historical Review,* XI (1924–1925), 190–99; and Richard E. Yates, "Governor Vance and the Peace Movement," in *North Carolina Historical Review,* XVII (1940), 1–25, 89–113.

For several of the states, separate studies of the secession movement have been made, among which these should be noted: Clarence P. Denman, *The Secession Movement in Alabama* (Montgomery, 1933): Percy L. Rainwater, *Mississippi, Storm Center of Secession, 1856–1861* (Baton Rouge, 1938); Henry T. Shanks, *The Secession Movement in Virginia, 1847–1861* (Richmond, 1934); and J. Carlyle Sitterson, *The Secession Movement in North Carolina* (Chapel Hill, 1939). A general discussion of secession is Dwight L. Dumond, *The Secession Movement, 1860–1861* (New York, 1931). The collections of secession editorials from Southern and Northern newspapers, by Dumond and Perkins, respectively, previously noted, should be recalled here. Among the many studies relating to the secession period are: John H. Aughey, *The Iron Furnace: or, Slavery and Secession* (Philadelphia, 1863); Lucius E. Chittenden, *A Report of the Debates and Proceedings in the Secret Sessions of the Conference Convention, for Proposing Amendments to the Constitution of the United States, Held at Washington, D.C., in February, A.D.*

1861 (New York, 1864); Arthur C. Cole, "Lincoln's Election an Immediate Menace to Slavery in the States?" in *American Historical Review,* XXXVI (1930–1931), 340–67; and its answer, Joseph G. de Roulhac Hamilton, "Lincoln's Election an Immediate Menace to Slavery in the States?" *ibid.,* XXXVII (1931–1932), 700–11; Samuel W. Crawford, *The Genesis of the Civil War. The Story of Sumter, 1860–1861* (New York, 1887); Rev. James W. Hunnicut, *The Conspiracy Unveiled. The South Sacrificed; or, The Horrors of Secession* (Philadelphia, 1863); Lillian A. Kibler, "Unionist Sentiment in South Carolina in 1860," in *Journal of Southern History,* IV (1938), 346–66; Frank L. Owsley, "The Fundamental Cause of the Civil War: Egocentric Sectionalism," in *Journal of Southern History,* VII (1941), 3–18; David M. Potter, *Lincoln and his Party in the Secession Crisis* (New Haven, 1942); Charles W. Ramsdell, "Lincoln and Fort Sumter," in *Journal of Southern History,* III (1937), 259–88; and John S. Tilley, *Lincoln Takes Command* (Chapel Hill, 1941). Reference should be made to a few pertinent items under the division of CONTEMPORARY PAMPHLETS AND LEAFLETS.

The best account of the part played by women is Francis B. Simkins and James W. Patton, *The Women of the Confederacy* (Richmond, 1936). Other items found useful are: Matthew P. Andrews (comp.), *The Women of the South in War Times* (Baltimore, 1920); Henry W. R. Jackson, *The Southern Women of the Second American Revolution* . . . (Atlanta, 1863); Mary E. Massey, "Southern Refugee Life during the Civil War," in *North Carolina Historical Review,* XX (1943), 1–21, 132–56; James W. Patton (ed.), *Minutes of the Proceedings of the Greenville Ladies' Association in Aid of the Volunteers of the Confederate Army* (Durham, 1937); Francis B. Simkins and James W. Patton, "The Work of Southern Women among the Sick and Wounded of the Confederate Armies," in *Journal of Southern History,* I (1935), 475–96; and Rev. John L. Underwood, *The Women of the Confederacy* . . . (New York, 1906). A controversial subject is dealt with in a scholarly manner in Dorothy M. and William R. Quynn, *Barbara Frietschie* (Baltimore, 1942).

Special accounts on a variety of subjects follow. Ella Lonn has made an excellent study in her *Desertion during the Civil War* (New York, 1928). Other works on this and the kindred subject of disloyalty are Bessie Martin, *Desertion of Alabama Troops from the Confederate Army; A Study in Sectionalism* (New York, 1932); Georgia Lee Tatum, *Disloyalty in the Confederacy* (Chapel Hill, 1934); and Joseph G. de Roulhac Hamilton (ed.), "The Heroes of America," in *Publications of the Southern History Association* (Washington, 1897–1907), XI (1907),

10–19. The standard work on Confederate diplomacy is Frank L. Owsley, *King Cotton Diplomacy; Foreign Relations of the Confederate States of America* (Chicago, 1931). Closely related to this subject are Ephraim D. Adams, *Great Britain and the American Civil War*, 2 vols. (London, 1925), and Donaldson Jordan and Edwin J. Pratt, *Europe and the American Civil War* (Boston, 1931). It should be noted here that the third volume of Series II of the *Official Records of the Union and Confederate Navies* is devoted to Confederate diplomatic correspondence. Competent studies on their respective subjects are Ella Lonn, *Foreigners in the Confederacy* (Chapel Hill, 1940), and Albert B. Moore, *Conscription and Conflict in the Confederacy* (New York, 1924).

Some of the Northern problems closely related to the Confederacy are taken up in these works: Wood Gray, *The Hidden Civil War; The Story of the Copperheads* (New York, 1942); George Fort Milton, *Abraham Lincoln and the Fifth Column* (New York, 1942); and James G. Randall, *Constitutional Problems under Lincoln* (New York, 1926).

Works on various other topics are: Annie H. Abel, "The Indians in the Civil War," in *American Historical Review*, XV, (1909–1910), 281–96; Milledge L. Bonham, Jr., *The British Consuls in the Confederacy* (New York, 1911); Paul Evans and Thomas P. Govan (eds.), "A Belgian Consul on Conditions in the South in 1860 and 1862," in *Journal of Southern History*, III (1937), 479–91; Margaret Leech, *Reveille in Washington, 1860–1865* (New York, 1941); Ella Lonn, *Salt as a Factor in the Confederacy* (New York, 1933); Robert D. Meade, "The Relations Between Judah P. Benjamin and Jefferson Davis," in *Journal of Southern History*, V (1939), 468–78; Charles W. Ramsdell, "The Texas State Military Board, 1862–1865," in *Southwestern Historical Quarterly*, XXVII (1923–1924), 253–75; William M. Robinson, Jr., "Prohibition in the Confederacy," in *American Historical Review*, XXXVII (1931–1932), 50–58; Madeline R. Robinton, *An Introduction to the Papers of the New York Prize Court, 1861–1865* (New York, 1945); James W. Silver, "Propaganda in the Confederacy," in *Journal of Southern History*, XI (1945), 487–503; Robert C. Wood, *Confederate Hand-Book; A Compilation of Important Data and Other Interesting and Valuable Matter Relating to the War Between the States, 1861–1865* (New Orleans, 1900); and Edward N. Wright, *Conscientious Objectors in the Civil War* (Philadelphia, 1931).

It probably ought to be stated that the foregoing bibliography does not claim to approach the vast limits of completeness nor does it claim to be the best select bibliography that could be constructed. Its purpose is to list with occasional criticism the items found available and used in this study.

INDEX

Manufacturers and Direct Trade Association of the Confederate States, 229

Manufacturers' Association of the Confederate States, 229 n.

Manufacturing and Direct Trade Association of the Confederate States, 212

March to the Sea, 360-61

Marietta, Ga., Sherman on burning of, 367 n.; robbery near, 423

Marine corps, 299

Marriages, 405

Marshall, Texas, meeting of governors at, 565-66

Marshall House, 72, 424

Marshallville, Ga., 431

Martin, George, 87 n.

Maryland, refuses to call secession convention, 3; effect of bombardment of Fort Sumter on, 44; Southern sympathizers of, flee to Virginia, 45; invasion of, by Lee, 355

Mason, James M., mentioned for presidency, 103; diplomatic career of, 186-87, 190, 195, 198

Masons, fraternal order, attempt to make peace, 546

Master William Mitten, 514

Matamoros, Mexico, 197

Matches, manufactures of, 215-16

Maury, Matthew F., in torpedo service, 300

Maximilian, 196, 197

Meade, George Gordon, 356

Meat, sources of supply of, 246

Mechanicsville, battle of, 355

Medals, for soldiers, 450-51

Medical Department, 430-31, 432 n., 434

Medicines, 430-31

Memminger, Christopher G., Unionism of, 3; on secession, 14; Secretary of the Treasury, 120, 149; characteristics of, 149-50; resigns, 163; opposes purchase of cotton crop by government, 166, 167 n.; on taxation, 173, 176, 181; asks for statistics on manufacturing, 212

Memphis, Tenn., seeks to be Confederate capital, 101; captured, 353

Memphis and Charleston Railroad, 26, 353

Memphis *Appeal,* wanderings of, 495-96

Memphis *Argus,* 496

Mercer, William, planter, 243

Mercer University, 519, 530

Merchants and Manufacturers Journal, 212

Mercier, Count Henri, visits Richmond, 191

Mercury, sources of, 205

Meridian, Miss., 26

Merrimac, government-owned blockade-runner, 290

Merrimac, ironclad, see *Virginia*

Methodists, 18, 521, 522, 524-25, 526, 528

Metropolitan, Richmond theater, 488, 489

Mexico, Confederate relations with, 196-97

Michigan, 7

Miles, George H., *see* Halphin, Ernest

Miles, William P., secessionist, 18; chairman of committee on flags, 117; continuous service in Congress, 134

Militarism, advocated in Confederacy, 65

Military policy, Confederate, in defending Missouri, 49; in locating capital in Richmond, 101-102; defensive, 342-43; offensive, 343-44, 347 n., 348 n.; leniency in invaded regions, 347; "scorched earth," 347-48; on holding territory, 348

Mill Springs, battle of, 353

Millen, Ga., 417

Millen Prison, 471

Miller's . . . Almanac, 516

Milton, Gov. John, on speculators, 224; on loyalty to Confederacy, 293-94; favors state troops, 310; commended by Davis, 398

Minnesota, 7

Minstrels, 489

Missionary Ridge, battle of, 360

Missionary Society of the Methodist Church, 527 n.

Mississippi, sends commissioners to South Carolina secession convention, 2; secedes, 2; sends commissioners to secession conventions of other states, 3;